EDUCATIONAL RESEARCH

Competencies for Analysis and Applications

EIGHTH EDITION

L. R. Gay
Late of Florida University

Geoffrey E. Mills
Southern Oregon University

Peter Airasian
Boston College

PEARSON

Merrill
Prentice Hall

Upper Saddle River, New Jersey
Columbus, Ohio

Library of Congress Cataloging in Publication Data

Gay, L. R.
  Educational research: compentencies for analysis and applications/L. R. Gay, Geoffrey
E. Mills, Peter Airasian—8th ed.
    p.cm.
  Includes bibliographical references and index.
  ISBN 0-13-118534-9
  1. Education—Research. I. Mills, Geoffrey E. II. Airasian, Peter W. III. Title.

LB1028.G37 2006
370'.7'2—dc22

2005048673

Vice President and Executive Publisher: Jeffery W. Johnston
Publisher: Kevin M. Davis
Development Editor: Autumn Crisp Benson
Editorial Assistant: Sarah Kenoyer
Production Editor: Mary Harlan
Copy Editor: Sue Snyder Kopp
Design Coordinator: Diane C. Lorenzo
Photo Coordinator: Lori Whitley

Text Design and Illustrations: Carlisle Publishers Services
Cover Design: Jason Moore
Cover Image: SuperStock
Production Manager: Laura Messerly
Director of Marketing: Ann Castel Davis
Marketing Manager: Autumn Purdy
Marketing Coordinator: Brian Mounts

This book was set in Berkeley by Carlisle Communications, Ltd. It was printed and bound by Courier Kendallville, Inc. The cover was printed by The Lehigh Press.

Photo Credits: p. 2, from *Dr. X*, Warner Bros./Photofest; p. 32, from The *Hunchback of Notre Dame*, RKO/Alex Kahle/The Kobal Collection; p. 70, from *Raiders of the Lost Ark*, Lucasfilm Ltd/Paramount/The Kobal Collection; p. 98, from *Gorgo*, King Brothers/The Kobal Collection; p. 120, from *Young Frankenstein*, Corbis/Bettmann; p. 158, from *Groundhog Day*, Columbia/Tri-Star/The Kobal Collection; p. 190, from *Gone With the Wind*, Selznick/MGM/The Kobal Collection; p. 216, from *Kissin' Cousins*, MGM/The Kobal Collection; pp. 232, 336, from *The Three Stooges*, The Kobal Collection; pp. 274, 440, from *The Wizard of Oz*, MGM/The Kobal Collection; p. 300, from *Madame Du Barry* (1919), UFA/The Kobal Collection; p. 384, from *A Beautiful Mind*, Dreamworks/Universal/Eli Reed/The Kobal Collection; p. 398, from *Some Like It Hot*, © Bettmann/Corbis; p. 412, from *I Love Lucy*, CBS-TV/The Kobal Collection; p. 428, from *The Shining*, Warner Bros/The Kobal Collection; p. 466, from *Sherlock Holmes: The Hound of the Baskervilles* (1959), Hammer/The Kobal Collection; p. 488, from *Frankenstein* (1931), Corbis/Bettmann; p. 498, from *The Blackboard Jungle*, MGM/The Kobal Collection; p. 514, from *Die Laughing*, Orion/The Kobal Collection; and p. 540, from *Charly*, Photofest.

Pearson Prentice Hall™ is a trademark of Pearson Education, Inc.
Pearson® is a registered trademark of Pearson plc
Prentice Hall® is a registered trademark of Pearson Education, Inc.
Merrill® is a registered trademark of Pearson Education, Inc.

Pearson Education Ltd.
Pearson Education Singapore Pte. Ltd.
Pearson Education Canada, Ltd.
Pearson Education–Japan

Pearson Education Australia Pty. Limited
Pearson Education North Asia Ltd.
Pearson Educación de Mexico, S. A. de C. V.
Pearson Education Malaysia Pte. Ltd.

10 9 8 7 6 5 4 3 2 1
ISBN: 0-13-118534-9

each chapter, the *Student Study Guide* contains key terms for students to explain, sample test items with answers, and a variety of examples, exercises, mini cases, and activities to support text content. Articles and portions of articles, as well as numerous examples from student research proposals, are included within the revised *Student Study Guide*. Although the exercises, examples, mini cases, and activities also facilitate factual-level content understanding, the primary objective of the *Student Study Guide* is to help students develop deeper understanding so that they can apply the concepts presented in the text. To that end, the *Student Study Guide* includes many tasks and activities that require higher-order thinking and transfer of content covered in the text. Sample responses with explanations are included. Examples that mirror the task activities in the text provide additional support for students as they apply the concepts presented in the text.

Instructor's Manual and Test Bank

The *Instructor's Manual and Test Bank* (0-13-118557-8) contains suggested activities, strategies for teaching each chapter, selected resources, and hundreds of newly written and tested test items. Suggestions are based on personal experience with teaching the course and conducting research. In addition, the more than 700 test items represent a variety of levels of multiple-choice items. New test items—in particular, questions related to qualitative research—have been added to reflect text additions and expansions.

TestGen

The computerized test bank software gives instructors electronic access to the test questions printed in the *Instructor's Manual and Test Bank* and allows them to create and customize exams. The computerized test bank is available in both Macintosh and PC/Windows (0-13-118554-3) versions.

SPSS Student Version

The text includes examples of SPSS calculations with screen images and output tables illustrating the calculations. To complement this new content, copies of SPSS Student Version are available at a discounted price when packaged with this textbook. Contact your local Prentice Hall representative for ordering information.

STATPAK Statistical Software

STATPAK statistical software computes all of the statistics that are calculated in the text and shows students the intermediate stages as well as the final answers. The STATPAK software has been upgraded for this edition and is available in both Macintosh (ISBN 0-13-013949-1) and PC/Windows versions. For Windows users, STATPAK is available for use from the Companion Website at **www.prenhall.com/gay**. Mac users may obtain a disk copy from their local Prentice Hall sales representative.

Companion Website

This upgraded site, located at **www.prenhall.com/gay**, allows students and professors using the text free access to a wealth of newly created online resources. Here students can review chapter objectives—and more specific learning objectives within each objective—and test their knowledge by taking chapter quizzes that provide hints and automatic feedback. (Items are graded with a percentage score and correct answers.) Students can apply their newly gained knowledge in "Applying What You Know" essay questions and can browse course topics on the Internet using well-screened and evaluated Web sites related to educational research.

Content changes reflect the inclusion of new topics and the expansion or clarification of existing topics. There are many improvements in this edition, and we describe the more significant highlights here:

1. We have broadened our coverage of qualitative research throughout the text. Five chapters now focus on qualitative research (Chapters 14–18); two of these chapters (Chapters 16 and 17) are new. Although the text still focuses mainly on quantitative research, this edition provides a more balanced view of qualitative and quantitative research methods. In particular, the first five chapters now reflect this balanced discussion of qualitative and quantitative research.

   In Chapter 14 we present an overview of qualitative research methods and discuss how qualitative researchers address validity, reliability, and generalizability.

   Chapter 15 focuses on data collection. We begin by discussing how to identify and select study participants. We then discuss collecting data through observations, interviews, and the examination of records.

   Chapter 16 focuses specifically on conducting narrative research, and Chapter 17 focuses on conducting ethnographic research.

   Finally, Chapter 18 describes the analysis and interpretation of qualitative data and presents strategies for writing narratives based on the research results.

   Throughout, our discussion of both qualitative and quantitative research is guided by a commitment to ethical research practice and to the competencies required to carry out the basic steps common to educational research.

2. Chapter 19 is a new and expanded discussion of mixed methods research designs. We describe three different mixed methods approaches and present criteria for identifying and evaluating them.

3. Chapter 20 is a new and expanded discussion of action research.

4. SPSS is a comprehensive, full-featured software application for analyzing quantitative research data. In Chapters 11 and 12, we illustrate our discussion of statistical data analysis by showing our calculations in two formats: a step-by-step hand analysis and a computer analysis using SPSS Student Version 12.0 for Windows.

5. The experimental research chapter has been separated into two chapters with the creation of a new chapter on single-subject research design (Chapter 10) that includes an example of a published single-subject design study.

In addition, we have added new tables and figures throughout the text. Every chapter has been edited and updated. References have been updated.

:: SUPPLEMENTARY MATERIALS

A number of ancillaries are available to complement the text, including a *Student Study Guide* and an *Instructor's Manual and Test Bank*. For each part and chapter in the text, there is a corresponding part in these two ancillaries. Other supplementary materials include Prentice Hall TestGen computerized testbank software, SPSS Student Version 12.0 statistical software, a free and expanded Companion Website with 10 modules and many opportunities to practice newly learned research skills, and a CD-ROM with interactive computer simulations of educational research concepts and scenarios, including research articles.

Student Study Guide

The *Student Study Guide* (0-13-171669-7) has been significantly revised to coordinate with the new edition. It provides students with opportunities to check their current understanding and extend their knowledge beyond definitions to application of the concepts presented in the text. For research approaches and to more fully understand how the nature of the research question influences the selection of a research method. Part II describes and discusses quantitative research methods and the data collection and analysis needs of each. Individual chapters are devoted to the statistical (sadistical!) approaches to the analysis and interpretation of quantitative data, as well as to a discussion of postanalysis procedures to organize and protect research data. Part III looks at qualitative research methods, differentiating between the common approaches and describing the collection, analysis, and interpretation of qualitative data. Part IV is a new part dedicated to the discussion, application, and analysis of mixed methods research designs. Part V, another new section, focuses on the design and implementation of action research and presents the Dialectic Action Research Spiral as a model for conducting such research. Part VI focuses on helping the student prepare a research report, either for the completion of a degree requirement or for publication in a refereed journal. Finally, in Part VII, the student applies the skills and knowledge acquired in Parts I through V and critiques a research report.

Strategy

This text represents more than just a textbook to be incorporated into a course; it is actually a total instructional system that includes stated objectives, or competencies, instruction, and procedures for evaluating each competency. The instructional strategy of the system emphasizes demonstration of skills and individualization within structure. The format for each chapter is essentially the same. Following a brief introduction, each task to be performed is described. Tasks require students to demonstrate that they can perform particular research functions. Because each student works with a different problem, each student demonstrates the competency required by a task as it applies to his or her own problem. With the exception of Chapter 1, an individual chapter is directed toward the attainment of only one task (occasionally, students have a choice between a quantitative and qualitative task). Each chapter begins with a list of chapter objectives that entail knowledge and skills that facilitate students' abilities to perform a related task. In many instances, objectives may be assessed either as written exercises submitted by students or by tests, whichever the instructor prefers. For some objectives the first option is clearly preferable.

Text discussion is intended to be as simple and straightforward as possible. Whenever feasible, procedures are presented as a series of steps, and concepts are explained in terms of illustrative examples. In a number of cases, relatively complex topics or topics beyond the scope of the text are presented at a very elementary level, and students are directed to other sources for additional, in-depth discussion. There is also a degree of intentional repetition; a number of concepts are discussed in different contexts and from different perspectives. Also, at the risk of eliciting more than a few groans, an attempt has been made to sprinkle the text with touches of humor. Each chapter includes a detailed, often lengthy, summary with headings and subheadings directly paralleling those in the chapter. The summaries are designed to facilitate both review and location of related text discussion. Finally, each chapter (or part) concludes with suggested criteria for evaluating the associated task and with an example of the task produced by a former introductory educational research student. Full-length articles, reprinted from the educational research literature, appear at the ends of several chapters and serve as illustrations of "real-life" research methodology.

▒ MAJOR REVISIONS FOR THIS EDITION

Like the seventh edition, the eighth edition reflects a combination of both unsolicited and solicited input. Positive feedback suggested aspects of the text and supplementary materials that should not be changed—the writing style and the focus on ethical practice, for example. Every effort, however, was made to incorporate suggestions from users and nonusers. For example, several users requested an increased focus on qualitative research and an integration of SPSS analysis.

Preface

:: PHILOSOPHY AND PURPOSE

This text is designed primarily for use in the introductory course in educational research that is a basic requirement for many graduate programs. Because the topic coverage of the text is relatively comprehensive, it also may be easily adapted for use in either a senior-level undergraduate course or a more advanced graduate-level course.

The philosophy that guided the development of the current and previous editions of this text was the conviction that an introductory research course should be more skill and application oriented than theory oriented. Thus, the purpose of this text is to have students become familiar with research mainly at a "how-to" skill and application level. The text does not mystify students with theoretical and statistical jargon. It strives to provide a down-to-earth approach that helps students acquire the skills and knowledge required of a competent consumer and producer of educational research. The emphasis is not just on what the student knows but also on what the student can do with what he or she knows. It is recognized that being a "good" researcher involves more than the acquisition of skills and knowledge; in any field, significant research is usually produced by those who through experience have acquired insights, intutions, and strategies related to the research process. Research of any worth, however, is rarely conducted in the absence of basic research skills and knowledge. A basic assumption of this text is that there is considerable overlap in the competencies required of a competent consumer of research and a competent producer of research, and that a person is in a much better position to evaluate the work of others after she or he has performed the major tasks involved in the research process.

:: ORGANIZATION AND STRATEGY

The overall strategy of the text is to promote students' attainment of a degree of expertise in research through the acquisition of knowledge and by involvement in actual research.

Organization

For the eighth edition, the text has undergone a substantial reorganization, primarily in response to feedback from the field. Part I discusses the scientific and disciplined inquiry approach and its application in education. It describes the main steps in the research process and the purpose and methods of the various approaches to research. In Part I, each student selects and delineates a research problem of interest that has relevance to his or her professional area. Throughout the rest of the text, the student then simulates the procedures that would be followed in conducting a study designed to investigate the problem; each chapter develops a specific skill or set of skills required for the execution of such a research study. Specifically, the student reviews and analyzes related literature and formulates hypotheses (Chapter 2), develops a research plan (Chapter 3), selects and defines samples (Chapter 4), and evaluates and selects measuring instruments (Chapter 5). Throughout Part I there are now parallel discussions of quantitative and qualitative research constructs that previously were separated out in Parts II and III. This new organization allows the student to see the similarities and differences in

Las Vegas; Rayne Sperling, Penn State University; and Paul Westmeyer, University of Texas at San Antonio. These reviewers' thoughtful and detailed comments and suggestions contributed greatly to the eighth edition. Their efforts are very much appreciated.

For the past 7 years I have been fortunate to work with Kevin Davis, Publisher at Merrill/Prentice Hall. Kevin has taught me a great deal about writing, and I will always be indebted to him for trusting me with stewardship of the eighth edition of this wonderful text. I believe that I have made a positive contribution to this text and added to the wisdom of earlier editions by L. R. Gay and Peter Airasian, and that the text continues to be nurtured under Kevin's watchful eye.

Also at Merrill/Prentice Hall, Autumn Benson and Mary Harlan ably shepherded the manuscript through development and production, kept me from falling behind, and helped me see the light at the end of the tunnel. My thanks to copy editor Sue Kopp, who demonstrated an amazing ability to bring consistency to a text that has evolved over a number of years. An author does not take on the task of a major revision of a text of this magnitude without the commitment and support of excellent editors. Autumn and Kevin were instrumental in the development of this edition and I sincerely thank them for their professionalism, patience, caring, and sense of humor.

I wish to thank my friend and colleague Dr. Tom Schram for his thoughtful comments and guidance on the new chapters on narrative research and ethnographic research. Also, Dr. Gregg Gassman provided invaluable aid with the SPSS 12.0 sections. I appreciate their help.

Finally, I want to thank my best friend and wife, Dr. Donna Mills, and my son, Jonathan, for their love, support, and patience. I am very much looking forward to spending weekends, evenings, and vacations together again!

Geoff Mills
Southern Oregon University

Other modules on the site can expand learners' skill base.

- "Evaluating Articles" gives students opportunities to read, deconstruct, and critique two qualitative and two quantitative articles via questions and suggested answers and evaluative checklists.
- "Analyzing Quantitative Data" presents a data set and leads students through a step-by-step analysis of the data, requiring them to run SPSS and generate descriptive and inferential statistics and summarize their findings.
- "Analyzing Qualitative Data" presents a narrative data set and asks students to segment, code, and categorize data.
- "Research Tools and Tips" is a series of read-only, printable topics—including links to helpful information on the Web, handy protocol forms, and references to products to aid research—that can make any research project easier and less confusing.
- The STATPAK statistical calculator tool is available for PC/Windows users in "Calculating Statistics."

The Companion Website also contains Message Board and Live Chat areas to encourage student interaction. For professors, the **Syllabus Builder**™ allows easy instructional planning and convenient online access for their course.

Computer Simulation Software

Simulations in Educational Psychology and Research, version 2.1 (0-13-113717-4), features five psychological/educational interactive experiments on a CD-ROM. Exercises and readings help students explore the research concepts and procedures connected to these experiments. Qualitative and quantitative designs are included. Instructors should contact their local Prentice Hall sales representative to order a copy of these simulations.

Where the Web Meets Textbooks for Student Savings!

SafariX Textbooks Online™ is an exciting new choice for students looking to save money. As an alternative to purchasing the print textbook, students can subscribe to the same content online and save up to 50% off the suggested list price of the print text. With a SafariX WebBook, students can search the text, make notes online, print out reading assignments that incorporate lecture notes, and bookmark important passages for later review. For more information, or to subscribe to the SafariX WebBook, visit **http://www.safarix.com**. The SafariX WebBook for this text is 0-13-171351-5.

⠿ ACKNOWLEDGEMENTS

I sincerely thank everyone who provided input for the development of this edition. The following individuals reviewed the current edition: Ernest W. Brewer, University of Tennessee, Knoxville; Sheryl Gowen, Georgia State University; Barbara Kawulich, University of West Georgia; Daniel Matthews, University of Illinois at Springfield; Joseph Maxwell, George Mason University; Dana L. Miller, Doane College; LeAnn Putney, University of Nevada, Las Vegas; Marcia L. Rosal, Florida State University; Thomas Schram, University of New Hampshire; Kaia Skaggs, Eastern Michigan University; E. Lea Witta, University of Central Florida; and Kenneth W. Wunderlich, University of Texas at San Antonio. The following individuals reviewed the previous edition: Chris Chiu, University of Pittsburgh; Clark J. Hickman, University of Missouri–St. Louis; Ann Mackenzie, Miami University; Malina Monaco, Georgia State University; Ron Oliver, California State University, Fullerton; LeAnn G. Putney, University of Nevada,

∷ EDUCATOR LEARNING CENTER: AN INVALUABLE ONLINE RESOURCE

Merrill Education and the Association for Supervision and Curriculum Development (ASCD) invite you to take advantage of a new online resource, one that provides access to the top research and proven strategies associated with ASCD and Merrill—the Educator Learning Center. At **www.educatorlearningcenter.com**, you will find resources that will enhance your students' understanding of course topics and of current educational issues, in addition to being invaluable for further research.

∷ HOW THE EDUCATOR LEARNING CENTER WILL HELP YOUR STUDENTS BECOME BETTER TEACHERS

With the combined resources of Merrill Education and ASCD, you and your students will find a wealth of tools and materials to better prepare them for the classroom.

Research

- More than 600 articles from the ASCD journal *Educational Leadership* discuss everyday issues faced by practicing teachers.
- A direct link on the site to Research Navigator™ gives students access to many of the leading education journals, as well as extensive content detailing the research process.
- Excerpts from Merrill Education texts give your students insights on important topics of instructional methods, diverse populations, assessment, classroom management, technology, and refining classroom practice.

Classroom Practice

- Hundreds of lesson plans and teaching strategies are categorized by content area and age range.
- Case studies and classroom video footage provide virtual field experience for student reflection.
- Computer simulations and other electronic tools keep your students abreast of today's classrooms and current technologies.

∷ LOOK INTO THE VALUE OF EDUCATOR LEARNING CENTER YOURSELF

A four-month subscription to Educator Learning Center is $25 but is **FREE** when packaged with any Merrill Education text. In order for your students to have access to this site, you must use this special value-pack ISBN number **WHEN** placing your textbook order with the bookstore: 0-13-225925-7. Your students will then receive a copy of the text packaged with a free ASCD pincode. To preview the value of this website to you and your students, please go to **www.educatorlearningcenter.com** and click on "Demo."

Brief Contents

Contents

Research Articles

Note: Every effort has been made to provide accurate and current Internet information in this book. However, the Internet and information posted on it are constantly changing, so it is inevitable that some of the Internet addresses listed in this textbook will change.

EDUCATIONAL RESEARCH

Competencies for Analysis and Applications

"Despite a popular stereotype that depicts researchers as spectacled, stoop-shouldered, elderly gentlemen who endlessly add chemicals to test tubes, every day thousands of men and women of all ages, shapes, and sizes conduct educational research in a wide variety of settings." (p. 5)

Introduction to Educational Research

OBJECTIVES

After reading Chapter 1, you should be able to do the following:

1. List and briefly describe the major steps involved in conducting a research study.
2. Describe the differences between quantitative and qualitative research.
3. Briefly define and state the major characteristics of these research approaches: action, descriptive, correlational, causal–comparative, experimental, narrative, and ethnographic.
4. For each research approach in Objective 3, briefly describe two appropriate research studies.
5. Given a published article, identify and state the
   a. Problem or topic chosen to study
   b. Procedures employed to conduct the study
   c. Method of analyzing collected data
   d. Major conclusion of the study

Completing Chapter 1 should enable you to perform the following tasks.

TASKS 1A, 1B

Identify and briefly state the following for both research studies at the end of this chapter:

1. The topic (purpose of the study)
2. The procedures
3. The method of analysis
4. The major conclusions

(See Performance Criteria, p. 20.)

TASK 1C

Classify given research studies based on their characteristics and purposes. (See Performance Criteria, p. 20.)

⠶ WELCOME!

If you are taking a research course because it is required in your program of studies, raise your right hand. If you are taking a research course because it seemed like it would be a really fun elective, raise your left hand. When you have stopped laughing, read on. No, you are not the innocent victim of one or more sadists. Your professors have several legitimate reasons for believing this research course is an essential component of your graduate education.

First, educational research findings significantly contribute to both educational theory and educational practice. For example, educational researchers have investigated the pros and cons of such practices as ability grouping, intelligence testing, and ways to work with non-English speaking pupils. It is important that you, as a professional, know how to access, understand, and evaluate the findings reported.

Second, whether or not you seek them out, you are constantly exposed to research findings in professional publications and, increasingly, in the media. For example, you have undoubtedly encountered research results on such recurrent educational issues as low student achievement scores and how to improve them, the use of statewide assessments to determine high school graduation, the effects of "high-stakes" tests on student achievement, and the effects of whole-language versus phonics instruction in reading. As a professional, you have a responsibility to be able to distinguish between legitimate research claims and ill-founded ones.

And third, believe it or not, research courses are a fruitful source of future researchers. A number of the authors' students have become sufficiently intrigued by the research process to pursue further education and careers in the field. A career in research opens the door to a variety of employment opportunities in universities, research centers, and business and industry.

We recognize that for many of you, educational research is a relatively unfamiliar discipline. To meaningfully learn about and carry out the research process, you must first develop a perspective into which you can integrate information and experiences. Therefore, the goal of Chapters 1–5 is to help you acquire a general understanding of research processes and strategies that will help you learn about specific research knowledge and skills. In succeeding chapters, you will systematically study and carry out specific components of the research process. We begin by examining the scientific method.

:: THE SCIENTIFIC METHOD

The goal of all scientific endeavors is to explain, predict, and/or control phenomena. This goal is based on the assumption that all behaviors and events are orderly and that they are effects which have discoverable causes. Progress toward the goal involves acquiring knowledge and developing and testing theories. The existence of a viable theory greatly facilitates scientific progress by simultaneously explaining many phenomena.

But how do we acquire the knowledge needed to develop and test viable theories? There are many sources of knowledge, such as experience, authority, inductive reasoning, and deductive reasoning. Although commonly used, each of these approaches to understanding has limitations. Some of the problems associated with experience and authority as sources of knowledge are graphically illustrated in a story told about Aristotle. According to the story, one day Aristotle caught a fly and carefully counted and recounted the legs. He then announced that flies have five legs. No one questioned the word of Aristotle. For years his finding was uncritically accepted. Of course, the fly that Aristotle caught just happened to be missing a leg! Whether or not you believe the story, it does illustrate the limitations of relying on personal experience and authority as sources of knowledge.

Both inductive and deductive reasoning are also of limited value when used exclusively. **Inductive reasoning** involves developing generalizations based on observation of a limited number of related events or experiences.

Observation: Every research textbook examined contains a chapter on sampling.

Generalization: Therefore, all research textbooks contain a chapter on sampling.

Deductive reasoning involves essentially the reverse process: arriving at specific conclusions based on general principles, observations, or experiences (generalizations).

Observations: All research textbooks contain a chapter on sampling. This book is a research text.

Generalization: Therefore, this book contains a chapter on sampling. (Does it?)

Although neither approach is entirely satisfactory, inductive and deductive reasoning are very effective when used together as integral components of the scientific method. Basically, the scientific method involves induction of hypotheses based on observation, deduction of implications of the hypotheses, testing of the implications, and confirmation or disconfirmation of the hypotheses. More precisely, the **scientific method** is an orderly process entailing a number of steps: recognition and definition of a problem; formulation of hypotheses; collection of data; analysis of data; and statement of conclusions regarding confirmation or disconfirmation of the hypotheses. (A researcher forms a **hypothesis**—an explanation for the occurrence of certain behaviors, phenomena, or events—as a way of predicting the results of a research study.) These steps can be applied informally in the solution of such everyday problems as the most efficient route to take from home to work or school, the best time to go to the bank's drive-in window, or the best kind of computer to purchase. The more formal application of the scientific method to the solution of problems is what research is all about.

Compared to other sources of knowledge, such as experience, authority, inductive reasoning, and deductive reasoning, application of the scientific method is undoubtedly the most efficient and reliable.

:: APPLICATION OF THE SCIENTIFIC METHOD IN EDUCATION

Research is the formal, systematic application of the scientific method to the study of problems. **Educational research** is the formal, systematic application of the scientific method to the study of educational problems. Its goal follows from the goal of all science: namely, to explain, predict, and/or control educational phenomena. The major difference between educational research and some other types of scientific research is the nature of the phenomena studied—human behaviors. It can be quite difficult to explain, predict, and control situations involving human beings, by far the most complex of all organisms. There are so many factors, known and unknown, operating in any educational environment that it is extremely difficult to generalize or replicate findings. The kinds of rigid controls that can be established and maintained in a biochemistry laboratory, for instance, are virtually impossible in an educational setting. Observation also poses problems in educational research. Observers may be subjective in recording behaviors, and persons observed may behave atypically just because they are being watched; chemical reactions, on the other hand, tend to be oblivious to the fact that they are being observed! Precise measurement is another challenge for educational researchers. Most measurement must be indirect; there are no instruments comparable to a barometer for measuring intelligence, achievement, or attitude.

Perhaps it is precisely the difficulty and complexity of educational research that makes it such a challenging and exciting field. Despite a popular stereotype that depicts researchers as spectacled, stoop-shouldered, elderly gentlemen who endlessly add chemicals to test tubes, every day thousands of men and women of all ages, shapes, and sizes conduct educational research in a wide variety of settings. Every year many millions of dollars are spent in the quest for knowledge related to the teaching–learning process. Educational research has contributed many findings concerning principles of behavior, learning, and retention of knowledge. In addition, significant contributions have been made related to curriculum, instruction, instructional materials, and assessment techniques. Both the quantity and quality of research are increasing. This is partly because of better trained researchers. In fact, a great many graduate education programs, in such diverse areas as physical education, art education, and English education, require a course in research for all students.

The steps for conducting educational research should look familiar since they directly parallel those of the scientific method:

1. *Selection and definition of a problem.* A problem is a hypothesis or question of interest to education that can be tested or answered through the collection and analysis of data.
2. *Execution of research procedures.* The procedures reflect all the activities involved in collecting data related to the problem (e.g., how data are collected and from whom). To a great extent, the design of the study dictates the specific procedures followed.
3. *Analysis of data.* Data analysis usually involves application of one or more statistical techniques; data are analyzed in a way that permits the researcher to test the research hypothesis or answer the research question. For some studies, data analysis involves verbal synthesis of narrative data; these studies typically share resulting insights, generate hypotheses, or both.
4. *Drawing and stating conclusions.* The conclusions are based on the results of data analysis. They should be stated in terms of the original hypothesis or question.

Conclusions should indicate, for example, whether the research hypothesis was supported or not. For studies involving verbal synthesis, conclusions are much more tentative.

As you begin to do research in later chapters, you will be introduced to smaller steps and tasks that fall within each of these four general groupings.

Other Ways of Knowing

As mentioned earlier, we need to acknowledge that there are not only a variety of ways of understanding our world but also other ways of knowing and constructing meaning about our daily experiences—in both our personal and professional lives. For example, at times we rely on tradition: This is the way we've always done things; why change now? At other times we rely on the opinions of people viewed as experts: A leading expert in the field says that this is what we should do. Finally, our own personal experiences and our ability to generalize and make predictions based on these experiences provide us with much of our understanding. Each of these ways of knowing has disadvantages, however.

Relying on tradition inhibits change in one's perspective, thus stifling exploration and eliminating potentially new and fruitful understandings. As for depending solely on experts, even experts are not infallible (recall our story of Aristotle). Personal experience can produce idiosyncratic interpretations and even prejudices. Moreover, most of us have relatively limited experience with many of the issues we might seek to understand.

Rather than relying on tradition, experts, or personal experience, professionals in the field of education turn to the scientific method to find answers to the important questions that concern them. In this text we will present a variety of ways research can be conducted to increase our understanding of a particular phenomenon. Research studies can be classified in a number of ways. Two major approaches are to classify by purpose and to classify by method.

:: CLASSIFICATION OF RESEARCH BY PURPOSE

Research methods can be classified by the degree of direct applicability of the research to educational practice or settings. When purpose is the classification criterion, all research studies fall into one of five categories: basic research, applied research, evaluation research, research and development (R&D), or action research.

Basic and Applied Research

It is difficult to discuss basic and applied research separately, as they really are on a single continuum. In its purest form, **basic research** is research conducted solely for the purpose of developing or refining a theory. Theory development is a conceptual process that requires many research studies conducted over time. Basic researchers may not be concerned with the immediate utility of their findings, because it might be years before basic research leads to a practical educational application.

Applied research, as the name implies, is conducted for the purpose of applying, or testing, a theory to determine its usefulness in solving practical problems. A teacher who asks, "Will the theory of multiple intelligences help improve my students' learning?" is seeking an answer to a practical classroom question. The teacher is not interested in building a new theory or even generalizing beyond her classroom; instead, she is seeking specific helpful information about the impact of a "promising practice" (a teaching strategy based on the theory of multiple intelligences) on student learning.

Educators and researchers disagree about which end of the basic–applied research continuum should be emphasized. Many educational research studies would be located on the

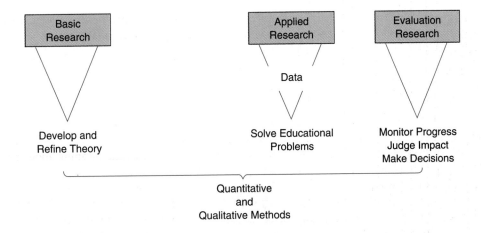

FIGURE 1.1

The educational
research continuum

applied end of the continuum; they are more focused on "what works best" than on finding out "why" it works as it does. However, both basic and applied research are necessary. Basic research provides the theory that produces the concepts for solving educational problems. Applied research provides data that can help support, guide, and revise the development of theory. Studies located in the middle of the basic–applied continuum seek to integrate both purposes. Figure 1.1 illustrates the educational research continuum.

Evaluation Research

At the far end of applied research is evaluation research, an important, widely used, and explicitly practical form of research. **Evaluation research** is the systematic process of collecting and analyzing data about the quality, effectiveness, merit, or value of programs, products, or practices. Unlike other forms of research that seek new knowledge or understanding, evaluation research focuses mainly on making decisions—decisions about those programs, products, and practices.

Some typical evaluation research questions are, "Is this special science program worth its costs?" "Is the new reading curriculum better than the old one?" "Did students reach the objectives of the diversity sensitivity program?" and "Is the new geography curriculum meeting the teachers' needs?" Note that the primary purpose of an evaluation is not to determine whether a program or practice is or is not worthwhile. The purpose is to make a decision based on the research findings. For example, a decision is made to continue a program or abandon it, to adopt a new curriculum or keep the current one.

Evaluations come in various forms and serve different functions.[1] An evaluation may be either formative or summative, for example. The function of **formative evaluation** is to form and improve a program or product under development so that weaknesses can be remedied during implementation. The function of **summative evaluation** is to sum up the overall quality or worth of a program or product at its completion.

Research and Development (R&D)

Research and development (R&D) is the process of researching consumer needs and then developing products specifically designed to fulfill those needs. The purpose of R&D efforts

---

[1] See *Evaluation Models: Viewpoints on Educational and Human Services Evaluation,* by D. Stufflebeam, G. Madaus, and T. Kellaghan, 2000, Norwell, MA: Kluwer Academic; *Program Evaluation,* by M. Gridler, 1996, Upper Saddle River, NJ: Prentice Hall; *The Program Evaluation Standards: How to Assess Evaluation of Education Programs* (2nd ed.), by Joint Committee on Standards for Educational Evaluation, 1994, Thousand Oaks, CA: Sage.

in education is not to formulate or test theory but to develop effective products for use in schools. Such products include teacher-training materials, learning materials, sets of behavioral objectives, media materials, and management systems. R&D efforts are generally quite extensive in terms of objectives, personnel, and time to completion. Products are developed according to detailed specifications. Once completed, products are field-tested and revised until a prespecified level of effectiveness is achieved. Although the R&D cycle is an expensive one, it does result in quality products designed to meet specific educational needs. School personnel who are the consumers of R&D endeavors may for the first time really see the value of educational research.

Action Research

Action research in education is any systematic inquiry conducted by teachers, principals, school counselors, or other stakeholders in the teaching–learning environment, to gather information about the ways in which their particular schools operate, the teachers teach, and the students learn. Its purpose is to provide teacher-researchers with a method for solving everyday problems in their own settings. Because the research is not characterized by the same kind of control evident in other categories of research, however, study results cannot be applied to other settings. The primary goal of action research is the solution of a given problem, not contribution to science. Whether the research is conducted in one classroom or in many classrooms, the teacher is very much a part of the process. The more research training the teachers involved have had, the more likely it is that the research will produce valid results.

The following are examples of action research:

- *A study to determine how mathematics problem-solving strategies are integrated into student learning and transferred to "real-life" settings outside the classroom.* An elementary teacher conducts the study in his own school.
- *The impact of a school grading policy change on student learning.* A team of high school teachers works collaboratively to determine how the elimination of number and letter grades (which have been replaced with narrative feedback) affects student learning and attitudes toward learning.

The value of action research is confined primarily to those conducting it. Despite this limitation, action research does represent a scientific approach to problem solving that is considerably better than change based on the alleged effectiveness of untried procedures, and infinitely better than no change at all. It is a means by which concerned school personnel can attempt to improve the educational process, at least within their environment. Of course, the value of action research to true scientific progress is limited. True progress requires the development of sound theories having implications for many classrooms, not just one or two. One sound theory that includes 10 principles of learning may eliminate the need for hundreds of would-be action research studies. Given the current status of educational theory, however, action research provides immediate answers to problems that cannot wait for theoretical solutions.

:: CLASSIFICATION OF RESEARCH BY METHOD

A research method comprises the overall strategy followed in collecting and analyzing data. Although there is some overlap, most research studies follow a readily identifiable strategy. The largest distinction we can make in classifying research by method is the distinction between quantitative and qualitative research. Quantitative and qualitative research, in turn, can be broken down into several distinct types or methods, each designed to answer a different kind of research question.

For much of the history of educational research, there were well-defined, widely accepted procedures for stating research topics, carrying out the research process, analyzing the resulting data, and verifying the quality of the study and its conclusions. For the most part, these research procedures were based on a quantitative approach to conducting and obtaining educational understandings.

Quantitative Research

Quantitative research is the collection and analysis of numerical data in order to explain, predict, and/or control phenomena of interest. But a quantitative research approach entails more than just the use of numerical data. Quantitative researchers must state the hypotheses to be examined and must specify the research procedures that will be used to carry out the study. They must also maintain control over contextual factors that might interfere with the data collected and use enough participants to provide statistically meaningful data. Quantitative researchers generally have little personal interaction with the participants they study, since most data are gathered using paper-and-pencil, noninteractive instruments.

Underlying quantitative research methods is the belief or assumption that we inhabit a relatively stable, uniform, and coherent world that we can measure, understand, and generalize about. This view, which the field of education adopted from the natural sciences, implies that the world and the laws that govern it are somewhat predictable and can be understood by scientific research and examination. In this quantitative perspective, claims about the world are not considered meaningful unless they can be verified through direct observation.

In the last 30 years, however, other, nonquantitative approaches to educational research have emerged and attracted many advocates.

Qualitative Research

Qualitative research is the collection, analysis, and interpretation of comprehensive narrative and visual (nonnumerical) data in order to gain insights into a particular phenomenon of interest. Qualitative research methods are based on different beliefs and purposes than quantitative research methods. For example, qualitative researchers do not accept the view of a stable, coherent, uniform world. They argue that all meaning is situated in a particular perspective or context, and because different people and groups often have different perspectives and contexts, there are many different meanings in the world, none of which is necessarily more valid or true than another.

Qualitative researchers often avoid stating hypotheses before data are collected. Qualitative research problems and methods tend to evolve as understanding of the research context and participants deepens. (Remember our discussion of inductive logic.) Qualitative researchers do not enter a research setting without any idea of what they intend to study, however. Rather, they commence their research with "foreshadowed problems."[2] Note the difference here—quantitative research tests a specific hypothesis; qualitative does not. It examines a particular phenomenon without a guiding statement about what might or might not be true about that phenomenon or its context. In qualitative research, context is not controlled or manipulated by the researcher. Additionally, the number of participants tends to be small, in part because of time-intensive data collection methods such as interviews and observations. Qualitative researchers analyze data inductively by categorizing and organizing the data into patterns that produce a descriptive, narrative synthesis. Finally, because of the

---

[2] *Argonauts of the Western Pacific* (p. 9), by B. Malinowski, 1922, London: Routledge.

TABLE 1.1	Overview of qualitative and quantitative research characteristics	
	Quantitative Research	**Qualitative Research**
Type of data collected	Numerical data	Nonnumerical narrative and visual data
Research problem	Hypothesis and research procedures stated before beginning the study	Research problems and methods evolve as understanding of topic deepens
Manipulation of context	Yes	No
Sample size	Larger	Smaller
Research procedures	Relies on statistical procedures	Relies on categorizing and organizing data into patterns to produce a descriptive, narrative synthesis
Participant interaction	Little interaction	Extensive interaction
Underlying belief	We live in a stable and predictable world that we can measure, understand, and generalize about.	Meaning is situated in a particular perspective or context that is different for people and groups; therefore, the world has many meanings.

Descriptive
Correlational
Causal - Comparative
Experimental   + Single Sub.

data collection methods and the effort to understand the participants' own perspective, researchers using qualitative methods often interact extensively and intimately with participants during the study. Table 1.1 provides an overview of quantitative and qualitative research characteristics.

Despite the differences between them, you should not consider quantitative and qualitative research to be oppositional. Taken together, they represent the full range of educational research methods. The terms *quantitative* and *qualitative* are used to conveniently differentiate one approach from the other. If you see yourself as a positivist, that does not mean you cannot use or learn from qualitative research methods. The same holds true for nonpositivist qualitative researchers. Depending on the nature of the question, topic, or problem to be investigated, one of these approaches will generally be more appropriate than the other. Note, however, that this does not preclude one approach borrowing from the other. In fact, both may be utilized in the same studies, as when the administration of a questionnaire (quantitative) is followed up by a small number of detailed interviews (qualitative) to obtain deeper explanations for the numerical data. Qualitative and quantitative approaches represent complementary components of the scientific method.

At this point, you should have a basic sense of the essence of the two approaches. However, to help you understand the field of educational research as a whole, let's look now at specific types of research that fall under the broad categories of quantitative and qualitative.

Quantitative Approaches

Quantitative research approaches are applied in order to describe current conditions, investigate relationships, and study cause–effect phenomena. Studies designed to describe current conditions are called *descriptive research*. Studies that investigate the relationship between two or more variables are referred to as *correlational* and *causal–comparative research*. Studies that provide information about cause–effect outcomes are called *experimental research*. Studies that focus on the behavior change an individual exhibits as a result of some intervention fall under the heading of *single-subject research.*

Descriptive Research

Descriptive research determines and reports the way things are; it involves collecting numerical data to test hypotheses or answer questions about the current status of the subject of study. One common type of descriptive research involves assessing the preferences, attitudes, practices, concerns, or interests of some group of people. A pre-election political poll and a survey about the public's perception of the quality of its local schools are examples. Descriptive research data are mainly collected through a questionnaire survey, an interview, or observation. Because descriptive research often involves a survey, it is also called *survey research.*

Although descriptive research sounds very simple, there is considerably more to it than just asking questions and reporting answers. Because researchers are often asking questions that have not been asked before, they usually have to develop their own measuring instrument for each specific descriptive study. Constructing questions for the intended respondents requires clarity, consistency, and tact. Other major challenges facing descriptive researchers are participants' failure to return questionnaires, to agree to be surveyed over the phone, and to attend scheduled interviews. If the response rate is low, valid, trustworthy conclusions cannot be drawn. For example, suppose you are doing a study to determine attitudes of principals toward research in their schools. You send a questionnaire to 100 principals and ask the question, "Do you usually cooperate if your school is asked to participate in a research study?" Forty principals respond and they all answer "Yes." Can you conclude that principals in general cooperate? No! Even though all those who responded said yes, those 60 principals who did not respond may never cooperate with researchers. After all, they didn't cooperate with you! Without more responses, it is not possible to generalize about how all principals feel about research in their schools.

The following are examples of questions that might be investigated in descriptive research studies:

- *How do second-grade teachers spend their teaching time?* Second-grade teachers would be asked to fill out a questionnaire, and results would probably be presented as percentages (e.g., teachers spent 50% of their time lecturing, 20% asking or answering questions, 20% in discussion, and 10% providing individual student help).
- *How will citizens of Yourtown vote in the next presidential election?* A sample of Yourtown citizens would complete a questionnaire or interview, and results would likely be presented as percentages (e.g., 70% said they will vote for Peter Pure, 20% named George Graft, and 10% are undecided).

Correlational Research

Correlational research involves collecting data to determine whether, and to what degree, a relationship exists between two or more quantifiable variables. A **variable** is a concept that can assume any one of a range of values; for example, intelligence, height, test score, and the like could be variables. The purpose of a correlational study may be to establish relationships or use existing relationships to make predictions. For example, a college admissions director might be interested in answering the question, "How do the SAT scores of high school seniors correspond to the students' first-semester college grades?" Is there a high relationship between students' SAT scores and their first-semester grades, suggesting that SAT scores might be useful in predicting how students will perform in their first year of college? Or is there a low correlation between the two variables, suggesting that SAT scores likely will not be useful?

When we talk about a **correlation**, we are referring to a quantitative measure of the degree of correspondence. The degree to which two variables are related is expressed as a **correlation coefficient**, which is a number between −1.00 and +1.00. Two variables that are not related will have a correlation coefficient near .00. Two variables that are highly correlated will have a correlation coefficient near −1.00 or +1.00. A number near +1.00 indicates a positive correlation: As one variable increases, the other variable also increases. A number near −1.00 indicates a negative correlation: As one variable increases, the other variable decreases. Since very few pairs of variables are perfectly correlated, predictions based on them are rarely perfectly positive or negative. At a minimum, correlation research requires information about at least two variables obtained from a single group of participants.

It is very important to note that the results of correlational studies do not suggest cause–effect relations between variables. Thus, a high correlation between, for example, self-concept and achievement does not imply that self-concept "causes" achievement or that achievement "causes" self-concept. The correlation indicates only that students with higher self-concepts tend to have higher levels of achievement and that students with lower self-concepts tend to have lower levels of achievement. We cannot conclude that one variable is the cause of the other.

The following are examples of correlational studies:

- *The relationship between intelligence and self-esteem.* Scores on an intelligence test and a measure of self-esteem would be acquired from each member of a given group. The two sets of scores would be correlated, and the resulting coefficient would indicate the degree of relationship.
- *Use of an algebra aptitude test to predict success in an algebra course.* Scores on the algebra aptitude test would be correlated with final exam scores in the algebra course. If the correlation were high, the aptitude test might be a good predictor of success in algebra.

Causal–Comparative Research

Causal–comparative research attempts to determine the cause, or reason, for existing differences in the behavior or status of groups of individuals. The cause, or **independent variable,** is a behavior or characteristic believed to influence some other behavior or characteristic. The change or difference in a behavior or characteristic that occurs as a result of the independent variable—that is, the effect—is known as the **dependent variable.** Put simply, causal–comparative research attempts to establish cause–effect relationships among groups.

The following are examples of causal–comparative studies. (Note that the word is *causal,* not *casual.*)

- *The effect of preschool attendance on social maturity at the end of the first grade.* The independent variable, or cause, is preschool attendance (students attending preschool and students not attending); the dependent variable, or effect, is social maturity at the end of the first grade. The researcher would identify a group of first graders who had attended preschool and a group who had not, gather data about their social maturity, and then compare the two groups.
- *The effect of having a working mother on school absenteeism.* The independent variable is the employment status of the mother (the mother works or does not work); the dependent variable is absenteeism, or number of days absent. The researcher would identify two groups (students who had working mothers and those who did not), gather information about their absenteeism, and compare the findings.

A weakness of causal–comparative studies is that, because the cause under study has already occurred, the researcher has no control over it. Suppose you wanted to investigate the effect of "heavy smoking" (the independent variable, or cause) on lung cancer (the dependent variable, or effect). You conduct a study comparing the frequency of lung cancer diagnoses in two groups, one consisting of long-time smokers and the other of nonsmokers. Because the groups are preexisting, you did not control the conditions under which the research participants smoked or did not smoke. Perhaps a large number of the long-time smokers, unknown to you, had lived in a smoggy, urban environment and that only a few of the nonsmokers did. If this were true, attempts to draw cause–effect conclusions in the study would be tenuous and tentative at best. Is it smoking that causes higher rates of lung cancer? Is it living in a smoggy, urban environment? Or is it some unknown combination of smoking and environment? A clear cause–effect link cannot be obtained.

Although causal–comparative research produces limited cause–effect information, it is an important form of educational research. True cause–effect relationships can be determined only through experimental research (discussed in the next section), in which the researcher maintains control of the independent variable; but in many cases, an experimental study would be inappropriate or unethical. The causal–comparative approach is chosen precisely because the independent variable either cannot be manipulated (e.g., as with gender, height, or year in school) or *should not* be manipulated (e.g., as with smoking or prenatal care). For example, to conduct the smoking study as an experiment, you would need to select a large number of participants who had never smoked and divide them into two groups, one directed to smoke heavily and one forbidden to smoke. Obviously, such a study would be unethical because of the potential harm to those forced to smoke. A causal–comparative study, which approximates cause–effect results without harming the participants, is the only reasonable approach. Like descriptive and correlational studies, however, causal–comparative research does not produce true experimental research outcomes.

Experimental Research

In **experimental research,** at least one independent variable is manipulated, other relevant variables are controlled, and the effect on one or more dependent variables is observed. True experimental research provides the strongest results of any of the quantitative research approaches because it provides clear evidence for linking variables. As a result, it also offers **generalizability,** or applicability of findings to settings and contexts different from the one in which they were obtained.

Unlike causal–comparative researchers, researchers conducting an experimental study can control the independent variable. They can select the participants for the study, divide the participants into two or more groups that have similar characteristics at the start of the research experiment, and then apply different treatments to the selected groups. They can also control the conditions in the research setting, such as when the treatments will be applied, by whom, for how long, and under what circumstances. Finally, the researchers can select tests or measurements to collect data about any changes in the research groups. It is the selection of participants from a single pool of participants and the ability to apply different treatments or programs to participants with similar initial characteristics that permit experimental researchers to draw conclusions about cause and effect. The essence of experimentation is control, although in many education settings it is not possible or feasible to meet the stringent control conditions required by experimental research.

The following are examples of experimental studies:

■ *The comparative effectiveness on computational skills of personalized instruction from a teacher versus computer instruction.* The independent variable is type of instruction (personalized teacher instruction versus computer instruction); the dependent variable is computational skills. A group of students who had never experienced either personalized teacher instruction or computer instruction would be selected and randomly divided into two groups, each taught by one of the methods. After a predetermined time, the students' computational skills would be measured and compared to determine which treatment, if either, produced higher skill levels.

■ *The effect of positive reinforcement on attitude toward school.* The independent variable is type of reinforcement (e.g., positive, negative, or no reinforcement); the dependent variable is attitude toward school. The researcher would randomly form three groups from a single large group of students. One group would receive positive reinforcement, another negative reinforcement, and the third no reinforcement. After the treatments were applied for a predetermined time, student attitudes toward school would be measured and compared for each of the three groups.

Single-Subject Research

Rather than compare the effects of different treatments (or treatment versus no treatment) on two or more groups of people, experimental researchers sometimes compare a single person's behavior before treatment to behavior exhibited during the course of the experiment. They may also study a number of individuals considered as one group. **Single-subject experimental designs** are those used to study the behavior change that an individual or group exhibits as a result of some intervention, or treatment. In these designs, the size of the **sample**—the individuals selected from a population for a study—is said to be one.

The following are examples of single-subject designs:

- *The effects of a training program with and without reinforced directed rehearsal as a correction procedure in teaching expressive sign language to nonverbal students with mental retardation.* Ten students with moderate to severe mental retardation were studied.[3]
- *The effects of instruction focused on assignment completion on the homework performance of students with learning disabilities.* A single-subject experiment design was used to determine how instruction in a comprehensive, independent assignment completion strategy impacted the quality of homework and the homework completion rate of eight students with learning disabilities.[4]

Qualitative Approaches

Qualitative research seeks to probe deeply into the research setting to obtain in-depth understandings about the way things are, why they are that way, and how the participants in the context perceive them. To achieve the detailed understandings they seek, qualitative researchers must undertake sustained in-depth, in-context research that allows them to uncover subtle, less overt, personal understandings.

Two qualitative approaches are narrative research and ethnographic research.

Narrative Research

Narrative research is the study of how different humans experience the world around them; it involves a methodology that allows people to tell the stories of their "storied lives."[5] The researcher typically focuses on a single person and gathers data by collecting stories about the person's life. The researcher and participant then construct a narrative (written account) about the individual's experiences and the meanings the individual attributes to the experiences. Because of the collaborative nature of narrative research, it is important for the researcher and participant to establish a trusting and respectful relationship. Another way to think of narrative research is that the narrative is the story of the phenomenon being investigated, and narrative

---

[3] "Effects of Reinforced Directed Rehearsal on Expressive Sign Language Learning by Persons With Mental Retardation," by A. J. Dalrymple and M. A. Feldman, 1992, *Journal of Behavioral Education, 2*(1), pp. 1–16.
[4] "Effects of Instruction in an Assignment Completion Strategy on the Homework Performance of Students With Learning Disabilities in General Education Classes," by C. A. Hughes, K. L. Ruhl, J. B. Schumaker, and D. D. Deshler, 2002, *Learning Disabilities Research and Practice, 17*(1), pp. 1–18.
[5] "Stories of Experience and Narrative Inquiry," by F. M. Connelly and D. J. Clandinin, 1990, *Educational Research, 19*(5), p. 2.

is also the method of inquiry being used by the researcher.[6] One of the goals of narrative research in education is to increase understanding of central issues related to teaching and learning through the telling, and retelling, of teachers' stories.

The following is an example of the narrative research approach:

> Kristy, an assistant professor of education, is frustrated by what she perceives as the "gender-biased distribution of resources" within the School of Education (SOE). Kristy shares her story with Winston, a colleague and researcher. In the course of their lengthy (tape-recorded) conversations, Kristy describes in great detail her view that the SOE dean, George, is allocating more resources for technology upgrades, curriculum materials, and conference travel to her male colleagues. Kristy also shares with Winston her detailed journals, which capture her experiences with George and other faculty members in interactions dealing with the allocation of resources. In addition, Winston collects artifacts—including minutes of faculty meetings, technology orders, and lists of curriculum materials ordered for the university's library—that relate to resource allocation.
>
> After collecting all of the data that will influence the "story," Winston reviews the information, identifies important elements (themes), and retells Kristy's story in a narrative form. After constructing the story with attention given to "time, place, plot and scene," he shares the story with Kristy, who collaborates on establishing its accuracy. In his interpretation of Kristy's unique story of gender bias, Winston describes themes related to power and influence in a hierarchical school of education and the struggles faced by beginning professors to establish their career paths in a culture that is remarkably resistant to change.

Ethnographic Research

Ethnographic research, or *ethnography,* is the study of the cultural patterns and perspectives of participants in their natural setting. Ethnography focuses on a particular site or sites that provide the researcher with a context in which to study both the setting and the participants who inhabit it. An ethnographic setting can be defined as anything from a bowling alley to a neighborhood, from a nomadic group's traveling range to an elementary principal's office. The participants are observed as they take part in naturally occurring activities within the setting.

The ethnographic researcher avoids making interpretations and drawing conclusions too early in the study. Instead, the researcher enters the setting slowly, learning to become accepted by the participants and gaining rapport with them. Then, over time, the researcher collects data in waves, making initial observations and interpretations about the context and participants, then collecting and examining more data in a second wave of refining the initial interpretation, then collecting another wave of data to further refine observations and interpretation, and so on, until the researcher has obtained a deep understanding of both the context and its participants' roles in it. Lengthy engagement in the setting is a key facet of ethnographic research. The researcher organizes the collected data and undertakes a cultural interpretation of the data. The result of the ethnographic study is a holistic description and cultural interpretation that represents the participants' everyday activities, values, and events. The study is written up and presented as a narrative, which, like the study from which it was produced, may also be referred to as an **ethnography.**

The following is an example of an ethnographic approach:

- *Study of the Hispanic student culture in an urban community college.* After selecting a general research question and a research site in a community college with Hispanic students, the researcher would first gain entry to the chosen college and establish rapport with the

---

[6] "Stories," Connelly and Clandinin, pp. 2–14.

ー

participants of the study. This might be a lengthy process, depending on the characteristics of the researcher (e.g., non-Hispanic vs. Hispanic; Spanish speaking vs. non-Spanish speaking). As is common in qualitative approaches, the researcher would simultaneously collect and interpret data to help focus the general research question initially posed.

Throughout data collection the researcher would identify recurrent themes, integrate them into existing categories, and add new categories as new themes or topics arose. The study's success would rely heavily on the researcher's skills in analyzing and synthesizing the qualitative data into coherent and meaningful descriptions. The research report would include a holistic description of the culture, the common understandings and beliefs shared by participants, how these relate to life in the culture, and how the findings compare to literature already published about similar groups. In a sense, the successful researcher would be providing guidelines that would enable someone not in the culture to know how to think and behave in the culture.

:: GUIDELINES FOR CLASSIFICATION

Determining which type of research is appropriate for a given study depends on the way the research problem is defined. The same general problem can often be investigated through several different types of research. For example, suppose you wanted to do a study in the general area of anxiety and achievement. You might conduct any one of the following studies:

- A survey of teachers to determine how and to what degree they believe anxiety affects achievement (descriptive)
- A study to determine the relationship between scores on an anxiety scale and scores on an achievement measure (correlational)
- A study to compare the achievement of a group of students with high anxiety to that of students with low anxiety (causal–comparative)
- A study to compare the achievement of two groups, one group taught in an anxiety-producing environment and another group taught in an anxiety-reducing enviroment (experimental)
- A study of six parents on the cultural patterns and perspectives related to how parents view the link between anxiety and achievement (ethnographic research)
- A study of a first-year teacher in a rural elementary school who struggles with establishing his teaching credibility on a teaching faculty dominated by female teachers and a female principal (narrative research)

Note that a research method should be chosen after, not before, the topic or question to be studied. It is the problem that determines which approach is appropriate, and as you can see in the preceding examples, clarifying the problem will help you narrow your choices.

Classifying a study by type will also help you when you review and evaluate others' research. If you identify a study as correlational, for instance, you'll be reminded to avoid making conclusions about cause and effect. Clearly, the more information you have about a study, the easier it'll be to categorize it. If you have only the title, you might determine the type of study from words such as *survey, comparison, relationship, historical, descriptive, effect,* and *qualitative.* If you have a description of the research strategy, you'll often be able to classify the study based on features such as the number of participants, qualitative or quantitative data, and statistical (correlational, descriptive, comparative) or nonstatistical (interpretive, participants' viewpoint) analysis.

The following examples should further clarify the differences among the various types of research. Can you label the type of research for each example? Can you state one characteristic that defines the type?

- *Teachers' attitudes toward unions.* The study is determining the current attitudes of teachers. Data are collected through use of a questionnaire or an interview.
- *The personal and educational interactions in a group of teachers developing social studies standards for a high school curriculum.* Teachers' interactions during the development of the standards are studied over time.
- *The relationship of Graduate Record Examination (GRE) scores to graduate student performance.* Participants' GRE scores are compared to their graduate school academic records (e.g., their grade point averages).
- *Characteristics of the drama–music clique in a suburban high school.* The researcher interviews and observes members and nonmembers of the clique to gather information about the beliefs and activities of those in the drama–music group. Participants are interviewed a number of times over the school year, and their behavior is periodically observed over the same time.

:: LIMITATIONS OF THE SCIENTIFIC METHOD

The steps in the scientific method guide researchers in planning, conducting, and interpreting research studies. However, it is important to recognize some of the limitations of such a "disciplined inquiry" approach. For example, it cannot provide answers to questions that seek to determine what should be done. A question such as "Should we adopt a new biology textbook or stay with the current one?" is not answerable by research studies. Collecting data will not resolve the question "Should we legalize euthanasia?" because the answer is also influenced by personal philosophy, values, and ethics. Simply put, *Should* questions are not researchable.

Secondly, research studies can never capture the full richness of the individuals and sites that they study. Although some research approaches lead to deeper understanding of the research context than others, no approach provides full comprehension of a site and its inhabitants. No matter how many variables one studies or how long one is immersed in a research context, there always will be other variables and aspects of context that were not examined. Thus, all research gives us a simplified version of reality, an abstraction from the whole.

Third, there are limits to our research technologies. Our data collection instruments and the available theories are primitive in comparison to the instruments and theories of, say, medicine. Our measuring instruments always have some degree of error. The variables we study are often proxies for the real behavior we seek to examine. For example, we use a multiple-choice test to assess a person's values and a 20-minute interview to decide whether to hire a teacher.

Finally, educational research is carried out with the cooperation of participants who agree to provide researchers with data. Because researchers deal with human beings, they must consider a number of ethical concerns and responsibilities to the participants. For example, they must shelter participants from real or potential harm. They must inform participants about the nature of the planned research and address the expectations of the participants.

All of these limitations will be addressed in later sections of this book. For now, bear in mind both the advantages and limitations of adopting the scientific method as your approach to educational research.

This chapter has provided a general introduction to fundamental aspects of scientific method. It provided examples of both quantitative and qualitative approaches and gave an overview of educational research strategies and methods. If the number of new terms and definitions seems overwhelming, you should know that most of these will be revisited and reviewed in succeeding chapters. In those chapters we will present more specific and detailed features needed to carry out, understand, and conduct useful educational research.

SUMMARY

The Scientific Method

1. The goal of all scientific endeavors is to explain, predict, and/or control phenomena.
2. Compared to other sources of knowledge, such as experience, authority, inductive reasoning, and deductive reasoning, application of the scientific method is undoubtedly the most efficient and reliable.
3. The scientific method is an orderly process that entails recognition and definition of a problem, formulation of hypotheses, collection of data, and statement of conclusions regarding confirmation or disconfirmation of the hypotheses.

Application of the Scientific Method in Education

4. Research is the formal, systematic application of the scientific method to the study of problems; educational research is the formal, systematic application of the scientific method to the study of educational problems.
5. The major difference between educational research and some other types of scientific research is the nature of the phenomena studied. It can be quite difficult to explain, predict, and control situations involving human beings, by far the most complex of all organisms.
6. The research process is made up of four main steps:
   a. Selection and definition of a problem
   b. Execution of research procedures
   c. Analysis of data
   d. Drawing and stating conclusions

Classification of Research by Purpose

Basic and Applied Research

7. Basic research is conducted to develop or refine theory, not to solve immediate practical problems. Applied research is conducted to find solutions to current practical problems.

Evaluation Research

8. The purpose of evaluation research is to help decision making about educational programs and practices.

Research and Development (R&D)

9. The major purpose of R&D efforts is not to formulate or test theory but to develop effective products for use in schools.

Action Research

10. The purpose of action research is to provide teacher researchers with a method for solving everyday problems in their own settings.

Classification of Research by Method

11. Although there is some overlap, most research studies follow a readily identifiable approach.
12. The largest distinction we can make in classifying research by method is the distinction between quantitative and qualitative research.

Quantitative Research

13. Quantitative research is the collection and analysis of numerical data in order to explain, predict, and/or control phenomena of interest.
14. Key features of quantitative research are hypotheses that predict the results of the research before the study begins; control of contextual factors that might influence the study; collection of data from sufficient samples of participants; and use of numerical, statistical approaches to analyze the collected data.
15. The quantitative approach views the world as relatively stable, uniform, and coherent.

Qualitative Research

16. Qualitative research is the collection, analysis, and interpretation of comprehensive narrative and visual (nonnumerical) data in order to gain insights into a particular phenomenon of interest.
17. Key features of qualitative research include defining the problem, but not necessarily at the start of the study; studying contextual factors in the participants' settings; collecting data from a small number of purposely selected participants; and using nonnumerical, interpretive approaches to provide narrative descriptions of the participants and their contexts.

18. An important belief that underlies qualitative research is that the world is neither stable, coherent, nor uniform, and therefore, there are many "truths."

Quantitative Approaches

19. Quantitative research approaches are intended to describe current conditions, investigate relationships, and study cause–effect phenomena.
20. Descriptive research involves collecting numerical data to answer questions about the current status of the participants of the study.
21. Correlational research examines the degree of relationship that exists between two or more variables. A variable is a measure—such as age, IQ, or height—that can take on different values.
22. The degree of relationship is measured by a correlation coefficient. If two variables are highly related, it does not mean that one is the cause of the other; there may be a third factor that "causes" both the related variables.
23. Causal–comparative research seeks to investigate relations between two or more different programs, methods, or groups. The activity thought to make a difference (the program, method, or group) is called the *independent variable, causal factor,* or *treatment.* The effect is called the *dependent variable.*
24. In most causal–comparative research studies, the researcher does not have control over the independent variable because it already has occurred or cannot be manipulated.
25. Causal–comparative research is useful in those circumstances when it is impossible or unethical to manipulate the independent variable.
26. True experimental research investigates causal relationships among variables.
27. The experimental researcher controls the selection of participants by choosing them from a single pool and assigning them at random to different causal treatments. The researcher also controls contextual variables that might interfere with the study.
28. Because participants are randomly selected and assigned into different treatments, experimental

research permits researchers to make true cause–effect statements.

29. Single-subject experimental designs are a type of experimental research that can be applied when the sample size is one. Used to study the behavior change an individual or group exhibits as a result of some intervention, or treatment.

Qualitative Approaches

30. Qualitative approaches include ethnographic research and narrative research. The focus of these methods is on deep description of aspects of people's everyday perspectives and context.
31. Narrative research is the study of how different humans experience the world. The researcher typically focuses on a single person and gathers data through the collection of stories.
32. Ethnographic research is the study of the cultural patterns and perspectives of participants in their natural setting. Ethnography focuses on a particular site or sites that provide the researcher with a context in which to study both the setting and the participants who inhabit the setting.

Guidelines for Classification

33. The type of research method needed for a given study depends on the problem to be studied. The same general problem can be investigated using many types of research. Knowing the type of research applied helps one identify the important aspects to examine in evaluating the study.

Limitations of the Scientific Method

34. Four main factors put limitations on the use of a scientific and disciplined inquiry approach: inability to answer *Should* questions, inability to capture the full richness of the research site and participants' complexity, limitations of measuring instruments, and the need to address participants' ethical needs and responsibilities.

Now go to the Companion Website at **www.prenhall.com/gay** to assess your understanding of chapter content with Practice Quiz, apply comprehension in Applying What You Know, broaden your knowledge about research in Web Links, and expand your research skills in Evaluating Articles, Analyzing Qualitative Data, Analyzing Quantitative Data, and Research Tools and Tips.

PERFORMANCE CRITERIA

TASK 1

Tasks 1a and 1b

Reprints of two published research reports appear on the following pages (Task 1a Quantitative Example and Task 1b Qualitative Example).

Read the reports and then state the following for each study:

- Topic studied
- Procedures used to gather data
- Method of data analysis
- Major conclusion

One sentence should be sufficient to describe the topic. Six sentences or less will adequately describe the major procedures of most studies. For the procedures used to gather data, briefly describe the participants, instrument(s), and major steps. As with the topic, one or two sentences will usually be sufficient to state the method of data analysis. You are expected only to identify the analysis, not explain it. The major conclusion that you identify and state (one or two sentences should be sufficient) should directly relate to the original topic. Statements like "more research is needed in this area" do not represent major conclusions.

Suggested responses to these tasks appear in Appendix C of this text. If your responses differ greatly from those suggested, study the reports again to see why you were in error.

Task 1c

Brief descriptions of six research studies follow these instructions. Read each description and decide whether the study represents an action, descriptive, correlational, causal–comparative, experimental, ethnographic, or narrative research approach. State the research approach for each topic statement, and indicate why you selected that approach. Your reasons should be related to characteristics that are unique to the type of research you have selected.

1. This study involved a group of teachers investigating ways to determine strategies to engage their students in math.
2. This study administered a questionnaire to determine how social studies teachers felt about teaching world history to fifth graders.
3. This study was conducted to determine whether the Acme Interest Test provided similar results to the Acne Interest Test.
4. This study compared the achievement in reading of fifth graders from single-parent families and those from two-parent families.
5. This study divided fifth-grade students in a school into two groups at random and compared the results of two methods of conflict resolution on students' aggressive behavior.
6. This study examined the culture of recent Armenian emigrants in their new setting.

Suggested responses appear in Appendix C. Additional examples for the tasks are included in the *Student Study Guide* that accompanies this text.

MOTIVATIONAL EFFECTS ON TEST SCORES
OF ELEMENTARY STUDENTS

STEVEN M. BROWN
Northeastern Illinois University

HERBERT J. WALBERG
University of Illinois at Chicago

ABSTRACT A total of 406 heterogeneously grouped students in Grades 3, 4, 6, 7, and 8 in three K through 8 Chicago public schools were assigned randomly to two conditions, ordinary standardized-test instructions (control) and special instructions, to do as well as possible for themselves, their parents, and their teachers (experimental). On average, students given special instructions did significantly better ($p < .01$) than the control students did on the criterion measure, the mathematics section of the commonly used Iowa Test of Basic Skills. The three schools differed significantly in achievement ($p < .05$), but girls and boys and grade levels did not differ measurably. The motivational effect was constant across grade levels and boys and girls, but differed significantly ($p < .05$) across schools. The average effect was moderately large, .303 standard deviations, which implies that the special instructions raise the typical student's scores from the 50th to the 62nd percentile.

Parents, educators, business people, politicians, and the general public are greatly concerned about U.S. students' poor performance on international comparisons of achievement. Policy makers are planning additional international, state, district, and school comparisons to measure progress in solving the national crisis. Some members of those same groups have also grown concerned about the effects of students' high or low motivational states on how well they score on tests.

One commonly expressed apprehension is that some students worry unduly about tests and suffer debilitating anxiety (Hill, 1980). Another concern is that too much testing causes students to care little about how well they do, especially on standardized tests that have no bearing on their grades. Either case might lead to poorer scores than students would attain under ideal motivational states; such effects might explain, in part, the poor performance of U.S. students relative to those in other countries or in relation to what may be required for college and vocational success.

Experts and practicing educators have expressed a variety of conflicting opinions about motivational effects on learning and test scores (Association for Supervision and Curriculum Development, 1991, p. 7). Given the importance of testing policies, there is surprisingly little research on the topic. The purpose of the present study is to determine the effect of experimentally manipulated motivational conditions on elementary students' mathematical scores.

As conceived in this study, the term *motivation* refers to the commonsense meaning of the term, that is, students' propensity to engage in full, serious, and sustained effort on academic tests. As it has been measured in many previous studies, motivation refers to students' reported efforts to succeed or to excel on academic tasks. It is often associated with self-concept or self-regard in a successful student or test taker. A quantitative synthesis of the correlational studies of motivation and school learning showed that nearly all correlations were positive and averaged about .30 (Uguroglu & Walberg, 1979).

Previous Research

The National Assessment Governing Board (NAGB, 1990) recently characterized the National Assessment of Educational Progress (NAEP) as follows:

> . . . as a survey exam which by law cannot be reported for individual students and schools. NAEP may not be taken seriously enough by students to enlist their best efforts. Because it is given with no incentives for good performance and no opportunity for prior study, NAEP may understate achievement (NAGB, p. 17).

To investigate such questions, NAEP is adding items to ask students how hard they tried in responding to future achievement tests.

Motivation questions can be raised about nearly all standardized commercial tests, as well as state-constructed achievement tests. The content of those tests is often unrelated to specific topics that students have been recently studying; and their performance on such tests ordinarily does not affect their grades, college, or job prospects. Many students know they will not see how well they have done.

Some students admit deficient motivation, but surveys show reasonably favorable attitudes toward tests by most students. Paris, Lawton, and Turner (1991), for example, surveyed 250 students in Grades 4, 7, and 10 about the Michigan Educational Assessment Program. They found that most students reported that they tried hard, thought they did well, felt the test was not difficult or confusing, and saw little or no cheating. However, Karmos and Karmos's (1984) survey of 360 sixth- through ninth-grade student attitudes toward tests showed that 47% thought they were a waste of time, 22% saw no good reason to try to do well, and 21% did not try very hard.

Kellaghan, Madaus, and Arisian (1982) found various small fractions of a sixth-grade Irish sample disaffected by standardized tests, even though they are uncommon in Ireland. When asked

Address correspondence to Steven M. Brown, 924 South Austin, Apt. 2, Oak Park, IL 60304.

about their experience with standardized tests, 29% reported feeling nervous; 19%, unconfident; 16%, bored; and 15% uninterested. Twenty-nine percent reported that they did not care whether they took the tests, and 16% said they did not enjoy the experience.

Paris, Lawton, and Turner (1991) speculated that standardized tests may lead both bright and dull students to do poorly: Bright students may feel heightened parental, peer, or self-imposed expectations to do well on tests, which makes them anxious. Slower, disadvantaged students may do poorly, then rationalize that school and tests are unimportant and, consequently, expend less effort preparing for and completing tests. Either case might lead to a self-reinforcing spiral of decelerating achievement.

Surveys, however, cannot establish causality. Poor motivation may cause poor achievement, or vice versa, or both may be caused by other factors such as deficiencies in ability, parental support of academic work, or teaching. To show an independent effect of motivation on achievement requires an experiment, that is, a randomized assignment of students to conditions of eliciting different degrees of motivation. Such was the purpose of our study.

METHOD

Sample

The subjects for the study included students from three K through 8 public schools in Chicago. The student populations of the schools are generally lower-middle, working class, mostly Hispanic and African-American. Two normal heterogeneous classes within the schools were sampled from Grades 3, 4, 6, 7, and 8; because of exigencies, we did not sample Grade 5 classes.

Instrument

We chose Form 7 of the Mathematics Concepts subtest of the Iowa Basic Skills (ITBS) 1978 edition, Levels 9–14, because it is a commonly used, highly reliable test. An earlier-than-contemporary edition was used so it would not interfere with current testing programs. In a review of the 1978 ITBS, Nitko (1985) judged that the reliability of its subtests is generally higher than .85 and that it contains content generally representative of school curriculum in Grades 3 though 9. "The ITBS," he concluded, "is an excellent basic skills battery measuring global skills that are likely to be highly related to the long-term goals of elementary schools" (p. 723).

Procedure

Pairs of classes at each grade level from each school were randomly chosen to participate. Classes were selected for experimental and control conditions by a flip of a coin.

The first author (Brown) met with all participating teachers in each school to explain the instructions from the ITBS test manual (see Appendix A). Then, the experimental teachers were retained for the following further instructions:

We are conducting a research study to determine the effects of telling students that the test they are going to take is very impor-

tant. It is extremely important that you read the brief script I have for you today EXACTLY as it is written to your students.

The following script was provided:

It is really important that you do as WELL as you can on this test. The test score you receive will let others see just how well I am doing in teaching you math this year.

Your scores will be compared to students in other grades here at this school, as well as to those in other schools in Chicago.

That is why it is extremely important to do the VERY BEST that you can. Do it for YOURSELF, YOUR PARENTS, and ME.

(Now read the instructions for the test.)

Following the administration of the test, teachers and the first author asked students for their reactions to the script that was read to them.

Analysis

An analysis of variance was run to test the effects of the experimental and normal conditions; the differences among the three schools and five grades; between boys and girls; and the interactions among the factors.

RESULTS

The analysis of variance showed a highly significant effect of experimental condition ($F = 10.59$, $p < .01$), a significant effect of school ($F = 3.35$, $p < .05$), and an interaction between condition and school ($F = 5.01$, $p < .05$). No other effects, including grade level, were significant. The means and standard deviations of selected factors are shown in Table 1.

The mean normal curve equivalent test score of the 214 students in the experimental group was 41.37 ($SD = 15.41$), and the mean of the control group was 36.25 ($SD = 16.89$). The motiva-

Table 1.
Normal Curve Equivalent Means and Standard Deviations

Grade	Condition	M	SD
3	Control	32.77	19.57
	Experimental	42.55*	16.59
4	Control	33.07	13.93
	Experimental	39.42*	13.12
6	Control	40.84	17.77
	Experimental	39.64	14.66
7	Control	43.21	16.07
	Experimental	41.21	16.48
8	Control	31.12	14.06
	Experimental	44.66**	15.94

*$p < .01$.
**$p < .001$.

tional effect is moderately large, .303 standard deviations, which implies that the special instructions raised the typical student's scores from the 50th to the 62nd percentile. The special instructions are comparable to the effects of better (though not the best) instructional practices over conventional classroom instruction (Walberg, 1986). If American students' average achievement in mathematics and science could be raised that much, it would be more comparable to that of students in other economically advanced countries.

The motivational effect was the same for boys and girls and constant across grade levels, but it differed among schools. Figure 1 shows a very large effect at School A, a large effect at School C, and the control group somewhat higher than the experimental group at School B.

Only 62 students (15% of the total sample) were tested at School B, which may account for the lack of effect in this school. At any rate, although the overall effect is moderately large and constant across grade levels and for boys and girls, the size of the effect varies from school to school. Such differences may depend on test-taking attitudes of teachers and students in the schools, motivational and cultural differences in the student populations, variations in conditions of administration, and other factors.

Several comments made by students and teachers during debriefing sessions illuminate the statistical findings. Student Comments 1, 2, and 3 illustrate students' motivation to do well to please their parents and teachers. Teacher Comments 1 and 2 also confirm the reasons for the effect. The last student and teacher comments, however, illustrate motivational states and conditions that diminish or vitiate the effect. When students are unthoughtful or when teachers keep constant pressures on for testing, special instructions may have little effect.

CONCLUSION

The results show that motivation can make a substantial difference in test scores. Students asked to try especially hard did considerably better than those who were given the usual standardized test instructions. The special conditions raised the typical student's score .303 standard deviation units, corresponding to a 12 percentile-point gain from the 50th to the 62nd percentile. Although the effect was the same for boys and girls and for students in different grade levels, it varied in magnitude among the three schools.

The results suggest that standardized commercial and state-constructed tests that have no bearing on students' grades may be underestimating U.S. students' real knowledge, understanding, skills, and other aspects of achievement. To the extent that motivation varies from school to school, moreover, achievement levels of some schools are considerably more underestimated than in others. Such motivational differences would tend to diminish the validity of comparisons of schools and districts.

We would be heartened to conclude that U.S. students' poor performance on achievement relative to students in other countries is attributable to the test-motivation effect. That conclusion is overly optimistic, however, because the effect may also operate

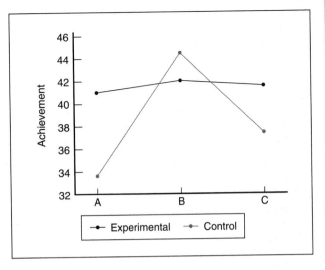

FIGURE 1. Means by condition and school

to a greater or lesser extent in other countries. Further research is obviously in order.

The motivation effect might be reduced in several ways. Highly motivating instructions could be given to all students. The content of school lessons and standardized tests could be brought into closer correspondence, making the tests more plausible to students, and perhaps justifying their use in grading. Some students, moreover, may be unmotivated because they never see the results. Providing timely, specific, and useful feedback to students, parents, and teachers on how well they have done might lead students to try harder.

APPENDIX A

Directions for Administering the Mathematics Concepts Subtest of the Iowa Test of Basic Skills (1979)

Now we are ready for the first mathematics test. Open your test booklets to page 73. (Pause) Find the section of your answer sheet for Test M-1: Mathematics Concepts. (Pause) Read the directions on page 73 silently while I read them aloud.

This is a test of how well you understand the number system and the terms and operations used in mathematics. Four answers are given for each exercise, but only one of the answers is right. You are to choose the one answer that you think is better than the others. Then, on the answer sheet, find the row of the answer numbered the same as the exercise. Fill in the answer space for the best answer.

Do not make any marks on the test booklet. Use your scratch paper for figuring. You will have 25 minutes for this test. If you finish early, recheck your work. Don't look at the other tests in the booklet. If you have questions, raise your hand, and I will help you after the others have begun. Now find your place to begin. (Pause)

Does everyone have the correct place? (Pause) Ready, BEGIN.

APPENDIX B

Selected Anecdotal Comments
Students

1. Third-Grade Girl: My teacher always tells us to get good scores on tests. I wanted to make her happy and my parents happy.
2. Fourth-Grade Boy: I think I did well. My teacher works hard with us. I also want my school to be the best.
3. Eighth-Grade Boy: I wanted to do really well for my teacher. She does a great job and I didn't want to let her down.
4. Seventh-Grade Girl: I just took the test, and really didn't think much about the instructions she gave.

Teachers

1. I don't know what the results will show but my gut feeling is that students in the experimental groups will do better. I think it's probably because of motivational reasons.
2. The script gives me a feeling of *family*. I think if we told students just how much we want them to do well, and that it will not only benefit themselves but the whole school, they will probably do better.
3. I think all the students (control and experimental) will probably do equally well, because we always stress how important the tests are.

REFERENCES

Association for Supervision and Curriculum Development (1991). *Update, 33*(1), 1–8.

Hill, K. T. (1980). Motivation, evaluation, and testing policy. In L. J. Fyans, Jr. (Ed.), *Achievement motivation: Recent trends in theory and research.* New York, NY: Plenum Press.

Iowa Test of Basic Skills normal curve equivalent norms (1978). Boston, MA: Houghton Mifflin.

Karmos, A. H., & Karmos, J. S. (1984, July). Attitudes toward standardized achievement tests and their relation to achievement test performance. *Measurement and Evaluation in Counseling and Development, 12,* 56–66.

Kelleghan, T., Madaus, G. F., & Arisian, P. M. (1982). *The effects of standardized testing.* Boston, MA: Kluwer-Nijhoff.

National Assessment Governing Board (1991). Issues for the 1994–1996 NAEP. Washington, DC: Author.

Nitco, A. J. (1985). Review of the Iowa Test of Basic Skills. In James V. Mitchell (Ed.), *The ninth mental measurements yearbook.* Lincoln, NE: Buros Institute.

Paris, S. G., Lawton, T. A., & Turner, J. C. (1991). Reforming achievement testing to promote students' learning. In C. Collins & Mangieri (Eds.), *Learning in and out of school.* Hillsdale, NJ: Lawrence Erlbaum Associates.

Uguroglu, M. E., & Walberg, H. J. (1979). Motivation and achievement: A quantitative synthesis. *American Educational Research Journal, 16,* 375–390.

Walberg, H. J. (1986). Synthesis of research on teaching. In M. C. Wittrock (Ed.), *Handbook of research on teaching.* New York, NY: Macmillan.

Source: The Journal of Educational Research, 86 *(3), pp.133–136, 1993. Reprinted with the permission of the Helen Dwight Reid Educational Foundation. Published by Heldref Publications, 1319 Eighteenth St., NW, Washington, DC 20036-1802. Copyright © 1993.*

A REALLY GOOD ART TEACHER WOULD BE LIKE YOU, MRS. C.: A QUALITATIVE STUDY OF A TEACHER AND HER ARTISTICALLY GIFTED MIDDLE SCHOOL STUDENTS

POLLY WOLFE

Ball State University

ABSTRACT In this paper, I examine the experiences of a teacher and her artistically gifted middle school students over the course of a school year in an attempt to add to the definition of effective teaching for that population. Identified as artistically gifted through a formal, multimethod process, the students experienced a five-phase curriculum rhythm (a construct devised to describe the chronology of the class content). The phases—image flood, reflection, art work, critique, and exhibition—enabled the veteran teacher to "translate" meaning in both the student world and the adult art world. The translation process influenced students' self-identification as artists and their abilities to reflect and to be more articulate about their art. Possible ramifications of this study include further exploration of the themes of curriculum rhythm and translation as components of art teacher effectiveness with artistically gifted and other student populations.

A really good art teacher would be like you, Mrs. C. She would do neat projects, like this mural. And we would learn all that stuff, like mixing colors. She would be funny, too. Oh yea, she'd let us drink cokes during class, too. (Kelly, transcript; December 9, 1993)[1]

This quote by a seventh-grade participant in an artistically gifted program presents his simplified view of an area infrequently addressed in research: definitions of excellent or effective teaching relevant to the needs of artistically gifted students. Within his statement, Kelly addresses both pedagogical actions (high-interest projects, technical instruction) and personal attributes (flexibility and a sense of humor), which are mentioned in the literature as central to art teacher effectiveness (Clark & Zimmerman, 1995; Saunders, 1989).

In education literature, extensive effort has been expended to describe or define excellence and/or effectiveness (Amidon & Flanders, 1967). Long lists of qualities are proffered as characteristics of effective teachers (Langlois & Zales, 1991). In art education, studies disclose teacher traits such as artistic competence (Bradley, 1984; Hathaway, 1980; Saunders, 1989; Zimmerman, 1991, 1992), and the concomitant ability to share that capability with students as important to art teacher effectiveness. Assuming a variety of roles, valuing art education, having organizational and evaluative skills, and being aware of student developmental and emotional needs exemplify the types of skills, knowledge, and behaviors that excellent art teachers exhibit (Capet, 1986; May, 1993; Saunders, 1989; Stokrocki, 1991; Thomas, 1992).

With the exception of two studies (Zimmerman, 1991, 1992), Clark and Zimmerman's (1984) statement that the "question of ideal teacher characteristics for students with superior abilities in the arts is virtually unexplored and unanswered at this time" (p. 94), still holds true. In learning more about effectiveness, there is a need to go beyond the "armchair lists" (Clark & Zimmerman, 1984) of teacher behaviors and characteristics. For example, what does artistic competence imply (Bradley, 1984; Hathaway, 1980; Saunders, 1989; Zimmerman, 1991)? How does a teacher use that competence with students?

Zimmerman (1991, 1992) studied painting instructors working with middle and high school artistically gifted students in a summer enrichment program. She noted one instructor who used storytelling to impart art history or technique information, allowing the reader a sense of the students' and teacher's intensity and learning atmosphere in the short-term program. However, no similar narratives of in-school artistically gifted programs and teachers exist. In this study, I explore what a group of artistically gifted students are doing, talking about, or thinking as their teacher plans and executes lessons directed toward their differentiated needs. Discerning how the teacher's and students' actions and reactions evolve as a year progresses has the potential to expand comprehension of teacher effectiveness beyond the listing of teachers' skills and characteristics.

RESEARCH FRAMEWORK

The theoretical framework of most qualitative research depends on the issues to be explored, the types of guiding questions asked by the researcher, the roles assumed by the researcher, and ways in which the study is written (Bresler, 1994; Ettinger, 1987; Jacob, 1987; Patton, 1990). Instead of generating hypotheses, as is common in quantitative research, broad-based open-ended guiding questions are developed for qualitative research. In this study such questions pertain to the teacher's role as instructional leader, the ways in which the teacher and students interact to construct meaning (or learn together), and the effects of the wider context

---

[1] Material which came directly from the collected data, such as Kelly's quote, is cited by type of data and date of data collection. The three types of data used were field notes, video notes, and transcripts. As unpublished raw data, these are not listed in the reference section.

(school, peers, family, and community) on learning. These questions reflect the broad-based focus of qualitative research. My intent in this study is to enhance the broad descriptive term *effectiveness* through the in-depth study of a teacher and her artistically gifted students.

Blumer's (1967) social interaction theory, which describes meaning-making as a social interactionary process modified through self and social interpretation, forms the theoretical basis of the study. Blumer posits that one learns through social interaction combined with internal dialogue and interpretation. In this study, I concentrated on the interactions between the teacher and students, between students and teacher and student, as well as students' internal dialogue revealed in their art work.

THE SETTING AND PARTICIPANTS

Criteria for site selection included conditions such as the presence of an ongoing artistically gifted program and a school district with administrative and community history of support for gifted and talented programming. The researcher selected the school district because it was one of the first in the state to act as a model site for gifted programs, initiating artistically gifted programs along with academic ones. The selected program began in 1987 as a pilot program for the school district.

The Community

The selected school is a largely middle-class community of 43,764 inhabitants (Department of Commerce, 1990) across the river from a university town of 25,907. With a low (3.8%) unemployment rate, the city has a varied economic base with 88% of the adults employed in manufacturing, service, government, and retail (Indiana Department of Work Force Development, 1993). The school district has one large high school (grades 9–12), two middle schools (grades 6–8), and 11 elementary schools (grades K–5). There are also 9 religion-based schools. A modest art museum, a historical museum, a performing and visual arts center, a library, a community orchestra, and the variety of offerings typical to a large university community provide opportunity for community arts involvement.

The School

Although school selection criteria were auxiliary to the teacher selection, administrative support for the artistically gifted program was central to the school site selection. The district and middle school administration supply the teacher with procedural aid in the gifted identification process, scheduling assistance, and funding for the teacher's inservice growth.

Sunnydale Middle School (a pseudonym, as are those of the teacher and students) is a typically midwestern set of brick rectangles, squatting in an "L" shape in an older section of the city. The middle school reflects the community both economically and ethnically. Of the students, 94% are Caucasian, 2% are African American, with the other 4% Hispanic, Asian, or "other." One third of all students receive the free or reduced-price lunch. Compared to students of similar economic constituency, the Sunnydale students score slightly better on the standardized tests than other middle schoolers across the state.

The Teacher

KC (or "Mrs. C." to her students) was selected because of her continuing educational pursuits, gifted and talented training (Feldhusen & Hansen, 1994), her activity in local and state art organizations, and community recognition as an active artist and teacher (Clark & Zimmerman, 1984, 1992; Zimmerman, 1991, 1992). Receiving a fellowship to attend Clark and Zimmerman's Artistically Talented Program in 1992, KC continually seeks ways to keep abreast of educational and artistic developments. She frequently mentors student- and first-year teachers. On the executive board of the state art education association, she is also active in several arts groups in the city.

The Students

All 26 students who participated in the program (called "Challenge Art") were part of the study. The sixth, seventh, and eighth graders were identified through a formal multimethod screening process based on self, teacher, and parent nomination forms, along with three drawing elements from the Clark's Drawing Abilities Test (Clark, 1989). An identification committee consisting of the teacher, the gifted-talented coordinator, and other art teachers rated the drawings and nomination forms, with the highest scoring students being invited to join the Challenge program. In 1993–1994, all of the Challenge Art students were Caucasian, although a few African-American and Asian students enrolled in prior Challenge Art classes. Fifty percent of the 1993–1994 students were also enrolled in one or more academic Challenge courses. First semester of the 1993–1994 year, the 21 students were evenly divided among grades six, seven, and eight. Five students dropped out second semester, and 5 new students were added, leaving a total of 9 seventh and eighth graders and 3 sixth graders. First semester there were 12 girls and 9 boys, while second semester there were 11 girls and 10 boys.

Researcher Role

In anthropology, the participant observer is one who attempts to become part of the target culture (Ettinger, 1987; Maitland-Gholson & Ettinger, 1994; Patton, 1990). Assuming that role, I attempted to blend with the Challenge Art class in order to experience things as they did.

Initially, I participated as a learner, sitting with different student social groups, who seemed to designate certain tables or room areas as their own. I listened, learned, drew, and painted with them, and they watched me struggle with similar decisions and problem solving. I asked their advice, and they reciprocated. As the year progressed, I shifted more into an assistant teacher role, circulating among the students, asking questions, coaching, and talking with participants. I also used that time to informally interview students, take notes, take photographs, and record class interactions on audio and video tape.

Beginning in October, the class met weekly after school for 1 to $2\frac{1}{2}$ hours. I attended 32 hours (95%) of the first semester meetings. Second semester I attended 29 hours (87%) of scheduled meetings. I met a few times with the summer school Challenge Art group, which contained many students who participated during the school year.

Data Sources and Collection

Primary data sources were field notes, taken during or shortly after class, audio or video tapes of observed classes, and interviews, along with slides and photos of student work. The video camera was placed to provide an overview of the entire classroom, while the audio recorder was placed on a table among 4 to 6 students, and moved to different tables each week. Since student social groups seemed to "claim" different areas of the room, or certain tables, moving the audio recorder allowed data collection from different social groups. Transcripts were made from both audio and video tapes, or notes taken while viewing video tapes. Multiple copies of transcripts were made, some of which were cut and placed in color-coded files to reflect analytic categories.

Slides, photos, and videos of art works became important data. These items were analyzed to reflect students' learning processes. Artifacts such as copies of student artwork, handouts, lesson plans, in-school bulletins, notes home, newspaper articles, and tapes of newscasts served as secondary data sources, augmenting the primary sources.

Data Analysis

Focusing on teacher-student, student-teacher, and student-student interactions, I began preliminary analysis within the first month of observation, using the constant comparison method of analysis, which involves combining inductive behavior coding with simultaneous comparison of all observed events (Glaser & Strauss, 1967; Strauss, 1987). The codes, which began as interaction descriptors, began to reveal patterns within the accumulation of coded transcripts. Using the coding system, 7 graduate and undergraduate art education students rated representative interaction behaviors in five video clips. Their coding reflected an interrater reliability of .91 with the codes I had assigned the same clips.

Linkages were sought between patterns, usually emerging from theoretical memos written as analysis progressed (Strauss, 1987). These codes, patterns, and linkages were triangulated with interview and secondary data information, and particularly scanned for disconfirming data, causing assertions to be revised to include that data.

CHALLENGE ART DESCRIPTION

The Teacher-Translator

The translation process is a construct the researcher developed to describe the complex phenomena of teacher and student behaviors, interaction patterns, and art work manifestations which reflect the intentional and unintentional classroom curricula in Challenge Art. Similar to Dillon's (1989) teacher as a cultural broker, the teacher-translator bridges the cultures/worlds of the artistically gifted middle school student and the art-world. The students' world includes school, peers, family, and community, while the artworld includes the local, regional, and international art world.

A translator is one who is fluent in more than one language. To translate efficiently, one must be able to clearly understand in one language, and almost simultaneously repeat the thought in another, retaining the same clarity, emphasis, and nuance. KC is a translator. Her "languages" are those of the artworld and the students' world. The artworld language is full of images, galleries, history, critical analyses, contact with other artists, aesthetic discussions, museums, books. The language of the students' world is full of references to the middle school culture of teachers, peers, who did what during lunch, who "likes" whom, who called whom last night, who got in trouble third period. . . .

KC is a veteran teacher. KC is an artist. She melds the two in a life-web which attracts artistically gifted middle school students around her in a bubble of giggly enthusiasm. "I have to do art," she says, and the kids begin to feel the love she has for her field. "My kids . . ." she says, and they know the beginning of trust. One cannot talk to her without hearing about one or the other—her kids, art. The synergy resulting from her dual passions of art and teaching forms the basis for KC's effectiveness as a teacher-translator.

KC's personal time is filled with the vocabulary of the artworld. Travel involves visits to galleries and museums, as she and her spouse deliver and retrieve his paintings from Chicago, or take their works to exhibitions in other Midwestern cities. She reads a number of art magazines regularly, feeling that it is important to be "on the cutting edge of our profession . . . as artists" (Transcript; December 2, 1992).

As part of the school world, KC operates successfully in both adult and student circles. With her colleagues, she serves on school and district committees, helps reading teachers by assisting on a bookmaking unit, is part of a Friday breakfast "club," and uses the Art Club to assist in school decoration and scenery construction for music and drama productions.

As part of the student world, KC interacts with the Challenge Art students as they burst through the door on Thursday afternoons, asking one how he did on an English test, another about a musical audition. Frequently snapping pictures, she tells them that "this one's for the yearbook," or "I want to show other art teachers what you're really like" (Transcript; March 3, 1994). The class milieu is full of energy and laughter. Even her disciplinary statements are humor-laced. "Tank, the Chumpette, forgot to put up his chair again," she says in mock desperation. "Poor Mrs. C." is the response (Video notes; December 9, 1993). The cheerful by-play is the background for the more serious work of artistic teaching-learning conducted through the translation process. This translation is conducted through the medium of KC's curriculum rhythm.

Curriculum Rhythm

Curriculum rhythm is a construct developed by the researcher to reflect what was observed in this classroom over time. KC's teaching has a pattern to it. Reflecting the need for differentiated instruction, the pattern used with her "regular" students is different from the one used with her Challenge Art students. KC gives her regular students a chronological overview of art history, an introduction to critical and aesthetic learning experiences combined with varied media experiences. Highly structured, her regular art classes extend 9 or 12 weeks, depending on grade level.

In Challenge Art, the thematic subject matter differs each semester, yet the pattern of learning and experience remains consistent. The thematic curriculum accommodates in-depth study and extended immersion in student-selected art projects. In Challenge Art, KC provides problem finding and problem solving. For the regular classes, KC's curriculum rhythm is staccato; for her Challenge Art class, the rhythm resembles a more sustained melody reflecting the differentiated needs of her high-interest students.

The curriculum rhythm is the medium through which KC translates the artworld to the students. Art teachers easily recognize the concept of the rhythm of an art class. If it is a production lesson, the students enter the room, put their backpacks, food, and assorted clothing aside, retrieve what they are working on, and settle down to listen to the teacher, who introduces or demonstrates the day's lesson. The students work on their projects, clean up and leave—a cycle repeated throughout the day for the teacher, throughout the term for the students.

KC employs that familiar rhythm for some Challenge Art classes, but her class rhythms fall within a larger overall pattern consisting of five phases. KC's Challenge Art classes are semester based, as is the duration of her curriculum rhythm cycle. The rhythm cycle is repeated each semester, differing in its thematic content. As the translation vehicle, each of the five phases serves to further meld the student world and the artworld. The five phases are: image flood, reflection, art work, critique, and exhibition. I observed two complete cycles and part of a third during this study. Each semester evidenced all five phases of the rhythmic cycle. Through these rhythmic cycles the translation process occurs as described here.

Phase one: The image flood. KC begins each cycle with a flood of images for her students. Assembling many books, slides, and visuals on the selected topic, she floods her students with visual images. The first semester of the study, KC selected the theme of American Western art for her Challenge Art curriculum. She showed slides and snapshots of a prior trip through the Southwest, had dozens of books and magazines (such as *Arizona Highways*) available to the students, while discussing the physical characteristics of the Southwest. She then showed slides of noted Southwestern artists' work. Some were 19th-century; some were current. She discussed various techniques used, along with color choices. Remington, T. C. Cannon, Victor Higgins, and O'Keeffe illustrate the exemplar variety. Following the slides, the students went to a museum specializing in Western art. Not one to overlook an instructional opportunity, KC distributed many of the books and magazines on Western art to the students on the bus, reiterating technique, subject matter, and style. At the museum, a capable, denim-clad docent discussed artists, painting, and historical context of the works. Finally, the students were allowed to explore. The 18 kids who attended the field trip went nose-close to works of interest, or sprawled on the floor to sketch. A museum patron commented to me about their keen absorption. When informed that they were middle schoolers, she expressed surprise. Informed that they were artistically gifted, she no longer wondered at their intensity (Field notes; October 13, 1993).

Winter semester, which centered on both public art and Victorian architecture, in preparation for painting a mural on a bridge underpass, included a similar image flood phase. Field trips included investigating community public art, visits to the city historical museum and a lovingly restored Victorian home, as well as a bus tour around the historic neighborhood. Experiences were supplemented with slides and with opportunities for students to photograph selected homes or architectural details for future reference. Student sketch books reveal gas lamps, intricate wrought iron fences, and replications of fish scale shingles. Along with visual stimulation, the students heard "stories" about the city founders who populated the neighborhood, providing a visual and verbal picture of 1800s life.

KC explained to a group of fellow art teachers the necessity of the image flood:

> As adults we have built a large store of images. We have looked at a lot of art. My students have limited experience. So it is my job to fill them with a wide variety of images to build up their imagic store. (Field notes; October 29, 1994)

As the students are bombarded with these images, they are also making critical choices in selecting images of interest and recording them either photographically or in their sketch books.

Phase two: Reflection. The second phase of the teaching-learning rhythm begins during the first, as the students select which images to sketch or photograph. This is the reflection phase wherein the students reflect upon what they have seen, and begin generating ideas for further development.

One student, intrigued with a tree seen at the Western art museum, began to sketch it at the museum. Upon returning to the classroom, Ward transferred that sketch to a masonite board as the centerpiece of his Western painting. His sketch book revealed that the texture of the tree was of greatest interest, while the form of the tree was altered and refined as he continued the painting and drawing process. That same semester, another sixth grade boy was drawn to the smooth surface of an O'Keeffe pueblo painting at the museum. Pursuing his interest in O'Keeffe, he found a black-and-white photo of a skull drawing showing an intricate antler structure. Using that as a springboard, Biker also used real bovine skulls as further reference for his drawing (Video notes; November 4, 1993).

As part of the reflective process, this combining and altering visual references occurred during the second semester as well, with a notable addition, that of written reflection. KC asked the students questions such as "Why did you choose your house or object? What style is it?" (Video notes; February 24, 1994). Sketchbook journaling included information such as chronological data about chosen buildings, architectural style, as well as stories about the object or building. Much of the resource information came from materials KC had photocopied at the historical museum. As work continued on the actual bridge murals, KC asked them to record how they felt about their work and the collaborative nature of the project. She indicated that the students should "have a record of what you did, so you can show your children someday" (Video notes; February 24, 1994). While the students laughed at the vision of their own progeny, the permanence of the project was impressed upon them.

The journals/sketchbooks were not only used in recording interesting images, developing ideas, and writing about personal and historic documentation, but were also used as references in later presentations. As the work on the mural progressed, the students were asked on numerous occasions to discuss their work with interested community groups and community media. The sketchbook material became a resource for those comments.

Phase three: Art work. As the students researched material for their art, using the abundant resources available, some generated ideas almost immediately. Others took more time, beginning with one idea, abandoning it and exploring another. KC helped them formulate ideas by referring them to the visual resources in the room (the slides, magazines, books, photos) and through technical instruction. Jack, a tall, bright, energetic seventh grader, talked about his Western art idea:

> I want it to represent all those old cowboy pictures. You know the ones where the cowboy rides off into the sunset. Only this is supposed to represent *all* the horses riding off into the sunset in *all* those movies. (Interview transcript; June 16, 1994)

Along with idea generation, two other components were central to the art-work phase, that of technical instruction and problem solving.

KC knew her students "wanted things to look real," so she gave them technique instruction which would aid them (Field notes; March 19, 1994). She used visual resources, demonstrated and repeatedly spoke of changing values to create the illusion of depth. "Those flat colors are a good start, Drake, now add some darker and some lighter right here" (Transcript; December 2, 1993). "See how this artist did that?" (Video notes; April 21, 1994). "Look at how these clouds are really flat on the bottom (referring to a photo), can you do that with yours?" (Transcript; December 9, 1993).

Formal and informal demonstrations were part of the mix. She spent two class periods in November discussing color theory and demonstrating scumbling, blending, and impressionistic paint strokes on her own painting. During the demonstration she discussed how painting was fun "because you can't make a mistake. You can let it dry and paint right over it" (Field notes; October 20 and 28, 1993).

In one-to-one situations, she would mix a bit of paint on the newspaper next to a painting, or add a little to a student's picture. The students seemed to regard this positively, as Elenie indicated: "Mrs. C. will start something on a little part of my painting, and then I get it" (Interview transcript; June 16, 1994). Most students did indeed "get it," demonstrating sophisticated layers of subtle shading in each semester's paintings.

When students encountered difficulty, they usually raised their hands or asked a friend. KC worked around the class clockwise, trying to touch base with each student as work sessions progressed. Students were confident in her help. Asked what they did when they had a problem, most responded, "I ask Mrs. C." If KC was unavailable, most indicated that they would wait until she was (Interview transcripts; June 21 and 22, 1994). Jack, however, admitted that he would "walk around and get noisy" until he figured out what to do (Interview transcript; June 21, 1994). Besides demonstrating, KC frequently referred students to the visual resources. "Why don't you look in . . ." "See if you can find the book where the picture of . . ." was a repeated song in Challenge Art. The book/visual reference table usually had two or three students thumbing through visuals to find their own help.

Informal peer instruction was common. However, it seemed limited to problems like color mixing or texture. "I mixed red and that dark blue and a little brown for this" (Video notes; March 10, 1994). They also sought affirmation from each other: "Clara, what do you think of this?" "It's great, Mildred, but you need some more of that dark stuff there. It's all the same" (Transcript, December 1, 1993). They sought this affirmation in the same tone as they asked about social things like "Do you like my new sweater?" From their friends, they expected positive answers. From KC they expected help.

While giving them tools to help them achieve realism, KC also encouraged individual styles. "Wow, that's surrealistic, Jack" (Transcript; December 21, 1993). "Your clouds have that impressionistic feel, Clara" (Transcript; December 21, 1993). The art history and stylistic references were not accidental; rather, she attempted to reinforce earlier learning along with providing affirmation.

Phase four: The critique. Two sorts of critical activities were evident in the Challenge Art class: in-process assessment and whole class critique. Documented in several studies (Stokrocki, 1991), in-process assessment occurs as a teacher helps a student decide how well he or she is progressing. Adler (1982) refers to the practice of facilitating the fine tuning of student skills as "coaching."

In the Challenge Art class it was difficult to separate the one-on-one technical instruction from in-process assessment, as the instructional and assessment comments were so interwoven. Students sought affirmation and direction at the same time. Clara said: "What do you think, Mrs. C?" KC replied: "Oh, Clara, it's beautiful. The way you have layered those colors is wonderful. Let's put it up there so you can see it from a distance" (Transcript; December 9, 1993). Balancing the painting on the chalk tray, KC and Clara discussed the contrast. Clara could see that her dark colors needed a little light to afford more clarity. Since she seemed to love thickly layered colors, she would happily continue, following KC's gentle suggestions. The chalkboard sessions would also be used to demonstrate a student's successful use of a technique to the class. Elenie's skull and cactus was used as an exemplar of skillful shading. The now familiar "dark-medium-light" exhortation was heard as KC showed how Elenie's highlighting and shading made her cactus seem real enough to prickle (Video notes; December 16, 1993).

At the end of the Western art unit, the students entered the room in a chorus of "oohs and aahs," discovering their paintings carefully balanced on drawers and counters along the north wall. As students perched on tables and chairs, KC announced that they would be "looking for things that work well, and for things that can be improved" (Transcript; December 21, 1993). Pointing out similarities and differences in technique and subject matter, KC had students point out evidences of scumbling, blending, and shading. She contrasted stylistic and color treatments of similar subject matter in discussing the several skull pastels and paintings. The effects of color on mood were tied to those who used Cannon's riotous colors and those who demonstrated "soft, velvety colors" (Transcript; December 21, 1993). Although teacher talk dominated, students were encouraged to voice opinions, make connections, and find further examples of concepts under discussion.

Phase five: Exhibition. The exhibition phase of KC's teaching/learning rhythm brings the students into the adult art-world. KC firmly believes in ensuring that her students' work is seen publicly. She takes slides of all finished work, using some slides to show her other students as exemplars, others for presentations at state and national conferences. Inevitably, she shows the students these slides before a presentation, telling them she is "showing them off to other art teachers" (Transcript; October 9,

1993; March 3, 1994). One major difference between this phase and the others is that it occurs beyond the semester framework. Thus, the work from the fall semester may be exhibited in the spring, depending on exhibition schedules. However, with the number of continuing students, and KC's consistency, each student knows his or her work will be exhibited.

KC organizes a county-wide K–8 art show, inviting friends and family to the opening. Two of the last three such exhibitions have shared space with adult artists. KC feels that this is important, as the arts community can recognize the quality of student work, while the students have the opportunity to interact with adult artists and their patrons (Interview transcript; December 2, 1992). A fall exhibition at a university gallery allowed students to explain how they had devised their sculptures to assembled friends, family, and art educators. Even the quietest students responded with alacrity to professors' questions, with answers like "I just stuffed the gloves with cotton and painted on them" (Video notes; October 30, 1993).

The second semester public art project gave students numerous opportunities to make public statements about their art. The first arose when they spoke to the local historic neighborhood association concerning their proposals for bridge murals. Using their sketch book information, students gave presentations on their drawings of buildings and events in the district, including historical information about the drawings' subjects. Mildred: "I did the circus wagon because they used to have a circus which would play in Murdock Park," followed by a bit she had written about circus day in the late 1800s. Two girls who had worked together on a drawing did a well-rehearsed presentation which included historical fact, architectural preference, and comments on their collaborative process. A blurb on the evening television news about the project was a precursor to other newscasts and newspaper features as the murals progressed. After the first newscast, KC made it a point to steer the reporters to the students, as she noted "they are the ones doing all the work" (Field notes; May 1, 1994).

The exhibitions, presentations, and news coverage had the effect of solidifying students' cognition about both art process and subject matter. The students' historical facts about local residences and events were well researched and accurately delivered. Describing their research and art process to an audience served to increase their identification as "real" artists among themselves, their peers, their families, and the community (Interview transcripts; June 16 and 21, 1994).

DISCUSSION AND IMPLICATIONS FOR FURTHER RESEARCH

Discussion

In this study, I attempted to describe how an effective art teacher and her artistically gifted students learn together over the course of a school year. Such description demonstrates how teacher and learning rhythms can impact a middle school class for artistically gifted students. The rhythm created by KC gave the students a familiarity with several art processes, both as observers and creators, as they absorbed, reflected upon, created, and interpreted art images. Through exhibition and their own explanations to various publics, the artistically gifted middle school students became part of the art world as they helped others interpret and understand their work. Finally, the circular, rhythmic translation process cemented students' self-identification as "real" artists with peers, family, and community.

Clark and Zimmerman (1984, 1988) and Zimmerman (1991, 1992) discussed the importance to artistically gifted students of peer interaction and substantive teaching. KC and her students extend the understanding of what substantive teaching may be.

The nature of qualitative research is a collaboration between researcher and researched, as interpretations are clarified, or transcriptions revisited. The research process itself has helped KC reflect upon her own practice. Discussing and watching the growth of her students, through her own and another's eyes, has made her more aware of the choices she makes as she plans, prepares for, and teaches these students. She recognizes the rhythmic nature of her curriculum. "That's what I do, all right" (Field notes; October 29, 1994). She comprehends the translation concept, linking it with Renzulli's (1977) real products for real audiences (Field notes; October 29, 1994). Reflecting and collaborating allowed KC to perceive the effects of the publicity surrounding the bridge murals from her students' point of view. As a result, she plans to continue community-based projects for her Challenge students. Included in her future plans are a sculpture for the school and murals for a local community center.

Implications for Research

KC and teacher effectiveness definitions. This study began in a quest to understand more about teacher effectiveness in conjunction with artistically gifted students. Reflecting the nature of qualitative study, the results of this research are idiosyncratic. Yet KC does demonstrate some characteristics noted in effective art teachers such as valuing art education, organizational skills, and awareness of students' developmental and social needs (Capet, 1986; May, 1993; Saunders, 1989; Stokrocki, 1991; Thomas, 1992). She also meets some of Clark and Zimmerman's (1988, 1992, 1995) recommendations for teaching artistically gifted students: substantive teaching, providing access to professional level visual resources, and solid technical instruction. Evidenced in the discussion of each of the five phases is the way in which KC combines these qualities as she translates student-artworld languages making her teaching and the learning of her students effective.

Translation. The translation concept may be potentially significant for those responsible for developing meaningful artistically gifted/talented programming. Teachers and administrators may be able to discern the importance of bringing the outside world to the gifted/talented classroom and vice versa. Particularly at the tumultuous middle-school age, self-identification is an important issue. Clark and Zimmerman (1988) discussed the effects of positive peer interaction in artistically gifted classes. KC's students reflected that positive peer, family, school, and teacher influence. It may be meaningful to continue to monitor the students' self-identification as artists to discern any long-lasting effects.

If teachers and administrators can develop programs that allow students to see themselves as real contributors, artistically gifted students may have a better understanding of the positive ramifications of their special abilities.

Curriculum rhythm. The concept of curricular rhythm has potential as a tool for understanding more about teacher effectiveness. Although the idea developed as a way of describing the chronology of content in one class, it is a concept with resonance. Research may determine other styles of rhythms which exist in effective art teaching. Patterns of common traits may be found in particularly effective curricular rhythms, or effective rhythms may be found to be idiosyncratic to class or teacher. Rhythm types may link with specific teaching styles or unique populations in effective classrooms. Cross-case analysis, the method by which many qualitative studies are analyzed, may provide more illumination into the possibilities of the rhythm concept and its relationship to teaching effectiveness.

Eisner (1993) called for "fine grained study, description, interpretation, and evaluation of what actually goes on in art classrooms" (p. 54). This paper is an attempt to heed that call. KC is a highly effective teacher, working with her school's "best artists." She demonstrates many qualities cited in research as part of being effective. However, through her unique translation process, involving a carefully developed curriculum rhythm conducted with her gifted students' needs at the forefront, KC has forged her own brand of effectiveness from which we each may take pieces to use in our own practical or theoretical applications.

REFERENCES

Adler, M. (1982). *The paideia proposal.* New York: Collier Books, MacMillan.

Amidon, E., & Flanders, N. (1967). *The role of the teacher in the classroom.* Minneapolis, MN: Paul Amidon and Associates.

Blumer, H. (1967/1986). *Symbolic interactionism: Perspective and method.* Englewood Cliffs, NJ: Prentice Hall.

Bradley, L. (1984). Legislative impact on art teacher certification standards. *Action in Teacher Education 6*(4), 43–46.

Bresler, L. (1994). Zooming in on the qualitative paradigm in art education: Educational criticism, ethnography, and action research. *Visual Arts Research, 20*(1), 1–21.

Capet, M. (1986). An exploratory study of teaching visual arts grades one through eight: A phenomenological account of teacher cues, assumptions, intuition, and dialog during a studio experience and their implications for future research. (Doctoral dissertation, University of California, Los Angeles, 1986). *Dissertation Abstracts International.* (University Microfilms no. ADD85-00582).

Clark, G. (1989). Screening and identifying students talented in the visual arts: Clark's Drawing Abilities Test. *Gifted Child Quarterly, 33*(3), 98–105.

Clark, G., & Zimmerman, E. (1984). *Educating artistically talented students.* Syracuse, NY: Syracuse University Press.

Clark, G., & Zimmerman, E. (1988). Views of self, family background, and school: Interviews with artistically talented students. *Gifted Child Quarterly, 32*(4), 340–346.

Clark, G., & Zimmerman, E. (1992). *Issues and practices related to identification of gifted and talented students in the visual arts.* Storrs, CT: The National Research Center on the Gifted and Talented.

Clark, G., & Zimmerman, E. (1995). Programming opportunities for students gifted and talented in the visual arts. *Translations: From theory to practice, 5*(1), 1–6.

Department of Commerce. (1990). *1990 Census of population and housing: Population and housing characteristics for census tracts and block numbering areas 1990 CPH-3-199, Lafayette-West Lafayette. IN MSA.* Washington, DC: U.S. Government Printing Office.

Dillon, D. (1989). Showing them that I want them to learn and that I care about who they are: A microethnography of the social organization of a secondary low track English reading classroom. *American Educational Research Journal, 26*(2), 227–259.

Eisner, E. (1993). The emergence of new paradigms for educational research. *Art Education, 46*(6), 50–55.

Ettinger, L. (1987). Styles of on-site descriptive research: A taxonomy for art educators. *Studies in Art Education, 28*(2), 79–95.

Feldhusen, J., & Hansen, J. (1994). A comparison of trained and untrained teachers of gifted students. *Gifted Child Quarterly, 38*(3), 115–123.

Glaser, B., & Strauss, A. (1967). *The discovery of grounded theory: Strategies for qualitative research.* Chicago: Aldine.

Hathaway, J. (Ed.). (1980). *Art education: Middle/junior high school* (3rd printing). Reston, VA: National Art Education Association, 59–63.

Indiana Work Force Development (1993). *Highlights: Tippecanoe County, 1993 edition.* Lafayette, IN: Indiana Work Force Development.

Jacob, E. (1987). Qualitative research traditions: A review. *Review of Educational Research, 57*(1), 1–50.

Langlois, D., & Zales, C. (1991). Anatomy of a top teacher. *American School Board Journal, 178,* 44–46.

Maitland-Gholson, J., & Ettinger, L. (1994). Interpretative decision making in research. *Studies in Art Education, 36*(1), 18–27.

May, W. (1993). Good teachers making the best of it: Case studies of elementary art and music teaching. *Elementary Subjects' Center Series No. 100.* East Lansing, MI: Office of Educational Research and Improvement, Washington, DC, Center for Learning and Teaching of Elementary Subjects. (ERIC Documentation Reproduction Service No. ED 360 230.)

Patton, M. (1990). *Qualitative evaluation and research methods* (2nd edition). Newbury Park, CA: Sage Publications.

Renzulli, J. (1977). *The Enrichment triad model: A guide for developing defensible programming for the gifted and talented.* Mansfield Center, CT: Creative Learning Press.

Saunders, H. (1989). How to select an effective art teacher. *NASSP Bulletin,* May 1989, 4, 54–69.

Stokrocki, M. (1991). A decade of qualitative research in art education: Methodology expansions and pedagogical explorations. *Visual Arts Research, 17*(1), 42–51.

Strauss, A. (1987). *Qualitative analysis for social scientists.* New York: Cambridge University Press.

Thomas, R. (1992). Art Education: Program evaluation report. Orlando, FL: Orange County Public Schools. (ERIC Document Reproduction Service No. ED 357 057.)

Zimmerman, E. (1991). Rembrandt to Rembrandt: A case study of a memorable painting teacher of artistically talented 13–16 year old students. *Roeper Review, 13*(2), 76–80.

Zimmerman, E. (1992). A comparative study of two painting teachers of talented adolescents. *Studies in Art Education, 33*(3), 174–185.

"Some graduate students spend many anxiety-ridden days and sleepless nights worrying about where they are going to find the problem they need for their thesis or dissertation." (p. 34)

Selecting and Defining a Research Topic

OBJECTIVES

After reading Chapter 2, you should be able to do the following:

1. Make a list of at least three educational topics on which you would be interested in conducting a research study.
2. Select one of the topics and identify 10 to 15 complete references (source works) that directly relate to the selected problem. The references should include a variety of source types (e.g., books, articles, Internet reports, etc.).
3. Distinguish between quantitative and qualitative methods of starting a research study.
4. Read and abstract the references you have listed.
5. Formulate a testable or descriptive hypothesis for your problem.

Note: These objectives will form the basis for Task 2.

Selection and definition of a research topic is the first step in applying the scientific method. Before you read more about this first step, a few comments about the research process seem appropriate. Textbooks tend to present the process and its steps in a simple, linear form: Do this and then this and then this, and ultimately you'll get to where you want to be. Although a linear format provides a necessary template for student learning, the reality of educational research is that progress is seldom so straightforward. Educational research is truly a process of trial and error. As you investigate and refine your research topic, for instance, you will find things that "don't fit" as expected, ideas that are not as clear on paper as they were in your head, or ideas that require considerable rethinking and rewriting. That is the reality of research. However, your ability to work through the challenges will be an important and satisfying measure of your understanding. Remember this as you embark on this learning experience.

The research topic (also called the *research question, problem,* or *purpose*) provides focus and structure for the remaining steps in the scientific method; it is the thread that binds everything together. When properly defined, the research topic reduces a study to a manageable size. A common difficulty among researchers is selecting a topic so broad and complex that the research is difficult to implement or complete. An initial topic often proves unmanageable for study, and the researcher must narrow its scope. Selecting and defining a topic is a very important component of the research process and should entail considerable thought.

The research topic that you ultimately select is the topic you will work with in succeeding chapters of this text. Therefore, it is important that you select a problem relevant to your area of study and of particular interest to you.

The goal of Chapter 2 is for you to identify and define a meaningful topic, conduct an adequate review of related literature, and state a testable hypothesis. A topic statement, a review of related literature, and a hypothesis are components of both a written research plan and research report. Completing Chapter 2 should enable you to perform the following task.

TASK 2

Write an introduction for a quantitative research plan. Include a statement of the research topic, a statement concerning the importance or significance of the topic, a brief review of related literature, and a testable hypothesis regarding the outcome of your study. Include definitions of terms where appropriate. (See Performance Criteria, p. 66.)

:: IDENTIFYING A TOPIC OR QUESTION TO RESEARCH

Throughout our school careers we are taught to solve problems of various kinds. Ask people to list the 10 most important outcomes of education, and most will invariably mention problem solving. Now, after many years of emphasis on solving problems, you face a research task that asks you to find, rather than solve, a problem. If you are like most people, you have had little experience doing this. For beginning researchers, selection of a problem is the most difficult step in the research process. Some graduate students spend many anxiety-ridden days and sleepless nights worrying about where they are going to find the problem they need for their thesis or dissertation.

The first step in selecting a research topic is to identify a general subject area that is related to your area of expertise and is of particular interest to you. Remember, you will be spending a great deal of time reading about and working with your chosen topic. Having one that interests you will help you maintain focus during the months of conducting and writing your study.

Sources of Research Topics

You may be asking yourself, "Where do research topics, questions, purposes, or problems come from? Where should I look to ferret out topics to study?" The four main sources of research topics are theories, personal experiences, previous studies that can be replicated, and library searches.

LISTSERVES

Researchers frequently use e-mail to solicit advice and feedback and conduct dialogue with peers and experts in their fields. The most common way to do so is by subscribing to an electronic mailing list service, commonly known as a *listserve*. A well-known example is Listserv, run by L-Soft International. Electronic mailing lists are designed by organizations or special interest groups to facilitate communication among their members. Through one of these lists, you can expect to receive announcements and bulletins related to your area of interest. In addition, you can post comments or questions on the listserve. Your messages will be read by members of the listserve, who have the option of responding to you personally or to the mailing list as a whole.

A listserve is a good resource to consult when you are devising a research question. You can ask listserve members what they think of a particular topic, if they know of other research pertaining to your topic, or for links (electronic or otherwise) to resources of interest. You can also bounce ideas off other listserve members at each stage of your research. You can even ask for volunteers to read your work in progress!

To subscribe to a listserve, you generally are required to send a short e-mail message to the listserve. Subscribed, you will receive detailed information about how to post messages, how to unsubscribe, etc. Examples of useful education listserves include the following:

American Educational Research Association List
  (lists.asu.edu)
AERA Division K Teaching and Teacher Education Forum
  (lists.asu.edu)
Educational Administration Discussion List
  (listserv.wvnet.edu)

A useful Web site to consult in your search for appropriate listserves is http://www.lsoft.com/lists/listref.html. This site, sponsored by L-Soft International, contains a catalog of Listserv lists. At this site, you can browse public lists on the Internet, search for mailing lists of interest, and get information about host sites. A recent search for education lists yielded hundreds of Listserv mailing lists.

Theories

Although there are several major sources of problems, the most meaningful ones are generally those derived from theories. A **theory** is an organized body of concepts, generalizations, and principles that can be subjected to investigation. Educationally relevant theories, such as theories of learning and behavior, can provide the inspiration for many research problems. For example, Jean Piaget posited that children pass through four stages of cognitive development: sensorimotor stage (birth to age 2), preoperational stage (ages 2 to 7), concrete operational stage (ages 7 to 11), and formal operational stage (ages 11 to adulthood). Piaget indicated what children could or could not do at each stage. Examining whether aspects of Piaget's theory operate as suggested could be the basis for many possible research topics. Research focused on aspects of a theory is not only conceptually rich, it also provides information that confirms or disconfirms one or more of those aspects and may suggest additional studies that would further test the theory. Take a moment now to think of two other theories that are popular in education and identify from them a few topics to investigate.

Personal Experiences

Another common way to identify research topics is to examine some of the questions we commonly ask ourselves about education. Such questions may arise when we participate in class discussion, read articles in local newspapers and educational journals, or interact with others. It is hard to imagine an educator who has never had a hunch concerning a better way to do something (e.g., increase learning or improve student behavior) or asked questions about a program or materials whose effectiveness was untested (for example, questioning why a writing program was successful or science materials were not). We observe or read about schools, teachers, and programs, and news articles about schooling, and we ask ourselves questions such as: "Why does that happen?" "What causes that?" "What would happen if . . . ?" and "How would a different group respond to this?" Normally we think briefly about such questions and get back to our everyday business. But such questions are probably the most common source of research topics because they capture our interest.

Studies That Can Be Replicated

An additional source of research topics is previous studies that can be replicated. A **replication** is a repetition of a study, using different subjects, or a retesting of its hypothesis. No single study, regardless of its focus or breadth, provides the certainty needed to assume that similar results will occur in all or most similar situations. Progress through research usually comes from accumulated understandings and explanations. Replication is a tool used to provide such accumulated information.

In most cases, a replication is not carried out in a way identical to the original study. Rather, some feature or features of the original study are altered in an attempt to "stretch" the original findings. Thus, the researcher might select a different sample of participants for the replication in the hope of determining whether the results obtained are the same as those of the original study. Or the researcher might examine a different kind of community or student, use a different questionnaire, or apply a different method of data analysis. There are a variety of interesting and useful ways to replicate studies in the many domains of education.

Library Searches

Another commonly cited source of research topics is a library search. Many students are encouraged to immerse themselves in the library and read voraciously in their area of study until a research topic emerges. Although some research topics do emerge from library immersion, they are considerably fewer than those emerging from theories, personal experiences, and previous studies. Trying to identify a topic amid the enormous possibilities in a library is akin to looking for a needle in a haystack; sometimes we find it, but not very often. Clearly libraries are essential sources of information in the research process. However, the library is most useful to the researcher after a topic has been narrowed (discussed shortly). Then library resources can provide information to place the topic in perspective, reveal what has already been done on the topic, and suggest methods for carrying out the topic's examination.

Narrowing the Topic

For most quantitative researchers and some qualitative researchers, the general topic area must be narrowed to a more specific, researchable one. A topic that is too broad can lead to grief. First, a broad topic enlarges the task of reviewing the related literature (discussed in the next section), likely resulting in many extra hours spent in the library. Second, broad topics complicate the organization of the review itself. Finally, and more importantly, a topic that is too broad tends to result in a study that is general, difficult to carry out, and difficult to interpret. Conversely, a well-defined, manageable problem results in a well-defined, manageable study.

Note that the appropriate time to narrow a topic differs for quantitative and qualitative approaches. Quantitative research typically requires that the researcher spell out a specific and manageable topic at the start of the research process. Conversely, for most qualitative research, it is desirable to enter the research setting with only a general topic area in mind. On the basis of what is observed in the research setting over a period of time, the qualitative researcher will formulate a narrowed research topic.

For ideas on narrowing your topic, you might begin by talking to your faculty advisors and to specialists in your area to solicit specific suggestions for study. You will also want to read sources that provide overviews of the current status of research in your topic area and search through handbooks that contain many chapters focused on research in a particular area (e.g., *Handbook of Research in Educational Administration, The Handbook of Educational Psychology, Handbook of Research on Curriculum, Handbook of Research on Teacher Education, Handbook of Sport Psychology, International Handbook of Early Child Education, International Handbook of Self-Study of Teacher Education Practices,* and many more). You could also check the *Encyclopedia of Educational Research* or journals such as the *Review of Educational Research,* which provide reviews of research in many areas. These sources often identify "next-step" studies that need to be conducted. For example, a study investigating the effectiveness of computer-assisted instruction in elementary arithmetic might suggest the need for similar studies in other curriculum areas. Bear in mind that at this stage in the research process, you seek general research overviews that describe the nature of research in an area and that can suggest more specific topics in your chosen area.

In narrowing your topic, you should select an aspect of the general problem area that is related to your area of expertise. For example, the general problem area "the use of reviews to increase retention" could generate many specific problems, such as "the comparative effectiveness of immediate versus delayed review on the retention of geometric concepts" and "the effect of review games on the retention of vocabulary words by second graders." In your efforts to sufficiently delineate a problem, however, be careful not to get carried away; a problem that is too narrow is just as bad as a problem that is too broad. A study such as "the effectiveness of pre-class reminders in reducing instances of pencil sharpening during class time" would probably contribute little, if anything, to education knowledge.

Selecting a good topic is well worth the time and effort. As mentioned previously, there is no shortage of significant educational problems that need to be researched; there is really no excuse for selecting a trite, overly narrow problem. Besides, it is generally to your advantage to select a worthwhile problem; you will certainly get a great deal more out of it professionally and academically. If the subsequent study is well conducted and reported, not only will you earn a good grade and make a contribution to knowledge, but you might also find your work published in a professional journal. The potential personal benefits to be derived from publication include increased professional status and job opportunities, not to mention tremendous self-satisfaction.

We look more closely at the characteristics of "good" topics next.

Characteristics of Good Topics

As already mentioned, working with an interesting topic helps a researcher stay motivated during months of study. Being interesting, however, is only one of the characteristics of a good research topic. A research topic, by definition, is an issue in need of investigation, so it follows that a fundamental characteristic of a good topic is that it is researchable. A researchable topic is one that can be investigated through collecting and analyzing data. Problems dealing with philosophical or ethical issues are not researchable. Research can assess how people "feel" about such issues, but it cannot resolve them. In education a number of issues make great topics for debate (e.g., "Should prayer be allowed in the schools?") but are not researchable problems; there is no way to resolve these issues through collecting and analyzing data. Generally, topics or questions that contain the word *should* cannot be answered by research of any kind, because they ultimately are matters of opinion.

Note, however, that one could carry out research studies that examine the effects on teachers and students of school prayer, grouping practices, or being held back in grade. Do you see how a slight wording change can create researchable topics? Such studies, as worded, can tell us about the varied consequences of these practices, but the decision of what should be done in a school or classroom involves issues that go beyond the abilities of any research study.

A third characteristic of a good research topic is that it has theoretical or practical significance. People's definitions of *significant* vary, but a general rule of thumb is that a significant study is one that contributes in some way to the improvement or understanding of educational theory or practice. A fourth major characteristic of a good topic is that it is a manageable topic for you. Choosing an interesting topic in an area in which you have expertise is not sufficient. You must choose a topic that you can adequately investigate, given your current level of research skill, the resources available to you, and the time you can commit to carrying out the study. The availability of appropriate participants and measuring instruments, for example, is an important consideration. A fifth important characteristic is that the research is ethical. That is, the research must not potentially harm the research participants. Harm encompasses not only physical danger but emotional danger as well. The characteristics of a good topic are summarized in Figure 2.1. As you assess a topic for its appropriateness and feasibility, you may wish to consult your faculty advisors for their opinions.

FIGURE 2.1

Characteristics of a good research topic

1. *The topic is interesting.* It will hold the researcher's interest throughout the entire research process.
2. *The topic is researchable.* It can be investigated through the collection and analysis of data, and it is not stated as an effort to determine what *should* be done.
3. *The topic is significant.* It contributes in some way to the improvement or understanding of educational theory or practice.
4. *The topic is manageable.* It fits the researcher's level of research skill, available resources, and time restrictions.
5. *The topic is ethical.* It does not involve practices or strategies that might embarrass or harm participants.

Stating the Research Topic

Once you have selected and narrowed your research topic, you will need to draft a written statement of that topic. The way in which a topic is stated varies according to the type of research undertaken and the preferences of the researcher. As with other parts of the research process, the approach differs somewhat for quantitative and qualitative studies.

Stating Quantitative Research Topics

For a quantitative study, a well-written **topic statement** generally describes the variables of interest, the specific relationship between those variables and, ideally, important characteristics of the participants (e.g., gifted students, fourth graders with learning disabilities, teenage mothers). An example of a problem statement might be: "The topic to be investigated in this study is the effect of positive reinforcement on the quality of 10th graders' English compositions." The variables to be examined in this study are "positive reinforcement" and "quality of English compositions." The participants will be 10th graders.

Other possible topic statements include the following:

- "The topic to be investigated in this study is secondary teachers' attitudes toward required afterschool activities."
- "The purpose of this study is to investigate the relationship between school entrance age and reading comprehension skills of primary-level students."
- "The problem to be studied is the effect of wearing required school uniforms on the self-esteem of socioeconomically disadvantaged sixth-grade students."

Try to identify the variable or variables in each of these examples and suggest the quantitative research approach that would likely be employed to carry out the study.

Stating Qualitative Research Topics

At this point in the research process, qualitative research topics often are stated in more general language than quantitative ones, because in many cases, the qualitative researcher needs to spend time in the research context for the focus of the study to emerge. Remember, the qualitative researcher usually is much more attuned to the specifics of the context in which the study takes place than is the quantitative researcher. Qualitative topic statements will eventually narrow as the researcher learns more about the research context and its inhabitants, and these more precise statements will appear in the research report. The following are examples of general statements that might be drafted in the earlier stages of the research process:

- "The purpose of this study is to describe the nature of children's engagement with mathematics. The intention is to gather details about children's ways of entering into and sustaining their involvement with mathematics."
- "This qualitative study examines how members of an organization identify, evaluate, and respond to organizational change. The study examines what events members of an organization identify as significant change events and whether different events are seen as significant by subgroups in the organization."
- "The purpose of this research is to study the social integration of children with disabilities in a general education third-grade class."

Placement and Nature of the Topic Statement in a Study

It's helpful to understand how the topic statement will be used in later stages of the research process. A statement of the topic is the first component of the introductory sections of both a research plan and the completed research report, and it gives direction to the remaining aspects of both the plan and report. The statement is accompanied by a presentation of the topic's background, a justification for the study (a discussion of its significance) and, often, a list of limitations of the study. The background includes information needed by readers to understand the nature of the topic.

To provide a justification of the study, the researcher must explain how investigation of the research topic might contribute to educational theory or practice. For example, suppose an introduction begins with this topic statement: "The purpose of this study is to compare the effectiveness of salaried paraprofessionals and nonsalaried parent volunteers with respect to the reading achievement of first-grade children." This statement might be followed by a discussion of (1) the role of paraprofessionals, (2) the increased utilization of paraprofessionals by schools, (3) the expense involved, and (4) the search for alternatives, such as parent volunteers. The significance of the problem would be that if parent volunteers and paid paraprofessionals are equally effective, volunteers can be substituted for salaried paraprofessionals at great savings. Any educational practice that might increase achievement at no additional cost is certainly worthy of investigation!

Thinking about the significance of your topic will help you develop a tentative hypothesis, or a prediction of research findings (you'll learn more about hypotheses later in this chapter). A researcher typically uses the tentative hypothesis as a guiding hypothesis during the process of reviewing literature related to the research topic. In the example just given, a tentative hypothesis would be that parent volunteers are equally as effective as salaried paraprofessionals. The tentative hypothesis is likely to be modified, even changed radically, as a result of the review of the literature. The hypothesis does, however, give direction to the literature search and helps the researcher narrow its scope to include only relevant topics.

:: REVIEW OF RELATED LITERATURE

Having happily found a suitable topic, the beginning researcher is usually "raring to go." Too often the review of related literature is seen as a necessary evil to be completed as fast as possible so that one can get on with the "real research." This perspective is due to a lack of understanding of the purposes and importance of the review and to a feeling of uneasiness on the part of students who are not sure exactly how to go about reporting on the literature. Nonetheless, the review of related literature is as important as any other component of the research process and can be conducted quite painlessly if approached in an orderly manner. Some researchers even find the process quite enjoyable!

Definition, Purpose, and Scope

The **review of related literature** involves the systematic identification, location, and analysis of documents containing information related to the research problem. The term is also used to describe the written component of a research plan or report that discusses the reviewed documents. These documents can include articles, abstracts, reviews, monographs, dissertations, books, other research reports, and electronic media. The literature review has several important purposes that make it well worth the time and effort. The major purpose of reviewing the literature is to determine what has already been done that relates to your topic. This knowledge not only prevents you from unintentionally duplicating another person's research, it also gives you the understanding and insight you need to place your topic within a logical framework. Put simply, the review tells you what has been done and what needs to be done. Previous studies can provide the rationale for your research hypothesis, and indications of what needs to be done can help you justify the significance of your study.

Another important purpose of reviewing the literature is to discover research strategies and specific data collection approaches that have or have not been productive in investigations of topics similar to yours. This information will help you avoid other researchers' mistakes and profit from their experiences. It may suggest approaches and procedures that you previously had not considered. For example, suppose your topic involved the comparative effects of a brand-new experimental method versus the traditional method on the achievement of eighth-grade science students. The review of literature might reveal 10 related studies that found no differences in achievement. Several of the studies, however, might suggest that the brand-new method may be more effective for certain kinds of students than for others. Thus, you might reformulate your topic to involve the comparative effectiveness of the brand-new method versus the traditional method on the achievement of a subgroup of eighth-grade science students: those with low aptitude.

Being familiar with previous research also facilitates interpretation of your study results. The results can be discussed in terms of whether and how they agree with previous findings. If the results contradict previous findings, you can describe differences between your study and the others, providing a rationale for the discrepancy. If your results are consistent with other findings, your report should include suggestions for the next step; if they are not consistent, your report should include suggestions for studies that might resolve the conflict.

Beginning researchers often have difficulty determining how broad their literature review should be. They understand that all literature directly related to their topic should be reviewed; they just don't know when to quit! They have trouble determining which articles are "related enough" to their topic to be included. Unfortunately, there is no formula that can be applied to solve the problem; you must base your decisions on your own judgment and the advice of your teachers or advisors. The following general guidelines, however, can assist you:

■ *Avoid the temptation to include everything you find in your literature review.* Bigger does not mean better. A smaller, well-organized review is definitely preferred to a review containing many studies that are more or less related to the problem.

■ *When investigating a heavily researched area, review only those works that are directly related to your specific problem.* You'll find plenty of references and should not have to rely on less-related studies. For example, the role of feedback in learning has been extensively researched for both animals and human beings, for verbal learning and nonverbal learning, and for a variety of different learning tasks. If you were concerned with the relationship between frequency of feedback and chemistry achievement, you would probably not have to review feedback studies related to animal learning.

■ *When investigating a new or little-researched problem area, review any study related in some meaningful way to your problem.* You'll need to gather enough information to develop a logical framework for the study and a sound rationale for the research hypothesis. For example, suppose you wanted to study the effects on GPA of an exam for non-English speaking students. The students must pass the exam to graduate. Your literature review would probably include any studies that involved English as a second language (ESL) classes and the effects of culture-specific grading practices, as well as studies that identified strategies to improve the learning of ESL students. In a few years from now, there will probably be enough research on the academic consequences of such an exam on non-English speaking students to permit a much more narrowly focused literature review.

A common misconception among beginning researchers is that the worth of a topic is a function of the amount of literature available on it. This is not the case. For many new and important areas of research, few studies have been published; the effects of high-stakes testing is one such area. The very lack of such research often increases the worth of its study. On the other hand, the fact that a thousand studies have already been done in a given problem area does not mean there is no further need for research in that area. Such an area will generally be very well developed, and subtopics that need additional research will be readily identifiable.

Qualitative Research and the Review of Related Literature

Unlike quantitative researchers, who spend a great deal of time examining the research on their topic at the outset of the study, some qualitative researchers will not delve deeply into their literature until their topic has emerged over time. There is disagreement among qualitative researchers about the role of the literature review in the research process. Some qualitative researchers have argued that reviewing the literature curtails inductive analysis—using induction to determine the direction of the research—and should be avoided at the early stages of the research process.[1] Others suggest that the review of related literature is important early in the qualitative research process because it serves the following functions:[2]

- The literature review demonstrates the underlying assumptions (propositions) behind the research questions that are central to the research proposal.
- The literature review provides a way for the novice researcher to convince the proposal reviewers that she is knowledgeable about the related research and the "intellectual traditions" that support the proposed study.[3]
- The literature review provides the researcher with an opportunity to identify any gaps that may exist in the body of literature and to provide a rationale for how the proposed study may contribute to the existing body of knowledge.
- The literature review helps the researcher to refine the research questions and embed them in guiding hypotheses that provide possible directions the researcher may follow.

We recommend that qualitative researchers conduct a review of related literature but also recognize that the review serves a slightly different purpose than the one outlined for quantitative researchers.

Identifying Keywords

Before you go marching off to the library to find resources, you should make a list of keywords to guide your literature search. Most of the initial source works you consult will have alphabetical subject indexes to help you locate information on your topic. You will look in these indexes under the keywords you have selected. For example, if your problem concerns the effect of interactive multimedia on the achievement of 10th-grade biology students, the logical keywords would be *interactive multimedia* and *biology*. You will also need to think of alternative words under which your topic might be listed. For example, references related to this problem might be found using the keywords *multimedia* or *interactive videodiscs*. Usually, the keywords will be obvious; sometimes you may have to play detective.

Some years ago a student was interested in the effect of artificial turf on knee injuries in football. He looked for references under every keyword he could think of, including *surface, playing surface, turf,* and *artificial turf*. He found nothing. Because he knew that studies had been done, he kept trying. When he finally did find a reference, it was listed under, of all things, *lawns!* Identifying keywords is usually not such a big deal. In looking at initial sources, you might identify additional keywords that will help you find succeeding sources. Giving a

---

[1] *Qualitative Research for Education: An Introduction to Theory and Methods* (3rd ed.), by R. C. Bogdan and S. K. Biklen, 1998, Boston: Allyn & Bacon.
[2] *Designing Qualitative Research* (2nd ed.), by C. Marshall and G. Rossman, 1995, Thousand Oaks, CA: Sage.
[3] Ibid., p. 28.

bit of thought to possible keywords should facilitate an efficient beginning to a task that requires organization. After identifying your keywords, you will be ready to find appropriate sources. But, first, let's discuss the general kinds of sources you will be searching for.

Identifying Your Sources

Eventually you will have to examine a range of sources that are pertinent to your topic. However, to start, it is best to consult pertinent educational encyclopedias, handbooks, and annual reviews found in libraries. These resources (some of which were mentioned earlier in the discussion on narrowing your topic) provide summaries of important topics in education and reviews of research on various topics. They allow you to get a picture of your topic in the broader context and help you understand where it fits in the field.

Following are some examples of handbooks, encyclopedias, and reviews relevant to educational research:

Encyclopedia of Educational Research
National Society for the Study of Education Yearbooks
Review of Educational Research
The Encyclopedia of Human Development and Education: Theory, Research, and Studies
The Handbook of Research on Teaching
The International Encyclopedia of Education: Research and Studies
The International Handbook on Self-Study of Teaching and Teacher Education Practices
Handbook of Research on Social Studies Teaching and Learning
Handbook of Research on Curriculum
Review of Research in Education

It's important to distinguish here between two types of sources used by educational researchers. A **secondary source** is secondhand information, such as a brief description of a study written by someone other than the person who conducted it. The reference works just listed contain secondhand information; the *Review of Educational Research,* for example, summarizes many research studies conducted on a given topic. One specific type of summary, an **abstract,** describes a study's most important hypotheses, procedures, results, and conclusions.

Because secondary sources usually give complete bibliographic information on the references cited, they can direct you to relevant primary sources, which are preferred over secondary sources. A **primary source** is firsthand information, such as an original document or a description of a study written by the person who conducted it. (Although in this context we're talking mostly about written works, primary sources can be any firsthand source of information, such as a relic or the testimony of an eyewitness.) You should not be satisfied with the information contained in secondary sources; the corresponding primary sources will be considerably more detailed and will give you information "straight from the horse's mouth." There is a difference between the opinion of an author and the results of an empirical study. The latter is more valued in a review.

Searching for Books on Your Topic in the Library

Having identified your keywords and some potential resources, it is a good time to make an initial foray into your university library. Because it will be a second home to you, at least for a while, you should become familiar with the library. Time spent initially will save more in the long run. You should find out what references are available and where they are located. Most libraries, especially university libraries, provide help and education in the use of their resources. You should be familiar with services offered by the library, as well as the rules and regulations regarding the use of library materials. It also might be useful to identify people who are actively conducting research in your topic area. You could then contact them to request copies of their recent articles on your topic and suggestions for useful references in the area.

Most university libraries have a librarian on duty to help with requests. It is not uncommon for a university to have an "education" librarian who has experience in both K–12 and graduate education and is very skilled in helping folks track down resources. Although significant technological advances have changed the way research is conducted in the library, individual libraries vary greatly in their ability to capitalize on increasingly available options. Librarians will usually be very willing to help you, but you should also learn to navigate the library on your own; the librarian might not be as cheerful the ninth time you approach as he was the first time! With or without a librarian's help, you can use the library catalog and browse the stacks to search for books on your topic.

Using Library Catalogs.   In nearly all libraries, the card catalogs of previous generations have been replaced with computer terminals that provide access to the library's resources. You may even be able to borrow from other libraries with whom your institution has reciprocal loan agreements if a particular reference is not available at your home library. These electronic catalogs are extremely user friendly and give you a good place to start your search for literature related to your area of focus.

To locate either secondary or primary sources, you need to conduct a search of the library's catalog. By typing in a title or author name, you'll quickly learn the availability of the item and its location (usually indicated by call number) in the library. If you don't know the author or title, you can search by subject or keyword. For example, to find summaries of research previously conducted in an area of psychology, you might enter the keywords *handbook* and *psychology*.

If you are at the beginning of your search for primary sources, you should conduct a keyword search. A keyword search may be narrow or broad; how narrow or broad depends on factors such as the purpose of the search and the amount of material available on your topic. If you need a relatively small number of references and if much has been published about your topic, a narrow search will likely be appropriate. If you need a relatively large number of references and very little has been published about your topic, a broad search will be better. If you do not have a sense of what is available, your best strategy is to start narrow and broaden as necessary. For example, if you find that there are very few references related to the effect of interactive multimedia on the achievement of 10th-grade biology students, you could broaden your search by including all sciences or all secondary students.

A useful way to narrow or broaden a keyword search is to use Boolean operators, words that tell the computer which keywords you want your search results to include or exclude. Common Boolean operators are the words *AND, OR,* and *NOT* (usually typed in capital letters). Put simply, using the connector *AND* or *NOT* between keywords narrows a search, whereas using the connector *OR* broadens one. If you type the phrase "Easter AND rabbit" into the keyword search box, for example, you will obtain a list of references that refer to both Easter and rabbit. If you type the phrase "Easter NOT rabbit," your search results will include references pertaining to Easter but will exclude references pertaining to rabbit. A search for "Easter OR rabbit" will produce a list of references that relate to either or both concepts. By using various combinations of the *AND* and *OR* connectors, you can vary your search strategy as needed. Table 2.1 gives other examples of searches with Boolean operators and describes additional ways to limit keyword searches. Note that it is difficult to develop a search model that can be followed in every library. You must get acquainted with your own library's unique search methods.

Browsing the Stacks.   With access to electronic catalogs, many young researchers may not consider an older strategy for locating books: browsing the stacks. This is similar to the kind of activity you might undertake at a public library when looking for a new fiction book to read. If you can locate the area of the library with books related to your area of focus, it can be productive to browse and pull interesting books off the shelves. You may also find leads to related materials, not necessarily uncovered in your electronic search, by looking at any given book's reference list.

TABLE 2.1	Summary of ways to limit keyword searches

Keyword Searches			
General	**Field Codes**	**Boolean Operators**	**Field Qualifiers**
k = assessment	k = dickonson.au	k = assessment AND alternative	k = 1990.dt1,dt2. and assessment (books on assessment published in 1990)
k = book review	k = criticism.su		
k = automa? (retrieves automatic, automation, automating, etc.)	k = research.ti	k = authentic OR alternative	
	Codes limit searches to specific areas or fields in the bibliographic record, such as author, title, and subject	k = assessment NOT standardized	k = curriculum and fre.la (books on curriculum in French)
Looks for word or phrase anywhere in a bibliographic record		Used to expand or limit a search	
		AND: retrieves records containing *both* terms	Used with Boolean operators to limit searches
Adjacency is assumed (i.e., words will be next to each other unless specified)		OR: retrieves records containing *either* term	Inquire in your library for available field qualifiers
? is used to retrieve singular, plural, or variant spellings		NOT: retrieves records containing one term and *not* the other	

Source: Adapted from Boston College Libraries Information System, "Guide to Using Quest." Used with permission of Trustees of Boston College.

Consulting Computer Databases to Locate Journals, Articles, Reports, and Other Publications

The electronic catalog found in a library is an example of a **database,** a sortable, analyzable collection of units of information maintained on a computer. Other types of computer databases are also used in research. Available online or on CD-ROMs, some are topic-specific indexes, some are collections of abstracts, and some—full-text databases—are compilations of articles or other documents. Available at most university and public libraries, computer databases provide an excellent way to identify primary sources.

The steps involved in searching a research database, be it online or on CD-ROM, are similar to those involved in a book search:

1. Identify keywords related to your topic.
2. Select the databases you wish to search.
3. Specify your search strategy.

The following sections describe some of the commonly used databases for searches of education literature.

Education Resources Information Center (ERIC).   Established in 1966 by the National Library of Education as part of the United States Department of Education's Office of Educational Research and Improvement, ERIC is the world's largest database on education. The online database provides information on subjects ranging from early childhood and elementary education to education for gifted children and rural and urban education. ERIC is used by more than 500,000 people each year, providing them with access to more than 1.1 million bibliographic citations and more than 107,000 full-text non-journal documents. In 2004 the ERIC system was restructured by the Department of Education. The new Web site, launched in September 2004, uses the most up-to-date retrieval methods in order to provide users access to the ERIC databases.

With its user-friendly features, ERIC is a quick, easy way to get access to the related literature. In addition, there is no charge associated with conducting an ERIC search from your home or school computer and accessing full-text ERIC documents.

The best starting point for your ERIC explorations is the ERIC home page at http://www.eric.ed.gov. (Internet addresses were checked for accuracy during the production of this text. Due to the rapidly changing nature of technology, some addresses and online procedures may be different at the time of your reading. The basic strategies for online searching, however, will remain the same.) The home page includes links to all other ERIC sites, most notably:

- ERIC search
- ERIC thesaurus, which includes a comprehensive listing of descriptive words ("descriptors") in numerous subject categories

You can conduct a search using ERIC online in several ways. The basic ERIC search prompts you to search using keywords, author only, title only, or ERIC document number.

The advanced ERIC search offers the same prompts as the basic search but also allows you to search by ISBN number, journal name, source institution, sponsoring agency, publication type (e.g., book, review, dissertation), ERIC thesaurus descriptor, publication date, and full-text availability.

The thesaurus page prompts you to search using your own descriptor, which is then matched to one or more ERIC descriptors (remember: garbage in, garbage out!). You must search ERIC using ERIC descriptors. For example, entering the term *achievement tests* results in a suggestion from ERIC to use a narrower search term such as *equivalency tests, mastery tests,* or *national competency tests.* You can also browse the thesaurus alphabetically or look for descriptors in the 40-plus subject categories provided by ERIC.

Once you have identified materials that you would like to examine, you need to access these materials. You may notice in your searches that documents are categorized with an ED or EJ designation. An ED designation is generally used for unpublished documents, such as reports, studies, and even lesson plans. ED references are available in university libraries through ERIC's microfiche collection or may be available as full-text online documents. An EJ designation is used for articles that have been published in professional journals. EJ articles are not available in full text from ERIC and must be tracked down in the periodicals collection of a library or purchased from article reprint companies.

Although ERIC is the largest computer database for searches of education literature, it is not the only source available. Other commonly used computer databases in education are described next.

Education Index. The Education Index is an electronic index of articles published in educational periodicals since 1983. It provides bibliographic information and abstracts of sources (some libraries subscribe to a full-text feature) pertaining to the topic(s) that have been researched. A sample result of an Education Index search is shown in Figure 2.2. In addition to article abstracts, the database includes citations for yearbooks and monograph series, videotapes, motion picture and computer program reviews, and law cases.

PsycINFO. The PsycINFO database is the online version of *Psychological Abstracts,* a print source that presents summaries of completed psychological research studies (see http://www.apa.org/psycinfo). Produced monthly, Psychological Abstracts contains summaries of journal

FIGURE 2.2	Results of an Education Index search

Record 1 of 1 in Education Abstracts 6/83-6/01
TITLE: **Developing academic confidence** to build literacy: what teachers can do
AUTHOR(S): Colvin,-Carolyn; Schlosser,-Linda-Kramer
SOURCE: Journal of Adolescent and Adult Literacy v 41 Dec 1997/Jan 1998 p. 272–81
ABSTRACT: A study examined how the classroom literacy behaviors of middle school students relate to their academic success and reinforce students' evolving sense of self. The participants were at-risk students, academically successful students, and teachers from a middle school in southern California. It was found that when academically marginal students call on literacy strategies, these strategies are limited in scope and offer little help. However, more academically successful students seem well aware of the behaviors that are likely to result in a successful literacy experience. The characteristics of academically marginal and successful students are outlined, and suggestions for helping teachers create classrooms where students behave with greater efficacy are offered.
DESCRIPTORS: Attitudes-Middle-school-students; Middle-school-students-Psychology; Self-perception; Language-arts-Motivation

Source: From Colvin, Carolyn, & Schlosser, Linda Kramer. (Dec 1997/Jan 1998). Developing academic confidence to build literacy: What teachers can do. *Journal of Adolescent & Adult Literacy, 41*(2), 272–281. Reprinted with permission of Carolyn Colvin and the International Reading Association. The International Reading Association makes no warranties as to the accuracy of this translation.

articles, technical reports, book chapters, and books in the field of psychology. It is organized by subject area according to the PsycINFO classification codes for easy browsing. The classification codes also serve as the table of contents for the Psychological Abstracts and can be accessed at http://www.apa.org/psycinfo/training/tips-classcodes.html. These classification codes allow you to retrieve abstracts for studies in a specific category—for example, Developmental Disorders and Autism (3250) or Speech and Language Disorders (3270).

Dissertation Abstracts.   Dissertation Abstracts contains bibliographic citations and abstracts from all subject areas for doctoral dissertations and master's theses completed at more than 1,000 accredited colleges and universities worldwide. The database dates back to 1861, with abstracts included from 1980 forward. If after reading an abstract you wish to obtain a copy of the complete dissertation, check to see if it is available in your library. If not, speak to a librarian about how to obtain a copy. The results of a Dissertation Abstracts search are shown in Figure 2.3.

Readers' Guide to Periodical Literature.   Readers' Guide to Periodical Literature is an index similar in format to the Education Index. Instead of professional publications, however, it indexes articles in nearly 200 widely read magazines. Articles located through the Readers' Guide will generally be nontechnical, opinion-type references. These can be useful in documenting the significance of your problem. The Readers' Guide lists bibliographic information for each entry. To obtain an article listed in the Readers' Guide, search your library's catalog for the magazine in which the article appears. If your library holds that magazine, it will be located in the periodicals department.

Annual Review of Psychology.   The Annual Review of Psychology includes reviews of psychological research that are often relevant to educational research. It provides bibliographic information and abstracts for such specific areas as child development, educational administration, exceptional child education, and language teaching.

Searching the Internet and the World Wide Web

The Internet and the World Wide Web provide information and resources on many educational topics. The World Wide Web is a service on the Internet that gives users access to text,

---

FIGURE 2.3 Results of a Dissertation Abstracts search

OCLC FirstSearch: Detailed Record
Your requested information from your library BOSTON COL

Dissertation Abstracts Online results for: kw: literacy. Record 2 of 5208

Mark: ☑

Database: Dissertations

Title: **Learning community: An ethnographic study of popular education and homeless women in a shelter-based adult literacy program**

Author(s): Rivera, Lorna

Degree: Ph.D.

Year: 2001

Pages: 00264

Institution: Northeastern University; 0160

Advisor: Adviser Gordana Rabrenovic

Source: DAI, 61, no. 09A (2001): p. 3511

Standard No: ISBN: 0-599-95181-8

Abstract: This dissertation studies the impact of popular education approaches on the lives of fifty homeless and formerly homeless women who participated in the Adult Learners Program at a shelter located in one of Boston's poorest neighborhoods. Data were collected between January 1995 and June 1998. The guiding research questions are: How do poor women interpret the value of education? What poverty-related barriers interfere with their participation in popular education classes? How do the principles and practices of popular education build a sense of community and collective social action?

This ethnographic study utilizes multiple research methods to illustrate how popular education approaches make it possible for poor women to become empowered individually and collectively. Popular education is a methodology of teaching and learning through dialogue that directly links curriculum content to people's lived experience. It's roots are in critical social theory and the work of Paulo Freire. This research shows that poor women place a high value on education. They believe that a high school diploma will provide access to better economic opportunities and they struggle to complete their formal education within the context of homelessness and family violence.

It is argued that popular education's potential to build community is strengthened by the Adult Learners Program's participatory organization and the support services it offers to homeless families. Further, it is argued that popular education had a positive impact on the women's lives, as evidenced by: the women's increased levels of participation in their children's education; the women's participation in efforts to help other poor women in the community; the women's reported increase in self-confidence and group esteem; and, the women becoming stronger advocates for their basic legal rights related to welfare, housing, health, and education.

The research data suggest that the 1995 Massachusetts welfare reform legislation poses a significant barrier to adult literacy for welfare recipients. It is argued that limiting access to education through "work-first" welfare reform policies reproduces social inequalities. This dissertation about homeless women and popular education provides strong evidence in support of the social, political, and economic benefits of popular education programs for the poor.

SUBJECT(S)

Descriptor: EDUCATION, SOCIOLOGY OF
SOCIOLOGY, PUBLIC AND SOCIAL WELFARE
EDUCATION, ADULT AND CONTINUING

Accession No: AAI9988499

Source: Screen capture retrieved from OCLC FirstSearch Web site: http://FirstSearch.oclc.org. FirstSearch electronic presentation and platform copyright © 1992–2001 by OCLC. Reprinted by permission. FirstSearch and WorldCat are registered trademarks of OCLC Online Computer Library Center, Inc.

---

graphics, and multimedia. You can access the Web using a computer with a modem that is hooked up to a telephone or cable line. Your computer will also need a browser (such as Netscape or Internet Explorer).

The resources you can find on the Web are almost limitless. With just a few clicks, you can access electronic educational journals that provide full-text articles, bibliographic information, and abstracts. You can also obtain up-to-the-minute research reports and information about educational research activities being undertaken at various research centers, and you can access education home pages that provide links to a range of education resources that other researchers have found especially valuable. But be warned—there is little quality control for much that is found on the Internet. At times, the sheer volume of information on the Web can be overwhelming. Be prepared to sift through piles of cyberspace junk to find the diamond in the rough. The best way to become adept at searching the Web efficiently is simply by surfing (browsing) it during your spare time. In this way, you will become familiar with maneuvering from site to site and implementing successful search strategies.

Following are some Web sites that are especially useful to educational researchers. Their Internet addresses are in parentheses. In addition, you can access other electronic indexing and abstracting sources by using your computer's search engine (e.g., Lycos, Infoseek, Yahoo, or Excite) to find some of your own addresses. Addresses containing *ed* or ending in *.edu* are related to educational institutions, and those ending in *.com* are related to commercial enterprises.

UnCover Periodical Index (http://www.unm.edu/~brosen/uncover.htm). UnCover is a database with brief descriptive information about articles from more than 17,000 multidisciplinary journals. If you register (for a fee) with UnCover REVEAL, an automated alerting service, you will receive monthly tables of contents from your favorite periodicals. The service also allows you to create search strategies for your research topics.

NewJour (http://gort.ucsd.edu/newjour/). This site provides an up-to-date list of journals and newsletters available on the Internet on any subject. Using NewJour's search option, you can do a title search to see if a specific journal is currently on the Web, or do a subject search to find out which journals in a particular subject are available on the Internet. Direct links are provided to available journals.

Education Week (http://www.edweek.org/). Full-text articles from *Education Week,* a periodical devoted to education reform, schools, and policy, are available at the site. In addition to current and past articles, the site provides background data to enhance current news, resources for teachers, and recommended Web sites to investigate for other information.

Journal of Statistics Education (http://www.amstat.org/publications/jse/). This electronic journal provides abstracts and full-text articles that have appeared since 1993. Interesting features of the journal are "Teaching Bits: A Resource for Teachers of Statistics" and "Datasets and Stories."

CSTEEP: The Center for the Study of Testing, Evaluation, and Educational Policy (http://www.csteep.bc.edu/). The Web site for this educational research organization contains information on testing, evaluation, and public policy studies on school assessment practices and international comparative research.

National Center for Education Statistics (http://www.nces.ed.gov/). This site contains statistical reports and other information on the condition of U.S. education. It also reports on education activities internationally.

Developing Educational Standards (http://www.edstandards.org/Standards.html). This site contains a wealth of up-to-date information regarding educational standards and curriculum frameworks from all sources (national, state, local, and other). Information on standards and frameworks can be linked to by subject area, state, governmental agency, or organization. Entire standards and frameworks are available.

Internet Resources for Special Education (http://specialed.miningco.com). This site provides links to a variety of topics, including teaching resources for regular education and special education teachers; Web sites for students to visit; disability information, resources, and research; disability laws; special education laws; assistive technology; clearinghouses; and information about current topics of interest.

U.S. Department of Education (http://www.ed.gov/). This site contains links to the U.S. government's education databases (including ERIC). It also makes available full-text reports on current findings on education. In addition, it provides links to research offices and organizations, as well as research publications and products. One Department of Education publication, *A Researcher's Guide to the Department of Education,* helps researchers access the various resources that the department has to offer.

It is entirely possible that you will want to access information on the World Wide Web that is not available on the Web sites just described. The easiest and quickest way to find interesting new sites is to use a search engine (such as Google, Yahoo!, Lycos, Excite, or Alta Vista) to look for Web pages containing keywords related to your topic. Once you have entered a keyword or keywords in the appropriate place on the search engine's home page, the search engine examines a selected large portion of the Internet (or a specific domain of the Internet, if you say so) for sites that contain your keyword(s).

To facilitate your search, most search engines offer you the option of narrowing a search so that only the most relevant sites are identified. An example using Yahoo! is shown in Figure 2.4. Clicking on the subcategory *Education* in the Yahoo! Web Directory (Figure 2.4a) will significantly narrow your search to relevant sources in the field of education. After selecting the *Education* subcategory, a very useful page, shown in Figure 2.4b, appears. Clicking on a subtopic such as *Early Childhood Education* will then take you to another Web page that provides links to numerous sites pertaining to your topic. Clicking on any of the links shown in Figure 2.4c will access all of the information that those particular sites have to offer.

Becoming a Member of Professional Organizations

Another way to access current literature related to your research topic is through membership in professional organizations. The following list gives the names of a few U.S.-based professional organizations that could be valuable resources for research reports and curriculum materials. In countries other than the United States, there are likely to be similar organizations that could also be accessed through an Internet search. This list of professional organizations is not intended to be comprehensive, for there are as many professional organizations as there are content areas (reading, writing, mathematics, science, social studies, music, health, and physical education, to name a few) and special interest groups (Montessori education, for example). A search of the Internet will provide a listing of more Web sites than you will have the time or energy to visit!

Association for Supervision and Curriculum Development (ASCD) (http://www.ascd.org/). Boasting 160,000 members in more than 135 countries, ASCD is one of the largest educational organizations in the world. ASCD publishes books, newsletters, audiotapes, videotapes, and some excellent journals that are a valuable resource for teacher researchers, including *Educational Leadership* and the *Journal of Curriculum and Supervision.*

National Council of Teachers of Mathematics (NCTM) (http://nctm.org). With nearly 100,000 members, NCTM is dedicated to the teaching and learning of mathematics and offers vision and leadership for mathematics educators at all age levels. NCTM provides regional and national professional development opportunities and publishes the following journals: *Teaching Children Mathematics, Mathematics Teaching in the Middle School, Mathematics Teacher, Online Journal for School Mathematics,* and the *Journal for Research in Mathematics Education.*

National Council for the Social Studies (NCSS) (http://www.ncss.org/). The NCSS supports and advocates social studies educations. Its resources for educators include the following journals: *Social Education* and *Social Studies and the Young Learner.*

National Science Teachers Association (NSTA) (http://nsta.org/). The NSTA, with more than 55,000 members, provides many valuable resources for science teachers. It develops the National Science Education Standards and publishes the following journals: *Science and Children, Science Scope, The Science Teacher,* and *Journal of College Science Teaching.*

International Reading Association (IRA) (http://www.reading.org/). The IRA provides resources to an international audience of reading teachers through its publication of the following journals: *The Reading Teacher, Journal of Adolescent and Adult Literacy,* and *Reading Research Quarterly.*

FIGURE 2.4   Sample search using Yahoo!

(a) Search options in opening screen; (b) search topics in Education category; (c) links in Early Childhood Education.

Source: Reproduced with permission of Yahoo! Inc. © 2005 by Yahoo! Inc. YAHOO! and the YAHOO! logo are trademarks of Yahoo! Inc.

Evaluating Your Sources

Once you have a source in hand, you will need to evaluate it. Obviously, the first thing to do is to determine if it really applies to your research topic. If it does, you then need to evaluate the quality of the information. For example, does the information come from a scholarly journal or a popular magazine? Is the information someone's personal opinion or the result of a research study? Clearly, sources of different types merit different weight in your review.

An initial appraisal of a source includes looking closely at the date of publication and where the source was found. Look at the copyright date of books that you find and the dates on which articles were published. Appropriate research in topic areas of current interest and continuing development generally require recent, up-to-date references.

Next, identify where the source was found. For instance, did you find your source in a refereed or a nonrefereed journal? In a **refereed journal,** articles are reviewed by a panel of experts in the field and are thus seen as more "scholarly" and "trustworthy" than articles from nonrefereed or popular journals. Research articles in refereed journals are required to comply with strict guidelines regarding not only format but also research procedures.

It is also important to verify that the information presented in a particular source is objective and impartial. Does the author present evidence to support the interpretations made? Does the content of the article consist mainly of an individual's opinion, or does it contain appropriately collected and analyzed data? Finally, does the source add to the information you have already gathered about your topic? If the source adds to your growing knowledge of your topic, it is useful and worth paying attention to.

Special care and caution must be taken when evaluating World Wide Web sources, because anyone can post information on the Web. Just because an Internet search identifies a particular source does not mean that the source is accurate or credible. Sources from the World Wide Web must be closely examined for bias, subjectivity, intent, and accuracy.

Conducting effective library and Internet searches will yield an abundance of useful information about your topic. By using both search methods, you will collect information that is both up-to-date and comprehensive. As time goes on and you become more experienced, you will be able from the beginning to conduct more efficient searches that are focused appropriately on your topic.

Abstracting

After you have identified the primary references related to your topic, you are ready to move on to the next phase of a review of related literature—abstracting the references. Basically, this involves creating abstracts by reviewing, summarizing, and classifying your references. Students sometimes ask why it is necessary to read and abstract original, complete articles (or reports, or whatever) if they already have perfectly good abstracts. There are two basic reasons. First, a provided abstract is not necessarily "perfectly good." It may not be a totally accurate summary of the article's contents. Second, there is a great deal of important information that you can obtain only by reading the complete article. (You'll see.)

To begin the abstracting process, arrange your articles and other sources in reverse chronological order. Beginning with the latest references is a good research strategy because the most recent research is likely to have profited from previous research. Also, recent references may cite preceding studies you may not have identified. For each reference, complete the following steps:

1. If the article has an abstract or a summary, which most do, read it to determine the article's relevancy to your problem.
2. Skim the entire article, making mental notes of the main points of the study.
3. On an index card or in a computer database, write a complete bibliographic reference for the work. (The word *reference* can mean either a reference work or a bibliographic reference—a note containing complete bibliographic information on a work.) Include the library call number on the card or in the database if the source work is a book. This is tedious but important. You will spend much more time trying to find the complete bibliographic information for an article or book you failed to abstract completely than you will abstracting it in the first place. If you know that your final report must follow a

particular editorial style, such as that described in the *Publication Manual of the American Psychological Association* (APA), put your bibliographic reference in that form. For example, an APA-style reference for a journal article would look like this:

Snurd, B. J. (1995). The use of white versus yellow chalk in the teaching of advanced calculus. *Journal of Useless Findings, 11,* 1–99.

In this example, 1995 is the data of publication, 11 is the volume number of the journal, and 1–99 are the page numbers. A style manual such as the APA's provides reference formats for all types of sources. Whatever format you use, use it consistently and be certain your bibliographic references are accurate. You never know when you might have to go back and get additional information from an article. (Chapter 21 provides detailed information about reference formats.)

4. Classify and code the article according to some system, and then add the code to the database entry or index card (or a photocopy) in a conspicuous place, such as an upper corner. The code should be one that can be easily accessed when you want to sort your notes into the categories you devise. Any coding system that makes sense to you will facilitate your task later when you have to sort, organize, analyze, synthesize, and write your review of the literature. Coding and keeping track of articles is key for organization. Useful computer programs that simplify coding and subsequent data retrieval are HyperRESEARCH[4] and EndNote.[5]

5. Abstract, or summarize, the reference (source work) by typing or neatly writing (you're going to have to read your abstracts later) its essential points. If the work is an opinion article, write the main points of the author's position—for example, "Jones believes parent volunteers should be used because [list the reasons]." If it is a study, state the problem, the procedures (including a description of participants and instruments), and the major conclusions. Make special note of any particularly interesting or unique aspect of the study, such as use of a new measuring instrument. Double-check the reference to make sure you have not omitted any pertinent information. If an abstract provided at the beginning of an article contains all the essential information (and that is a big *if*), by all means use it.

6. Indicate any thoughts that come to your mind, such as points on which you disagree (mark them with an *X,* for example) or components that you do not understand (mark with a "?"). For example, if an author stated that he or she had used a double-blind procedure, and you were unfamiliar with that technique, you would put a question mark next to that statement, either in your database entry, on your index card, or on a photocopy of the page. Later, you could find out what it is.

7. Indicate any statements that are direct quotations or personal reactions. Plagiarism (intentional or not) is an absolute no-no, with the direst of consequences. If you do not put quotation marks around direct quotations on your card or database entry, for example, you might not remember later which statements are, and which are not, direct quotations. You must also record the exact page number of the quotation in case you use it later in your paper. You will need the page number when citing the source in your paper. Incidentally, direct quotations should be kept to a minimum in your research plan and report; both should be in *your* words, not those of other researchers. Occasionally, however, a direct quotation may be quite appropriate and useful. Be sure, however, that you record all bibliographic information required by your style manual. (You may choose to photocopy entries from other researchers' reference lists, but the main disadvantage of this is cost.)

---

[4] HyperRESEARCH 2.6 [Computer software], 2003, Randolph, MA: ResearchWare, Inc.
[5] EndNote 8 [Computer software], 2004, Berkeley, CA: ISI ResearchSoft.

Whatever approach you use, guard your notes with your life. Make a copy and put it away in a safe place. When you have completed your reviewing task, those notes will represent many hours of work. Students have been brought to tears because they left their notes "on the bus" or "on a table in the cafeteria" or, even worse, lost all their files to a computer virus! Beyond being sympathetic, your instructor can do little more than to tell you to start over (ouch!). Also, when the research report is completed, the cards or computer information can be filed (photocopies can be placed in notebooks) and saved for future reference and future studies (nobody can do just one!).

Analyzing, Organizing, and Reporting the Literature

For beginning researchers, the hardest part of writing the literature review for a plan or report is thinking about how hard it is going to be to write the literature review. More time is spent worrying about doing it than actually doing it. This hesitancy stems mostly from a lack of previous experience with the type of writing needed in a literature review. A literature review requires a technical form of writing that is unlike most of the writing we do. In technical writing, facts must be documented and opinions substantiated. For example, if you say that Ohio's high school dropout percentage has increased in the last 10 years, you must provide a source for this information. Technical writing is precise, requiring clarity of definitions and consistency in the use of terms. If the term *achievement* is important in your review, you must indicate what you mean by it and be consistent in using that meaning throughout the written review. Figure 2.5 summarizes these and other important technical writing guidelines useful in a literature review.

If you have efficiently abstracted the literature related to your problem, and if you approach the task in an equally systematic manner, then analyzing, organizing, and reporting the literature will be relatively painless. To get warmed up, you should read quickly through your notes. This will refresh your memory and help you identify references that no longer seem sufficiently related to your topic. Do not force references into your review that do not really "fit"; the review forms the background and rationale for your hypothesis and should contain only references that serve this purpose. The following guidelines—based on experience acquired the hard way—should be helpful to you:

Make an outline. Don't groan; your eighth-grade teacher was right about the virtues of an outline. However you construct it, an outline will save you time and effort in the long run and will increase your probability of having an organized review. The outline does not have to be excessively detailed. Begin by identifying the main topics and the order in which they

---

FIGURE 2.5 **Guidelines for technical writing**

- *Document facts and substantiate opinions.* Cite references to support your facts and opinions. Note that facts are usually based on empirical data, while opinions are not. In the hierarchy of persuasiveness, facts are more persuasive than opinions. Differentiate between facts and opinions in the review.
- *Define terms clearly, and be consistent in your use of terms.*
- *Organize content logically.*
- *Direct your writing to a particular audience.* Usually the literature review is aimed at a relatively naive reader, one who has some basic understanding of the topic but requires additional education to understand the topic or issue being studied. Do not assume your audience knows as much as you do about the topic and literature! They don't, so you have to write to educate them.

- *Follow an accepted manual of style.* The manual of style indicates the style in which chapter headings are set up, how tables must be constructed, how footnotes and bibliographies must be prepared, and the like. Commonly used manuals and their current editions are *Publication Manual of the American Psychological Association,* Fifth Edition, and *The Chicago Manual of Style,* Fifteenth Edition.
- *Evade affected verbiage and eschew obscuration of the obvious.* In other words, limit big words; avoid jargon.
- *Start each major section with a brief overview of the section.* The overview might begin like this: " In this section, three main issues are examined. The first is. . . ."
- *End each major section with a summary of the main ideas.*

should be presented. For example, the outline of the review for the problem concerned with salaried paraprofessionals versus parent volunteers might begin with these headings: "Literature on Salaried Paraprofessionals," "Literature on Parent Volunteers," and "Literature Comparing the Two." Note that you can always add or remove topics in the outline as your work progresses. The next step is to differentiate each major heading into logical subheadings. In our outline for this chapter, for example, the section "Review of Related Literature" was subdivided as follows:

Review of Related Literature

Definition, Purpose, and Scope
Qualitative Research and the Review of Literature
Identifying Keywords
Identifying Your Sources
Evaluating Your Sources
Abstracting
Analyzing, Organizing, and Reporting the Literature

The need for further differentiation will be determined by your topic; the more complex it is, the more subheadings you will require. When you have completed your outline, you will invariably need to rearrange, add, and delete topics. It is much easier, however, to reorganize an outline than it is to reorganize a document written in paragraph form.

Analyze each reference in terms of your outline. In other words, determine the subheading under which each reference fits. Then sort your references into appropriate piles. If you end up with references without a home, there are three logical possibilities: (1) there is something wrong with your outline, (2) the references do not belong in your review and should be discarded, or (3) the references do not belong in your review but do belong somewhere else in your research plan and report introduction. Opinion articles or reports of descriptive research often will be useful in the introduction, whereas formal research studies will be most useful in the review of related literature section.

Analyze the references under each subheading for similarities and differences. If three references say essentially the same thing, you will not need to describe each one; it is much better to make one summary statement and cite the three sources, as in this example:

> Several studies have found white chalk to be more effective than yellow chalk in the teaching of advanced mathematics (Snurd, 1995; Trivia, 1994; Ziggy, 1984).

Give a meaningful overview of past research. Don't present a series of abstracts or a mere list of findings (Jones found A, Smith found B, and Brown found C). Your task is to organize and summarize the references in a meaningful way. Do not ignore studies that are contradictory to most other studies or to your personal bias. Analyze and evaluate contradictory studies and try to determine a possible explanation. For example,

> Contrary to these studies is the work of Rottenstudee (1998), who found yellow chalk to be more effective than white chalk in the teaching of trigonometry. However, the size of the treatment groups (two students per group) and the duration of the study (one class period) may have seriously affected the results.

Discuss the references least related to your problem first and those most related to your problem just prior to the statement of the hypothesis. Think of a big V. At the bottom of the V is your hypothesis; directly above your hypothesis are the studies most directly related to it, and so forth. The idea is to organize and present your literature in such a way that it leads logically to a tentative, testable conclusion, namely, your hypothesis. Highlight or summarize important aspects of the review to help readers identify them. If your problem has more than one major aspect, you may have two Vs or one V that logically leads to two tentative, testable conclusions.

Conclude the review with a brief summary of the literature and its implications. The length of this summary depends on the length of the review. It should be detailed enough to clearly show the chain of logic you have followed in arriving at your implications and tentative conclusions.

One way to summarize the results of the literature is to conduct a meta-analysis.

Meta-Analysis

A **meta-analysis** is a statistical approach to summarizing the results of many quantitative studies that have investigated basically the same problem. It provides a numerical way of expressing the "average" result of a group of studies.

As you may have noticed when you reviewed the literature related to your problem, numerous variables have been the subject of literally hundreds of studies; ability grouping, for example, is one such variable. Traditional attempts to summarize the results of many related studies have basically involved classifying the studies in some defined way, noting the number of studies in which a variable was and was not significant, and drawing one or more conclusions. Thus, it might be stated that in 45 of 57 studies the Warmfuzzy approach resulted in greater student self-esteem than the No-nonsense approach, and therefore the Warmfuzzy approach appears to be an effective method for promoting self-esteem. Two major problems are associated with the traditional approach to summarizing studies. The first is that subjectivity is involved. Different authors use different criteria for selecting the studies to be summarized, use different review strategies, and often come to different (sometimes opposite) conclusions. Thus, for example, some reviewers might conclude that the Warmfuzzy method is superior to the No-nonsense method, whereas other reviewers might conclude that the results are inconclusive. The second problem is that as the number of research studies available on a topic increases, so does the difficulty of the reviewing task. During the 1970s, the need for a more efficient and more objective approach to research integration, or summarization, became increasingly apparent.

Meta-analysis is the alternative that was developed by Gene Glass and his colleagues.[6] Although much has been written on the subject, Glass's *Meta-Analysis in Social Research* remains the classic work in the field. It delineates specific procedures for finding, describing, classifying, and coding the research studies to be included in a meta-analytic review, and for measuring and analyzing study findings. A central characteristic that distinguishes meta-analysis from more traditional approaches is the emphasis placed on making the review as inclusive as possible. Thus, reviewers are encouraged to include results typically excluded, such as those presented in dissertation reports and unpublished works. Critics of meta-analysis claim that this strategy results in the inclusion in a review of a number of "poor" studies. Glass and his colleagues counter that there is no evidence to support this claim; final conclusions are not negatively affected by including the studies; and further, evidence suggests that on average, dissertations, for example, exhibit higher design quality than many published journal articles. Glass and his colleagues also note that experimental effects reported in journals are generally larger than those presented in dissertations; thus, if dissertations are excluded, effects will appear to be greater than they actually are.

The key feature of meta-analysis is that each study's results are translated into an effect size. *Effect size* is a numerical way of expressing the strength or magnitude of a reported relationship, be it causal or not. For example, in an experimental study the effect size expresses how much better (or worse) the experimental group performed on a task or test as compared to the control group.

After effect size has been calculated for each study, the results are averaged, yielding one number that summarizes the overall effect of the studies. Effect size is expressed as a decimal

---

[6] *Meta-Analysis in Social Research*, by G. V. Glass, B. McGaw, and M. L. Smith, 1981, Beverly Hills, CA: Sage.

number, and although numbers greater than 1.00 are possible, they do not occur very often. An effect size near .00 means that, on average, experimental and control groups performed the same; a positive effect size means that, on average, the experimental group performed better; and a negative effect size means that, on average, the control group did better. For positive effect sizes, the larger the number, the more effective the experimental treatment.

Although there are no hard and fast rules, it is generally agreed that an effect size in the twenties (e.g., .28) indicates a treatment that produces a relatively small effect, whereas an effect size in the eighties (e.g., .81) indicates a powerful treatment. Just to give you a couple of examples, Walberg[7] has reported that for cooperative learning studies the effect size is .76. This indicates that cooperative learning is a very effective instructional strategy. Walberg also reports that the effect size for assigned homework is .28, and for graded homework, .79. This suggests that homework makes a relatively small difference in achievement but that graded homework makes a big difference. (Many of you can probably use this information to your advantage!)

As suggested earlier, meta-analysis is not without its critics. It must be recognized, however, that despite its perceived shortcomings, it still represents a significant improvement over traditional methods of summarizing literature. Further, it is not a fait accompli, but rather an approach in the process of refinement.

Now that you have systematically developed your literature review, you are ready to state your hypothesis.

:: FORMULATING AND STATING A HYPOTHESIS

Earlier you prepared a tentative hypothesis to guide you in your search for literature. Before you proceed to the actual execution of your research study, you will need to refine and finalize that hypothesis. A written statement of your hypothesis will be part of your research plan and report. Both quantitative and qualitative researchers deal with hypotheses, but the nature of each approach differs. We will first discuss the quantitative use of hypotheses and then discuss the qualitative counterpart.

Quantitative Definition and Purpose of Hypotheses

As mentioned previously, a **hypothesis** is a researcher's prediction of the research findings. It states the researcher's expectations about the relationship between the variables in the research topic. Many studies contain a number of variables, and it is not uncommon to have more than one hypothesis for a research topic. Note that the researcher does not set out to prove a hypothesis but rather collects data that either support or do not support it. Hypotheses are essential to all quantitative research studies, with the possible exception of some descriptive studies whose purpose is to answer certain specific questions.

Hypotheses are typically derived from theories or from knowledge gained while reviewing the related literature. The literature often leads one to expect a certain relationship. For example, studies finding white chalk to be more effective than yellow chalk in teaching mathematics would lead a researcher to expect it to be more effective in teaching physics, if there were not other findings to the contrary. Similarly, a theory that suggested that the ability to think abstractly was quite different for 10-year-olds versus 15-year-olds might suggest a hypothesis stating that 10- and 15-year-olds would perform differently on a test of abstract reasoning.

---

[7] "Improving the Productivity of America's Schools," by H. J. Walberg, 1984, *Educational Leadership, 41*(8), pp. 19–27.

A quantitative researcher formulates a hypothesis before conducting the study because the nature of the study is determined by the hypothesis. Every aspect of the research is affected by the hypothesis, including participants, measuring instruments, design, procedures, data analysis, and conclusions. Although all hypotheses are based on theory or previous knowledge and are aimed at extending knowledge, they are not all of equal worth. There are a number of criteria that can be, and should be, applied to determine the value of a given hypothesis.

Criteria for Hypotheses

In quantitative research a good hypothesis has the following characteristics:

1. It is based on sound reasoning that is consistent with theory or previous research.
2. It provides a reasonable explanation for the predicted outcome.
3. It clearly states the expected relationship between defined variables.
4. It is testable within a reasonable time frame.

By now it should be clear that a hypothesis should be based on a sound rationale. It should derive from previous research or theory and its confirmation or disconfirmation should contribute to educational theory or practice. Therefore, a major characteristic of a good hypothesis is that it is consistent with theory or previous research. The chances are slim that you'll be a Christopher Columbus of educational research who shows that something believed to be "flat" is really "round"! Of course, in areas of research where results are conflicting, your hypothesis won't be consistent with every study, but it should follow from the rule, not from the exception. A good hypothesis provides a reasonable explanation for the predicted outcome. If your telephone is out of order, you might hypothesize that butterflies are sitting on your telephone wires, but such a hypothesis would not be a reasonable explanation. A more reasonable hypothesis might be that you forgot to pay your bill or that a repair crew is working outside. A hypothesis suggesting that schoolchildren with freckles attend longer to tasks than schoolchildren without freckles would not be a reasonable explanation for children's attention behavior. On the other hand, a hypothesis suggesting that children who eat a nutritious breakfast pay attention longer than children who have no breakfast is more reasonable.

A good hypothesis states as clearly and concisely as possible the expected relationship (or difference) between two variables and defines those variables in operational, measurable terms. A simply but clearly stated hypothesis makes the relationship easier for readers to understand, is simpler to test, and facilitates the formulation of conclusions. The relationship between two variables may be expressed as a correlational or a causal one. For example, the variables anxiety and math achievement might be hypothesized to be significantly related; the hypothesis would be that there is a significant *correlation* between anxiety and math achievement. Or, it might be hypothesized that high anxiety *causes* students to perform better than low-anxiety students on math problems.

This example also illustrates the need for operational definitions that clearly describe variables. To define the variables in these studies, a researcher must ask such questions as "What kind of math problems?" "What does it mean to 'perform better'?" "What observable characteristics define a high-anxiety student?" In this example, "high-anxiety student" might be defined as any student whose score on the Acme Anxiety Inventory is in the upper 30% of student scores. "Low-anxiety student" might be defined as any student who scores in the lowest 30% of students. "Better" performance on math problems might be defined in terms of certain math subtest scores on the California Achievement Test. Operational definitions clarify important terms in a study so that all readers will understand the precise meaning the researcher intends.

If you can operationally define your variables within the actual hypothesis statement without making it unwieldy, you should do so. If not, you should state the hypothesis and define the appropriate terms immediately after. Of course, if all necessary terms have already been defined, either within or immediately following the topic statement, there is no need to repeat the definitions in the statement of the hypothesis. The general rule of thumb is to define terms the first time you use them, but it does not hurt to occasionally remind readers of these definitions.

A well-stated and defined hypothesis must also be testable (and it will be if it is well formulated and stated). It should be possible to test the hypothesis by collecting and analyzing data. It would not be possible to test a hypothesis that indicated that some students behave better than others because some have an invisible little angel on their right shoulder and some have an invisible little devil on their left shoulder. There would be no way to collect data to support the hypothesis. In addition to being testable, a good hypothesis should normally be testable within some reasonable period of time. For example, the hypothesis that first-grade students who brush their teeth after lunch every day will have fewer false teeth at age 60 would obviously take a very long time to test. The researcher would very likely be long gone before the study was completed, and the educational significance of the hypothesis would be negligible! A more manageable hypothesis with the same theme might be that first-grade children who brush their teeth after lunch every day will have fewer cavities at the end of the first grade than those who don't brush.

Types of Hypotheses

Hypotheses can be classified in terms of how they are derived (inductive versus deductive hypotheses) or how they are stated (directional versus null hypotheses). If you recall the discussion of inductive and deductive reasoning in Chapter 1, you may guess that an **inductive hypothesis** is a generalization based on specific observations. The researcher observes that certain patterns or associations among variables occur in a number of situations and uses these tentative observations to form an inductive hypothesis. For example, a researcher observes that in some eighth-grade classrooms students who are given essay tests appear to show less testing stress than those who are given multiple-choice tests. This observation could become the basis for an inductive hypothesis. A **deductive hypothesis** is derived from theory and provides evidence that supports, expands, or contradicts the theory.

A **research hypothesis** states an expected relationship or difference between two variables. In other words, it specifies the relationship the quantitative researcher expects to verify in the research study. Research hypotheses can be nondirectional or directional. A **nondirectional hypothesis** states simply that a relationship or difference exists between variables. A **directional hypothesis** states the expected direction of the relationship or difference. For example, a nondirectional hypothesis might state the following:

> There is a significant difference in the achievement of 10th-grade biology students who are instructed using interactive multimedia and those who receive regular instruction only.

The corresponding directional hypothesis might read as follows:

> Tenth-grade biology students who are instructed using interactive multimedia achieve at a higher level than those who receive regular instruction only.

The nondirectional hypothesis states that there will be a difference between the 10th-grade groups, whereas the directional hypothesis states that there will be a difference and that the difference will favor interactive media instruction. A directional hypothesis should be stated only if you have a basis for believing that the results will occur in the stated direction. Nondirectional and directional hypotheses involve different types of statistical tests of significance, as will be examined in Chapter 12.

Finally, a **null hypothesis** states that there is no significant relationship or difference between variables. For example, a null hypothesis might state the following:

> There is no significant difference in the achievement level of 10th-grade biology students who are instructed using interactive multimedia and those who receive regular instruction.

The null hypothesis is the hypothesis of choice when there is little research or theoretical support for a hypothesis. Also, statistical tests for the null hypothesis are more conservative than they are for directional hypotheses. The disadvantage of null hypotheses is that they rarely express the researcher's true expectations based on literature, insights, and logic. Given that few studies are really designed to verify the nonexistence of a relationship, it seems logical that most studies should be based on a nonnull hypothesis. Hypotheses are critical aspects of quantitative research approaches; they focus the study on the methods and strategies needed to collect data to test the hypotheses.

Stating the Hypothesis

A good hypothesis is stated clearly and concisely, expresses the relationship between two variables, and defines those variables in measurable terms. A general model for stating hypotheses for experimental studies is as follows:

> P who get X do better on Y than
>
> P who do not get X (or get some other X)

Although this model is an oversimplification and may not always be appropriate, it should help you to understand the statement of a hypothesis. Further, this model, sometimes with variations, will be applicable in many situations. In the model,

> P = the participants
> X = the treatment, the causal or independent variable (IV)
> Y = the study outcome, the effect or dependent variable (DV)

Study the following topic statement, and see if you can identify the P, X, and Y:

> The purpose of this study is to investigate the effectiveness of 12th-grade mentors on the absenteeism of low-achieving 10th graders.

In this example,

> P = low-achieving 10th graders
> X = presence or absence of a 12th-grade mentor (IV)
> Y = absenteeism (days absent or, stated positively, days present) (DV)

A review of the literature might indicate that mentors have been found to be effective in influencing younger students. Therefore, the directional hypothesis resulting from this topic might read,

> Low-achieving 10th graders (P) who have a 12th-grade mentor (X) have less absenteeism (Y) than low-achieving 10th graders who do not.

As another example, consider this topic statement:

The purpose of the proposed research is to investigate the effectiveness of different conflict resolution techniques in reducing the aggressive behaviors of high school students in an alternative educational setting.

For this topic statement,

P = high school students in an alternative educational setting
X = type of conflict resolution (punishment or discussion) (IV)
Y = instances of aggressive behaviors (DV)

The related nondirectional hypothesis might read,

There will be a difference in the number of aggressive behaviors of high school students in an alternative educational setting who receive either punishment or discussion approaches to conflict resolution.

Of course, in all of these examples there are terms that require operational definition (e.g., "aggressive behaviors").

Got the idea? Let's try one more. Here is the topic statement:

This study investigates the effectiveness of token reinforcement, in the form of free time given for the completion of practice worksheets, on the math computation skills of ninth-grade general math students.

P = ninth-grade general math students
X = token reinforcement in the form of free time for completion of practice worksheets
Y = math computation skills

The hypothesis might be this:

Ninth-grade general math students who receive token reinforcement in the form of free time when they complete their practice worksheets have higher math computation skills than ninth-grade general math students who do not receive token reinforcement for completed worksheets.

The null hypothesis for the preceding topic statement would take this form:

There is no difference on Y (the outcome of the study) between P_1 (Treatment A) and P_2 (Treatment B).

P_1 (Treatment A) = free time
P_2 (Treatment B) = no free time

See if you can write the null hypothesis for the following problem statement:

The purpose of this study is to assess the impact of formal versus informal preschool reading instruction on first graders' reading comprehension at the end of the first grade.

Testing the Hypothesis

The researcher selects the sample, measuring instruments, design, and procedures that will enable her to collect the data necessary to test the hypothesis. During the course of a research study, collected data are analyzed in a manner that permits the researcher to determine whether the hypothesis is supported. Note that analysis of the data does not lead to a hypothesis being proven or not proven, only supported or not supported for this particular study. The results of analysis indicate whether a hypothesis was supported or not supported for the particular participants, context, and instruments involved. Many beginning researchers have the misconception that if their hypothesis is not supported by their data, then their study is a failure, and conversely, if it is supported, then their study is a success. Neither of these beliefs is true. It is just as important to know what variables are not related as it is to know what variables are related. If a hypothesis is not supported, a valuable contribution may be made in the form of a revision of some aspect of a theory; such revision will generate new or revised hypotheses. Thus, hypothesis testing contributes to education primarily by expanding, refining, or revising its knowledge base.

Qualitative Definition and Purpose of Hypotheses

As noted, the aims and strategies of qualitative researchers differ substantially from those of quantitative researchers. As a general rule, qualitative researchers do not state formal hypotheses before conducting a study. They seek to understand the nature of their participants and contexts before stating a research focus or hypothesis. However, as noted earlier, the qualitative researcher may develop guiding hypotheses for their proposed research. Rather than testing a hypothesis, qualitative researchers are much more likely to generate new hypotheses as a result of their studies. The inductive process widely used in qualitative research is based on observing patterns and associations in the participants' natural setting without prior hunches or hypotheses of what researchers will study and observe. Note that qualitative researchers' reluctance to immediately start identifying variables and predictions stems from their view that contexts and participants differ and must be understood on their own terms before hypothesizing or judging. Thus, qualitative researchers have more discretion in determining when and how to examine or narrow a topic.

Identifying patterns and associations in the setting often helps the reseacher discover ideas and questions that lead to new hypotheses. For example, the repeated observation that early in the school year first-grade students can accurately identify who are the "smart" and who are the "not smart" students in class might suggest a hypothesis related to how teachers' actions and words communicate students' status in the classroom. In simple terms, it is generally appropriate to say that a strength of qualitative research is in generating hypotheses. not testing hypotheses.

Having identified a guiding hypothesis, the qualitative researcher may "operationalize" the hypothesis through the development of research questions that provide the researcher with a focus for data collection. Qualitative research questions encompass a range of topics, but most focus on participants' understanding of meanings and social life in a particular context. Note, however, that these general topics must necessarily be more focused to become useful and researchable questions. For example, the topic, "What are the cultural patterns and perspectives of this group in its natural setting?" could be narrowed by asking, "What are the cultural patterns and perspectives of teachers during lunch in the teachers' lounge?" Similarly, the topic, "How do people make sense of their everyday activities in order to behave in socially acceptable ways?" might be narrowed by asking, "How do rival gang members engage in socially acceptable ways when interacting with each other during the school day?" Clearly there are many ways to restate these questions to make them viable and focused research questions. In most cases, the purpose of narrowing questions is to reduce aspects of the topic, much as a hypothesis does for quantitative research, because most researchers overestimate the proper scope of a study.

SUMMARY

Identifying a Topic or Question to Research

1. The first step in selecting a research topic is to identify a general subject that is related to your area of expertise and is of particular interest to you.

Sources of Research Topics

2. The four main sources of research topics are theories, personal experiences, previous studies that can be replicated, and library searches.

3. Theories are composed of organized bodies of concepts, generalizations, and principles. Research studies often study particular aspects of a theory to determine its applicability or generalizability.

4. A researcher's personal experiences and concerns often lead to useful and personally rewarding studies. Common questions, such as "Why does that happen?" and "What would happen if . . . ?" can be rich topic sources if followed up.

5. Existing studies are a common source of research topics. Replication, or repetition, of a study usually involves some feature differing from the original study.

6. Library immersion in the literature in a problem area is generally not an efficient way to identify a research topic. Handbooks, encyclopedias, and yearbooks that cover many topics briefly are more useful. Of course, library resources will be invaluable once you have identified a topic to study.

Narrowing the Topic

7. Once an initial topic is identified, it often needs to be narrowed and focused into a manageable topic to study.

8. Qualitative and quantitative research often differ in the timing of narrowing their topics. Quantitative research topics are usually narrowed quickly. Qualitative research topics are not usually narrowed until the researcher has more information about the participants and their setting.

Characteristics of Good Topics

9. A basic characteristic of a research problem is that it is researchable using the collection and analysis of data. Topics related to philosophical and ethical issues (*should* questions) are not researchable.

10. A good problem has theoretical or practical significance; its solution contributes in some way to improving the educational process.

11. A good topic must be a topic that can be adequately investigated given your (1) current level of research skill, (2) available resources, and (3) time and other restrictions.

12. A good topic is one that is ethical, that is, a study that does not harm participants in any way.

Stating the Research Topic

13. A well-written topic statement for a quantitative study generally indicates the variables of interest to the researcher, the specific relationship between those variables that is to be investigated and, ideally, the type of participants involved.

14. A well-written quantitative topic statement also defines all relevant variables, either directly or operationally; operational definitions define concepts in terms of measurable characteristics.

15. The statement of the problem should indicate the background of the problem, including a justification for the study in terms of its significance.

16. Qualitative research topics usually are stated later than quantitative research topics because qualitative researchers need to become attuned to the research context before narrowing their topic.

17. The topic statement is the first item in the introductory section of a research plan and report and provides direction for the remaining aspects of both.

18. A researcher typically develops a tentative hypothesis that guides the process of reviewing literature.

Review of Related Literature

Definition, Purpose, and Scope

19. The review of related literature involves systematically identifying, locating, and analyzing documents pertaining to the research topic.

20. The major purpose of reviewing the literature is to identify information that already exists about your topic. Qualitative researchers usually review the literature later than quantitative researchers.

21. The literature review can point out research strategies, procedures, and instruments that have and have not been found to be productive in investigating your topic.

22. A smaller, well-organized review is preferred to a review containing many studies that are more or less related to the problem.

23. Heavily researched areas usually provide enough references directly related to a topic to eliminate the need for reporting less related or secondary studies. Little-researched topics usually require review of any study related in some meaningful way in order to develop a logical framework and rationale for the study.

24. A common misconception is the idea that the worth of a problem is a function of the amount of literature available on the topic. Unfortunately, there is no formula that indicates how much literature has to be reviewed for a given topic.

25. Both qualitative and quantitative researchers construct literature reviews. Qualitative researchers are more likely to construct their review after starting their study, whereas quantitative researchers are more likely to construct the review prior to starting their study.

Qualitative Research and the Review of Related Literature

26. There is disagreement among qualitative researchers about the role of the literature review in the qualitative research process.

27. The qualitative research review of related literature may serve the following functions: to demonstrate the underlying assumptions behind the research questions, to convince proposal reviewers that the researcher is knowledgeable about "intellectual traditions," to provide the researcher with an opportunity to identify any gaps in the body of literature and how the proposed study may contribute to the existing body of knowledge, and to help the qualitative researcher to refine research questions.

Identifying Keywords

28. It is important to make a list of keywords to guide your literature search. Most of the sources you consult will have alphabetical subject indexes to help you locate information on your topic.

Identifying Your Sources

29. A good way to start a review of related literature is with a narrow search of pertinent educational encyclopedias, handbooks, and annual reviews found in libraries. These resources provide broad overviews of issues in one or many subject areas.

30. A study written by the person who conducted it is a primary source; a brief description of a study written by someone other than the original researcher is a secondary source. Primary sources are preferred in the review.

Searching for Books on Your Topic in the Library

31. Most libraries use an electronic catalog system that indexes all of the sources in the library by author, title, and subject. You should familiarize yourself with your library and its resources.

32. If you are at the beginning of a literature search for primary references, you might not have identified specific titles or authors to search for. A keyword search uses terms or phrases pertinent to your topic to search for and identify potentially useful literature sources.

33. Keyword searches can be focused by using the Boolean operators AND, OR, and NOT. Using AND or NOT narrows a search and the number of sources identified; using OR broadens the search and acquired sources. It is often best to start with a narrow search.

Consulting Computer Databases

34. Computer databases can facilitate the identification of relevant primary sources. Among the most used are ERIC, Education Index, PsycINFO (Psychological Abstracts), and Dissertation Abstracts. Most of these sources provide abstracts of literature.

35. ERIC is the world's largest database on education and is used by more than 500,000 people each year.

Searching the Internet and the World Wide Web

36. The Internet links organizations and individuals all over the world. The World Wide Web is on the Internet.

37. To access the Internet, you need a computer with a modem hooked to a telephone or cable line and a browser to get you onto the Web. Alternatively, you can access the Internet at most libraries.

38. The available resources on the World Wide Web are virtually limitless, so the best way to become familiar with its use is to "surf around" in your spare time. Talk to other Internet users when you have a question.

39. The Web contains a variety of sites relevant to an educational researcher. Each site is reached by using

its Internet address. Addresses containing *ed* or ending in *.edu* are related to educational institutions, and those ending in *.com* are related to commercial enterprises.

Using a Search Engine to Find Information Sources

40. Search engines allow the user to search the Internet. Most search engines list a variety of topics that can be used to focus a search. Search engines also allow keyword searches that encompass large portions of the World Wide Web.

Becoming a Member of Professional Organizations

41. Another way to access current literature related to your research topic is through membership in professional organizations. The Web sites for professional organizations maintain links to current research, or "hot topics," in a particular discipline.

42. Popular professional organizations include the following: Association for Supervision and Curriculum Development, National Council of Teachers of Mathematics, National Council for the Social Studies, National Science Teachers Association, and the International Reading Association.

Evaluating Your Sources

43. All identified sources must be evaluated for quality and applicability. Are sources up to date? Are they from refereed journals? Do they pertain directly to the research topic?

44. It cannot be overemphasized that material on the World Wide Web is not screened for quality, honesty, bias, or authenticity. Virtually anyone can put anything on the Web. Thus, users must be careful not to assume that all material obtained from the Web is useful or accurate just because it comes from the Internet.

45. Combining a library search with a Web search will probably produce the most useful material.

Abstracting

46. Abstracting involves creating abstracts by locating, reviewing, summarizing, and classifying your references.

47. The main advantage of beginning with the latest references on your topic is that the most recent studies are likely to have profited from previous research. Also, references in more recent studies often contain references to other studies you had not identified.

48. For each source work, list the complete bibliographic record, including author's name, date of publication, title, journal name or book title, volume number, issue number, page numbers, and library call number. Briefly list main ideas. Put quotation marks around quotes taken from the source, and don't forget to get page numbers of the quote. Keep all references in the format required for research reports or dissertations.

49. Make a copy of your references and put it in a safe place.

Analyzing, Organizing, and Reporting the Literature

50. Describing and reporting research call for a different style of writing than commonly used. Technical writing requires documenting facts and substantiating opinions, clarifying definitions and using them consistently, using an accepted style manual, and starting sections with an introduction and ending them with a brief summary.

51. The following guidelines should be helpful: Make an outline; sort your references into appropriate topic piles; analyze the similarities and differences between references in a given subheading; do not present your references as a series of abstracts or annotations; discuss references least related to the problem first; and conclude with a brief summary of the literature and its implications.

Meta-Analysis

52. Meta-analysis is a statistical approach to summarizing the results of many quantitative studies that have investigated basically the same problem. It provides a numerical way of expressing the "average" result of the studies.

53. A central characteristic that distinguishes meta-analysis from more traditional approaches is the emphasis placed on making the review as inclusive as possible.

54. The key feature of meta-analysis is that each study's results are translated into an effect size. Effect size is a numerical way of expressing the strength or magnitude of a reported relationship, be it causal or not.

Formulating and Stating a Hypothesis

55. A hypothesis is a researcher's prediction of the research findings. Hypotheses are more common in quantitative than qualitative research.

56. Researchers do not set out to "prove" a hypothesis but rather collect data that either support or do not support it.
57. A hypothesis is formulated based on theory or on knowledge gained while reviewing the related literature. The hypothesis logically follows the literature review and is based on the implications of previous research.

Criteria for Hypotheses

58. A critical characteristic of a good hypothesis is that it is based on a sound rationale. A hypothesis is a reasoned prediction, not a wild guess. It is a tentative, but rational, explanation for the predicted outcome.
59. A good hypothesis states as clearly and concisely as possible the expected relationship (or difference) between variables. Variables should be stated in measurable terms.
60. A well-stated and defined hypothesis must be testable.

Types of Hypotheses

61. An inductive hypothesis is a generalization made from a number of observations. A deductive hypothesis is derived from theory and is aimed at providing evidence that supports, expands, or contradicts aspects of a given theory. Deductive, quantitative hypotheses are more common than inductive, qualitative hypotheses.
62. A research hypothesis states the expected relationship (or difference) between two variables. It states the relationship the researcher expects to verify through the collection and analysis of data.

63. A nondirectional hypothesis indicates that a relationship or difference exists but does not indicate the direction of the difference; a directional hypothesis indicates that a relationship or difference exists and indicates the direction of the difference. A null hypothesis states that there will be no significant relationship (or difference) between variables.

Stating the Hypothesis

64. A general paradigm, or model, for stating hypotheses for experimental studies is as follows: *P* who get *X* do better on *Y* than *P* who do not get *X* (or get some other *X*). *P* refers to participants, *X* refers to the treatment or independent variable (IV), and *Y* refers to the outcome or dependent variable (DV).

Testing the Hypothesis

65. Hypotheses are tested using statistical analyses of data gathered in the study.
66. It is just as important to know which variables are not related as it is to know which variables are.

Qualitative Definition and Purpose of Hypotheses

67. As a general rule, qualitative researchers do not state formal hypotheses prior to the study.
68. However, a qualitative researcher may develop guiding hypotheses for their proposed research.
69. Rather than testing an hypothesis, qualitative researchers are much more likely to generate new hypotheses as a result of their studies.

Now go to the Companion Website at **www.prenhall.com/gay** to assess your understanding of chapter content with Practice Quiz, apply comprehension in Applying What You Know, broaden your knowledge about research in Web Links, and expand your research skills in Evaluating Articles, Analyzing Qualitative Data, Analyzing Quantitative Data, and Research Tools and Tips.

PERFORMANCE CRITERIA

The introduction that you develop for Task 2 will be the first part of the research report required for Task 10 (Chapter 21). Therefore, it may save you some revision time later if, when appropriate, statements are expressed in the past tense ("the topic investigated was" or "it was hypothesized," for example). Your introduction should include the following subheadings and contain the following types of information:

Introduction (Background and significance of the problem)
Statement of the Problem (Problem statement and necessary definitions)
Review of the Literature (Don't forget the big V)
Statement of the Hypothesis(es)

As a guideline, three typed pages will generally be a sufficient length for Task 2. Of course, for a real study you would review not just 10 to 15 references but all relevant references, and the introduction would be correspondingly longer.

One final note: The hypothesis you formulate now will influence all further tasks—that is, who will be your participants, what they will do, and so forth. In this connection, the following is an informal observation based on the behavior of thousands of students, not a research-based finding. All beginning research students fall someplace on a continuum of realism. At one extreme are the Cecil B. Demise students who want to design a study involving a cast of thousands, over an extended period of time. At the other extreme are the Mr. Magi students who will not even consider a procedure unless they know for sure they could actually execute it in their work setting, with their students or clients. You do not have to actually execute the study you design, so feel free to operate in the manner most comfortable for you. Keep in mind, however, that there is a middle ground between Demise and Magi.

The Task 2 example that follows illustrates the format and content of an introduction that meets the criteria just described. (See Task 2 Example.) This task example, with few modifications, represents the task as submitted by a former student in an introductory educational research course (Sara Jane Calderin of Florida International University). Although an example from published research could have been used, the example given more accurately reflects the performance that is expected of you at your current level of expertise.

Additional examples for the tasks are included in the *Student Study Guide* that accompanies this text.

:: TASK 2 Example

Effect of Interactive Multimedia on the Achievement of 10th-Grade Biology Students

Introduction

One of the major concerns of educators and parents alike is the decline in student achievement (as measured by standardized tests). An area of particular concern is science education where the high-level thinking skills and problem solving techniques so necessary for success in our technological society need to be developed (Smith & Westhoff, 1992).

Research is constantly providing new proven methods for educators to use, and technology has developed all kinds of tools ideally suited to the classroom. One such tool is interactive multimedia (IMM). IMM provides teachers with an extensive amount of data in a number of different formats including text, sound, and video, making it possible to appeal to the different learning styles of the students and to offer a variety of material for students to analyze (Howson & Davis, 1992).

When teachers use IMM, students become highly motivated, which results in improved class attendance and more completed assignments (O'Connor, 1993). Students also become actively involved in their own learning, encouraging comprehension rather than mere memorization of facts (Kneedler, 1993; Reeves, 1992).

Statement of the Problem

The purpose of this study was to investigate the effect of interactive multimedia on the achievement of 10th-grade biology students. Interactive multimedia was defined as "a computerized database that allows users to access information in multiple forms, including text, graphics, video and audio" (Reeves, 1992, p. 47).

Review of Related Literature

Due to modern technology, students receive more information from visual sources than they do from the written word, and yet in school the majority of information is still transmitted through textbooks. While textbooks cover a wide range of topics superficially, IMM provides in-depth information on essential topics in a format that students find interesting (Kneedler, 1993). Smith and Westhoff (1992) note that when student interest is sparked, curiosity levels are increased and students are motivated to ask questions. The interactive nature of multimedia allows the students to seek out their own answers and by so doing they become owners of the concept involved. Ownership translates into comprehension (Howson & Davis, 1992).

Many science concepts are learned through observation of experiments. Using multimedia, students can participate in a variety of experiments that are either too expensive, too lengthy, or too dangerous to carry out in the laboratory (Howson & Davis, 1992; Leonard, 1989; Louie, Sweat, Gresham, & Smith, 1991). While observing the experiments the students can discuss what is happening and ask questions. At the touch of a button teachers are able to replay any part of the proceedings, and they also have random access to related information that can be used to completely illustrate the answer to the question (Howson & Davis, 1992). By answering students' questions in this detailed way the content will become more relevant to the needs of the student (Smith & Westhoff, 1992). When knowledge is relevant students are able to use it to solve problems and, in so doing, develop higher-level thinking skills (Helms & Helms, 1992; Sherwood, Kinzer, Bransford, & Franks, 1987).

A major challenge of science education is to provide students with large amounts of information that will encourage them to be analytical (Howson & Davis, 1992; Sherwood et al., 1987). IMM offers electronic access to extensive information allowing students to organize, evaluate and use it in the solution of problems (Smith & Wilson, 1993). When information is introduced as an aid to problem solving, it becomes a tool with which to solve other problems, rather than a series of solitary, disconnected facts (Sherwood et al., 1987).

Although critics complain that IMM is entertainment and students do not learn from it (Corcoran, 1989), research has shown that student learning does improve when IMM is used in the classroom (Sherwood et al., 1987; Sherwood & Others, 1990). A 1987 study by Sherwood et al., for example, showed that seventh- and eighth-grade science students receiving instruction enhanced with IMM had better retention of that information, and O'Connor (1993) found that the use of IMM in high school mathematics and science increased the focus on students' problem solving and critical thinking skills.

Statement of the Hypothesis

The quality and quantity of software available for science classes has dramatically improved during the past decade. Although some research has been carried out on the effects of IMM on student achievement in science, due to promising updates in the technology involved, further study is warranted. Therefore, it was hypothesized that 10th-grade biology students whose teachers use IMM as part of their instructional technique will exhibit significantly higher achievement than 10th-grade biology students whose teachers do not use IMM.

References

Corcoran, E. (1989, July). Show and tell: Hypermedia turns information into a multisensory event. *Scientific American, 261,* 72, 74.

Helms, C. W., & Helms, D. R. (1992, June). Multimedia in education (Report No. IR-016-090). Proceedings of the 25th Summer Conference of the Association of Small Computer Users in Education. North Myrtle Beach, SC (ERIC Document Reproduction Service No. ED 357 732).

Howson, B. A., & Davis, H. (1992). Enhancing comprehension with videodiscs. *Media and Methods, 28,* 3, 12–14.

Kneedler, P. E. (1993). California adopts multimedia science program. *Technological Horizons in Education Journal, 20,* 7, 73–76.

Lehmann, I. J. (1990). Review of National Proficiency Survey Series. In J. J. Kramer & J. C. Conoley (Eds.), *The eleventh mental measurements yearbook* (pp. 595–599). Lincoln: University of Nebraska, Buros Institute of Mental Measurement.

Leonard, W. H. (1989). A comparison of student reaction to biology instruction by interactive videodisc or conventional laboratory. *Journal of Research in Science Teaching, 26,* 95–104.

Louie, R., Sweat, S., Gresham, R., & Smith, L. (1991). Interactive video: Disseminating vital science and math information. *Media and Methods, 27,* 5, 22–23.

O'Connor, J. E. (1993, April). Evaluating the effects of collaborative efforts to improve mathematics and science curricula (Report No. TM-019-862). Paper presented at the Annual Meeting of the American Educational Research Association, Atlanta, GA (ERIC Document Reproduction Service No. ED 357 083).

3

Reeves, T. C. (1992). Evaluating interactive multimedia. *Educational Technology, 32,* 5, 47–52.

Sherwood, R. D., Kinzer, C. K., Bransford, J. D., & Franks, J. J. (1987). Some benefits of creating macro-contexts for science instruction: Initial findings. *Journal of Research in Science Teaching, 24,* 417–435.

Sherwood, R. D., & Others (1990, April). An evaluative study of level one videodisc based chemistry program (Report No. SE-051-513). Paper presented at a Poster Session at the 63rd. Annual Meeting of the National Association for Research in Science Teaching, Atlanta, GA (ERIC Document Reproduction Service No. ED 320 772).

Smith, E. E., & Westhoff, G. M. (1992). The Taliesin project: Multidisciplinary education and multimedia. *Educational Technology, 32,* 15–23.

Smith, M. K., & Wilson, C. (1993, March). Integration of student learning strategies via technology (Report No. IR-016-035). Proceedings of the Fourth Annual Conference of Technology and Teacher Education. San Diego, CA (ERIC Document Reproduction Service No. ED 355 937).

"Part of good planning is anticipating potential problems and then doing what you can to prevent them." (p. 72)

Preparing and Evaluating a Research Plan

OBJECTIVES

After reading Chapter 3, you should be able to do the following:

1. Briefly describe three ethical considerations involved in conducting and reporting educational research.
2. Describe two major pieces of legislation affecting educational research.
3. Briefly describe each of the components of a quantitative research plan.
4. Briefly describe each of the components of a qualitative research plan.
5. Briefly describe two major ways in which a research plan can be evaluated.

The next task in the research process is to develop a research plan that delineates the methods and procedures you will use to carry out your study. Although research plans rarely are executed as initially stated, having a plan gives you an overview of your study.

Developing a complete research plan requires expertise in a number of areas. Research plans, regardless of whether they are for quantitative or qualitative studies, generally include the following: an introduction (which includes the review of related literature), a discussion of the research design and procedures, and information about data analysis. In this chapter we expand on this general framework and provide specific outlines (and examples) for quantitative and qualitative research plans.

The goal of Chapter 3 is to help you understand the importance of developing a research plan and to familiarize you with the components of a plan. Completing Chapter 3 should enable you to perform the following task.

TASK 3A

For the hypothesis you have formulated (Task 2), develop the remaining components of a research plan for a study you would conduct to test that hypothesis. Create brief sections using the following headings:

- Method
  Participants ✓
  Instruments ✓
  Design
  Procedure
- Data Analysis
- Time Schedule

In addition, include assumptions, limitations, and definitions where appropriate. (See Performance Criteria, p. 94.)

TASK 3B

Formulate a research topic and develop a research plan for a qualitative study you would conduct. Include the components from Figure 3.5 (p. 86) in your plan. In addition, include assumptions, limitations, and definitions where appropriate. (See Performance Criteria, p. 94.)

DEFINITION AND PURPOSE OF A RESEARCH PLAN

A **research plan** is a detailed description of a proposed study designed to investigate a given problem. It includes justification for hypotheses or exploration of posed research questions, and a detailed presentation of the research steps you will follow in collecting, choosing, and analyzing data. A research plan may be relatively brief and informal, such as the one that you will develop for Task 3a, or very lengthy and formal, such as the proposals submitted to obtain governmental and private research funding.

Most colleges and universities require that a proposal or prospectus be submitted for approval before the execution of a thesis or dissertation study. Students are expected to demonstrate that they have a reasonable research plan before being allowed to begin the study. Playing it by ear is all right for the piano, but not for conducting research.

After you have completed the review of related literature and formulated your hypothesis or research questions, you are ready to develop the rest of the research plan. In quantitative research the hypothesis will be the basis for determining the participant group, measuring instruments, design, procedures, and statistical techniques used in your study. In qualitative research the researcher's questions will be the basis for gaining entrance to the research context, identifying research participants, spending time in the field, determining how to gather data, and interpreting and narrating the data collected. In this chapter we describe, in general, how these tasks fit into the research plan; succeeding chapters will provide details about conducting the tasks.

The research plan serves several important purposes. First, it forces you to think through every aspect of the study. The very process of getting it down on paper usually helps you think of something you might otherwise have overlooked. A second purpose of a written plan is that it facilitates evaluation of the study, by you and others. Sometimes great ideas do not look so great after they have been written down and considered. In creating the plan, you may discover certain problems or find that some aspect of the study is infeasible. Others, too, can identify flaws and make suggestions about ways to improve the plan. Such suggestions are as important for "old hands" as they are for beginning researchers. A third and fundamental purpose of a research plan is that it provides detailed procedures to guide conduct of the study. Also, if something unexpected occurs that alters some phase of the study, you can refer to the plan to assess the overall impact on the rest of the study. For example, suppose you order 60 copies of a test to administer on May 1. If on April 15 you receive a letter saying that, due to a shortage of available tests, your order cannot be filled until May 15, your study might be seriously affected. At the very least, it would be delayed several weeks. The deadlines in your research plan might indicate that you cannot afford to wait. Therefore, you might decide to use an alternate measuring instrument or to contact another vendor.

A well thought-out plan saves time, provides structure for the study, reduces the probability of costly mistakes, and generally results in higher quality research. If your study is a disaster because of poor planning, you lose. If something that could have been avoided goes wrong, you might have to redo the whole study at worst, or somehow salvage the remnants of a less-than-ideal study at best. Murphy's law states, essentially, that "if anything can go wrong, it will, and at the worst possible time." Our law states that "if anything can go wrong, it will—unless you make sure that it doesn't!"

Part of good planning is anticipating potential problems and then doing what you can to prevent them. For example, you might anticipate that some principals will be less than open to your using their students as participants in your study (a common occurrence). To deal with this contingency, you should work up the best, but most honest, sales pitch possible. Do not ask, "Hey, can I use your kids for my study?" Instead, tell principals how the study will benefit their students or their schools. If there is still opposition, you might tell principals how enthusiastic central administration is about the study. Got the idea? To avoid many problems and to obtain strategies for overcoming them, it is extremely useful to talk to more experienced researchers.

You may get frustrated at times because you cannot do everything the way you would like to because of real or bureaucratic constraints. Don't let such obstacles exasperate you. Just relax and do your best. On the positive side, a sound plan critiqued by others is likely to result in a sound study conducted with a minimum of grief. You cannot guarantee that your study will be executed exactly as planned, but you can guarantee that things will go as smoothly as possible.

:: GENERAL CONSIDERATIONS IN A RESEARCH PLAN

We have already noted a number of factors you should consider in planning your research. Two additional factors are important to all research studies. First is the ethics of conducting research. As a researcher, you have the responsibility to behave ethically and to uphold the rights of study participants. For example, any potential participant in your study should have the right to refuse to participate and the right to stop involvement at any time during the study. Some participant rights are protected by law. For example, legal restrictions concerning access to educational records are a way to safeguard students' privacy. The second factor to consider is your approach to human relations. To achieve your study aims, you will need to know strategies for achieving and maintaining cooperation from school personnel. You'll put these strategies to work as you attempt to gain entry to the research site. Your research plan may not specifically address either of these factors, but the plan's chance of being properly and ethically executed will be increased if you are aware of them.

The Ethics of Research

Ethical considerations play a role in all research studies. Therefore, all researchers must be aware of and attend to the ethical considerations related to their studies. In research the ends do not justify the means, and researchers must not put their need to carry out a study above their responsibility to maintain the well-being of the study participants. Research studies are built on trust between the researcher and the participants, and researchers have a responsibility to behave in a trustworthy manner, just as they expect participants to (for example, by providing data that can be trusted).

Many professional organizations have developed codes of ethical conduct for their members. Figure 3.1 presents the general principles from the American Psychological Association's *Ethical Principles of Psychologists and Code of Conduct*. Note that the code provides additional guidelines and contains much more specific ethical standards in the following ten categories: (1) Resolving Ethical Issues, (2) Competence, (3) Human Relations, (4) Privacy and Confidentiality, (5) Advertising and Other Public Statements, (6) Record Keeping and Fees, (7) Education and Training, (8) Research and Publication, (9) Assessment, and (10) Therapy. You may read the full text online at the American Psychological Association's Web site (http://www.apa.org/ethics/code2002.html). Most other professional organizations, such as the American Educational Research Association and the American Sociological Society, have similar codes for ethical research.

In 1974 the U.S. Congress put the force of law behind codes of ethical research. The need for legal restrictions was graphically illustrated by a number of studies in which researchers lied to or put research participants in harm's way in order to carry out their studies. For example, in a study on the effects of group pressure (conducted some years ago), researchers lied to participants while they participated in and watched what they thought was actual electric shocking of other participants.[1] In another study, men known to be infected with syphilis were not treated for their illness because they were part of a control group in a comparative study.[2] Studies such as these prompted governmental regulations regarding research studies.

---

[1] "Group Pressure and Action Against a Person," by S. Milgram, 1964, *Journal of Abnormal and Social Psychology, 69,* 137–143.
[2] *The Tuskegee Syphilis Experiment,* by J. H. Jones, 1998, New York: Free Press.

FIGURE 3.1	General ethical principles

PRINCIPLE A: BENEFICENCE AND NONMALEFICENCE

Psychologists strive to benefit those with whom they work and take care to do no harm. In their professional actions, psychologists seek to safeguard the welfare and rights of those with whom they interact professionally and other affected persons, and the welfare of animal subjects of research. When conflicts occur among psychologists' obligations or concerns, they attempt to resolve these conflicts in a responsible fashion that avoids or minimizes harm. Because psychologists' scientific and professional judgments and actions may affect the lives of others, they are alert to and guard against personal, financial, social, organizational, or political factors that might lead to misuse of their influence. Psychologists strive to be aware of the possible effect of their own physical and mental health on their ability to help those with whom they work.

PRINCIPLE B: FIDELITY AND RESPONSIBILITY

Psychologists establish relationships of trust with those with whom they work. They are aware of their professional and scientific responsibilities to society and to the specific communities in which they work. Psychologists uphold professional standards of conduct, clarify their professional roles and obligations, accept appropriate responsibility for their behavior, and seek to manage conflicts of interest that could lead to exploitation or harm. Psychologists consult with, refer to, or cooperate with other professionals and institutions to the extent needed to serve the best interests of those with whom they work. They are concerned about the ethical compliance of their colleagues' scientific and professional conduct. Psychologists strive to contribute a portion of their professional time for little or no compensation or personal advantage.

PRINCIPLE C: INTEGRITY

Psychologists seek to promote accuracy, honesty, and truthfulness in the science, teaching, and practice of psychology. In these activities psychologists do not steal, cheat, or engage in fraud, subterfuge, or intentional misrepresentation of fact. Psychologists strive to keep their promises and to avoid unwise or unclear commitments. In situations in which deception may be ethically justifiable to maximize benefits and minimize harm, psychologists have a serious obligation to consider the need for, the possible consequences of, and their responsibility to correct any resulting mistrust or other harmful effects that arise from the use of such techniques.

PRINCIPLE D: JUSTICE

Psychologists recognize that fairness and justice entitle all persons to access to and benefit from the contributions of psychology and to equal quality in the processes, procedures, and services being conducted by psychologists. Psychologists exercise reasonable judgment and take precautions to ensure that their potential biases, the boundaries of their competence, and the limitations of their expertise do not lead to or condone unjust practices.

PRINCIPLE E: RESPECT FOR PEOPLE'S RIGHTS AND DIGNITY

Psychologists respect the dignity and worth of all people, and the rights of individuals to privacy, confidentiality, and self-determination. Psychologists are aware that special safeguards may be necessary to protect the rights and welfare of persons or communities whose vulnerabilities impair autonomous decision making. Psychologists are aware of and respect cultural, individual, and role differences, including those based on age, gender, gender identity, race, ethnicity, culture, national origin, religion, sexual orientation, disability, language, and socioeconomic status and consider these factors when working with members of such groups. Psychologists try to eliminate the effect on their work of biases based on those factors, and they do not knowingly participate in or condone activities of others based upon such prejudices.

Source: From "Ethical Principles of Psychologists and Code of Conduct," by American Psychological Association, 2002, *American Psychologist, 57,* pp. 1060–1073. Copyright © 2002 by the American Psychological Association. Reprinted with permission.

Informed Consent and Protection From Harm

Perhaps the most basic and important ethical issues in research are concerned with participants' right to informed consent and freedom from harm. Researchers obtain *informed consent* by making sure that research participants enter the research of their free will and with understanding of the nature of the study and any possible dangers that may arise. This requirement is intended to reduce the likelihood that participants will be exploited by a researcher persuading them to participate when they do not fully know what the study's requirements are. Researchers ensure *freedom from harm* by not exposing participants to undue risks. This requirement involves issues of confidentiality (protecting participants from embarrassment or ridicule) and issues related to personal privacy. Collecting information on participants or observing them without their knowledge or without appropriate permission is not ethical. Furthermore, any information or data that are collected, either from or about a person, should be strictly confidential, especially if it is at all personal. Access to data should be limited to persons directly involved in conducting the research. An individual participant's performance should not be reported or made public using the participant's name, even for an innocuous measure such as an arithmetic test. For example, individuals identified as members of a group that performed poorly on a research instrument might be subjected to ridicule, censure by parents, or lowered teacher expectations.

The use of confidentiality or anonymity to avoid privacy invasion and potential harm is common. **Anonymity** is what study participants have when their identities are kept hidden from the researcher. It is often confused with **confidentiality,** which is what researchers protect when they know the identities of study participants but do not disclose that information. If the researcher knows participants' identities, there can be confidentiality, but no anonymity. Removing names or coding records is one commonly used way to maintain anonymity. When planning your study, you must indicate to participants whether you will provide confidentiality (you'll know but won't tell) or anonymity (you will not know the participants' names) and be sure they know the difference. Sometimes researchers seek access to data from a previous study to examine new questions based on the old data. In such cases, the original researcher has the responsibility to maintain the confidentiality or anonymity promised the participants of the original study.

Two major pieces of legislation affecting educational research are the National Research Act of 1974 and the Family Educational Rights and Privacy Act of 1974. The **National Research Act of 1974** requires that to ensure protection of participants, proposed research activities involving human participants be reviewed and approved by an authorized group before the execution of the research. Protection of participants is broadly defined and requires that they not be harmed in any way (physically or mentally) and that they participate only if they freely agree to do so (informed consent). If participants are not of age, informed consent must be given by parents or legal guardian.

Most colleges and universities have a review group, usually called the Human Subjects Review Board or Institutional Review Board (IRB). By law, this board must consist of at least five members, not all of one gender; include one nonscientist; and include one (or more) member who is mainly concerned with the welfare of the participants. Persons who might have a conflict of interest are excluded.

Typically, the researcher submits a proposal to the chair of the board, who distributes copies to all the members. They evaluate the proposed treatment of participants. If there is any question as to whether participants might be harmed in any way, the researcher is usually asked to meet with the review group to answer questions and clarify the study's procedures. When the review group is satisfied that the participants will not be placed at risk (or that potential risk is minimal compared to the potential benefits of the study), the committee members sign the approval forms. Members' signatures on the approval forms signify that the proposal is acceptable with respect to participant protection. We recommend that you contact the IRB at your university to learn its guidelines for the protection of human subjects. You should obtain any forms required for human-subjects research and consider how you would complete the paperwork given the ethical guidelines presented in this chapter.

The **Family Educational Rights and Privacy Act of 1974,** usually referred to as the *Buckley Amendment,* was designed to protect the privacy of students' educational records. Among its provisions is the specification that data that actually identify a student may not be made available unless written permission is acquired from the student (if of age) or a parent or legal guardian. The consent must indicate what data may be disclosed, for what purposes, and to whom. If part of your study required obtaining information from individual elementary students' school record files, you would need to obtain written permission from *each* student's parent or guardian, not a blanket approval from the school principal or classroom teacher. Note that if you were interested in using only class averages (in which no individual student was identified), consent from the principal would likely suffice. However, if you planned to calculate the class average from information provided in individual student records, permission from each student would be required because you'd need access to individual records.

There are some exceptions to the requirement for written consent. For example, school personnel with a "legitimate educational interest" in a student would not need written consent to examine student records. In other cases, the researcher could request that a teacher or guidance counselor either remove names from students' records completely or replace them with a coded number or letter. The researcher could then use the records without knowing the names of the individual students.

Deception

Another ethical dilemma occurs when a researcher poses a topic that, if disclosed completely to potential participants, would likely influence or change their responses. For example, studies concerned with participants' racial, gender, cultural, or medical orientation or attitudes are especially susceptible to such influences, so researchers often hide the true nature of the topic of study. Or a researcher might want to study how teachers interact with high- and low-achieving students. If the teachers know the aim of the study, they are likely to change their normal behaviors more than they would if told that the study is about "how high- and low-achieving students perform on oral questioning." Lying about the real focus is intended to deceive study participants. Research that plans to deceive participants must be seriously scrutinized on ethical grounds. Some researchers believe that any study that requires deceitful practice should not be carried out. Others recognize that some important studies cannot be undertaken without deception. We recommend that you do your initial research studies on a topic that does not require deception. If you do choose such a topic, your advisor and the Human Subjects Review Board or IRB at your institution will provide suggestions about ethical ways to carry out your research plan. Note that the primary researcher (usually you) is responsible for maintaining ethical standards in the research.

Ethical Issues in Qualitative Research

The ethical issues and responsibilities discussed thus far pertain to both quantitative and qualitative research plans. However, some features of qualitative research raise additional issues not typically encountered in quantitative research.

Qualitative research differs from quantitative in at least two major ways that produce additional ethical concerns. First, qualitative research plans typically evolve and change as the researcher's immersion in and understanding of the research setting grows. In a real sense, the research plan is "in process" and only generally formed when presented to the Human Subjects Review Board. As the plan evolves with added understanding of the context and participants, there is increased likelihood that unanticipated and unreviewed ethical issues will arise and need to be resolved on the spot. For example, as participants become more comfortable with the researcher, they often will ask to see what has been written about them. They feel entitled to this, even though seeing what has been written may cause personal or data collection problems. Second, qualitative researchers typically are personally engaged in the research context. Data collection methods such as interviews, debriefings, and the like bring the researcher and participants in close, personal contact. The closeness between participants and researcher helps to provide deep and rich data, but it may also create unconscious influences that raise issues for objectivity and data interpretation.

The focus on immersion and detailed knowledge of the research context often leads the qualitative researcher to observe illegal or unprofessional behavior. (This can occur in quantitative research also but is less common because of the researcher's less-personal contact with participants and their context.) The qualitative researcher might observe a janitor illegally loading school supplies into her car, for example. Or the researcher might observe a teacher continually ridiculing a particular student for his speech impediment. In these and other similar situations, what is the researcher to do? Should the researcher report the observations, knowing that it likely will end the study because participants will no longer be certain of the researcher's promise of confidentiality? Or should the researcher keep silent on the assumption that the system will eventually identify and correct the problems? If there is clear likelihood of physical or psychological danger, the researcher obviously has a strong mandate to inform the school authorities. Unfortunately, not all situations present ethically clear actions.

To respond appropriately when faced with ethical decisions, qualitative researchers must ensure that their professional ethical perspective is closely aligned with their personal ethical perspective. This may seem like a statement of the obvious, except for this caveat: Qualitative researchers may find themselves in situations that require an immediate response—the very essence of which may threaten the success of the research. If your personal and research ethical perspectives are aligned, you will in all likelihood respond to ethical challenges in an appropriate, professional fashion that will not threaten the ongoing conduct of your research.

The sources and advice noted in this chapter will help you conceive and conduct ethical studies. The suggestions provided do not cover all the ethical issues you are likely to encounter in your research. Perhaps the fundamental ethical rule is that participants should not be harmed in any way, real or possible, in the name of science. Respect and concern for your own integrity and for your participants' dignity and welfare are the bottom lines of ethical research.

Gaining Entry to the Research Site

Very rarely is it possible to conduct educational research without the cooperation of a number of people. An initial step in acquiring the needed cooperation is to identify and follow required procedures for gaining approval to conduct the study in the chosen site. In schools, research approval is usually granted by the superintendent, school board, or some other high-level administrator, such as the associate superintendent for instruction. In other settings, such as hospitals or industry, an individual or a committee is typically charged with examining and then approving or denying requests to do research at the site. Regardless of the site, the researcher must complete one or more forms that describe the nature of the research, the specific request being made of the site personnel, and the benefits to the site. Before the request is approved, the researcher may need to obtain permission from others as well; for example, a superintendent or school board may require that permission be granted from the principal or principals whose schools will be involved. Even if such approval is not required, it should be sought, both as a courtesy and for the sake of a smoothly executed study. Of course, as discussed earlier, participants in the study must give their consent. Depending on the nature of the study, permission, or at least acceptance, should be obtained from the teachers who will participate in the study. If students under 18 are to be involved, written parental approval will be needed.

Given the potential complexity of obtaining permission to conduct your research at the chosen site or sites, you should not assume that permission will be granted easily ("we're too busy") or quickly (bureaucracies move slowly). Thus, you should think carefully about how you will explain your study to all those who must provide permission and approval. The key to gaining approval and cooperation is good planning, and the key to good planning is a well-designed, carefully thought-out study and research plan. Some superintendents and principals are "gun-shy" about people doing research in their schools because of a previous bad experience. They don't want anyone else running around their schools, disrupting classes, administering poorly constructed questionnaires, or finding problems. It is up to you to convince school personnel that what you are proposing is of value, that your study is carefully designed, and that you will work with teachers to minimize inconvenience.

Achieving full cooperation, and not just approval on paper, requires that you invest as much time as is necessary to discuss your study with the principal, the teachers, and perhaps even parents. These groups have varying levels of knowledge and understanding regarding the research process. Their concerns will focus mainly on the perceived value of the study, its potential impact on participants, and the actual logistics of carrying it out. The principal, for example, will probably be more concerned with whether you are collecting any data that might be viewed as objectionable by the community than with the specific design you will be using. All groups will be interested in what you might be able to do for them. You should fully explain any potential benefits to be derived by the students, teachers, or principal as a result of your study. Your study, for example, might involve special instructional materials that are to be shared with the teachers and left with them after the study has ended. Even if all parties are favorably impressed, however, the spirit of cooperation will quickly dwindle if your study involves considerable extra work or inconvenience on their part. Bear in mind that principals and teachers are accommodating you, and they are helping you complete your study without relief from their normal responsibilities. As long as you do not adversely affect your work or its results, you should make any changes you can in the study to better preserve participants' normal routines. No change should be made solely for the sake of the compromise, without considering its impact on the study as a whole.

It is not unusual for the principal or teachers to want something in return for their participation. The request may be related to your study, as when a principal asks to review your final report draft for accuracy, asks you to return to the school to brief teachers on your findings, or requests that your results not be disseminated without the principal's approval. The first two requests are more easily agreed to than the third, which probably should be refused, but with an offer to discuss the principal's concerns, if any. It is common to ask the researcher to provide a session or two of professional development for teachers in the school.

Figure 3.2 presents a letter written by a principal to inform parents of a doctoral student's proposed study. The student appears to have shared the potential benefits of the study with the principal and, as a result, secured not only the principal's permission but also her strong support and cooperation. The parental consent form that accompanied the letter (Figure 3.3) addresses many of the ethical and legal concerns discussed in this chapter.

Clearly, human relations are an important factor in conducting research in applied settings. That you should be your usual charming self goes without saying. But you should keep in mind that you are dealing with sincere, concerned educators who may not have your level of research expertise. Therefore, you must make a special effort to discuss your study in plain English (it is possible!) and to never give school personnel the impression that you are talking down to them. Also, your task is not over once the study begins. The feelings of involved persons must be monitored and responded to throughout the duration of the study if the initial level of cooperation is to be maintained.

:: COMPONENTS OF THE QUANTITATIVE RESEARCH PLAN

Although they may go by other names, quantitative research plans typically include an introduction, a method section, a description of proposed data analyses, a time schedule, and sometimes a budget. The basic format for a typical research plan is shown in Figure 3.4.

Other headings may also be included, as needed. For example, if special materials are being developed for the study, or special equipment is being used (such as computer terminals),

---

THE SCHOOL BOARD OF KNOX COUNTY, MASSACHUSETTS

Oak Street Elementary School
Gwen Gregory, Principal
113 Oak Street
Clover, Massachusetts
555-555-5555

January 23, 2005

Dear Parent/Guardian:

Oak Street Elementary School has been chosen to participate in a research study. Our school was selected out of the entire country as a result of our outstanding students and computer program. All third- and fifth-grade students will be able to participate. The results of this study will enable our teachers and parents to discover and understand the learning styles of our students. This knowledge will enable teachers and parents to provide special instruction and materials to improve student learning. It will also provide valuable information for the future development of effective professional computer software.

This study will take place from January 29 to March 30, 2005. It will be conducted by Mrs. Joleen Levine, a recognized and experienced computer educator. She has been Director of Computer Education at Northern University for six years. During that time she has participated in many projects in Knox County that involved teacher training, computer curriculum development, and computer assisted instruction implementation.

I have reviewed this research study and feel that it is a very worthwhile endeavor for our students and school. Please review the information on the following page in order to make a decision concerning parental consent for your child to participate in this study.

Sincerely,

Gwen Gregory

Gwen Gregory
Principal

FIGURE 3.2

Principal's letter to parents concerning a proposed research study

---

then headings such as "Materials" or "Apparatus" might be included under "Method" and before "Design."

Introduction Section

If you have completed Task 2, you are very familiar with the content of the introduction section: a statement of the topic, a review of related literature, and a statement of the hypothesis.

Statement of the Topic

Because the topic sets the stage for the rest of the plan, it should be stated as early as possible. The statement should be accompanied by a description of the background of the topic and a rationale for its significance.

PARENTAL CONSENT FORM

The information provided on this form and the accompanying cover letter is presented to you in order to fulfill legal and ethical requirements for Northwest Eaton College (the institution sponsoring this doctoral dissertation study) and the Department of Health and Human Services (HHS) regulations for the Protection of Human Research Subjects as amended on March 26, 1989. The wording used in this form is utilized for all types of studies and should not be misinterpreted for this particular study.

The dissertation committee at Northern University and the Research Review Committee of Knox County Public Schools have both given approval to conduct this study, "The Relationships Between the Modality Preferences of Elementary Students and Selected Instructional Styles of CAI as They Affect Verbal Learning of Facts." The purpose of this study is to determine the effect on achievement scores when the identified learning styles (visual, audio, tactile/kinesthetic) of elementary students in grades 3 and 5 are matched or mismatched to the instructional methods of specifically selected computer assisted instruction (CAI).

Your child will be involved in this study by way of the following:

1. Pretest on animal facts.
2. Posttest on animal facts.
3. Test on learning styles.
4. Interaction with computer-assisted instruction (CAI-software on the computer)—visual, audio, tactile CAI matching the student's own learning style.

All of these activities should not take more than two hours per student. There are no foreseeable risks to the students involved. In addition, the parent or researcher may remove the student from the study at any time with just cause. Specific information about individual students will be kept *strictly confidential* and will be obtainable from the school principal if desired. The results that are published publicly will not reference any individual students since the study will only analyze relationships among groups of data.

The purpose of this form is to allow your child to participate in the study, and to allow the researcher to use the information already available at the school or information obtained from the actual study to analyze the outcomes of the study. Parental consent for this research study is strictly voluntary without undue influence or penalty. The parent signature below also assumes that the child understands and agrees to participate cooperatively.

If you have additional questions regarding the study, the rights of subjects, or potential problems, please call the principal, Ms. Gwen Gregory, or the researcher, Ms. Joleen Levine (Director of Computer Education, Northern University, 555-5554).

_____

Student's Name

_____   _____

Signature of Parent/Guardian   Date

FIGURE 3.4   Components of a quantitative research plan

1. Introduction
   a. Statement of the topic
   b. Review of related literature
   c. Statement of the hypothesis
      (if appropriate)

2. Method
   a. Participants
   b. Instruments
   c. Design
   d. Procedure

3. Data Analysis
4. Time Schedule
5. Budget (if appropriate)

Review of Related Literature

The review of related literature should provide an overview of the topic and present references related to what is known about the topic. The literature review should lead logically to a testable conclusion, your hypothesis. The review should conclude with a brief summary of the literature and its implications.

Statement of the Hypothesis

For research plans that have one or more hypotheses, each hypothesis should have an underlying explanation for its prediction. That is, there should be some literature that supports the hypothesis. It should clearly and concisely state the expected relationship (or difference) between the variables in your study and should define those variables in operational, measurable, or common-usage terms. The people reading your plan (and especially those reading your final report) may not be as familiar with your terminology as you are. Finally, each hypothesis should be clearly testable within a reasonable period of time.

Method Section

The specific method of research your study represents will affect the format and content of your method section. The method section for an experimental study, for example, typically includes a description of the experimental design, whereas the design and procedure sections may be combined in a plan for a descriptive study. In general, however, the method section includes a description of the research participants, measuring instruments, design, and procedure.

Research Participants

The description of participants should identify the number, source, and characteristics of the sample (Chapter 4 describes the process of sampling participants). It should also define the **population,** that is, the larger group from which the sample will be selected. In other words, what are members of the population like? How large is it? For example, a description of participants might include the following:

> Participants will be selected from a population of 157 students enrolled in an algebra I course at a large urban high school in Miami, Florida. The population is tricultural, being composed primarily of Caucasian non-Hispanic students, African American students, and Hispanic students from a variety of Latin American backgrounds.

> In general, quantitative research samples tend to be large and broadly representative.

Instruments

The instruments section of a research plan describes the particular instruments to be used in the study and how they will measure the variables stated in your hypothesis. An **instrument** is a test or tool used for data collection. (You'll learn more about the nature of measures and instruments in Chapter 5.) If you use instruments that are published, such as a standardized test, you should provide information about (1) the appropriateness of the chosen instruments for your study and sample, (2) the measurement properties of the instruments (especially their validity and reliability[3]), and (3) the process of administering and scoring the instruments. If

---

[3] *Validity* is concerned with whether the data or information being gathered is relevant to the decision being made; *reliability* is concerned with the stability or consistency of the data or information. Both concepts are discussed fully in Chapter 5.

you are going to develop your own instrument, you should describe how the instrument will be developed, what it will measure, how you plan to evaluate its validity and reliability, and how it relates to your hypothesis and participants.

Of course, if more than one instrument is used—a common occurrence in many studies—each should be described separately and in detail. At this stage in your research, you may not yet be able to identify by name or fully describe the instrument you would use in your study. Consequently, in Task 3a you should describe the kind of instrument you would use rather than name a specific instrument. For example, you might say that your instrument will be a questionnaire about teacher unions that will allow teachers to express different degrees of agreement or disagreement in response to statements about teacher unions. While planning or even conducting your research, you may discover that an appropriate instrument for collecting the needed data is not available. If this occurs, you will need to decide whether to alter the hypothesis, change the selected variable, or develop your own instrument.

Materials/Apparatus

If special materials (such as booklets, training manuals, or computer programs) are to be developed for use in the study, they also should be described in the research plan. Also, if special apparatus (such as computer terminals) are going to be used, they should be described.

Design

A **design** is a general strategy or plan for conducting a research study. The description of the design indicates the basic structure and goals of the study. The nature of the hypothesis, the variables involved, and the constraints of the "real world" all contribute to the selection of the research design. For example, if the hypothesis involves comparing the effectiveness of high-impact versus low-impact aerobic exercises with respect to exercise-related injuries, the study would involve comparing the number of injuries occurring in the two groups over some period of time. Thus, the design would involve two groups receiving different treatments and being compared in terms of number of exercise-related injuries. Depending upon whether participants were randomly assigned to treatment or already in treatment before the study, the design would be, respectively, an experiment or a causal–comparative design. There are a number of basic research designs to select from and a number of variations within each design. Quantitative research designs will be discussed in more detail in later chapters.

Procedure

The procedure section describes all the steps that will be followed in conducting the study, from beginning to end, in the order in which they will occur. This section typically begins with a detailed description of the technique to be used to select the study participants. If the design includes a pretest, the procedures for its administration—when it will be administered and how—will usually be described next. Any other measure to be administered at the beginning of the study will also be discussed. For example, in addition to a pretest on current skill in reading music, a researcher studying the effect of a music-reading strategy might administer a general musical achievement test in order to check for the initial equivalence of groups. For a study designed to compare two different methods of teaching reading comprehension to third graders, the procedure section might state the following:

> In September, one week following the first day of school, the Barney Test of Reading Comprehension, Form A, will be administered to both reading method groups.

In research plans that do not include a separate instrument section, relevant information about the instrument is presented in the procedure section.

The remainder of the section describes procedures for carrying out all the other major components of in the study; for example, it might describe procedures for gaining entry to the research site and those for collecting and storing data. The nature of what will occur in a study, however, depends greatly on the kind of research study planned. The procedures for conducting an experiment are different from those for conducting a survey or a historical study. These differences are examined in detail in later chapters.

The procedure section should include any assumptions and limitations that have been identified by the researcher. An **assumption** is any important "fact" presumed to be true but not actually verified. For example, in a study involving reading instruction for pre-school children, it might be assumed that, given the population, none of the children had received reading instruction at home. Limitations in the study also should be noted. A **limitation** is some aspect of the study that the researcher knows may negatively affect the results of the study but over which the researcher has no control. Two common limitations are less-than-ideal sample size and length of the study. A research plan might state one of the following, for example:

Only one class of 30 students will be available for participation.

Ideally, participants should be exposed to the experimental treatment for a longer period of time in order to more accurately assess its effectiveness; however, permission has been granted to the researcher to be in the school for a maximum of two weeks.

Such limitations should be openly and honestly stated so readers can judge for themselves how seriously the limits might affect the study results.

The procedure section should be as detailed as possible, and any new terms should, of course, be defined. The writing should be so precise that a person reading your plan would be able to conduct the study exactly as you intended it to be conducted. Without detailed information on how a study will be carried out, external readers cannot make reasonable judgments about the usefulness of the potential results. It is the appropriateness of the procedures that permits readers to judge the quality of the study.

Data Analysis

The research plan must include a description of the technique or techniques that will be used to analyze study data. For certain descriptive studies, data analysis may involve little more than simple tabulation and presentation of results. For most studies, however, one or more statistical methods will be required. Identification of appropriate analysis techniques is extremely important. Very few situations cause as much "weeping and gnashing of teeth" as collecting data only to find that there is no appropriate analysis or that the appropriate analysis requires sophistication beyond the researcher's level of competence. Once the data are collected, it usually is too late to resolve the problem. That is one reason you should submit a detailed research plan before beginning your study.

The hypothesis of a study determines the nature of the research design, which in turn determines the analysis. An inappropriate analysis does not permit a valid test of the research hypothesis. Which available analysis technique should be selected depends on a number of factors, such as how the groups will be formed (e.g., by random assignment, by using existing groups), how many different treatment groups will be involved, how many variables will be involved, and the kind of data to be collected (e.g., counts of the number of times fifth-grade students fail to turn in their homework on time, a student's test score, or students' placement into one of five socioeconomic categories). Although you may not be familiar with a variety of specific analytic techniques, you probably can describe in your research plan the kind of analysis you would need. For example, you might say,

An analysis will be used that is appropriate for comparing the achievement, on a test of reading comprehension, of two randomly formed groups of second-grade students.

By the time you get to Task 7, you will know exactly what you need (honest!).

Time Schedule

A realistic time schedule is equally important for both beginning researchers working on a thesis or dissertation and for experienced researchers working under the deadlines of a research grant or contract. Researchers infrequently have unlimited time to complete a study. The existence of deadlines typically necessitates careful budgeting of time. Basically, a time schedule includes a listing of major activities or phases of the proposed study and an expected completion time or date for each activity. Such a schedule in a research plan enables the researcher to assess the feasibility of conducting a study within existing time limitations. It also helps the researcher to stay on schedule during the execution of the study. In developing a time frame, do not make the mistake of "cutting it too thin" by allocating a minimum amount of time for each activity. Allow yourself more time than you initially planned to account for unforeseen delays. (Some call *research* a process designed to take 3 to 6 months longer than the researcher thinks it will.) For example, your advisor might not be available when needed, your computer might malfunction and take days or weeks to be repaired, or the teacher who agreed to let you collect data in her class might become ill and be out of school for a month. You should also plan to set the completion date for your final study sometime *before* your actual deadline. Also recognize that your schedule will not necessarily be a series of sequential steps that require one activity to be completed before another is begun. For example, while the study is being conducted, you may also be working on the first part of the research report.

Budget

Proposals submitted to governmental or private agencies for research support almost always require the inclusion of a tentative budget. Researchers not seeking external funding for their research are not required to create a budget; however, it is useful to anticipate costs that might be incurred in the study. For example, costs related to computer programs, travel, printing, and mailing are common research expenses. Although you do not need to have a detailed budget for these and similar expenses, you should recognize that conducting your study will require some personal expenditures.

⠶ COMPONENTS OF THE QUALITATIVE RESEARCH PLAN

A qualitative research plan is a much less structured document than a quantitative research plan. Because qualitative research is an intimate and open-ended endeavor that must be responsive to the context and setting under study, the plan must be flexible. This does not mean, however, that the qualitative researcher is excused from creating a plan in the first place! Far from it. The qualitative researcher must be able to craft a conceptually sound and persuasive (if not elegant) document that provides reviewers with an argument for supporting the proposed study. As Bogdan and Biklen[4] warn, this sometimes places graduate students and contract researchers at odds with Institutional Review Boards and funding agencies who are more

---

[4] *Qualitative Research for Education: An Introduction to Theory and Methods* (3rd ed.), by R. C. Bogdan and S. K. Biklen, 1998, Boston: Allyn & Bacon.

accustomed to dealing with traditional quantitative proposals. Therefore, writing a qualitative research plan requires skill in crafting a document that ultimately provides the "intellectual glue"[5] for the entire proposal and research process.

Prior Fieldwork

Qualitative researchers disagree about the need to undertake some kind of preliminary *fieldwork*, or data collection (discussed further in Chapter 15), before writing a research plan. The purpose of such pre-proposal fieldwork is to provide background that will prepare researchers for what they might expect to find in the research setting. At a very practical level, however, it may be difficult for a qualitative researcher to obtain permission from a school district to conduct fieldwork when the researcher has not yet received approval from the IRB to undertake research in public schools (or elsewhere). Furthermore, pre-proposal fieldwork conflicts with the long traditions established in universities—institutions that are not well recognized for being responsive to change!

Our recommendation is that if it is possible for the researcher to undertake some informal pre-proposal fieldwork that will yield a better understanding of the sociocultural context of the research setting, then it should be done. Otherwise, the researcher will have to rely on the literature review and life's experiences to gain a perspective from which to craft the proposal.

A well-written qualitative research proposal includes details under the headings shown in Figure 3.5.

Title

In qualitative research the title of a study provides the researcher with a frame of reference for continuous reflection. As qualitative researchers immerse themselves in the contexts of their studies, they become increasingly attuned to key issues of their research—issues they may have been unaware of before starting the research. This may lead a researcher to shift the focus of the research and, as a result, change the title of the study to more accurately reflect the new focus.

Similarly, the title serves as a "conceptual point of reference"[6] for readers of the study as well. By conveying in the title the key concepts of study, the researcher attracts the attention of interested readers and enables the work to be correctly catalogued based on the title alone.[7]

Introduction Section

The introduction section of the research plan should include subsections that give the following information: the purpose of the research study; a framing of the study as a larger theoretical, policy, or practical problem; initial research questions; and related literature that helps to frame the research questions.

Purpose of the Research

The statement of purpose sets the stage for everything that follows in the research plan. It should be written as clearly as possible and be a "bite-sized" statement that can be retained by the reader and researcher alike.

---

[5] *Designing Qualitative Research* (2nd ed., p. 31), by C. Marshall and G. Rossman, 1995, Thousand Oaks, CA: Sage.
[6] *Conceptualizing Qualitative Inquiry: Mindwork for Fieldwork in Education and the Social Sciences* (p. 112), by T. H. Schram, 2003, Upper Saddle River, NJ: Merrill/Prentice Hall.
[7] *Writing Up Qualitative Research* (2nd ed.), by J. F. Wolcott, 2001, Thousand Oaks, CA: Sage.

| **FIGURE 3.5** | Components of a qualitative research plan |

1. Title of the Study
2. Introduction to the Study
   a. Describe the purpose of the research study
   b. Frame the study as a larger theoretical, policy, or practical problem
   c. Pose initial research questions
   d. Describe related literature that helps to frame the research questions
3. Research Procedures
   a. Overall approach and rationale for the study
   b. Site and sample selection
   c. The researcher's role (entry to the research site, reciprocity, and ethics)
   d. Data collection methods
   e. Data management strategies
   f. Data analysis strategies
   g. Trustworthiness features
   h. Ethical considerations
4. Potential Contributions of the Research
5. Limitations of the Study
6. Appendixes (one or more of the following, if needed)
   a. Timeline for the research
   b. Proposed table of contents for the study
   c. Consent forms, IRB approval
   d. Samples of structured surveys or questionnaires

Sources: Qualitative Research for Education: An Introduction to Theory and Methods (3rd ed.), by R. C. Bogdan and S. K. Biklen, 1998, Boston: Allyn & Bacon; *Designing Qualitative Research* (2nd ed.), by C. Marshall and G. Rossman, 1995, Thousand Oaks, CA: Sage; and *Conceptualizing Qualitative Inquiry: Mindwork for Fieldwork in Education and the Social Sciences,* by T. H. Schram, 2003, Upper Saddle River, NJ: Merrill/Prentice Hall.

Framing the Study

In this subsection the researcher should demonstrate the relevancy of the proposed study to a frame of reference that the reader will be able to relate to. Where appropriate, the researcher should indicate how the proposed study will contribute to existing theory, educational policy, or the solution of a practical problem.

Initial Research Questions

Posing initial research questions (which may include guiding hypotheses) in a qualitative research plan can be tricky business if the researcher is to maintain the flexibility that is inherent in undertaking qualitative research. We suggest that these initial questions be closely linked to theories, policies, and practical problems outlined in the "Framing the Study" discussion (as well as to the related literature).

Review of Related Literature

The review of related literature should describe the assumptions and theories that underlie your initial research questions and proposed study. In so doing, the review should persuade the reader of your preparedness to undertake a qualitative study, identify potential gaps in the existing literature that may be filled by the proposed study and, if appropriate, suggest a promising educational practice that will address an identified teaching and learning need. As discussed earlier, the review of related literature helps the researcher refine the research questions and embed the questions in "guiding hypotheses" that provide possible directions the researcher may follow.

Research Procedures Section

The procedures section in a qualitative study may have varying forms and degrees of specificity depending on whether or not the researcher has been able to undertake any pre-proposal fieldwork. In general, however, this section includes a description of the overall approach and rationale for the study, the site and sample selection, the researcher's role, data collection methods, data management strategies, data analysis strategies, trustworthiness features, ethical considerations, potential contributions of the research, and limitations of the study.

Overall Approach and Rationale for the Study

This part of the procedures section provides the researcher with an opportunity to classify the overall qualitative research approach (action research, narrative research, ethnographic research) to be used in the research; to provide a rationale for why the particular approach is appropriate, given the purpose of the study; and to provide a link to the appropriate literature on research methods. For example, Mills[8] linked his proposed study of educational change to the literature on educational change as well as to the anthropological literature on cultural change; at the same time, he provided a rationale for the appropriateness of an ethnographic approach to studying the processes and functions of educational change.

Site and Sample Selection

In contrast to quantitative research, qualitative research samples tend to be small and not necessarily broadly representative of the phenomenon being investigated. For example, it is not uncommon for qualitative researchers to claim a sample size of one—even though the sample may be one classroom of children or one school district! In this subsection the qualitative researcher should briefly describe the rationale for choosing a particular sample. Similarly, the researcher should explain why a site was chosen, specifically noting the likelihood of gaining entry to the site and of building sound relationships with the study participants.

In his research plan, for example, Mills[9] discusses the selection of a single school district as his sample; the rationale behind choosing three specific "case study" sites from among the 15 elementary schools in the district; his access to the site made possible by personal relationships with district administrators, teachers, and student teachers; and the expectation that the study would yield credible data. The sites are then discussed in terms of their "representativeness" of the schools in the district but no claims are made as to the generalizability of the findings of the study.

The Researcher's Role

In this part of the procedures section the researcher should describe any negotiations that will need to be undertaken to obtain entry to the research site, any expectations of reciprocity that the research participants may have, and any ethical dilemmas that may face the researcher. Marshall and Rossman[10] suggest that these issues can be sorted into "technical" ones that address entry to the research site and "interpersonal" ones that deal with the ethical (and personal) dilemmas that arise in qualitative research, although rarely are the technical and interpersonal issues mutually exclusive. For example, in order to gain entry to McKenzie School District, Mills[11] met with the district's administrative team, explained the purpose of the proposed study and how his role in the district would be defined, and answered questions from principals and central office personnel. Interpersonal issues were an important aspect of this presentation—the researcher had to convince the administrators that he was trustworthy, sensitive to ethical issues, and a good communicator. In qualitative research, where the "researcher is the instrument," it is critical to the success of the study that the researcher establish his "OKness" with the study's participants.

[8] *Managing and Coping With Multiple Educational Change: A Case Study and Analysis,* by G. E. Mills, 1988, unpublished doctoral dissertation, University of Oregon, Eugene.
[9] Ibid.
[10] *Designing Qualitative Research* (p. 59), Marshall and Rossman.
[11] *Managing and Coping,* Mills.

Data Collection Methods

This part of the procedures section provides the qualitative researcher with an opportunity to briefly describe the specific fieldwork techniques or tools that will be used to collect data to answer the research questions. The researcher should provide examples of the multiple data sources that will be used for each research question. For example, the plan may include samples of structured interview schedules, surveys, and so on, that may be used in the study. In short, the researcher must convince the reader that he knows how he will collect his data!

Data Management Strategies

One of the pervasive images of qualitative researchers is that they are literally buried knee deep in data, surrounded by field notes, transcriptions of taped interviews, artifacts, videotapes, portfolios, and the like. For this reason, it is important for qualitative researchers to provide some insights into how they intend to manage various data sources. For example, the research plan should describe how *field notes* (see Chapter 15), audiotapes, videotapes, photographs, and so on, will be stored and when (giving dates and times, if appropriate) materials will be collected (e.g., "Videotapes will be collected from classrooms weekly"). The importance of attention to detail in managing data will become evident to the qualitative researcher when it's time to write up the research!

Data Analysis Strategies

Qualitative research sometimes combines qualitative and quantitative (e.g., test scores) data in studies, resulting in the need for statistical analysis. However, most qualitative research is heavily weighted toward interpretive, not statistical, data analysis. The researcher analyzes the qualitative data from interviews, field notes, observations, and the like by organizing and interpreting the data. Thus, in the research plan the qualitative researcher should describe the procedures for collating the various forms of data collected and the manner in which the data will be categorized (often by emergent themes in the data). For example, you might state that you will use an analysis that allows field notes and interview data to be organized into a limited number of concepts or issues.

Trustworthiness Features

In qualitative research, trustworthiness features consist of any efforts by the researcher to address the more traditional quantitative issues of validity (the degree to which something measures what it purports to measure) and reliability (the consistency with which it measures it over time). For example, one way that you might address the trustworthiness of your data collection is through the use of *triangulation,* the use of multiple data sources to address each of your research questions (see Chapter 15).

Ethical Considerations

As discussed earlier, demonstrating sensitivity to possible ethical issues that may arise in conducting the study is critical to the success of the qualitative research plan. In qualitative research the most pervasive ethical issues relate to informed consent and the researcher's ability to have closely aligned personal and professional ethical perspectives. Therefore, in your research plan you should include a description of the process you will use to obtain informed consent (including any forms participants will complete) as well as a statement describing your personal/professional ethical perspective for addressing difficult issues that may arise. Addressing such issues can be tricky business. For example, in Mills' study of educational change, [12] he was surprised to find himself questioned by principals about the teaching effectiveness of individual teachers participating in the study—after all, he was from the university and must be an expert on teaching! Commenting on the instructional practices would have been an obvious violation of the participants' right to confidentiality. It was critical for the researcher to respond sensitively to the requests while educating the principals about the researcher's role in the district and revisiting the conditions under which the study's conduct had been negotiated. The qualitative researcher is well advised to include a discussion of ethics in the research plan.

Potential Contributions of the Research

In this section of the plan, the researcher should be prepared to answer the question "So what?"—a common challenge made of a qualitative researcher who has just explained that a proposed study will contribute to one's "understanding" of the phenomenon under investigation. In elaborating on your study's significance, you have an excellent opportunity to link the possible implications of your research back to the broader ideas about theory, policy, and practical solutions discussed in the review of related literature. If you are tempted to make claims about the generalizability of your potential findings, you should think again about the specificity of your research context. It is usually prudent to make modest claims about how a qualitative study will contribute to the existing body of knowledge.

Limitations of the Study

The limitations section of the research plan need not be extensive—you don't want to talk yourself out of conducting the study! You should focus your discussion on any perceived limitations, over which you have no control, that could affect your ability to conduct the proposed research. For example, if the research participants with whom you negotiated entry to the setting leave, you may find yourself without a place to conduct your research! Discuss possible roadblocks to your work in an open and honest fashion so that the readers of your plan can judge for themselves whether the limitations might affect the study's results.

Appendixes

The appendixes of a qualitative research plan typically include one or more of the following: a timeline for the research, a proposed table of contents for the research report (it's never to early to start writing!), sample consent forms to be used with research participants, IRB approval (if already obtained), and samples of structured surveys or questionnaires to be used in the research. You should consider including in your research plan any material that will help the reader determine your preparedness to conduct the research.

As noted previously, there are many differences and distinctions between qualitative and quantitative research. Table 3.1 provides a contrast between the two approaches based on the discussed components of the research process and written plan. As you look at the table, also note the similarities among the components.

:: REVISING AND IMPROVING THE RESEARCH PLAN

Judging the adequacy of a research plan can involve both informal and formal assessment. Informally, the plan should be reviewed and critiqued by you, your advisor, and another experienced researcher. A research plan should be reviewed by at least one skilled researcher and

---

[12] Ibid.

	Quantitative Research	Qualitative Research
TABLE 3.1	Comparison of quantitative and qualitative research components	
Purpose of the research/statement of a topic	Topic stated at the beginning to guide the research process	Statement of purpose may be preceded by fieldwork to learn context of the research; purpose guides study; study framed as part of theoretical, policy, or practical problem; narrower topic may emerge after immersion in setting
Review of the literature	Review conducted early in the study to identify related research, potential hypotheses, and methodological approaches	Review may lead to guiding hypotheses and/or promising practices; links study to underlying assumptions and theories; if not needed for a research plan, may be conducted after study onset
Hypotheses	Hypothesis usually related to review of literature; states researcher's hunches about the relations between the study variables; stated in operational terms; is more specific than the topic statement	Formal hypothesis rarely stated; initial research questions used in plan and are closely linked to theories, policies, and practical problems; understanding is ongoing, shifting
Research participants	Participants chosen from a defined population, usually randomly, at the start of study; samples often large	Small group of participants purposefully selected from research context; participants provide detailed data about themselves and life in context
Data collection and instruments	Data consist of results from tests, questionnaires, and other paper–pencil instruments; collection requires little direct interaction between researcher and participants	Data consist of notes from observations, interviews, examination of artifacts; collection requires substantial interaction between researcher and participants; researcher must manage variety of data sources
Special materials or apparatus	Chosen and used as needed	Chosen and used as needed
	Clear, well-ordered sequence of steps used to conduct research; designs specific to common quantitative approaches, such as correlational, descriptive, causal—comparative, experimental, and single-subject research	Formats vary and are flexible and changeable during research; designs specific to common qualitative approaches, such as ethnographic and narrative research
Research design	Research designs may include both quantitative and qualitative methods; the two approaches are not totally independent of each other	
Research procedures	Procedures describe what occurs in a study; despite many different emphases, most procedures pertinent to both quantitative and qualitative research; concerns include research limits (inability to obtain needed participants or gain access to setting) and lack of research control (inability to obtain needed data or data being lost); maintaining description of procedures being used is critical if other researchers are to judge process and results later	
Time schedule	Research usually completed in relatively short time; data collected and analyzed relatively quickly; planning of time schedule very useful	Research usually occupies lengthy time period; much time needed to collect data in field and interact with participants over time; planning of time schedule very useful
Budget	Budget depends on nature of study and researcher's resources, including time; realistic assessment of budget will help guide choice of a reasonable research topic	
Data analysis	Quantitative methods used to collect primarily numerical data; analysis based on numerical and statistical analyses; validity and reliability measures ensure data trustworthiness	Qualitative methods used to collect primarily descriptive narrative and visual data; analysis based on identifying themes and patterns; triangulation used to ensure trustworthiness of data
Final report	Report heavily focused on statistical analyses	Report heavily focused on narrative description

at least one expert in the study's area of investigation. Any researcher, no matter how long she or he has been a researcher, can benefit from the insight of others. Rereading your own plan several days after having written it can help you identify flaws or weaknesses.

Aspects of the research plan can be field-tested in a **pilot study**, a small-scale trial of a study conducted before the full-scale study. Think of the pilot study as a dress rehearsal.

For all or part of the study, every procedure is followed in order to identify unanticipated problems or issues. You can gain valuable experience from conducting a pilot study. Your research plan will almost always be modified as a result of the pilot study, and in some cases it may be substantially overhauled. One reason, aside from time, that more large-scale pilot studies are not conducted is lack of available participants. Any pilot study, however—even a small one—should be considered a very worthwhile use of your time.

SUMMARY

Definition and Purpose of a Research Plan

1. A research plan is a detailed description of a proposed study; it includes justification for the study, a description of the steps that will be followed in the study, and information about the analysis of the collected data. The plan provides a guide for conducting the study.

2. Most quantitative studies test a hypothesis that influences decisions about the participation, measuring instruments, design, procedures, and statistical techniques used in the study.

3. A written research plan helps you to think through the aspects of your study, facilitates evaluation of the proposed study, and generally improves the quality of the research.

4. Part of good planning is anticipation. Try to anticipate potential problems that might arise, do what you can to prevent them, and plan your strategies for dealing with them if they do occur.

General Considerations in a Research Plan

The Ethics of Research

5. Ethical considerations play a role in all research studies, and all researchers must be aware of and attend to ethical considerations in their research.

6. Many professional organizations have developed ethical principles for their members, and the federal government has enacted laws to protect research participants from harm and invasion of privacy.

7. Probably the most definitive source of ethical guidelines for researchers is *Ethical Principles of Psychologists and Code of Conduct*, prepared for and published by the American Psychological Association (APA).

8. The two most overriding rules of ethics are that participants should not be harmed in any way (physically or mentally) and that researchers obtain the participants' informed consent.

9. Most colleges and universities, as well as the U.S. government, require that proposed research activities involving human subjects be reviewed and approved by an authorized group in an institution, prior to the execution of the research, to ensure protection of the participants.

10. The Family Educational Rights and Privacy Act of 1974, referred to as the Buckley Amendment, protects the privacy of the educational records of students. It stipulates that data that identify participants by name may not be made available to the researcher unless written permission is granted by the participants.

11. Studies involving deception of participants are sometimes unavoidable but should be examined critically for unethical practices.

12. Both quantitative and qualitative research are subject to ethical guidelines. Qualitative researchers, because of their closeness to participants, must be aware of ethical issues and view informed consent as a process that evolves and changes throughout the study.

Gaining Entry to the Research Site

13. It is rarely possible to conduct research without the cooperation of many people. The first step in acquiring needed cooperation is to follow required procedures in the setting you seek to conduct your research in.

14. A formal approval process usually involves the completion of one or more forms describing the nature of the research and the specific request being made of the school or other system.

15. The key to gaining approval and cooperation is good planning and a well-designed, carefully thought-out study.

16. Once formal approval for the study is granted, you should invest the time necessary to explain the study to the principal, the teachers, and perhaps even parents. If these groups do not cooperate, you likely will not be able to do your study.

17. If changes in the study are requested and can be made to better accommodate the normal routine of the participants, these changes should be made unless the research will suffer as a consequence.

18. The feelings of participants should be monitored and responded to throughout the study if the initial level of cooperation is to be maintained. Human relations is an important aspect of conducting research in applied research settings.

Components of the Quantitative Research Plan

19. Quantitative research plans typically include an introduction, a method section, a data analysis description, and a time schedule.

Introduction Section

20. The introduction includes a statement of the topic or question, a review of related literature, and a statement of the hypothesis with variables stated in operational terms.

Method Section

21. The specific method of research your study represents influences the content of your method section. Particular research approaches (e.g., narrative, ethnographic, descriptive, correlational, causal–comparative, and true experimental) use different methods to carry out their unique purposes.

Research Participants

22. The description of participants should clearly define the number, source, and characteristics of the sample, as well as the population the sample was drawn from.

Instruments

23. One part of the method section should provide a description of the particular measures, instruments, and approaches that will be used to collect data. It should include a rationale for the specific selection of the instruments.

24. If you are going to develop your own instrument, you should describe how the instrument will be developed, what it will measure, and how you plan to determine its validity and reliability.

Design

25. A design is a general strategy for conducting a research study. Depending on the nature of the study's topic or question, the hypothesis (if appropriate), variables, and participants, the researcher selects an appropriate research design to carry the study. Both qualitative and quantitative researchers rely on research designs.

Procedure

26. The procedure section describes all the steps that will be followed in conducting the study, from beginning to end, in the order in which they will occur. The procedure will differ for qualitative and quantitative approaches.

27. The procedure section typically begins with a description of the strategy for selecting the sample or samples. If the study includes a pretest, the procedure and timing of it should be described next.

28. The procedure section will describe exactly what is going to occur in the study. The nature of what will occur depends on the kind of research study planned, since the procedures for different research approaches are different.

29. The procedure section should also include any identified assumptions and limitations. An assumption is a "fact" presumed to be true but not actually verified, whereas a limitation is some aspect of the study that the researcher knows may alter the results.

30. The procedure section should be precise to the point that someone else could read your plan and execute your study exactly as you intended it to be conducted.

Data Analysis

31. The research plan must include a description of the techniques that will be used to analyze study data.

32. The hypothesis in a quantitative study determines the design, which in turn determines the data analysis.

33. Selecting an analysis technique depends on a number of factors, such as how the groups will be formed, how many there are, the number of variables that will be studied, and the kind of data to be collected.

Time Schedule

34. The construction of a time schedule listing major research activities and their corresponding expected completion is a useful planning aid.

35. Allow for more time than you think you will need to complete your study. Plan for downtime, and set your finishing date earlier than the final deadline for completion.

Components of the Qualitative Research Plan

36. A qualitative research plan is a much less structured document than a quantitative plan because the research must be responsive to the context and setting under study.
37. If possible, qualitative researchers should undertake some informal pre-proposal fieldwork to better understand the sociocultural context of the research setting.

Introduction Section

38. The introduction includes the purpose of the study, a framing of the study as a larger problem, the initial research questions, a guiding hypothesis (if appropriate), and a review of related literature that helps to frame the research questions.

Research Procedures Section

39. The research procedures section includes a description of the overall approach for the study, the site and sample, the researcher's role, data collection methods, data management strategies, data analysis strategies, trustworthiness features, ethical considerations, potential contributions of the research, and study limitations.
40. The question in a qualitative study determines the design, which in turn determines the data analysis.
41. Qualitative researchers are their own instruments, gathering data through observations, field notes, and interviews. They describe in detail the nature of the data and method of collection and pay particular attention to the use of multiple data sources. They review their narrative data, organize it into categories and themes, and interpret it in terms of the context and participants' perspectives.

Revising and Improving a Research Plan

42. A written research plan permits the researcher and others to carefully examine the quality of the plan and make suggestions for how to improve it.
43. If possible, a researcher should carry out a small-scale pilot study to help in refining or changing planned procedures. A pilot study can examine the viability of the research plan before it is fully conducted.

Now go to the Companion Website at **www.prenhall.com/gay** to assess your understanding of chapter content with Practice Quiz, apply comprehension in Applying What You Know, broaden your knowledge about research in Web Links, and expand your research skills in Evaluating Articles, Analyzing Qualitative Data, Analyzing Quantitative Data, and Research Tools and Tips.

PERFORMANCE CRITERIA

The purpose of Task 3 is to have you construct brief research plans for a quantitative (Task 3a) and a qualitative (Task 3b) study. For a quantitative study, you have already created the introduction section of the plan (Task 2). You should now provide information about the methods you will employ to carry out your study, including information on the research participants (sample), instruments (questionnaires, surveys), design, and procedure; a short statement about the way in which data will be analyzed; and a time schedule. For a qualitative study, you will need to first develop a research topic. You can then complete a preliminary plan that includes the components outlined in Figure 3.5, p. 86.

Although it is expected that each of your plans contain all the components of a research plan, it is not expected that your plan be extensive or technically accurate. In later chapters you will learn ways to formulate each of a research plan's components. Feedback from your instructor concerning your research plan will also help you identify and critique aspects of a plan.

An example that illustrates the performance called for by Task 3a appears on the following pages. (See Task 3a Example.) The task in the example was submitted by the same student whose Task 2 work was previously presented. Thus, in this example the research plan is a continuation of the introduction. Keep in mind that the proposed activities described in this example do not necessarily represent ideal research procedure. Research plans are usually more detailed. The example given, however, does represent what you ought to be able to do at this point.

Additional examples for the tasks are included in the *Student Study Guide* that accompanies this text.

::: TASK 3A Example

Effect of Interactive Multimedia on the Achievement of 10th-Grade Biology Students

Method

Participants

Participants for this study will be 10th-grade biology students in an upper-middle-class, all-girl Catholic high school in Miami, Florida. Forty students will be selected and divided into two groups.

Instrument

The effectiveness of interactive multimedia (IMM) will be determined by comparing the biology achievement of the two groups as measured by a standardized test, if there is an acceptable test available. Otherwise, one will be developed.

Design

There will be two groups of 20 students each. Students in both groups will be posttested in May using a test of biology achievement.

Procedure

At the beginning of the school year, 40 10th-grade biology students will be selected from a population of approximately 200. Selected students will be divided into two groups, and one group will be designated to be the experimental group. The same teacher will teach both classes.

During the school year, the nonexperimental group of students will be taught biology using traditional lecture and discussion methods. The students in the experimental group will be taught using IMM. Both groups will cover the same subject matter and use the same text. The groups will receive biology instruction for the same amount of time and in the same room, but not at the same time, as they will be taught by the same teacher.

Academic objectives will be the same for each class and all tests measuring achievement will be identical. Both classes will have the same homework reading assignments. In May, a biology achievement test will be administered to both classes at the same time.

Data Analysis
The scores of the two groups will be compared statistically.

	August	September . . . April	May	June
		Time Schedule		
Select Participants	___			
Pretest	_____			
Execute Study		_____		
Posttest			___	
Analyze Data				___
Write Report			_____	

"... every individual has the same probability of being selected, and selection of one individual in no way affects selection of another individual." (p. 101)

Selecting a Sample

OBJECTIVES

After reading Chapter 4, you should be able to do the following:

1. Identify and describe four random sampling techniques.
2. Select a random sample using a table of random numbers.
3. Identify three variables that can be stratified.
4. Select stratified samples, cluster samples, and systematic samples.
5. Identify and describe three nonrandom sampling techniques.
6. Identify and briefly describe two major sources of sample bias.
7. Describe quantitative and qualitative sampling strategies.

The purpose of selecting a sample is to gain information concerning a population. For example, if you were interested in the effect of daily homework assignments on the test scores of ninth-grade algebra students, you would not be able to include all ninth-grade algebra students in the United States in your study. You would need to select a smaller group that represents the characteristics of the larger group, the population. Thus, a sample is used to make an inference about the performance of the larger group. As you will see in this chapter, sampling strategies depend on the researcher's purpose and the selection of a research design. Although all research involves the use of samples, the nature, size, and method of selecting samples vary with the research aim.

The goal of Chapter 4 is to help you to understand the importance of selecting an appropriate sample and to introduce you to various sampling techniques. The first section of the chapter deals with quantitative sampling, the second with qualitative sampling. Completing Chapter 4 should enable you to perform the following task.

TASK 4A

Having selected a topic and having formulated one or more testable quantitative hypotheses (Task 2), describe a sample appropriate for evaluating your hypotheses. Include the following in your description:

1. A definition of the population from which the sample would be drawn
2. The procedural technique for selecting the sample and, if necessary, for forming it into two or more groups
3. Sample sizes
4. Possible sources of sampling bias (See Performance Criteria, p. 118.)

TASK 4B

Having selected a topic and having formulated initial research questions (Task 3b), describe the process and context for selecting a purposive sample for a qualitative research study. (See Performance Criteria, p. 118.)

▓ QUANTITATIVE SAMPLING

Sampling is the process of selecting a number of participants for a study in such a way that they represent the larger group from which they were selected. A **sample** is made up of the individuals, items, or events selected from a larger group referred to as a *population*. Rarely do studies gather data from the entire population. In fact, not only is it generally not feasible to study the whole population, it is also not necessary. If the population of interest is large or geographically scattered, studying this population would likely not be feasible due to prohibitive cost, substantive time, or both. If a quantitative sample is well selected, the research results based on it will be generalizable to the population.

As an example, suppose the superintendent of a large school system wanted to find out how the 5,000 teachers in that system felt about teacher unions, whether they would join one, and for what reasons. Interviews were determined to be the best way to collect the desired data. Clearly, it would take a very long time to interview each and every teacher: Even if each interview took only 15 minutes, it would take a minimum of 1,250 hours—more than 31 full-day workweeks—to collect data from all 5,000 teachers. On the other hand, if 10%, or 500, of the teachers were interviewed, it would take only 125 hours, or about 3 weeks to collect data. Assuming that the superintendent needed the information "now, not next year," the latter approach would definitely be preferable if it would yield the same information. If the sample of 500 teachers is correctly selected, the conclusions based on their interviews should be the same or very close to the conclusions based on interviews of all the teachers. Of course, selecting just any 500 teachers would not do. For example, selecting and interviewing 500 elementary teachers would not be satisfactory. In the first place, the number of elementary teachers who are female is highly disproportionate to the total number of female teachers in the district, and males might feel differently about unions. In the second place, opinions of elementary teachers might not be the same as those of junior high or senior high teachers. How about interviewing 500 teachers who are members of the National Education Association (NEA)? Although they would probably be more representative of all 5,000 teachers, they still would not do. Many teachers who are members of the NEA are already members of a union affiliated with that organization. It is reasonable to assume that the opinions toward unions of members and nonmembers of the NEA would be different. How, then, can we obtain an adequate representative sample?

Give up? Don't! There are several relatively simple sampling techniques that could be applied to select a representative sample of teachers. These procedures do not guarantee that the sample will be perfectly representative of the population, but they definitely increase the odds. Use of the procedures would also allow the superintendent to speak more confidently about the generalizability of the study's findings.

In the sections that follow, we will discuss defining a population, selecting a random sample, determining sample size, avoiding sampling error and bias, and selecting a nonrandom sample. The sections will guide you through the necessary steps for selecting a representative sample for your research.

Defining a Population

The first step in sampling is to define the population to which results will be generalizable. Examples of populations are all 10th-grade students in the United States, all gifted elementary school children in Utah, and all first-grade students in Utopia County who have physical disabilities and have participated in preschool training. These examples illustrate two important points about populations. First, populations may be virtually any size and may cover almost any geographical area. Second, the entire group of interest to the researcher is rarely available. Thus, a distinction is made between the population to which the researcher would *ideally* like to generalize study results, the **target population,** and the population from which the researcher can realistically select subjects, which is known as the **accessible population** or *available population.* In most studies the chosen population is generally a realistic choice (i.e., accessible), not an idealistic one (i.e., target).

Suppose you decide to do a study of high school principals' opinions about having their students attend school 6 days a week. Suppose, also, that you wish to generalize your results to all high school principals in the United States. You quickly realize the difficulty of getting information from every high school principal in the United States, so you decide to obtain a representative sample of all U.S. principals. But obtaining even this sample would be a difficult, time-consuming, and expensive effort. Your research plan must be brought into line with cold, hard reality, so you decide to study only principals in your home state. By selecting from a more narrowly defined population, you will save time and money, but you will also lose the ability to generalize about the target population. Your results will be directly generalizable to all high school principals in your home state, but not to all high school principals in the United States. The key is to define your population in enough detail that others can determine how applicable your findings are to their situation.

A description of the sample you ultimately choose should include the number of participants and demographic information about the sample (e.g., average number of years teaching, percentage of each gender or racial group, level of education, achievement level). The type of demographic information reported depends on the sample; the information used to describe a sample of teachers would be different from that used to describe a sample of students, parents, or administrators.

Selecting a Random Sample

Selecting a sample is a very important step in conducting a research study, particularly for quantitative researchers. The "goodness" of the sample determines the meaningfulness and generalizability of the results. As discussed, a good sample is one that is representative of the population from which it was selected. As we saw with our superintendent who needed to assess teachers' attitudes about unions, selecting a representative sample is not a haphazard process. There are several appropriate techniques for selecting a sample. Certain techniques are more appropriate for certain situations, and not all of the techniques provide the same level of assurance concerning representativeness. However, as with populations, we sometimes have to compromise the ideal for what is feasible.

The following sections describe four basic techniques or procedures for selecting a *random* sample: simple random sampling, stratified sampling, cluster sampling, and systematic sampling. These techniques are referred to as **probability sampling** techniques because they permit the researcher to specify the probability, or chance, that each member of a defined population will be selected for the sample. Each of the techniques requires the same basic steps: identify the population, determine the required sample size, and select the sample.

Simple Random Sampling

Simple random sampling is the process of selecting a sample in such a way that all individuals in the defined population have an equal and independent chance of being selected for the sample. The selection of the sample is completely out of the researcher's control; instead, a random, or chance, procedure selects the sample. In other words, every individual has the same probability of being selected, and selection of one individual in no way affects selection of another individual. You may recall times in physical education class when the teacher formed teams by having the class line up and count off by twos—1, 2, 1, 2, and so on. With this method you could never be on the same team as the person next to you. This selection process was not random, because whether you were on one team or another was determined by your place in line and the team of the person next to you. If selection of teams had been random, you would have had an equal (50–50) chance of being on either team, regardless of which team the person next to you was on.

Random sampling is the best single way to obtain a representative sample. Although no technique, not even random sampling, guarantees a representative sample, the probability of achieving one is higher for this procedure than for any other. In most cases, the differences between the sample and the intended population are small. For example, you might not expect the exact same ratio of males to females in a sample as in a population, but random sampling assures that the ratio will be close and that the probability of having too many females is the same as the probability of having too many males. In any event, differences that do occur are a result of chance and are not the result of the researcher's conscious or unconscious bias in selection.

Another point in favor of random sampling is that it is required in many statistical analyses. These analyses permit the researcher to make inferences about a population based on the behavior of a sample.[1] If samples are not randomly selected, then one of the major assumptions of many statistical analyses is violated, and inferences made from the research can be rendered suspect.

Steps in Simple Random Sampling.   In general, random sampling involves defining the population, identifying each member of the population, and selecting individuals for the sample on a completely chance basis. One way to do this is to write each individual's name on a separate slip of paper, place all the slips in a hat or other container, shake the container, and select slips from the container until the desired number of participants is selected. This procedure is not exactly satisfactory if a population has 1,000 or more members. One would need a very large hat—and a strong writing hand! A much more satisfactory approach is to use a **table of random numbers** (also called a *table of random digits*). In essence, a table of random numbers selects the sample for you, with each member being selected on a purely random, or chance, basis. Such tables are included in the appendix of most statistics books and some educational research books; they usually consist of columns of five-digit numbers that have been randomly generated by a computer to have no defined patterns or regularities (see Table A.1 in Appendix A for an example). Using a table of random numbers to select a sample involves the following specific steps:

1. Identify and define the population.
2. Determine the desired sample size.
3. List all members of the population.
4. Assign all individuals on the list a consecutive number from zero to the required number, for example, 000 to 799 or 00 to 89. Each individual must have the same number of digits as each other individual.
5. Select an arbitrary number in the table of random numbers. (Close your eyes and point!)
6. For the selected number, look at only the number of digits assigned to each population member. For example, if a population had 800 members, you would look at only the last 3 digits of the number in the table; if a population had 90 members, you would look at the last 2 digits.
7. If the number corresponds to a number assigned to an individual in the population, then that individual is in the sample. For example, if a population had 500 members and the number selected was 375, the individual assigned 375 would be in the sample; if a population had only 300 members, then 375 would be ignored.
8. Go to the next number in the column, and repeat steps 6 and 7 until the desired number of individuals has been selected for the sample.

Once the sample has been selected, it may be used as is for descriptive or correlational studies or randomly subdivided into two or more subgroups for use in experimental or causal–comparative studies. If there will be only two subgroups, the full sample may be divided by flipping a coin—heads for one group, tails for the other. Actually, the random selection process is not as complicated as the preceding explanation might suggest. The following example should make the procedure clear.

An Example of Simple Random Sampling.   It is now time to help our long-suffering superintendent who wants to select a sample of teachers so that their attitudes toward unions

---

[1] In Chapter 12 you will learn how to select and apply several commoly used *inferential statistics*. Don't you dare groan. You will be amazed at how easy statistics really is.

can be determined. We will apply each of the eight random sample steps described to the superintendent's problem:

1. The population is all 5,000 teachers in the superintendent's school system.
2. The desired sample size is 10% of the 5,000 teachers, or 500 teachers.
3. The superintendent has supplied a directory that lists all teachers in the system.
4. The teachers in the directory are each assigned a number from 0000 to 4999.
5. A table of random numbers is entered at an arbitrarily selected number, such as the one underlined here.

   59058
   11859
   <u>53634</u>
   48708
   71710
   83942
   33278
   etc.

6. The population has 5,000 members, so we are concerned only with the last four digits of the number, 3634.
7. There is a teacher assigned the number 3634; that teacher is therefore in the sample.
8. The next number in the column is 48708. The last four digits are 8708. Because there are only 5,000 teachers, there is no teacher assigned the number 8708. The number is therefore skipped.
9. Applying these steps to the remaining random numbers shown, teachers 1710, 3942, and 3278 are included. This procedure would be continued in succeeding columns until 500 teachers were selected.

At the completion of this process, the superintendent would, in all probability, have a representative sample of all the teachers in the system. The 500 selected teachers could be expected to appropriately represent all relevant subgroups of teachers, such as elementary teachers, older teachers, male teachers, and so on. With simple random sampling, however, representation of specific subgroups is probable but not guaranteed. If you flip a quarter 100 times, the probable outcome is 50 heads and 50 tails. You might get 53 heads and 47 tails, or 45 heads and 55 tails, but most of the time you can expect to get close to a 50–50 split. (You try!) Other, more deviant outcomes are also possible, but relatively infrequent. In tossing a quarter 100 times, 85 heads and 15 tails is a possible but low-probability outcome. Similarly, if 55% of the 5,000 teachers were female and 45% were male, we would expect roughly the same percentages in the random sample of 500. Just by chance, however, the sample might turn out to be 30% females and 70% males.

The superintendent might not be willing to leave accurate representation to chance. If there were one or more variables that the superintendent believed might be highly related to attitudes toward unions, she might adopt a different sampling approach. For example, she might decide that teaching level (elementary, middle, high) would be a significant variable and that elementary teachers might feel differently toward unions than middle or senior high school teachers. She would want a sample that would guarantee appropriate representation of the three teaching levels. To accomplish this, she would probably use stratified sampling rather than simple random sampling.

Stratified Sampling

Stratified sampling is the process of selecting a sample in such a way that identified subgroups (strata) in the population are represented in the sample in the same proportion in which they exist in the population. (A subgroup, or **stratum,** is a variable that can be divided into groups. For example, the variable *gender* can be divided into a male group and a female group; the variable *politicians* can be divided into groups of Democrat, Republican, Independent, and others; and the variable *level of education* can be divided into various groups—elementary, high school, college, and higher.) *Proportional stratified sampling,* as this variation of the method is called, would be appropriate if you were going to take a survey before a national election in order to predict the probable winner. You would want your sample to represent the voting population. Therefore, the proportion of Democrats and Republicans in your sample would need to be the same as in the population. If Democrats made up 63 percent of registered voters and Republicans made up 37 percent, you would want 63 percent of the sample to be Democrats and 37 percent to be Republicans. Other likely variables for proportional stratification might include race, gender, socioeconomic status, and level of education.

Stratified sampling can also be used to select equal-sized (nonproportional) samples from each of a number of subgroups if subgroup comparisons are desired. Suppose, for example, that you were interested in comparing the achievement of students of different ability levels (high, average, and low) being taught by two methods of mathematics instruction (teacher and computer). Simply selecting a random sample of students and assigning one half of the sample to each of the two methods would not (as you know!) guarantee equal representation of each of the ability levels in each method. In fact, just by chance, one of the methods might not have any students from one of the three ability levels. However, randomly selecting students from each ability level, and then assigning half of each selected group to each of the methods, would guarantee equal representation of each ability level in each method. That is the purpose of stratified sampling—to guarantee desired representation of relevant subgroups within the sample.

Steps for Equal-Sized Groups in Stratified Sampling.

The steps in stratified sampling are similar to those in random sampling except that selection is from subgroups in the population rather than the population as a whole. In other words, random sampling is done more than once; it is done for each subgroup. Stratified sampling involves the following steps:

1. Identify and define the population.
2. Determine desired sample size.
3. Identify the variable and subgroups (strata) for which you want to guarantee appropriate representation.
4. Classify all members of the population as members of one of the identified subgroups.
5. Randomly select (using a table of random numbers) an "appropriate" number of individuals from each of the subgroups. *Appropriate* in this case means an equal number of individuals.

As with simple random sampling, once the samples from each of the subgroups have been randomly selected, each may be randomly assigned to two or more treatment groups. If we were interested in the comparative effectiveness of two methods of mathematics instruction for different levels of ability, the steps in sampling might be as follows:

1. The population is all 300 eighth-grade students enrolled in general math at Central Middle School.
2. The desired sample size is 45 students in each of the two methods.
3. The variable is ability, and the desired subgroups are three levels of ability—high, average, and low.
4. Classification of the 300 students indicates that there are 45 high-ability students, 215 average-ability students, and 40 low-ability students.

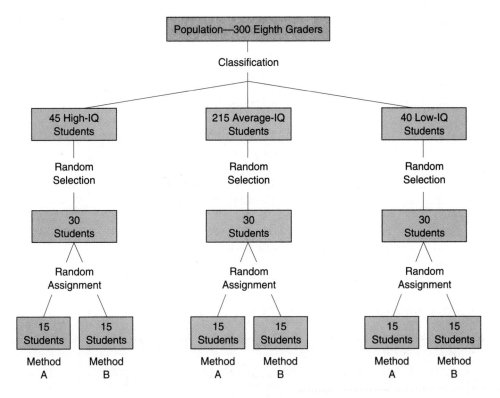

FIGURE 4.1

Procedure for
selecting a stratified
sample based on IQ
for a study designed
to compare two
methods (A and B) of
mathematics
instruction

5. Using a table of random numbers, 30 students are randomly selected from each of the ability subgroups; that is, 30 high-, 30 average-, and 30 low-ability students are selected. This gives us three samples, one for each ability group.
6. The 30 students in each sample are randomly assigned to one of the two methods; that is, 15 of each 30 are randomly assigned to one of the two methods. Therefore, each method contains 45 students—15 high-ability students, 15 average-ability students, and 15 low-ability students (Figure 4.1).

As you may have guessed, stratification can be done on more than one variable. In this example we could have stratified on math interest or prior math grades. The following example, based on a familiar situation, should help to further clarify the process of stratified sampling.

An Example of Proportional Stratified Sampling.   Let us suppose that our old friend the superintendent wanted to guarantee proportional representation of teaching level in the sample of teachers. We will apply each of the five steps previously described for selecting a stratified sample:

1. The population is all 5,000 teachers in the superintendent's school system.
2. The desired sample size is 10% of the 5,000 teachers, or 500 teachers.
3. The variable of interest is teaching level, and there are three subgroups—elementary, middle, and high.
4. We classify the teachers into the subgroups. Of the 5,000 teachers, 65%, or 3,250, are elementary teachers; 20%, or 1,000, are middle teachers; and 15%, or 750, are senior high teachers.

5. We want 500 teachers. Because we want proportional representation, 65% of the sample (325 teachers) should be elementary teachers, 20% (100 teachers) should be junior high teachers, and 15% (75 teachers) should be senior high teachers.

Therefore, using a table of random numbers, we randomly select 325 of the 3,250 elementary teachers (makes sense, since we want a total sample of 10%), 100 of the 1,000 junior high teachers, and 75 of the 750 senior high teachers.

At the completion of this process, the superintendent would have a sample of 500 teachers (325 + 100 + 75), or 10% of the 5,000, and each teaching level would be proportionally represented. Note that using proportionally sized groups requires that you have accurate information about the size of each group. Without this information, proportional group studies are not recommended.

So far we have discovered two ways in which the superintendent could get a sample of teachers, simple random sampling and stratified sampling. Both of these techniques, however, would result in a sample scattered over the entire district. The interviewer would have to visit many, many schools, some of them containing only one or two teachers in the sample. In the event that the superintendent wanted the information quickly, a more expedient method of sampling would be needed. For the sake of convenience, cluster sampling might be used.

Cluster Sampling

In **cluster sampling,** intact groups, not individuals, are randomly selected. All the members of selected groups have similar characteristics. For example, instead of randomly selecting from all fifth-graders in a large school district, you could randomly select fifth-grade classrooms and use all the students in each classroom. Cluster sampling is more convenient when the population is very large or spread out over a wide geographic area. It may be the only feasible method of selecting a sample when the researcher is unable to obtain a list of all members of the population. Also, educational researchers frequently cannot select and assign individual participants, as they may like. For example, if your quantitative study's population were 10th-grade biology students, it is very unlikely that you would obtain administrative approval to randomly select and remove a few students from different classrooms for your study. You would have a much better chance of securing permission to use several intact classrooms.

Any location within which we find an intact group of similar characteristics (population members) is a **cluster.** Examples of clusters are classrooms, schools, city blocks, hospitals, and department stores. Cluster sampling usually involves less time and expense and is generally more convenient than other techniques. As the previous example of 10th-grade biology students illustrated, it is easier to obtain permission to work with all the students in several classrooms than to work with a few students in many classrooms. Similarly, in a descriptive study it is easier to survey all the people in a limited number of city blocks than a few people in many city blocks. In each case, cluster sampling would be more convenient (though not necessarily as good, as we shall see later!) than either simple random sampling or stratified sampling.

Steps in Cluster Sampling.   The steps in cluster sampling are not very different from those in random sampling. The major difference, of course, is that groups (clusters), not individuals, are randomly selected. Cluster sampling involves the following steps:

1. Identify and define the population.
2. Determine the desired sample size.
3. Identify and define a logical cluster (neighborhood, school, city block, etc.).
4. List all clusters (or obtain a list) that make up the population of clusters.
5. Estimate the average number of population members per cluster.
6. Determine the number of clusters needed by dividing the sample size by the estimated size of a cluster.

7. Randomly select the needed number of clusters (using a table of random numbers).
8. Include in your study all population members in each selected cluster.

Cluster sampling can be carried out in stages, involving selection of clusters within clusters. This process is called *multistage sampling*. For example, a district in a state, then schools in the district, and then classrooms in the schools could be randomly selected to sample classrooms for a study.

One common misconception about cluster sampling is that it is appropriate to randomly select only a single cluster. It is not uncommon, for example, for some researchers to define a population as all fifth graders in Knox County, to define a cluster as a school, and to randomly select only one school in the population. However, these same "researchers" would not dream of randomly selecting only one student! The principle is the same. Keeping in mind that a good sample is representative of the population from which it is selected, it is highly unlikely that one randomly selected student could ever be representative of an entire population. Similarly, it is unlikely that one randomly selected school could be representative of all schools in a population. Thus, one would normally have to select a number of clusters for the results of a study to be generalizable to the population. The following example should make the procedures involved in cluster sampling clear.

An Example of Cluster Sampling.   Let us see how our superintendent would get a sample of teachers if cluster sampling were used. We will follow the steps previously listed:

1. The population is all 5,000 teachers in the superintendent's school system.
2. The desired sample size is 500.
3. A logical, useful cluster is a school.
4. The superintendent has a list of all the schools in the district; there are 100 schools.
5. Although the schools vary in the number of teachers per school, there is an average of 50 teachers per school.
6. The number of clusters (schools) to be selected equals the desired sample size, 500, divided by the average size of a cluster, 50. Thus, the number of schools needed is (500 ÷ by 50) = 10.
7. Therefore, 10 of the 100 schools are randomly selected by assigning a number to each school and using a table of random numbers.
8. All the teachers in each of the 10 schools are in the sample (10 schools, 50 teachers per school on average, equals the desired sample size).

Thus, the researcher could conduct interviews at 10 schools and interview all teachers in each school instead of traveling to a possible 100 different schools.

Although the advantages of cluster sampling are evident, it does have several drawbacks. For one thing, the chances are greater of selecting a sample that is not representative of the population. The smaller the sample size, the more likely that the sample selected may not represent the population. For example, the teachers in this example are from a limited number of schools. The possibility exists that the 10 schools selected are somehow different (e.g., in socioeconomic level of the students, or teacher experience) from the other 90 schools in the district. One way to compensate for this problem is by selecting a larger sample of clusters, thus increasing the likelihood that the schools selected adequately represent all the schools.

As another example, suppose our population was all fifth-graders in 10 schools (each school having an average of 120 students in four classes of 30 students each), and we wanted a sample of 120 students. We might select our sample in any number of ways. For example, we could (1) randomly select one school and use all the fifth-graders in that school, (2) randomly select two classes from each of two schools, or (3) randomly select 120 students from the 10 schools. In each case we would wind up with 120 students, but the samples would probably not be equally "good." In the first case, we would have students from only one school. It is very likely that this school would be different from the other nine in some significant way. In the second case, we would be doing a little better, but we would still only have 2 of the 10 schools represented. Only in the third case would we have a chance of selecting a sample containing students from all or most of the schools, and the classes within those schools. If random sampling were not feasible, as is often the case, selecting two classes from each of two schools would be preferable to selecting all the students in one school. Actually, if cluster sampling were used, it would be even better to select one class each from four of the schools. One way we could attempt to compensate for the loss of representativeness associated with cluster sampling would be to select more than four classes.

Another problem is that commonly used statistical methods are not appropriate for analyzing data resulting from a study using cluster sampling. Such statistics generally require randomly formed groups, not those selected in a whole cluster. The statistics that are available and appropriate for cluster samples are generally less sensitive to differences that may exist between groups. Thus, one should carefully weigh the advantages and disadvantages of cluster sampling before choosing this method of sampling. There is one more type of random sampling with which you should be familiar, systematic sampling.

Systematic Sampling

Systematic sampling is not used very often, but it is appropriate in certain situations. In some instances, it is the only feasible way to select a sample. **Systematic sampling** is sampling in which individuals are selected from a list taking every Kth name. So what's a "Kth" name? That depends on what K is. If $K = 4$, selection involves taking every 4th name; if $K = 10$, every 10th name is taken, and so forth. The "list" referred to is a list of the individuals in the population, and K is determined by dividing the number of individuals on the list by the number of subjects desired for the sample. The major difference between systematic sampling and the other types of sampling discussed is that all members of the population do not have an independent chance of being selected for the sample. Once the first name is selected, all the rest of the individuals to be included in the sample are automatically determined.

Even though choices are not independent, a systematic sample can be considered a random sample if the list of the population is randomly ordered. One or the other has to be random—either the selection process or the list. Because randomly ordered lists are rarely available, systematic sampling is rarely as "good" as random sampling. Although some researchers argue this point, the major objection to systematic sampling of a nonrandom list is the possibility that the process will cause certain subgroups of the population to be excluded from the sample. A classic example is that many people who share a nationality have distinctive last names that tend to group together under certain letters of the alphabet; if K is at all large, taking every Kth name from an alphabetized list makes it possible to completely skip over these subgroups of people.

Steps in Systematic Sampling.   Systematic sampling involves the following steps:

1. Identify and define the population.
2. Determine the desired sample size.
3. Obtain a list of the population.
4. Determine K by dividing the size of the population by the desired sample size.
5. Start at some random place in the population list. Close your eyes and stick your finger on a name.
6. Starting at that point, take every Kth name on the list until the desired sample size is reached.
7. If the end of the list is reached before the desired sample is reached, go back to the top of the list.

Now let us see how our superintendent would use systematic sampling.

An Example of Systematic Sampling.   If our superintendent used systematic sampling, the process would be as follows:

1. The population is all 5,000 teachers in the superintendent's school system.
2. The desired sample size is 500.
3. The superintendent has a directory that lists all teachers in the system in alphabetical order. The list is not randomly ordered, but it is the best available.
4. K is equal to the size of the population, 5,000, divided by the desired sample size, 500. Thus $K = (5,000 \div 500) = 10$.
5. Select one random name in the list of teachers.
6. Every 10th name after that point is automatically in the sample. For example, if the teacher selected in Step 5 were the 3rd name on the list, then the sample would include the 13th name, the 23rd, the 33rd, the 43rd, and so forth.

In this case, due to the nonrandom nature of the list, the sample might not be as representative as the samples resulting from application of the other techniques. Table 4.1 summarizes characteristics of the four quantitative random sampling approaches.

Determining Sample Size

The sampling question most frequently asked by beginning researchers is probably, "How large should my sample be?" And the answer is, "large enough!" This answer may not be very comforting or precise, but the question is a difficult one. If the sample is too small, the results of the study may not be generalizable to the population, regardless of how well the sample is selected. Suppose, for example, the population were 300 first graders. If we randomly selected

4 Quantitative Random Sampling Approaches

TABLE 4.1	Random sampling strategies		
Type	**Process**	**Advantages**	**Disadvantages**
Simple random sampling	Select desired number of sample members using a table of random numbers.	Easy to conduct; strategy requires minimum knowledge of the population to be sampled.	Need names of all population members; may over- or underrepresent sample members; difficult to reach all selected in sample.
Stratified random sampling	Divide population into separate levels, or strata, and randomly sample from the separate strata.	More precise sample; can be used for both proportions and stratification sampling; sample represents the desired strata.	Need names of all population members; difficult to reach all selected in sample; researcher must have names of all populations.
Cluster sampling	Select groups, not individuals; identify clusters and randomly select them to reach desired sample size.	Efficient; clusters are most likely to be used in school research; don't need names of all population members; reduces travel to sites.	Fewer sampling points make it less likely to produce a representative sample.
Systematic sampling	Using list of population, pick a name on list at random and select each Kth person on the list to the desired sample size.	Sample selection is simple.	All members of population do not have an equal chance to be selected; Kth person may be related to a periodic order in the population list, producing unrepresentativeness in the sample.

only one student, clearly that student could not represent all the students. Nor could two, three, or four students, even if randomly selected, adequately represent the population. On the other hand, we would all agree that a sample of 299, 298, or 297 students would represent the population. How about 10? Too small, you say. OK, how about 30? 75? 100? At what point does the sample size stop being "too small" and become "big enough"? That is a question without an easy answer.

Knowing that the sample should be as large as possible helps some but still does not give any specific guidance as to an adequate size. In many cases, the researcher does not have access to large numbers of potential research participants. In fact, obtaining permission to involve students in a study, or finding adults willing to participate in a study, is generally not an easy task. Usually the problem is too few participants rather than too many. In any event, there are some guidelines you can be apply to determine what size sample is "big enough."

In general, the minimum sample size depends on the type of research involved. Some cite a sample size of 30 as a guideline for correlational, causal–comparative, and true experimental research. For correlational studies, at least 30 participants are needed to establish the existence or nonexistence of a relationship. For causal–comparative and true experimental studies, a minimum of 30 participants in each group (e.g., treatment and nontreatment groups) is recommended, although in some cases it might be difficult to attain this number. However, the larger the sample, the more likely one would be to detect a difference between the different groups. We would not be very confident about the results of a single study based on small samples, but if a number of such studies obtained similar results, our confidence in the findings would generally be higher. What is important for you to understand is the consequences of a small quantitative sample size.

For descriptive research, it is common to sample 10% to 20% of the population, although this guideline can be misleading. In reality, the appropriate sample size depends on such factors as the specific type of descriptive research involved, the size of the population, and whether data will be analyzed for given subgroups. For descriptive as well as other types of research, statistical techniques and related software are available for determining sample size in a precise way that takes into account relevant variables. A more general approach is illustrated in Table 4.2. Based on a formula originally developed by the United States Office of Education, Krejcie and Morgan generated the appropriate sample sizes listed. For a given population size (N), Table 4.2 indicates the sample size (S) needed for the sample to be representative, assuming one is going to survey a random sample. Although in certain respects Table 4.2 represents an oversimplified approach to determining sample size, the table does suggest some general rules of thumb.

The data in Table 4.2 suggest that the following general rules are helpful in determining sample size:

- The larger the population size, the smaller the percentage of the population required to get a representative sample.
- For smaller populations, say, $N = 100$ or fewer, there is little point in sampling; survey the entire population.
- If the population size is around 500 (give or take 100), 50% should be sampled.
- If the population size is around 1,500, 20% should be sampled.
- Beyond a certain point (about $N = 5,000$), the population size is almost irrelevant and a sample size of 400 will be adequate. Thus, the superintendent from our previous examples would be relatively safe with a sample of 400 teachers, but would be even more confident with a sample of 500.

Of course, these numbers or percentages are suggested minimums. If it is at all possible to obtain more participants, you should do so. Even very large samples, however, can lead to

TABLE 4.2		Sample sizes (S) required for given population sizes (N)							
N	**S**	**N**	**S**	**N**	**S**	**N**	**S**	**N**	**S**
10	10	100	80	280	162	800	260	2800	338
15	14	110	86	290	165	850	265	3000	341
20	19	120	92	300	169	900	269	3500	346
25	24	130	97	320	175	950	274	4000	351
30	28	140	103	340	181	1000	278	4500	354
35	32	150	108	360	186	1100	285	5000	357
40	36	160	113	380	191	1200	291	6000	361
45	40	170	118	400	196	1300	297	7000	364
50	44	180	123	420	201	1400	302	8000	367
55	48	190	127	440	205	1500	306	9000	368
60	52	200	132	460	210	1600	310	20000	370
65	56	210	136	480	214	1700	313	15000	375
70	59	220	140	500	217	1800	317	20000	377
75	63	230	144	550	226	1900	320	30000	379
80	66	240	148	600	234	2000	322	40000	380
85	70	250	152	650	242	2200	327	50000	381
90	73	260	155	700	248	2400	331	75000	382
95	76	270	159	750	254	2600	335	100000	384

Source: From R. V. Krejcie and D. W. Morgan, "Determining Sample Size for Research Activities," *Educational and Psychological Measurement, 30*, p. 608, copyright © 1970 by Sage Publications, Inc. Reprinted by permission of Sage Publications, Inc.

erroneous conclusions. We turn now to the many forms of sampling bias that can affect a study regardless of sample size.

Avoiding Sampling Error and Bias

Selecting random samples does not guarantee that they will be representative of the population. Error, beyond that within the control of the researcher, is a reality of random sampling. Of course, no sample will have a composition precisely identical to that of the population. However, if well selected and sufficiently large, the chances are that the sample will closely represent the population. Occasionally, however, just by chance (remember, *random* means out of the researcher's control and at the mercy of chance), a sample will differ significantly from the population on some important variable. This expected, chance variation in variables is called **sampling error.** If there is a variable for which the sample is greatly underrepresented, the researcher should stratify (create a new sample using stratified sampling) on that variable because stratification can provide proportional or equal-sized samples.

In contrast to sampling error, which results from random differences between samples and populations, **sampling bias** is systematic sampling error that is generally the fault of the researcher. It occurs when some aspect of the sampling creates a bias in the data. For example, suppose a researcher who wished to study college students' attitudes toward alcohol stood outside bars and asked patrons leaving the bars to answer questions regarding their attitudes toward alcohol. This would be a biased sample. Remember, the study was to be about the attitudes of college students—all types of college students. By sampling outside bars, the researchers systematically omitted college students who don't go to bars. The sampling bias in the study makes the study conclusions invalid. Similarly, when a survey researcher gets a return of only 45 percent of questionnaires sent out, the large number of nonreturns introduces a potential response bias in the results. As these examples illustrate, sample bias greatly affects the trustworthiness of a study.

Researchers should be aware of sources of sampling bias and do their best to avoid it. We've already mentioned that securing administrative approval to involve students in educational research studies is not easy. Of necessity, researchers often are forced to use whatever samples they can get (you'll read more about this problem in the section "Convenience Sampling") and whatever methods teachers and administrators will allow. Cooperating with teachers and administrators is, of course, advisable, but not at the expense of good research. If your study cannot be conducted properly under the administrators' restrictions, try hard to convince the administration to allow the study to be conducted in a way that will provide viable results. If this fails, you should look elsewhere for participants.

If it is not possible to avoid sampling bias, you must decide whether the bias is so severe that the study results will be seriously affected. If you decide to continue with the study, with full awareness of the existing bias, such bias should be completely reported in the final research report. This allows the consumers of the research to decide for themselves how serious the bias is.

Selecting a Nonrandom Sample

Although random sampling techniques provide the best opportunity to obtain unbiased samples, it is not always possible for researchers to use random sampling. For example, teachers or administrators often select the students or classes they want researchers to study to ensure a good impression or result in the outcome, or researchers might not find many people willing to participate in their study. These and similar factors can introduce sampling bias. **Nonprobability sampling,** also called *nonrandom sampling,* is the process of selecting a sample using a technique which does *not* permit the researcher to specify the probability, or chance, that each member of a population has of being selected for the sample. Nonrandom sampling methods do not have random sampling at any stage of sample selection.

When nonrandom samples are used, it is usually difficult, if not impossible, to describe the population from which a sample was drawn and to whom results can be generalized. To compensate for this problem, the researcher may wish to obtain information from nonrespondents. Oftentimes, follow-up contact with nonrespondents will provide the researcher with insights about potential bias provided by the respondents. For example, the researcher may determine that the majority of nonrespondents were people for whom English is a second language. They were unable to respond to the research request because of a language barrier. This becomes important information for the researcher concerned about possible bias in a study.

Nonrandom sampling approaches include convenience sampling, purposive sampling, and quota sampling. Of these methods, convenience sampling is the most used in educational research and is therefore the major source of sampling bias in educational research studies.

Convenience Sampling

Convenience sampling, also referred to as *accidental sampling* and *haphazard sampling,* is the process of using as the sample whoever happens to be available at the time. Two examples of convenience sampling are the use of volunteers and the use of existing groups just because "they are there." For example, have you ever been stopped on the street or in a grocery store by someone who wants your opinion of an event or of a new kind of muffin? Those who volunteer to answer are usually different from nonvolunteers. They may be more motivated or more interested in the particular study. Because the total population is composed of both volunteers and nonvolunteers, the results of a study based solely on volunteers are not likely generalizable to the entire population. Suppose you send a questionnaire to 100 randomly selected people and ask the question, "How do you feel about questionnaires?" Suppose that

40 people respond, and all 40 indicate that they love questionnaires. Should you then conclude that the group from which the sample was selected loves questionnaires? Certainly not. The 60 who did not respond may not have done so simply because they hate questionnaires!

Purposive Sampling

In **purposive sampling**, also referred to as *judgment sampling*, is the process of selecting a sample that is *believed* to be representative of a given population. In other words, the researcher selects the sample using his experience and knowledge of the group to be sampled. For example, if a researcher planned to study exceptional high schools, he would choose schools to study based on his knowledge of exceptional schools. Prior knowledge or experience might lead the researcher to select exceptional high schools that meet certain criteria, such as a high proportion of students going to four-year colleges, a large number of AP students, extensive computer facilities, and a high proportion of teachers with advanced degrees. Notice that there is an important difference between convenience sampling, in which participants who happen to be available are chosen, and purposive sampling, in which the researcher deliberately identifies criteria for selecting the sample. Clear criteria provide a basis for describing and defending purposive samples. The main weakness of purposive sampling is the potential for inaccuracy in the researcher's criteria and resulting sample selections.

Quota Sampling

Quota sampling is the process of selecting a sample based on required, exact numbers, or *quotas*, of persons of varying characteristics. It is most often used in descriptive research when it is not possible to list all members of the population of interest. When quota sampling is involved, data gatherers are given exact characteristics and quotas of persons to be interviewed (e.g., 35 working women with children under the age of 16, 20 working women with no children under the age of 16). This sampling technique is widely used in large-scale surveys. Obviously, when quota sampling is used, data are obtained from easily accessible individuals. Thus, people who are less accessible (more difficult to contact, more reluctant to participate, and so forth) are underrepresented.

:: QUALITATIVE SAMPLING

Qualitative sampling is the process of selecting a small number of individuals for a study in such a way that the individuals chosen will be able to help the researcher understand the phenomenon under investigation. The purpose of qualitative sampling is to choose participants who will be good "key informants" (collaborators, coresearchers) who will contribute to the researcher's understanding of a given phenomenon. The characteristics of a good key informant include the ability to be reflective and thoughtful, to communicate (orally, in writing, or both) effectively with the researcher, and to be comfortable with the researcher's presence at the research site.

Qualitative research samples are generally different, smaller, and less "representative" compared to those of quantitative research because the two approaches have different aims and needs. Because of the interest in participants' perspectives, immersion in the setting, and the research topic being studied, qualitative research requires more in-depth data collection than that typically needed in quantitative research. Whereas a quantitative researcher might ask, "What teacher behaviors are correlated with the amount of time students will continue on a task?" a qualitative researcher might ask, "What meanings do students and teachers create together about time on task, and how are the perspectives of different students manifested when working on tasks?" To obtain the desired depth of information required by such topics, qualitative researchers must almost always deal with small samples, normally interacting over a long period of time and in great depth.

Remember, one of the basic tenets of qualitative research is that each research setting is unique in its own mix of people and contextual factors. The researcher's intent is to describe a particular context in depth, not to generalize to a context or population. Representativeness is secondary to the participants' ability to provide the desired information about self and setting.

Selecting Research Participants: Purposive Sampling Approaches

Because many potential participants are unwilling to undergo the lengthy demands of participation, sampling in qualitative research is almost always purposive. The researcher relies on experience and insight to select a sample; randomness is rarely part of the process. One reason qualitative researchers spend time in the research setting before selecting a sample is to observe and obtain information that can be generally used to select participants whom they judge to be thoughtful, informative, articulate, and experienced with the research topic and setting. Within the domain of qualitative purposive sampling, there are a number of specific approaches that are used in qualitative research. Table 4.3 illustrates the range of qualitative sampling approaches, providing an example of use and a sample strategy for each of five common types.

In many qualitative studies, combinations of the approaches in Table 4.3 and other purposive sampling approaches may be used to identify and narrow a sample. For example, qualitative researchers can test the robustness of their findings by purposefully selecting a few new participants and determining whether they provide similar information and perspectives as the original group of participants.

It should be noted that simply stating the name of a purposive sampling technique in a research plan or report will not tell readers what they need to know about members of the sample. Both qualitative and quantitative researchers who use these techniques must provide detailed information about research participants and how they were chosen. This brings to mind another important point. When choosing a sampling technique and the sample itself, researchers need to remember a primary goal: selecting participants who can best add to the understanding of the phenomenon under study, not participants who necessarily represent some larger population. The participants' perspectives, as described by the researcher, form the very core of a qualitative research study.

When identifying a potential participant, the researcher should meet with the person firsthand. The initial communication is the start of a relationship that may continue throughout the study. Establish a day and time when you can meet to discuss the study. It will usually be more convenient to hold the visit in the research setting. This face-to-face meeting will give you a view of the setting and will allow you to demonstrate your interest in the potential participant and your desire to start the research relationship off in a positive and professional way. It will also help you determine whether the person is able to provide the data you seek. Finally, if the potential participant is interested, understands your expectations, and can provide appropriate data, then you can arrange additional times and places for interviewing, observing, and meeting.

Determining Sample Size

Inevitably all qualitative researchers face the question: How many participants are enough? As is usually the case with such questions, the answer is, "It depends." There are no hard and fast

TABLE 4.3	Examples of qualitative sampling	
Type	**Example**	**Sample Strategy**
Intensity sampling	Selecting participants who permit study of different levels of the research topic; for example, the researcher might select some good and poor students, experienced and inexperienced teachers, or teachers with small and large classes.	Compare differences of two or more levels of the topic (e.g., good versus bad students); select two groups of about 20 participants from each of the two levels.
Homogeneous sampling	Selecting participants who are very similar in experience, perspective, or outlook; this produces a narrow, homogeneous sample and makes data collection and analysis simple.	Select a small group of participants who fit a narrow, homogeneous topic; collect data from the chosen participants.
Criterion sampling	Selecting all cases that meet some set of criteria or have some characteristic; the researcher might pick students who have been held back in two successive years or teachers who left the profession to raise children and then returned to teaching.	Identify participants who meet the defined criterion; select a group of five or so participants to collect data from.
Snowball sampling	Selecting a few people who fit a researcher's needs, then using those participants to identify additional participants, and so on, until the researcher has a sufficient number of participants. (Snowballing is most useful when it is difficult to find participants of the type needed.)	Decide how many participants are needed; let initial participants recruit additional participants that fit the researcher's requirements until the desired number is reached.
Random purposive sampling	Selecting more participants than needed for the study; for example, if 25 participants were purposively selected by the researcher but only 10 participants could take part in the study, a random sample of 10 from 25 potential participants would be chosen; this strategy adds credibility to the study, although the initial sample is based on purposive selection. (This approach is typically used with small samples.)	Given a pool of participants, decide how many of them can reasonably be dealt with in the study, and randomly select this number to participate. (This strategy is intended to deal with small samples.)

rules for determining the "correct" number of participants. Qualitative studies can be carried out with a single participant or with as many as 60 or 70 participants representing multiple contexts. However, qualitative studies with more than 20 or so participants are rare, and many studies will have fewer. The qualitative researcher's time, money, participant availability, participant interest, and other factors will influence the number of participants engaged in a research sample. Remember, in qualitative research, more "subjects" does not necessarily mean "better."

Two general indicators are commonly used to determine when the number of participants is sufficient. The first is the extent to which the selected participants represent the range of potential participants in the setting. For example, if the research setting is a school with kindergarteners to sixth graders and the researcher includes only teachers from grades K, 1, and 2, the selected participants do not represent those in the chosen setting. To rectify this problem, the researcher could change the focus to the lower grades or add participants at the higher grade levels. The second indicator is the redundancy of the information gathered from the participants. When the researcher begins to hear the same thoughts, perspectives, and responses from most or all of the participants, she will know that little more is being learned and additional participants are not needed, at least for that particular topic or issue. This point is commonly known as **data saturation**.

SUMMARY

Quantitative Sampling

1. Sampling is the process of selecting a number of individuals for a study in such a way that the individuals represent the larger group from which they were selected.

2. The purpose of sampling is to gain information about a larger population. A population is the group to which a researcher would like the results of a study to be generalizable.

3. The population that the researcher would ideally like to generalize results to is referred to as the *target population;* the population that the researcher realistically selects from is referred to as the *accessible population* or *available population.*

4. The degree to which the selected sample represents the population is the degree to which the research results are generalizable to the population.

Selecting a Random Sample

5. Regardless of the specific technique used, the steps in sampling include identifying the population, determining required sample size, and selecting the sample.

Simple Random Sampling

6. Simple random sampling is the process of selecting a sample in such a way that all individuals in the defined population have an equal and independent chance of being selected for the sample. It is the best single way to obtain a representative sample.

7. Random sampling involves defining the population, identifying each member of the population, and selecting individuals for the sample on a completely chance basis. Usually a table of random numbers is used to select the sample.

Stratified Sampling

8. Stratified sampling is the process of selecting a sample in such a way that identified subgroups in the population are represented in the sample in the same proportion in which they exist in the population.

9. Stratified sampling can also be used to select equal-sized samples from each of a number of subgroups if subgroup comparisons are desired.

10. The steps in stratified sampling are similar to those in random sampling except that selection is from subgroups in the population rather than the population as a whole. In other words, random sampling is done for each subgroup.

Cluster Sampling

11. Cluster sampling is sampling in which groups, not individuals, are randomly selected. Clusters can be communities, states, school districts, and so on.

12. The steps in cluster sampling are similar to those in random sampling except that the random selection of groups (clusters), not individuals, is involved. Both stratified and cluster sampling often use multistage sampling.

Systematic Sampling

13. Systematic sampling is sampling in which individuals are selected from a list by taking every Kth name, where K equals the number of individuals on the list divided by the number of participants desired for the sample.

Determining Sample Size

14. Samples in quantitative studies should be as large as possible; in general, the larger the sample, the more representative it is likely to be, and the more generalizable the results of the study will be.

15. Minimum, acceptable sample sizes depend on the type of research, but there are no universally accepted minimum sample sizes.

Avoiding Sampling Error and Bias

16. Sampling error is beyond the control of the researcher and occurs as part of random selection procedures.

17. Sampling bias is systematic and is generally the fault of the researcher. Bias can result in research findings being invalid. A major source of bias is the use of nonrandom sampling techniques.

18. Any sampling bias present in a study should be fully described in the final research report.

Selecting a Nonrandom Sample

19. Researchers cannot always select random samples and occasionally must rely on nonrandom selection procedures.

20. When nonrandom sampling techniques are used, it is not possible to specify what probability each member of a population has of being selected for the sample; in addition, it is often difficult to even

describe the population from which a sample was drawn and to whom results can be generalized.

21. Three types of nonrandom sampling are convenience sampling, which involves using as the sample whoever happens to be available; purposive sampling, which involves selecting a sample the researcher believes to be representative of a given population; and quota sampling, which involves giving interviewers exact numbers, or *quotas*, of persons of varying characteristics who are to be interviewed.

Qualitative Sampling

22. Qualitative sampling is the process of selecting a small number of individuals ("key informants") for a study in such a way that the individuals chosen will be able to help the researcher understand the phenomenon under investigation.

23. Qualitative research most often deals with small, purposive samples. The researcher's insights through first-hand experience in the research setting guide the selection of participants.

Selecting Research Participants: Purposive Sampling Approaches

24. The purpose of qualitative sampling is to choose participants who will be good informants and contribute to the researcher's understanding a given phenomenon.

25. A variety of purposive sampling approaches are used in qualitative research, including intensity sampling, homogeneous sampling, criterion sampling, snowball sampling, and random purposive sampling.

26. The use of purposive sampling requires that the researcher describe in detail the methods used to select a sample.

Determining Sample Size

27. There are no hard and fast numbers that represent the correct number of participants in a qualitative study.

28. Qualitative studies can be carried out with a single participant or, when studying multiple contexts, may have as many as 60 or 70 participants.

Now go to the Companion Website at **www.prenhall.com/gay** to assess your understanding of chapter content with Practice Quiz, apply comprehension in Applying What You Know, broaden your knowledge about research in Web Links, and expand your research skills in Evaluating Articles, Analyzing Qualitative Data, Analyzing Quantitative Data, and Research Tools and Tips.

PERFORMANCE CRITERIA

The definition of the quantitative population should describe its size and relevant characteristics (such as age, ability, and socioeconomic status). The description of the qualitative context should be stated.

The procedural technique for selecting study participants should be described in detail. For example, do not just say that stratified sampling will be used; indicate on what basis population members will be stratified and how they (and how many) will be selected from each subgroup. Or do not just say that snowball sampling will be used; explain how and why it was chosen. For quantitative studies, describe how selected participants will be placed into treatment groups (e.g., by random assignment).

Include a summary statement that indicates the resulting sample size for each group. For example, the following statement might appear in a quantitative plan:

> There will be two groups with a sample size of 30 each; each group will include 15 participants with above-average motivation and 15 participants with below-average motivation.

A qualitative plan might include a statement such as this one:

> There will be six participants available for in-depth interviews and observations over a period of 6 months. Participants will be chosen for their knowledge of the research context and their lengthy experience in the context studied.

Any identifiable source of sampling bias (e.g., small sample sizes) should also be discussed.

An example that illustrates the quantitative performance called for by Task 4 appears on the following pages. (See Task 4A Example.) Again, the task in the example was submitted by the same student whose Task 2 and Task 3a work was previously presented.

Additional examples for the tasks are included in the *Student Study Guide* that accompanies this text.

:: TASK 4A Example

Effect of Interactive Multimedia on the Achievement of 10th-Grade Biology Students

Participants in this study will be selected from the population of 10th-grade biology students at an upper-middle-class all-girl Catholic high school in Miami, Florida. The student population is multicultural, reflecting the diverse ethnic groups in Dade County. The student body is composed of approximately 90% Hispanic students from a variety of Latin American backgrounds, the major one being Cuban; 9% Caucasian non-Hispanic students; and 1% African American students. The population is anticipated to contain approximately 200 biology students.

Prior to the beginning of the school year, before students have been scheduled, 60 students will be randomly selected (using a table of random numbers) and randomly assigned to 2 classes of 30 each; 30 is the normal class size. One of the classes will be randomly chosen to receive IMM instruction and the other will not.

"Regardless of the type of research you conduct, you must collect data." (p. 122)

Selecting Measuring Instruments

OBJECTIVES

After reading Chapter 5, you should be able to do the following:

1. State the links or relationships among a construct, a variable, and an operationalized variable.
2. Describe different types of variables: nominal, ordinal, interval, and ratio; categorical and quantitative; dependent and independent.
3. Explain various testing terms: standardized test, assessment, measurement, selection, supply, performance assessment, raw score, norm- and criterion-referenced scoring.
4. Describe the purposes of various types of tests: achievement, aptitude, attitude, interest, value, personality, projective, nonprojective, and self-report.
5. Describe various scales used to collect data for cognitive and affective variables.
6. Familiarize yourself with measuring instruments, and select those suited for varied research needs.
7. Describe the purposes of and ways to determine content, criterion-related, construct, and consequential validity.
8. Describe the purposes of and ways to determine stability, equivalence, equivalence and stability, internal consistency, and scorer/rater reliability.
9. Define or describe standard error of measurement.
10. Know useful sources for finding information about specific tests.
11. State a strategy for test selection.
12. Identify and briefly describe three sources of test information.

Whether you are testing hypotheses or seeking understanding, you must decide on a method or methods to collect your data. In many cases, this is a matter of selecting the best existing instrument. Sometimes, how-ever, you may have to develop your own instrument for data collection. At still other times, you will be your own "instrument," observing, discussing, and interacting with research participants. (A discussion of the validity and reliability of qualitative data collection instruments is included in Chapter 14, and Chapter 15 will focus on qualitative data collection.) You must consider several factors when selecting a method or instrument. The major point to remember, however, is that you should select or construct an approach that will provide pertinent data about the topic of your study.

The general goals of Chapter 5 are for you to (1) understand the link among constructs, variables, and instruments; (2) know criteria for selecting appropriate instruments; and (3) be able to select the best instrument for a given study from those available. Completing Chapter 5 should enable you to perform the following task.

TASK 5

For a quantitative study, you have stated a topic to investigate, formulated one or more hypotheses, and described a sample (Tasks 2 and 4a). Now describe three instruments appropriate for collecting data pertinent to your study. In the description of each instrument, include the following:

1. Name, publisher, and cost
2. A brief description of the purpose of the instrument
3. Validity and reliability data
4. The group for whom the instrument is intended
5. Administration requirements
6. Information on scoring and interpretation
7. Reviewers' overall impressions

On the basis of this information, indicate which instrument is most acceptable for your quantitative study, and why. (See Performance Criteria, p. 155.)

:: CONSTRUCTS

Regardless of the type of research you conduct, you must collect data. **Data** are the pieces of information you collect and use to examine your topic, hypotheses, or observations. The scientific method is based on the collection, analysis, and interpretation of data. Before you can collect data, however, you must determine what kind of data to collect. To do this, you must understand the relationships among constructs, variables, and instruments.

A **construct** is an abstraction that cannot be observed directly; it is a concept invented to explain behavior. Examples of educational constructs are intelligence, personality, teacher effectiveness, creativity, ability, achievement, and motivation. In order to be measurable, constructs must be operationally defined—that is, defined in terms of processes or operations that can be observed and measured. To measure a construct, it is necessary to identify the scores or values it can assume. For example, the construct "personality" could be made measurable by defining two personality types, introverts and extroverts, as measured by scores on a 30-item questionnaire, with a high score indicating a more introverted personality and a low score indicating a more extroverted personality. Similarly, the construct "teacher effectiveness" might be operationally defined by observing a teacher in action and judging effectiveness based on four levels: unsatisfactory, marginal, adequate, and excellent. When constructs are operationally defined, they become variables.

:: VARIABLES

In Chapter 1 we defined **variable** as a concept that can assume any one of a range of values. The concept, or construct, must be able to take on at least two or more values or scores. We deal with variables in all our research studies. Height, weight, hair color, test score, age, and teacher experience are all variables; people differ on them.

There are many different approaches to measuring a variable and many instruments for doing so. (In educational research, an **instrument** is a tool used to collect data.) For example, to measure sixth-grade students' mathematics achievement, we can choose from a number of existing measuring instruments, such as the Stanford Achievement Test or the Iowa Tests of Basic Skills. We could also use a teacher-made test to measure math achievement.

Can you identify the variables in the following research topics and hypotheses?

1. Is there a relationship between middle school students' grades and their self-confidence in science and math?
2. What do high school principals consider to be the most pressing administrative problems they face?
3. Do students learn more from our new social studies program than from the previous one?
4. What were the effects of the GI Bill on state colleges in the Midwest in the 1950s?
5. How do the first 5 weeks of school in Ms. Foley's classroom influence student activities and interactions in succeeding months?
6. There will be a statistically significant relationship between teachers' number of years teaching and their interest in taking new courses.
7. There will be a statistically significant difference in attitudes toward science between ninth-grade girls and boys.

The variables in these examples are as follows: (1) grades and self-confidence, (2) administrative problems, (3) learning and the new social studies program (note that the social studies program has two forms—new and old—and thus is also a variable), (4) effects of the GI Bill, (5) student activities and student interactions, (6) years teaching and interest in taking new courses, and (7) attitudes toward science. Variables indicate what will be examined in a research study. The researcher will select or develop an appropriate instrument for each variable. Information about the instruments should be included in the procedure section of the research plan.

Variables themselves differ in many ways. For example, variables can be represented by different kinds of measurements, they can be identified as categorical or quantitative, or they can be classified as dependent or independent.

Measurement Scales and Variables

There are four types of measurement scales and associated variables: nominal, ordinal, interval, and ratio. A **measurement scale** consists of a group of several related statements that participants select from to indicate their degree of agreement or lack of agreement. In other words, the scale is the instrument used to obtain the actual range of values or scores for each variable. Each type of scale may be used to express one or more of the variable types. It is important to know which type of scale is represented in your data because, as we shall see in later chapters, different scales require different methods of statistical analysis. We discuss each of the four variable types in the following subsections.

Nominal Variables

A **nominal variable**, also called a *categorical variable*, represents the lowest level of measurement. It simply classifies persons or objects into two or more categories. Nominal variables include gender (female, male), employment status (full time, part time, unemployed), marital status (married, divorced, single), and type of school (public, private, charter). For identification purposes, nominal variables are often represented by numbers. For example, the category "male" may be represented by the number 1 and "female" by the number 2. It is critically important to understand that such numbering of nominal variables does not indicate that one category is higher or better than another. That is, representing male with a 1 and female with a 2 does not indicate that males are lower or worse than females. The numbers are only labels for the groups. To avoid such confusion, it is often better to label nominal variables with letters (A, B, C, etc.), not numbers.

Ordinal Variables

An **ordinal variable** not only classifies persons or objects, it also ranks them. In other words, ordinal variables put persons or objects in order from highest to lowest or from most to least. If 50 people were ranked from 1 to 50 on the ordinal variable *height*, the person with Rank 1 would be the tallest and the person with Rank 50 would be the shortest. Rankings make it possible to say that one person is taller or shorter than another. Class rank or order of finishing a marathon are ordinal variables. Although ordinal variables permit us to describe performance as higher, lower, better, or worse, they do not indicate how much higher one person performed compared to another. In other words, intervals between ranks are not equal; the difference between Rank 1 and Rank 2 is not necessarily the same as the difference between Rank 2 and Rank 3. Consider the ranking of these three heights:

Rank	Height
1	6 ft 5 in.
2	6 ft 0 in.
3	5 ft 11 in.

The difference in height between Rank 1 and Rank 2 is 5 inches; the difference between Rank 2 and Rank 3 is 1 inch. Thus, although an ordinal variable can be used to rank persons or objects, it does not have equal scale intervals. This characteristic limits the statistical methods used to analyze ordinal variables.

Interval Variables

An **interval variable** has all the characteristics of nominal and ordinal variables, but it also has equal intervals. Most of the tests used in educational research, such as achievement, aptitude, motivation, and attitude tests, are treated as interval variables. When variables have equal intervals, it is assumed that the difference between a score of 30 and a score of 40 is essentially the same as the difference between a score of 50 and a score of 60, and the difference between 81 and 82 is about the same as the difference between 82 and 83. Interval scales, however, do not have a true zero point. Thus, if Roland's science achievement test score is 0 on a scale of 0 to 100, his score does not indicate the total absence of science knowledge. Nor does Gianna's score of 100 indicate complete mastery. Thus, we can say that a test score of 90 is 45 points higher than a score of 45, but we cannot say that a person scoring 90 knows twice as much as a person scoring 45. For most educational measurement, it is sufficient to know only the score each person attained. Variables that have or are treated as having equal intervals are subject to an array of statistical data analysis methods.

Ratio Variables

A **ratio variable** represents the highest level of measurement; it has all the properties of the previous three types of variables and, in addition, has a true zero point. Height, weight, time, distance, and speed are examples of ratio scales. The concept of "no weight," for example, is a meaningful one. Because of the true zero point, we can say not only that the difference between a height of 3 ft 2 in. and a height of 4 ft 2 in. is the same as the difference between 5 ft 4 in. and 6 ft 4 in. but also that a person 6 ft 4 in. is twice as tall as one 3 ft 2 in. Thus, with ratio variables we can say that Frankenstein is tall and Igor is short (nominal scale), Frankenstein is taller than Igor (ordinal scale), Frankenstein is 7 feet tall and Igor is 5 feet tall (interval scale), and Frankenstein is seven fifths as tall as Igor (ratio scale). Because ratio variables encompass mainly physical measures, they are not used very often in educational research. Table 5.1 contrasts types of measurement scales.

TABLE 5.1	Comparison of measurement scales	
Scale	**Description**	**Examples**
Nominal	Categorical	Northerners, Southerners Republicans, Democrats Eye color Male, female Public, private Gifted student, typical student
Ordinal	Rank order, unequal units	Scores of 5, 6, 10 are equal to scores of 1, 2, 3
Interval	Rank order and interval units but no zero point	A score of 10 and a score of 30 have the same degree of difference as a score of 60 and a score of 90
Ratio	All of the above and a defined zero point	A person is 5 feet tall and her friend is two thirds as tall as she

Qualitative and Quantitative Variables

Nominal or categorical variables do not provide quantitative information about how people or objects differ. They provide information about qualitative differences only. Nominal variables permit persons or things that represent different qualities (e.g., eye color, religion, gender, political party) but not different quantities.

Quantitative variables are ones that exist on a continuum that ranges from low to high, or less to more. Ordinal, interval, and ratio variables are all quantitative variables, because they describe performance in quantitative terms. Examples are test scores, heights, speed, age, and class size.

Dependent and Independent Variables

As you may recall from chapter 1, a **dependent variable** is the variable hypothesized to depend on or be caused by another variable, the **independent variable.**

Recall this research topic from Chapter 1:

What is the effect of positive versus negative reinforcement on elementary students' attitudes toward school?

You probably had little trouble identifying *attitudes toward school* as a variable—and as a dependent variable—but did you also identify *type of reinforcement* as a variable? This variable contains two levels or methods of reinforcement, positive and negative. Notice that *attitudes toward school* is a quantitative variable because it is measured in terms of more or less attitude. Notice, also, that *type of reinforcement* is a categorical variable because it represents categories (positive reinforcement versus negative reinforcement), not numbers. Independent and dependent variables are primarily used in causal–comparative and experimental research studies. The independent variable (also called the *experimental variable,* the *manipulated variable,* the *cause,* or the *treatment*) is the intended cause of the dependent variable (also called the *criterion variable,* the *effect,* the *outcome,* or the *posttest*). The independent variable is manipulated by the researcher, whereas the dependent variable is not. In the preceding example, the researcher "manipulated" the two treatments by selecting them and then assigning participants to them. The dependent variable, attitudes toward school, is dependent on how well the two types of reinforcement function. The independent variable is the cause, and the dependent variable is the effect. It is important to remember that the independent variable must have at least two levels or treatments. Two or more levels make up a variable. Thus, neither positive nor negative reinforcement is a variable by itself. It is only when both are included in the general variable (type of reinforcement) that we have two levels or treatments that vary and thus make up a variable.

Try to identify the independent and dependent variables in this research topic:

Older teachers are less likely to express approval of new teaching strategies than younger teachers.

:: CHARACTERISTICS OF MEASURING INSTRUMENTS

In this section we examine the range of measuring instruments used to collect data in qualitative and quantitative research studies. There are three major ways to collect research data:

1. Administer a standardized instrument.
2. Administer a self-developed instrument.
3. Record naturally occurring or already available data (for example, make observations in a classroom or record existing grade point averages).

This chapter is concerned with published, standardized tests and teacher-prepared tests, the first two listed items. Although using naturally occurring or existing data requires a minimum of effort and sounds very attractive, there are not many quantitative studies for which existing data are appropriate. (Qualitative studies, such as ethnographic studies, often are built around the idea that the researcher will work with naturally occurring or existing data.) Even when appropriate, using available data can lead to other problems. For example, the same grade given by two different teachers may not necessarily represent the same level of achievement, and conclusions based on the data may not be trustworthy. Developing a high-quality instrument also has drawbacks. It requires considerable effort and skill and greatly increases the total time needed to conduct the study. At a minimum, you would need a course in measurement to gain the skills needed for proper instrument development. At times, however, constructing your own instrument will be necessary, especially if your research topic and concepts are original or relatively unresearched.

Selecting an appropriate standardized or other instrument invariably takes less time than developing an instrument yourself. Standardized instruments tend to be developed by experts, who possess needed test construction skills. From a research point of view, an additional advantage of using a standardized instrument is that results from different studies using the same instrument can be compared.

There are thousands of published and standardized instruments available that yield a variety of data for a variety of variables. Major areas for which numerous measuring instruments have been developed include achievement, personality, attitude, interest, and aptitude. Each of these can, in turn, be further divided into many subcategories. Personality instruments, for example, can be classified as nonprojective or projective. *Nonprojective instruments* include measures of attitude and interest. A *projective instrument* provides respondents with an unstructured stimulus to respond to; an example is an ink blot test. Choosing an instrument for a particular research purpose involves identifying and selecting the most appropriate instrument from among alternatives. To do this intelligently, researchers must be familiar with a variety of instruments and know the criteria they should apply in selecting the best alternatives.

Instrument Terminology

Given the array of instruments in educational research, it is important to know some of the basic terminology used to describe them. We start with the terms *test, assessment,* and *measurement*.

A **test** is a formal, systematic, usually paper-and-pencil procedure for gathering information about peoples' cognitive and affective characteristics. (A **cognitive characteristic** is simply a mental characteristic related to intellect, such as achievement; an **affective characteristic** is a mental characteristic related to emotion, such as attitude.) Tests typically produce numerical scores. A **standardized test** is one that is administered, scored, and interpreted in the same way no matter where or when it is used. For example, the SAT, ACT, Iowa Tests of Basic Skills, Stanford Achievement Test, and other nationally used tests have been crafted to ensure that all test takers experience the same conditions when taking them. Such *standardization* allows comparisons among test takers from across the nation. You may remember taking national standardized achievement tests in school. They were the ones with a stop sign every few pages that warned you, "Stop! Do not turn the page until instructed." These "stops" were used to ensure that all test takers were given the same amount of time for each part of the test.

Assessment is a broader term than *test* or *instrument* and encompasses the entire process of collecting, synthesizing, and interpreting information, whether formal or informal, numerical or textual. Tests are a subset of assessment, as are observations and interviews. **Measurement** is the process of quantifying or scoring performance on an assessment instrument. Measurement occurs after data are collected.

Quantitative and Qualitative Data Collection Methods

Researchers typically use paper-and-pencil methods, observations, or interviews to collect data. Observation and interviewing are used predominantly by qualitative researchers (and will be discussed in detail in Chapter 15), whereas paper-and-pencil methods are favored by quantitative researchers.

Paper-and-pencil methods are divided into two general categories: selection and supply. *Selection methods* (or *selection items* on an instrument) include multiple choice, true–false, and matching (the test taker has to select from among the given answers). *Supply methods* (or *supply items*) include fill in the blank, short answer, and essay (the test taker has to supply an answer). Current emphasis on supply methods in schools has spawned the rise of so-called performance assessments. A **performance assessment,** also known as an *authentic* or *alternative assessment,* is a type of assessment that emphasizes a student process (lab demonstration, debate, oral speech, or dramatic performance) or product (an essay, a science fair project, a research report). By asking students to do or create something, educators seek to assess more complex tasks than memorization. If a researcher is conducting research in schools, it is likely that performance assessments will be one of the data collection methods that are used.

Interpreting Instrument Data

Performance on an assessment can be reported and interpreted in various ways. A **raw score** is the number or point value of items a person answered correctly on an assessment. If Leron got 78 of 100 points on a test, his raw score would be 78. In most quantitative research, raw scores are the basic data analyzed. By themselves, however, raw scores don't give us much information. To learn more, we must put the scores into a context; in other words, we must interpret the scores in some way.

Norm-referenced, criterion-referenced, and self-referenced scoring approaches represent three ways of interpreting performance on tests and measures. In **norm-referenced scoring,** a student's performance on an assessment is compared to the performance of others. For example, if we ask how well Rita did in science compared to other students in her grade from across the nation, we are asking for norm-referenced information. The interpretation of Rita's score will be based on how she performed compared to her class or a national group of students in her grade. Norm-referenced scoring is also called *grading on the curve,* where the curve is a bell-shaped distribution of the percentages of students who can receive each grade. Standardized tests and assessments frequently report norm-referenced scores in the form of derived scores such as *percentile ranks* or *stanines* (discussed in detail in Chapter 11, "Descriptive Statistics"). In **criterion-referenced scoring,** an individual's performance on an assessment is compared to a predetermined, external standard, rather than to the performance of others. For example, a teacher may say that test scores of 90 to 100 are an A, scores of 80 to 89 are a B, scores of 70 to 79 are a C, and so on. A student's score is compared to the preestablished performance levels—to preestablished *criteria*—to determine the grade. Anyone who scores between 90 and 100 will get an A. If no one scores between 90 to 100, no one will get an A. If all students get between 90 and 100, they all will get As. This could not happen in norm-referenced scoring, which requires that different scores, even very close ones, must get different grades. **Self-referenced scoring** approaches involve measuring how an individual student's performance on a single assessment changes over time. Student performances at different times are compared to determine improvement or regression.

:: TYPES OF MEASURING INSTRUMENTS

There are many different kinds of tests available and many different ways to classify them. The Mental Measurements Yearbooks (MMYs), published by the Buros Institute of Mental Measurements, are a major source of test information for educational researchers. The yearbooks, which can be found in most large libraries, provide information and reviews of published tests in various school subject areas (such as English, mathematics, and reading) as well as personality, intelligence, aptitude, speech and hearing, and vocational tests. The Web addresses for the Buros Institute and its catalogs are http://www.unl.edu/buros/ and http://www.unl.edu/buros/catalog.html.

Cognitive Tests

A **cognitive test** measures intellectual processes, such as thinking, memorizing, problem solving, analyzing, reasoning, and applying information. Most of the tests school pupils take are cognitive achievement tests.

Achievement Tests

An **achievement test** measures an individual's current proficiency in given areas of knowledge or skill. Typically administered in school settings, achievement tests are designed to provide information about how well test takers have learned what they have been taught in school. The tests are standardized, and an individual's performance is usually determined by comparing it to the *norm*, the performance of a national group of students in the individual's grade or age level who took the same test. Thus, these tests can provide comparisons of a given student to similar students nationally. Standardized achievement tests typically cover a number of different curriculum areas, such as reading, vocabulary, language, and mathematics. A standardized test that measures achievement in several curriculum areas is called a *test battery*, and each test is called a *subtest*. The California Achievement Test, Stanford Achievement Tests, TerraNova, and the Iowa Tests of Basic Skills are examples of cognitive achievement tests commonly used in American classrooms. Depending on the number of subtests and other factors, standardized achievement batteries can take from 1 to 5 hours to complete.

Some achievement tests, such as the Gates-MacGinitie Reading Tests, focus on achievement in a single subject area. Single-subject tests are sometimes used as diagnostic tests. A **diagnostic test** yields multiple scores for each area of achievement measured in order to facilitate identification of a student's weak and strong areas. The Stanford Diagnostic Reading Test and the Key Math Diagnostic Inventory of Essential Mathematics Test are examples of widely used diagnostic achievement instruments.

Aptitude Tests

An **aptitude test** is commonly used to predict how well an individual is likely to perform in a future situation. It includes cognitive measures, but ones that are not normally part of classroom tests. Tests of general aptitude are also referred to as *scholastic aptitude tests* and *tests of general mental ability*. Aptitude tests are standardized and are often administered as part of a school testing program. They also are used extensively in job hiring.

General aptitude tests require a participant to respond to a variety of verbal and nonverbal tasks intended to measure the individual's ability to apply knowledge and solve problems. Such tests often yield three scores: an overall score, a verbal score, and a quantitative score. A commonly used group-administered battery is the Columbia Mental Maturity Scale (CMMS). The CMMS has six versions and can be administered to school-age children, college students, and adults. It includes 12 subtests representing five aptitude factors: logical reasoning, spatial relations, numerical reasoning, verbal concepts, and memory. Another frequently administered group aptitude test is the Otis-Lennon School Ability Test, which has versions designed for children in grades k–12. The Otis-Lennon School Ability Test measures four factors: verbal comprehension, verbal reasoning, figurative reasoning, and quantitative reasoning. The Differential Aptitude Tests, on the other hand, include tests on space relations, mechanical reasoning, and clerical speed and accuracy, among other areas, and are designed to predict success in various job areas.

If there is a reason to question the appropriateness of a group of tests for particular test takers (e.g., very young children or students with disabilities), an individual test should be used. Probably the most well known of the individually administered tests are the Stanford-Binet Intelligence Scale and the Wechsler scales. The Stanford-Binet is appropriate for young children and adults. Wechsler scales are available to measure the intelligence of persons from the age of 2 to adulthood: the Wechsler Preschool and Primary Scale of Intelligence—Third Edition (WPPSI–III), ages 2 to 7; the Wechsler Intelligence Scale for Children—Fourth Edition (WISC–IV), ages 6 to 17; and the Wechsler Adult Intelligence Scale—Third Edition (WAIS–III), older adolescents and adults. As an example, the WISC is a scholastic aptitude test that includes verbal tests (e.g., general information, vocabulary) and performance tests (e.g., picture completion, object assembly). Other commonly used individually administered aptitude tests are the McCarthy Scales of Children's Abilities and the Kaufman Assessment Battery for Children.

Affective Tests

An **affective test** is an assessment designed to measure affective characteristics—mental characteristics related to emotion, such as attitude, interest, and value. Affective tests are often used in educational research and exist in many different formats. Most are nonprojective; that is, they are self-report measures in which the test taker responds to a series of questions or statements about himself. For example, a question may ask, "Which would you prefer, reading a book or playing basketball? Circle your answer." Self-report tests are frequently used in survey (descriptive) studies (e.g., to describe the personality structure of various groups, such as high school dropouts), correlational studies (e.g., to determine relationships between various personality traits and other variables, such as achievement), and experimental studies (e.g., to investigate the comparative effectiveness of different instructional methods for different personality types).

Instruments that examine values, attitudes, interests, and personalities tap the test takers' emotions and perceptions. *Values* are deeply held beliefs about ideas, persons, or objects. For example, we may value our free time, our special friendships, or a vase given by our great-grandmother. *Attitudes* indicate what things we feel favorable or unfavorable about; they reflect our tendencies to accept or reject groups, ideas, or objects. For example, Greg's attitude toward brussels sprouts is much more favorable than his attitude toward green beans (which puts Greg in a distinct minority). *Interests* indicate the degree to which we seek out or participate in particular activities, objects, and ideas. For example, one of this text's authors has very little interest in having his nose pierced (nor does he value or have a positive attitude toward nose piercing). *Personality,* also called *temperament,* is made up of a number of characteristics that represent a person's typical behaviors; it describes what we do in our natural life circumstances.

Attitude Scales

An **attitude scale** determines what an individual believes, perceives, or feels about self, others, activities, institutions, or situations. Five basic types of scales are used to measure attitudes: Likert scales, semantic differential scales, rating scales, Thurstone scales, and Guttman scales. The first three are the most often used.

Likert Scales.   A **Likert scale** asks an individual to respond to a series of statements by indicating whether he or she strongly agrees (SA), agrees (A), is undecided (U), disagrees (D), or strongly disagrees (SD). Each response is assigned a point value, and an individual's score is determined by adding the point values of all the statements. For example, the following point values are typically assigned to positive statements: SA = 5, A = 4, U = 3, D = 2, SD = 1. An example of a positive statement is, "Short people are entitled to the same job opportunities as tall people." A score of 5 or 4 on this item would indicate a positive attitude toward equal opportunity for short people. A high total score across all items on the test would be indicative of an overall positive attitude. For negative statements, the point values would be reversed—that is, SA = 1, A = 2, U = 3, D = 4, and SD = 5. An example of a negative statement is, "Short people are not entitled to the same job opportunities as tall people." On this item, scores should be reversed; "disagree" or "strongly disagree" would indicate a positive attitude toward opportunities for short people.

Semantic Differential Scales.   A semantic differential scale asks an individual to indicate his or her attitude about a topic (e.g., property taxes) by selecting a position on a continuum that ranges from one bipolar adjective (e.g., fair) to another (e.g., unfair). Each position on the continuum has an associated score value. For example, a scale concerning attitudes toward property taxes might include the following items and values:

Necessary								Unnecessary
	3	2	1	0	−1	−2	−3	
Fair								Unfair
	3	2	1	0	−1	−2	−3	
Better								Worse
	3	2	1	0	−1	−2	−3	

The scale is typical of semantic differential scales, which usually have 5 to 7 intervals with a neutral attitude assigned a score value of 0. A person who checked the first interval (i.e., a score of 3) on each of these items is indicating a very positive attitude toward property taxes (fat chance!). Totaling the score values for all items yields an overall score. Usually, summed scores (interval data) are used in statistical data analysis.

Rating Scales.   A **rating scale** may also be used to determine a respondent's attitudes—toward self, others, activities, institutions, or situations. One form of rating scale provides descriptions of performance or preference and asks the individual to check the most appropriate description.

> Select the choice that best describes your actions in the first five minutes of the classes you teach.
>
> _____ State lesson objectives and overview at start of the lesson
>
> _____ State lesson objectives but no overview at start of the lesson
>
> _____ Don't state objectives or give overview at start of the lesson

A second type of rating scale asks the individual to rate performance or preference using a numerical scale similar to a Likert scale.

> Circle the number that best describes the degree to which you state lesson objectives and give an overview before teaching a lesson. 5 = always, 4 = almost always, 3 = about half the time, 2 = rarely, 1 = never
>
> 1   2   3   4   5

Note that Likert, semantic differential, and rating scales are similar, requiring the respondent to self-report along a continuum of choices. Note, also, that in certain situations, such as observing performance or judging teaching competence, Likert, semantic differential, and rating scales can be used by others (a researcher, a principal, a colleague) to collect information about study participants. For example, in some studies it might be best to have the principal, rather than the teacher, use a Likert, semantic differential, or rating scale to collect data about that teacher.

Thurstone and Guttman Scales.   A *Thurstone scale* asks participants to select from a list of statements that represent different points of view on a topic. Each item has an associated point value between 1 and 11; point values for each item are determined by averaging the values of the items assigned by a number of judges. An individual's attitude score is the average point value of all the statements checked by that individual. A *Guttman scale* also asks respondents to agree or disagree with a number of statements; it, however, attempts to determine whether an attitude is *unidimensional*. An attitude is unidimensional if it produces a cumulative scale in which an individual who agrees with a given statement also agrees with all related preceding statements. For example, if you agree with Statement 3, you also agree with Statements 2 and 1.

Interest Inventories

An *interest inventory* asks participants to indicate personal likes and dislikes, such as the kinds of activities they prefer. The respondent's pattern of interest is compared to the interest patterns typical of successful persons in various occupational fields. Interest inventories are widely used to suggest the fields in which respondents might be most happy and successful.

Two frequently used inventories are the Strong-Campbell Interest Inventory and the Kuder Preference Record–Vocational. The Strong-Campbell Interest Inventory examines areas of interest in occupations, school subjects, activities, leisure activities, and day-to-day interactions with various types of people. Test takers are presented with many topics related to these five areas and are asked to indicate whether they like (L), dislike (D), or are indifferent (I) to each topic. A second part of the Strong-Campbell inventory consists of a choice between two options such as "dealing with people" or "dealing with things" and a number of self-descriptive statements that the individual responds to by choosing *Yes (like me), No (not like me),* or *? (not sure).*

The Kuder Occupational Interest Survey addresses 10 broad categories of interest: outdoor, mechanical, computational, scientific, persuasive, artistic, literary, musical, social service, and clerical. Individuals are presented with three choices related to these categories and must select the one they most like and the one they least like. For example, an individual might be presented with this item:

> Would you rather: dig a hole, read a book, or draw a picture? Choose the one that you most would like to do and the one that you least would like to do.

The Strong-Campbell and the Kuder are both self-report instruments that provide information about persons' interests. Scoring the instruments requires sending data to the testing companies who produce them for computer analysis. *You cannot score them yourself.* Information on the Strong-Campbell, the Kuder, and other attitudinal, value, and personality instruments may be found in the *Mental Measurements Yearbook.*

Values Tests

The Study of Values instrument (Riverside Publishing Co.) is old but is still used. It measures the relative strength of an individual's valuing of six different areas: theoretical (discovery of truth, empirical approach), economic (practical values), aesthetic (symmetry, form, and harmony), social (altruism, philanthropic), political (personal power, influence), and religious (unity of experience, cosmic coherence). Individuals are presented with items consisting of either two or four choices and are asked to allocate points to the alternatives according to how much they value them. For example, a two-alternative item might be the following:

> Suppose you had the choice of reading one of two books first. If the books were titled *Making Money in the Stock Market* and *The Politics of Political Power,* which would you read first?

Respondents allocate points to the two choices, indicating degree of preference. By counting up the points given to each of the six areas, the scorer can obtain an indication of an individual's preference among the six categories. A second form of scoring provides four choices that the respondent must rank from 4 to 1 in order of preference. The Study of Values is used primarily in research studies to categorize individuals or measure the value orientation of different groups such as scientists and newspaper writers.

Personality Inventories

A *personality inventory* lists questions or statements that describe behaviors characteristic of certain personality traits. Respondents indicate whether each statement describes them. Some inventories are presented as checklists; respondents simply check items they feel characterize them. An individual's score is based on the number of responses characteristic of the trait being measured. An introvert, for example, would be expected to respond yes to the statement, "Reading is one of my favorite pastimes," and no to the statement, "I love large parties." Personality instruments may measure only one trait or many.

General inventories frequently used in educational research studies include the Personality Adjective Checklist, California Psychological Inventory, Minnesota Multiphasic Personality Inventory, Mooney Problem Checklist, Myers-Briggs Type Indicator, and the Sixteen Personality Factor Questionnaire. The Minnesota Multiphasic Personality Inventory (MMPI) alone has been utilized in hundreds of educational research studies. Its items were originally selected on the basis of response differences between psychiatric and "normal" patients. The MMPI measures many personality traits, such as depression, paranoia, schizophrenia, and social introversion. It contains more than 370 items to which a test taker responds *True (of me), False (of me),* or *Cannot Say.* It also has nearly 200 items that form additional scales for anxiety, ego strength, repression, and alcoholism.

Self-report general personality instruments such as the MMPI are complex and require a substantial amount of knowledge of both measurement and psychology to score. Beginning researchers should avoid their use unless they have more than a passing knowledge of these areas.

Problems With Self-Report Instruments

Because they are generally self-report instruments, attitude, interest, values, and personality scales suffer from some problems. The researcher can never be sure that individuals are expressing their true attitude, interest, values, or personality, as opposed to a "socially acceptable" response. Every effort should be made, therefore, to increase honesty of response by giving appropriate directions to those completing the instruments.

Another problem when forced-choice items are used is that of accurate responses. Scores are meaningful only to the degree that respondents are honest and select choices that truly characterize them. A common problem is the existence of a **response set,** the tendency of an individual to continually respond in a particular way to a variety of instruments. One common response set occurs when an individual selects responses that she believes are the most socially acceptable, even if they are not necessarily characteristic of her. Another form of a response set is when a test taker continually responds *yes, agree,* or *true* to items because she believes that is what the researcher desires. Thus, in studies utilizing affective tests, every effort should be made to increase the likelihood that valid test results are obtained. One strategy to overcome the problem of response sets is to allow participants to respond anonymously.

Both affective and cognitive instruments are subject to **bias,** distortion of research data that renders the data suspect or invalid. Bias is present when respondents' characteristics—such as ethnicity, race, gender, language, or religious orientation—distort their performance or responses. For example, low scores on reading tests by students who speak little English or nonstandard forms of English are probably due in large part to language disadvantages, not reading difficulties. If one's culture discourages competition, or making eye contact, or speaking out, the responses on self-report instruments can differ according to cultural background, not personality, values, attitudes, or interests. For these students, test performance means something different than it does to English-fluent students who also took the test. These issues need to be recognized in selecting and interpreting the results of both cognitive and affective instruments.

Projective Tests

Projective tests were developed in part to eliminate some of the problems inherent in the use of self-report and forced-choice measures. Projective tests are ambiguous and not obvious to respondents. Because the purpose of the test is not clear, conscious dishonesty of response is reduced. Such tests are called projective because respondents *project* their true feelings or thoughts onto the ambiguous stimulus. The classic example of a projective test is the Rorschach inkblot test. Respondents are shown a picture of an inkblot and are asked to describe what they see in it. The inkblot is really just that—an inkblot made by putting a dab of ink on a paper and folding the paper in half. There are no right or wrong answers to the question, "What do you see in the inkblot?" (It's only an inkblot—honest.) The test taker's descriptions of such blots are a "projection" of his feelings and personality, which the administrator interprets.

The most commonly used projective technique is the method of association. Presented with a stimulus such as a picture, inkblot, or word, participants respond with a reaction or interpretation. Word-association tests are probably the most well known of the association techniques (How many movie psychiatrists deliver the line, "I'll say a word and you tell me the first thing that comes to your mind"?). Similarly, in the Thematic Apperception Test, the individual is shown a series of pictures and is asked to tell a story about what is happening in each picture.

In the past, all projective tests were required to be administered individually. There have been some recent efforts, however, to develop group projective tests. One such test is the Holtzman Inkblot Technique, which is intended to measure the same variables as the Rorschach Test.

From the preceding comments, it should not be a surprise that projective tests are used mainly by clinical psychologists and very infrequently by educational researchers. Administering, scoring, and interpreting projective tests require lengthy and specialized training. Because of the training required, projective testing is not recommended for beginning researchers.

There are other types and formats of measuring instruments beyond those discussed here. The intent of this section is to provide an overview of different types of tests, different formats for gathering data, different scoring methods, different interpretation strategies, and different limitations. To find more information about the specific tests described in this chapter and many other tests we have not described, refer to the Mental Measurement Yearbooks.

:: CRITERIA FOR GOOD MEASURING INSTRUMENTS

If researchers' interpretations of data are to be valuable, the measuring instruments used to collect those data must be both valid and reliable. The following sections give an overview of both validity and reliability; more specific information on these topics and on testing in general can be found in the *Standards for Educational and Psychological Testing.*[1]

Validity of Measuring Instruments

Validity is the most important characteristic a test or measuring instrument can possess. **Validity** is the degree to which a test measures what it is supposed to measure and, consequently, permits appropriate interpretation of scores. When we test, we test for a purpose. For example, a researcher may administer a questionnaire to find out about participants' opinions of increasing funding for education. Or the researcher in an experimental study may give a general science test to compare learning for science students taught by Method A and Method B. A key question for these and other such test users is, "Does this test or instrument permit me to make the interpretation I wish to make?" That is, will responses to the opinion questionnaire or the science test allow the researchers to make appropriate interpretations about the respondents' attitudes or learning?

Validity is important in all forms of research and all types of tests and measures. In some situations a test or instrument is used for a number of different purposes. For example, a high school chemistry achievement test may be used to assess students' end-of-year chemistry learning, to predict students' future performance in science courses, and even to select students for advanced placement chemistry. Each of these uses calls for a different interpretation of the chemistry test scores. Therefore, each intended use requires its own validation. Further, the same test may be given to groups of respondents with significant differences (e.g., one group who has studied the test material and one who has not); the differences may or may not have been considered when the test was developed. Thus, validity is specific to the interpretation being made and to the group being tested. In other words, we cannot simply say, "This test is valid." Rather, we must say, "This test is valid for this particular interpretation and this particular group." It is also important to understand that validation does not exist on an all-or-nothing basis. Validity is best thought of in terms of degree: highly valid, moderately valid, and generally invalid. Validation begins with an understanding of the interpretation(s) to be made from the selected tests or instruments. It then requires the collection of evidence to support the desired interpretation.

There are four types of test validity: content validity, criterion-related validity, construct validity, and consequential validity. They are viewed as interrelated, not independent, aspects of validity. We look at each type next.

Content Validity

Content validity is the degree to which a test measures an intended content area. Content validity requires both item validity and sampling validity. **Item validity** is concerned with whether the test items are relevant to the measurement of the intended content area. **Sampling validity** is concerned with how well the test samples the total content area being tested. A test designed to measure knowledge of biology facts could have good item validity, because all the items are relevant to biology, but poor sampling validity, because all the test items are about vertebrates. If, instead, the test adequately sampled the full content of biology, it would be said

---

[1] *Standards for Educational and Psychological Testing,* by American Education Research Association, American Psychological Association, and National Council on Measurement in Education, 1999, Washington, DC: American Psychological Association.

to have good content validity. This is important because we cannot possibly measure each and every test item in a content area, and yet we do wish to make inferences about test takers' performance on the entire content area. Such inferences are possible only if the test items adequately sample the domain of possible items. For this reason, you should clearly identify and examine for completeness the bounds of the content area to be tested before constructing or selecting a test or measuring instrument.

Content validity is of particular importance for achievement tests. A test score cannot accurately reflect a student's achievement if it does not measure what the student was taught and is supposed to have learned. Content validity will be compromised if the test covers topics not taught or if it does *not* cover topics that have been taught. Achievement test validity has been a problem in a number of research studies. Early studies that compared the effectiveness of "new" math with the "old" math are classic cases. These studies invariably found no achievement differences between students learning under the two approaches. The problem was that the "new" math was emphasizing concepts and principles, but the achievement tests were emphasizing computational skills. When tests were developed that contained an adequate sampling of items measuring concepts and principles, studies began to find that the two approaches to teaching math resulted in essentially equal computational ability but that the "new" math resulted in better conceptual understanding. The moral of the story is, take care that your test measures what the students were expected to learn in the treatments. That is, be sure that the test is content valid for your study and for your research participants.

Content validity is determined by expert judgment. There is no formula or statistic by which it can be computed, and there is no way to express it quantitatively. Often experts in the topic covered by the test are asked to assess its content validity. These experts carefully review the process used to develop the test as well as the test itself, and then they make a judgment about how well items represent the intended content area. In other words, they compare what was taught and what is being tested. When the two coincide, the content validity is strong.

The term *face validity* is sometimes used to describe the content validity of tests. Although its meaning is somewhat ambiguous, **face validity** basically refers to the degree to which a test appears to measure what it claims to measure. Although determining face validity is not a psychometrically sound way of estimating validity, the process is sometimes used as an initial screening procedure in test selection. It should be followed up by content validation.

Criterion-Related Validity

Criterion-related validity is determined by relating performance on a test to performance on a second test or other measure. The second test or measure is the criterion against which the validity of the initial test is judged. Criterion-related validity has two forms: concurrent validity and predictive validity.

Concurrent Validity. **Concurrent validity** is the degree to which scores on one test are related to scores on a similar, preexisting test administered in the same time frame or to some other valid measure available at the same time. Often, for example, a test is developed that claims to do the same job as some other tests, except easier or faster. One way to determine whether the claim is true is to administer the new and the old test to a group and compare the scores.

Concurrent validity is determined by establishing a relationship or discrimination. The relationship method involves determining the correlation between scores on the test under study (e.g., a new test) and scores on some other established test or criterion (e.g., grade point average). The steps are as follows:

1. Administer the new test to a defined group of individuals.
2. Administer a previously established, valid criterion test (the criterion) to the same group, at the same time, or shortly thereafter.

3. Correlate the two sets of scores.
4. Evaluate the results.

The resulting correlation, or *validity coefficient,* indicates the degree of concurrent validity of the new test; if the coefficient is high (near 1.0), the test has good concurrent validity. For example, suppose Professor Jeenyus developed a 5-minute group test of children's interest in school. If scores on this test correlated highly with scores on the Almost Never Ending Interest Test (which must be administered to one child at a time and takes at least an hour), then Professor Jeenyus's test would definitely be preferable in a great many situations.

The discrimination method of establishing concurrent validity involves determining whether test scores can be used to discriminate between persons who possess a certain characteristic and those who do not or who possess it to a greater degree. For example, a test of personality disorder would have concurrent validity if scores resulting from it could be used to correctly classify institutionalized and noninstitutionalized persons.

Predictive Validity.   **Predictive validity** is the degree to which a test can predict how well an individual will do in a future situation. If an algebra aptitude test administered at the start of school can fairly accurately predict which students will perform well or poorly in algebra at the end of the school year (the criterion), the aptitude test has high predictive validity.

Predictive validity is extremely important for tests that are used to classify or select individuals. An example many of you are all too familiar with is the use of Graduate Record Examination (GRE) scores to select students for admission to graduate school. Many graduate schools require a minimum score for admission, often 1000, in the belief that students who achieve that score have a higher probability of succeeding in graduate school than those scoring lower than 1000. Other tests used to classify or select people include those used to determine eligibility for special education services and the needs of students receiving such services. It is imperative in these situations that decisions about appropriate programs be based on the results of predictively valid measures. Consequential validity (discussed shortly) should be considered as well.

The predictive validity of an instrument may vary depending on a number of factors, including the curriculum involved, textbooks used, and geographic location. The Mindboggling Algebra Aptitude Test, for example, may predict achievement better in courses using the *Brainscrambling Algebra I* text than in courses using other texts. Likewise, studies on the GRE have suggested that although the test appears to have satisfactory predictive validity for success in some areas of graduate study (such as English), its validity in predicting success in other areas (such as art education) appears to be questionable. Thus, if a test is to be used for prediction, it is important to compare the description of its validation with the situation in which it is to be used.

No test, of course, will have perfect predictive validity. Therefore, predictions based on the scores of any test will be imperfect. However, predictions based on a combination of several test scores will invariably be more accurate than predictions based on the scores of any single test. Therefore, when important classification or selection decisions are to be made, they should be based on data from more than one indicator.

In establishing the predictive validity of a test (called the **predictor** because it is the variable upon which the prediction is based), the first step is to identify and carefully define the **criterion,** or predicted variable, which must be a valid measure of the performance to be predicted. For example, if we wished to establish the predictive validity of an algebra aptitude test, final examination scores at the completion of a course in algebra might be considered a valid criterion. As another example, if we were interested in establishing the predictive validity of a given test for forecasting success in college, grade point average at the end of the first year would probably be considered a valid criterion, but number of extracurricular activities in which the student participated probably would not. Once the criterion has been identified and defined, the procedure for determining predictive validity is as follows:

1. Administer the predictor variable to a group.
2. Wait until the behavior to be predicted, the criterion variable, occurs.
3. Obtain measures of the criterion for the same group.
4. Correlate the two sets of scores.
5. Evaluate the results.

The resulting correlation, or validity coefficient, indicates the predictive validity of the test; if the coefficient is high, the test has good predictive validity. You may have noticed that the procedures for determining concurrent validity and predictive validity are very similar. The major difference has to do with when the criterion measure is administered. In establishing concurrent validity, the criterion measure is administered at about the same time as the predictor. In establishing predictive validity, the researcher usually has to wait for a longer period of time to pass before criterion data can be collected. In the discussion of both concurrent and predictive validity, we have noted that a high coefficient indicates that the test has good validity. You may have wondered, "How high is high?" Although there is no magic number that a coefficient should reach, a high number (close to 1.0) is best.

Construct Validity

Construct validity is the degree to which a test measures an intended hypothetical construct. It is the most important form of validity because it asks the fundamental validity question: What is this test really measuring? We have seen that all variables derive from constructs and that constructs are nonobservable traits, such as intelligence, anxiety, and honesty, "invented" to explain behavior. Constructs underlie the variables that researchers measure. You cannot see a construct; you can only observe its effect. Constructs, however, do an amazingly good job of explaining certain differences among individuals. For example, it was always observed that some students learn faster than others, learn more, and retain information longer. To explain these differences, scientists hypothesized that there is a construct called intelligence that is related to learning and that everyone possesses to a greater or lesser degree. A theory of intelligence developed. Tests were developed to measure how much intelligence a person has. As it happens, students whose scores indicate that they have a "lot" of it—that is, students who have high intelligence scores—tend to do better in school and other learning environments than those who have less of it.

Research studies involving a construct are valid only to the extent that the instrument used actually measures the intended construct and not some unanticipated, intervening variable. Determining construct validity is by no means easy. It usually involves gathering a number of pieces of evidence to demonstrate validity. If we wished, for example, to determine whether the Big Bob Intelligence Test was construct valid, we could carry out all or most of the following validation studies. First, we could see whether students who scored high on the Big Bob test learned faster, more, and with greater retention than low scorers. We could correlate scores on the Big Bob test taken at the beginning of the school year with students' grades at the end of the school year. We could also correlate performance on the Big Bob test with performance on other, well-established intelligence tests to see whether the correlations were high. We could have scholars in the field of intelligence examine the Big Bob test items to judge whether they represented typical topics in the field of intelligence. In addition to confirmatory evidence such as this, we could seek disconfirmatory validity information. For example, we would not expect scores on an intelligence test to correlate highly with self-esteem or height. If we correlated the Big Bob Intelligence Test with self-esteem and height and found low or moderate correlations, we could conclude that the Big Bob test is measuring something different from self-esteem or height. Thus, we would have evidence that the Big Bob test correlates highly with other intelligence tests (confirmatory validation) and does not correlate highly with self-esteem and height (disconfirmatory validation). Notice how content and criterion-related forms of validity are used in studies to determine a test's construct validity. No single validation study can establish the construct validity of a test.

Consequential Validity

Consequential validity, as the name suggests, is concerned with the consequences that occur from tests. As more and more tests are being administered to more and more individuals, and as the consequences of testing are becoming more important, concern over the consequences of testing has increased. All tests have intended purposes (I mean, really, who would create these things for *fun?*), and in general, the intended purposes are valid and appropriate. There are, however, some testing instances that produce (usually unintended) negative or harmful consequences to the test takers. **Consequential validity,** then, is the extent to which an instrument creates harmful effects for the user. Examining consequential validity allows researchers to ferret out and identify tests that may be harmful to students, teachers, and other test users, whether the problem is intended or not.

The key issue in consequential validity is the question, "What are the effects on teachers or students from various forms of testing?" For example, how does testing students solely with multiple-choice items affect students' learning as compared with assessing them with other, more open-ended items? Should non-English speakers be tested in the same way as English speakers? Can people who see the test results of non-English speakers, but do not know about their lack of English, make harmful interpretations for such students? Although most tests serve their intended purpose in nonharmful ways, consequential validity reminds us that testing can and sometimes does have negative consequences for test takers or users. Table 5.2 summarizes the four forms of validity.

Factors That Threaten Validity

A number of factors can diminish the validity of tests and instruments used in research, including the following:

- Unclear test directions
- Confusing and ambiguous test items

TABLE 5.2	Forms of validity	
Form	**Method**	**Purpose**
Content validity	Compare content of the test to the domain being measured.	To what extent does this test represent the general domain of interest?
Criterion-related validity	Correlate scores from one instrument to scores on a criterion measure, either at the same (concurrent) or different (predictive) time.	To what extent does this test correlate highly with another test?
Construct validity	Amass convergent, divergent, and content-related evidence to determine that the presumed construct is what is being measured.	To what extent does this test reflect the construct it is intended to measure?
Consequential validity	Observe and determine whether the test has adverse consequences for test takers or users.	To what extent does the test create harmful consequences for the test taker?

- Using vocabulary too difficult for test takers
- Overly difficult and complex sentence structures
- Inconsistent and subjective scoring methods
- Untaught items included on achievement tests
- Failure to follow standardized test administration procedures
- Cheating, either by participants or by someone teaching the correct answers to the specific test items

These factors diminish the validity of tests because they distort or produce atypical test performance, which in turn distorts the desired interpretation of the test scores.

Validity is the most important characteristic a test or measure can have. Without validity, the desired interpretations of the variables measured have inappropriate meaning. There are multiple ways to establish the various forms of test validity. In the end, the test user makes the final decision about the validity and usefulness of a test or measure. The bases for that decision should be described in the procedure section of your research plan.

Reliability of Measuring Instruments

In everyday English, *reliability* means dependability or trustworthiness. The term means the same thing when describing measurements. **Reliability** is the degree to which a test consistently measures whatever it is measuring. The more reliable a test is, the more confidence we can have that the scores obtained from the test are essentially the same scores that would be obtained if the test were readministered to the same test takers. If a test is unreliable (i.e., if it provides inconsistent information about performance), then scores would be expected to be quite different every time the test was administered. For example, if an attitude test is unreliable, then a student getting a total score of 75 today might score 45 tomorrow and 95 the day after tomorrow. If the test is reliable, and if the student's total score is 75, then we would not expect the student's score to vary much on retesting. Of course, we also should not expect the student's score to be exactly the same on other retestings. The reliability of test scores is similar to the reliability of golf, bowling, or shot-putting scores. Golf, bowling, or shot-putting rarely produce the identical scores time after time after time. An individual's health, motivation, anxiety, guessing luck, attitude, and attention change from time to time and influence performance of these activities, just as they affect performance on tests. All test scores have some degree of measurement error, and the smaller the amount of error, the more reliable the scores and the more confidence we have in the consistency and stability of test takers' performances.

Reliability is expressed numerically, usually as a *reliability coefficient*, which is obtained by using correlation. A high reliability coefficient indicates high reliability. A perfectly reliable test would have a reliability coefficient of 1.00, meaning that students' scores perfectly reflected their true status with respect to the variable being measured. However, alas and alack, as noted, no test is perfectly reliable. High reliability indicates minimum error—that is, that the effect of errors of measurement is small.

Validity tells test users about the appropriateness of a test, and reliability tells about the consistency of the scores produced. Both are important for judging the suitability of a test or measuring instrument. However, *a valid test is always reliable, but a reliable test is not always valid.* In other words, if a test is measuring what it is supposed to be measuring, it will be reliable, but a reliable test can consistently measure the wrong thing and be invalid! Suppose an instrument that intended to measure social studies concepts actually measured only social studies facts. It would not be a valid measure of concepts, but it could certainly measure the facts very consistently. For example, suppose the reported reliability coefficient for a test was .24, which is definitely quite low. Would this tell you anything about the test's validity? Yes, it would. It would tell you that the validity was not high because if it were, the reliability would be higher. What if the reported reliability coefficient were .92 (which is definitely good)? Would this tell you any-thing about the validity? Not really. The coefficient would tell you only that the validity *might* be good, because the reliability is good; in truth, the test could be consistently measuring the wrong thing. To review, reliability is necessary but not sufficient for establishing validity. Got it?

As with validity, there are different types of reliability, each of which deals with a differ-ent kind of test consistency and is established in a different manner. The following sections describe five general types of reliability: stability, equivalence, equivalence and stability, in-ternal consistency, and scorer/rater reliability.

Stability

Stability, also called **test–retest reliability,** is the degree to which scores on the same test are consistent over time. It provides evidence that scores obtained on a test at one time (test) are the same or close to the same when the test is readministered some other time (retest). The more similar the scores on the test over time, the more stable the test scores. Test stability is especially important for tests used to make predictions, because these predictions are based heavily on the assumption that the scores will be stable over time.

The procedure for determining test–retest reliability is basically quite simple:

1. Administer the test to an appropriate group.
2. After some time has passed, say 2 weeks, administer the same test to the same group.
3. Correlate the two sets of scores.
4. Evaluate the results.

If the resulting coefficient, referred to as the *coefficient of stability,* is high, the test has good test–retest reliability. A major problem with this type of reliability is the difficulty of knowing how much time should elapse between the two testing sessions. If the interval is too short, the students may remember responses they made on the test the first time; if they do, the es-timate of reliability will be artificially high. If the interval is too long, students may improve on the test due to intervening learning or maturation; if they do, the estimate of reliability will be artificially low. Generally, although not universally, a period of from 2 to 6 weeks is used to determine a test's stability. When stability information about a test is given, the stability co-efficient and the time interval between testings also should be given.

Equivalence

Equivalence, also called **equivalent-forms reliability,** is the degree to which two similar forms of a test produce similar scores from a single group of test takers. The two forms meas-ure the same variable, have the same number of items, the same structure, the same difficulty level, and the same directions for administration, scoring, and interpretation. Only the specific items are not the same, although they do measure the same topics or objectives. The equiva-lent forms are constructed by randomly sampling two sets of items from the same, well-described population. If there is equivalence, the two tests can be used interchangeably. It is reassuring to know that a person's score will not be greatly affected by the particular form ad-ministered. In some research studies, two forms of a test are administered to the same group, one as a pretest and the other as a posttest.

The procedure for determining equivalent-forms reliability is similar to that for deter-mining test–retest reliability:

1. Administer one form of the test to an appropriate group.
2. At the same session, or shortly thereafter, administer the second form of the test to the same group.
3. Correlate the two sets of scores.
4. Evaluate the results.

If the resulting *coefficient of equivalence* is high, the test has good equivalent-forms reliability. Equivalent-forms reliability is the most commonly used estimate of reliability for most tests used in research. The major problem with this method of estimating reliability is the difficulty of constructing two forms that are essentially equivalent. Even though equivalent-forms reliability is considered to be a very good estimate of reliability, it is not always feasible to administer two different forms of the same test. Imagine telling your students that they had to take two final examinations!

Equivalence and Stability

This form of reliability combines equivalence and stability. If the two forms of the test are administered at two different times (the best of all possible worlds!), the resulting coefficient is referred to as the *coefficient of stability and equivalence*. In essence, this approach assesses stability of scores over time as well as the equivalence of the two sets of items. Because more sources of measurement error are present, the resulting coefficient is likely to be somewhat lower than a coefficient of equivalence or a coefficient of stability. Thus, the coefficient of stability and equivalence represents a conservative estimate of reliability.

The procedure for determining equivalence and stability reliability is as follows:

1. Administer one form of the test to an appropriate group.
2. After a period of time, administer the other form of the test to the same group.
3. Correlate the two sets of scores.
4. Evaluate the results.

Internal Consistency Reliability

Internal consistency reliability is the extent to which items in a single test are consistent among themselves and with the test as a whole. It is obtained through three different approaches: split-half, Kuder-Richardson, or Cronbach's alpha. Each provides information about items in a single test that is taken only once. Because internal consistency approaches require only one test administration, some sources of measurement errors, such as differences in testing conditions, are eliminated.

Split-Half Reliability. **Split-half reliability** is a measure of internal consistency that involves dividing a test into two halves and correlating the scores on the two halves. It is especially appropriate when a test is very long or when it would be difficult to administer either the same test at two different times or two different forms to a group. The procedure for determining split-half reliability is as follows:

1. Administer the total test to a group.
2. Divide the test into two comparable halves, or subtests, most commonly by selecting odd items for one subtest and even items for the other subtest.
3. Compute each participant's score on the two halves—each participant will have a score for the odd items and a score for the even items.
4. Correlate the two sets of scores.
5. Apply the Spearman-Brown correction formula.
6. Evaluate the results.

The odd–even strategy for splitting the test works out rather well regardless of how a test is organized. Suppose, for example, we have a 20-item test in which the items get progressively more difficult. Items 1, 3, 5, 7, 9, 11, 13, 15, 17, and 19 as a group should be approximately as difficult as Items 2, 4, 6, 8, 10, 12, 14, 16, 18, and 20. In effect, we are artificially creating two equivalent forms of a test and computing equivalent-forms reliability.

In split-half reliability the two equivalent forms just happen to be parts of the same test—thus the label *internal consistency reliability.*

Notice that the procedure does not stop after the two sets of scores are correlated. Because longer tests tend to be more reliable and the split-half reliability coefficient represents the reliability of a test only half as long as the actual test, a correction formula must be applied to determine the reliability of the whole test. The correction formula used is the Spearman-Brown prophecy formula. For example, suppose the split-half reliability coefficient for a 50-item test were .80. The .80 would be based on the correlation between scores on 25 even items and 25 odd items and would therefore be an estimate of the reliability of a 25-item test, not a 50-item test. The Spearman-Brown formula provides an estimate of the full 50-item test. The formula is very simple and is applied to our example in the following way:

$$r_{\text{total test}} = \frac{2r_{\text{split half}}}{1 + r_{\text{split half}}}$$

$$r_{\text{total test}} = \frac{2(.80)}{1 + .80} = \frac{1.60}{1.80} = .89$$

Kuder-Richardson and Cronbach's Alpha Reliabilities. Kuder-Richardson 20 (KR-20) and **Cronbach's alpha** estimate internal consistency reliability by determining how all items on a test relate to all other test items and to the total test. When a test's items or tasks are measuring similar things, they are internally consistent. Cronbach's alpha is a general formula of which the KR-20 formula is a special case. Both provide reliability estimates that are equivalent to the average of the split-half reliabilities computed for all possible halves. KR-20 is a highly regarded method of assessing reliability but is useful only for items, such as multiple-choice items, that are scored dichotomously (given one of two scores—one for the right answer, one for the wrong answer). If items can have more than two scores (e.g., 0, 1, 2, 3), then Cronbach's alpha should be used. Many affective instruments and performance tests are scored using more than two choices. For example, Likert scales are commonly used in many affective instruments. If numbers are used to represent the response choices, analysis for internal consistency can be accomplished using Cronbach's alpha.

Kuder and Richardson provided an alternative, more easily computed form of their formula, called Kuder-Richardson 21 (KR-21). It requires less time than any other method of estimating reliability, although its results are a more conservative estimate of reliability. The KR-21 formula is as follows:

$$r_{\text{total test}} = \frac{(K)(SD^2) - \bar{X}(K - \bar{X})}{(SD^2)(K - 1)}$$

where

K = the number of items in the test

SD = the standard deviation of the scores

$\bar{X}$ = the mean of the scores

In a later chapter you will learn how to compute the mean and standard deviation of a set of scores. For the moment, let it suffice to say that the mean ($\bar{X}$) is the average score on the test for the group that took it, and the standard deviation (SD) is an indication of the amount of score variability, or how spread out the scores are. For example, assume that you have administered a 50-item test and have calculated the mean to be 40 ($\bar{X} = 40$) and the standard deviation to be 4 ($SD = 4$). The reliability of the test (which in this example turns out to be not too hot) would be calculated as follows.

$$r_{\text{total test}} = \frac{(50)(4^2) - 40(50 - 40)}{(4^2)(50 - 1)}$$

$$= \frac{(50)(16) - 40(10)}{(16)(49)} = \frac{800 - 400}{784} = \frac{400}{784} = .51$$

Figure 5.1 summarizes the previously discussed methods of estimating reliabilities.

Scorer/Rater Reliability

Reliability also must be investigated when scoring tests. Subjectivity occurs when a single scorer over time or different scorers do not agree on the scores of a single test. Essay tests, short-answer tests, performance and product tests, projective tests, and observations—almost any test that calls for more than a one-word response—raise concerns about the reliability of scoring. **Interjudge reliability** refers to the consistency of two or more independent scorers, raters, or observers; **intrajudge reliability** refers to the consistency of one individual's scoring, rating, or observing over time (a kind of test–retest reliability).

Subjective scoring is a major source of errors of measurement, so it is important to determine the reliability of those who score open-ended tests. It is especially important to determine scorer/rater reliability when performance on a test has serious consequences for the test taker; for example, some tests are used to determine who will be awarded a high school diploma or promoted to the next grade. The more open-ended test items are, the more important it is to seek consensus in scoring among judges. Subjective scoring reduces reliability and, in turn, diminishes the validity of the interpretations one wished to make from the scores. Table 5.3 summarizes the five types of reliability.

Reliability Coefficients

What constitutes an acceptable level of reliability? The minimum level of acceptability differs among test types. For example, standardized achievement and aptitude tests should have high reliability, often higher than .90. On the other hand, personality measures and other projective tests do not typically report such high reliabilities (although certainly some do), and one would therefore be satisfied with a reliability somewhat lower than expected from an achievement test. Moreover, when tests are developed in new areas, reliability is often low initially. You can get an idea of the level of reliability to expect in a test that you are using by getting information about what's typical for that type of test. It is good practice to always report reliability information in your research plan.

If a test is composed of several subtests that will be used individually in a study, then the reliability of each subtest should be evaluated. Because reliability is a function of test length, the reliability of any particular subtest is typically lower than the reliability of the total test.

Researchers must also be sure to report reliability for their own research participants. Reliability, like validity, is dependent on the group being tested. The more heterogeneous the

Number of Different Tests

		1	2
Number of Administration Times	1	Split-half KR-21	Equivalent-forms
	2	Test–retest	Stability and equivalence

FIGURE 5.1

Summary of methods for estimating reliability

TABLE 5.3	Five types of reliability	
Name	**What Is Measured**	**Description**
Stability (test-retest)	Stability of scores over time	Give one group the same test at two different times, and correlate the two scores.
Equivalence (alternative forms)	Relationship between two versions of a test intended to be equivalent	Give alternative test forms to a single group, and correlate the two scores.
Equivalence and stability	Relationship between equivalent versions of a test given at two different times	Give two alternative tests to a group at two different times, and correlate the scores.
Internal consistency	The extent to which the items in a test are similar to one another in content	Give tests to one group, and apply split-half, Kuder-Richardson, or Cronbach's alpha to estimate the internal consistency of the test items.
Scorer/rater	The extent to which independent scorers or a single scorer over time agree on the scoring of an open-ended test	Give copies of a set of tests to independent scorers or a single scorer at different times, and correlate or compute the percentage of scorer agreement.

test scores of a group, the higher the reliability will be. Thus, if Group A and Group B both took the same test, but Group A was made up of valedictorians and Group B was made up of students ranging from low to high performers, the test would be more reliable for Group B than for Group A.

Standard Error of Measurement

Reliability can also be expressed by stating the standard error of measurement. You should be familiar with this concept, because such data are often reported for a test. Basically, the **standard error of measurement** is an estimate of how often one can expect errors of a given size in an individual's test score. Thus, a small standard error of measurement indicates high reliability, and a large standard error of measurement indicates low reliability.

If a test were perfectly reliable (which no test is), a person's test score would be her true score—the score she'd obtain under ideal conditions. However, we know that if you administered the same test over and over to the same individual, the scores would vary, like the golf, bowling, and shot-put scores discussed previously. The amount of variability would be a function of the test's reliability. The variability would be small for a highly reliable test and large for a test with low reliability. If we could administer a test many times to the same individual or group of individuals, we could see how much variation actually occurred. Of course, realistically we can't do this, but it is possible to estimate this degree of variation (the standard error of measurement) using the data from the administration of a single test. In other words, the standard error of measurement allows us to estimate how much difference there might be between a person's obtained score and true score. The size of this difference is a function of the reliability of the test. We can estimate the standard error of measurement using the following simple formula:

$$SEm = SD\sqrt{1 - r}$$

where

SEm = standard error of measurement

SD = the standard deviation of the test scores

r = the reliability coefficient

For example, for a 25-item test we might calculate the standard deviation of a set of scores to be 5 ($SD = 5$) and the reliability coefficient to be .84 ($r = .84$). The standard error of measurement would then be calculated as follows:

$$SEm = SD\sqrt{1 - r} = 5\sqrt{1 - .84} = 5\sqrt{.16} = 5(.4) = 2.0$$

As this example illustrates, the size of the SEm is a function of both the SD and the reliability coefficient. Higher reliability is associated with a smaller SEm, and a smaller SD is associated with a smaller SEm. If the reliability coefficient in the previous example was .64, would you expect SEm to be larger or smaller? It would be larger: 3.0. If the standard deviation in the example was 10, what would you expect to happen to SEm? Again, it would be larger: 4.0. Although a small SEm indicates less error, it is impossible to say how small is "good." This is because the size of the SEm is relative to the size of the test. Thus, an SEm of 5 would be large for a 20-item test but small for a 200-item test. In our example an SEm of 2.0 would be considered moderate. To facilitate better interpretation of scores, some test publishers do not just present the SEm for the total group but also give a separate SEm for each of a number of identified subgroups.

:: SELECTING A TEST

A very important guideline for selecting a test is this: Do not stop with the first test you find that appears to measure what you want, say "Eureka, I have found it!" and blithely use it in your study! Instead, identify a group of tests that are appropriate for your study, compare them on relevant factors, and select the best one. If you become knowledgeable concerning the qualities a test should possess and familiar with the various types of tests that are available, then selecting an instrument will be a very orderly process. Assuming that you have defined the purpose of your study and identified the research participants, the first step in choosing a test is to determine precisely what type of test you need. The next step is to identify and locate appropriate tests. Finally, you must do a comparative analysis of the tests and select the best one for your needs.

Sources of Test Information

Mental Measurements Yearbooks

Once you have determined the type of test you need (e.g., a test of reading comprehension for second graders or an attitude measure for high schoolers), a logical place to start looking for specific tests to meet your needs is the Mental Measurements Yearbooks (MMYs). Currently produced by the Buros Institute of Mental Measurements at the University of Nebraska–Lincoln, the MMYs have been published periodically since 1938, and they represent the most comprehensive source of test information available to educational researchers. The *Fifteenth Mental Measurements Yearbook* is the latest publication in a series that includes the MMYs, *Tests in Print*, and many other related works such as *Vocational Tests and Reviews*. An MMY is published every few years, and supplements were published between major revisions in the years from 1988 to 1999. Most university libraries contain the MMYs. The MMYs are expressly designed to assist users in making informed test selection decisions. The stated purposes are to provide (1) factual information on all known new or revised tests in the English-speaking world, (2) objective test reviews written specifically for the MMYs, and (3) comprehensive bibliographies, for specific tests, of related references from published literature. (Some of this information is available free of charge from the Buros Institute Web site, http://www.unl.edu/buros/, but a fee is charged for the test reviews.)

Getting maximum benefit from the MMYs requires, at the very least, that you familiarize yourself with the organization and the indexes provided. Perhaps the most important thing to know in using the MMYs is that the numbers given in the indexes are test numbers, not page numbers. For example, in the Classified Subject Index, under "Achievement," you will find the following entry (among others): Wechsler Individual Achievement Test—Second Edition; Ages 4–85 years; 275. The 275 means that the description of the Wechsler Individual Achievement Test is entry 275 in the main body of the volume; it does not mean that it is on page 275.

The MMY provides six indexes to help you find information about tests: Index of Titles, Index of Acronyms, Classified Subject Index (alphabetical list of test subjects), Publishers Directory and Index (names and addresses of publishers), Index of Names (names of test developers and test reviewers), and Score Index (types of scores obtained from the tests). So, for example, if you heard that Professor Jeenyus had developed a new interest test, but you did not know its name, you would look in the Index of Names under "Jeenyus"; there you would be given test numbers for all tests developed by Professor Jeenyus that were included in the volume.

If you are looking for information on a particular test, you can find it easily by using the alphabetical organization of the most recent MMYs. If you are not sure of a test's title or know only the general type of test you need, you may use the following procedure:

1. If you are not sure of a test's title, look through the Index of Titles for possible variants of the title or consult the appropriate subject area in the Classified Subject Index for that particular test or related ones.
2. If you know the test publisher, consult the Publishers Directory and Index and look for the test you seek.
3. If you are looking for a test that yields a particular type of score, search for tests in that category in the Score Index.
4. Using the entry numbers listed in all of the sections described previously, locate the test descriptions in the Tests and Reviews section (the main body of the volume).

An example of an MMY entry is shown in Figure 5.2. Note that the entry contains the suggested ages of the participants, the author and publisher, a review by a researcher in the subject area, information about the validity and reliability, and other useful information about the test.

Tests in Print

A very useful supplemental source of test information is *Tests in Print (TIP)*. *TIP* is a comprehensive bibliography of all known commercially available tests that are currently in print. It also serves as a master index of tests that directs the reader to all original reviews that have appeared in the MMYs to date. It is most often used to determine a test's availability. Once you know that a test is available, you can look it up in the MMY to find out if it is appropriate for your purpose. The main body of the latest *TIP* edition is organized alphabetically.

Thus, *TIP* provides information on many more tests than the MMYs, but the MMYs contain more comprehensive information for each test.

Pro-Ed Publications

Some other sources of test information come from Pro-Ed Publications. *Tests: A Comprehensive Reference for Assessments in Psychology, Education, and Business* (T. Maddox, Ed.), now in its fifth edition, provides descriptions of more than 2,000 tests. Although no reviews are

| FIGURE 5.2 | Sample entry from the *Mental Measurements Yearbook* |

[183]

The Hundred Pictures Naming Test.

Purpose: "A confrontation naming test designed to evaluate rapid naming ability."

Population: Ages 4-6 to 11-11.

Publication Date: 1992.

Acronym: HPNT.

Scores, 3: Error, Accuracy, Time.

Administration: Individual.

Price Data, 1992: $195 per complete kit including manual (84 pages), test book, and 25 response forms; $10 per 25 response forms.

Time: (6) minutes.

Authors: John P. Fisher and Jennifer M. Glenister.

Publisher: Australian Council for Educational Research Ltd. [Australia]

Review of The Hundred Pictures Naming Test by JEFFREY A. ATLAS, Deputy Chief Psychologist and Assistant Clinical Professor, Bronx Children's Psychiatric Center, Albert Einstein College of Medicine, Bronx, NY:

The Hundred Pictures Naming Test (HPNT) is introduced in its test manual as "a confrontation naming test designed to evaluate rapid naming ability across age groups" (manual, p. 1). Given this stated purpose, the HPNT seems to qualify as a "test," and a valuable one, for "preparatory" (preschooler) boys and girls aged 5 to 6½, a grouping that constituted roughly 66% of the test reference group of 275 children. The remaining group cells have too few children to provide truly normative data, but may be suggestive in screening subjects who may have language disability or in evaluating recovery of function after brain injury.

The manual and test plates are attractively packaged and sturdy (except for the cardboard test container which will likely be discarded after several uses), but a bit overpriced at $195 for a test with restricted norms and limited generalizability. My sample package contained repeats of the manual pages 1–6 and test plate 18. These are minor distractors that I hope do not reflect overall quality control.

The reference group has nearly equal sex distribution, satisfactory city-suburban-country stratification (64%, 25%, and 11%), but scant socioeconomic information. The fact the test was developed in Australia seems not to have resulted in much content sampling bias. Preliminary inspection for test items that might prompt minor concern suggest "unicorn" and "rake" are words that may be absent from the linguistic environment of preschoolers living in cinder-block projects in New York City, and "koala" and "crown" reflect Australian versus other English-speaking nationality locales.

The mean "accuracy" score for the reference group was 74.34 (*sd* = 15.67), with a range of 23 to 98. These numbers comprise expectable figures for a 100-item examination and the linearity of increased test scores by age was impressive, permitting some normative evaluation, especially for preschoolers. Useful indicators for evaluating poor test performance, with some error categories indicating the need for speech therapy, some response categories indicating psychological intervention (e.g., for Selective Mutism), and overall poor lexicon indicating language remediation. The inclusion of 31 speech-language problem youngsters in the reference group provides suggestive screening norms but the low sample number and uneven linearity of scores limits the usefulness of the HPNT as a test for this group. Similarly, the division of the reference group into English First, English Main(ly), and English Only is helpful in qualitative assessment of performance but inadequate in providing test norms.

A useful aspect of the HPNT may be as a monitor of recovery of function after brain injury. Test-retest data (*r* = .98, after about 1 month for a bit over a fifth of the reference pool) and interrater reliability (*r* = .97 using a little over a tenth of the pool) furnish adequate criteria for retest using the HPNT. A sample protocol in the manual illustrates 6-year-old Warren's notable improvements in accuracy and significant error reduction, reflecting good recovery of function approximately 7 months following brain injury suffered in a car accident.

In summary, The Hundred Pictures Naming Test offers a useful test of English-only preschoolers' expressive speech accuracy, of recovery of speech function in some aphasias, and a screening device for psychological, environmental, and second-language interferences. As such it represents itself as a useful addition to the armamentarium of speech-language pathologists, early childhood educators, and in a more limited way, English-as-Second-Language instructors.

Source: Conoley, J. C., and Impara, J. C. (Eds.), *The Twelfth Mental Measurements Yearbook,* pp. 380–81. Lincoln, NE: Buros Institute of Mental Measurements.

included, complete information about test publishers is provided to enable users to call or write for additional information. In addition, tests appropriate for individuals with physical, visual, and hearing impairments are listed, as are tests that are available in a variety of languages. A complementary Pro-Ed publication, the multi-volume *Test Critiques* (D. Keyser and R. Sweetland, Eds.), contains extensive reviews for more than 800 tests widely used in psychology, education, and business. Information on *Tests* and *Test Critiques* can be found in Pro-Ed's online catalog at http://proedinc.com/store/index.php. In addition to these reference works, Pro-Ed publishes numerous tests, which are also described in the catalog.

ETS Test Collection Database

A joint project of the Educational Testing Service and the ERIC Clearinghouse on Assessment and Evaluation, the ETS Test Collection Database is an online searchable database containing descriptions of more than 20,000 tests and research instruments in virtually all fields. In contrast to the MMYs, the database includes unpublished as well as published tests but provides much less information on each test. To access the ETS Test Collection Database, go to http://www.ets.org/testcoll/index.htm/ on the Web. There you will be able to search for tests and research instruments by title or keyword. For each test included in the database, the following information is given: title, author, publication date, target population, publisher or source, and an annotation describing the purpose of the instrument.

Professional Journals

A number of journals, many of which are American Psychological Association publications, regularly publish information of interest to test users. For example, *Psychological Abstracts* is a potential source of test information. Using the monthly or annual index, you can quickly determine if *Psychological Abstracts* contains information on a given test. Other journals of interest to test users include *Journal of Applied Measurement, Journal of Consulting Psychology, Journal of Educational Measurement,* and *Educational and Psychological Measurement.*

Test Publishers and Distributors

After narrowing your search to a few acceptable tests, a good source of additional information on tests is the manuals for the tests, which are available from the tests' publishers. A manual typically includes detailed technical information, a description of the population for whom the test is intended to be appropriate, a detailed description of norming procedures, conditions of administration, detailed scoring instructions, and requirements for score interpretation. Final selection of a test usually requires examining the actual test. A test that appears from all descriptions to be exactly what you need may have one or more problems. For example, it may contain many items measuring content not covered, or its language level may be too high or low for your participants. Above all, remember that in selecting tests you must be a good consumer, one who finds an instrument that fits your needs.

Selecting From Alternatives

Once you have narrowed the number of test candidates and acquired relevant information, you must make a comparative analysis of the tests. Although there are a number of factors to be considered in choosing a test, these factors are not of equal importance. For example, the least expensive test is not necessarily the best test! As you undoubtedly know by now, the most important factor to be considered in test selection is validity. Is one of the tests more appropriate for your sample? If you are interested in prediction, does one of the tests have a significantly higher validity coefficient? If content validity is of prime importance, are the items of one test more relevant to the topic of your study than other tests? These are typical questions to ask. If, after the validity comparisons, there are still several tests that seem appropriate, the next factor to consider is reliability.

You would presumably select the test with the highest reliability, but there are other considerations, such as ease of test use. For example, a test that can be administered during one class period would be considerably more convenient than a 2-hour test. Shorter tests generally are also preferable because they are less tiring and more motivating for test takers. However, a shorter test will tend to be less reliable than a longer one. If one test takes half as long to administer as another and is only slightly less reliable, the shorter test is probably better.

By the time you get to this point, you will have probably made a decision. The test you choose will probably be a group-administered rather than an individually administered one. Some intelligence and personality tests must be individually administered, but individually administered tests are usually required only in certain situations, such as when a person is tested for a disability. Of course, if the nature of your research study requires it, by all means use an individually administered test, but be certain you have the qualifications needed to administer, score, and interpret the results. If you do not, can you afford to acquire the necessary personnel? If, after all this soul searching, by some miracle you still have more than one test in the running, by all means pick the cheapest one!

Two additional considerations in test selection have nothing to do with their psychometric qualities. Both are related to the use of tests in schools. If you are planning to use schoolchildren in your study, you should check to see what tests they have already taken. You would not want to administer a test with which test takers are already familiar. Second, you should be sensitive to the fact that some parents or administrators might object to a test that contains "touchy" items. Certain attitude, values, and personality tests, for example, contain questions related to the personal beliefs and behaviors of the respondents. If there is any possibility that the test contains potentially objectionable items, either choose another test or acquire appropriate permissions before administering the test.

Constructing Tests

On rare occasions you may not be able to locate a suitable test. One logical solution is to construct your own test. Good test construction requires a variety of skills. If you don't have them, get some help. As mentioned previously, experience at least equivalent to a course in measurement is needed. You should buy and read one of the many useful classroom assessment test books. If you do develop your own test, you must collect validity and reliability data. A self-developed test should not be utilized in a research study unless it has first been pretested by a group of 5 to 10 persons similar to the group you will be collecting data from in the actual study. The following discussion gives an overview of some guidelines to follow if you need to construct a test to administer to schoolchildren.

Writing Your Own Paper-and-Pencil Test Items

To create a paper-and-pencil test, you will need to determine what type or types of test items to include. Selection items include multiple choice, true–false, and matching. Supply items include short-answer items, completion items, and essays. Note that scoring or judging responses is much more difficult for essays than the other types of test items. Get help if needed.

The following suggestions provide elementary strategies for constructing your own paper-and-pencil test items.[2] Figure 5.3 presents further suggestions for preparing items.

- Avoid wording and sentence structure that is ambiguous and confusing.
  Poor: All but one of the following items are not elements. Which one is not?
  Better: Which one of the following is an element?
- Use appropriate vocabulary.
  Poor: The thesis of capillary execution serves to illuminate how fluids are elevated in small tubes.   True   False
  Better: The principle of capillary action helps explain how liquids rise in small passages.
      True   False

---

[2] Test items on these pages are from *Classroom Assessment: Concepts and Applications* (4th ed., pp. 182–190), by P. W. Airasian, 2001, New York: McGraw Hill. Copyright 2001 by The McGraw-Hill Companies, Inc. Reprinted with Permission.

FIGURE 5.3

Suggestions for preparing test items

Source: From *Classroom Assessment: Concepts and Applications* (4th ed., p. 192), by P. W. Airasian, 2001, New York: McGraw-Hill. Copyright 2001 by The McGraw-Hill Companies, Inc. Reprinted with permission.

Multiple-Choice Items
- Set pupils' task in the item stem.
- Include repeated words in the stem.
- Avoid grammatical clues.
- Use positive wording if possible.
- Include only plausible options.
- Avoid using "all of the above" or "none of the above."

Matching Items
- Use a homogeneous topic.
- Put longer options in left column.
- Provide clear direction.
- Use unequal numbers of entries in the two columns.

Essay Items
- Use several short-essay questions rather than one long one.
- Provide a clear focus in questions.
- Indicate scoring criteria to pupils.

True-False Items
- Make statements clearly true or false.
- Avoid specific determiners.
- Do not arrange responses in a pattern.
- Do not select textbook sentences.

Completion and Short-Answer Items
- Provide a clear focus for the desired answer.
- Avoid grammatical clues.
- Put blanks at the end of the item.
- Do not select textbook sentences.

- Write items that have only one correct answer.
  Poor: Ernest Hemingway wrote _____.
  Better: The author of *The Old Man and the Sea* is _____.
- Give information about the nature of the desired answer.
  Poor: Compare and contrast the North and South in the Civil War. Support your views.
  Better: What forces led to the outbreak of the Civil War? Indicate in your discussion the economic, foreign, and social conditions. You will be judged in terms of these three topics. Your essay should be five paragraphs in length, and spelling and grammar will count in your grade.
- Do not provide clues to the correct answer.
  Poor: A figure that has eight sides is called an
  a. pentagon
  b. quadrilateral
  c. octagon
  d. ogive
  Better: Figures that have eight sides are called
  a. pentagons
  b. quadrilaterals
  c. octagons
  d. ogives

Be sure to assess only content that has been taught. Aligning instruction and assessment will help you ensure valid results. We strongly suggest that you try out any test you construct yourself in a research setting. It is not necessary to have a large number of persons to find out if your test is valid and clear. Ask four or five insightful teachers or individuals experienced in test-item writing to critique your test for clarity and logic. On the basis of their suggestions, you can improve your test.

Test Administration

You should be aware of several general guidelines for test administration. First, if testing is to be conducted in a school setting, arrangements should be made beforehand with the appropriate persons. Consultation with the principal should result in agreement as to when the testing will take place, under what conditions, and with what assistance from school personnel. The principal can be very helpful in supplying such information as dates for which testing is inadvisable (e.g., assembly days and days immediately preceding or following holidays). Second, whether you are testing in the schools or elsewhere, you should do everything you can to ensure ideal testing conditions; a comfortable, quiet environment is more conducive to participant cooperation. You should monitor test takers carefully to minimize cheating. Also, if testing is to take place in more than one session, the conditions of the sessions should be as identical as possible. Third, follow the Boy Scout motto and be prepared. Be thoroughly familiar with the administration procedures presented in the test manual, and follow the directions precisely. If they are at all complicated, practice beforehand. Administer the test to some group, or stand in front of a mirror and give it to yourself!

As with everything in life, good planning and preparation usually pay off. If you have made all necessary arrangements, secured all necessary cooperation, and are very familiar and comfortable with the administration procedures, the actual testing situation should go well. If some unforeseen catastrophe, such as an earthquake or a power failure, occurs during testing, make careful note of the incident. If it is serious enough to invalidate the testing, you may have to try again another day with another group. At minimum, note the occurrence of the incident in your final research report. You cannot predict every problem that might arise, but you can greatly increase the probability of all going well if you adequately plan and prepare for the big day.

SUMMARY

Constructs

1. All types of research require collecting data; the scientific method depends on the collection, analysis, and interpretation of data. Data are pieces of evidence used to examine a research topic or hypothesis.
2. Constructs are mental abstractions such as personality, creativity, and intelligence that cannot be observed or measured directly. Constructs become variables when they are stated in terms of operational definitions.

Variables

3. Measurement scales describe four different levels of variable: nominal, ordinal rank, interval, and ratio.
4. Categorical variables are nonnumerical (nominal); quantitative variables are numerical (ordinal, interval, and ratio).
5. An independent variable is the treatment or cause, and the dependent variable is the outcome or effect of the independent variable.

Characteristics of Measuring Instruments

6. There are three main ways to collect data for research studies: administer an existing instrument, construct one's own instrument, and record naturally occurring events (observation) or collect existing data.

7. The time and skill it takes to select an appropriate instrument are invariably less than the time and skill it takes to develop one's own instrument.
8. There are thousands of standardized and nonstandardized instruments available for researchers. A standardized test is one that is administered, scored, and interpreted in the same way no matter when and where it is administered.
9. Most quantitative tests are paper-and-pencil ones, whereas most qualitative research collects data by observation and oral questioning.
10. Raw scores indicate the number of items or points a person got correct. They can be transformed into derived scores such as percentile ranks, stanines, and standard scores. Derived scores are most often used with standardized tests.
11. Norm-referenced scoring compares a student's test performance to the performance of other test takers; criterion-referenced scoring compares a student's test performance to predetermined standards of performance.

Types of Measuring Instruments
Cognitive Tests

Achievement Tests
12. Achievement tests measure the current status of individuals on school-taught subjects.

13. Most standardized achievement tests are scored using norm-referencing approaches.

Aptitude Tests

14. Aptitude tests are used to predict how well a test taker is likely to perform in the future. They are standardized and used extensively in job hiring. General aptitude tests typically ask the test taker to perform a variety of verbal and nonverbal tasks.

15. Readiness tests are administered before instruction to determine whether and to what degree a student is ready for a given level of instruction.

Affective Tests -emotion

16. Affective tests are assessments designed to measure characteristics related to emotion.

17. Most affective tests are nonprojective; that is, they are self-report measures in which the individual responds to a series of questions about himself.

18. Five basic types of scales are used to measure attitudes: Likert scales, semantic differential scales, rating scales, Thurstone scales, and Guttman scales. The first three are the most used.

19. Attitude scales ask respondents to state their feelings about various objects, persons, and activities. Likert scales are responded to by indicating *strongly agree, agree, undecided, disagree,* and *strongly disagree;* semantic differential scales present a continuum of attitudes on which the respondent selects a position to indicate the strength of attitude; and rating scales present statements that respondents must rate on a continuum from high to low. These are all self-report measures.

20. Interest inventories ask individuals to indicate personal likes and dislikes. Responses are generally compared to existing interest patterns.

21. Values are deeply held beliefs about ideas, persons, and objects.

22. Personality, also called *temperament,* describes characteristics that represent a person's typical behavior. Personality inventories present respondents with lists of statements describing human behaviors, and they must indicate whether each statement pertains to them.

23. Personality inventories may be specific to a single trait (introversion–extroversion) or may be general and measure a number of traits.

24. Use of self-report measures create the concern about whether an individual is expressing his or her true attitude, values, interests, or personality.

25. Test bias in both cognitive and affective measures can distort the data obtained. Bias is present when one's ethnicity, race, gender, language, or religious orientation influences test performance.

Projective Tests

26. Projective tests present an ambiguous situation and require the test taker to "project" her or his true feelings on the ambiguous situation.

27. Association is the most commonly used projective technique and is exemplified by the inkblot test. Only the specially trained can administer and interpret projective tests.

Criteria for Good Measuring Instruments

Validity of Measuring Instruments

28. Validity is the degree to which a test measures what it is supposed to measure, thus permitting appropriate interpretations of test scores.

29. A test is not valid per se; it is valid for a particular interpretation and for a particular group. Each intended test use requires its own validation. Tests are not simply valid or invalid; they are highly valid, moderately valid, or generally invalid.

30. The four main forms of validity are content, criterion-related, construct, and consequential. They are viewed as interrelated, not independent aspects of validity.

Content Validity

31. Content validity assesses the degree to which a test measures an intended content area. It requires both item validity and sampling validity. Item validity is concerned with whether the test items are relevant to the intended content area; sampling validity is concerned with how well the test sample represents the total content area. Content validity is of prime importance for achievement tests.

32. Content validity is determined by expert judgment of item and sample validity, not by statistical means.

Criterion-Related Validity

33. Criterion-related validity has two forms, concurrent and predictive. Concurrent validity is the degree to which the scores on a test are related to scores on another test administered at the same time or to another measure available at the same time. Predictive validity is the degree to which scores on a test are related to scores on another test administered in the future. In both cases, a single group must take both tests.

34. Concurrent and predictive validity are determined by correlating one test with another test or measure, either at the same time or in the future.

Construct Validity

35. Constructs underlie research variables, and construct validity seeks to determine whether the construct underlying a variable is actually being measured.

36. Construct validity is determined by a series of validation studies that can include content and criterion-related approaches. Both confirmatory and disconfirmatory evidence are used to determine construct validation.

37. The validity of any test or measure can be diminished by such factors as unclear test directions, inappropriate teaching, subjective scoring, and failing to follow administration procedures.

Consequential Validity

38. Consequential validity is concerned with the potential of tests to create harmful effects for test takers. This is a new but important form of validity.

Reliability of Measuring Instruments

39. Reliability is the degree to which a test consistently measures whatever it measures. Reliability is expressed numerically, usually as a coefficient ranging from 0.0 to 1.0; a high coefficient indicates high reliability.

40. Reliability provides information about the inevitable fluctuations in scores due to person and test factors. No test is perfectly reliable, but the smaller the measurement error, the more reliable the test.

41. The five general types of reliability are stability, equivalence, equivalence and stability, internal consistency, and scorer/rater.

42. Stability, also called test–retest reliability, is the degree to which test scores are consistent over time. It is determined by correlating scores.

43. Equivalence, also called equivalent-forms reliability, is the degree to which two similar forms of a test produce similar scores from a single group of test takers.

44. Equivalence and stability determine the degree to which two forms of a test given at two different times produce similar scores as measured by correlations.

45. Internal consistency deals with the reliability of a single test taken at one time. It measures the extent to which the items in the test are consistent among

themselves and with the test as a whole. Split-half, Kuder-Richardson 20 and 21, and Cronbach's alpha are four main approaches to obtaining internal consistency.

46. Split-half reliability is determined by dividing a test into two equivalent halves (odd–even), correlating the two halves, and using the Spearman-Brown formula to determine the reliability of the whole test.

47. Kuder-Richardson reliability deals with the internal consistency of tests that are scored dichotomously (right, wrong), whereas Cronbach's alpha deals with the internal consistency of tests that are scored with more than two choices (agree, neutral, disagree or 0, 1, 2, 3).

48. Scorer/rater reliability is important when scoring tests that are potentially subjective. Interjudge reliability refers to the reliability of two or more independent scorers, whereas intrajudge reliability refers to the reliability of a single individual's scorings over time.

49. Estimates of interjudge or intrajudge reliability are obtained from correlating scores or computing the percentage of agreement.

Reliability Coefficients

50. What constitutes an acceptable level of reliability differs among test types, with standardized achievement tests having very high reliabilities and projective tests having considerably lower reliabilities.

51. If a test is composed of several subtests that will be used individually in a study, the reliability of each subtest should be determined and reported.

Standard Error of Measurement

52. The standard error of measurement is an estimate of how often one can expect test score errors of a given size. A small standard error of measurement indicates high reliability; a large standard error of measurement, low reliability.

53. The standard error of measurement allows us to estimate how much difference there is between a person's obtained and true score. Big differences indicate low reliability.

Selecting a Test

54. Do not choose the first test you find that appears to meet your needs. Identify a few appropriate tests and compare them on relevant factors.

Sources of Test Information

55. The Mental Measurement Yearbooks (MMYs) are the most comprehensive sources of test information available. They provide factual information on all known or revised tests, test reviews, and comprehensive bibliographies and indexes. The numbers given in the indexes are test numbers, not page numbers.

56. *Tests in Print (TIP)* is a comprehensive bibliography of all tests that have appeared in preceding MMYs. Pro-Ed Publications' *Tests* describes more than 2,000 tests in education, psychology, and business; reviews of many of these are found in *Test Critiques*.

57. The ETS Test Collection Database describes more than 20,000 tests, published and unpublished.

58. Other sources of test information are professional journals and test publishers or distributors.

Selecting From Alternatives

59. The three most important factors to consider in selecting a test are its validity, reliability, and ease of use.

Constructing Tests

60. Self-constructed tests should be pretested before use to determine validity, reliability, and feasibility. Pretesting is important for researcher-constructed tests.

61. Be certain to align instruction and assessment to ensure valid test results.

Test Administration

62. Every effort should be made to ensure ideal test administration conditions. Failing to administer procedures precisely, or altering the administration procedures, especially on standardized tests, lowers the validity of the test.

63. Monitor test takers to minimize cheating.

Now go to the Companion Website at **www.prenhall.com/gay** to assess your understanding of chapter content with Practice Quiz, apply comprehension in Applying What You Know, broaden your knowledge about research in Web Links, and expand your research skills in Evaluating Articles, Analyzing Qualitative Data, Analyzing Quantitative Data, and Research Tools and Tips.

PERFORMANCE CRITERIA

All the information required for the descriptions of the tests can be found in the Mental Measurements Yearbooks. Following the descriptions, you should present a comparative analysis of the three tests that forms a rationale for your selection of the "most acceptable" test for your study. As an example, you might indicate that all three tests have similar reliability coefficients reported but that one of the tests is more appropriate for your participants.

An example that illustrates the performance called for by Task 5 appears on the following pages. (See Task 5 Example.) The task in the example was submitted by the same student whose work for Tasks 2, 3a, and 4a were previously presented.

Additional examples for the tasks are included in the *Student Study Guide* that accompanies this text.

:: TASK 5 Example

Effect of Interactive Multimedia on the Achievement of 10th-Grade Biology Students

Test One (from an MMY, test #160)

a) High-School Subject Tests, Biology—1980–1990

American Testronics

$33.85 per 35 tests with administration directions; $13.25 per 35 machine-scorable answer sheets; $19.45 per Teacher's Manual ('90, 110 pages).

b) The Biology test of the High-School Subject Tests is a group-administered achievement test that yields 10 scores (Cell Structure and Function, Cellular Chemistry, Viruses/Monerans/Protists/Fungi, Plants, Animals, Human Body Systems and Physiology, Genetics, Ecology, Biological Analysis and Experimentation).

c) Reviewers state that reliability values (KR-20s) for the various subject tests ranged from .85 to .93, with a median of .88. Content validity should be examined using the classification tables and objective lists provided in the teacher's manual so that stated test objectives and research objectives can be matched.

d) Grades 9–12.

e) Administration time is approximately 40 minutes.

f) Scoring services are available from the publisher.

g) Reviewers recommend the test as a useful tool in the evaluation of instructional programs, recognizing that the test fairly represents the content for biology in the high school curriculum. However, they do caution that a match should be established between stated test objectives and local objectives.

Test Two (from an MMY, test #256)

a) National Proficiency Survey Series: Biology (NPSS:B)—1989

The Riverside Publishing Company

$34.98 per 35 test booklets including directions for administration; $19.98 per 35 answer sheets; $9 per technical manual (26 pages) (1990 prices)

b) The NPSS:B is a group-administered achievement test with 45 items designed to measure "knowledge about the living world ranging from single-celled organisms to the human body."

c) Content validity is good; items were selected from a large item bank provided by classroom teachers and curriculum experts. The manual alerts users that validity depends in large measure upon the purpose of the test. Although the standard error of measurement is not given for the biology test, the range of KR-20s for the entire battery is from .82 to .91, with a median of .86.

d) Grades 9–12.

e) Administration time is approximately 45 minutes.

f) Tests can be machine scored or self-scored. A program is available on diskette so that machine scoring may be done on site. Both percentile rank and NCE scores are used. NCEs allow users to make group comparisons.

g) The reviewer finds the reliability scores to be low if the test is to be used to make decisions concerning individual students. However, he praises the publishers for their comments regarding content validity, which state that "information should always be interpreted in relation to the user's own purpose for testing."

Test Three (from an MMY, test #135)

a) End of Course Tests (ECT) – 1986

CTB/McGraw-Hill

$21 per complete kit including 35 test booklets (Biology 13 pages) and examiner's manual.

b) The ECT covers a wide range of subjects in secondary school. Unfortunately, detailed information is not available for individual subjects. The number of questions range from 42 to 50 and are designed to measure subject matter content most commonly taught in a first-year course.

c) No statistical validity evidence is provided for the ECT and no demographic breakdown is provided to understand the representativeness of the standardization samples. However, reliability estimates were given and ranged from .80 to .89 using the KR-20 formula.

d) Secondary school students.

e) Administration time is from 45 to 50 minutes for any one subject test.

f) Both machine scoring and hand scoring are available. A Class Record Sheet is provided in the manual to help those who hand score to summarize the test results.

g) Users must be willing to establish local norms and validation evidence for effectual use of the ECT, since no statistical validity evidence is provided.

Conclusion

All three batteries have a biology subtest; The High-School Subject Tests (HSST) and the NPSS:B are designed specifically for 10th-grade students, while the ECT is course, rather than grade, oriented. It is acknowledged that more data are needed for all three tests, but reported validity and reliability data suggest that they all would be at least adequate for the purpose of this study (i.e., to assess the effectiveness of the use of interactive multimedia in biology instruction).

Of the three tests, the least validity evidence is provided for the ECT, so it was eliminated from contention first. Both the HSST and the NPSS:B provide tables and objective lists in their manuals that may be used to establish a match between stated test objectives and research objectives. The HSST and the NPSS:B both have good content validity but the HSST does not cross-index items to objectives, as does the NPSS:B. Also, norming information indicates that Catholic school students were included in the battery norm group. Therefore, of the three tests, the NPSS:B seems to be the most valid for the study.

With respect to reliability, all three tests provide a comparable range of KR-20 values for battery subtests. While specific figures are not given for the biology subtests, the reported ranges (low eighties to low nineties) suggest that they all have adequate internal consistency reliability.

The NPSS:B appears to be the most appropriate instrument for the study. The items (which were provided by both classroom teachers and curriculum experts) appear to match the objectives of the research study quite well. The KR-20 reliability is good, both in absolute terms and as compared to that of the other available tests. Both machine- and self-scoring are options, but an added advantage is that machine scoring can be done on site using a program provided by the publisher.

Thus, the NPSS:B will be used in the current study. As a cross-check, internal consistency reliability will be computed based on the scores of the subjects in the study.

"The respondent may give biased answers that are affected by her
reaction to the interviewer . . . " (p. 173)

Descriptive Research

OBJECTIVES

After reading Chapter 6, you should be able to do the following:

1. Briefly state the purpose of descriptive research.
2. List the major steps involved in designing and conducting a descriptive research study.
3. Briefly describe the main types of self-report research.
4. List and briefly describe the steps involved in conducting a questionnaire study.
5. Identify and briefly describe four major differences between an interview study and a questionnaire study.

Completing Chapter 6 should enable you to perform the following task.

TASK 6A

For a quantitative study, you have created research plan components (Tasks 2, 3a), described a sample (Task 4a), and considered appropriate measuring instruments (Task 5). If your study involves descriptive research, now develop the methods section of the research report. Include a description of participants, data collection methods, and research design. (See Performance Criteria at the end of Chapter 10, p. 287.)

▚ DESCRIPTIVE RESEARCH: DEFINITION AND PURPOSE

As you may recall from Chapter 1, **descriptive research**, also referred to as *survey research,* determines and describes the way things are. It may also compare how subgroups (such as males and females or experienced and inexperienced teachers) view issues and topics. We dis-

cuss descriptive research in some detail for two major reasons. First, a high percentage of research studies rely on surveys for data and, as a result, are descriptive in nature. Descriptive research influences what television programs we see, the type of automobiles that will be produced, the foods found on grocery shelves, the fashions we wear, and what issues and topics we will be confronted with. Second, the descriptive method is useful for investigating a variety of educational problems and issues. Typical descriptive studies are concerned with assessing attitudes, opinions, preferences, demographics, practices, and procedures. Examples of educational descriptive research topics are, "How do teachers in our school district rate the qualities of our new teacher evaluation program?" and "What do high school principals consider their most pressing administrative problems?" Descriptive data are usually collected by questionnaire surveys, telephone surveys, interviews, or observation.

It is important to note that some methods used in descriptive research, mainly interviews and observations, are also used in qualitative research. However, interviews and observations serve different purposes in qualitative and quantitative approaches. For example, when qualitative researchers interview and observe research participants, they do so primarily to identify what participants believe are the important issues to study. In quantitative research the researcher predetermines what variables will be surveyed before selecting or observing the research participants; interviews and observations are then used to gather data. The two approaches have a different conception of whose view is more important, the researcher's (quantitative) or the participants' (qualitative). Quantitative and qualitative researchers simply take different yet viable approaches to descriptive research.

:: THE DESCRIPTIVE RESEARCH PROCESS

Although descriptive research sounds very simple, there is considerably more to it than just asking questions and reporting answers. Descriptive studies involve a number of unique problems. For example, self-report studies, such as those utilizing questionnaires or interviews, often suffer from lack of participant response; many potential participants do not return mailed questionnaires or attend scheduled interviews. This makes it difficult to interpret findings, because people who do not respond may feel very differently than those who do. Twenty percent of survey participants might feel very negatively about the year-round school concept and might avail themselves of every opportunity to express their unhappiness, including on your questionnaire. The other 80%, who feel neutrally or positively, might not be as motivated to respond. Thus, if researchers consider only the opinions of those who responded, they might draw very wrong conclusions about the population's feelings toward year-round schooling. Further, questionnaire researchers must be very careful to write or select questions that are clear and unambiguous. The researcher seldom has an opportunity to explain to participants who are filling out a questionnaire what a particular question or word really means. Descriptive studies that utilize observational techniques also involve complex tasks, such as developing recording forms that permit data to be collected objectively and reliably.

A set of basic steps should guide descriptive research studies, just as it does other types of research studies. Each step must be conscientiously executed: identify a topic or problem, review the literature, select an appropriate sample of participants, collect valid and reliable data, analyze data, and report conclusions.

Within the basic steps are a number of substeps. Once you have defined a descriptive research problem, reviewed related literature and, if appropriate, stated hypotheses or questions, you must give careful thought to selection of the research participants and data collection procedures. Identifying the population that has the desired information, for example, is not always easy and must be thought through ahead of time. Finding the most appropriate method for collecting data also requires careful consideration. Suppose, for example, that your problem concerned how elementary school teachers spend their time during the school day. You might hypothesize that they spend one quarter of their time on noninstructional activities, such as collecting book money and maintaining order. Your first thought might be to mail to a sample of principals a questionnaire about how teachers spend their time. Doing this, however, assumes that principals know how teachers spend their daily time. Although principals would of course be familiar with the duties and responsibilities of their teachers, it is not likely that they could provide the data needed for the study. Thus, directly asking the teachers themselves would probably result in more accurate information. However, it is possible that teachers might tend to subconsciously exaggerate the amount of time they spend on activities they consider distasteful, such as grading papers or other clerical tasks. After further thought, you might decide that direct observation (though time-consuming) would yield the most accurate data or that allowing teachers to respond anonymously to a questionnaire would increase the likelihood of accurate answers.

After you have decided on a target population and a data collection strategy, your next steps are to identify your accessible population, determine needed sample size, select an appropriate sampling technique, and select or develop a data collection instrument. Because descriptive studies often seek information that is not already available, researchers usually need to develop an appropriate instrument. If a valid and reliable instrument is available, you can certainly use it, but using an instrument just "because it is there" is not a good idea. If you want the appropriate answers, you have to ask the appropriate questions. If you do develop an instrument, you should try it out and revise it as needed before using it in the actual study.

Once you have selected or developed a valid data collection instrument, you must then carefully plan and execute the specific procedures of the study (when the instrument will be administered, to whom, and how) and analyze the data. In general, the basic steps in conducting a descriptive study will be similar across studies, with specific details such as the research question, the participants, and data collection instruments differing across studies.

:: CLASSIFYING DESCRIPTIVE RESEARCH

The most common way to classify descriptive research is according to how the data are collected. Descriptive data are collected in two main ways: through self-report and through observation. This chapter will focus on self-report research, and observation will be discussed in detail in Chapter 15.

As noted in Chapter 5, self-report approaches require individuals to respond to a series of statements or questions about themselves. For example, a survey about local schools might ask respondents a questions such as this: "Do you believe the cost for the education of children in our community is too high?" Respondents would self-report their views by marking *Yes, Uncertain,* or *No.* Conversely, in an observation study, individuals are not directly asked for information; rather, the researcher obtains the desired data by watching participants. With observation, the researcher can choose various levels of involvement, ranging from participant observer (very involved) to nonparticipant observer (least involved). Also, the descriptive researcher typically observes predetermined activities, unlike the qualitative (narrative, ethnographic) researcher, who usually does not have predetermined topics to observe. It is possible, but not typical, for a descriptive (survey) study to employ both self-report and observation methods.

Self-Report Research

There are several major types of self-report research studies. The most well known and often used is probably survey research, which generally utilizes questionnaires or interviews to collect data. Surveys are often viewed with some disdain because many people have encountered poorly planned and poorly executed survey studies that utilize poorly developed instruments. You should not condemn survey research, however, just because it is often misused. Survey research at its best can provide very valuable data.

Types of Surveys

Surveys are used in many fields, including political science, sociology, economics, and education. They come in a variety of types, many of which are familiar to most people. Several types are described in the following paragraphs. It's important to note that a single survey can be classified in more than one way. For example, the same survey can be both a school survey and a sample survey; another can be both a developmental survey and a longitudinal survey.

School Surveys.   In education, surveys are most commonly used for the collection of data by schools or about schools. Surveys conducted by schools are usually prompted by a need for certain kinds of information related to the instruction, facilities, or student population. For example, school surveys may examine such variables as community attitudes toward schools, institutional and administrative personnel, curriculum and instruction, finances, and physical facilities. School surveys can provide necessary and valuable information to both the schools studied and to other agencies and groups whose operations are school related.

Sample Surveys.   The results of various public opinion polls are frequently reported by the media. Such polls represent an attempt to determine how all the members of a population (be it the American public in general or citizens of Skunk Hollow) feel about political, social, educational, or economic issues. Public opinion polls are almost always sample surveys. A **sample survey** is research in which information about a population is inferred based on the responses of a sample selected from that population. A sample is selected to properly represent a relevant subgroup (which shares characteristics such as socioeconomic status, gender, or geographic location), and results are often reported separately for that subgroup as well as for the total group.

Developmental Surveys. A *developmental survey* is concerned primarily with variables that characterize children at different levels of age, growth, or maturation. Developmental studies may investigate progression along a number of dimensions, such as intellectual, physical, emotional, or social development. The children studied may be a relatively heterogeneous group, such as fourth graders in general, or a more narrowly defined homogeneous group, such as children who are academically gifted. Knowledge of developmental patterns of various student groups can be used to make curriculum and instruction more appropriate and relevant for students. Knowing that 4-year-old and 5-year-old children typically enjoy skill-testing games (such as jumping rope and bouncing balls) but do not enjoy competitive group activities would certainly be helpful to a preschool teacher in developing lesson plans.

Cross-Sectional and Longitudinal Surveys. Some of the survey types already mentioned might also be classified as either cross-sectional or longitudinal. A **cross-sectional survey** is one in which data are collected from selected individuals in a single time period (however long it takes to collect data from the participants). It is a single, stand-alone study. One limitation of cross-sectional studies is that often a single point in time does not provide sufficient perspective to make needed decisions. Another major concern in a cross-sectional study is selecting samples of children that truly represent children at their level. A further related problem is selecting samples at different levels that are comparable on relevant variables such as intelligence. However, the advantage of the cross-sectional study is convenience. When a cross-sectional study attempts to collect data from each and every member of a population, as in the U.S. census, the survey is called, oddly enough, a **census survey.**

A **longitudinal survey** is a survey in which data are collected at two or more times to measure change or growth over time. Developmental surveys frequently rely on longitudinal data to measure growth or development. There are four kinds of longitudinal surveys. All collect data multiple times, but they collect it from different samples and groups. To illustrate the differences among the four types, consider how each could be used to collect information about California female valedictorians' attitudes toward female/male equality.

1. A *trend survey* would sample from the general population of female valedictorians in California. To provide information about the trend of the valedictorians' attitudes, the researcher would annually select a sample of the female valedictorians in the current year. Each succeeding annual sample would be made up of that year's female valedictorians. A trend survey focuses on different groups and different samples over time.

2. A *cohort survey* would select a specific population of female California valedictorians, such as the valedictorians in 1997. Over time, the researcher would select samples of the 1997 valedictorians. Each sample would be composed of different valedictorians, but all samples would be selected only from the 1997 valedictorian group. The members would stay the same, but different groups of them would be sampled over time. A cohort survey focuses on the same group but different samples from that group over time.

3. A *panel survey* would select a single sample of valedictorians from a particular year and study the attitudes of that sample over time. If the researcher were conducting a 3-year panel study, the same individuals would respond in each of the 3 years of the study. A panel survey focuses on the same group and the same sample over time. A frequent

problem with panel studies and, to a lesser degree, cohort studies is loss of individuals from the study because of their relocation, name change, lack of interest, or death. This is especially problematic the longer the longitudinal survey continues.

4. A *follow-up survey* is similar to a panel study, except that it is undertaken after the panel study is completed and seeks to examine subsequent development or change in a group after some period of time. For example, a researcher who wished to study female valedictorians in California a number of years after the original study was concluded would find individuals from the study and survey them to examine changes in their attitudes. Follow-up studies are often conducted by educational institutions for the purpose of internal or external evaluation of their instructional program. Colleges and accreditation agencies, for example, typically require systematic follow-up of their graduates. Such efforts seek objective information on the current status of former students (Such as, Are you presently employed?) as well as attitudinal and opinion data concerning graduates' perceptions of the adequacy of their education. If a majority of graduates indicated that the career counseling they received at old Alma Mater University was poor, this would suggest an area for improvement.

Longitudinal surveys are useful for studying the dynamics of a topic or issue over time. Suppose, for example, you were interested in studying the development of abstract thinking in elementary school students in grades 1 to 4. If you used a cross-sectional approach, you could study samples of children at each of the four grade levels, first graders to fourth graders. The children studied at one grade level would be different children from those studied at another grade level. If you used a longitudinal approach, such as a panel study, you could select a sample of first graders and study the development of their abstract thinking as they progressed from grade to grade; the children who were studied at the fourth-grade level would be the same children who were studied in the first, second, and third grades. In longitudinal studies, samples tend to shrink as time goes by; keeping track of participants over time can be difficult, as can maintaining their participation in the study. An advantage of the longitudinal method is that this latter concern about comparability is not a problem in that the same group is involved at each level. A major disadvantage of the longitudinal method is that an extended commitment must be made by the researcher, the subjects, and all others involved.

:: CONDUCTING SELF-REPORT RESEARCH

Self-report research requires the collection of standardized, quantifiable information from all members of a population or sample. To obtain comparable data from all participants, the researcher must ask them each the same questions. A written collection of self-report questions to be answered by a selected group of research participants is called a **questionnaire.** Many of the types of tests described in Chapter 5 are used in survey self-report research studies and could also be classified as questionnaires. An **interview** is an oral, in-person question-and-answer session between a researcher and an individual respondent. The procedures for conducting both questionnaire and interview studies are described in the following sections.

Conducting a Questionnaire Study

Most criticisms of questionnaires are related not to their use but to their misuse. Carelessly and incompetently constructed questionnaires have unfortunately been administered and distributed too often. Development of a sound questionnaire requires both skill and time. The use of a paper-and-pencil questionnaire has some definite advantages over other methods of collecting data. In comparison to an interview, for example, a questionnaire requires less time, is less expensive, and permits collection of data from a much larger sample.

Questionnaires may be individually administered to each respondent, but for efficiency they are usually mailed. Although a personally administered questionnaire has some of the same advantages as an interview, such as the opportunity to establish rapport with respondents and explain unclear items, it also has some drawbacks. It is very time-consuming, especially if the number of respondents is large and geographically scattered. An often-used alternative to the mailed questionnaire is the telephone interview. The steps in conducting a questionnaire study are essentially the same as for other types of research, although data collection involves some unique considerations.

Stating the Problem

The problem or topic studied and the contents of the questionnaire must be of sufficient significance both to motivate potential respondents to respond and to justify the research effort in the first place. Questionnaires dealing with trivial issues, such as the color of pencils preferred by fifth graders or the make of car favored by teachers, usually end up in potential respondents' circular file. In defining the topic, the researcher should set specific objectives indicating the kind of information needed. Specific aspects of the topic, as well as the kind of questions to be formulated, should be described.

Suppose a school superintendent wants to know how high school teachers perceive their schools. He wants to conduct a study to help identify areas in the high schools that might be improved. Because a survey questionnaire is made up of a number of questions related to the research topic, it would be useful for the superintendent to identify important aspects of his general question. For example, he might focus the study on the following four subareas of the topic: (1) respondent demographics (to compare the perceptions of males and females, experienced and new teachers, and teachers in different departments), (2) teacher perceptions of the quality of teaching, (3) teacher perceptions of available educational resources, and (4) teacher perceptions of the school curriculum. Breaking the general topic into a few main areas helps to focus the survey and aid decision making in succeeding steps in the research sequence.

Selecting Participants

Survey participants should be selected using an appropriate sampling technique. Although simple random and stratified random sampling are most commonly used in survey research, cluster, systematic, and nonrandom samples are also used. (Refresh your memory about these types of samples by reviewing Chapter 4.) In some rare cases, when the population is small, the entire group may make up the sample. The selected research participants must be able to provide the desired information sought and be willing to provide it to the researcher. Individuals who possess the desired information but are not sufficiently interested, or for whom the topic under study has little meaning, are not likely to respond. It is sometimes worth the effort to do a preliminary check of a few potential respondents to determine their receptivity.

The target population for our superintendent's study is likely to be all high school teachers in the state. Such a group is too large a group to reasonably survey, so the superintendent must select participants from the accessible population. In this case, the likely accessible population would be high school teachers from the schools in the superintendent's district. A sample, perhaps stratified by gender and department, would be randomly selected and asked to complete the questionnaire.

Sometimes it is useful to send the questionnaire to a person of authority, rather than directly to the person with the desired information. If a person's boss passes along a questionnaire and asks the person to complete and return it, that person may be more likely to do so than if the researcher asked. This strategy is a good idea only if the boss cares enough to pass the questionnaire along and if the boss's request will not influence the respondent's responses.

Constructing the Questionnaire

As a general guideline, the questionnaire should be attractive, brief, and easy to respond to. Respondents are turned off by sloppy, crowded, misspelled, and lengthy questionnaires, especially ones that require long written responses to each question. Turning people off is certainly not the way to get them to respond. To meet this guideline, you must carefully plan both the content and the format of the questionnaire. No item should be included that does not directly relate to the topic of the study; and structured, selection-type items should be used if at all possible. It is easier to respond by circling a letter or word than writing out a lengthy response. Identifying subareas of the research topic can greatly help in developing the questionnaire. For example, the four areas our superintendent identified could make up the four sections of a questionnaire.

An important decision faced by all descriptive researchers is, what method should I use to collect data? There are five approaches: mail, e-mail, telephone, personal administration, and interview. Each approach has its advantages and disadvantages. The bulk of educational surveys rely on mailed questionnaires. Although they are inexpensive, easily standardized, confidential, and easy to score, they are also subject to low response rates and suffer from the researcher's inability to ask probing or follow-up questions. Sending questionnaires by e-mail has recently become a popular alternative. In addition to being speedy and efficient, this method shares both the advantages and disadvantages of mail questionnaires, with the additional disadvantage that not all potential respondents have e-mail service. Telephone surveys tend to have high response rates and allow data to be collected fairly quickly, but they require lists of target phone numbers and administrator training. Personal administration of a prepared questionnaire is efficient if participants are closely situated, but it is time-consuming and also requires administrator training. Personal interviews allow rich, more complete responses, but they have the least standardization and take the longest to administer. Table 6.1 summarizes the strengths and weaknesses of the five methods.

Many types of items are commonly used in questionnaires, including scaled items (Likert and semantic differential), ranked items ("Rank the following activities in order of their importance"), checklist items ("Check all of the following that characterize your principal"),

TABLE 6.1	Comparison of survey data collection methods	
Method	**Advantages**	**Disadvantages**
Mail	Inexpensive Can be confidential or anonymous Easy to score most items Standardized items and procedures	Response rate may be small Cannot probe, explain, or follow up items Limited to respondents who can read Possibility of response sets
E-mail	Speedy results Easy to target respondents Other advantages same as mail	Not everyone has e-mail Possibility of multiple replies from single participant Other disadvantages same as mail
Telephone	High response rates Quick data collection Can reach a range of locations and respondents	Requires phone number lists Difficult to get in-depth data Administrators must be trained
Personal administration	Efficient when respondents are closely situated	Time-consuming Administrators must be trained
Interview	Can probe, follow up, and explain questions Usually high return rate May be recorded for later transcription and analysis Flexibility of use	Time-consuming No anonymity Possible interviewer bias Complex scoring of unstructured items Administrators must be trained

and free response items ("Write in your own words the main reasons you became a teacher"). These item types are all self-report measures. Most surveys consist of structured items. A **structured item** (also called a *closed-ended item*) is any item that asks the respondent to choose among the provided response options (e.g., by circling a letter, checking a list, or numbering preferences).

Questionnaires rarely contain large numbers of free response items, but they may include one or two to give respondents the opportunity to add information not tapped by the closed-ended items. An **unstructured item** format, in which the respondent has complete freedom of response (questions are posed and the respondent must construct a response), is sometimes defended on the grounds that it permits greater depth of response and insight into the reasons for responses. Although this may be true, and unstructured items are simpler to construct, their disadvantages generally outweigh their advantages. Heavy reliance on free response items creates several problems for the researcher: Many respondents won't take the time to respond to free response items or will give unclear or useless responses, and scoring such items is more difficult and time-consuming than scoring closed-ended items. For certain topics or purposes, some unstructured items may be necessary. In general, however, structured items are preferred.

Consider our superintendent, who wishes to conduct a survey to identify areas in high schools that could be improved. He is interested in four areas: the demographics of high school teachers and teachers' perceptions of teaching quality, educational resources, and school curriculum. He might develop questionnaire items like those shown in Figure 6.1. Each group of items relates to one of the superintendent's areas of interest. Note that these items are examples and that the full questionnaire would likely have more items (and would

---

FIGURE 6.1   Sample questionnaire items in a survey of high school teachers

DEMOGRAPHIC INFORMATION

For each of the following items, put an X beside the choice that best describes you.
1. Gender: Male ___ Female ___
2. Total years teaching: 1–5 ___ 6–10 ___ 11–15 ___ 16–20 ___ 21–25 ___ more than 25 ___
3. Department (please list) _____

CHECKLIST

Below is a list of educational resources. Put a check in front of each resource you think is adequately available in your school.
4. ___ up-to-date textbooks
5. ___ VCRs
6. ___ classroom computers
7. ___ games
8. ___ trade books

LIKERT

Following are a number of statements describing a school's curriculum. Read each statement and circle whether you strongly agree (SA), agree (A), are uncertain (U), disagree (D), or strongly disagree (SD) that it describes your school.
In my school the curriculum:

9. is up to date	SA	A	U	D	SD
10. emphasizes outcomes more complex than memory	SA	A	U	D	SD
11. is familiar to all teachers	SA	A	U	D	SD
12. is followed by most teachers	SA	A	U	D	SD
13. can be adapted to meet student needs	SA	A	U	D	SD

FREE RESPONSE

14. Circle how you would rate the quality of teaching in your school:
    very good   good   fair   poor
15. Write a brief explanation of why you feel as you do about the quality of teaching in your school.
16. Please make any additional comments you have about this topic.

not have the headings in the figure). It is also desirable to include an open-ended question that asks, "Do you have any additional comments or information you would like to share?"

In addition to the suggestions just provided, the following guidelines should help you as you construct your questionnaire:

- *Include only items that relate to the objectives of the study.*
- *Collect demographic information about the sample if you plan to make comparisons between different subgroups.*
- *Focus each question on a single concept.*

Consider this item:

> Although labor unions are desirable in most fields, they have no place in the teaching profession. Agree or disagree?

The researcher is really asking two questions: Do you agree or disagree that labor unions are desirable, and do you agree or disagree that there should be no teachers' unions? This creates a problem for both respondent and researcher. If respondents agree with one part of the item but disagree with the other, how should they respond? Also, if a respondent selects "agree," can the researcher assume that means agreement to both statements or to only one—and which one?

- *Define or explain ambiguous terms.* Any term or concept that might mean different things to different people should be defined or restated. What does *usually* or *several* mean? Be specific! Do not ask, "Do you spend a lot of time each week preparing for your classes?" because one teacher might consider one hour per day "a lot," whereas another might consider one hour per week "a lot." Instead, ask, "How many hours per week do you spend preparing for your classes?" or

> How much time do you spend per week preparing for your classes?
>
> a. less than 30 minutes
> b. between 30 minutes and an hour
> c. between 1 and 3 hours
> d. between 3 and 5 hours
> e. more than 5 hours

Underlining (in a typed questionnaire) or italicizing (in a printed one) key phrases may also help to clarify questions.

- *Include a point of reference to guide respondents in answering questions.* This suggestion is similar to the last, in that it is a way of soliciting specific answers. If you were interested in not only how many hours were actually spent in preparation but also in teachers' perceptions concerning that time, you would not ask, "Do you think you spend a lot of time preparing for classes?" Instead, you would ask, "Compared to other teachers in your department, do you think you spend a lot of time preparing for your classes?" If you don't provide a point of reference, different respondents will use different points, thereby making responses more difficult to interpret.
- *Avoid leading questions, which suggest that one response may be more appropriate than another.* Don't use items that begin, "Don't you agree with the experts that . . . " or "Would you agree with most people that. . . . "
- *Avoid touchy questions to which the respondent might not reply honestly or at all.* For example, asking teachers if they set high standards for achievement is like asking parents if they love their children; no matter what the truth is, the answer is going to be "of course!"
- *Don't ask a question that assumes a fact not necessarily true.* Unwarranted assumptions may be subtle and difficult to spot. For example, a questionnaire item sent to high school foreign language teachers in a state asked, "How many hours per week do you use your

foreign language laboratory?" This question assumed that all the high schools in the state had a foreign language lab. A researcher could instead ask, "Does your school have a language lab?" and "If so, how many hours per week it is used?"

Remember that the questionnaire must stand on its own. In most cases, you will not be present to explain to respondents what you meant by a particular word or item. That is why it is important to make your questions clear and unambiguous.

After you have constructed the questionnaire items, you must place them in the questionnaire and write directions for respondents. Even though respondents will receive a cover letter (described shortly) along with the questionnaire, it is good practice to include a brief statement describing the study and its purpose at the top of the questionnaire. To structure the questionnaire, ask general items first and then move to more specific items. Start with a few interesting and nonthreatening items. If possible—and it often is not—put similar item types together. Provide information about how to respond to items; typical directions include the following:

Select the choice that you most agree with.
Circle the letter of choice.
Rank the choices from 1 to 5, where 1 is the most desirable and 5 the least.
Darken your choice on the answer sheet provided. Please use a pencil to record your choices.

Standardized directions promote standardized, comparable responses. If an item format is unusual, you can provide a completed example. Don't jam items together; leave sufficient space whenever respondents must write an answer. If possible, keep an item and its response options together on a page. Number pages and items to help with organizing your data for analysis. Don't put very important questions at the end; respondents often do not finish questionnaires. Figure 6.2 summarizes important aspects of constructing a questionnaire.

Preparing the Cover Letter

Every mailed questionnaire must be accompanied by a cover letter that explains what is being asked of the respondent and why. The letter should be brief, neat and, if at all possible, addressed specifically to a specific person ("Dear Dr. Jekyll," not "Dear Sir"). Mercifully, there are database management computer programs that can assist you with the chore of personalizing your letters. However, recognize that it is not always possible to identify each potential respondent by name. The cover letter should explain the purpose of the study, emphasizing its importance and significance. Give the respondent a good reason for cooperating—the fact that you need the data for your thesis or dissertation is *not* a good reason. Good reasons relate to how the data gathered will help the respondent and the field in general. If at all possible, the letter should state a commitment to share the results of the study when completed. Include a mailing address, phone number, or e-mail address where you can be reached in case potential

---

FIGURE 6.2   Guidelines for constructing a questionnaire

- Make the questionnaire attractive and brief.
- Know what information you need and why.
- Include only items that relate to your study's objectives.
- Collect demographic information, if needed.
- Focus items on a single topic or idea.
- Define or explain ambiguous terms.
- Word questions as clearly as possible.
- Avoid leading questions.

- Avoid or carefully word items that are potentially controversial or embarrassing.
- Organize items from general to specific.
- Use examples if item format is unusual.
- If using open-ended items, leave sufficient space for respondents to write their responses.
- Try to keep items and response options together.
- Subject items to a pretest review of the questionnaire.

respondents want to ask questions. In some cases, you may want to contact potential research participants before sending out the questionnaire and cover letter. A brief letter or phone call can alert people that they will be receiving a request for participation in a study. You should briefly note the nature of the study, explain who you and fellow researchers are, and give an indication of when the formal request is likely to arrive.

You can add credibility to your study by obtaining the endorsement of an organization, institution, group, or administrator that the respondent is likely to know or recognize. For example, if you are seeking principals as respondents, you should try to get a principals' professional organization or the state's chief school officer to endorse your study. If you are seeking parents as respondents, then school principals or school committees would be helpful endorsers. Ideally, you would like to have endorsers cosign the cover letter or at least agree to let you mention their support in the letter. If the planned respondents are very heterogeneous, or have no identifiable affiliation in common, you might make a general appeal to professionalism.

If the survey questions are at all threatening (for example, if items deal with gender or attitudes toward colleagues or the local administrators), anonymity or confidentiality of responses must be assured. If the responses are anonymous, that means that no one, including the researcher, knows who completed a given questionnaire. If they are confidential, that means that the researcher knows who completed each survey but promises not to divulge that information. We highly recommend that one of these approaches be used and explained in the cover letter. The promise of anonymity or confidentiality will increase the truthfuless of responses as well as the percentage of returns. One way to promise anonymity and still be able to utilize follow-up efforts with nonrespondents is to include a preaddressed stamped postcard with the questionnaire. People can be asked to sign their name on the postcard and mail it separately from the questionnaire. The postcards tell the researcher who has and has not responded, but they don't reveal who completed each of the separately mailed questionnaires. If responses are anonymous and the researcher wishes to make subgroup comparisons later, specific demographic information should be requested in the questionnaire.

You should give respondents a specific deadline date by which to return the completed questionnaire. Choose a date that will give participants enough time to respond but discourage procrastination; 2 to 3 weeks will usually be sufficient. Sign individually each letter you send. When many questionnaires are to be sent, individually signing each letter will admittedly take more time than making copies of one signed letter, but it adds a personal touch that might make a difference in a potential respondent's decision to comply or not comply. Finally, the act of responding should be made as painless as possible. Include a stamped, addressed, return envelope; if you do not, your letter and questionnaire will very likely be placed into the circular file along with the mail addressed to "Occupant"! Figure 6.3 shows an example of a cover letter.

Pretesting the Questionnaire

Before distributing the questionnaire to participants, try it out in a pilot study. The cover letter can be pilot tested at the same time. Few things are more disconcerting and injurious to a survey than sending out a questionnaire only to discover that participants didn't understand the directions or many of the questions. Pretesting the questionnaire provides information about deficiencies and suggestions for improvement. Having three or four individuals read the cover letter and complete the questionnaire will help identify problems. Choose individuals who are thoughtful and critical, as well as similar to the research participants. That is, if research participants are superintendents, then individuals critiquing the cover letter and questionnaire should be superintendents. Encourage your pretest group to make comments and state suggestions concerning the survey directions, recording procedures, and specific items. They should note issues of both commission and omission. For example, if they feel that certain important questions have been left out or that some existing topics are not relevant, they

FIGURE 6.3

Sample cover letter

SCHOOL OF EDUCATION

BOSTON COLLEGE

January 17, 2005

Mr. Dennis Yacubian
Vice-Principal
Westside High School
Westside, MA 00001

Dear Mr. Yacubian,

The Department of Measurement and Evaluation at Boston College is interested in determining the types of testing, evaluation, research, and statistical needs high school administrators in Massachusetts have. Our intent is to develop a master's level program that provides graduates who can meet the methodological needs of high school administrators. The enclosed questionnaire is designed to obtain information about your needs in the areas of testing, evaluation, research, and statistics. Your responses will be anonymous and seriously considered in developing the planned program. We will also provide you a summary of the results of the survey so that you can examine the responses of other high school administrators. This study has been approved by the university's Human Subjects Review Committee.

We would appreciate your completion of the questionnaire by January 31. We have provided a stamped, addressed envelope for you to use in returning the questionnaire. You do not need to put your name on the questionnaire, but we request that you sign your name on the enclosed postcard and mail it separately from the questionnaire. That way we will know you have replied and will not have to bother you with follow-up letters.

We realize that your schedule is busy and your time is valuable. However, we hope that the 15 minutes it will take you to complete the questionnaire will help lead to a program that will provide a useful service to school administrators.

Thank you in advance for your participation. If you have questions about the study, you can contact me at 555-555-4444.

Yours truly,

James Jones
Department Chair

---

should note this. Having reviewers examine the completeness of the questionnaire is one way to determine its content validity. All feedback provided should be carefully studied and considered. The end product of the pretest will be a revised instrument and cover letter ready to be mailed to the already selected research participants.

Conducting Follow-up Activities

Not everyone to whom you send a questionnaire is going to return it (what an understatement!). Some recipients will have no intention of completing it; others mean to but put it off so long that they either forget it or lose it. It is mainly for this latter group that follow-up activities are conducted. The higher your percentage of returned questionnaires, the better your data. Although you should not expect a 100% response rate, you should not be satisfied with whatever you get after your first mailing. Given all the work you have already done, it makes no sense to end up with a study of limited value because of low returns when some additional effort on your part can make a big difference.

An initial follow-up strategy is to simply send out a reminder postcard. Remember, if you decide on anonymity in your survey, you will have to send out reminders and questionnaires to all participants, unless you use some procedure (such as the postcard system previously mentioned) that allows you to know who has responded, but not what their responses were. If responses are confidential but not anonymous, you can mail cards only to those who have not responded. Receiving a reminder will prompt those who meant to fill out the questionnaire but put it off and have not yet lost it! Include a statement like the ones used by finance companies: "If you have already responded, please disregard this reminder. Thank you for your cooperation."

Full-scale follow-up activities are usually begun shortly after the cover letter deadline for responding has passed. A second questionnaire, new cover letter, and another stamped envelope can be sent to each person who has not responded. The new letter might suggest that you know the recipient meant to respond but may have misplaced the questionnaire. Perhaps the questionnaire was never received. In other words, do not scold your potential respondents; provide them with an acceptable reason for their nonresponse. Repeat the significance and purpose of the study, and reemphasize the importance of their input. The letter should suggest subtly that many others are responding, thus implying that their peers have found the study to be important and so should they.

If the second mailing does not result in an overall acceptable percentage of return, be creative. Magazine subscription agencies have developed follow-up procedures to a science and have become very creative, using gentle reminders and "sensational one-time-only offers," as well as phone calls from sweet-voiced representatives suggesting that your mail was apparently not getting through since you failed to renew your subscription. The point is that phone calls, if feasible, may be used with any other method of written, verbal, or personal communication that might induce additional participants to respond. They may grow to admire your persistence!

If your topic is of interest, your questionnaire well constructed, and your cover letter well written, you should get at least an adequate response rate. Research suggests that first mailings will typically result in a 30% to 50% return rate, and a second mailing will increase the percentage by about 20%; mailings beyond a second are generally not cost-effective, in that they each increase the percentage by about 10% or less. After a second mailing, it is usually better to use other approaches to obtain an acceptable percentage of returns.

Dealing With Nonresponse

Despite all your efforts and follow-ups, you may find yourself with an overall response rate of 60%. This raises concern about the generalizability of results, because you do not know how well the 60% responding represent the population from which the sample was originally selected or from the sample actually surveyed. If you knew that those responding were quite similar to the total sample, there would be no problem with generalizablilty; but you do not know that. Those who responded may be different in some systematic way from the nonrespondents. After all, they chose not to reply, which already makes them different. They may be better educated, feel more strongly about the issue, or be more concerned about other issues than those responding.

The usual approach to dealing with such nonrespondents is to try to determine if they are different from respondents in some systematic way. This can be done by randomly selecting a small sample of nonrespondents and interviewing them, either in person or by phone. This allows you to not only obtain responses to questionnaire items but also gather demographic information to determine if nonrespondents are similar to respondents. If responses are essentially the same for the two groups, you may assume that the response group is representative of the whole sample and that the results are generalizable. If the groups are significantly different, the generalizability across both groups is not present and must be discussed in the research report. Information describing the return rate and its impact on study interpretations should be provided in the final report.

In addition to nonresponse to the questionnaire in general, you may also encounter non-response to individual items in the questionnaire. If respondents do not understand an item or find it offensive in some way, they may not respond to it. Nonresponse to the entire questionnaire is usually more frequent and more critical than individual item nonresponse. The best defense for item nonresponse is careful examination of the questionnaire during your pretest. It is at that time that problems with items are most likely to show up. If you follow the item-writing suggestions in Figure 6.2 and subject the questionnaire to rigorous examination, item nonresponses will be few and will pose no problem in analysis.

Tabulating Questionnaire Responses

The easiest way to tabulate questionnaire responses is to have participants mark responses to closed-ended questions on a scannable answer sheet. This option involves locating a scanner and possibly paying a fee to have questionnaires scanned. If scannable answer sheets are not an option, then each respondent's answers will have to be entered one by one into a computer spreadsheet (e.g., Excel or Lotus) or a statistical program (e.g., SPSS or SAS). Remember this when designing your questionnaire. Make sure that the format is easy to follow and allows respondents to mark answers clearly. This will ensure that you can enter data quickly, without having to search for information.

If your questionnaire contains open-ended questions, you will need to code answers according to patterns in the responses provided. With a qualitative software program, you can examine your textual data, code it, and generate information regarding the frequency and nature of various codes. Many qualitative software programs also allow the researcher to export coded qualitative data into statistical programs, where advanced statistical analyses can be performed.

Analyzing Results

When presenting the results of a questionnaire study, you should include the response rate for each item as well as the total sample size and the overall percentage of returns, since not all respondents will answer all questions. The simplest way to present the results is to indicate the percentage of respondents who selected each alternative for each item, as in this example: "On Item 4 dealing with possession of a master's degree, 50% said yes, 30% said no, and 20% said they were working on one." In addition to simply determining choices, you can investigate comparisons in your data by examining the responses of different subgroups in the sample. For example, in the previous study it might be determined that 80% of those reporting possession of a master's degree expressed favorable attitudes toward personalized instruction, whereas only 40% of those reporting lack of a master's degree expressed a favorable attitude. Thus, possible explanations for certain attitudes and behaviors can be explored by identifying factors that seem to be related to certain responses. As note earlier, such comparison can be made only if demographic information about the respondents is collected on the questionnaire.

Although item-by-item descriptions are a simple way to report the results of a survey, they can produce an overload of information that is difficult to absorb and condense. A better way to report is to group items into clusters that address the same issue and develop total scores across an item cluster. For example, recall the four issues of concern to our school superintendent and the item types chosen for his questionnaire (Figure 6.1). Instead of reporting the response to each Likert or checklist item separately, the scores for each item type can be summed into a total score. For example, if the Likert items were scored from 5 (SA) to 1 (SD), a score for each item could be obtained and the scores summed across the Likert items. The total scores or their average could be reported, and demographic comparisons could be made by presenting the average score of each subgroup of interest (for instance, males and females). Not only does developing and analyzing clusters of items related to the same issue make a report of survey results more meaningful, it also improves the reliability of the scores themselves—in general, the more items, the higher the reliability.

Conducting an Interview Study

Conducting a question-and-answer session with each member of a sample—conducting an interview—has a number of unique advantages and disadvantages. An interview can produce in-depth data not possible with a questionnaire; on the other hand, it is expensive and time-consuming. The interview is most appropriate for asking questions that cannot effectively be structured into a multiple-choice format, such as questions of a personal nature or those that require lengthy responses. In contrast to the questionnaire, the interview is flexible; the interviewer can adapt the questions to fit each participant. An interviewer doesn't ask just anything that pops into mind, however, an effective interviewer follows a written protocol that has been prepared in advance (you'll learn more about that shortly). By establishing rapport and a trust, the interviewer can often obtain data that respondents would not give on a questionnaire. The interview may also result in more accurate and honest responses because the interviewer can explain and clarify both the purposes of the research and individual questions. Another advantage of the interview is that it allows the researcher to follow up on incomplete or unclear responses by asking additional probing questions. Reasons for particular responses can also be determined.

Direct interviewer–interviewee contact also has disadvantages. The respondent may give biased answers that are affected by her reaction to the interviewer, especially if she has not known the interviewer for very long. For example, she may become hostile or uncooperative if the interviewer reminds her of the dentist who performed five root canals on her last Wednesday! In contrast, another respondent may try hard to please the interviewer because she looks like her sister. Another disadvantage is that interviews are time-consuming and expensive, and as a consequence the number of respondents is generally a great deal fewer than the number that can be surveyed with a questionnaire. Interviewing 500 people would be a monumental task compared to mailing 500 questionnaires.

Also, the interview requires a level of skill usually beyond that of the beginning researcher. It requires not only research skills, such as knowledge of sampling and instrument development, but also a variety of communication and interpersonal relations skills.

A widely used alternative to face-to-face interviewing is telephone interviewing. The telephone interview is most useful and effective when the interview is short, specific, and not too personal and contains mainly selection-type questions. Some advantages of telephone interviews are that they are less expensive because there is no travel; they can be used to gather data from national samples; and they allow data to be collected and summarized easily in a single location. Telephone interviews also have some drawbacks. For example, it is difficult to build rapport with the interviewee; it is difficult to obtain detailed information over the telephone; interviewees are often bombarded by phone interviews and unwilling to participate. In general, telephone interviews, like face-to-face interviews, require a clear set of interview questions and training for interviewers.

The steps in conducting an interview study are basically the same as for a questionnaire study, with some unique differences. The process of selecting and defining a problem and formulating hypotheses is essentially the same. Potential respondents who possess the desired information are selected using an appropriate sampling method. An extra effort must be made to get a commitment of cooperation from selected respondents; their failure to attend interviews is more serious because the interview sample size is small to begin with. The major differences between an interview study and a questionnaire study are the nature of the instrument involved (an interview guide versus a questionnaire), the need for human relations and communication skills, the methods of recording responses, and the nature of pretest activities.

Constructing the Interview Guide

The interviewer must have a written protocol, or guide, that indicates what questions are to be asked, in what order, and how much additional prompting or probing is permitted. To obtain standardized, comparable data from each respondent, all interviews must be conducted in essentially the same manner. As with a questionnaire, each question in the interview should relate to a specific study topic. Also, as with a questionnaire, interview questions may be structured, semistructured, or unstructured. Using only structured questions defeats the purpose of an interview. Completely unstructured questions, such as "What do you think about life in general?" or "Tell me about yourself," allow absolute freedom of response but can be time-consuming and unproductive. Therefore, most interviewers use mostly semistructured questions and seek to guide respondents toward more narrow questions and issues. Sometimes it is useful to ask a structured question to focus in on a desired topic and then use semistructured questions to follow up on the structured question. For example, the question "Are you in favor of or against the death penalty?" is followed with "Why do you feel that way?" The answers to semistructured questions may help the researcher understand and explain the responses to the structured question. Thus, a combination of objectivity and depth can be obtained, and results can be tabulated as well as explained.

Many of the guidelines for constructing questionnaires apply to constructing interview guides. The interview should be reasonably brief, and questions should be worded as clearly as possible. Terms should be defined when necessary and a point of reference given when appropriate. Also, leading questions should be avoided, as should questions based on the assumption of a fact not in evidence ("Tell me, are you still stealing from the church poor box?").

Communicating During the Interview

Effective communication during the interview is critical, and interviewers should be well trained before the study begins. Getting the interview "off on the right foot" is important. Before asking the first formal question, you should spend some time establishing rapport and putting the interviewee at ease. Explain the purpose of the study, and give assurance that responses will be kept strictly confidential. Note that it is hard to provide anonymity when you are face-to-face with the respondent. As the interview proceeds, make full use of the advantages of the interview situation. You can, for example, explain the purpose of any question that is unclear to the respondent. You should also be sensitive to the reactions of the respondent and proceed accordingly. For example, if a respondent appears to be threatened by a particular line of questioning, move on to other questions and return to the threatening questions later, when perhaps the interviewee is more relaxed. Or if the person gets carried away with a question and gets "off the track," gently guide the conversation back to the appropriate topic. Above all, avoid words or actions that may make the respondent unhappy or feel threatened. Frowns and disapproving looks have no place in an interview!

Recording Responses

Responses made during an interview can be recorded manually by the interviewer or mechanically by a recording device. If the interviewer writes the responses, space on the interview form should be provided after each question. Responses can be written during the interview or shortly after the interview is completed. Writing responses during the interview may tend to slow things down, especially if responses are at all lengthy. It also may make some respondents nervous to have someone writing down the words they say. If responses are written after the interview, the interviewer is not likely to recall every response exactly as given, especially if many questions have been asked. On the other hand, if an audiocassette recorder or video camcorder is used, the interview moves more quickly, and responses are recorded exactly as given. If a response needs clarifying, several persons can listen to or view the recordings independently and make judgments about the response. Of course, a recorder or VCR may make respondents nervous, but most will forget its presence as the interview progresses. In general, mechanical recording leads to more objective interpretations and scoring. Before a device is used, the respondent must be informed and must agree to be recorded or filmed.

Pretesting the Interview Procedure

Before the main study begins, the interview guide, procedures, and planned analysis should be tried out with a small group from the same or a very similar population to the one being studied. As with written questionnaires, feedback from a small pilot study can be used to add, remove, or revise interview questions. Insights into better ways to handle certain questions can also be acquired. Finally, the pilot study will determine whether the resulting data can be quantified and analyzed in the manner intended. Feedback should be sought from the pilot group as well as from the interviewers. As always, a pretest is a good use of the researcher's time. (For further discussion of interviewing techniques see Chapter 17, "Ethnographic Research.")

An example of descriptive research appears at the end of this chapter. Note that the study involved a stratified random sample, a mailed questionnaire, a procedure for assuring anonymity of responses, a follow-up mailing, and telephone interviews to assess response bias (i.e., differences between mail—respondents and nonrespondents).

SUMMARY

Descriptive Research: Definition and Purpose

1. Descriptive research, or survey research, determines and describes the way things are. It involves collecting data to test hypotheses or to answer questions about people's opinions on some topic or issue.
2. A high percentage of all research studies are descriptive in nature. Surveys are used in many fields, including education, political science, sociology, and economics.

The Descriptive Research Process

3. Descriptive research is not as simple as it appears.

Classifying Descriptive Research

4. Descriptive studies are commonly classified according to how data are collected, through self-report or observation. The most often used type of self-report research, survey research, uses questionnaires or interviews to collect data.
5. Surveys can be categorized as cross-sectional or longitudinal. Cross-sectional studies collect data at one point in time, whereas longitudinal studies collect data at more than one time in order to measure growth or change.

Conducting Self-Report Research

6. Self-report research requires the collection of standardized, quantifiable information from all members of a population or sample.
7. A questionnaire is written collection of self-report questions to be answered by a selected group of research participants. An interview is an oral, in-person question-and-answer session between a researcher and an individual respondent.

Conducting a Questionnaire Study

8. In comparison to an interview, a questionnaire is much more efficient in that it requires less time, is less expensive, and permits collection of data from a much larger sample.
9. Questionnaires may be administered to respondents by mail, telephone, or in person. Mailing questionnaires is usually the most efficient.

Stating the Problem

10. The problem under investigation, and the topic of the questionnaire, must be of sufficient significance to motivate subjects to respond.
11. The problem must be defined in terms of specific objectives or subtopics concerning the kind of information needed; questions must be formulated

and every item on the questionnaire should directly relate to them.

Selecting Participants

12. Participants should be selected using an appropriate sampling technique (or an entire population may be used), and identified participants must be persons who have the desired information and are willing to give it.

Constructing the Questionnaire

13. As a general guideline, the questionnaire should be attractive, brief, and easy to respond to. No item should be included that does not directly relate to the objectives of the study.
14. Structured, or closed-ended, items should be used if at all possible. A structured item provides a list of alternative responses from which the respondent selects. In addition to facilitating responses, structured items also facilitate data analysis; scoring is very objective and efficient.
15. Common structured items used in questionnaires are scaled items (Likert and semantic differential), ranked items, and checklists.
16. In an unstructured item format, respondents have complete freedom of response; questions are asked but respondents must construct their own answers. Unstructured items permit greater depth of response that may permit insight into the reasons for responses, but they often are difficult to analyze and interpret.
17. Often it is useful to obtain demographic information about the participants (e.g., gender, occupation, years teaching) to make comparisons of the respondents in different subgroups.
18. The number one rule in item construction is that each question should focus on a single concept and be worded as clearly as possible. Any term or concept that might mean different things to different people should be defined.
19. Avoid leading questions, questions that assume a fact not necessarily in evidence, and questions that do not indicate a point of reference.

Preparing the Cover Letter

20. Every mailed questionnaire must be accompanied by a cover letter that explains what is being asked of the respondent and why. The cover letter should be brief, neat, and addressed to a specific individual, if possible.

21. The letter should explain the purpose of the study, emphasizing its importance and significance, and give the respondent a good reason for cooperating.
22. It usually helps to obtain the endorsement of an organization, institution, group, or administrator with which the respondent is associated or views with respect (such as a professional organization).
23. It should be made clear whether anonymity or confidentiality of responses is assured.
24. A specific deadline date by which the completed questionnaire is to be returned should be given. Include a stamped, addressed envelope for the respondents to return their surveys.

Pretesting the Questionnaire

25. The questionnaire and cover letter should be tried out in a field test using a few respondents who are similar to those who will respond to the questionnaire.
26. Pretesting the questionnaire yields data concerning instrument deficiencies as well as suggestions for improvement. Omissions or unclear or irrelevant items should be revised.
27. A too-often-neglected procedure is validation of the questionnaire to determine if it measures what it was developed to measure.

Conducting Follow-up Actvities

28. If your percentage of returns is low, the validity of your conclusions may be weak. An initial follow-up strategy is to simply send out a reminder postcard.
29. Full-scale follow-up activities are usually begun shortly after the deadline for responding has passed.

Dealing With Nonresponse

30. If your total response rate is low, you may have a problem with the generalizability of your results. You should try to determine if the persons who did not respond are similar to the persons who did respond. This can be done by randomly selecting a small subsample of nonrespondents and interviewing them, either in person or by phone.

Analyzing Results

31. The simplest way to present the results is to indicate the percentage of respondents who selected each alternative for each item. However, analyzing summed item clusters—groups of items focused on the same issue—is more meaningful and reliable.
32. Relationships between variables can be investigated by comparing the summed cluster scores of different subgroups (e.g., male–female).

Conducting an Interview Study

33. When well conducted, an interview can produce in-depth data not possible with a questionnaire; but it is expensive and time-consuming and generally involves smaller samples.

Constructing the Interview Guide

34. The interviewer must have a protocol, a written guide that indicates what questions are to be asked, in what order, and what additional prompting or probing is permitted. To obtain standardized, comparable data from each subject, all interviews must be conducted in essentially the same manner.

35. As with a questionnaire, each question in the interview should relate to a specific study objective. Most interviews use a semistructured approach, first asking structured questions and following them up with explanatory, open-ended questions.

36. Many of the guidelines for constructing a questionnaire apply to constructing interview guides.

Communicating During the Interview

37. Before the first formal question is asked, some time should be spent establishing rapport and putting the interviewee at ease. The interviewer should also be sensitive to the reactions of the respondent and proceed accordingly.

Recording Responses

38. Responses made during an interview can be recorded manually by the interviewer or mechanically by a recording device. In general, mechanical recording is more objective and efficient. Respondents must both be aware of and consent to being recorded or filmed.

Pretesting the Interview Procedure

39. Feedback from a small pilot study can be used to revise questions in the interview guide. Insights into better ways to handle certain questions can also be acquired.

40. The pilot study will determine whether the resulting data can be quantified and analyzed in the manner intended.

Now go to the Companion Website at **www.prenhall.com/gay** to assess your understanding of chapter content with Practice Quiz, apply comprehension in Applying What You Know, broaden your knowledge about research in Web Links, and expand your research skills in Evaluating Articles, Analyzing Qualitative Data, Analyzing Quantitative Data, and Research Tools and Tips.

READING INSTRUCTION:
PERCEPTIONS OF ELEMENTARY SCHOOL PRINCIPALS

JOHN JACOBSON
The University of Texas at Arlington

D. RAY REUTZEL
Brigham Young University

PAUL M. HOLLINGSWORTH
Brigham Young University

ABSTRACT   A stratified random sample of 1,244 U.S. elementary public school principals was surveyed to determine perceptions of their understanding of current issues in elementary reading instruction and the information sources that they use to learn about current issues in reading. The principals reported four major unresolved reading issues: (a) whole language versus basal approaches; (b) assessment of students' reading progress; (c) the use of tradebooks in place of basals; and (d) ability grouping students for reading instruction. Principals' priority ranking of the four most important unresolved reading issues were (a) whole language versus basal approaches; (b) effective alternative assessment of students' reading progress; (c) alternatives to ability grouping students for reading instruction; and (d) the necessity of phonics instruction as a prerequisite to formal reading instruction. The most frequently consulted reading information sources used by elementary school principals within the past 12 months included (a) professional education magazines, (b) personal contacts with specialists and colleagues, and (c) newspapers. Although college classes were the least used information resource of U.S. elementary school principals within the past 12 months, college courses in reading education rated high in utility along with personal contacts with reading specialists. The study concluded that U.S. elementary school principals report awareness of the important reading issues of the day, but that they may need readily accessible and practical information to significantly impact implementation of the current innovations in reading education.

No other area of the curriculum receives as much attention and generates as much debate as does reading instruction. For many years, research and practice have indicated that the success or failure of a school's reading program depends largely upon the quality of school principals' knowledge of and involvement in the school reading program (Ellis, 1986; McNinch & Richmond, 1983; McWilliams, 1981; Weber, 1971). One may conclude, then, that it is important for elementary principals to be informed, active participants in the national conversation about reading instructional issues. It is also an ipso facto conclusion that the quality of school principals' instructional leadership in school reading programs is directly linked to the quality of their knowledge about reading instruction (Barnard & Hetzel, 1982; Kean, Summers, Raivetz, & Tarber, 1979; McNinch & Richmond, 1983; Nufrio, 1987; Rausch & Sanacore, 1984). When principals lack necessary understanding of reading instruction, they tend to shun or delegate responsibility to others for the school reading program (Nufrio). Even worse, some researchers have determined that principals who lack sufficient knowledge of reading instruction tend to resort to misguided means for making decisions instead of grounding their decisions in reliable information and research (Roser, 1974; Zinski, 1975).

A synthesis of past and current research strongly suggests that elementary school principals should bear a major responsibility for the school reading program and have an ethical and professional obligation to be conversant in the same curriculum areas as those expected of elementary classroom teachers (Wilkerson, 1988). To do this, elementary school administrators must stay abreast of current critical reading issues to be effective instructional leaders in their own school's reading programs.

Past research related to elementary school principals' understanding of reading instruction has been based primarily on surveys of teachers' impressions of principals' reading leadership capabilities. In other related studies, elementary school administrators have been queried about their familiarity with specific reading instructional concepts, their professional reading instruction preparation, and the amount of their own classroom reading teaching experience. Some past research has determined that principals understand reading instructional concepts fairly well (Aldridge, 1973; Gehring, 1977; Panchyshyn, 1971; Shelton, Rafferty, and Rose, 1990), while other research concluded that principals' reading instructional understanding is insufficient and their preparation inadequate to assume leadership roles for elementary school reading programs (Berger & Andolina, 1977; Kurth, 1985; Laffey & Kelly, 1983; Lilly, 1982; Moss, 1985; Nufrio, 1987; Rausch & Sanacore, 1984; Zinski, 1975).

Several problems have been associated with past attempts to research principals' knowledge of reading instruction. First, most past studies have been limited to a local area or single state. Few past studies go beyond state lines, and none of them have attempted to describe elementary school principals' perceived knowledge of reading instructional issues nationwide. Second, past survey studies have generally had marginally acceptable return rates, and no checks for response bias by comparing responders with nonresponders were made, thus severely limiting the generalizability of their conclusions.

Address correspondence to Paul M. Hollingsworth, Brigham University, Department of Elementary Education, 215 McKay Building, Provo, UT 84602.

An exhaustive search of the extant literature indicated that no national research study of principals' perceived knowledge of current critical issues in reading education has been conducted to date. Thus, little is known about the state of contemporary elementary school administrators' perceptions of current, critical issues in reading education. Furthermore, no research data are available on how these important leaders of school reading programs commonly access information regarding current issues in reading education. Thus, the purpose of this study focused on three research questions: (a) What do practicing elementary principals perceive are the critical and unresolved issues in reading education? (b) What level of understanding do practicing elementary principals perceive that they have of each issue? (c) What sources do practicing elementary principals use and find helpful to inform themselves about current issues in reading education?

METHOD

Survey Instrument

A survey questionnaire consisting of several sections was constructed (see Appendix A). The first section requested the following standard demographic information from the elementary school principals surveyed: (a) school size and type (I–299, 300–599, or 600 or more students, and Grades K–3, K–6, etc.), (b) years of experience as a principal and educator, (c) state, and (d) type of reading approaches used in their schools. The second section of the survey instrument included three tasks. Task 1 presented principals with 11 reading issues and asked them to indicate whether each issue was resolved, unresolved, or never had been an issue in their own minds, experiences, or schools.[1] Task 2 requested that principals rank order from 1 to 3 the top three issues that they had classified as unresolved in Task 1. Task 3 requested that the principals perform a self-rating of their understanding level of each reading issue on a 4-point forced-choice scale: (a) understand well enough to describe underlying issues and give a reasoned argument, (b) understand most of the underlying issues and give a rationale in taking a position, (c) know problem exists, but not sure of basic issue, and (d) not aware of a problem.

In the third section of the questionnaire, Task 4 listed 16 different information sources that principals could use to learn about current reading instructional issues and related research. Principals were asked to respond whether they "had" or "had not" used each of the 16 information sources within the past 12 months. Finally, Task 5 asked principals to rate the usefulness of each reading information resource that they had used on a 3-point forced-choice scale: (1) quite helpful, (2) moderately helpful, and (3) not very helpful.

Procedures

Subjects for this study were randomly selected from a computerized list obtained from Quality Educational Data (QED) of elementary public school principals in the United States during the 1989–90 school year. A total of 1,261 principals from a possible population of 41,467 were selected. The sample represented approximately 3% of the total target population. A stratified random sampling design was used to increase the precision of variable estimates (Fowler, 1988). Elementary school principals were proportionately selected from school size and school types to yield 95% confidence intervals of within ± 1% for the total population from schools with a population of 1 through 299, 300 through 599, and 600 or more. Other subject schools included those having only Grades K through 3 and K through 6 (Fowler, 1988, p. 42).

To track the responses anonymously, we included a postcard (giving the principal's name and a code indicating the size of school) in the mailing. Respondents were asked to return the questionnaire and postcard to separate return addresses. The first mailing was sent in February 1990. Four weeks later, a second mailing (with an updated cover letter and survey form) was sent to those who had not responded to the initial mailing (Heberlein & Baumgartner, 1981).

Return rates on mailed educational survey instruments are frequently in the 40 to 60% range (Could-Silva & Sadoski, 1987). An unbiased final sample of 500 responses would still yield 95% confidence intervals of within ± 3% for the entire target population of U.S. elementary school administrators surveyed (Asher, 1976). To check for response bias among responders, a trained graduate student randomly selected and interviewed over the telephone a sample of 31 (5%) of the nonrespondents (Frey, 1989). The telephone interview consisted of 16 questions selected from the mailed questionnaire (11 questions relating to reading issues and 5 questions on reading information sources used). Telephone responses were then compared with mailed responses by using chi-square analyses of each item to learn if any systematic differences existed between the answers of the two groups. If significant differences were not found between the two groups, then responses for those who returned their survey by mail may be generalizable to the larger population of elementary school principals (Borg & Gall, 1989).

RESULTS

Of the 1,261 surveys sent, 17 were returned because of inaccurate addresses. Thus, a total of 1,244 possible responses remained. Thirty percent (373) of the principals responded to the first mailing. The second mailing yielded an additional 17% or 208 principals, giving a total response rate of 47%, or 581 principals. In Table 1, we report the number of principals receiving and returning questionnaires from each state.

Because a 47% survey return rate is a figure that is minimally adequate to accurately reflect the perceptions of the target population (Dillman, 1978), a follow-up telephone interview of 5% of the nonrespondents was conducted. Responses to the telephone interview were compared with the mailed responses by constructing contingency tables from the responses of the two groups (responders and nonresponders). Chi-square statistics were calculated for each of the 16 questions. No significant differences ($p < .05$) were found for responses on 7 of 11 reading issues and 4 of 5 reading information sources. In other words, 64% of the responses between those who responded by telephone and those who responded by mail did

Table 1.
Number of Principals Receiving and Returning Questionnaires, by State

State	Sent	Returned	State	Sent	Returned	State	Sent	Returned
Alabama	21	5	Kentucky	16	8	North Dakota	4	1
Alaska	5	3	Louisiana	23	8	Ohio	62	28
Arizona	14	6	Maine	9	3	Oklahoma	21	10
Arkansas	17	6	Maryland	24	12	Oregon	21	8
California	125	38	Massachusetts	32	11	Pennsylvania	57	30
Colorado	23	12	Michigan	56	24	Rhode Island	7	3
Connecticut	18	7	Minnesota	24	12	South Carolina	17	5
Delaware	2	0	Mississippi	12	6	South Dakota	17	4
District of Columbia	3	2	Missouri	29	16	Tennessee	22	8
Florida	39	16	Montana	7	3	Texas	92	45
Georgia	27	16	Nebraska	17	7	Utah	10	7
Hawaii	4	3	Nevada	6	2	Vermont	7	2
Idaho	9	8	New Hampshire	7	4	Virginia	21	10
Illinois	53	30	New Jersey	36	13	Washington	24	12
Indiana	33	19	New Mexico	11	8	West Virginia	19	10
Iowa	25	12	New York	68	27	Wisconsin	23	11
Kansas	22	7	North Carolina	31	12	Total	1,244[a]	581

not vary significantly on the 11 reading issues. And 80% of the responses between those who responded by telephone and those who responded by mail did not vary significantly on the sources of information that principals use to remain informed about reading issues. The differences between responders and nonresponders are described in Table 2.

In addition, chi-square analyses of responders from the first and second mailings yielded no significant differences, nor were measurable differences found between respondents resulting from school type or size ($p < .05$). Overall, the similarities between the two groups were determined sufficient to enable reasonably confident generalizations to the target population to be made by using the mail responses only (deVaus, 1986). Therefore, only the mail response data are reported.

Summary of Research Questions

Research Question 1: What do practicing elementary school principals perceive are the critical and unresolved issues in reading education? Of the 11 issues surveyed, 40% or more of the principals perceived 6 issues as *unresolved:* (a) use of whole language approaches instead of basal-reader approaches (73%); (b) assessment of students' reading progress (63%); (c) use of trade books instead of basal readers (56%); (d) use of ability grouping for reading instruction (48%); (e) whether kindergarten children should pass a screening test to enter kindergarten (46%); (f) whether at-risk readers should spend increased time reading or practicing skills (40%).

Of the 11 issues, 40% or more of the principals surveyed perceived the following 6 issues as *resolved:* (a) whether reading skills should be taught in isolation or integrated with the remaining language arts (63%); (b) whether phonics should be taught as a prerequisite to formal reading instruction (48%); (c) whether at-risk

readers should spend increased time reading or practicing skills (47%); (d) whether reading instruction should be mastery based (46%); (e) use of ability grouping for reading instruction (43%); and (f) whether schools should be required to use the same reading instructional program in all grades (41%).

In 24% or more of the principals' responses, they indicated that certain reading issues had never been an issue in their perception. In order of *never been an issue,* the principals indicated (a) whether schools should be required to adopt basal reading series (26%); (b) whether tradebooks should be used in place of basal readers (25%); (c) whether kindergarten children should pass a screening test to enter kindergarten (25%); and (d) whether schools should be required to use the same reading instructional program in all grades (24%).

Of the issues that principals rated as unresolved, the top four items receiving the highest *priority ranking* in terms of their relative importance to improving reading instruction were (a) use of whole language approaches instead of basal reader approaches; (b) assessment of students' reading progress; (c) use of ability grouping for reading instruction; and (d) whether phonics should be taught as a prerequisite to formal reading instruction. Of the 11 reading issues surveyed, the principals perceived the issue of requiring schools to use the same program in all grades (e.g., the same basal series) to be the issue of least importance. Table 3 gives the rankings of the surveyed elementary school principals for each reading issue.[2]

In summary, from among the 11 reading issues surveyed, elementary school principals rated the following as the single most important *unresolved* issue: use of whole language approaches instead of basal reader approaches (73%). The issue that the principals perceived as most *resolved* was whether reading skills should be taught in isolation or integrated with the remaining language arts (63%). The *unresolved* issue that the

Table 2.
Percentage of Responders and Nonresponders Whose Answers Differed Significantly
(Chi-Square) for the Resolvedness Question About Reading

Issue	Unresolved (%)	Resolved (%)	Never an issue (%)	No response	Total
Should schools be required to adopt a basal series?					
Responders	38.9	35.1	26.0	3	581
Nonresponders	48.4	51.6	.0	0	31
Should reading instruction be mastery based?					
Responders	37.3	46.0	16.7	5	581
Nonresponders	38.7	61.3	0.0	0	31
Should children's entry into kindergarten be delayed until they perform successfully on a screening test?					
Responders	45.7	29.1	25.3	3	581
Nonresponders	45.2	48.4	6.5	0	31
Should schools be required to use the same program in all grades (e.g., same basal series)?					
Responders	35.0	41.1	23.9	7	581
Nonresponders	51.6	45.2	3.2	0	31

Note. Critical value of chi-square $= 5.99$, $df = 2$, $p < .05$.

principals ranked highest in relative importance was use of whole language approaches instead of basal reader approaches. Finally, the issue that most of the principals felt had *never been an issue* was whether schools should be required to adopt basal reading series (26%).

Research Question 2: What level of understanding do practicing elementary principals perceive they have of each issue? After the principals were asked to rank order the unresolved issues in terms of importance, we requested that they rate their understanding level for each of the 11 reading issues using a 4-point scale (1 being the highest). Therefore, the lower the mean score, the higher the principals rated their personal understanding of each reading issue. Percentages, along with means and standard deviations, are also presented in Table 3.

Principals expressed *greatest* understanding of the following four issues: (a) teaching reading skills in isolation or integrated with other language arts curriculum ($M = 1.34$); (b) grouping students by reading ability for instruction in reading ($M = 1.42$); (c) teaching phonics as a prerequisite to reading instruction ($M = 1.42$); and (d) assessing students' reading progress. Principals expressed *least* confidence in their understanding of the following three issues: (a) using tradebooks in place of basals ($M = 1.93$); (b) using mastery-based reading instruction ($M = 1.76$); and (c) requiring schools to adopt a basal series ($M = 1.72$). Though principals reported a lack of confidence in their understanding of certain reading education issues, an overall mean score of 1.59 indicated that, generally, elementary school principals believed they understood most of the underlying issues, but, according to the survey criteria, they did not feel confident enough in their understanding of reading issues to give a good rationale for taking one side or the other.

Research Question 3: What sources do practicing elementary principals use and find helpful to inform themselves about current issues in reading education? Sixteen different information sources were listed on the questionnaire. Principals were to indicate if they had used each of the information sources in the past 12 months. They were asked also to rate the helpfulness of the sources that they had used. Percentages, along with means and standard deviations, were calculated and are reported in Table 4.

The principals reported that the top four reading information sources *used most* were (a) magazines for professional educators that carry articles about reading and literacy (96.6%); (b) personal contacts with specialists in the field (95.9%); (c) newspaper articles about reading issues (93.6%); and (d) magazines or newsletters focusing on reading issues (88.6%). The five reading information sources *used least* were, in order, (a) college or university reading courses (14.3%); (b) college textbooks focused on reading (24.9%); (c) reading articles in professional handbooks (38.8%); (d) reading reports from research agencies (42.3%); and (e) journal research articles (49.3%).

Also shown in Table 4 are the principals' rankings of the relative helpfulness of each used source. To calculate means and standard deviations for the relative helpfulness rating of each information resource, we converted category responses to numeric values, using a 3-point scale. The closer each mean approximated the value of 1, the higher the mean helpfulness utility rating for the information source. From an examination of the means, the following five reading information sources were reported as *most helpful;* (a) personal contacts with specialists in the field ($M = 1.2$); (b) workshops or organized study groups focused on reading ($M = 1.3$); (c) attendance at professional

Table 3.

Classification, Rating, and Ranking of Reading Issues by U.S. Elementary School Principals

Reading issues	Unresolved (%)	Resolved (%)	Never an issue (%)	Issue ranking	Understanding of the issues[a]					
					1 (%)	2 (%)	3 (%)	4 (%)	M	SD
How should student reading progress be assessed?	65	26	9	2	60	33	5	2	1.48	.68
Should the whole language approach be used instead of the basal reader approach?	73	21	6	1	52	39	8	1	1.58	.67
Should tradebooks be used in place of basals?	56	19	25	7	43	15	31	11	1.93	1.0
Should reading skills be taught in isolation or integrated with other language arts curriculum?	23	63	14	8	76	18	3	3	1.34	.70
Should phonics be taught as a prerequisite to formal reading instruction?	39	48	13	4	67	27	4	2	1.42	.67
Should students be grouped by ability for reading instruction?	48	43	9	3	67	28	2	3	1.42	.69
Should schools be required to adopt a basal series?	39	35	26	10	57	26	6	11	1.72	1.0
Should at-risk readers spend more time reading connected text or on practicing isolated reading skills?	40	47	13	6	57	33	8	2	1.54	.71
Should reading instruction be mastery based?	37	46	17	9	45	39	11	5	1.76	.84
Should children's entrance into kindergarten be delayed until they perform successfully on a screening test?	46	29	25	5	58	28	9	5	1.62	.86
Should schools be required to use the same program in all grades (e.g., the same basal series)?	35	41	24	11	61	24	5	10	1.64	.96

[a]1 = understand well enough to describe underlying issues and give a reasoned argument; 2 = understand most of underlying issues and give a rationale in taking a position; 3 = know problem exists, but not sure of basic issue; 4 = not aware of problem.

association conventions ($M = 1.4$); (d) literacy articles in magazines for professional educators ($M = 1.4$); and (e) college or university reading courses ($M = 1.4$). Three information sources rated *least helpful* by elementary principals were (a) reading articles in popular national magazines ($M = 2.1$); (b) watching or listening to TV or radio broadcasts about reading issues ($M = 2.1$); and (c) reading newspaper articles about reading issues ($M = 2.1$).

DISCUSSION

Among elementary school principals surveyed across the United States, the most unresolved reading issue is the controversy between the whole language versus basal approaches to reading instruction. The reading education issue rated least understood by

principals was the use of tradebooks in place of basals. These findings are most interesting because of their immediate relationship to each other and to the whole language versus basal reader approaches to reading instruction issue. Explaining this finding is difficult because principals were not asked *why* they indicated that this issue is unresolved. One speculation might be that, in the minds of principals, part of the problem associated with deciding whether to implement tradebooks in reading instruction is the question of *how* to use tradebooks either to supplant or supplement the basal reader. However, further research is needed to determine the reasons *why* the issue surrounding the use of whole language versus basal readers is an issue of such great importance.

Also of note, the principals ranked as the second and third most important *unresolved* national reading issues, assessment of reading progress and use of ability grouping. Yet, when asked to rank their understanding of reading issues, the principals gave the

Table 4.
Utility of Reading Education Information Sources as Rated by U.S. Elementary School Principals

Source	Percentage used	Rated utility in percentages				
		Quite	Moderately	Not very	M	SD
Personal contacts with specialists in the field	95.9	79.1	20.7	.2	1.2	.41
Professional association conventions	61.0	62.0	35.4	2.5	1.4	.54
Magazines or newsletters focusing on reading issues	88.6	52.5	46.3	1.2	1.5	.52
Literacy articles in magazines for professional educators	96.6	61.3	36.6	2.1	1.4	.53
Reading articles in magazines focused on techniques and instructional methods	81.3	46.2	51.5	2.3	1.6	.54
Reading articles in popular national magazines	74.4	17.6	55.4	27.0	2.1	.66
Journal articles reporting results of research	49.3	53.3	42.1	4.6	1.5	.59
Reading articles in professional handbooks	38.8	50.0	46.4	3.6	1.5	.57
College textbooks focused on reading	24.9	42.0	49.0	9.1	1.7	.64
Books about reading published by popular press	64.4	36.3	53.8	9.9	1.7	.63
TV or radio broadcasts about reading issues	77.7	19.3	55.6	25.1	2.1	.67
Newspaper articles about reading issues	93.6	18.3	55.8	25.9	2.1	.66
Reading reports from research agencies	42.3	49.6	46.7	3.7	1.5	.57
Reading reports and publications sponsored by governmental agencies	76.2	47.0	46.6	6.4	1.6	.61
College or university reading courses	14.3	61.3	35.0	3.8	1.4	.57
Workshops or organized study groups focused on reading issues	67.5	71.5	27.9	.5	1.3	.47

Note. Data represent only those principals who reported using the information resources in the past 12 months.

second and most important unresolved issue, assessment of student reading progress, the fourth highest rating of understanding, indicating that although it is an unresolved issue, they understand it well. Additionally, the third most important unresolved issue, ability grouping students for reading instruction, received the second highest rating of understanding. Though principals rated their perceived understanding of the issue of ability grouping as being high, it remains an unresolved issue in the minds of principals nationally. Again, these issues share close philosophical proximity with the whole language versus basal reader issue. Because tradebook use calls into question accepted assessment practices and the use of ability groups, one can understand that these issues would loom as critical issues in the minds of U.S. principals.

Principals' perceived lack of understanding and priority rating of the whole language versus basal reader issue as unresolved reflects a widespread concern among principals nationally regarding this issue. One positive sign that principals may be attempting to deal with the whole language versus basal reader issue is the fact that only 77% of the principals surveyed reported that their schools used the basal reader as the major approach for reading instruction, as compared with other recent estimates indicating that basal reader use in American schools exceeds 90% (Goodman, Shannon, Freeman, & Murphy, 1988).

Although the principals rated their understanding of the whole language versus basal reader issue as one of the least understood issues, they reported less use of basal readers and greater use of trade-

books in schools than previous national estimates indicated. This finding suggests that the principals' perceived lack of understanding regarding the whole language versus basal reader issue may not be precluding their attempts to make greater use of tradebooks in their school reading programs. The means by which principals are learning to make these changes *may* be related to their use of reading information resources.

With respect to the information resources used and valued most by principals, this study revealed that the majority of principals surveyed relied on (a) professional education magazines, (b) personal contacts with specialists in reading, and (c) newspapers as their major sources for gaining information about reading education issues and practices. Nearly 90% of those principals surveyed indicated that they had used one of those top three information sources about reading education in the past 12 months. Of note, those sources tend to be interpretive sources and may give only surface-level information, as opposed to more in-depth original research sources. However, considering the constraints exigent upon principals' time, less formal research synthesis may be the most pragmatic means of acquiring current information regarding critical reading instructional issues and promising practices. This fact is substantiated in part by the information sources that the principals used last.

During the past 12 months, the information sources that principals used least were (a) college or university reading courses, (b) college textbooks on reading, (c) articles in professional handbooks, and (d) research reports from research agencies. Those sources tend to focus on theories, practices, techniques, and approaches verified by in-depth original research studies, and they require greater time commitments than do the less formal information resources used most by practicing principals. The finding that enrolling in college or university reading courses was least used was rather curious when juxtaposed against principals' rankings of the most helpful information sources. Although the principals tended not to enroll in college and university reading course work during the past 12 months, they ranked college and university reading courses in the top four reading information sources as most helpful ($M = 1.4$, on a 3-point, with 1 being the highest).

In summary, the principals chose print informational sources that were interpretive, informal, and less technical information sources, that is, newsletters, newspaper articles, and magazines. They tended not to use detailed research reports found in texts, journals, handbooks, and reading reports from research agencies. However, the principals' selection and use of less technical, more interpretive reading information sources, as well as accessible reading specialists, seems logical given the constraints upon their time. Although the principals tended to rate college courses as extremely helpful, enrolling in university course work might not always be accessible, convenient, or even feasible for many practicing principals.

IMPLICATIONS

From this study, one might conclude that the vast majority of U.S. elementary school principals do attempt to keep current on issues related to reading education. Although principals appear to be aware of current trends and issues in reading education, they may not feel sufficiently confident about their understanding of the issues to implement innovative changes in school reading programs. This conclusion is sustained by the principals' ranking of the issue regarding using whole language versus basal readers as the most unresolved issue while also ranking this issue as least understood.

The conclusion of this study, that U.S. elementary school principals prefer obtaining information about critical reading issues and practices from practical and accessible sources, suggests that authors of educational literature and reading specialists should be aware that principals not only need to understand the issues but also to receive specific guidance on *how* to select promising reading practices for use in their schools and *how* to implement reading program changes.

One paradoxical finding should give strong signals to colleges and universities. Although the principals valued university-level reading courses, many of them had not used that information resource within the past 12 months. This finding may indicate a need for institutions of higher learning to design more accessible means for disseminating current, practical information into schools and classrooms.

In conclusion, the majority of U.S. elementary principals perceived that they were aware of current, critical, and unresolved issues in reading education, that is, tradebooks, reading assessment, and ability grouping. However, according to the survey criteria, many principals did not have enough confidence in their understanding of reading issues to give a reasoned rationale for taking one side or the other. Finally, if principals are to remain informed, information related to innovative reading practices must be disseminated in easily accessible and understandable ways.

APPENDIX A

Reading Education in the United States: Elementary Principals' Involvement
Elementary School Principals' Questionnaire
(This questionnaire takes approximately 10–15 minutes to complete)

Section 1. Important Demographic Information
Please complete the following:
(Check)

School Size: _____1–299   _____300–599   _____6001
School Type: _____K–3   _____K–6   _____Other _____
                                                 (Specify)

Years of experience as an elementary school principal_____
Total years of experience as an educator_____
State in which your school is located_____
Give, in percentage, the kinds of reading approaches that are currently being used in your school.
(e.g., 70% basal   20% literature based   10% whole language   _____other_____)
_____basal   _____literature based   _____whole language   _____other _____
                                                                  (Specify)

SECTION 2. THIS SECTION ASKS YOU TO CONSIDER ELEVEN READING INSTRUCTION ISSUES. YOU WILL BE ASKED TO COMPLETE THREE TASKS RELATED TO THESE ELEVEN ISSUES.

Task 1. Classify
Eleven reading education issues are listed below. In your mind, which of these are:
UI: An Unresolved Issue (research is conclusive—was once an issue but is no longer)
NI: Never has been an issue as far as I am concerned.
For each concern, circle the letter which designates the category you selected.

Task 2. Rank
After you have classified each statement, rank order the top three unresolved issues in terms of their relative importance to improving reading instruction from your point of view. Use the number "1" to indicate the issue which you believe is most important. Then use the numbers "2," "3," and so on to indicate the issues that are second, third. . . . Rank only the issues you classified as unresolved.

Task 3. Rate
Please rate your understanding of each issue (including any issues you added) as follows:
A. I understand this problem well enough to describe the underlying issues and can give a reasoned argument explaining my position.
B. I believe that I understand most of the underlying issues, but I can't give a good rationale for taking one side or the other.
C. I know that this problem exists, but I'm unsure of what the basic issues are.
D. I'm not aware of any problems in this area.

Reading Issues:

	Task 1: Classify			Task 2: Rank	Task 3: Rate
1. How should students' reading progress be assessed?	UI	RI	NI	___	___
2. Should the whole language approach be used instead of the basal reader approach?	UI	RI	NI	___	___
3. Should tradebooks be used in place of basals?	UI	RI	NI	___	___
4. Should reading skills be taught in isolation or integrated with other language arts curriculum?	UI	RI	NI	___	___
5. Should phonics be taught as a prerequisite to reading instruction?	UI	RI	NI	___	___
6. Should students be grouped by reading ability for instruction in reading?	UI	RI	NI	___	___
7. Should schools be required to adopt a basal reading series?	UI	RI	NI	___	___
8. Should at-risk readers spend more time on reading connected text or on practicing isolated reading skills?	UI	RI	NI	___	___
9. Should reading instruction be mastery based?	UI	RI	NI	___	___
10. Should children's entry into kindergarten be delayed until they perform successfully on a screening test?	UI	RI	NI	___	___
11. Should schools be required to use the same program in all grades (e.g., the same basal series)?	UI	RI	NI	___	___
12. (Other)_____	UI	RI	NI	___	___

SECTION 3. THIS SECTION ASKS YOU TO CONSIDER SIXTEEN READING INFORMATION SOURCES AVAILABLE TO PRINCIPALS. YOU WILL BE ASKED TO DO TWO TASKS IN THIS SECTION.

Task 4

Which of the activities listed below have you personally participated in during the past 12 months as a means of keeping yourself informed about current issues in reading. Mark an "X" in the blank "Have Done" or "Have Not Done" for each source.

Task 5

After completing Task 4, rate the degree to which each source you have used was helpful by placing an "X" in the blank "Quite Helpful," "Moderately Helpful," or "Not Very Helpful." **DO NOT** rate sources that you have not used in the last 12 months. Sources:

	Task 4		Task 5		
	Have Done	Have Not Done	Quite Helpful	Moderately Helpful	Not Very Helpful
1. Personal contacts with specialists in the field (e.g., informal contacts with friends, colleagues, professors, and educators who have specialized in reading education)	___	___	___	___	___
2. Attendance at conventions of professional associations (e.g., local, state, or national: International Reading Association, National Reading Conference)	___	___	___	___	___
3. Reading magazines or newsletters which focus on reading issues (e.g., Language Arts, Reading Teacher, Journal of Reading, Reading Horizons)	___	___	___	___	___
4. Reading articles about literacy issues in magazines for professional educators (e.g., Phi Delta Kappan, The Principal, Elementary School Journal, Educational Leadership)	___	___	___	___	___
5. Reading articles in magazines focused on teaching techniques and instructional methods (e.g., Instructor, Teacher, K–12 Learning)	___	___	___	___	___

	Task 4		Task 5		
	Have Done	Have Not Done	Quite Helpful	Moderately Helpful	Not Very Helpful

6. Reading articles in popular national magazines (e.g., Atlantic Monthly, Time, U.S. News, Reader's Digest, Parents, Family Circle)
7. Reading journal articles which focus on reporting the results of reading research (e.g., Reading Research Quarterly, Journal of Reading Behavior, Journal of Educational Psychology, Journal of Educational Research)
8. Reading articles in professional handbooks (e.g., Handbook of Reading Research, Handbook of Research on Teaching, Encyclopedia of Educational Research, Review of Research in Education)
9. Reading college textbooks focused on reading (e.g., Books on teaching language arts, reading)
10. Books about reading which have been published by popular press (e.g., Cultural Literacy, Illiterate American, Why Johnny Still Can't Read, Closing of the American Mind, All I Ever Needed to Know I Learned in Kindergarten)
11. Watching or listening to radio and television broadcasts about reading issues (e.g., news reports, documentaries, debates, interviews, commentaries)
12. Reading newspaper articles about reading issues.
13. Reading reports about reading from research agencies (e.g., Center for the Study of Reading, regional labs)
14. Reading reports and publications about reading sponsored by governmental agencies (e.g., What Works, Becoming a Nation of Readers)
15. Enrollment in college or university courses related to reading education.
16. Participation in college or university courses related to reading education.
17. Other:_____

NOTES

1. The 11 issues included in the survey were selected by a panel of reading experts. Issues were selected based on attention that each has received in the recent reading education and research literature.
2. In the ranking of the reading issues, some respondents did not follow directions. They ranked all issues, instead of ranking only issues that they felt were unresolved. To adjust for the problem, we included only unresolved issues in the data analysis.

REFERENCES

Aldridge, T. (1973). *The elementary principal as an instructional leader for reading instruction.* Unpublished doctoral dissertation, University of Missouri.

Asher, J. W. (1976). *Educational research and evaluation methods.* Boston: Little, Brown.

Barnard, D., & Hetzel, R. (1982). *Principals handbook to improve reading instruction.* Lexington, MA: Ginn and Company.

Berger, A., & Andolina, C. (1977). How administrators keep abreast of trends and research in reading. *Journal of Reading, 21,* 121–125.

Borg, W. R., & Gall, M. D. (1989). *Educational research, 5th ed.* New York: Longman.

Could-Silva, C., & Sadoski, M. (1987). Reading teachers' attitudes toward basal reader use and state adoption policies. *Journal of Educational Research, 81* (1), 5–16.

deVaus, D. A. (1986). *Surveys in social research.* Boston: George Allen and Unwin.

Dillman, D. A. (1978). *Mail and telephone surveys: The total design method.* New York: Wiley.

Ellis, T. (1986). The principal as instructional leader. *Research-Roundup, 3*(1), 6.

Fowler, F. J. (1988). *Survey research methods.* Newbury Park, CA: Sage.

Frey, J. H. (1989). *Survey research by telephone* (2nd ed.). Newbury Park, CA: Sage.

Gehring, R. (1977). *An investigation of knowledge of Clark County, Nevada, elementary school principals about the teaching of reading in primary grades.* Unpublished doctoral dissertation, University of Colorado, Boulder.

Goodman, K., Shannon, P., Freeman, Y., & Murphy, S. (1988). *Report card on basal readers.* Katonah, NY: Richard C. Owen Publishers.

Heberlein, T. A., & Baumgartner, R. (1981). Is a questionnaire necessary in a second mailing? *Public Opinion Quarterly, 45,* 102–108.

Kean, M., Summers, A., Raivetz, M., & Tarber, I. (1979). *What works in reading.* Office of Research and Evaluation, School Districts of Philadelphia, PA.

Kurth, R. J. (1985, December). *Problems court: The role of the reading educator in the training of elementary school principals.* Paper presented at the annual meeting of the American Reading Forum, Sarasota, FL.

Laffey, J., & Kelly, D. (1983). Survey of elementary principals. *The Journal of the Virginia State Reading Association* (a special edition), James Madison University, Harrisonburg, VA.

Lilly, E. R. (1982, September). *Administrative leadership in reading: A professional quagmire.* Paper presented at the meeting of the District of Columbia Reading Council of the International Reading Association, Washington, DC.

McNinch, G. H., & Richmond, M. G. (1983). Defining the principals' roles in reading instruction. *Reading Improvement, 18,* 235–242.

McWilliams, D. R. (1981). *The role of the elementary principal in the management of the primary reading program.* Unpublished doctoral dissertation, University of Pittsburgh, PA.

Moss, R. K. (1985). *More than facilitator: A principal's job in educating new and experienced reading teachers.* Paper presented at the annual meeting of the National Council of Teachers of English Spring Conference, Houston, TX. (ERIC Document Reproduction Service No. ED 253 856)

Nufrio, R. M. (1987). *An administrator's overview for teaching reading.* Opinion paper. (ERIC Document Reproduction Service No. ED 286 287)

Panchyshyn, R. (1971). *An investigation of the knowledge of elementary school principals about the teaching of reading in primary grades.* Unpublished doctoral dissertation, University of Iowa, Iowa City.

Rausch, S., & Sanacore, J. (1984). The administrator and the reading program: An annotated bibliography on reading leadership. *Reading World, 23,* 388–393.

Roser, N. L. (1974, February). Evaluation and the administrator: How decisions are made. *Journal of Education, 156,* 48–49.

Shelton, M., Rafferty, C., & Rose, L. (1990, Winter). The state of reading: What Michigan administrators know. *Michigan Reading Journal, 23,* 3–14.

Weber, G. (1971). *Inner-city children can be taught to read: Four successful schools.* New York: Council for Basic Education, Occasional Papers No. 18.

Wilkerson, B. (1988). A principal's perspective. In J. L. Davidson (Ed.), *Counterpoint and beyond: A response to becoming a nation of readers.* Urbana, IL: National Council of Teachers of English.

Zinski, R. (1975). *The elementary school principals and the administration of a total reading program.* Unpublished doctoral dissertation, University of Wisconsin, Madison.

Source: The Journal of Educational Research, 85, pp. 370–380, 1992. Reprinted with permission of the Helen Dwight Reid Educational Foundation. Published by Heldref Publications, 1319 Eighteenth St., NW, Washington, DC 20036-1802. Copyright © 1992.

"Correlational research involves collecting data to determine whether, and to what degree, a relationship exists. . . " (p. 191)

Correlational Research

OBJECTIVES

After reading Chapter 7, you should be able to do the following:

1. Briefly state the purpose of correlational research.
2. List and briefly describe the major steps involved in basic correlational research.
3. Describe the size and direction of values associated with a correlation coefficient.
4. Describe how the size of a correlation coefficient affects its interpretation with respect to (1) statistical significance, (2) its use in prediction, and (3) its use as an index of validity and reliability.
5. State two major purposes of relationship studies.
6. Identify and briefly describe the steps involved in conducting a relationship study.
7. Briefly describe four different types of correlation and the nature of the variables they are used to correlate.
8. Describe the difference between a linear and a curvilinear relationship.
9. Identify and briefly describe two factors that may contribute to an inaccurate estimate of relationship.
10. Briefly define or describe predictor variables and criterion variables.
11. State purposes of prediction studies.
12. State the major difference between data collection procedures in a prediction study and a relationship study.

Completing Chapter 7 should enable you to perform the following task.

TASK 6B

For a quantitative study, you have created research plan components (Tasks 2, 3a), described a sample (Task 4a), and considered appropriate measuring instruments (Task 5). If your study involves correlational research, now develop the methods section of a research report. Include a description of participants, data collection methods, and research design. (See Performance Criteria at the end of Chapter 10, p. 287.)

⚏ CORRELATIONAL RESEARCH: DEFINITION AND PURPOSE

Correlational research is sometimes treated as a type of descriptive research, primarily because it does describe an existing condition. However, the condition it describes is distinctly different from the conditions typically described in survey or observational studies. As you learned in Chapter 1, **correlational research** involves collecting data to determine whether, and to what degree, a relationship exists between two or more quantifiable variables. The degree of relationship is expressed as a correlation coefficient. If a relationship exists between two variables, it means that scores within a certain range on one variable are associated with scores within a certain range on the other variable. For example, there is a relationship between intelligence and academic achievement; persons who get high scores on intelligence tests tend to have high grade point averages, and persons who get low scores on intelligence tests tend to have low grade point averages.

The purpose of a correlational study may be to determine relationships between variables (relationship studies) or to use these relationships to make predictions (prediction studies). Correlational studies typically investigate a number of variables believed to be related to a major, complex variable, such as achievement. Variables found not to be highly related to achievement will be dropped from further examination, whereas variables that are highly related to achievement may be examined in causal–comparative or experimental studies to determine the nature of the relationships.

As noted in Chapter 1, the fact that there is a high correlation between two variables does not imply that one causes the other. A high correlation between self-concept and achievement does not mean that achievement causes self-concept or that self-concept causes achievement. However, even though correlational relationships are not cause–effect ones, the existence of a high correlation does permit prediction. For example, high school grade point average (GPA) and college GPA are highly related; students who have high GPAs in high school tend to have high GPAs in college, and students who have low GPAs in high school tend to have low GPAs in college. Therefore, high school GPA can be and is used in college admission to predict college GPA. As discussed in Chapter 5, correlational procedures are also used to determine various types of validity and reliability.

Correlational studies provide a numerical estimate of how related two variables are. Clearly, the higher the correlation, the closer the relationship between the two variables and the more accurate are predictions based on the relationship. Rarely are two variables perfectly correlated or perfectly uncorrelated, but many are sufficiently related to permit useful predictions.

:: THE CORRELATIONAL RESEARCH PROCESS

Although relationship and prediction studies have unique features that differentiate them, their basic processes are very similar.

Problem Selection

Correlational studies may be designed either to determine whether and how a set of variables are related or to test hypotheses regarding expected relationships. Variables to be correlated should be selected on the basis of some rationale. That is, the relationship to be investigated should be a logical one, suggested by theory or derived from experience. Having a theoretical or experiential basis for selecting variables to be correlated makes interpretation of results more meaningful. Correlational "treasure hunts" in which the researcher correlates all sorts of variables to see "what turns up" are strongly discouraged. This research strategy (appropriately referred to as a "shotgun" or "fishing" approach) is very inefficient and makes findings difficult to interpret.

Participant and Instrument Selection

The sample for a correlational study is selected by using an acceptable sampling method, and 30 participants are generally considered to be a minimally acceptable sample size. There are, however, some factors that influence the size needed for the sample. The higher the validity and reliability of the variables to be correlated, the smaller the sample can be, but not less than 30. If validity and reliability are low, a larger sample is needed, because errors of measurement may mask the true relationship. As in any study, it is important to select or develop valid and reliable measures of the variables being studied. The measuring instruments to be used in a correlational study must be carefully selected. If the measures used do not represent the intended variables, the resulting correlation coefficient will not accurately indicate the degree of relationship. Suppose, for example, you wanted to determine the relationship between achievement in mathematics and achievement in physics. If you administered a valid, reliable test of math computational skill and a valid, reliable test of physics achievement, the resulting correlation coefficient would not be an accurate estimate of the intended relationship, because computational skill is only one aspect of mathematical achievement. The resulting coefficient would indicate the relationship between physics achievement and only one aspect of mathematical achievement, computational skill. Thus, care must be taken to select measures that are valid and reliable for your purposes.

Design and Procedure

The basic correlational research design is not complicated; scores for two (or more) variables of interest are obtained for each member of the sample, and the paired scores are then correlated. The result is expressed as a correlation coefficient that indicates the degree of relationship between the two variables. Some studies investigate more than two variables, and some utilize complex statistical procedures, but the basic design is similar in all correlational studies.

Data Analysis and Interpretation

When two variables are correlated, the result is a correlation coefficient, which is a decimal number ranging from -1.00 to 0.00 to $+1.00$. The correlation coefficient indicates the size and direction of the relationship between variables. A coefficient near $+1.00$ has a high size (it represents a high degree of relationship) and a positive direction. This means that a person with a high score on one of the variables is likely to have a high score on the other variable, and a person with a low score on one variable is likely to have a low score on the other. An increase on one variable is associated with an increase on the other variable. If the coefficient is near .00, the variables are not related. This means that a person's score on one variable provides no indication of what the person's score is on the other variable. A coefficient near -1.00 has a high size and a negative or inverse direction. This means that a person with a high score on one variable is likely to have a low score on the other variable, and a person with a low score on one is likely to have a high score on the other. An increase on one variable is associated with a decrease on the other variable, and vice versa. Note that equal correlations near $+1.00$ and near -1.00 represent the same size of relationship. The plus and minus represent different directions of relationship.

Table 7.1 presents four scores for each of eight 12th grade students: IQ, GPA, weight, and errors on a 20-item final exam. The table shows that IQ is highly and positively related to GPA ($r = +.95$), not related to weight ($r = +.13$), and negatively, or inversely, related to errors ($r = -.89$). The students with progressively higher IQs have progressively higher GPAs. On the other hand, students with higher IQs tend to make fewer errors (makes sense!). The relationships are not perfect, but then again, variables rarely are perfectly related or unrelated. One's GPA, for example, is related to other variables besides intelligence, such as motivation. The data do indicate, however, that IQ is one major variable related to both GPA and examination errors. The data also illustrate an important concept that is often misunderstood. A

TABLE 7.1 Hypothetical sets of data illustrating a high positive relationship between two variables, no relationship, and a high negative relationship

	High Positive Relationship		No Relationship		High Negative Relationship	
	IQ	GPA	IQ	Weight	IQ	Errors
1. Iggie	85	1.0	85	156	85	16
2. Hermie	90	1.2	90	140	90	10
3. Fifi	100	2.4	100	120	100	8
4. Teenie	110	2.2	110	116	110	5
5. Tiny	120	2.8	120	160	120	9
6. Tillie	130	3.4	130	110	130	3
7. Millie	135	3.2	135	140	135	2
8. Jane	140	3.8	140	166	140	1
Correlation	$r = +.95$		$r = +.13$		$r = -.89$	

FIGURE 7.1

Data points for scores presented in Table 7.1 illustrating a high positive relationship (IQ and GPA), no relationship (IQ and weight), and a high negative relationship (IQ and errors)

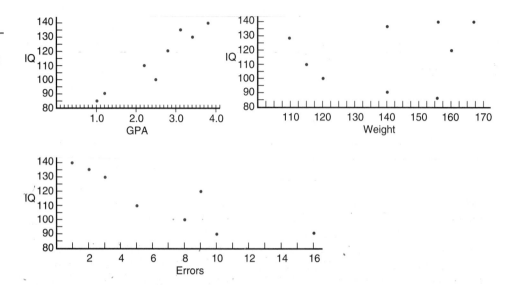

high negative relationship is just as strong as a high positive relationship; −1.00 and +1.00 indicate equally perfect relationships. They represent the same degree but different directions of relationship. A coefficient near .00 indicates no relationship; the farther away from .00 the coefficient is, in either direction, the stronger the relationship. Both high positive and high negative relationships are equally useful for making predictions; knowing that Iggie has a low IQ score would enable you to predict both a low GPA and a high number of errors.

Figure 7.1 shows a scatterplot for each of the three correlations shown in Table 7.1. The top left scatterplot shows that students who score low on IQ also tend to score low on GPA and that students who score high on IQ also tend to score high on GPA. This pattern illustrates a high positive correlation. The bottom scatterplot shows that students who score high on IQ tend to score low on errors and that students who score low on IQ tend to score high on errors. This pattern illustrates a high negative correlation. The lack of any systematic relationship between IQ and weight in the top right scatterplot illustrates a lack of relation between the two variables.

One way to interpret correlation coefficients is this:

Coefficient	Relationship Between Variables
Lower than +.35 or −.35	Low or none
Between +.35 and +.65 or between −.35 and −.65	Moderate
Higher than +.65 or −.65	High

These figures are approximations and should not be blindly used. A correlation coefficient much lower than plus or minus .50 is generally useless for either group prediction or individual prediction, although a combination of several variables in this range may yield a reasonably satisfactory prediction. Coefficients of plus or minus .60 or .70 are usually considered adequate for group prediction purposes, as are coefficients of plus or minus .80 and higher for individual prediction purposes. A correlational criterion-related validity of .60 for an affective measuring instrument may be considered high, because many affective instruments have lower validities. Conversely, we would consider a stability reliability of .74 for an achievement test to be low. A researcher would be very happy with observer reliabilities in the .90s, satisfied with the .80s, minimally accepting of the .70s, and would be progressively more unhappy with the .60s, .50s, and so forth. Thus, a correlation coefficient of .40, for example, would be considered useful in a relationship study, not useful in a prediction study, and terrible in a reliability study. A coefficient of .60 would be considered useful in a prediction study but would still probably be considered unsatisfactory as an estimate of reliability.

What a correlation coefficient means is difficult to explain. However, one thing it does not indicate is the percentage of relationship between variables. Unfortunately, many beginning researchers erroneously think that a correlation coefficient of .50 means that two variables are 50% related. Not true. In research talk, a correlation coefficient squared indicates the amount of common variance shared by the variables (What?!). Now, in English. When two or more variables are correlated, each variable will have a range of scores. Each variable will have score variance; that is, everyone will not get the same score. In Table 7.1, for example, IQ scores vary from 85 to 140 and GPAs from 1.0 to 3.8. **Common variance** (or *shared variance*) is the variation in one variable (e.g., in scores) that is attributable to it tendency to vary with another variable. It indicates the extent to which variables vary in a systematic way. The more systematically two variables vary, the higher the correlation coefficient. If two variables do not systematically vary, then the scores on one variable are unrelated to the scores on the other variable; there is no common variance, and the correlation coefficient will be near .00. If two variables are perfectly related (positively or negatively), then the variability of one set of scores is very similar to the variability in the other set of scores. There is a great deal of common variance, and the correlation coefficient will be near plus or minus 1.00. In other words, the more the common variance, the higher the correlation coefficient. In Table 7.1 a great deal of the score variance of IQ and GPA and IQ and errors is common, whereas the common variance of IQ and weight is quite small.

To determine common variance, you simply square the correlation coefficient. A correlation coefficient of .80 indicates $(.80)^2$ or .64, or 64% common variance. As you can see, the percentage of common variance is *less than* the numerical value of the correlation coefficient when the coefficient is not .00 or 1.00. (A correlation coefficient of .00 indicates $[.00]^2$ or .00, or 00% common variance, and a coefficient of 1.00 indicates $[1.00]^2$ or 1.00, or 100% common variance.) Thus, a correlation coefficient of .50 may look pretty good at first, but it actually means that the variables have 25% common variance; 75% of the variance is unexplained, not common, variance.

Interpretation of a correlation coefficient depends how it is to be used. In other words, how large it needs to be in order to be useful depends on the purpose for which it was computed. In a prediction study, the value of the correlation coefficient in facilitating accurate predictions is important. In a study designed to explore or test hypothesized relationships, a correlation coefficient is interpreted in terms of its statistical significance. Heads up! **Statistical significance,** the conclusion that results are unlikely to have occurred by chance, is an important new concept that you will be seeing more of in the next few chapters. (In addition, in Chapter 12 the concepts of statistical significance, level of significance, and degrees of freedom will be discussed in depth.) To be statistically significant, an obtained correlation coefficient must truly be different from a correlation of zero, or no relation. That is, the correlation must reflect a true statistical relationship, not a chance one with no meaning. Decisions concerning statistical significance are made at a given level of probability. Based on a correlation with a sample of a given size, a statistical significance test does not allow you to determine with perfect certainty that there is or is not a true, meaningful relationship between the variables. However, the statistical test does indicate the probability that there is or is not a significant, true relationship. To determine statistical significance, you simply have to consult a table that tells you how large your coefficient must be to be significant at a given probability level and given sample size. (See Table A.2 in Appendix A. See also the article at the end of this chapter, especially Tables 2 and 3.)

Statistical significance depends on the sample size. To demonstrate a true relationship, the correlation coefficients for small samples sizes must be higher than those for large sample sizes. This is because we can generally have a lot more confidence in a correlation coefficient based on 100 participants than one based on only 10 participants. Thus, for example, to be 95% confident that a correlation represents a true relationship (not a chance one), with a sample of 12 participants you would need a correlation of at least .58. On the other hand, with a sample of 102 participants you would need a correlation of only .19 to conclude that the relationship is significant.[1] This concept makes sense if you consider a situation in which you could collect data on every member of a population. No inference would be needed because the whole population was in the sample. Thus, regardless of how small the actual correlation coefficient was, it would represent the true degree of relationship between the variables *for that population*. Even if the coefficient were only .11, for example, it would still indicate the existence of a significant relationship. As noted, the larger the sample, the more closely it approximates the population and therefore the more probable it is that a given correlation coefficient represents a significant relationship.

You may also have noticed that for a given sample size, the value of the correlation coefficient needed for significance increases as the level of confidence increases (see Table A.2). The level of confidence, commonly called the *significance level,* indicates how confident we wish to be that we have a significant relationship. Usually we choose a significance level of .05 or .01, meaning that we wish to be 95% or 99% sure that we have a real, significant relationship.

Table A.2 shows that at the 95% confidence level ($p = .05$), the required coefficient for a sample of 12 ($df = 10$) is .58. At the 99% confidence level ($p = .01$), the required correlation rises to .71. In other words, the more confident you wish to be that your decision concerning significance is the correct one, the larger the coefficient must be. Beware, however, of confusing significance with strength. No matter how significant a coefficient is, a low coefficient represents a low degree of association between two variables. The level of significance indicates only the probability that a given relationship, whether weak or strong, is a true relationship.

When interpreting a correlation coefficient, you must always keep in mind that you are talking about relationship, not causality. When one observes a high relationship between two variables, it is often very tempting to conclude that one variable "causes" the other. In fact, it may be that neither one is the cause of the other; there may be a third variable that "causes" both of them. The existence of a positive relationship between self-concept and achievement could mean one of three things: a higher self-concept leads to higher achievement; higher achievement leads to higher self-concept; or another factor, such as parent–child interaction, is responsible for both self-concept and higher achievement. A significant correlation coefficient may suggest a cause–effect relationship but does not establish one. As you carry on your correlation and causal–comparative research (discussed in the next chapter), recognize that neither correlation nor causal–comparative research provides true experimental data. The only way to establish a cause–effect relationship is by conducting experimental research (the subject of Chapter 9).

:: RELATIONSHIP STUDIES

A **relationship study** attempts to gain insight into variables, or factors, that are related to a complex variable. Some examples of complex variables in educational research are academic achievement, motivation, and self-concept. For example, a researcher may be interested in whether a variable such as hyperactivity is related to motivation or whether parental punish-

---

[1] In case you are trying to read Table A.2, a 95% level of confidence corresponds to $p = .05$. Degrees of freedom, *df,* are equal to the number in the sample minus 2. For 12 cases, $df = 10$. For 102 cases, $df = 100$. With this information, you can find the correlation coefficients in the body of the table.

ment is related to elementary school children's self-concept. Relationship studies serve several purposes. First, they help researchers identify related variables suitable for subsequent examination in causal–comparative and experimental studies. Experimental studies are costly and often time-consuming, so the use of relationship studies to suggest potentially productive experimental studies is efficient. Second, relationship studies give researchers information about what variables to control for in both causal–comparative and experimental research studies. If researchers can identify variables that might be related to performance on the dependent variable, they can remove their influence so that the variables will not be confused with that of the independent variable. If you were interested in comparing the effectiveness of different methods of reading instruction on first graders, for example, you would probably want to control for initial differences in reading readiness. You could do this by selecting first graders who were homogeneous in reading readiness or by using stratified sampling to ensure similar levels of reading readiness in each method.

The strategy of attempting to understand a complex variable such as self-concept by identifying variables correlated with it has been more successful for some variables than others. For example, whereas a number of variables correlated with achievement have been identified, factors significantly related to success in such areas as administration and teaching have not been as easy to pin down. Relationship studies that have not uncovered useful relationships have nevertheless identified variables that can be excluded from future studies, a necessary step in science.

Data Collection

In a relationship study, the researcher first identifies the variables to be correlated. For example, if you were interested in factors related to self-concept, you might identify the variables introversion, academic achievement, and socioeconomic status. As noted previously, you should have a reason for selecting variables in the study. A shotgun approach is inefficient and often misleading. Also, the more correlation coefficients that are computed at one time, the more likely it is that some wrong conclusions about the existence of a relationship will be reached. Computing only 10 or 15 correlation coefficients generally doesn't cause a problem. Computing 100 coefficients, on the other hand, greatly increases the chance for error. Thus, a smaller number of carefully selected variables is much preferred to a larger number of carelessly selected variables.

After identifying variables, the next step in data collection is identifying an appropriate population of participants from which to select a sample. The population must be one for which data on each of the identified variables can be collected. Although data on some variables, such as past achievement, can be collected without direct access to participants, many relationship studies require the administration of one or more instruments and, in some cases, observations. Any of the types of measuring instruments discussed so far in this text (see Chapter 5) can be used in a relationship study. One advantage of a relationship study is that all the data may be collected within a relatively short period of time. Instruments may be administered at one session or at several sessions in close succession. In studies where schoolchildren are the subjects, time demands on students and teachers are relatively small compared to those required for experimental studies, and it is usually easier to obtain administrative approval.

Data Analysis and Interpretation

In a relationship study, the scores for one variable are correlated with the scores for another variable. If a number of variables are to be correlated with some particular variable of primary interest, each of the variables would be correlated with that variable; each correlation coefficient then represents the relationship between a particular variable and the variable of primary interest. The end result of data analysis is a number of correlation coefficients, ranging between -1.00 and $+1.00$. There are a number of different methods of computing a correlation coefficient. Which is appropriate depends on the type of data represented by each variable. The most common technique uses the *product moment correlation coefficient,* usually referred to as the **Pearson r**, a measure of correlation appropriate when both variables to be correlated are expressed as continuous (i.e., ratio or interval) data. Because most scores from instruments used in education, such as achievement measures and personality measures, are classified as interval data, the Pearson *r* is usually the appropriate coefficient for determining relationship. Further, because the Pearson *r* results in the most precise estimate of correlation, its use is preferred even when other methods may be applied.

If the data for at least one variable are expressed as rank or ordinal data, the appropriate correlation coefficient to use is the *rank difference correlation*, usually referred to as the **Spearman rho.** Rank data is found in studies where participants are arranged in order of score and assigned a rank from 1 to however many subjects there are. For a group of 30 participants, for example, the subject with the highest score would be assigned a rank of 1, the subject with the second highest score 2, and the subject with the lowest score 30. When two subjects have the same score, their ranks are averaged. Thus, two participants with the identical high score are assigned the average of Rank 1 and Rank 2, namely 1.5. If only one of the variables to be correlated is in rank order, the other variable or variables to be correlated with it must also be expressed as rank data in order to use the Spearman rho technique. For example, if class standing (rank data) were to be correlated with intelligence, students would have to be ranked from high to low in terms of intelligence. Actual IQ scores (continuous data) could not be used in calculating the correlation coefficients.

Although the Pearson *r* is more precise, with a small number of subjects (fewer than 30) the Spearman rho is much easier to compute and results in a coefficient very close to the one that would have been obtained had a Pearson *r* been computed. When the number of subjects is large, however, the process of ranking becomes more time-consuming and the Spearman rho loses its only advantage over the Pearson *r.*

There are also a number of other correlational techniques that are encountered less often but that should be used when appropriate. A *phi coefficient* is used when both variables can be expressed only in terms of a categorical dichotomy, such as gender (male or female), political affiliation (Democrat versus Republican), smoking status (smoker versus nonsmoker), or educational status (high school graduate versus high school dropout). These dichotomies are considered "true" because a person is or is not a female, a Democrat, a smoker, or a high school graduate. The two categories typically are labeled 1 and 0 or 1 and 2. Recall that for nominal variables, a 2 does not mean more of something than a 1, and a 1 does not mean more of a something than a 0. The numbers indicate different categories, not different amounts.

Other correlational techniques are appropriate when one or both variables are expressed as artificial dichotomies. Artificial dichotomies are created by operationally defining a midpoint and categorizing subjects as falling above it or below it. For example, participants with test scores of 50 or higher could be classified as "high achievers" and those with scores lower than 50 as "low achievers." Such artificial classifications are typically translated into "scores" of 1 and 0. These dichotomies are called "artificial" because variables that were ordinal, interval, or ratio are artificially turned into nominal variables. Table 7.2 describes a number of different correlations and the conditions under which they are used.

Most correlational techniques are based on the assumption that the relationship being investigated is a **linear relationship,** one in which an increase (or decrease) in one variable is associated with a corresponding increase (or decrease) in another variable. Plotting the scores of two variables that have a linear relationship results in a straight line. If a relationship is perfect ($+1.00$ or -1.00), the line will be perfectly straight, but if there is no relationship, the points will form a scattered, random plot. Refer back to Figure 7.1, which plots the data presented in Table 7.1. The top left and bottom scatterplots illustrate the concept of a linear relationship. Not all relationships, however, are linear; some are curvilinear. In a **curvilinear relationship,** an increase in one variable is associated with a corresponding in-

TABLE 7.2	Types of correlation coefficients		
Name	**Variable 1**	**Variable 2**	**Comments**
Pearson r	Continuous	Continuous	Most common correlation
Spearman's rho, or rank difference	Rank	Rank	Easy to compute for small samples
Kendall's tau	Rank	Rank	Used with samples of fewer than 10
Biserial	Artificial dichotomy	Continuous	Used to analyze test items; may have r greater than 1.00 if score distribution is oddly shaped
Point biserial	True dichotomy	Continuous	Maximum when dichotomous variable split 50–50
Tetrachoric	Artificial dichotomy	Artificial dichotomy	Should not be used with extreme splits or sample
Phi coefficient	True dichotomy	True dichotomy	Used in determining inter-item relationships
Intraclass	Continuous	Continuous	Useful in judging rater agreement
Correlation ratio, or eta	Continuous	Continuous	Used for nonlinear relationships

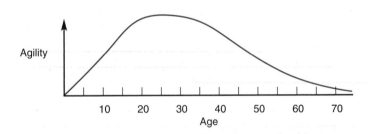

FIGURE 7.2

The curvilinear relationship between age and agility

crease in another variable up to a point, at which further increase in the first variable results in a corresponding decrease in the other variable (or vice versa). Plotting the scores of the two variables produces a curve. For example, the relationship between age and agility is a curvilinear one. As Figure 7.2 illustrates, agility increasingly improves with age, peaks or reaches its maximum somewhere in the twenties, and then progressively decreases as age increases. Two other examples of curvilinear relationships are age of car and dollar value, and anxiety and achievement. A car decreases in value as soon as it leaves the lot, it continues to do so over time until it becomes an antique (!), and then it increases in value as time goes by. In contrast, increases in anxiety are associated with increases in achievement to a point; but at some point, anxiety becomes counterproductive and interferes with learning in that as anxiety increases, achievement decreases. If a relationship is suspected of being curvilinear, then an *eta coefficient* is appropriate. If you try to use a correlational technique that assumes a linear relationship when the relationship is in fact curvilinear, your measure of the degree of relationship will be way off base. Use of a linear correlation coefficient to determine a curvilinear correlation will reveal little or no relationship.

In addition to computing correlation coefficients for a total participant group, researchers sometimes find it useful to examine relationships separately for certain defined subgroups. For example, the relationship between two variables may be different for females and males, college graduates and non–college graduates, or high-ability and low-ability students. When the subgroups are lumped together and correlated, differential relationships may be obscured. However, regardless of whatever worthwhile knowledge may come from subdividing a sample and correlating the subgroups separately, a few cautions must be recognized.

For example, subdivision and correlation can be carried out only if the original sample is large enough to permit sufficient numbers in the subgroups. Suppose a researcher starts with a sample of 30 participants (15 males and 15 females) and subsequently wishes to compare separately the correlations of males and females on the selected variables. Subgroups of only 15 participants are too small to yield stable results. Sometimes researchers recognize this problem and select a larger sample to permit analysis of subgroups. However, if there are unequal numbers in the subgroups (for example, 55 females and 15 males), comparative analyses still cannot be carried out. If you think you want to study subgroups of your sample, select larger samples and use stratified samples to ensure similar numbers in the subgroups.

Other factors also may contribute to inaccurate estimates of relationship. **Attenuation,** for example, is the reduction in correlation coefficients that tends to occur if the measures being correlated have low reliability. In correlational studies a correction for attenuation (unreliability) can be applied that provides an estimate of what the coefficient would be if both measures were perfectly reliable. If such a correction is used, it must be kept in mind that the resulting coefficient does not represent what was actually found. Such a correction should not be used in prediction studies because predictions must be based on existing measures, not hypothetical, perfectly reliable measures. Another factor that may lead to a correlation coefficient being an underestimate of the true relationship between two variables is a restricted range of scores. The more variability (spread) there is in each set of scores, the higher the coefficient is likely to be. The correlation coefficient for IQ and grades, for example, tends to decrease as these variables are measured at higher educational levels. Thus, the correlation will not be as high for college seniors as for high school seniors. The reason is that there are not many college seniors with low IQs; individuals with low IQs either do not enter college or drop out long before their senior year. In other words, the range of IQ scores is smaller, or more restricted, for college seniors, and a correlation coefficient based on a narrow range of scores will tend to be lowered. There is also a correction for restriction in range that may be applied to obtain an estimate of what the coefficient would be if the range of scores were not restricted. The resulting coefficient should be interpreted with the same caution as that produced after the correction for attenuation since it, too, does not represent what was actually found.

:: PREDICTION STUDIES

If two variables are highly related, scores on one variable can be used to predict scores on the other variable. High school grades, for example, can be used to predict college grades. Or scores on a teacher certification exam can be used to predict principals' evaluation of teachers' classroom performance. The variable used to predict (high school grades or certification exam) is called the **predictor,** and the variable that is predicted (college grades or principals' evaluations) is a complex variable called the **criterion.** A **prediction study** is an attempt to determine which of a number of variables are most highly related to the criterion variable. Prediction studies are conducted to facilitate decision making about individuals, to aid in various types of selection, and to determine the predictive validity of measuring instruments. Typical prediction studies include those used to predict an individual's likely level of success in a specific course (such as first-year algebra), those that predict which of a number of individuals are likely to succeed in college or in a vocational training program, and those that predict the area of study in which an individual is most likely to be successful. Thus, the results of prediction studies are used not only by researchers but also by counselors, admissions directors, and employers.

More than one variable can be used to make predictions. If several predictor variables each correlate well with a criterion, then a prediction based on a combination of those variables will be more accurate than a prediction based on any one of them. For example, a prediction of probable level of GPA success in college based on high school grades will be less predictive than a prediction based on high school grades, rank in graduating class, and scores on college entrance exams. Although there are several major differences between prediction studies and relationship studies, both involve determining the relationship among a number of identified variables.

Data Collection

As in all correlational studies, research participants must be able to provide the desired data and be available to the researcher. Valid measuring instruments should be selected to represent the variables. It is especially important that the measure used as the criterion variable be valid. If the criterion were "success on the job," the researcher would have to carefully define "success" in quantifiable terms in order to carry out the prediction study. For example, size of desk would probably not be a valid measure of job success (although you never know!), whereas number of promotions or salary increases probably would be. The major difference in data collection procedures for a relationship study and a prediction study is that in a relationship study all variables are collected within a relatively short period of time, whereas in a prediction study the predictor variables are generally obtained earlier than the criterion variable. Sometimes the researcher must have data that spans a lengthy time period, which in turn can create problems of participant loss. In determining the predictive validity of a physics aptitude test, for example, success in physics would probably be measured by end-of-course grade, whereas the aptitude test itself would be administered some time before the beginning of the course.

Once the strength of the predictor variable is established, the predictive relationship is tested on a new group of participants to determine how well it will predict for other groups. An interesting characteristic of prediction studies is **shrinkage,** the tendency of a prediction equation (discussed shortly) to become less accurate when used with a group other than the one on which the equation was originally developed. The reason for shrinkage is that an initial equation may be the result of chance relationships that will not be found again with another group of participants. Thus, any prediction equation should be subject to **cross-validation,** validation of the equation with at least one other group. Variables no longer found to be related to the criterion measure should then be taken out of the equation.

Data Analysis and Interpretation

As in a relationship study, each predictor variable in a prediction study is correlated with the criterion variable. Data analysis in prediction studies differs somewhat from that of relationship studies, however. It is beyond the scope of this text to discuss the statistical processes related to the analysis of prediction studies, but we will provide examples of how to interpret them. There are two types of prediction studies: single prediction studies and multiple prediction studies. A single prediction study predicts using a single predictive variable, and a multiple prediction study predicts using more than one predictive variable. In both cases, data analysis is based on a prediction equation. For single variable predictions, the form of the prediction equation is

$$Y = a + bX$$

where

Y = the predicted criterion score for an individual

X = an individual's score on the predictor variable

a = a constant calculated from the scores of all participants

b = a coefficient that indicates the contribution of the predictor variable to the criterion variable

Suppose, for example, that we wished to predict a student's college GPA using high school GPA. We know that the student's high school grade average is 3.0, the coefficient *b* is .87, and the constant *a* is .15. The student's predicted score would be calculated as follows:

$$Y = .15 + .87 (3.0) = .15 + 2.61 = 2.76 \text{ predicted college GPA}$$

We can compare the student's predicted college GPA to the student's actual college GPA at some subsequent time to determine how accurate the prediction equation is.

Because a combination of variables usually results in a more accurate prediction than any one variable, a prediction study often results in a multiple regression equation. A **multiple regression equation** (also called a *multiple prediction equation*) is a prediction equation using two or more variables that individually predict a criterion to make a more accurate prediction. For example, suppose we wished to predict college GPA from high school GPA, SAT verbal score, and the rated quality of the student's college admission essay. The student's high school GPA is 3.0, SAT verbal score is 450, and the rating for the admission essay is 10. If *a* is .15 and the coefficients *b* for the three predictors are .87, .0003, and .4, the multiple regression equation would be as follows:

$$Y = .15 + .87 (3.0) + .0003 (450) + .4 (10)$$
$$= .15 + 2.61 + .135 + .2 = 3.095 \text{ predicted college GPA}$$

We would validate the accuracy of the equation by comparing the predicted GPA of 3.095 to the student's actual college GPA.

Predictive studies are influenced by factors that affect the accuracy of prediction. For example, if the predictor and criterion variables are not reliable, error of measurement is introduced and the accuracy of the prediction is diminished. Also, the longer the length of time between the measurement of the predictor and the criterion, the lower the prediction accuracy. This is because many intervening variables that influence the link between predictor and criterion variables can occur over time. An **intervening variable** is one that alters the relationship between an independent variable and a dependent variable but which cannot be directly observed or controlled. Finally, general criterion variables such as success in business or teacher effectiveness tend to have lower prediction accuracy than narrower criterion variables because so many factors make up broad, general criterion variables.

Because relationships are rarely perfect, predictions made by single or multiple prediction equations are not perfect. Thus, predicted scores are generally reported as a range of predicted scores using a statistic called the *standard error*. For example, a predicted college GPA of 2.20 might be placed in an interval of 1.80 to 2.60. In other words, students with a predicted GPA of 2.20 would be predicted to earn a GPA somewhere in the range between 1.80 and 2.60. Thus, for most useful interpretation, the prediction should be viewed as a range of possible scores, not as a single score. A college that does not accept all applicants will probably as a general rule fail to accept any applicants with such a projected GPA range even though it is very likely that some of those students would be successful if admitted. Although the predictions for any given individual might be way off (either too high or too low), for the total group of applicants predictions are quite accurate on the whole; most applicants predicted to succeed, do so. As with relationship studies, and for similar reasons, prediction equations may be formulated for each of a number of subgroups as well as for a total group.

As in relational studies, predictive studies can provide an indication of the common variance shared by the predictor(s) and the criterion variables. This statistic, called the *coefficient of determination,* indicates the percentage of variance in the criterion variable that is predicted by the predictor(s) variable. The coefficient of determination is the squared correlation of the predictor and the criterion. For example, if the correlation between high school GPA and college GPA is .80, the coefficient of determination is .80 × .80 = .64, or 64%. This is a moderately high coefficient of determination, and the higher the coefficient of determination, the better the prediction.

:: OTHER CORRELATION-BASED ANALYSES

Many sophisticated statistical analyses are based on correlational data. We will briefly describe a number of these, recognizing that they are statistically complex. Discriminant function analysis is quite similar to multiple regression analysis, with one major difference: the criterion variable is categorical, not continuous. In multiple regression, continuous predictor variables are used to predict a continuous criterion variable. In *discriminant function analysis,* continuous predictor variables are used to predict a categorical variable, such as introverted/extroverted, high anxiety/low anxiety, or achiever/nonachiever. Thus, the predictions made are about categorical group membership. For example, on the basis of the predictor variables, discriminant function analysis allows us to classify whether an individual manifests the characteristics of an introvert or an extrovert. Having identified groups who are introverts and extroverts, a researcher might want to compare the two groups on other variables.

Path analysis allows us to see the relationships and patterns among a number of variables. The outcome of a path analysis is a diagram that shows how variables are related to one another. Suppose, for example, that we wanted to examine the connections (paths) between variable X and variables A, B, and C. A path analysis based on the correlations among the variables will produce a path diagram such as that shown in Figure 7.3. In this diagram, single arrows indicate connections among variables and double arrows (A to B) indicate no direct link. Thus, variables A and B are individually linked to D, and A and B are linked to variable C. Variable C is not linked to D. Path analyses are useful both for showing what variables influence a given variable (like X) and also for testing theories about the ways in which groups of variables are related to a given variable. An extension of path analysis that is more sophisticated and powerful is called *structural equation modeling,* or LISREL, for the computer program used to perform the analysis. This approach provides more theoretical validity and statistical precision in the model diagrams it produces than those of path analysis. Like path analysis, it clarifies the direct and indirect interrelations among variables relative to a given variable.

Canonical analysis is an extension of multiple regression analysis. As noted, multiple regression uses multiple predictors to predict a single criterion variable. *Canonical analysis* produces a correlation based on a group of predictor variables and a group of criterion variables. For example, if we had a group of predictors related to achievement (GPA, SAT scores, teachers' ratings of ability, and number of AP courses passed) and we wanted to see how these predictors related to a group of criterion variables also related to achievement (job success, work income, and college GPA), we would use canonical analysis. Such analysis produces a single correlation that indicates the correlation among both groups of variables.

Trying to make sense of a large number of variables is difficult, simply because there are so many variables to be considered. *Factor analysis* is a way to take a large number of variables

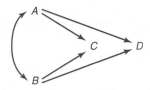

FIGURE 7.3

Example of a path analysis model: The connections of variables A, B, and C to variable D

and group them into a smaller number of clusters called *factors.* Factor analysis computes the correlations among all the variables and then derives factors by finding groups of variables that are correlated highly among each other, but lowly with other variables. The factors identified, not the many individual items within the factors, are then used as variables. Factor analysis produces a manageable number of factor variables to deal with and analyze.

:: PROBLEMS TO CONSIDER IN INTERPRETING CORRELATION COEFFICIENTS

The quality of the information provided in correlation coefficients depends on the data they are calculated from. It is important to ask the following questions when interpreting correlation coefficients:

- Was the proper correlation method used to calculate the correlation? (See Table 7.2.)
- Do the variables being correlated have high reliabilities? Low reliabilities lower the chance of finding significant relationships.
- Is the validity of the variables strong? Invalid variables produce meaningless results.
- Is the range of scores to be correlated restricted or extended? Narrow or restricted score ranges lower correlation coefficients, whereas broad or extended score ranges raise them.
- How large is the sample size? The larger the sample size, the smaller the value needed to reach statistical significance. Large sample sizes may be statistically significant but practically unimportant.

An example of correlational research appears at the end of the chapter. Note that the alpha reliability coefficients for the instruments used are given and they are satisfactory.

SUMMARY

Correlational Research: Definition and Purpose

1. Correlational research involves collecting data to determine whether and to what degree a relationship exists between two or more variables. The degree of relationship is expressed as a correlation coefficient.
2. If a relationship exists between two variables, it means that the scores on the variables vary in some nonrandom, related way.
3. The fact that there is a relationship between variables does not imply that one is the cause of the other. Correlations do not describe causal relationships. You cannot prove that one variable causes another with correlational data.

4. If two variables are highly related, a correlation coefficient near +1.00 (or −1.00) will be obtained; if two variables are not related, a coefficient near .00 will be obtained. The more highly related two variables are, the more accurate are predictions based on their relationship.

The Correlational Research Process

Problem Selection

5. Correlational studies may be designed either to determine which variables of a list of likely candidates are related or to test hypotheses regarding expected relationships. The variables to be correlated should be selected on the basis of some rationale suggested by theory or experience.

Participant and Instrument Selection

6. A common, minimally accepted sample size for a correlational study is 30 participants. However, if the variables correlated have low reliabilities and validities or if the participants will be subdivided and correlated, a higher sample size is necessary.

Design and Procedure

7. In the basic correlational design, scores for two (or more) variables of interest are obtained for each member of a selected sample, and the paired scores are correlated.

Data Analysis and Interpretation

8. A correlation coefficient is a decimal number between +1.00 and −1.00. It describes both the size and direction of the relationship between two variables. If the correlation coefficient is near .00, the variables are not related.

9. A correlation coefficient near +1.00 indicates that the variables are highly and positively related. A person with a high score on one variable is likely to have a high score on the other variable, and a person with a low score on one is likely to have a low score on the other. An increase on one variable is associated with an increase on the other.

10. If the correlation coefficient is near −1.00, the variables are highly and negatively or inversely related. A person with a high score on one variable is likely to have a low score on the other variable, and a person with a low score on one is likely to have a high score on the other. An increase on one variable is associated with a decrease on the other variable.

11. Correlations of +1.00 and −1.00 represent the same high degree but different directions of relationship.

12. A correlation coefficient much lower than .50 is not generally useful for either group prediction or individual prediction. However, using a combination of correlations below .50 may yield a useful prediction.

13. Coefficients in the .60s and .70s are usually considered adequate for group prediction purposes, and coefficients in the .80s and higher are adequate for individual prediction purposes.

14. Although all reliabilities in the .90s are acceptable, for certain kinds of instruments, such as

personality measures, a reliability in the low .70s might be acceptable.

15. Squaring the correlation coefficient indicates the common variance, the extent of shared variation between the variables. The higher the common variance, the higher the correlation.

16. How large a correlation coefficient must be to be useful depends on the purpose for which it was computed. Exploring or testing hypothesized relationships, predicting future performance, or determining validity and reliability each require different correlation sizes.

17. Statistical significance refers to whether the obtained coefficient is really different from zero and reflects a true relationship, not a chance relationship. To determine how large your correlation coefficient needs to be, to be statistically significant, you find the value in a table from which you can choose a level of significance and the size of your sample.

18. For a given level of significance, the smaller the sample size, the larger the coefficient required. For a given sample size, the value of the correlation coefficient needed for significance increases as the level of confidence increases.

19. No matter how significant a coefficient is, a low coefficient represents a low degree of association between the variables.

20. When interpreting any correlation coefficient, you must always keep in mind that you are talking only about an association between variables, not a cause–effect relationship.

Relationship Studies

21. A relationship study is conducted to gain insight into the variables, or factors, that are related to a complex variable, such as academic achievement, motivation, or self-concept. Such studies give direction to subsequent causal–comparative and experimental studies.

Data Collection

22. In a relationship study, the researcher first identifies, either inductively or deductively, the variables to be related. A smaller number of carefully selected variables is much to preferred to a large number of carelessly selected variables.

23. The population must be one for which data on each of the identified variables can be collected, and one whose members are available to the

researcher. One advantage of a relationship study is that all the data may be collected within a relatively short time period.

Data Analysis and Interpretation

24. In a relationship study, the scores for each variable are correlated among themselves or with the scores of a complex variable of interest.
25. There are many types of correlation, distinguished mainly by the type of data that are being correlated. The most commonly used correlation is the product moment correlation coefficient (Pearson *r*), which is used when both variables are expressed as continuous (i.e., ratio or interval) data. The Spearman rho correlation is used when ordinal data (ranks) are being correlated.
26. Most correlational techniques are concerned with investigating linear relationships. If a relationship is instead curvilinear, an increase in one variable is associated with a corresponding increase in another variable to a point, at which point further increase in the first variable results in a corresponding decrease in the other variable (or vice versa).
27. In addition to computing correlation coefficients for a total sample group, researchers may wish to examine relationships separately for certain defined subgroups. To obtain reliable results, you must begin with a large enough sample.
28. Attenuation is the reduction in correlation coefficients that tends to occur if the measures being correlated have low reliability. In relationship studies a correction for attenuation can be applied that indicates what the correlation coefficient would be if both measures were perfectly reliable.
29. A narrow or restricted range of scores is another factor that can lead to a correlation coefficient underrepresenting the true relationship. A correction for restriction in range may be applied to obtain an estimate of what the coefficient would be if the range of scores were not restricted.

Prediction Studies

30. If two variables are highly related, scores on one variable can be used to predict scores on the other variable. Prediction studies are often conducted to facilitate decision making about individuals or to aid in the selection of individuals.

31. The variable on which the prediction is made is referred to as the *predictor,* and the variable predicted is referred to as the *criterion.*
32. If several predictor variables each correlate well with a criterion, then a prediction based on a combination of those variables will be more accurate than a prediction based on any one of them.

Data Collection

33. As with a relationship study, participants must be selected from whom the desired data can be collected and who are available to the researcher.
34. In a relationship study, data on all variables are collected within a relatively short period of time. In contrast, in a prediction study, predictor variables are measured well before the criterion variable is measured.
35. Shrinkage is the tendency of a prediction equation to become less accurate when used with a group other than the one on which the equation was originally formulated. Thus, any prediction equation should be validated with at least one other group to assess shrinkage.
36. A prediction equation should be cross-validated on a new group of participants to determine its usefulness for groups other than the original one.

Data Analysis and Interpretation

37. As with a relationship study, each predictor variable is correlated with the criterion variable.
38. There are two types of prediction studies: single prediction studies and multiple prediction studies.
39. Because a combination of variables usually results in a more accurate prediction than any one variable, a prediction study often results in a prediction equation referred to as a multiple regression equation. A multiple regression equation uses all variables that individually predict the criterion to make a more accurate prediction.
40. The accuracy of prediction can be lowered by unreliable variables, length of time between gathering data about the predictor(s) and the criterion variable, and broadness of the criterion.
41. Because relationships are not perfect, predictions made by multiple regression equations are not perfect. Predicted scores should be interpreted as intervals, not as a single number.

42. As with relationship studies, and for similar reasons, prediction equations may be used for both the total group and subgroups.

43. Predictive studies can provide an indication of the common variance shared by the predictor(s) and the criterion variables by using the coefficient of determination.

Other Correlation-Based Analyses

44. There are a number of more complex correlation-based analyses, including discriminant function analysis, path analysis, canonical analysis, and factor analysis.

Now go to the Companion Website at **www.prenhall.com/gay** to assess your understanding of chapter content with Practice Quiz, apply comprehension in Applying What You Know, broaden your knowledge about research in Web Links, and expand your research skills in Evaluating Articles, Analyzing Qualitative Data, Analyzing Quantitative Data, and Research Tools and Tips.

EXPLORATIONS IN PARENT-SCHOOL RELATIONS

KATHLEEN V. HOOVER-DEMPSEY
OTTO C. BASSLER
JANE S. BRISSIE
Peabody College of Vanderbilt University

ABSTRACT   Grounded in Bandura's (1976, 1986) work, parent efficacy was defined as a parent's belief that he or she is capable of exerting a positive influence on children's school outcomes. Parents' sense of efficacy and its relationship to parent involvement were examined in this study. Parents ($n = 390$) of children in kindergarten through fourth grade in a metropolitan public school district responded to questionnaires assessing parent efficacy and parent involvement in five types of activities: help with homework, educational activities, classroom volunteering, conference participation, and telephone calls with teachers. Teachers ($n = 50$) from the same schools also participated, responding to questionnaires assessing teacher efficacy, perceptions of parent efficacy, and estimates of parent involvement. Findings revealed small but significant relationships between self-reported parent efficacy and three of the five indicators of parent involvement. Results for teachers revealed significant relationships among teacher efficacy, teacher perceptions of parent efficacy, and teacher reports of parent involvement in four areas. Results are discussed in relation to the patterns of involvement activities reported by parents and implications for research and intervention in parent-school relationships.

Bandura's (1977, 1984, 1986) work on personal efficacy considers the influence of beliefs that one is capable of achieving specific outcomes on behavior choices. In general, his work suggests that persons higher in efficacy will be more likely to engage in behaviors leading to a goal and will be more persistent in the face of obstacles than will persons with a lower sense of efficacy.

Hoover-Dempsey, Bassler, and Brissie (1987) earlier examined relationships between teacher efficacy and parent involvement. Building on Bandura's work and studies of the role of teacher efficacy in various educational outcomes (Ashton, Webb, & Doda, 1983; Dembo & Gibson, 1985), the authors defined teacher efficacy as "teachers' certainty that their instructional skills are effective" (p. 425). Hoover-Dempsey, Bassler, and Brissie found that teacher efficacy was significantly related to teacher reports of parents' involvement in conferences, volunteering, and home tutoring, as well as teacher perceptions of parent support.

Examination of specific parent variables often related to children's school performance suggests a complementary avenue of exploration in efforts to understand and improve parent-school relations. Some evidence that *parent* efficacy beliefs may be important in parent behaviors and child outcomes are reported in

Baumrind's (1971, 1973) work on parenting styles, which established clear linkages between patterns of parenting behaviors and patterns of children's social and cognitive development. For example, the characteristics of Baumrind's authoritative style include consistent parental willingness to give reasons and explanations for requests and to consider and discuss alternative points of view. Because children of authoritative parents have consistent access to their parents' thinking—and because authoritative parents listen and take into account their children's reasoning—the children tend to develop higher levels of social and cognitive competence than do peers raised in other parenting styles.

Dornbusch, Ritter, Leiderman, Roberts, and Fraleigh (1987) recently demonstrated another specific outcome of an authoritative parenting style; they found that adolescents raised by authoritative parents, when compared with adolescents raised by authoritarian parents, have higher levels of academic performance in high school. In a related line of inquiry, Mondell and Tyler (1981) reported significant positive relationships between elements of parental competence and characteristics of parents' teaching interactions with their children, for example, more competent parents treat the child as an "origin," offer more approval and acceptance, and offer more helpful problem-solving questions and strategies.

In each set of findings, the qualities of parental behavior suggest the presence of strong parental beliefs in the abilities and "worthiness" of the child, for example, giving children reasons for requests and treating them as capable of solving problems. These behaviors suggest that parents believe in the abilities of the child and have confidence in their own ability to guide the child's learning. Such attitudes and the behaviors that they enable are central to a parental sense of efficacy—parents' belief and knowledge that they can teach their children (content, processes, attitudes, and values) and that their children can learn what they teach.

Applied in this manner, Bandura's (1977, 1984, 1986) theory suggests that parents will hold personal efficacy beliefs about their ability to help their children learn. These efficacy beliefs will influence their decisions about the avenues and timing of efforts to become involved in their children's education. For ex-

Address correspondence to Kathleen V. Hoover-Dempsey, Department of Psychology and Human Development, Box 512, Peabody College, Vanderbilt University, Nashville, TN 37203.

ample, parents with a strong sense of efficacy are more likely than low-efficacy parents are to help their children resolve a misunderstanding with the teacher, because they believe that they are capable of offering, and helping their child to act on, appropriate guidance. Overall, parents most likely become involved when they believe that their involvement will "make a difference" for their children.

Following Bandura's (1986) suggestion that assessments of perceived self-efficacy are appropriately "tailored to the domains of functioning being analyzed" (p. 360), the present study was designed to explore parent efficacy and the nature of its relationship to specific indicators of parents' involvement in their elementary school children's education. Although parent efficacy is likely only one of several contributors to parents' involvement decisions (Bandura 1986), we believe that it may operate as a fundamentally important mechanism, explaining variations in involvement decisions more fully than do some of the more frequently referenced status variables (e.g., parent income, education, employment). We believe that self-efficacy is more significant than such status variables because self-efficacy beliefs, far more than variables describing an individual's status, "function as an important set of proximal determinants of human motivation, affect, and action" (Bandura, 1989, p. 1175). Support for this position comes from related bodies of work, for example, Greenberger and Goldberg's (1989) findings that adults' commitment to parenting is "more consequential" for other parenting practices than is their involvement in work (30).

We also explored the replicability of previous results indicating a significant positive relationship between teachers' sense of efficacy and parent involvement. That relationship is grounded in the logical probability that teachers with a higher sense of personal teaching efficacy, being more confident of their teaching skills, are more likely to invite parent involvement and to accept parents' initiation of involvement activities (Hoover-Dempsey et al., 1987). Finally, we explored teachers' perceptions of parents' efficacy and involvement, based, in part, on earlier findings of a significant relationship between an "other's" perceptions of teacher efficacy and selected teacher outcomes (Brissie, Hoover-Dempsey, & Bassler, 1988). In general, we expected that higher levels of parent involvement would be associated with higher levels of parent efficacy, teacher efficacy, and teacher perceptions of parent efficacy. We expected to find those relationships because higher efficacy parents and teachers, being more confident of their skills and abilities related to children's learning, would more likely initiate and invite parent involvement in children's school-related learning activities.

Sample, Methods, and Procedures

Four elementary schools in a large public school district participated in the study. The schools varied in geographic location within the district, size (300 to 500 students), and mean annual family income reported by parents ($15,000 to $37,000). Because the purpose of the study was to examine a group of parents across varied school settings, data are not reported for individual schools.

We contacted principals from each school and obtained permission to solicit parent and teacher participation. Letters describing the study were put in teacher mailboxes at each school. Teachers choosing to participate were asked to complete a questionnaire that contained all teacher data needed for the study and to leave it in a sealed envelope in a collection box in the school office. All the teachers at each school, whether they choose to participate in the study or not, were asked to send parent letters and questionnaire packets home with students in their classes. The letter explained the study, solicited voluntary participation, and asked parents to complete an accompanying questionnaire and return it to school in a sealed envelope. We collected the sealed return envelopes from parents and teachers at the schools.

Parent Sample

Three hundred ninety parents participated in the study. The number represented approximately 30% of the children served by the four schools. Individual school response rates ranged from 24% to 36%. Given the relatively low response rate, the results must be interpreted with caution. It seemed probable that bias in the sample favored participation by parents who had stronger opinions about the issues involved. As a check on that possibility, we reviewed parents' comments at the end of the questionnaire (in a "comments" space used by approximately half of the participants). The comments revealed a wide range of positive and negative statements, indicating a varied set of parent experiences and attitudes (e.g., "I would appreciate more news on what the children are doing and why from teachers to parents, plus how to assist with that at home." "Conference times are inaccessible to people who work. Teachers do not like phone calls from parents in their off time and I understand this. You never hear from the schoolteacher unless they have a complaint or want something." "Our son's teacher this year and last has been a very positive influence on him. We're grateful for her caring the way she does." "She never has homework. What is this teacher's problem? Is she too lazy to grade extra papers? My child is making Cs and Ds. Please help.") Although the respondents may have had a higher-than-average level of interest in parent involvement issues, the variety of experiences reflected in their comments suggested that their reports would be useful in understanding many parents' patterns of school-related involvement.

In general, the respondents appeared to be an average group of elementary school parents (Table 1). Most of the respondents were mothers, most were married, and most were employed outside of the home. Education and income levels spanned a wide range. A comparison of that group with national data suggests that those parents were typical of many public school districts' parent population (e.g., compare Table 1 figures with national percentages for marital status in 1987—63% married, 36% not married—and for education—among the 25- to 34-year-old age group in 1984, 34% had a high school education and 16% had a college degree; U.S. Bureau of the Census, 1989).

Teacher Sample

Fifty teachers in the four schools (63% of the total possible) participated in the study and returned usable questionnaires. All the teachers were women, and their class enrollments averaged 21.06 (SD = 5.20). They had been teaching for an average

Table 1.
Parent Characteristics

Elementary school parents	n	% of sample
Sex		
Female	326	84
Male	54	14
No response	8	2
Education		
Grade school	27	7
High school	131	34
Some college	125	32
BA/BS degree	50	13
Some graduate work	22	6
Graduate degree (MA/MS, PhD/MD)	24	7
No response	9	2
Marital status		
Married	259	67
Not married (includes single, separated, divorced, widowed)	124	32
No response	5	1
Employment status		
Employed out of the home	253	65
Not employed out of the home	118	30
No response	17	4
Family income		
≤ $5,000	25	6
$5,001–$10,000	42	11
$10,001–$20,000	78	20
$20,001–$30,000	76	20
$30,001–$40,000	75	20
$40,001–$50,000	36	9
$50,001 +	23	6
No response	10	8
Age of respondent	$M = 33.37$	$SD = 6.61$

of 15.76 years ($SD = 7.57$) and had been in their present schools for approximately 6.5 years ($SD = 5.73$). Their average age was 41.21 years ($SD = 8.73$). The majority of the teachers held a master's degree, and many had credits beyond the MA/MS degrees.

Measures

All data on the parents and teachers were derived from questionnaires returned by the respondents. The questionnaire for each set of respondents contained demographic items, a set of requests for estimates of participation in specific parent involvement activities, and a series of items designed to assess respondents' perceptions of parent or teacher efficacy.

Parent Questionnaire. The Parent Questionnaire asked participants to give specific information about themselves (employment status, education, family income, marital status, age, and sex) and estimates of their levels of involvement in various forms of parent-school activities—help with homework (hours in average week); other educational activities with children (hours in average week); volunteer work at school (hours in average week); telephone calls with teachers (number in average month); and parent-teacher conferences (average number in semester). Similar estimation procedures have been used successfully in other investigations (Grolnick & Ryan, 1989; Hoover-Dempsey, et al., 1987; Stevenson & Baker, 1987).

The Parent Questionnaire contained Likert-scale response items designed to assess parents' perceptions of their own efficacy. We developed the 12-item Parent Perceptions of Parent Efficacy Scale on the basis of the teaching efficacy and parenting literature cited earlier. Although efforts to develop an assessment of general parenting efficacy have been reported (Johnston & Mash, 1989), the teaching efficacy literature was used as the basis for this measure because interest in this study focused on parents' perceptions of personal efficacy specifically in relation to children's school learning. The scale included such items as "I know how to help my child do well in school" and "If I try hard, I can get through to my child even when he/she has trouble understanding something." Following the model set by previously reported scales of teacher efficacy, items in this scale focused on assessment of parents' general abilities to influence children's school outcomes and specific effectiveness in influencing children's school learning. Items were scored on a 5-point scale ranging from *strongly disagree* (1) to *strongly agree* (5). Negatively worded items were subsequently rescored so that higher scores uniformly reflected higher efficacy. Possible total scores for the scale ranged from 12 to 60. Similarity to selected items of the Teacher Perceptions of Efficacy Scale (see below) and its grounding in related literature support the validity of this scale. Alpha reliability for this sample, .81, was judged satisfactory.

Teacher Questionnaire. The Teacher Questionnaire asked for specific information about teachers and their classes (grade, enrollment, percentage of students qualifying for free lunch, total years taught, years at present school, highest degree earned, sex, and age). Teachers were also asked to estimate the number of students in their classes whose parents participated in scheduled conferences, volunteer work at school, regular assistance with homework, regular involvement in other educational activities with children (e.g., reading and playing games), and telephone calls with the teacher. Again, such procedures have been used successfully in other investigations (Hoover-Dempsey et al., 1987; Stevenson & Baker, 1987).

We developed a seven-item Teacher Perceptions of Parent Efficacy Scale on the basis of the literature cited earlier. Items included such statements as "My students' parents help their children learn," and "My students' parents have little influence on their children's academic performance." All the items were scored on a scale ranging from *strongly disagree* (1) to *strongly agree* (5); negatively worded items were rescored so that higher scores consistently reflected more positive teacher perceptions of parent efficacy. Possible scores for the scale ranged from 7 to 35. Similarity to selected items of the Parent Perceptions of Parent Efficacy Scale and its grounding in the literature reviewed earlier support the validity of this scale. Alpha reliability of .79 for this sample was adequate.

Items on the 12-item Teacher Perceptions of Teacher Efficacy Scale (Hoover-Dempsey et al., 1987) included such statements as "I am successful with the students in my class" and "I feel that I am making a significant educational difference in the lives of my students." Items were scored on a scale ranging from *strongly disagree* (1) to *strongly agree* (5); negatively worded items were subsequently rescored so that higher scores uniformly reflected higher efficacy. Total scale scores ranged from 12 to 60. The scale's grounding in related literature, and its earlier successful use after substantial pretesting for clarity and content, support the validity of the scale. An alpha reliability of .83 for the scale with this sample was judged satisfactory.

RESULTS

Correlations between parent efficacy and three indicators of parent involvement were statistically significant. Higher levels of parent efficacy were associated with more hours of classroom volunteering, more hours spent in educational activities with children, and fewer telephone calls with the teacher (see Table 2).

Parent efficacy scores did not reveal significant variations related to parents' sex, marital status, employment status, or family income. Parent education, however, was linked to some variations in efficacy scores, $F(5, 353) = 4.59$, $p < .01$. Parents with a grade school education had significantly lower efficacy scores than did parents with all levels of college education,

and parents with a high school education were significantly lower than parents with some college work beyond the bachelor's degree.

Parent reports of involvement were linked to some parent status characteristics. More hours of classroom volunteering were reported by females (0.74 hours per week v. 0.25 for males, $F[1, 352] = 8.53$, $p < .01$), married parents (0.81 hours per week v. 0.32 for not married, $F[1, 352] = 7.90$, $p < .01$), and unemployed parents (1.27 hours per week v. 0.34 for employed, $F[1, 352] = 8.82$, $p < .01$). More hours of homework help were reported by parents with lower education (high school at 4.80 hours per week v. college degree at 3.33, $F[5, 348] = 3.18$, $p < .01$), lower family income (3 lower income groups = 6.52 − 5.33 hours per week v. 3 higher income groups = 3.62 − 3.09, $F[6, 326] = 7.97$, $p < .01$), and single parent status (not married = 5.51 hours per week v. married = 4.05, $F[1, 352] = 13.83$, $p < .01$). More phone calls were reported by the lowest income parents (lowest income group = 1.38 calls per month v. 0.58 − 0.20 for all other income groups, $F[6, 326] = 3.90$, $p < .01$).

Teacher efficacy and teacher perceptions of parents' efficacy were both positively linked to teacher reports of parent involvement in homework, educational activities, volunteering, and conference participation (see Table 3). Teacher efficacy was also positively linked to teacher perceptions of parent efficacy. Although teacher efficacy did not show a significant relationship with the number of students qualifying for free lunch ($r = −.16$, *ns*), teacher perceptions of parent efficacy were significantly linked to the free lunch figure ($r = −.59$, $p < .01$).

Table 2.
Means, Standard Deviations, and Intercorrelations: Parent Involvement Variables and Parent Efficacy ($n = 354$)

	Homework	Educational activities	Volunteering	Telephone calls	Conferences	Parent efficacy
Homework (hours per week)	—					
Educational activities (hours per week)	.38**	—				
Volunteering (hours per week)	.07	.14**	—			
Telephone calls (number per month)	.09	.02	.02	—		
Conferences (number per semester)	.10*	.08	.08	.34**	—	
Parent efficacy	.06	.11*	.15**	−.14**	.02	—
M	4.54	4.84	.66	.49	1.45	45.71
SD	3.58	3.58	.21	1.06	1.99	5.82

*$p < .05(.11)$. ** $p < .01(.14)$.

Table 3.
Means, Standard Deviations, and Intercorrelations Among Teacher Variables

	Homework	Educational activities	Volunteering	Telephone calls	Conferences	Free lunch	Teacher efficacy	Perceptions of parent efficacy
Parents help with homework (number of students)	—							
Parents engage in educational activities with children (number of students)	.69**	—						
Parents do volunteer work at school (number of students)	.58**	.67**	—					
Telephone calls with parents (average number per month)	.25	.30	.12	—				
Parents attend scheduled conferences (number of students)	.62**	.52**	.49**	.10	—			
Number of students qualifying for free lunch	−.34*	−.48**	−.45**	−.25	−.38**	—		
Teacher efficacy	.42**	.39**	.54**	.17	.41**	−.16	—	
Perceptions of parent efficacy	.56**	.75**	.65**	.27	.59**	.44**	−.59**	—
M	8.72	8.06	2.96	4.74	9.98	9.94	43.28	24.09
SD	4.59	4.58	2.48	5.03	5.83	8.39	6.38	4.57

*$p < .05$ (.30). **$p < .11$ (.38).

DISCUSSION

The finding that parent efficacy is related, at modest but significant levels, to volunteering, educational activities, and telephone calls suggests that the construct may contribute to an understanding of variables that influence parents' involvement in decisions and choices. Defined as a set of beliefs that one is capable of achieving desired outcomes through one's efforts and the effects of those efforts on others, parent efficacy appears to facilitate increased levels of parent activity in some areas of parent involvement. The correlational nature of our results suggests that just as efficacy may influence involvement choices, these varied forms of involvement may influence parents' sense of efficacy (e.g., parents may feel increased effectiveness when they observe, during their involvement activities, that their children are successful). Regardless of the direction of influence, however, the observed linkages seem logically based in dynamic aspects of the relationship between many parents and teachers.

Classroom volunteering, for example, may be linked to efficacy, because the decision to volunteer requires some sense that one has educationally relevant skills that can and will be used effectively. Similarly, the experiences implicit in classroom volunteering may offer parents new and positive information about their effectiveness with their own child. The decision to engage in educational activities with one's children at home may reflect a sense of personal efficacy ("I will do this because it will help my child learn."); in like manner, the activities undertaken may show up, from the parent's perspective, in improved school perfor-

mance that, in turn, may enhance parent efficacy. The negative relationship between efficacy and telephone calls probably reflects the still-prevalent reality that calls to and from the school signal child difficulties. Lower efficacy parents, less certain of their ability to exert positive influence on their children's learning, may seek contact more often. Similarly, more school-initiated calls may signal to the parent that he or she is offering the child less-than-adequate help.

Overall, our findings suggest that the construct of parent efficacy warrants further investigation. Grounded in the teaching efficacy literature and theoretical work on personal efficacy, the Parent Perceptions of Parent Efficacy Scale achieved satisfactory reliability with this sample and emerged, as predicted, with modest but significant relationships with some indicators of parent involvement. Parents' average efficacy score, 45.71 (SD = 5.82) in a scale range of 12 to 60, indicated that those parents as a group had relatively positive perceptions of their own efficacy. The variations in efficacy by parental status characteristics suggested that, at least in this group, sex, marital status, employment status, and family income were *not* related to efficacy. The finding that parental education was significantly linked to efficacy is not surprising, given the probability that parents' own school experiences contribute to their sense of school-focused efficacy in relation to their children.

Parent efficacy may differ from parent education in the way it operates, however. Whereas higher levels of education may give parents a higher level of skill and knowledge, efficacy—a set of attitudes about one's ability to get necessary resources and offer effective help—increases the likelihood that a parent will *act* on his or her knowledge (or seek more information when available resources are insufficient). The explanatory function of efficacy is suggested by the finding that parent education was related to fewer and different outcomes than parent efficacy was. Parent efficacy was related to educational activities, volunteering and telephone calls, whereas education was significantly linked to homework alone. In that finding, parents with a high school education reported spending more time helping their children with homework than did parents with a college education. The fact that a group with lower education reported *more* homework help may reflect several different possibilities: the lower efficacy parents may be more determined to see their children succeed; they may use a set of less efficient helping strategies; or they may be responding to a pattern of greater school difficulty experienced by their children.

Although our data do not permit an assessment of those possibilities, we suspect that the finding reflects less adequate knowledge of effective helping strategies. Because many of our low-education parents were also unemployed, the finding may also reflect that they simply had more time for their children's homework activities than did the other parent groups. Whatever the explanations, the finding that education was related to fewer and different outcomes than efficacy suggests that the construct of parent efficacy warrants further investigation, perhaps particularly as it is distinguished from parent education.

Results for teachers support earlier findings (Hoover-Dempsey et al., 1987) of significant positive relationships between teacher efficacy and teacher reports of parent involvement. The general pattern—higher efficacy teachers reported high levels of parent participation in help with homework, educational activities, volunteering, and conferences—suggests that higher efficacy teachers may invite and receive more parent involvement or, conversely, that teachers who perceive and report higher levels of parent involvement develop higher judgments of personal teaching efficacy. It is also possible that both perceptions are operating. The absence of a significant positive relationship between teacher efficacy and the number of students in a school using the free lunch program also supports previous findings, suggesting again that teachers' personal efficacy judgments are to some extent independent of school socioeconomic status (SES). We suspect that the absence of a significant relationship reflects the probability that teacher judgments of personal ability to "make a difference" are related more powerfully to variables other than the status characteristics of their students—for example, teaching skills, organizational support, and relations with colleagues (Brissie et al., 1988).

The strong positive linkages between teacher judgments of parents' efficacy and teacher reports of parent involvement likely point to the important role that parents' involvement efforts (and perhaps the visibility of those efforts) play in teachers' judgments of parents' effectiveness. In contrast to the absence of a significant relationship between teacher efficacy and school SES, teachers' judgments of *parent* efficacy were strongly and positively linked to school SES. Thus, although teachers appeared to distinguish between their own efficacy and the socioeconomic circumstances of the families that they serve, they did not appear to draw such boundaries between parents' SES and their judgments of parents' efficacy.

The further linkage between teacher efficacy and teacher judgments of parent efficacy suggests both that teachers with higher efficacy were likely to judge parents as more efficacious and that teachers who see their students' parents as more effective experience higher levels of efficacy themselves. We suspect that this relationship is an interactive one in reality, because, for example, high efficacy in each party would tend to allow each to act with more confidence and less defensiveness in the many forms of interaction that parents and teachers often routinely undertake.

The relationships between parent efficacy and some parent involvement outcomes, as well as those between teacher perceptions of parent efficacy and teacher efficacy, suggest the potential importance of intervention strategies designed to increase parents' sense of efficacy and involvement. Bandura's (1977, 1984, 1986) work offers specific points of entry into the development of such interventions. For example, parents' *outcome expectancies*—their general beliefs that engaging in certain involvement behaviors will usually yield certain outcomes—should be examined in relation to parents' *personal efficacy* expectancies (beliefs that one's *own* involvement behaviors will yield desired outcomes). Future investigations might focus on parents' expectations about the outcomes of involvement, for example, do most parents really believe that their involvement is directly linked to child outcomes? If they believe so, what makes parents think that their own involvement choices are—or are not—important?

The findings reported here suggest the possibility that high-efficacy parents are more likely than those with low efficacy to believe that their efforts pay off. Therefore, the schools' best interests may be served by designing parent involvement approaches that focus specifically on increasing parents' sense of positive influence in their children's school success. This could be accomplished in a number of ways. For example, schools might regularly send home relatively specific instructions for parents about strategies for helping children with specific types of homework assignments. Schools might issue specific invitations related to volunteering for specific assignments (e.g., making posters, doing classroom aide work) and follow up with brief notes of thanks for a valued job well done. Teachers might routinely link some student accomplishments and positive characteristics to parent efforts as they conduct scheduled conference discussions. Many schools already engage in such practices, but the frequency and focus of such efforts might be increased in other schools as one means of communicating a basic efficacy-linked message to parents: "We think you're doing a good job of _____, and this is helping your child learn."

Similarly, the role and functions of teacher efficacy in the parent involvement process should be explored further. Is it the case, for instance, that higher efficacy teachers—more secure in and confident of their own roles in children's learning—invite (explicitly and implicitly) more frequent and significant parent involvement? Do more efficacious teachers, aware of children's specific learning needs, offer more specific suggestions or tasks for parent-child interaction? It may be true that teachers in schools with stronger parent involvement programs tend to receive more (and more positive) feedback on the value and impact of their teaching efforts. Also, teachers with varying levels of teaching efficacy perceive parent involvement and comments from parents differently (e.g., high-efficacy teachers may hear legitimate questions in a parent comment, whereas low-efficacy teachers hear criticism and threat).

The role and function of teachers' perceptions of parent efficacy also appear to warrant further examination. Teachers in this sample appeared able to give reliable estimates of their assessments of parents' efficacy. Of future interest would be an examination of the bases on which teachers make such evaluations and the role of those evaluations in teacher interactions with parents. Lightfoot (1978) suggested that parents and teachers participate in children's schooling with different interests and roles; the roles often engender conflict, but they may also be construed as complementary. Implicit in these relationships, whatever their form, is the assumption that parents and teachers watch and evaluate the actions of the other, equally essential, players in the child's school success. Closer examination of teachers' and parents' perceptions of their own roles and the "others'" roles in children's learning may yield information about an important source of influence on parent involvement and its outcomes.

The many calls over recent decades for increased parent involvement in children's education (Hess & Holloway, 1984; Hobbs, Dokecki, Hoover-Dempsey, Moroney, Shayne, & Weeks, 1984; Phi Delta Kappa, 1980) appear to have produced public and professional belief that parent involvement is one means of increasing positive educational outcomes for children. As yet, however, there has been little specific examination of the ways in which parent involvement—in general or in its varied forms—functions to produce those outcomes. With few exceptions (Epstein, 1986), little information on patterns of specific forms of parent involvement is available, underscoring the relatively unexamined nature of the causes, manifestations, and outcomes of parent involvement. The findings of this study suggest that further examination of parents' and teachers' sense of efficacy in relation to children's educational outcomes may yield useful information as both sets of participants work to increase the probabilities of children's school success.

NOTES

We appreciate the cooperation and support of the parents, teachers, principals, and other administrators who participated in this research.

We also gratefully acknowledge support from the H. G. Hill Fund of Peabody College, Vanderbilt University.

REFERENCES

Ashton, P. T., Webb, R. B., & Doda, N. (1983). *A study of teachers' sense of efficacy: Final report, executive summary.* Gainesville, FL: University of Florida.

Bandura, A. (1977). Self-efficacy: Toward a unifying theory of behavioral change. *Psychological Review, 84,* 191–215.

Bandura, A. (1984). Recycling misconceptions of perceived self-efficacy. *Cognitive Therapy and Research, 8,* 231–255.

Bandura, A. (1986). The explanatory and predictive scope of self-efficacy theory. *Journal of Social and Clinical Psychology, 4,* 359–373.

Bandura, A. (1989). Human agency in social cognitive theory. *American Psychologist, 44,* 1175–1184.

Baumrind, D. (1971). Current patterns of parental authority. *Developmental Psychology Monographs, 4,* 1–103.

Baumrind, D. (1973). The development of instrumental competence through socialization. In A. D. Pick (Ed.), *Minnesota Symposium on Child Psychology, Vol. 7,* 3–46. Minneapolis, MN: University of Minnesota Press.

Brissie, J. S., Hoover-Dempsey, K. V., & Bassler, O. C. (1988). Individual and situational contributors to teacher burnout. *Journal of Educational Research, 82,* 106–112.

Dembo, M. H., & Gibson, S. (1985). Teachers' sense of efficacy: An important factor in school achievement. *The Elementary School Journal, 86,* 173–184.

Dornbusch, S. M., Ritter, P. L., Leiderman, P. H., Roberts, D. F., & Fraleigh, M. J. (1987). The relation of parenting style to adolescent school performance. *Child Development, 58,* 1244–1257.

Epstein, J. L. (1986). Parents' reactions to teacher practices of parent involvement. *Elementary School Journal, 86,* 277–294.

Greenberger, E., & Goldberg, W. A. (1989). Work, parenting and the socialization of children. *Developmental Psychology, 25,* 22–35.

Grolnick, W. S., & Ryan, R. M. (1989). Parent styles associated with children's self-regulation and competence in school. *Journal of Educational Psychology, 81,* 143–154.

Hess, R. D., & Holloway, S. D. (1984). Family and school as educational institutions. In R. D. Parke, R. M. Emde, H. P. McAdoo, & G. P. Sackett (Eds.), *Review of child development research: Vol. 7. The family* (pp. 179–222). Chicago: University of Chicago Press.

Hobbs, N., Dokecki, P. R., Hoover-Dempsey, K. V., Moroney, R. M., Shayne, M. W., & Weeks, K. A. (1984). *Strengthening families.* San Francisco: Jossey-Bass.

Hoover-Dempsey, K. V., Bassler, O. C., & Brissie, J. S. (1987). Parent involvement: contributions of teacher efficacy, school socioeconomic status, and other school characteristics. *American Educational Research Journal, 24,* 417–435.

Johnston, C., & Mash, E. J. (1989). A measure of parenting satisfaction and efficacy. *Journal of Clinical Child Psychology, 18,* 167–175.

Lightfoot, S. L. (1978). *Worlds apart: Relationships between families and schools.* New York: Basic Books.

Mondell, S., & Tyler, F. B. (1981). Parental competence and styles of problem-solving/play behavior with children. *Developmental Psychology, 17,* 73–78.

Phi Delta Kappa (1980). *Why do some urban schools succeed?* Bloomington, IN: Author.

Stevenson, D. L., & Baker, D. P. (1987). The family-school relation and the child's school performance. *Child Development, 58,* 1348–1357.

U.S. Bureau of the Census (1989). *Statistical abstract of the United States.* Washington, DC: U.S. Government Printing Office.

"... the resulting matched groups are identical or very similar with respect to the identified extraneous variable." (p. 222)

Causal–Comparative
Research

OBJECTIVES

After reading Chapter 8, you should be able to do the following:

1. Briefly state the purpose of causal–comparative research.
2. State the major differences between causal–comparative and correlational research.
3. State one major way in which causal–comparative and experimental research are the same and one major way in which they are different.
4. Diagram and describe the basic causal–comparative design.
5. Identify and describe three types of control procedures that can be used in a causal–comparative study.
6. Explain why the results of causal–comparative studies must be interpreted very cautiously.

Completing Chapter 8 should enable you to perform the following task.

TASK 6C

For a quantitative study, you have created research plan components (Tasks 2, 3a), described a sample (Task 4a), and considered appropriate measuring instruments (Task 5). If your study involves causal–comparative research, now develop the methods section of a research report. Include a description of participants, data collection methods, and research design. (See Performance Criteria at the end of Chapter 10, p. 287.)

▓ CAUSAL–COMPARATIVE RESEARCH: DEFINITION AND PURPOSE

Like correlational research, causal–comparative research is sometimes treated as a type of descriptive research be-
cause it too describes conditions that already exist. Causal–comparative research, however, also attempts to determine reasons, or causes, for the existing condition. This emphasis, as well as differences in research procedures, qualifies causal–comparative as a unique type of research.

As you learned in Chapter 1, in **causal–comparative research,** or *ex post facto research,* the researcher attempts to determine the cause, or reason, for existing differences in the behavior or status of groups of individuals. In other words, it is observed that groups are different on some variable, and the researcher attempts to identify the major factor that has led to this difference. Such research is referred to as *ex post facto* (Latin for "after the fact") because both the effect and the alleged cause have already occurred and must be studied in retrospect. For example, a researcher might hypothesize that participation in preschool education is the major factor contributing to differences in the social adjustment of first graders. To examine this hypothesis, the researcher would select a sample of first graders who had participated in preschool education and a sample of first graders who had not and then would compare the social adjustment of the two groups. If the group that did participate in preschool education exhibited a higher lever of social adjustment, the researcher's hypothesis would be supported. Thus, the basic causal–comparative approach involves starting with an effect and seeking possible causes.

A variation of the basic approach starts with a cause and investigates its effect on some variable; such research is concerned with questions of "What is the effect of X?" For example, a researcher might wish to investigate the long-range effect that failure to be promoted to the seventh grade has on the self-concept of children not promoted. The researcher might hypothesize that children who are "socially promoted" have higher self-concepts at the end of the seventh grade than children who are retained or "held back" and made to repeat the sixth grade.

At the end of a school year, the researcher would identify a group of seventh graders who had been socially promoted to the seventh grade the year before and a group of sixth graders who had been made to repeat the sixth grade. The self-concepts of the two groups would be compared. If the socially promoted group exhibited a higher level of self-concept, the researcher's hypothesis would be supported. The basic approach, which involves starting with effects and investigating causes, is sometimes referred to as **retrospective causal–comparative research**. The variation, which starts with causes and investigates effects, is called **prospective causal–comparative research**. Retrospective causal–comparative studies are by far more common in educational research.

Beginning researchers often confuse causal–comparative research with both correlational research and experimental research. Correlational and causal–comparative research are probably confused because of the lack of variable manipulation common to both and the similar cautions regarding interpretation of results. There are definite differences, however. Causal–comparative studies *attempt* to identify cause–effect relationships; correlational studies do not. Causal–comparative studies typically involve two (or more) groups and one independent variable, whereas correlational studies typically involve two (or more) variables and one group. Also, causal–comparative studies involve comparison, whereas correlational studies involve relationship. A common misconception that beginning and even more experienced researchers have is that causal–comparative research is "better" or more rigorous than correlational research. Perhaps it is because the term *causal–comparative* sounds more "research- ey" than *correlation*, as if it might prove the cause of something. We all have heard the research mantra: "Correlation does not imply causation." In fact, *both* causal–comparative and correlation methods fail to produce true experimental data—a point to remember as you continue your causal–comparative and correlational research.

It is understandable that causal–comparative and experimental research are at first difficult to distinguish; both *attempt to establish* cause–effect relationships, and both involve group comparisons. In an experimental study, the researcher selects a random sample from a population and then randomly divides the sample into two or more groups. These groups are assigned to the treatments by the researcher, and the study is carried out. In causal–comparative research there is also a comparison, but individuals are not randomly assigned to treatment groups because they already were selected into groups before the research began. To put it as simply as possible, the major difference is that in experimental research the independent variable, the alleged cause, is manipulated by the researcher, whereas in causal–comparative research the independent variable is not manipulated because it has already occurred. In experimental research the researcher can randomly form groups and manipulate the independent variable; that is, the researcher can determine "who" is going to get "what" treatment of the independent variable. In causal–comparative research the groups are *already formed* and already differ in terms of the independent variable. The difference was not brought about by the researcher.

Independent variables in causal–comparative studies are variables that cannot be manipulated (such as socioeconomic status), should not be manipulated (such as number of cigarettes smoked per day), or simply are not manipulated but could be (such as method of reading instruction). There are a number of important educational problems for which it is impossible or not feasible to manipulate the independent variable. For instance, the variable may be an **organismic variable**, a characteristic of a subject or organism that cannot be directly controlled; age and sex are common organismic variables. Ethical considerations often prevent manipulation of a variable that *could be* manipulated but *should not be*, particularly when the manipulation might cause physical or mental harm to participants. For example, suppose a researcher were interested in determining the effect of mothers' prenatal care on the developmental status of their children at age 1. Clearly, it would not be ethical to deprive a group of mothers-to-be of prenatal care for the sake of a research study when such care is considered to be extremely important to the health of both mothers and children. Thus, causal–comparative research permits investigation of a number of variables that cannot be studied experimentally.

FIGURE 8.1	Examples of independent variables investigated in causal–comparative studies

ORGANISMIC VARIABLES	PERSONALITY VARIABLES	FAMILY-RELATED VARIABLES	SCHOOL-RELATED VARIABLES
Age	Anxiety level	Family income	Preschool attendance
Sex	Introversion/extroversion	Socioeconomic status	Size of school
Ethnicity	Aggression level	Employment status (of)	Type of school (e.g., public
	Self-concept	Student	vs. private)
ABILITY VARIABLES	Self-esteem	Mother	Per pupil expenditure
Intelligence	Aspiration level	Father	Type of curriculum
Scholastic aptitude	Brain dominance	Marital status of parents	Leadership style
Specific aptitudes	Learning style (e.g.,	Family environment	Teaching style
Perceptual ability	field independence/	Birth order	Peer pressure
	field dependence)	Number of siblings	

Note: A few of the variables *can be* manipulated (e.g., type of curriculum), but are frequently the object of causal–comparative research.

Figure 8.1 shows independent variables often studied in causal–comparative research. These variables are used to compare two or more levels of a dependent variable. For example, a causal–comparative researcher might compare the retention of facts in participants younger than 50 to the retention of facts in participants older than 50; the attention span of students with high anxiety to that of students with low anxiety; or the achievement of first graders who attended preschool to the achievement of first graders who did not attend preschool. In each case, preexisting participant groups are compared on a dependent variable.

As mentioned previously, experimental studies are costly in more ways than one and should be conducted only when there is good reason to believe the effort will be fruitful. Like correlational studies, causal–comparative studies help to identify variables worthy of experimental investigation. In fact, causal–comparative studies are sometimes conducted solely for the purpose of identifying the probable outcome of an experimental study. Suppose, for example, a superintendent was considering implementing computer-assisted remedial math instruction in his school system. Before implementing the instructional program, the superintendent might consider trying it out on an experimental basis for a year in a number of schools or classrooms. However, even such limited adoption would require costly new equipment and teacher training. Thus, as a preliminary measure, to inform his decision, the superintendent might conduct a causal–comparative study to compare the math achievement of students in school districts currently using computer-assisted remedial math instruction with the math achievement of students in school districts or classrooms not currently using it. Because most districts have yearly testing programs to assess student achievement in various subject areas, including math, obtaining information on math achievement would not be difficult. If the results indicated that the students learning through computer-assisted remedial math instruction were achieving higher scores, the superintendent would probably decide to go ahead with an experimental tryout of computer-assisted remedial math instruction in his own district. If no differences were found, the superintendent would probably not go ahead with the experimental tryout, preferring not to waste time, money, and effort.

Despite its many advantages, causal–comparative research does have some serious limitations that should be kept in mind. Because the independent variable has already occurred, the same kinds of controls cannot be exercised as in an experimental study. Extreme caution must be applied in interpreting results. An apparent cause–effect relationship may not be as it appears. As with a correlational study, only a relationship is established, not necessarily a causal connection. The alleged cause of an observed effect may in fact be the effect itself, or there may be a third variable that has "caused" both the identified cause and the effect. For example, suppose a researcher hypothesized that self-concept is a determinant of reading achievement. The researcher would compare the achievement of two groups: one group with high self-concepts and one group with low self-concepts. If the high self-concept group did indeed perform better on reading measures, the temptation would be to conclude that self-concept influences high reading achievement. However, this conclusion would be unwarranted. Because both the independent and dependent variables would have already occurred, it would not be possible to determine which came first and, thus, which influences the other. If the study was reversed, and a group of high achievers was compared with a group of low achievers, it might well be that they would be different on self-concept, thus suggesting that achievement causes self-concept. It would even be possible (in fact, very plausible) that some third variable, such as parental attitude, might be the main influence on *both* self-concept and achievement. Parents who praise and encourage their children might produce high self-concept and high academic achievement. Thus, caution must be exercised in claiming cause–effect relationships based on causal–comparative research. Only in experimental research is the degree of control sufficient to establish cause–effect relationships. Only in experimental research does the researcher randomly assign participants to treatment groups. In causal–comparative research the researcher cannot assign participants to treatment groups because they are already in those groups. However, despite these limitations, causal–comparative studies *do* permit investigation of variables that cannot or should not be investigated experimentally, facilitate decision making, provide guidance for experimental studies, and are less costly on all dimensions.

:: CONDUCTING A CAUSAL–COMPARATIVE STUDY

The basic causal–comparative design is quite simple, and although the independent variable is not manipulated, there are control procedures that can be exercised to improve interpretation of results. Causal–comparative studies also involve a wider variety of statistical techniques than the other types of research thus far discussed.

Design and Procedure

The basic causal–comparative design involves selecting two groups differing on some independent variable and comparing them on some dependent variable (Table 8.1). As Table 8.1 indicates, the researcher selects two groups of participants, which are referred to as *experimental* and *control groups* but should more accurately be referred to as *comparison groups*. The groups may differ in two ways. Either one group possesses a characteristic that the other

TABLE 8.1	The basic causal–comparative design		
	Group	Independent Variable	Dependent Variable
Case A	(E)	(X)	O
	(C)		O
Case B	(E)	(X_1)	O
	(C)	(X_2)	O

Symbols:
  (E) = Experimental group; ( ) indicates no manipulation
  (C) = Control group
  (X) = Independent variable
  O = Dependent variable

does not (Case A), or one group has the characteristic but to differing degrees or amounts (Case B). An example of Case A would be a comparison of two groups, one composed of brain-injured children and the other composed of non–brain-injured children. An example of Case B would be a comparison of two groups, one composed of high self-concept individuals and the other composed of low self-concept individuals. Another Case B example is a comparison of the algebra achievement of two groups, one that had learned algebra via traditional instruction and one that had learned algebra via computer-assisted instruction. In both Case A and Case B designs, the performance of the groups would be compared using some valid dependent variable measure selected from the types of instruments discussed in Chapter 5.

Definition and selection of the comparison groups are very important parts of the causal–comparative procedure. The independent variable differentiating the groups must be clearly and operationally defined, since each group represents a different population. The way in which the groups are defined will affect the generalizability of the results. If a researcher wanted to compare a group of students with an "unstable" home life to a group of students with a "stable" home life, the terms *unstable* and *stable* would have to be operationally defined. An unstable home life could refer to any number of things, such as life with a parent who abuses alcohol, who is violent, or who neglects the child. It could refer to a combination of these or other factors. Operational definitions help define the populations and guide sample selection.

Random selection from the defined populations is generally the preferred method of participant selection. The important consideration is to select samples that are representative of their respective populations. Note that in casual–comparative research the researcher samples from two already existing populations, not from a single population as in experimental research. This difference is key in differentiating the two approaches. As in experimental studies, the goal is to have groups that are as similar as possible on all relevant variables except the independent variable. To determine the equality of groups, information on a number of background and current status variables may be collected and compared for each group. For example, information on age, years of experience, gender, prior knowledge, and the like, may be obtained and examined for the groups being compared. The more similar the two groups are on such variables, the more homogeneous they are on everything but the independent variable. This makes a stronger study and reduces the possible alternative explanations of the research findings. There are a number of control procedures to correct for identified inequalities on such variables.

Control Procedures

Lack of randomization, manipulation, and control are all sources of weakness in a causal–comparative study. Random assignment of participants to groups is probably the single best way to try to ensure equality of groups. This is not possible in causal–comparative studies because the groups already exist and have already received the independent variable. A problem already discussed is the possibility that the groups are different on some other important variable (e.g., gender, experience, age) besides the identified independent variable. It may be this other variable is the real cause of the observed difference between the causal–comparative groups.

For example, if a researcher simply compared a group of students who had received preschool education to a group who had not, she might draw the conclusion that preschool education results in higher first-grade reading achievement. However, what if all preschool programs in the region in which the study was conducted were private and required high tuition? If this were the case, the researcher would really be investigating the effects not just of preschool education but also of membership in a well-to-do family. It might very well be that parents in such families provide early informal reading instruction for their children. This could make it very difficult to disentangle the effects of preschool education from the effects of affluent families on first-grade reading. A researcher aware of the situation, however, could control for this variable by studying only children of well-to-do parents. Thus, the two groups to be compared would be equated with respect to the extraneous variable of parents' income level. The preceding example is but one illustration of a number of statistical and nonstatistical methods that can be applied in an attempt to control for extraneous variables. The following sections describe three control techniques: matching, comparing homogeneous groups or subgroups, and analysis of covariance. These and other techniques are discussed in more detail in Chapter 9, "Experimental Research."

Matching

Matching is a technique for equating groups on one or more variables. If a researcher has identified a variable likely to influence performance on the dependent variable, he may control for that variable by *pair-wise matching* of participants. In other words, for each participant in one group, the researcher finds a participant in the other group with the same or very similar score on the control variable. If a participant in either group does not have a suitable match, the participant is eliminated from the study. Thus, the resulting matched groups are identical or very similar with respect to the identified extraneous variable. For example, if a researcher matched participants in each group on IQ, a participant in one group with an IQ of 140 would have a matched participant with an IQ at or near 140. As you may have deduced (if you have an IQ of 140!), a major problem with pair-wise matching is that invariably some participants will have no match and must therefore be eliminated from the study. The problem becomes even more serious when the researcher attempts to simultaneously match participants on two or more variables.

Comparing Homogeneous Groups or Subgroups

Another way to control extraneous variables is to compare groups that are homogeneous with respect to the extraneous variable. In the study about preschool attendance and first-grade achievement, the decision to compare only children of well-to-do families would be an attempt to control extraneous variables by comparing homogeneous groups. If, in another situation, IQ were an identified extraneous variable, the researcher might limit groups to only subjects with IQs between 85 and 115 (average IQ). This procedure may lower the numbers of participants in the study and also limits the generalizability of the findings because only a limited range of IQ participants was studied.

A similar but more satisfactory approach is to form subgroups within each group that represent all levels of the control variable. For example, each group might be divided into high (116 and above), average (85 to 115), and low (84 and below) IQ subgroups. The existence of comparable subgroups in each group controls for IQ. In addition to controlling for the variable, this approach also permits the researcher to determine whether the independent variable affects the dependent variable differently at different levels of IQ, the control variable. That is, the researcher can examine whether the effect on the dependent variable is different for the different subgroups. If this information is of interest, the best approach is not to do separate analyses for each of the subgroups but to build the control variable right into the research design and analyze the results with a statistical technique called factorial analysis of variance. A **factorial analysis of variance** (discussed further in Chapter 12) allows the researcher to determine the effect of the independent variable and the control variable on the dependent variable both separately and in combination. In other words, it permits him to determine if there is an interaction between the independent variable and the control variable such that the independent variable operates differently at different levels of the control variable. For example, IQ might be a control variable in a causal–comparative study of the effects of two different methods of learning fractions. It might be found that a method involving manipulation of blocks is more effective for students with lower IQs who may have difficulty thinking abstractly.

Analysis of Covariance

Analysis of covariance is used to adjust initial group differences on variables used in causal–comparative and experimental group studies. In essence, **analysis of covariance** adjusts scores on a dependent variable for initial differences on some other variable related to performance on the dependent variable. For example, suppose we were doing a study to compare two methods, X and Y, of teaching fifth graders to solve math problems. When we gave the two groups a pretest of math ability, we found that the group to be taught by Method Y scored much higher than the group to be taught by Method X. This difference suggests that the Method Y group will be superior to the Method X group at the end of the study just because members of the group began with higher math ability than members of the other group. Analysis of covariance statistically adjusts the scores of the Method Y group to remove the initial advantage so that at the end of the study the results can be fairly compared as if the two groups started equally.

Data Analysis and Interpretation

Analysis of data in causal–comparative studies involves a variety of descriptive and inferential statistics. All of the statistics that may be used in a causal–comparative study may also be used in an experimental study, and a number of them will be described in Chapters 11 and 12. Briefly, however, the most commonly used descriptive statistics are the *mean,* which indicates the average performance of a group on a measure of some variable, and the *standard deviation,* which indicates how spread out a set of scores is around the mean—that is, whether the scores are relatively homogeneous or heterogeneous around the mean (see Chapter 11). The most commonly used inferential statistics are the *t test,* used to determine whether the means of two groups are significantly different from one another; *analysis of variance,* used to determine if there is significant difference among the means of three or more groups; and *chi square,* used to compare group frequencies—that is, to see if an event occurs more frequently in one group than another (see Chapter 12).

As repeatedly pointed out, interpreting the findings in a causal–comparative study requires considerable caution. Due to lack of randomization, manipulation, and control factors, it is difficult to establish cause–effect relationships with any great degree of confidence. The cause–effect relationship may in fact be the reverse of the one hypothesized (the alleged cause may be the effect and vice versa), or a third factor may be the underlying cause of both the independent and dependent variables.

Reversed causality is not a reasonable alternative in every case, however. For example, preschool training may "cause" increased reading achievement in third grade but reading achievement in third grade cannot "cause" preschool training. Similarly, one's gender may affect one's achievement in mathematics, but one's achievement in mathematics certainly does not affect one's gender! When reversed causality is more plausible, it should be investigated. For example, it is equally plausible that excessive absenteeism produces, or leads to, involvement in criminal activities as it is that involvement in criminal activity produces, or leads to, excessive absenteeism. The way to determine the correct order of causality—which variable caused which—is to determine which one occurred first. If, in the preceding example, it could be demonstrated that a period of excessive absenteeism was frequently followed by a student getting in trouble with the law, then it could more reasonably be concluded that excessive absenteeism leads to involvement in criminal activities. On the other hand, if it were determined that a student's first involvement in criminal activities was preceded by a period of good attendance but followed by a period of poor attendance, then the hypothesis that involvement in criminal activities leads to excessive absenteeism would be more reasonable.

The possibility of a third, common explanation is plausible in many situations. Recall the example of parental attitude affecting both self-concept and achievement. As mentioned, one way to control for a potential common cause is to compare homogeneous groups. For example, if students in both the high self-concept group and low self-concept group could be selected from parents who had similar attitudes, the effects of parents' attitudes would be removed because both groups would have been exposed to the same parental attitudes. It is clear that to investigate or control for alternative hypotheses, the researcher must be aware of them and must present evidence that they are not in fact the true explanation for the behavioral differences being investigated.

An example of causal–comparative research appears at the end of the chapter. Note that even though survey forms were used to collect data, the study was not descriptive because its purpose was to investigate existing differences between groups.

SUMMARY

Causal–Comparative Research: Definition and Purpose

1. In causal–comparative, or ex post facto, research the researcher attempts to determine the cause, or reason, for existing differences in the behavior or status of groups.

2. The basic causal–comparative approach is retrospective; that is, it starts with an effect and seeks its possible causes. A variation of the basic approach is prospective—that is, starting with a cause and investigating its effect on some variable.

3. An important difference between causal–comparative and correlational research is that causal–comparative studies involve two or more groups and one independent variable whereas correlational studies involve two or more variables and one group. *Neither* causal–comparative nor correlational research produce true experimental data.

4. The major difference between experimental research and causal–comparative research is that in experimental research the independent variable, the alleged cause, is manipulated, and in causal–comparative research it is not, because it has already occurred. In experimental research the researcher can randomly form groups and manipulate the independent variable. In causal–comparative research the groups are already formed and already divided on the independent variable.

5. Independent variables in casual–comparative studies are variables that cannot be manipulated (such as socioeconomic status), should not be manipulated (such as number of cigarettes smoked per day), or simply are not manipulated but could be (such as method of reading instruction).

6. Causal–comparative studies identify relationships that may lead to experimental studies, but only a relationship is established. Cause–effect relationships established through causal–comparative research are at best tenuous and tentative. Only experimental research can truly establish cause–effect relationships.

7. The alleged cause of an observed causal–comparative effect may in fact be the effect, the supposed cause, or a third variable that has "caused" both the identified cause and effect.

Conducting a Causal–Comparative Study

Design and Procedure

8. The basic causal–comparative design involves selecting two groups differing on some independent variable and comparing them on some dependent variable.

9. The groups may differ in one of two ways. One group may possess a characteristic that the other does not, or one group may possess more of a characteristic than the other.

10. It is important to select samples that are representative of their respective populations and similar with respect to critical variables other than the independent variable.

Control Procedures

11. Lack of randomization, manipulation, and control are all sources of weakness in a causal–comparative design. It is possible that the groups are different on some other major variable besides the identified independent variable, and it is this other variable that is the real cause of the observed difference between the groups.

12. A number of strategies are available to overcome problems of initial group differences on an

extraneous variable. Three approaches to overcoming such group differences are matching, comparing homogeneous groups or subgroups, and analysis of covariance.

13. Analysis of covariance adjusts scores on a dependent variable for initial differences on some other variable related to performance on the dependent variable.

Data Analysis and Interpretation

14. Analysis of data in causal–comparative studies involves a variety of descriptive and inferential statistics.

15. The descriptive statistics most commonly used in causal–comparative studies are the mean, which indicates the average performance of a group on a measure of some variable, and the standard deviation, which indicates how spread out a set of scores is—that is, whether the scores are relatively close together and clustered around the mean or widely spread out around the mean.

16. The inferential statistics most commonly used in causal–comparative studies are the t test, which is used to see if there is a significant difference between the means of two groups; analysis of variance, which is used to determine if there is a significant difference among the means of three or more groups; and chi square, which is used to compare group frequencies—that is, to see if an event occurs more frequently in one group than another.

17. As repeatedly pointed out, interpreting the findings in a causal–comparative study requires considerable caution. The alleged cause–effect relationship may be the effect, and vice versa. There may be a third factor that is the real "cause" of both the independent and dependent variable.

18. The way to determine the correct order of causality—which variable caused which—is to determine which one occurred first.

19. One way to control for a potential common cause is to equate groups on the suspected variable.

Now go to the Companion Website at **www.prenhall.com/gay** to assess your understanding of chapter content with Practice Quiz, apply comprehension in Applying What You Know, broaden your knowledge about research in Web Links, and expand your research skills in Evaluating Articles, Analyzing Qualitative Data, Analyzing Quantitative Data, and Research Tools and Tips.

Differing Opinions on Testing Between Preservice and Inservice Teachers

KATHY E. GREEN
University of Denver

ABSTRACT   Studies of teachers' use of tests suggest that classroom tests are widely used and that standardized test results are rarely used. What is the genesis of this lack of use? A previous comparison of pre- and inservice teachers' attitudes toward assessment suggested no differences. This study assessed the different opinions among sophomores ($n = 84$), seniors ($n = 152$), and inservice teachers ($n = 553$) about the use of classroom and standardized tests. Significant differences were found; preservice teachers had less favorable attitudes toward classroom testing than teachers did and more favorable attitudes toward standardized testing.

This study assessed differences among college students entering a teacher education program, students finishing a teacher education program, and inservice teachers concerning their opinions of some aspects of classroom and standardized testing. Although numerous studies of inservice teachers' attitudes toward testing have been conducted, little research is available regarding preservice teachers' views of testing and of the genesis of teachers' views of testing.

Interest in this topic stemmed from research findings suggesting that the results of standardized tests are not used by most teachers. If standardized testing is to continue, the failure to use results is wasteful. Other studies have identified some of the reasons for the lack of use. This study's purpose was to determine whether opinions about the usefulness of standardized and other tests were negative for students before they even entered the teaching profession. When were those attitudes developed? Are attitudes fixed by students' educational experiences *prior* to entry into a teacher education program? Are preservice teachers socialized by their educational programs into resistance to testing? Do negative attitudes appear upon entry into the profession because of socialization into the school culture? Or do they appear after several years of service as a teacher because of personal experiences in the classroom?

I found only one study that addressed differences in opinions of pre- and inservice teachers (Reeves & Kazelskis, 1985). That study examined a broad range of issues salient to first-year teachers; only one item addressed testing specifically. Reeves and Kazelskis found no significant differences between pre- and inservice teachers' opinions about testing, as measured by that item. In this study, I sought more information pertinent to the development of opinions about testing.

Test use in U.S. schools has been and continues to be extensive. It has been estimated that from 10 to 15% of class time is spent dealing with tests (Carlberg, 1981; Newman & Stallings, 1982). Gullickson (1982) found that 95% of the teachers he surveyed gave tests at least once every 2 weeks. The estimated percentage of students' course grades that are based on test scores is 40 to 50%, ranging from 0 to 100% (Gullickson, 1984; McKee & Manning-Curtis, 1982; Newman & Stallings). Classroom tests, thus, are used frequently and may, at times, be used almost exclusively in determining students' grades.

In contrast, a review of past practice suggests minimal teacher use of *standardized* test results in making instructional decisions (Fennessey, 1982; Green & Williams, 1989; Lazar-Morrison, Polin, Moy, & Burry, 1980; Ruddell, 1985). Stetz and Beck (1979) conducted a national study of over 3,000 teachers' opinions about standardized tests. They noted that 41% of the teachers surveyed reported making little use of test results, a finding consistent with that of Goslin (1967) from several decades ago and that of Boyd, McKenna, Stake, and Yachinsky (1975). Test results were viewed as providing information that was supplemental to the wider variety of information that the teachers already possessed. Reasons offered for why standardized tests are given but results not always used by teachers include resistance to a perceived narrowing of the curriculum, resistance to management control, accountability avoidance (Darling-Hammond, 1985), and a limited understanding of score interpretation resulting from inadequate preservice training (Cramer & Slakter, 1968; Gullickson & Hopkins, 1987). Marso and Pigge (1988) found that teachers perceive a lower need for standardized testing skills than for classroom testing skills. They also found that teachers reported lower proficiencies in standardized test score use and interpretation than in classroom test score use and interpretation.

The results of those studies suggest that inservice teachers use classroom tests extensively but make little use of standardized test results. This suggests that inservice teachers, in general, hold positive attitudes toward classroom tests and less positive attitudes toward standardized tests. The literature does not lead to any predictions about preservice teachers' attitudes toward tests.

Address correspondence to Kathy E. Green, University of Denver, School of Education, Denver, CO 80208.

This study assessed differences between preservice and inservice teachers' opinions about testing and test use. The following research hypotheses were formulated to direct the study.

H1. There are significant differences in opinions about the testing and test use between preservice and inservice teachers.

H2. There are significant differences in opinions about testing between students beginning their preparation (sophomores) and students finishing their preparation (seniors).

H3. There are significant differences among inservice teachers with differing years of experience.

METHOD

Samples

Three samples were drawn for this study. They were samples of (a) practicing teachers, (b) college sophomores beginning a teacher education program, and (c) college seniors completing a teacher education program (but prior to student teaching). For the first sample, survey forms were mailed in a rural western state to 700 teachers randomly selected from the State Department of Education list of all licensed educators. During the spring semester of 1986, teachers were sent a letter explaining the nature of the study, a survey form, and a stamped return envelope. With two follow-up mailings, a total of 555 questionnaires were received, or 81% of the deliverable envelopes. (Twelve questionnaires were undeliverable, 4 persons refused to respond, and 133 persons did not reply.) No compulsory statewide standardized testing program was in place in the state.

The second sample was a convenience sample of three sections of an educational foundations class typically taken by college sophomores who have just enrolled in a teacher preparation program (n = 84). The course examines educational thought and practice in the United States. The classes were taught in an 8-week block, meeting for 50 min per day, 4 days per week. Survey forms were distributed in class and completed during class time.

The third sample was also a convenience sample of four sections of a tests and measurement class taken by college seniors (n = 152). The course is typically taken after coursework is almost complete, but prior to student teaching. The course provides instruction in basic statistics, classroom test construction and analysis, and standardized test use and interpretation. The course was also taught in an 8-week block, with the same schedule as the foundations course. Survey forms were distributed during the first week of class and completed during class time. Survey forms took from 10 to 30 min to complete. Responses were anonymous. Both sophomores and seniors were attending a public university in a small western town.

Table 1 presents descriptive information for the three samples.

Instruments

Three different forms with overlapping questions were used in this study. The survey form sent to the teachers contained questions regarding training in tests and measurement, subject and grades taught, tests given, and attitudes toward both standardized and classroom tests. The questionnaire was two pages in length, double-sided and contained 49 questions. The form given to the sophomores had 43 questions and was one page in length, double-sided. The form given to the seniors was three pages in length, single-sided. The latter two forms differed by the inclusion of an evaluation anxiety scale and items eliciting importance of contemporary measurement practices for the seniors. Although different formats may have affected responses to some extent, all the forms began with several demographic questions followed by the items relevant to this study. Any form differences would, then, likely be minimized for those initial items.

There were 18 items common to the three forms. Sixteen of the items were Likert items with a 1 to 6 (*strongly disagree* to *strongly agree*) response format. Likert-scale items were drawn from a previously developed measure of attitudes toward both standardized and classroom testing (Green & Stager, 1986). Internal consistency reliabilities of the measures ranged from .63 to .75. The remaining two items asked how many hours per week teachers spend in testing activities and how much of a student's grade should be based on test results. The study examined differences found among groups on those items. Item content is presented in Table 2, in which items are grouped by content (opinions about standardized tests, classroom tests, and about personal liking for tests).

Data were analyzed using multivariate analyses of variance, followed by univariate analyses of variance. If univariate results were significant, I used Tukey's HSD test to assess the significance of pairwise post hoc differences. Samples of both items and persons were limited; therefore, results may not be widely generalizable.

Results

Significant multivariate differences were found across opinion items (Wilks's lambda = .70, $p < .001$) when the three samples were compared (Table 2). Hypothesis 1 was supported. Differences were found between teachers and students for all items, with significance levels varying from .02 to .001 for individual items. Opinions were not consistently more positive across all items for teachers or for students. For instance, whereas teachers were most likely to feel that standardized tests address important educational outcomes, teachers were least likely to find that standardized tests serve a useful purpose. In general, though, students favored use of standardized tests for student or

Table 1.
Description of Samples

Item	Sophomores (n = 84)	Seniors (n = 152)	Teachers (n = 553)
Percentage female	84	152	553
Mean age	73.0	75.9	63.6
Age range	18–33	20–45	—
Mean years in teaching	—	—	12

Table 2.
Means and Standard Deviations for Opinions About Testing by Group

Variable	Sophomores (n = 84)	Seniors (n = 152)	Teachers (n = 553)	p	1	2	3
Hours spent in testing/week	10.43 (6.72)	9.18 (6.43)	4.37 (4.05)	.001	*	*	—
Percentage grade based on test	49.63 (15.48)	46.94 (18.71)	41.31 (22.68)	.001	*	*	—
Standardized test items							
Standardized tests are the best way to evaluate a teacher's effectiveness.	2.79 (1.03)	2.83 (1.10)	2.12 (1.18)	.001	*	*	—
Teachers whose students score higher on standardized tests should receive higher salaries.	2.53 (1.07)	2.33 (1.17)	1.74 (1.01)	.001	*	*	—
Requiring *students* to pass competency tests would raise educational standards.	4.14 (1.13)	3.89 (1.09)	3.69 (1.26)	.001	*	*	—
Requiring *teachers* to pass competency tests would raise educational standards	4.35 (.90)	4.09 (1.27)	3.30 (1.34)	.001	*	*	—
Standardized tests assess important educational outcomes.	3.47 (1.04)	3.54 (.87)	3.95 (.88)	.001	*	*	—
Standardized tests serve a useful purpose.	4.02 (.83)	3.97 (.81)	2.93 (.97)	.001	*	*	—
Standardized tests force teachers to "teach to the test."	3.05 (1.19)	2.74 (.98)	3.11 (1.22)	.02	—	*	—
Classroom test items							
Test construction takes too much teacher time.	4.57 (1.02)	4.36 (.85)	3.97 (.88)	.001	*	*	—
Test scores are a fair way to grade students.	3.42 (1.02)	3.32 (1.13)	4.04 (.84)	.001	*	*	—
Testing has a favorable impact on student motivation.	4.00 (.71)	3.88 (1.00)	4.16 (.88)	.01	—	*	—
Tests are of little value in identifying learning problems.	1.76 (.96)	1.43 (.84)	1.44 (1.05)	.01	*	—	*
It is relatively easy to construct tests in my subject area.	4.11 (1.25)	3.51 (1.34)	4.35 (.89)	.001	—	*	*
Tests measure only minor aspects of what students can learn.	2.92 (1.13)	3.01 (1.13)	3.24 (1.00)	.01	*	—	—
Personal reflections							
I do(did) well on tests.	4.05 (1.04)	4.00 (1.10)	4.46 (.94)	.001	*	*	—
I personally dislike taking tests.	3.13 (1.35)	3.12 (1.14)	3.46 (1.16)	.01	—	*	—
The tests I have taken were generally good assessments of my knowledge of an area.	3.65 (1.08)	3.41 (1.10)	4.09 (.82)	.001	*	*	—

Note. For opinion items, the scale ranged from *strongly disagree* (1) to *strongly agree* (6). Standard deviations are presented in parentheses. Asterisks (*) indicate significant ($p < .05$) differences between groups: 1 = teachers versus sophomores, 2 = teachers versus seniors, 3 = sophomores versus seniors.

teacher evaluation more than teachers did. Although the students were less likely to say that they do well on tests and that tests previously taken were good assessments of their ability, the students were also less likely to say that they disliked taking tests. Students' opinions about classroom testing were less favorable than were teachers' opinions for all but one item. Differences were also found between teachers and students in estimates of time spent in testing and in the percentage of students' grades based on test scores.

Hypothesis 2 was not supported. Only two significant differences in means were found between the sophomores and the seniors. One difference was found for the item "It is relatively easy to construct tests in my subject area." Sophomores tended to agree with that statement more than the seniors did. Because the seniors were required to complete a task involving test construction, the impending course requirement may have influenced their opinions. The second difference was found for the item "Tests are of little value in identifying learning problems," with more positive opinions expressed by seniors than by sophomores.

Hypothesis 3 was tested by dividing teachers into three groups: 0 to 1 years, 2 to 5 years, and 5+ years of experience as a teacher. No significant multivariate or univariate differences were found, so Hypothesis 3 was not supported. However, there were few teachers with 0 to 1 years of experience in the sample. Because of the small number of teachers with 0 to 1 years of teaching (46 teachers; 8.7% of the data file), groups were reformed as follows: 0 to 3 years, 4 to 6 years, and 6+ years of experience. Still, no significant multivariate or univariate differences were found. (In addition, no differences were found between teachers with 0 to 3 years of experience and those with 6 or more years of experience.)

DISCUSSION

This study was undertaken to examine whether differences in opinions about testing would be discerned between preservice and inservice teachers and whether those differences would suggest a progression. The differences found suggest that teacher education students are less favorable to classroom testing and more favorable to standardized testing than teachers are. Differences were *not* found between sophomores and seniors, however. Nor were opinions about testing found to depend upon years of experience in teaching. Those results do not reflect a developmental progression. The shift in opinion seems to occur when beginning a teaching position, suggesting effects that result from job requirements or socialization as a teacher more than from a developmental trend. Differences between students and teachers, then, seem likely to be caused by direct teacher experience with creating, administering, and using tests or by acculturation into life as a teacher in a school. That conclusion suggests that if one wishes to affect teachers' opinions about testing, provision of inservice experiences may be a more profitable avenue than additional preservice education.

Test use. The teachers sampled in this study reported spending an average of about 11% of their time in testing, which is consistent with estimates reported in the literature (10 to 15%). The finding in this study that an average of 41% of the students' grades was based on test results is also consistent with estimates reported in the literature (40 to 50%). Estimates of the time needed for testing activities obtained from students sampled in this study were much higher (23% and 26% for seniors and sophomores, respectively) than the estimates obtained from the teachers' reports. Although students' estimates of the percentage of grade based on test scores were significantly higher than those of teachers, they were within the range reported in the literature. Students, then, who lack an experiential base, seem either to have exaggerated views regarding the time that teachers spend on testing-related activities or think that it will take them longer to construct tests.

Beginning teachers also lack an experiential base. One might ask whether beginning teachers spend more time in test-related activities than do teachers with more experience, because beginning teachers may not have files of tests to draw upon. Mean reported time spent in testing was higher for first- and second-year teachers (means of 5.4 and 5.7 hours per week) than for teachers with more experience (mean for third year = 2.3, 4th year = 2.8, 5th year = 3.8). Thus, students may be accurate in their perception of the time needed by novices for testing-related activities.

Standardized testing. The students' opinions ranged from neutral to positive regarding the use of standardized tests and were, on average, significantly more positive than the teachers' opinions. One explanation for the positive opinions may be that students have extremely limited personal experience with standardized tests (their own or their friends) and so have a limited basis upon which to judge test effectiveness. By college level, most students have taken a number of standardized tests but may not be aware of the results, may not have been directly affected by the results, or may have been affected by the results at a time when they were too young to understand or argue. Students may believe that the tests must be useful because "authorities and experts" sanction their administration. Students' opinions may, then, be shaped by the positive *public* value placed on tests, as well as by their educational programs. The tests and measurement course taken by many preservice teachers emphasizes how tests can be valuable if used properly. One can argue that most students view themselves as intending to use tests properly. In contrast, many teachers are required to give standardized tests, and they may also be required to take them.

Preservice–inservice differences might be even more extreme in states where the stakes attached to standardized test use are higher—where the teacher's job or salary depends upon test results. Teachers develop a broader base of experience with standardized testing, and they may be more aware of the limitations of the tests and of the controversy surrounding standardized testing. The measurement profession is unclear about the value of standardized testing; it is not surprising that teachers also have reservations.

Classroom testing. Differences were also found between teachers and teacher education students for most classroom test items, though differences were not as pronounced for these items. The result is in contrast to Reeves and Kazelski's (1985) finding of no differences between similar groups. The result of somewhat less favorable opinions of preservice than inservice teachers toward classroom testing may have stemmed from the frequent test taking by students versus the frequent use of tests by teachers. By the time students are seniors in college, they will have taken a larger number of classroom tests than standardized tests and thus will have considerably more experience in evaluating their effectiveness. Students undoubtedly encounter classroom tests and test questions that they consider to be unfair assessments of their knowledge. Such experiences may temper their opinions toward classroom tests. In contrast, because most teachers rely to some extent on test results in assigning grades and in evaluating instruction, opinions may change to conform with this behavior. Teachers' opinions may also be influenced by an experiential understanding of testing gained through learning how informative test results can be.

Because it is unlikely that the widespread use of classroom and standardized tests will diminish, teachers will continue to be called upon to use tests to make decisions that are important in the lives of students. Teachers need to be competent in test construction and interpretation. However, if tests are to be used effectively as part of the instructional process, teachers must perceive the positive aspects of test use. If a teacher finds that task impossible, that teacher should discontinue traditional test use and seek alternative assessment techniques, within the boundaries allowed by the district. Teachers should communicate positive feelings about the tests they give to their students. Teachers will probably be more likely to do so if they have positive opinions of tests. Tests are often viewed as evaluative; they may more effectively be viewed as informative and prescriptive.

If teacher educators wish to affect prospective teachers' views, they may need to both clarify their own views about the place of testing in instruction and clearly present arguments about testing, pro and con, to their classes. Well-constructed classroom assessments, whether paper-and-pencil, portfolio, or performance measures, provide diagnostic and prescriptive information about the students' progress and about the effectiveness of instruction. This information is valuable. Poorly constructed or standardized measures that do not address the curriculum provide little information of use in the classroom. The reasons for giving tests that do not provide information useful in instruction must be clearly explained. Such tests may be mandated to provide legitimate administrative, state, or national information.

But to what extent can teacher educators shape *prospective* teachers' views? The results of this study suggest that opinions held prior to and following preservice instruction may not survive the transition to the real world of the classroom. If this is the case, the preservice course—no matter how good it is—would be ineffective in influencing attitudes. (It may, however, be highly effective in influencing the quality of testing practices by providing basic skills in test construction and interpretation.) Inservice instruction may be a better vehicle to use to produce attitude change.

This study was cross-sectional in design. A longitudinal study that examined opinions over time (from preservice to inservice) is required to identify the extent to which opinions are shaped by school requirements. Additional information regarding school characteristics affecting preservice and inservice teachers' attitudes toward testing would be of interest, as would information about differences in testing skill levels between pre- and inservice teachers.

NOTES

An earlier version of this paper was presented at the 1990 annual meeting of the National Council on Measurement in Education, held April 1990 in Boston.

Appreciation is expressed to the *Journal of Educational Research* reviewers for their helpful suggestions.

REFERENCES

Boyd, J., McKenna, B. H., Stake, R. E., & Yachinsky, J. (1975). *A study of testing practices in the Royal Oak (MI) public schools.* Royal Oak, MI: Royal Oak City School District. (ERIC Reproduction Service No. 117 161)

Carlberg, C. (1981). South Dakota study report. Denver, CO: Midcontinent Regional Educational Laboratory.

Cramer, S., & Slakter, M. (1968). A scale to assess attitudes toward aptitude testing. *Measurement and Evaluation in Guidance, 1*(2).

Darling-Hammond, L., & Wise, A. E. (1985). Beyond standardization: State standards and school improvement. *Elementary School Journal, 85,* 315–336.

Fennessey, D. (1982). Primary teachers' assessment practices: Some implications for teacher training. Paper presented at the annual conference of the South Pacific Association for Teacher Education, Frankston, Victoria, Australia.

Goslin, D. A. (1967). *Teachers and testing.* New York: Russell Sage Foundation.

Green, K. E., & Stager, S. F. (1986–87). Testing: Coursework, attitudes, and practices. *Educational Research Quarterly, 11*(2), 48–55.

Green, K. E., & Stager, S. F. (1986). Measuring attitudes of teachers toward testing. *Measurement and Evaluation in Counseling and Development, 19,* 141–150.

Green, K. E., & Williams, E. J. (1989, March). Standardized test use by classroom teachers: Effects of training and grade level taught. Paper presented at the annual meeting of the National Council on Measurement in Education, San Francisco.

Gullickson, A. R. (1982). The practice of testing in elementary and secondary schools. (ERIC Reproduction Service No. ED 229 391)

Gullickson, A. R. (1984). Teacher perspectives of their instructional use of tests. *Journal of Educational Research, 77,* 244–248.

Gullickson, A. R., & Hopkins, K. D. (1987). The context of educational measurement instruction for preservice teachers: Professor perspectives. *Educational Measurement: Issues and Practice, 6,* 12–16.

Karmos, A. H., & Karmos, J. S. (1984). Attitudes toward standardized achievement tests and their relation to achievement test performance. *Measurement and Evaluation in Counseling and Development, 17,* 56–66.

Lazar-Morison, C., Polin, L., Moy, R., & Burry, J. (1980). A review of the literature on test use. Los Angeles: Center for the Study of Evaluation, California State University. (ERIC Reproduction Service No. 204 411)

Marso, R. N., & Pigge, F. L. (1988). Ohio secondary teachers' testing needs and proficiencies: Assessments by teachers, supervisors, and principals. *American Secondary Education, 17,* 2–9.

McKee, B. G., & Manning-Curtis, C. (1982, March). Teacher-constructed classroom tests: The stepchild of measurement research. Paper presented at the National Council on Measurement in Education annual conference, New York.

Newman, D. C., & Stallings, W. M. (1982). Teacher competency in classroom testing, measurement preparation, and classroom testing practices. Paper presented at the American Educational Research Association annual meeting. New York. (ERIC Reproduction Service No. ED 220 491)

Reeves, C. K., & Kazelskis, R. (1985). Concerns of preservice and inservice teachers. *Journal of Educational Research, 78,* 267–271.

Ruddell, R. B. (1985). Knowledge and attitudes toward testing: Field educators and legislators. *Reading Teacher, 38,* 538–543.

Stetz, F. P., & Beck, M. D. (1979). Comments from the classroom: Teachers' and students' opinions of achievement tests. Paper presented at the annual meeting of the National Council on Measurement in Education, San Francisco.

"When well conducted, experimental studies produce the soundest evidence concerning cause–effect relationships." (p. 234)

Experimental Research

OBJECTIVES

After reading Chapter 9, you should be able to do the following:

1. Briefly state the purpose of experimental research.
2. List the basic steps involved in conducting an experiment.
3. Explain the purpose of control.
4. Briefly define or describe internal validity and external validity.
5. Identify and briefly describe eight major threats to the internal validity of an experiment.
6. Identify and briefly describe six major threats to the external validity of an experiment.
7. Briefly discuss the purpose of experimental design.
8. Identify and briefly describe five ways to control extraneous variables (and you'd better not leave out randomization!).
9. For each of the pre-experimental, true experimental, and quasi-experimental group designs discussed in this chapter, (1) draw a diagram, (2) list the steps involved in its application, and (3) identify major problems of invalidity.
10. Briefly define and describe the purpose of a factorial design.
11. Briefly explain what is meant by the term *interaction*.

Completing Chapter 9 should enable you to perform the following task.

TASK 6D

For a quantitative study, you have created research plan components (Tasks 2, 3a), described a sample (Task 4a), and considered appropriate measuring instruments (Task 5). If your study involves experimental research, now develop the methods section of a research report. Include a description of participants, data collection methods, and research design. (See Performance Criteria at the end of Chapter 10, p. 287.)

:: EXPERIMENTAL RESEARCH: DEFINITION AND PURPOSE

Experimental research is the only type of research that can test hypotheses to establish cause–effect relationships. It represents the strongest chain of reasoning about the links between variables. You may recall from Chapter 1 that in **experimental research** the researcher manipulates at least one independent variable, controls other relevant variables, and observes the effect on one or more dependent variables. The researcher determines "who gets what"; that is, she has control over the selection and assignment of groups to treatments. The manipulation of the independent variable is the one characteristic that differentiates experimental research from other types of research. The independent variable, also called the *treatment, causal,* or *experimental variable,* is that treatment or characteristic believed to make a difference. In educational research, independent variables that are frequently manipulated include method of instruction, type of reinforcement, arrangement of learning environment, type of learning materials, and length of treatment. This list is by no means exhaustive. The dependent variable, also called the *criterion, effect,* or *posttest variable,* is the outcome of the study, the change or difference in groups that occurs as a result of the independent variable. It gets its name because it is "dependent" on the independent variable. The dependent variable may be measured by a test or some other quantitative measure (e.g., attendance, number of suspensions, time on task). The only restriction on the dependent variable is that it represents a measurable outcome.

Experimental research is the most structured of all research types. When well conducted, experimental studies produce the soundest evidence concerning cause–effect relationships. The results of experimental research permit prediction, but not the kind that is characteristic of correlational research. A correlational study predicts a particular score for a particular individual. Predictions based on experimental findings are more global and often take the form, "If you use Approach X, you will probably get better results than if you use Approach Y." Of course, it is unusual for a single experimental study to produce broad generalization of results, because any single study is limited in context and participants. However, replications of a study using different contexts and participants often produce cause–effect results that can be generalized widely.

The Experimental Process

The steps in an experimental study are basically the same as in other types of research: selecting and defining a problem, selecting participants and measuring instruments, preparing a research plan, executing procedures, analyzing the data, and formulating conclusions. An experimental study is guided by at least one hypothesis that states an expected causal relationship between two variables. The experiment is conducted to confirm (support) or disconfirm (refute) the experimental hypothesis. In an experimental study, the researcher is in on the action from the very beginning. He selects the groups, decides what treatment will go to which group, controls extraneous variables, and measures the effect of the treatment at the end of the study.

It is important to note that the experimental researcher controls both the selection and the assignment of the research participants. That is, the researcher randomly selects participants from a single, well-defined population and then randomly assigns these participants into the different treatment conditions. It is the ability to randomly select and randomly assign participants to treatments that makes experimental research unique. The random assignment of participants to treatments, which is also called the *researcher's manipulation of the treatments,* is the distinguishing aspect of experimental research and the feature that distinguishes it from causal–comparative research. It is important for you to understand the difference between random selection and random assignment. Experimental research has both, whereas causal–comparative research has only random selection, not assignment, because causal–comparative participants are obtained from two already-existing populations. There can be no random assignment to a treatment from a single population in causal–comparative studies.

An experiment typically involves a comparison of two groups (although as you will see later, there may be only one group or even three or more groups). The experimental comparison is usually one of three types: (1) comparison of two different approaches (A versus B), (2) comparison of a new approach and the existing approach (A versus no A), and (3) comparison of different amounts of a single approach (a little of A versus a lot of A). An example of an A versus B comparison would be a study that compared the effects of a computer-based and a teacher-based approach to teaching first-grade reading. An example of an A versus no A comparison would be a study that compared a new handwriting method and the classroom teachers' existing handwriting approach. An example of a little of A versus a lot of A comparison would be a study that compared the effect of 20 minutes of daily science instruction versus 40 minutes of daily science instruction on fifth graders' attitudes toward science. Experimental designs may get quite complex and involve simultaneous manipulation of several independent variables. At this stage of the game, however, we recommend that you stick to just one!

The group that receives the new treatment is often called the **experimental group**, and the group that receives a different treatment or is treated as usual is called the **control group**.

An alternative to using these terms is to simply describe the treatments as comparison groups, treatment groups, or Groups A and B. The terms are used interchangeably. A common misconception is that a control group always receives no treatment. This is not true and would hardly provide a fair comparison. For example, if the independent variable was type of reading instruction, the experimental group might be instructed with a new method, and the control group might continue, instruction with the currently used method. The control group would still receive reading instruction; members would not sit in a closet while the study was being conducted. Otherwise, you would not be evaluating the effectiveness of a new method as compared to that of a traditional method; you'd be comparing a new method to no reading instruction at all! Any method of instruction is bound to be more effective than no instruction.

The groups that are to receive the different treatments should be equated on all variables that might influence performance on the dependent variable. For example, in the previous example, initial reading readiness should be very similar in each treatment group at the start of the study. The researcher must make every effort to ensure that the two groups start as equivalently as possible on all variables except the independent variable. The main way that groups are equated is through simple random or stratified random sampling (see Chapter 4).

After the groups have been exposed to the treatment for some period, the researcher collects data on the dependent variable from the groups and determines whether there is a real or significant difference between their performance. In other words, using statistical analysis, the researcher determines whether the treatment made a real difference. Chapters 11 and 12 discuss statistical analysis of experimental studies in detail. For now, suppose that at the end of an experimental study one group had an average score of 29 on the dependent variable and the other group had an average score of 27. There clearly is a difference between the groups, but is a 2-point difference a meaningful or significant difference, or is it just a chance difference produced by measurement error? Statistical analysis helps answer this question.

Experimental studies in education often suffer from two problems: a lack of sufficient exposure to treatments and failure to make the treatments substantially different from each other. In most cases, no matter how effective a treatment is, it is not likely to be effective if students are exposed to it for only a brief period. To adequately test a hypothesis concerning the effectiveness of a treatment, the experimental group would need to be exposed to it over a period of time so that the treatment is given a fair chance to work. Also of concern is the difference between treatments. In a study comparing team teaching and traditional lecture teaching, it would be vital that team teaching be operationalized in a manner that clearly differentiated it from the traditional method. If team teaching meant two teachers taking turns lecturing, it would not be very different from traditional teaching and the researcher would be very unlikely to find a meaningful difference between the two study treatments. Also, if teachers using different treatments converse with and borrow from each other's treatments, the original treatments become diluted and similar to each other. These problems have detrimental effects on the outcome of the study.

Manipulation and Control

Direct manipulation by the researcher of at least one independent variable is the one single characteristic that differentiates experimental research from other types of research. Manipulation of an independent variable is often a difficult concept to grasp. Quite simply, it means that the researcher decides what treatments will make up the independent variable and which group will get which treatment. For example, if the independent variable was number of annual teacher reviews, the researcher might decide to form three groups: one group receiving no review, a second group receiving one review, and a third group receiving two reviews.

In addition, having selected research participants from a single, well-defined population, the researcher would randomly assign participants to treatments. Thus, manipulation means being able to select the number and type of treatments and to randomly assign participants to treatments.

Independent variables in education are either manipulated (active variables) or not manipulated (assigned variables). You can manipulate such variables as method of instruction, number of reviews, and size of group. You cannot manipulate variables such as gender, age, or socioeconomic status. You can place participants into one method of instruction or another (active variable), but you cannot place participants into male or female categories because they already are male or female (assigned variable). Although the design of an experimental study may or may not include assigned variables, at least one active variable must be present.

Control refers to the researcher's efforts to remove the influence of any variable other than the independent variable that might affect performance on the dependent variable. In other words, the researcher wants the groups to be as similar as possible, so that the only major difference between them is the treatment variables as manipulated. To illustrate the importance of research control, suppose you conducted a study to compare the effectiveness of student tutors versus parent tutors in teaching first graders to read. Student tutors might be older children from higher grade levels, and parent tutors might be members of the PTA. Suppose also that student tutors helped each member of their group for 1 hour per day for a month, whereas the parent tutors helped each member of their group for 2 hours per week for a month. Would the comparison be fair? Certainly not. Participants with the student tutors would have received 2½ times as much help as that provided to the parents' group (5 hours per week versus 2 hours per week). Thus, one variable that would need to be controlled would be amount of tutoring. If this variable were not controlled, you could be confronted with a dilemma. If the student tutors produced higher reading scores than the parent tutors, you would not know whether this result indicated that student tutors were more effective than parent tutors, that longer periods of tutoring were more effective than shorter periods, or that type and amount of tutoring combined were more effective. To make the comparison fair and interpretable, both students and parents would tutor for the same amount of time. Then time of tutoring would be controlled, and you could truly compare the effectiveness of student and parent tutors.

A researcher must consider many factors when attempting to identify and control extraneous variables. Some variables that need controlling may be relatively obvious; as the researcher in the preceding study, you would need to examine such variables as reading readiness and prior reading instruction in addition to time spent tutoring. Some variables that need to be controlled may not be as obvious; for example, you would also need to ensure that both groups used similar reading texts and materials. Thus, there are really two different kinds of variables that need to be controlled: participant variables and environmental variables. A **participant variable** (such as reading readiness) is one on which participants in different groups in a study might differ; an **environmental variable** (such as learning materials) is a variable in the setting of the study that might cause unwanted differences between groups. The researcher strives to ensure that the characteristics and experiences of the groups are as equal as possible on all important variables except the independent variable. If relevant variables can be controlled, group differences on the dependent variable can be attributed to the independent variable.

Control is not easy in an experiment, especially in educational studies, where human beings are involved. It certainly is a lot easier to control solids, liquids, and gases! Our task is not an impossible one, however, because we can concentrate on identifying and controlling only those variables that might really affect—or interact with—the dependent variable. An

interaction occurs when different values of the independent variable are differentially effective depending upon the level of the control variable. For example, if two groups had significant differences in shoe size or height, such differences would probably not affect the results of most education studies. Techniques for controlling those extraneous variables that do matter will be presented later in this chapter.

:: THREATS TO EXPERIMENTAL VALIDITY

As noted, any uncontrolled extraneous variables affecting performance on the dependent variable are threats to the validity of an experiment. An experiment is valid if results obtained are due only to the manipulated independent variable and if they are generalizable to individuals or contexts beyond the experimental setting. These two criteria are referred to, respectively, as the internal validity and external validity of an experiment.

Internal validity is the degree to which observed differences on the dependent variable are a direct result of manipulation of the independent variable, not some other variable. In other words, an examination of internal validity focuses on threats or rival explanations that influence the outcomes of an experimental study but are not part of the independent variable. In the example of student and parent tutors, a plausible threat or rival explanation for the research results would have been the differences in the amount of time the two groups tutored. The degree to which experimental research results are attributable to the independent variable and not to some other rival explanation is the degree to which the study is internally valid.

External validity, also called *ecological validity,* is the degree to which study results are generalizable, or applicable, to groups and environments outside the experimental setting. In other words, an examination of external validity focuses on threats or rival explanations that would not permit the results of a study to be generalized to other settings or groups. A study conducted with groups of gifted ninth graders, for example, should produce results that are applicable to other groups of gifted ninth graders. If research results were never generalizable outside the experimental setting, then no one could profit from research. Each and every study would have to be reestablished over and over and over. An experimental study can contribute to educational theory or practice only if its results and effects are replicable and generalize to other places and groups. If results cannot be replicated in other settings by other researchers, the study has low external, or ecological, validity.

So, all one has to do in order to conduct a valid experiment is to maximize both internal and external validity, right? Wrong. Unfortunately, a Catch-22 complicates the researcher's experimental life. To maximize internal validity, the researcher must exercise very rigid controls over participants and conditions, producing a laboratory-like environment. However, the more a research situation is narrowed and controlled, the less realistic and generalizable it becomes. A study can contribute little to educational practice if its techniques, which have been proven effective in a highly controlled setting, will not also be effective in a less controlled classroom setting. On the other hand, the more natural the experimental setting becomes, the more difficult it is to control extraneous variables. It is very difficult, for example, to conduct a well-controlled study in an actual classroom. Thus, the researcher must strive for balance between control and realism. If a choice is involved, the researcher should err on the side of control rather than realism,[1] since a study that is not internally valid is worthless. A useful

---

[1] This is a clear distinction between the emphases of quantitative and qualitative research.

strategy to address this problem is to first demonstrate an effect in a highly controlled environment (with maximum internal validity) and then redo the study in a more natural setting (to examine external validity). In the final analysis, however, the researcher must seek a compromise between a highly controlled and highly natural environment.

In the following pages we describe many threats to internal and external validity. Some extraneous variables are threats to internal validity, some are threats to external validity, and some may be threats to both. How potential threats are classified is not of great importance; what is important is that you be aware of their existence and how to control for them. As you read, you may begin to feel that there are just too many threats for one little researcher to control. However, the task is not as formidable as it may at first appear, since there are a number of experimental designs that do control many or most of the threats you are likely to encounter. Also, remember that each threat is a potential threat only—it may not be a problem in a particular study.

Threats to Internal Validity

Probably the most authoritative source on experimental design and threats to experimental validity is the work of Donald Campbell and Julian Stanley, and Thomas Cook and Donald Campbell.[2] They identified eight main threats to internal validity: history, maturation, testing, instrumentation, statistical regression, differential selection of participants, mortality, and selection–maturation interaction. However, before describing these threats to internal validity, we would like to note the role of experimental research in overcoming these threats. You are not rendered helpless when faced with them. Quite the contrary, the use of random selection of participants, the researcher's assignment of participants to treatments, and control of other variables are powerful approaches to overcoming the threats. As you read about the threats, note how experimental research's random selection and assignment to treatments can control most threats.

History

When discussing threats to validity, **history** refers to any event occurring during a study that is not part of the experimental treatment but may affect the dependent variable. The longer a study lasts, the more likely it is that history will be a threat. A bomb scare, an epidemic of measles, or even general current events are examples of events that could produce a history effect. For example, suppose you conducted a series of in-service workshops designed to increase the morale of teacher participants. Between the time you conducted the workshops and the time you administered a posttest measure of morale, the news media announced that, due to state-level budget problems, funding to the local school district was going to be significantly reduced and promised pay raises for teachers would likely be postponed. Such an event could easily wipe out any effect the workshops might have had, and posttest morale scores might well be considerably lower than they otherwise might have been (to say the least!).

Maturation

Maturation refers to physical, intellectual, and emotional changes that naturally occur within individuals over a period of time. In a research study, these changes may affect participants' performance on a measure of the dependent variable. Especially in studies that last a long time,

---

[2] *Experimental and Quasi-Experimental Designs for Research,* by D. T. Campbell and J. C. Stanley, 1971, Chicago: Rand McNally; *Quasi-Experimentation: Design and Analysis Issues for Field Settings,* T. D. Cook and D. T. Campbell, 1979, Chicago: Rand McNally.

participants may become older, more coordinated, unmotivated, anxious, or just plain bored. Maturation is more likely to be a problem in a study designed to test the effectiveness of a psychomotor training program on 3-year-olds than in a study designed to compare two methods of teaching algebra. Young participants would typically be undergoing rapid biological changes during the training program, raising the question of whether changes were due to the training program or to maturation.

Testing

Testing, also called *pretest sensitization,* refers to the threat of improved performance on a posttest being a result of having taken a pretest. Taking a pretest may improve participants' scores on a posttest, regardless of whether they received any treatment or instruction in between. Testing is more likely to be a threat when the time between testings is short; taking a pretest taken in September is not likely to affect performance on a posttest taken in June. The testing threat to internal validity is more likely to occur in studies that measure factual information that can be recalled. For example, taking a pretest on algebraic equations is less likely to improve posttest performance than taking a pretest on multiplication facts would.

Instrumentation

The **instrumentation** threat refers to unreliability, or lack of consistency, in measuring instruments that may result in an invalid assessment of performance. Instrumentation may threaten validity in several different ways. A problem may occur if the researcher uses two different tests, one for pretesting and one for posttesting, and the tests are not of equal difficulty. For example, if the posttest is more difficult than the pretest, it may mask improvement that is actually present. Alternatively, if the posttest is less difficult than the pretest, it may indicate improvement that is not really present. If data are collected through observation, the observers may not be observing or evaluating behavior in the same way at the end of the study as at the beginning. In fact, if they are aware of the nature of the study, they may "see" and record only what they know the researcher is hypothesizing. If data are collected through the use of a mechanical device, the device may be poorly calibrated, resulting in inaccurate measurement. Thus, the researcher must take care in selecting tests, observers, and mechanical devices to measure the dependent variable.

Statistical Regression

Statistical regression usually occurs in studies where participants are selected on the basis of their extremely high or extremely low scores. **Statistical regression** is the tendency of participants who score highest on a test (a pretest) to score lower on a second, similar test (a posttest), and of subjects who score lowest on a pretest to score higher on a posttest. The tendency is for scores to regress, or move, toward a mean (average) or expected score. Thus, extremely high scorers regress (move lower) toward the mean, and extremely low scorers regress (move higher) toward the mean. For example, suppose a researcher wished to determine the effectiveness of a new method of instruction on the spelling ability of poor spellers. The researcher might administer a 100-item, 4-alternative, multiple-choice spelling pretest. Each question might read, "Which of the following four words is spelled incorrectly?" The researcher might then select for the study the 30 students who scored lowest. Now suppose none of the pretested students knew any of the words and guessed on every single question. With 100 items, and 4 choices for each item, a student would be expected to receive a score of 25 just by guessing. Some students, however, just due to rotten guessing, would receive scores much lower than 25, and other students, equally by chance, would receive much higher scores than 25. If they were administered the test a second time, without any instruction intervening, their expected score would still be 25. Thus, students who scored very low the first time would be expected to have a second score closer to 25, and students who scored very high the first time would also be expected to score closer to 25 the second time. Whenever participants are selected on the basis of their extremely high or extremely low performance, statistical regression is a viable threat to internal validity.

Differential Selection of Participants

Differential selection of participants is the selection of subjects who have differences before the start of a study that may at least partially account for differences found in a posttest. The threat that the groups were different before the study even began is more likely when a researcher is comparing already-formed groups. Suppose, for example, you receive permission to use two of Ms. Hynee's English classes in your study. You have no guarantee that the two classes are at all equivalent. If your luck is really bad, one class might be the honors English class and the other class might be the remedial English class. It would not be too surprising if the first class does much better on the posttest! The use of already-formed groups should be avoided if possible. If they must be used, the researcher should select groups that are as similar as possible and should administer a pretest to check for initial equivalence.

Mortality

First, let us make it perfectly clear that the mortality threat has nothing to do with subjects dying! **Mortality,** or *attrition,* refers to a reduction in the number of research participants that occurs over time as individuals drop out of a study. Mortality creates problems with validity particularly when different groups drop out for different reasons and with different frequency. The change in the characteristics of the groups due to mortality can have a significant effect on the results of the study. For example, participants who drop out of a study may be less motivated or uninterested in the study than those who remain. This is especially a problem when volunteers are used or when a study compares a new treatment to an existing treatment. Participants rarely drop out of control groups or existing treatments because few or no additional demands are made on them. However, volunteers or participants using the new, experimental treatment may drop out because too much effort is required for participation. The experimental group that remains at the end of the study then represents a more motivated group than the control group. As another example of mortality, suppose Suzy Shiningstar (a high IQ and all that student) got the measles and dropped out of your control group. Before Suzy dropped out, she managed to infect her friends in the control group. Since birds of a feather often flock together, Suzy's control-group friends might also be the "high IQ and all that" type students. The experimental group might end up looking pretty good when compared to the control group simply because many of the good students dropped out of the control group. The researcher cannot assume that participants drop out of a study in a random fashion and should, if possible, select a design that controls for mortality.

A researcher can assess the mortality of groups by obtaining demographic information about the participant groups before the start of the study and then determining if the makeup of the groups has changed at the end of the study. One way to reduce mortality is to provide some incentive to participants to remain in the study. Another approach is to identify the kinds of participants who drop out of the study and remove similar portions from the other groups.

Selection–Maturation Interaction and Other Interactive Effects

The effects of differential selection may also interact with the effects of maturation, history, or testing to cause a threat to internal validity. What this means is that if already-formed groups are used, one group may profit more (or less) from a treatment or have an initial advantage (or

TABLE 9.1	Threats to internal validity
Threat	**Description**
History	Unexpected events occur between the pre- and posttest, affecting the dependent variable.
Maturation	Changes occur in the participants, from growing older, wiser, more experienced, etc., during the study.
Testing	Taking a pretest alters the result of the posttest.
Instrumentation	The measuring instrument is changed between pre- and posttesting, or a single measuring instrument is unreliable.
Statistical regression	Extremely high or extremely low scorers tend to regress to the mean on retesting.
Differential selection of participants	Participants in the experimental and control groups have different characteristics that affect the dependent variable differently.
Mortality	Different participants drop out of the study in different numbers, altering the composition of the treatment groups.
Selection–maturation interaction	The participants selected into treatment groups have different maturation rates. Selection interactions also occur with history and instrumentation.

disadvantage) because of maturation, history, or testing factors. The most common of these interactive effects is **selection–maturation interaction,** which would exist if participants selected into the treatment groups matured at different rates during the study. To get a better idea of these effects, suppose, for example, that you received permission to use two of Ms. Hynee's English classes and that both classes were average and apparently equivalent on all relevant variables. Suppose, however, that for some reason Ms. Hynee had to miss one of her classes but not the other (maybe she had to have a root canal) and Ms. Alma Mater took over Ms. Hynee's class. As luck would have it, Ms. Mater proceeded to cover much of the material now included in your posttest (remember history?). Unbeknownst to you, your experimental group would have a definite advantage to begin with, and it might be this initial advantage, not the independent variable, that caused posttest differences in the dependent variable. Thus, a researcher must select a design that controls for potential problems such as this or make every effort to determine if they are operating in the study. Table 9.1 summarizes the threats to internal validity.

Threats to External Validity

There are several major threats to external validity that can limit generalization of experimental results to other populations. Building on the work of Campbell and Stanley, Bracht and Glass[3] refined and expanded discussion of threats to external validity. Bracht and Glass classified these threats into two categories. Threats affecting "generalizing to whom"—that is, threat affecting the groups to which research results be generalized—make up threats to population validity. Threats affecting "generalizing to what"—that is, threats affecting the settings, conditions, variables, and contexts to which results can be generalized—make up threats to ecological

---

[3] "The External Validity of Experiments," by G. H. Bracht and G. V. Glass, 1968, *American Educational Research Journal, 5,* pp. 437–474.

validity. The following discussion incorporates the contributions of Bracht and Glass into Campbell and Stanley's original (1971) conceptualizations.

Pretest–Treatment Interaction

Pretest–treatment interaction occurs when participants respond or react differently to a treatment because they have been pretested. Pretesting may sensitize or alert subjects to the nature of the treatment, potentially making the treatment effect different than it would have been had subjects not been pretested. Thus, the research results would be generalizable only to other pretested groups. The results would not even generalizable to the unpretested population from which the sample was selected.

The seriousness of the pretest–treatment interaction threat depends on the research participants, the nature of the independent and dependent variables, and the duration of the study. Studies involving self-report measures, such as attitude scales and interest inventories, are especially susceptible to this threat. Campbell and Stanley illustrate this effect by pointing out the probable lack of comparability of between two groups: one that views the antiprejudice film *Gentleman's Agreement* right after taking a lengthy pretest dealing with anti-Semitism and another that views the movie without a pretest. Individuals not pretested could conceivably enjoy the movie as a good love story and be unaware that it deals with a social issue. Pretested individuals would be much more likely to see a connection between the pretest and the message of the film. In contrast, taking a pretest on algebraic algorithms would probably have very little impact on a group's responsiveness to a new method of teaching algebra. The pretest–treatment interaction would also be expected to be minimized in studies involving very young children, who would probably not see or remember a connection between the pretest and the subsequent treatment. Similarly, for studies conducted over a period of months or longer, the effects of the pretest would probably have worn off or been greatly diminished by the time a posttest was given. Thus, for some studies the potential interactive effect of a pretest is a more serious consideration than others. In such cases, researchers should select a design that either controls for the effect or allows them to determine the magnitude of the effect. In studies in which pretest sensitization is a strong possibility, the researcher should (if it's feasible) make use of **unobtrusive measures,** ways to collect data that do not intrude on, or require interaction with, research participants. For example, data can be gathered from school records, transcripts, and other written sources.

Multiple-Treatment Interference

Sometimes the same research participants receive more than one treatment in succession. **Multiple-treatment interference** occurs when carryover effects from an earlier treatment make it difficult to assess the effectiveness of a later treatment. Suppose you were interested in comparing two different approaches to improving classroom behavior: behavior modification and corporal punishment (admittedly an extreme example used to make a point!). For 2 months, behavior modification techniques were systematically applied to the participants, and at the end of this period you found behavior to be significantly better than before the study began. For the next 2 months, the same participants were physically punished (with hand slappings, spankings, and the like) whenever they misbehaved, and at the end of the 2 months behavior was equally as good as after the 2 months of behavior modification. Could you then conclude that behavior modification and corporal punishment are equally effective methods of behavior control? Certainly not. In fact, the goal of behavior modification is to produce self-maintaining behavior—that is, behavior that continues after direct intervention is stopped. Thus, the good behavior exhibited by the participants at the end of the corporal punishment period could well be due to the effectiveness of previous exposure to behavior modification and exist in spite of, rather than because of, exposure to corporal punishment. If it is not possible to select a design in which each group receives only one treatment, the researcher should try to minimize potential multiple-treatment interference by allowing sufficient time to elapse between treatments and by investigating distinctly different types of independent variables.

Multiple-treatment interference may also occur when participants who have already participated in a study are selected for inclusion in another, apparently unrelated study. If the accessible population for a study is one whose members are likely to have participated in other studies (psychology majors, for example), then information on previous participation should be collected and evaluated before subjects are selected for the current study. If any members of the accessible population are eliminated from consideration because of previous research activities, a note should be made of this limitation in the research report.

Selection–Treatment Interaction

Selection–treatment interaction, like the "differential selection of participants" problem associated with internal invalidity, mainly occurs when participants are not randomly selected for treatments. Interaction effects aside, the very fact that participants are not randomly selected from a population severely limits the researcher's ability to generalize, because what population the sample represents is in question. Even if intact groups are randomly selected, the possibility exists that the experimental group is in some important way different from the control group, the larger population, or both.

When the use of nonrepresentative groups results in study findings that apply only to the groups involved and are not representative of the treatment effect in the extended population, this is **selection–treatment interaction,** another threat to population validity. This interaction occurs when actual study participants at one level of a variable react differently to a treatment than other potential participants in the population, at another level, would have reacted. For example, a researcher might conduct a study on the effectiveness of microcomputer-assisted instruction on the math achievement of junior high students. Classes available to the researcher (the accessible population) may represent an overall ability level at the lower end of the ability spectrum for all junior high students (the target population). If a positive effect is found, it may be that it would not have been found if the subjects were truly representative of the target population. And similarly, if an effect is not found, it might have been. Thus, extra caution must be taken in stating conclusions and generalizations based on studies involving existing, nonrandomized groups.

Selection–treatment interaction is also an uncontrolled variable in designs involving randomization. For example, the accessible population is often quite different from the researcher's target population, which creates another population validity problem when that researcher attempts to generalize the results of the accessible population to the target population. Thus, the way a given population becomes available to a researcher may make generalizability of findings questionable, no matter how internally valid an experiment may be. Suppose that, in seeking a sample, a researcher is turned down by 9 school systems and finally accepted by a 10th. The accepting system is very likely to be different from both the other 9 systems and the population of schools to which the researcher would like to generalize the results. Administrators and instructional personnel in the 10th school likely have higher morale, less fear of being inspected, and more zeal for improvement than personnel in the other 9 schools. In the research report, researchers should describe any problems they encountered in acquiring participants, including the number of times they were turned down, so that the reader can judge the seriousness of a possible selection–treatment interaction.

Specificity of Variables

Like selection–treatment interaction, specificity of variables is a threat to generalizability of research results regardless of the particular experimental design used. Any given study has **specificity of variables;** that is, the study is conducted with a specific kind of participant, using specific measuring instruments, at a specific time, and under a specific set of circumstances. We have discussed the need to describe research procedures in sufficient detail to permit another researcher to replicate the study. Such detailed descriptions also permit interested readers to assess how applicable findings are to their situation. Experimental procedures require operational definition of the variables. When studies that supposedly manipulated the same independent variable get quite different results, it is often difficult to determine the reasons for the differences because researchers have not provided clear, operational descriptions of their independent variables. When operational descriptions are available, they often reveal that two independent variables with the same name were in fact defined quite differently in the separate studies, thus explaining why results differed. Because such terms as *discovery method, whole language,* and *computer-based instruction* mean different things to different people, it is impossible to know what a researcher means by these terms unless they are defined. Without operationalized descriptions, it is not clear to what populations a study can be generalized. Generalizability of results is also tied to the clear definition of the dependent variable, although in most cases performance on a specific measure (e.g., the Baloney Achievement Test) is the operational definition. When there are a number of dependent variable measures to select from, questions about the comparability of these instruments must be raised.

Generalizability of results may also be affected by short- or long-term events that occur while the study is taking place. This threat is referred to as the *interaction of history and treatment effects.* It describes the situation in which events extraneous to the study alter the research results. Short-term, emotion-packed events, such as the firing of a superintendent, the release of district test scores, or the impeachment of a president might affect the behavior of participants. Usually, however, the researcher is aware of such happenings and can assess their possible impact on results. Of course, accounts of such events should also be included in the research report. The impact of longer term events, such as wars and economic depressions, however, is more subtle and tougher to evaluate.

Another threat to external validity is the *interaction of time of measurement and treatment effect.* This threat results from the fact that posttesting may yield different results depending on when it is done. A posttest administered immediately after the treatment might provide evidence for an effect that does not show up on posttest given some time after treatment. Conversely, a treatment may have a long-term, but not a short-term, effect. Thus, the only way to assess the generalizability of findings over time is to measure the dependent variable at various times following treatment.

To deal with the threats associated with specificity, the researcher must (1) operationally define variables in a way that has meaning outside the experimental setting and (2) be careful in stating conclusions and generalizations.

Treatment Diffusion

Treatment diffusion occurs when different treatment groups communicate with and learn from each other. Knowledge of each other's treatments often leads to the groups borrowing aspects from each other so that the study no longer has two distinctly different treatments, but two overlapping ones. The integrity of each treatment is diffused. Often, it is the more desirable treatment—the experimental treatment or the treatment with additional resources—that is diffused into the less desirable treatment. For example, suppose Mr. Darth's and Ms. Vader's classes were trying out two different treatments to improve spelling. Mr. Darth's class received videos, new and colorful spelling texts, and prizes for improved spelling. Ms. Vader's class received the traditional approach to spelling—the students were asked to list words on the board, copy them into notebooks, use each word in a sentence, and study at home. After the first week of treatments, the students began talking to their teachers about the different ways spelling was being taught. Ms. Vader heard about Mr. Darth's spelling treatment and asked if she could try out the videos in her class. Her students liked them so well that she incorporated them into her spelling program. The diffusion of Mr. Darth's treatment into Ms. Vader's treatment produced two overlapping treatments that did not represent the initial intended treatments. To reduce treatment diffusion, a researcher might ask teachers who are implementing different treatments not to communicate with each other about the treatments until the study is completed or might carry out the study in more than one location, thus allowing only one treatment per school.

Experimenter Effects

Researchers themselves also present potential threats to the external validity of their own studies. A researcher's influences on participants or on study procedures are known as **experimenter effects.** Passive experimenter effects occur as a result of characteristics or personality traits of the experimenter, such as gender, age, race, anxiety level, and hostility level. These influences are collectively called *experimenter personal-attributes effects.* Active experimenter effects occur when the researcher's expectations of the study results affect her behavior and actually contribute to producing certain research outcomes. This effect is referred to as the **experimenter bias effect.** Thus, an experimenter may unintentionally affect study results, typically in the direction desired by the researcher, simply by looking, feeling, or acting a certain way. One form of experimenter bias occurs when the researcher affects participants' behavior, or is inaccurate in evaluating their behavior, because of previous knowledge of the participants. Suppose a researcher hypothesizes that a new reading approach will improve reading skills. If the researcher knows that Suzy Shiningstar is in the experimental group and that Suzy is a good student, she may give Suzy's reading skills a higher rating than they actually warrant. This example illustrates another way a researcher's expectations may actually contribute to producing those outcomes: Knowing which participants are in the experimental and control groups may cause the researcher to unintentionally evaluate their performances differently.

It is difficult to identify experimenter bias in a study, which is all the more reason for researchers to be aware of its consequences on the external validity of their study. The moral is that the researcher should strive to avoid communicating emotions and expectations to participants in the study. Experimenter bias effects can be reduced by "blind" scoring in which the researcher doesn't know whose performance is being evaluated.

Reactive Arrangements

Reactive arrangements, also called *participant effects,* are threats to validity that are associated with the way in which a study is conducted and the feelings and attitudes of the participants involved. As discussed previously, in order to maintain a high degree of control and thus obtain internal validity, a researcher may create an experimental environment that is highly artificial and hinders generalizability to nonexperimental settings; this is a reactive arrangement. Another type of reactive arrangement results from participants' knowledge that they are involved in an experiment or their feeling that they are in some way receiving "special" attention. The effect that such knowledge or feelings can have on the participants was demonstrated at the Hawthorne Plant of the Western Electric Company in Chicago some years ago. Studies were conducted to investigate the relationship between various working conditions and productivity. As part of their study, researchers investigated the effect of light intensity and worker output. The researchers increased light intensity and production went up. They increased it some more and production went up some more. The brighter the place became, the more production rose. As a check, the researchers decreased the light intensity, and guess what, production went up! The darker it got, the more workers produced. The researchers soon realized that it was the attention given the workers, and not the illumination, that was affecting production. To this day, the term **Hawthorne effect** is used to describe any situation in which participants' behavior is affected not by the treatment per se, but by their knowledge of participating in a study.

A related reactive effect, known as *compensatory rivalry* or the **John Henry effect**, occurs when members of a control group feel threatened or challenged by being in competition with an experimental group and they perform way beyond what would normally be expected. Folk hero John Henry, you may recall, was a "steel drivin' man" who worked for a railroad. When he heard that a steam drill was going to replace him and his fellow steel drivers, he challenged, and set out to beat, the machine. Through tremendous effort he managed to win the ensuing contest, dropping dead at the finish line. When research participants are told that they will form the control group for a new, experimental method, they act like John Henry. They decide to challenge the new method by putting extra effort into their work, essentially saying (to themselves), "We'll show them that our old ways are as effective as their newfangled ways!" By doing this, however, the control group performs atypically and their performance provides a rival explanation for the study results. When the John Henry effect occurs, the treatment under investigation does not appear to be very effective, because posttest performance of the experimental group is not much (if at all) better than that of the control group.

As an antidote to the Hawthorne and John Henry effects, educational researchers often attempt to achieve a "placebo effect." The term comes from medical researchers who discovered that any "medication," even sugar and water, could make subjects feel better; any beneficial effect caused by a person's expectations about a treatment rather than the treatment itself became known as the **placebo effect.** To counteract this effect, a placebo approach was developed in which half of the subjects receive the true medication and half receive a placebo (sugar and water, for example). The use of a placebo is, of course, not known by the participants; both groups think they are taking a real medicine. The application of the placebo effect in educational research is that all groups in an experiment should appear to be treated the same. Suppose, for example, you have four groups of ninth graders, two experimental and two control, and the treatment is a film designed to promote a positive attitude toward a vocational career. If the experimental participants are to be excused from several of their classes to view the film, then the control participants should also be excused and shown another film whose content is unrelated to the purpose of the study (*Drugs and You: Just Say No!* would do). As an added control, you might have all the participants told that there are two movies and that eventually everyone will see both movies. In other words, it should appear as if all the students are doing the same thing.

Another reactive arrangement, or participant effect, is the **novelty effect,** which refers to the increased interest, motivation, or engagement participants develop simply because they are doing something different. In other words, a treatment may be effective because it is different, not because it is better. To counteract the novelty effect, a researcher should conduct a study over a period of time long enough to allow the treatment "newness" to wear off. This is especially advisable if the treatment involves activities very different from the subjects' usual routine. Table 9.2 summarizes the threats to external validity.

TABLE 9.2	Threats to external validity
Threat	**Description**
Pretest–treatment interaction	The pretest sensitizes participants to aspects of the treatment and thus influences posttest scores.
Selection–treatment interaction	The nonrandom or volunteer selection of participants limits the generalizability of the study.
Multiple-treatment interference	When participants receive more than one treatment, the effect of prior treatment can affect or interact with later treatments, limiting generalizability.
Specificity of variables	Poorly operationalized variables make it difficult to identify the setting and procedures to which the variables can be generalized.
Treatment diffusion	Treatment groups communicate and adopt pieces of each other's treatment, altering the initial status of the treatments' comparison.
Experimenter effects	Conscious or unconscious actions of the researcher affect participants' performance and responses.
Reactive arrangements	The fact of being in a study affects participants so that they act in ways different from their normal behavior. The Hawthorne and John Henry effects are reactive responses to being in a study.

Obviously there are many internal and external threats to the validity of an experimental (or causal–comparative) study. You should be aware of likely threats and strive to nullify them. One main way to overcome many threats to validity is to choose a research design that controls for such threats. We examine some of these designs in the following sections.

:: GROUP EXPERIMENTAL DESIGNS

The validity of an experiment is a direct function of the degree to which internal and external variables are controlled. If such variables are not controlled, it is difficult to interpret the results of a study and the groups to which results can be generalized. The term *confounding* is sometimes used to describe an intertwining of the effects of the independent variable with those of extraneous variables that makes it difficult to determine the unique effects of each. This is what experimental design is all about: the control of extraneous variables. Good designs control many sources of invalidity; poor designs control few. If you recall, two types of extraneous variables in need of control are participant variables and environmental variables. Participant variables include both organismic variables and intervening variables (introduced in Chapters 8 and 7, respectively). Organismic variables are characteristics of the participants that cannot be altered but can be controlled for; the sex of a participant is an example. Intervening variables intervene between the independent and the dependent variable and cannot be directly observed but can be controlled for; anxiety and boredom are examples.

Control of Extraneous Variables

Randomization is the best single way to simultaneously control for many extraneous variables. Thus, randomization should be used whenever possible; participants should be randomly selected from a population and randomly assigned to treatment groups. To ensure random selection and assignment, researchers use methods that rely on pure chance, usually consulting a table of random numbers. Other randomization methods are also available. For example, a researcher could flip a coin or use odd and even numbers on a die to assign participants to two treatments; heads or an even number would signal assignment to Treatment 1, and tails or an odd number would signal assignment to Treatment 2.

Randomization is effective in creating equivalent, representative groups that are essentially the same on all relevant variables. As noted, the use of randomly formed treatment groups is a unique characteristic of experimental research; it is a control factor not possible with causal–comparative research. The underlying rationale for randomization is that if subjects are assigned at random (by chance) to groups, there is no reason to believe that the groups will be greatly different in any systematic way. Thus, the groups would be expected to perform essentially the same on the dependent variable if the independent variable makes no difference. Therefore, if the groups perform differently at the end of the study, the difference can be attributed to the independent variable. It is important to remember that the larger the groups, the more confidence the researcher can have in the effectiveness of randomization. Randomly assigning 6 participants to two treatments is much less likely to equalize extraneous variables than assigning 50 participants to two treatments. In addition to equating groups on participant variables such as ability, gender, or prior experience, randomization can also equalize groups on environmental variables. Teachers, for example, can be randomly assigned to treatment groups so that the experimental groups will not have all the "Carmel Kandee" teachers or all the "Hester Hartless" teachers (and likewise for the control groups). Clearly, the researcher should use as much randomization as possible. If subjects cannot be randomly selected, those available should at least be randomly assigned. If participants cannot be randomly assigned to groups, then at least treatment conditions should be randomly assigned to the existing groups.

In addition to randomization, there are other ways to control for extraneous variables. Certain environmental variables, for example, can be controlled by holding them constant for all groups. Recall the example of the student tutor versus parent tutor study. In that example, help time was an important variable that had to be held constant, that is, made the same for both groups for them to be fairly compared. Other such variables that might need to be held constant include learning materials, prior exposure, meeting place and time (students might be more alert in the morning than in the afternoon), and years of teacher experience. Controlling participant variables is critical. If the groups are not the same to start with, you have not even given yourself a fighting chance to obtain valid, interpretable research results. Even if groups cannot be randomly formed, there are a number of techniques that can be used to try to equate groups. These include matching, comparing homogeneous groups or subgroups, using participants as their own controls, and analysis of covariance; several of these concepts were introduced in Chapter 8 in the discussion of equating groups in causal–comparative studies.

Matching

As you may recall from Chapter 8, matching is a technique for equating groups on one or more variables, usually ones highly related to performance on the dependent variable. The most commonly used approach to matching involves random assignment of pairs, one participant to each group. In other words, the researcher attempts to find pairs of participants similar on the variable or variables to be controlled. If the researcher is matching on gender, obviously the matched pairs must be of the same gender. However, if the researcher is matching on variables such as pretest, GRE, or ability scores, the pairing can be based on similarity of scores. Unless the number of participants is very large, it is unreasonable to try to make exact matches or matches on more than one or two variables. Once a matched pair is identified, one member of the pair is randomly assigned to one treatment group and the other member to the other treatment group. A participant who does not have a suitable match is excluded from the study. The resulting matched groups are identical or very similar with respect to the variable being controlled. As mentioned in Chapter 8, a major problem with such matching is that there are invariably participants who do not have a match and must be eliminated from the study. This may cost the researcher many subjects, especially if matching is attempted on two or more variables (imagine trying to find a match for a male with an IQ near 140 and a GPA between 1.00 and 1.50!). Of course, one way to combat loss of participants is to match less stringently. For example, the researcher might decide that if two ability test scores are within 20 points, they will constitute an acceptable match. This approach may increase the number of subjects, but it tends to defeat the purpose of matching.

A related matching procedure is to rank all of the participants, from highest to lowest, based on their scores on the variable to be matched. The two highest ranking participants, regardless of score, are the first pair. One member of the first pair is randomly assigned to one group and the other member to the other group. The next two highest ranked participants (third and fourth ranked) are the second pair, and so on. The major advantage of this approach is that no participants are lost. The major disadvantage is that it is a lot less precise than pair-wise matching. Advanced statistical procedures, such as analysis of covariance, have greatly reduced the research use of matching.

Comparing Homogeneous Groups or Subgroups

Another previously discussed way to control an extraneous variable is to compare groups that are homogeneous with respect to that variable. For example, if IQ were an identified extraneous variable, the researcher might select only participants with IQs between 85 and 115 (average IQ). The researcher would then randomly assign half the selected participants to the experimental group and half to the control group. Of course, this procedure also lowers the number of participants in the population and additionally restricts the generalizability of the findings to participants with IQs between 85 and 115. As noted in the discussion of causal–comparative research (Chapter 8), a similar, more satisfactory approach is to form different subgroups representing all levels of the control variable. For example, the available participants might be divided into high (116 or above), average (85 to 115), and low (84 and below) IQ subgroups. Half of the participants from each of the subgroups could then be randomly assigned to the experimental group and half to the control group. This procedure should sound familiar, since it describes stratified sampling. (You knew that!) If the researcher is interested not just in controlling the variable but also in seeing if the independent variable affects the dependent variable differently at different levels of IQ, the best approach is to build the control variable right into the design. Thus, the research design would have six cells: two treatments by three IQ levels. Draw the design for yourself, and label each cell with its treatment and IQ level.

Using Participants as Their Own Controls

Using participants as their own controls involves exposing a single group to different treatments one treatment at a time. This strategy helps to control for participant differences, because the same participants get both treatments. Of course, this approach is not always feasible; you cannot teach the same algebraic concepts to the same group twice using two different methods of instruction (well, you could, but it would not make much sense). A problem with this approach is a carryover effect from one treatment to the next. To use a previous example, it would be very difficult to evaluate the effectiveness of corporal punishment in improving behavior if the group receiving corporal punishment was the same group that had previously been exposed to behavior modification. If only one group was available, a better approach, if feasible, would be to randomly divide the group into two smaller groups, each of which would receive both treatments but in a different order. Thus, the researcher could at least get some idea of the effectiveness of corporal punishment because there would be a group that received it before behavior modification. In situations in which the effect of the dependent variable disappears quickly after treatment, or in which a single participant is the focus of the research, participants can be used as their own controls.

Analysis of Covariance

The analysis of covariance is a statistical method for equating randomly formed groups on one or more variables. As you learned in Chapter 8, in essence, analysis of covariance adjusts scores on a dependent variable for initial differences on some other variable, such as pretest scores, IQ, reading readiness, or musical aptitude. The covariate variable should be one related to performance on the dependent variable. Although analysis of covariance can be used in studies when groups cannot be randomly formed, its use is most appropriate when randomization is used. In spite of randomization, it might be found that two groups still differ significantly in terms of pretest scores. Analysis of covariance can be used in such cases to "correct" or adjust posttest scores for initial pretest differences. However, analysis of covariance is not universally useful. For example, the relationship between the independent and covariate variables must be linear (represented by a straight line). If the relationship is curvilinear, analysis of covariance is not useful. Also, analysis of covariance is often used when a study deals with intact groups, uncontrolled variables, and nonrandom assignment to treatments, all of which weaken its results. Calculation of an analysis of covariance is a complex procedure.

Types of Group Designs

The experimental design you select to a great extent dictates the specific procedures of your study. Selection of a given design influences factors such as whether there will be a control group, whether participants will be randomly selected and assigned to groups, whether the groups will be pretested, and how data will be analyzed. Particular combinations of such factors produce different designs that are appropriate for testing different types of hypotheses. Designs vary widely in the degree to which they control various threats to internal and external validity. Of course, there are certain threats to validity, such as experimenter bias, that no design can control for. However, some designs clearly do a better job than others. In selecting a design, you first determine which designs are appropriate for your study and for testing your hypothesis. You then determine which of these are also feasible given the constraints under which you may be operating. If, for example, you must use existing groups, a number of designs will automatically be eliminated. From the designs that are appropriate and feasible, you select the one that will control the most sources of internal and external invalidity and will yield the data you need to test your hypothesis or hypotheses.

There are two major classes of experimental designs: single-variable designs and factorial designs. A **single-variable design** is any design that involves one manipulated independent variable; **factorial design** is any design that involves two or more independent variables with at least one being manipulated.

Single-variable designs are classified as pre-experimental, true experimental, or quasi-experimental, depending on the degree of control they provide for threats to internal and external invalidity. *Pre-experimental designs* do not do a very good job of controlling threats to validity and should be avoided. In fact, the results of a study based on a pre-experimental design are so questionable they are not useful for most purposes except, perhaps, to provide a preliminary investigation of a problem. *True experimental designs* provide a very high degree of control and are always to be preferred. *Quasi-experimental designs* do not control as well as true experimental designs but do a much better job than the pre-experimental designs. If we were to assign letter grades to experimental designs, true experimental designs would get an A, quasi-experimental designs would get a B or a C (some are better than others), and pre-experimental designs would get a D or an F. Thus, if you have a choice between a true experimental design and a quasi-experimental design, select the true design. If your choice is between a quasi-experimental design, and a pre-experimental design, select the quasi-experimental design. If your choice is between a pre-experimental design or not doing the study at all, do not do the study at all, or do a follow-up study using an acceptable (C or better!) design. The less useful designs are discussed here only so that you will know what not to do and so that you will recognize their use in published research reports and be appropriately critical of their findings.

Factorial designs are basically elaborations of single-variable experimental designs except that they permit investigation of two or more variables, individually and in interaction with each other. After an independent variable has been investigated using a single-variable design, it is often useful to then study the variable in combination with one or more other variables. Some variables work differently when paired with different levels of another variable. The designs discussed next represent the basic designs in each category. Campbell and Stanley and Cook and Campbell[4] present a number of variations (for those of you who are getting hooked on research).

Pre-Experimental Designs

Here is a research riddle for you: Can you do an experiment with only one group? The answer is . . . yes, but not a really good one. As Figure 9.1 illustrates, none of the pre-experimental designs does a very good job of controlling extraneous variables that jeopardize validity.

The One-Shot Case Study.   The **one-shot case study** (it even sounds shoddy) involves a single group that is exposed to a treatment (X) and then posttested (O). None of the sources of invalidity are controlled in this design. As Figure 9.1 indicates, the only threats to validity that are controlled are those that are automatically controlled because they are irrelevant in this design. None of the validity threats that are relevant, such as history, maturation, and mortality, are controlled. Even if the research participants score high on the posttest, you cannot attribute their performance to the treatment because you do not even know what they knew before you administered the treatment. So, if you have a choice between using this design and not doing a study—select another study.

The One-Group Pretest–Posttest Design.   The **one-group pretest–posttest design** involves a single group that is pretested (O), exposed to a treatment (X), and posttested (O). The success of the treatment is determined by comparing pretest and posttest scores. This design controls some areas of invalidity not controlled by the one-shot case study, but a number of additional factors relevant to this design are not controlled. If participants do significantly better on the posttest than on the pretest, it cannot be assumed that the improvement is due to the treatment. History and maturation are not controlled. Something may happen to the participants that makes them perform better the second time, and the longer the study takes, the more likely it is that this "something" will threaten validity. Testing and instrumentation also are not controlled; the participants may learn something on the pretest that helps them

---

[4] *Experimental and Quasi-Experimental Designs for Research*, by D. T. Campbell and J. C. Stanley, 1971, Chicago: Rand McNally; *Quasi-Experimentation: Design and Analysis Issues for Field Settings*, T. D. Cook and D. T. Campbell, 1979, Chicago: Rand McNally.

FIGURE 9.1

Sources of invalidity
for pre-experimental
designs

Designs	Sources of Invalidity									
	Internal								External	
	History	Maturation	Testing	Instrumentation	Regression	Selection	Mortality	Selection Interactions	Pretest-X Interaction	Multiple-X Interference
One-Shot Case Study *X O*	–	–	(+)	(+)	(+)	(+)	–	(+)	(+)	(+)
One-Group Pretest–Posttest Design *O X O*	–	–	–	–	–	(+)	+	(+)	–	(+)
Static-Group Comparison *X₁ O* *X₂ O*	+	–	(+)	(+)	(+)	–	–	–	(+)	(+)

Each line of *X*s and *O*s represents a group.

Note: Symbols: *X* or X_1 = unusual treatment; X_2 = control treatment; *O* = test, pretest, or posttest; + = factor controlled for; (+) factor controlled for because not relevant; and – = factor not controlled for.

    Figures 9.1 and 9.2 basically follow the format used by Campbell and Stanley and are presented with a similar note of caution: The figures are intended to be supplements to, not substitutes for, textual discussions. You *should not* totally accept or reject designs because of their pluses and minuses; you *should* be aware that the design most appropriate for a given study is determined not only by the controls provided by the various designs but also by the nature of the study and the setting in which it is to be conducted.

    Although the symbols used in these figures, and their placement, vary somewhat from Campbell and Stanley's format, the intent, interpretations, and textual discussions of the two presentations are in agreement (personal communication with Donald T. Campbell, April 22, 1975).

on the posttest, or unreliability of the measures may be responsible for the apparent improvement. Statistical regression is also not controlled. Even if subjects are not selected on the basis of extreme scores (high or low), it is possible that a group may do very poorly on the pretest, just by poor luck. For example, participants may guess badly just by chance on a multiple-choice pretest and improve on a posttest simply because, this time, their guessing produces a score that is more in line with an expected score. The external validity threat pretest–treatment interaction is also not controlled. Pretest–treatment interaction may cause participants to react differently to the treatment than they would have if they had not been pretested.

    To illustrate the problems associated with this design, let us examine a hypothetical study. Suppose a professor teaches a very "heavy" statistics course and is concerned that the high anxiety level of students interferes with their learning. The kindly professor (aren't they all?) prepares a 100-page booklet that explains the course, tries to convince students that they will have no problems, and promises all the help they need to successfully complete the course, even if they have a poor math background. The professor wants to see if the booklet "works." At the beginning of the term, she administers an anxiety test and then gives each student a copy of the booklet with instructions to read it as soon as possible. Two weeks later she administers the anxiety scale again, and sure enough, the students' scores indicate much less anxiety than at the beginning of the term. The professor is satisfied and prides herself on the booklet's effectiveness in reducing anxiety. But wait, is this self-satisfaction warranted? If you think about it, you will see that a number of alternative factors or threats might explain the students' decreased anxiety. For example, students are typically more anxious at the beginning of a course because they do not know exactly what they are in for (fear of the unknown!). After being in a course for a couple of weeks, students usually find that it is not as bad as they imagined (right?), or they have dropped it (remember mortality?). Also, the professor doesn't even know whether the students read her masterpiece! The only situations for which the one-group pretest–posttest design is even remotely appropriate is when the behavior to be measured is not likely to change all by itself. Certain prejudices, for example, are not likely to change unless a concerted effort is made.

The Static-Group Comparison. The **static-group comparison** involves at least two nonrandomly formed groups: one that receives a new or unusual treatment (the experimental treatment) and another that receives a traditional treatment (the control treatment). Both groups are posttested. In this case, although the terms *experimental* and *control* are commonly used to describe the groups, it is probably more appropriate to call them both *comparison groups,* because each really serves as the comparison for the other. Each group receives some form of the independent variable (the treatments). So, for example, if the independent variable is type of drill and practice, the "experimental" group (X_1) may receive computer-assisted drill and practice, and the "control" group may receive worksheet drill and practice. Occasionally, but not often, the experimental group may receive something while the control group receives nothing. For example, a group of teachers may receive some type of in-service education while the comparison group of teachers does not. In this case, X_1 is in-service training, and X_2 is no in-service training. The purpose of a control group is to indicate what the performance of the experimental group would have been if it had not received the experimental treatment. Of course, this purpose is fulfilled only to the degree that the control group is equivalent to the experimental group.

The static-group comparison design can be expanded to deal with any number of groups. For three groups, the design would take the following form:

X_1 O
X_2 O
X_3 O

Which group is the control group? Basically, each group serves as a control or comparison group for the other two. For example, if the independent variable were number of minutes of review at the end of math lessons, then X_1 might represent 6 minutes of review, X_2 might represent 3 minutes of review, and X_3 no minutes of review. Thus X_3 (no minutes) would help us to assess the impact of X_2 (3 minutes), and X_2 would help us to assess the impact of X_1 (6 minutes). As already emphasized, but worthy of repeating, the degree to which the groups are equivalent is the degree to which their comparison is reasonable. In this design, participants are not randomly assigned to groups and there are no pretest data; thus, it is difficult to determine just how equivalent the groups are. That is, it is possible that posttest differences are due to initial group differences in maturation, selection, and selection interactions, rather than the treatment effects. Mortality is also a problem; if you lose participants from the study, you have no information about what you have lost because you have no pretest data. On the positive side, the presence of a comparison group does control for history, since it is assumed that events occurring outside the experimental setting will equally affect both groups.

In spite of its limitations, the static-group comparison design is occasionally employed in a preliminary or exploratory study. For example, one semester, early in the term, a teacher wondered if the kind of test items given to educational research students affects their retention of course concepts. For the rest of the term, students in one section of the course were given multiple-choice tests, and students in another section were given short-answer tests. At the end of the term, group performances were compared. The group receiving short-answer test items had higher total scores than the multiple-choice item group. On the basis of this exploratory study, a formal investigation of this issue was undertaken (with randomly formed groups and everything!).

True Experimental Designs

True experimental designs control for nearly all sources of internal and external invalidity. As Figure 9.2 indicates, all of the true experimental designs have one characteristic in common that none of the other designs have: random assignment of participants to treatment groups. Ideally, participants should be randomly selected and randomly assigned; however, to qualify as a true experimental design, at least random assignment (R) must be involved. Notice too that all the true designs have a control group (X_2). Finally, although the posttest-only control group design looks like the static-group comparison design, random assignment in the former makes it very different in terms of control.

The Pretest–Posttest Control Group Design.   The **pretest–posttest control group design** requires at least two groups, each of which is formed by random assignment; both groups are administered a pretest, each group receives a different treatment, and both groups are posttested at the end of the study. Posttest scores are compared to determine the effectiveness of the treatment. The pretest–posttest control group design may also be expanded to include any number of treatment groups. For three groups, for example, this design would take the following form:

$$
\begin{array}{cccc}
R & O & X_1 & O \\
R & O & X_2 & O \\
R & O & X_3 & O
\end{array}
$$

The combination of random assignment and the presence of a pretest and a control group serve to control for all sources of internal invalidity. Random assignment controls for regression and selection factors; the pretest controls for mortality; randomization and the control group control for maturation; and the control group controls for history, testing, and instrumentation. Testing is controlled because if pretesting leads to higher posttest scores, the advantage should be equal for both the experimental and control groups. The only weakness in this design is a possible interaction between the pretest and the treatment, which may make the results generalizable only to other pretested groups. The seriousness of this potential weakness depends on the nature of the pretest, the nature of the treatment, and the length of the study. When this design is used, the researcher should assess and report the probability of a pretest–treatment interaction. For example, a researcher might indicate that possible pretest interaction was likely to be minimized by the nonreactive nature of the pretest (chemical equations) and by the length of the study (9 months).

There are a number of ways in which the data from this and other experimental designs can be analyzed to test the research hypothesis regarding the effectiveness of the treatments. The best way to analyze these data is to compare the posttest scores of the two treatment groups. The pretest is used to see if the groups are essentially the same on the

Designs	Sources of Invalidity									
	Internal								External	
	History	Maturation	Testing	Instrumentation	Regression	Selection	Mortality	Selection Interactions	Pretest-X Interaction	Multiple-X Interference
TRUE EXPERIMENTAL DESIGNS										
1. Pretest–Posttest Control Group Design $R\ O\ X_1\ O$ $R\ O\ X_2\ O$	+	+	+	+	+	+	+	+	−	(+)
2. Posttest-Only Control Group Design $R\quad X_1\ O$ $R\quad X_2\ O$	+	+	(+)	(+)	(+)	+	−	+	(+)	(+)
3. Solomon Four-Group Design $R\ O\ X_1\ O$ $R\ O\ X_2\ O$ $R\quad X_1\ O$ $R\quad X_2\ O$	+	+	+	+	+	+	+	+	+	(+)
QUASI-EXPERIMENTAL DESIGNS										
4. Nonequivalent Control Group Design $O\ X_1\ O$ $O\ X_2\ O$	+	+	+	+	−	+	+	−	−	(+)
5. Time-Series Design $O\ O\ O\ O\ X\ O\ O\ O\ O$	−	+	+	−	+	(+)	+	(+)	−	(+)
6. Counterbalanced Design $X_1 O\ X_2 O\ X_3 O$ $X_3 O\ X_1 O\ X_2 O$ $X_2 O\ X_3 O\ X_1 O$	+	+	+	+	+	+	+	−	−	−

Note: Symbols: X or X_1 = unusual treatment; X_2 = control treatment; O = test, pretest, or posttest; R = random assignment of subjects to groups; + = factor controlled for; (+) = factor controlled for because not relevant; and − = factor not controlled for. This figure is intended to be a supplement to, not substitute for, textual discussions. See note that accompanies Figure 9.1.

FIGURE 9.2

Sources of invalidity for true experimental designs and quasi-experimental designs dependent variable at the start of the study. If they are, posttest scores can be directly compared using a statistic called the *t* test (discussed further in Chapter 12). If the groups are not essentially the same on the pretest (random assignment does not guarantee equality), posttest scores can be analyzed using analysis of covariance. Recall that covariance adjusts posttest scores for initial differences on any variable, including pretest scores. This approach is superior to using gain or difference scores (posttest minus pretest) to determine the treatment effects.

A variation of the pretest–posttest control group design involves random assignment of members of matched pairs to the treatment groups, in order to more closely control for one or more extraneous variables. There is really no advantage to this technique, however, because any variable that can be controlled through matching can be better controlled using other procedures such as analysis of covariance.

Another variation of this design involves one or more additional posttests. For example:

$$R \qquad O \qquad X_1 \qquad O \qquad O$$
$$R \qquad O \qquad X_2 \qquad O \qquad O$$

This variation has the advantage of providing information about the effect of the independent variable both immediately following treatment and at a later date. Recall that the interaction of time of measurement and treatment effects is a threat to external validity because posttesting may yield different results depending on when it is done. A treatment effect (or lack of same) that is based on the administration of a posttest immediately following the treatment may not be found if a delayed posttest is given after treatment. Although the variation described does not completely solve the problem, it does greatly minimize it by providing information about group performance subsequent to the initial posttest.

The Posttest-Only Control Group Design. The **posttest-only control group design** is exactly the same as the pretest–posttest control group design except there is no pretest; participants are randomly assigned to at least two groups, exposed to the different treatments, and posttested. Posttest scores are then compared to determine the effectiveness of the treatment. As with the pretest–posttest control group design, the posttest-only control group design can be expanded to include more than two groups.

The combination of random assignment and the presence of a control group serves to control for all sources of internal invalidity except mortality. Mortality is not controlled because of the absence of pretest data on participants. However, mortality may or may not be a problem, depending on the duration of the study. If it isn't a problem, the researcher may report that although mortality is a potential threat to validity with this design, it did not prove to be a threat because the group sizes remained constant or nearly constant throughout the study. If the probability of differential mortality is low, the posttest-only design can be very effective. However, if there is any chance that the groups may be different with respect to pretreatment knowledge related to the dependent variable, the pretest–posttest control group design should be used. Which design is "best" depends on the study. If the study is to be short, and if it can be assumed that neither group has any knowledge related to the dependent variable, then the posttest-only design may be the best choice. If the study is to be lengthy (good chance of mortality), or if there is a chance that the two groups differ on initial knowledge related to the dependent variable, then the pretest–posttest control group design may be the best.

What if, however, you face the following dilemma?

1. The study is going to last 2 months.
2. Information about initial knowledge is essential.
3. The pretest is an attitude test, and the treatment is designed to change attitudes.

This is a classic case where pretest–treatment interaction is probable. Do we throw our hands up in despair? Of course not. One solution is to select the lesser of the two evils by taking our chances that mortality will not be a threat. Another solution, if enough participants are available, is to use the Solomon four-group design, which we will discuss next. As Figure 9.2 shows, the Solomon four-group design is simply a combination of the pretest–posttest control group design (the top two lines) and the posttest-only control group design (the third and fourth lines). A variation of the posttest-only control group design involves random assignment of matched pairs to the treatment groups, one member to each group, to control for one or more extraneous variables. However, there is really no advantage to this technique, because any variable that can be controlled by matching can better be controlled using other procedures.

The Solomon Four-Group Design. The **Solomon four-group design** involves random assignment of participants to one of four groups; two of the groups are pretested and two are not; one of the pretested groups and one of the unpretested groups receive the experimental treatment; and all four groups are posttested with the dependent variable. This design is a combination of the pretest–posttest control group design and the posttest-only control group design, each of which has its own major source of invalidity (pretest–treatment interaction and mortality, respectively). The combination of these two designs results in a design that controls for pretest-treatment interaction and for mortality.

The correct way to analyze data resulting from application of the Solomon four-group design is to use a 2 × 2 (two by two) factorial with treatment and control groups crossed with pretesting and nonpretesting (factorial analysis of variance is discussed further in Chapter 12). There are two independent variables in this design: treatment/control and pretest/no pretest. The 2 × 2 factorial analysis tells the researcher whether the treatment is effective and whether there is an interaction between the treatment and the pretest. To put it simply, if the pretested experimental group performs differently on the posttest than the unpretested experimental group, there is probably a pretest–treatment interaction. If no pretest–treatment interaction is found, then the researcher can have more confidence in the generalizability of treatment differences across pretested and nonpretested treatments.

A common misconception is that because the Solomon four-group design controls for so many sources of invalidity, it is always the best design to choose. This is not true. For one thing, this design requires twice as many participants as most other true experimental designs, and participants are often hard to find. Further, if mortality is not likely to be a problem and pretest data are not needed, then the posttest-only design may be the best choice. If pretest–treatment interaction is unlikely and testing is a normal part of the subjects' environment (such as when classroom tests are used), then the pretest–posttest control group design may be best. Thus, which design is the best depends on the nature of the study and the conditions under which it is to be conducted.

Quasi-Experimental Designs

Sometimes it is just not possible to randomly assign individual participants to groups. For example, to receive permission to use schoolchildren in a study, a researcher often has to agree to keep existing classrooms intact. Thus, entire classrooms, not individual students, are assigned to treatments. When random assignment is not possible, a researcher still may choose from a number of quasi-experimental designs that provide adequate control of sources of invalidity. Although there are many quasi-experimental designs, we discuss only three of the major ones here. Keep in mind that designs such as these are to be used only when it is not feasible to use a true experimental design.

The Nonequivalent Control Group Design.   This design should be familiar to you since it looks very much like the pretest–posttest control group design. The only difference is that it involves random assignment of intact groups to treatments, not random assignment of individuals. In **nonequivalent control group design,** two (or more) treatment groups are pretested, administered a treatment, and posttested. For example, suppose a school volunteered six intact classrooms for a study. Three of six classrooms may be randomly assigned to the experimental group (X_1) and the remaining three assigned to the control group (X_2). The inability to randomly assign individuals to treatments (we're stuck with whole classes) adds validity threats such as regression and interactions between selection, maturation, history, and testing. The more similar the intact groups are, the stronger the study, so the researcher should make every effort to use groups that are as equivalent as possible. Comparing an advanced algebra class to a remedial algebra class, for example, would not be comparing equivalent groups. If differences between the groups on any major extraneous variable are identified, analysis of covariance can be used to statistically equate the groups. An advantage of this design is that because classes are selected "as is," possible effects from reactive arrangements are minimized. Groups may not even be aware that they are involved in a study. As with the pretest–posttest control group design, the nonequivalent control group design may be extended to include more than two groups.

The Time-Series Design.   This design is actually an elaboration of the one-group pretest–posttest design. In the **time-series design,** one group is repeatedly pretested until pretest scores are stable; then the group is exposed to a treatment and, after treatment implementation, repeatedly posttested. If a group scores essentially the same on a number of pretests and then significantly improves following a treatment, the researcher can be more confident about the effectiveness of the treatment than if just one pretest and one posttest were administered. To use a former example, if our statistics professor measured anxiety several times before giving the students her booklet, she would be able to see if anxiety was declining naturally, and thus not a result of the booklet per se. History is still a problem with the time-series design because some event or activity might occur between the last pretest and the first posttest. Instrumentation may also be a problem, but only if the researcher changes measuring instruments during the study. Pretest–treatment interaction is certainly a possibility; if one pretest can interact with a treatment, more than one pretest can only make matters worse. If instrumentation or pretest–treatment interaction threaten validity, however, you will probably be aware of the problem because scores will change prior to treatment.

Although statistical analyses appropriate for a time-series design are quite advanced, determining the effectiveness of the treatment basically involves analysis of the pattern of the test scores. Figure 9.3 illustrates some of the possible patterns that might be found. The vertical line between O_4 and O_5 indicates the point at which the treatment was introduced. Pattern A does not indicate a treatment effect; performance was increasing before the treatment was introduced and continued to increase at the same rate following introduction of the treatment. In fact, Pattern A represents the reverse situation to that encountered by our statistics professor with her anxiety-reducing booklet. Patterns B and C do indicate a treatment effect, with Pattern C more permanent than in Pattern B. Pattern D does not indicate a treatment effect even though student scores are higher on O_5 than O_4. The pattern is too erratic to make a decision about treatment effect. Scores appear to be fluctuating up and down, so the O_4 to O_5 fluctuation cannot be attributed to the treatment. These four patterns illustrate that just comparing O_4 and O_5 is not sufficient; in all four cases, O_5 indicates a higher score than O_4, but in only two of the patterns does it appear that the difference is due to a treatment effect.

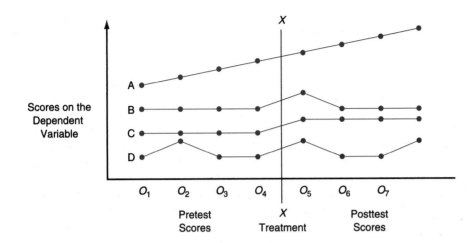

FIGURE 9.3

Possible patterns for the results of a study based on a time-series design

A variation of the time-series design is the **multiple time-series design**, which involves the addition of a control group to the basic design, as shown:

$$O \qquad O \quad O \quad O \quad X_1 \quad O \quad O \quad O \quad O$$
$$O \qquad O \quad O \quad O \quad X_2 \quad O \quad O \quad O \quad O$$

This variation eliminates history and instrumentation as validity threats and thus represents a design with no likely sources of internal invalidity. The multiple time-series design can be more effectively used in situations where testing is a naturally occurring event, such as in research involving school classrooms.

Counterbalanced Designs.   In a **counterbalanced design**, all groups receive all treatments but in a different order, and groups are posttested after each treatment. Although the counterbalanced design in Figure 9.2, p. 255, uses three groups and three treatments, any number of groups more than one may be studied. The only restriction is that the number of groups be equal to the number of treatments. The order in which the groups receive the treatments is randomly determined. Although participants may be pretested, this design is usually employed when intact groups must be used and when administration of a pretest is not possible. The pre-experimental static group comparison also can be used in such situations, but the counterbalanced design controls several additional sources of invalidity.

Figure 9.2 shows the sequence for three treatment groups and three treatments. The first horizontal line indicates that Group A receives Treatment 1 and is posttested, then receives Treatment 2 and is posttested, and finally receives Treatment 3 and is posttested. The second line indicates that Group B receives Treatment 3, then Treatment 1, and then Treatment 2, and is posttested after each treatment. The third line indicates that Group C receives Treatment 2, then Treatment 3, then Treatment 1, and is posttested after each treatment. To put it another way, the first column indicates that at Time 1, while Group A is receiving Treatment 1, Group B is receiving Treatment 3 and Group C is receiving Treatment 2. All three groups are posttested and the treatments are shifted to produce the second column. The second column indicates that at Time 2, while Group A is receiving Treatment 2, Group B is receiving Treatment 1 and Group C is receiving Treatment 3. The groups are then posttested again and the treatments are again shifted so that at Time 3, Group A is receiving Treatment 3, Group B is receiving Treatment 2, and Group C is receiving Treatment 1. All groups are posttested again. (Note that this design is not a research variation of the old comedy routine "Who's on

First?") To determine the effectiveness of the treatments, the average performance of the groups on each treatment can be calculated and compared. In other words, the posttest scores for all the groups for the first treatment can be compared to the posttest scores of all the groups for the second treatment, and so forth, depending on the number of groups and treatments.

A unique weakness of the counterbalanced design is potential multiple-treatment interference that results when the same group receives more than one treatment. Thus, a counterbalanced design should really be used only when the treatments are such that exposure to one will not affect the effectiveness of another. Unfortunately, there are not too many situations in education where this condition can be met. You cannot, for example, teach the same geometric concepts to the same group using several different methods of instruction. Sophisticated analysis procedures that are beyond the scope of this text can be applied to determine both the effects of treatments and the effects of the order of treatments.

Factorial Designs

As mentioned earlier in the chapter, factorial designs involve two or more independent variables, at least one of which is manipulated by the researcher. Factorial designs are basically elaborations of single-variable true experimental designs that permit investigation of two or more variables individually and in interaction with each other. In education, variables rarely operate in isolation. After an independent variable has been investigated using a single-variable design, it is often useful to study that variable in combination with one or more other variables. Some variables work differently at different levels of another variable. For example, one method of math instruction may be more effective for high-aptitude students, whereas a different method may be more effective for low-aptitude students. The term *factorial* refers to a design that has more than one independent variable, or factor. In the preceding example, method of instruction is one factor and student aptitude is another. The factor "method of instruction" has two levels because there are two types of instruction, and the factor "student aptitude" also has two levels, high aptitude and low aptitude. Thus, a 2×2 (two by two) factorial design has two factors, and each factor has two levels. This four-celled design is the simplest possible factorial design. As another example, a 2×3 factorial design has two factors; one factor has two levels, and the other factor has three levels (such as high, average, and low aptitude). Suppose we have three independent variables, or factors: homework (required homework, voluntary homework, no homework), ability (high, average, low), and gender (male, female). How would you symbolize this study? Right, it is a $3 \times 3 \times 2$ factorial design. Note that multiplying the factors yields the total number of cells in the factorial design. For example, a 2×2 design will have four cells, and a $3 \times 3 \times 2$ design will have 18 cells.

Figure 9.4 illustrates the simplest 2×2 factorial design. One factor, type of instruction, has two levels: personalized and traditional. The other factor, IQ, also has two levels: high

FIGURE 9.4

An example of the basic 2×2 factorial design

		Type of Instruction	
		Personalized	Traditional
IQ	High	Group 1	Group 2
	Low	Group 3	Group 4

and low. Each of the groups in the four design cells represents a combination of a level of one factor and a level of the other factor. Thus, Group 1 is composed of high-IQ students receiving personalized instruction (PI), Group 2 is composed of high-IQ students receiving traditional instruction (TI), Group 3 is composed of low-IQ students receiving PI, and Group 4 is composed of low-IQ students receiving TI. To implement this design, high-IQ students would be randomly assigned to either Group 1 or Group 2, and a similar number of low-IQ students would be randomly assigned to either Group 3 or Group 4. This approach should be familiar, since it involves stratified sampling. Also, in case the question crossed your mind, the study shown in Figure 9.4 would not necessarily require four classes; there could be two classes, the personalized class and the traditional class, and each of these two classes could be subdivided to obtain similar numbers of high- and low-IQ students. In a 2 × 2 design, both variables may be manipulated, or one may be a manipulated variable and the other a nonmanipulated variable. The nonmanipulated variable is often referred to as a **control variable.** Control variables are usually physical or mental characteristics of the subjects (such as gender, years of experience, or aptitude); in Figure 9.4, IQ is a nonmanipulated control variable. When describing and symbolizing factorial designs, the manipulated variable is traditionally placed first. Thus, a study with two independent variables, type of instruction (three types, manipulated) and gender (male, female), would be symbolized as 3 × 2, not 2 × 3.

The purpose of a factorial design is to determine whether the effects of an independent variable are generalizable across all levels or whether the effects are specific to particular levels. A factorial design also can demonstrate relationships that a single-variable design cannot. For example, a variable found not to be effective in a single-variable study may be found to interact significantly with another variable. The second example in Figure 9.5 illustrates this possibility.

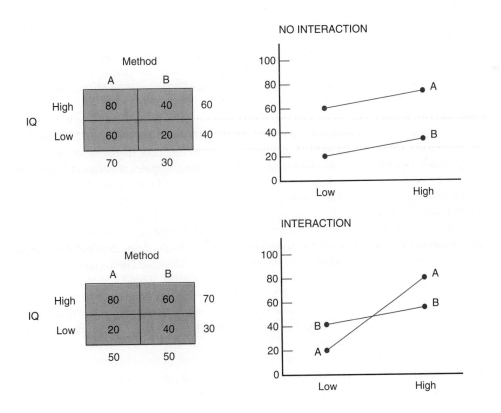

FIGURE 9.5

Illustration of interaction and no interaction in a 2 × 2 factorial experiment

Figure 9.5 represents two possible outcomes for an experiment involving a 2 × 2 factorial design. The number in each box, or cell, represents the average posttest score of that group. Thus, the high-IQ students under Method A had an average posttest score of 80, and the low-IQ students under Method B had an average score of 20. The row and column numbers outside the boxes represent average scores across boxes, or cells. Thus, in the top example, the average score for high-IQ students was 60 (found by averaging the scores for all high-IQ subjects regardless of treatment; 80 + 40 = 120/2 = 60), and the average score for low-IQ students was 40. The average score for students under Method A was 70 (found by averaging the scores of all the subjects under Method A regardless of IQ level; 80 + 60 = 140/2 = 70), and for students under Method B, 30. By examining the cell averages, we see that Method A was better than Method B for high-IQ students (80 versus 40), and Method A was also better for low-IQ students (60 versus 20). Thus, Method A was better, regardless of IQ level; there was no interaction between method and IQ. The high-IQ students in each method outperformed the low-IQ students in each method (no big surprise), and the subjects in Method A outperformed the subjects in Method B at each IQ level. The graph to the right of the results illustrates the lack of interaction.

In the bottom example of Figure 9.5, which method was better, A or B? The answer, as is frequently the case, is "It depends!" On what? On which IQ level we are talking about. For high-IQ students, Method A was better (80 versus 60); for low-IQ students, Method B was better (20 versus 40). Even though high-IQ students did better than low-IQ students regardless of method, how well they did depended on which method they were in. It cannot be said that either method was generally better; it can only be said that one or the other method was better for a particular IQ level. Now suppose the study had not used a factorial design but had simply compared two groups of subjects, one group receiving Method A and one group receiving Method B. High- and low-IQ students were not separated as in the factorial design. What would the researcher have concluded? The researcher would have concluded that Method A and Method B were equally effective, because the overall average score for both Methods A and B was 50! Using a factorial design allowed the researcher to determine that an interaction existed between the variables such that the methods were differentially effective depending on the IQ level of the participants. The crossed lines in the graph to the right of the results illustrate the interaction.

Many factorial designs are possible, depending on the nature and the number of independent variables. Theoretically, a researcher could simultaneously investigate 10 factors in a 2 × 2 × 2 × 2 × 2 × 2 × 2 × 2 × 2 × 2 design. In reality, however, more than 3 factors are rarely used because each additional factor increases the number of participants needed to fill the cells. Four cells are easier to fill than 10 cells. A 2 × 2 design with 20 participants per cell (a relatively small number) requires at least 80 participants (2 × 2 = 4 × 20 = 80). It is easy to see that as the number of cells increases things quickly get out of hand, and the results of studies with small sample sizes in each cell require extra-cautious interpretations. Moreover, when too many factors are included, resulting interactions become difficult, if not impossible, to interpret. Interpretation of a two-way interaction, such as the one illustrated in the second example in Figure 9.5, is relatively straightforward. But how, for example, would you interpret a five-way interaction between teaching method, IQ, gender, aptitude, and anxiety? Not only is it difficult to graph five-way interactions, they also tend to be uninterpretable! When used reasonably, factorial designs are very effective for testing research hypotheses that cannot be tested with a single-variable design.

An example of experimental research appears at the end of this chapter. See if you can figure out which experimental design was used. Hint: Students were randomly assigned to one of three treatment groups. Also, don't be concerned because you don't understand the statistics; focus on the problem, the procedures, and the conclusions.

SUMMARY

Experimental Research: Definition and Purpose

1. In an experimental study, the researcher manipulates at least one independent variable, controls other relevant variables, and observes the effect on one or more dependent variables.

2. The independent variable, also called the *experimental variable, cause,* or *treatment,* is that process or activity believed to make a difference in performance. The dependent variable, also called the *criterion variable, effect,* or *posttest,* is the outcome of the study, the measure of the change or difference resulting from manipulation of the independent variable.

3. When conducted well, experimental studies produce the soundest evidence concerning hypothesized cause–effect relationships.

The Experimental Process

4. The steps in an experimental study are basically the same as for other types of research: selecting and defining a problem, selecting participants and measuring instruments, preparing a research plan, executing procedures, analyzing the data, and formulating conclusions.

5. An experimental study is guided by at least one hypothesis that states an expected causal relationship between two treatment variables.

6. In an experimental study, the researcher forms or selects the groups, decides what treatments each group receives, controls extraneous variables, and observes or measures the effect on the groups at the end of the study.

7. The experimental group typically receives a new treatment, and the control group either receives a different treatment or is treated as usual.

8. The two groups that are to receive different treatments are equated on all other variables that might be related to performance on the dependent variable.

9. After the groups have been exposed to the treatment for some period, the researcher administers the dependent variable and then determines whether a significant difference exists between the groups.

Manipulation and Control

10. Direct manipulation by the researcher of at least one independent variable is the one single characteristic that differentiates experimental research from other types of research.

11. The three different forms of the independent variable are presence versus absence (A versus no A), presence in varying degrees (a lot of A versus a little A), and presence of one kind versus presence of another kind (A versus B).

12. *Control* refers to efforts to remove the influence of any variable (other than the independent variable) that might affect performance on the dependent variable.

13. Two different kinds of variables need to be controlled: participant variables, on which participants in the different groups might differ, and environmental variables, variables in the setting that might cause unwanted differences between groups.

Threats to Experimental Validity

14. Any uncontrolled extraneous variables that affect performance on the dependent variable are threats to the validity of an experiment. An experiment is valid if results obtained are due only to the manipulated independent variable and if they are generalizable to situations outside the experimental setting.

15. Internal validity is the degree to which observed differences on the dependent variable are a direct result of manipulation of the independent variable, not some other variable. External validity is the degree to which study results are generalizable to groups and environments outside the experimental setting.

16. The researcher must strive for a balance between control and realism, but if a choice is involved, the researcher should err on the side of control.

Threats to Internal Validity

17. History refers to any event occurring during a study that is not part of the experimental treatment but may affect performance on the dependent variable.

18. Maturation refers to physical, intellectual, and emotional changes that naturally occur within individuals over a period of time. These changes may affect participants' performance on a measure of the dependent variable.

19. Testing refers to the threat of improved performance on a posttest being a result of participants having taken a pretest.

20. Instrumentation refers to unreliability, or lack of consistency, in measuring instruments that may result in invalid assessment of performance.

21. Statistical regression usually occurs when participants are selected on the basis of their extreme scores and refers to the tendency of participants who score highest on a pretest to score lower on a posttest and the tendency of those who score lowest on a pretest to score higher on a posttest.

22. Differential selection is the selection of subjects who have differences at the start of a study that may influence posttest differences. It usually occurs when already-formed groups are used.

23. Mortality, or attrition, refers to a reduction in the number of research participants that occurs as individuals drop out of a study. Mortality can affect validity because it may alter the characteristics of the treatment groups.

24. Selection may also interact with factors related to maturation, history, and testing. This means that if already-formed groups are used, one group may profit more (or less) from a treatment or have an initial advantage (or disadvantage) because of maturation, history, or testing factors.

Threats to External Validity

25. Threats affecting to whom research results can be generalized make up threats to population validity.

26. Pretest–treatment interaction occurs when subjects respond or react differently to a treatment because they have been pretested. The pretest may provide information that influences the posttest results.

27. Multiple-treatment interference occurs when the same subjects receive more than one treatment in succession and when the carryover effects from an earlier treatment influence a later treatment.

28. Selection–treatment interaction occurs when subjects are not randomly selected for treatments and results of the study apply only to the groups involved. Interaction effects aside, the very fact that subjects are not randomly selected from a population severely limits the researcher's ability to generalize, because representativeness of the sample is in question.

29. Specificity is a threat to generalizability when the treatment variables are not clearly operationalized, making it unclear to whom the variables generalize.

30. Generalizability of results may be affected by short-term or long-term events that occur while the study is taking place. This potential threat is referred to as *interaction of history and treatment effects*.

31. Interaction of time of measurement and treatment effects results from the fact that posttesting may yield different results depending on when it is done.

32. Passive and active researcher bias or expectations can influence participants. Examples of experimenter effects are when the researcher affects participants' behavior or is unintentionally biased when scoring different treatment groups.

33. Reactive arrangements are threats to external validity that are associated with participants performing atypically because they are aware of being in a study. The Hawthorne, John Henry, and novelty effects are examples of reactive arrangements.

34. The placebo effect is sort of the antidote for the Hawthorne and John Henry effects. Its application in educational research is that all groups in an experiment should appear to be treated the same.

Group Experimental Designs

35. The validity of an experiment is a direct function of the degree to which extraneous variables are controlled.

36. Participant variables include organismic variables and intervening variables. Organismic variables are characteristics of the subject or organism that cannot be directly controlled but can be controlled for; the sex of a participant is an example. Intervening variables intervene between the independent variable and the dependent variable and cannot be directly observed but can be controlled for; anxiety and boredom are examples.

Control of Extraneous Variables

37. Randomization is the best single way to control for extraneous variables. Randomization is effective in creating equivalent, representative groups that are essentially the same on all relevant variables thought of by the researcher, and probably even a few not thought of. The use of randomly formed groups is a characteristic unique to experimental research; it is a control factor not possible with causal–comparative research.

38. Randomization should be used whenever possible; participants should be randomly selected from a population and be randomly assigned to groups, and treatments should be randomly assigned to groups.

39. Certain environmental variables can be controlled by holding them constant for all groups. Controlling participant variables is critical.

40. Matching is a technique for equating groups. The most commonly used approach to matching involves finding pairs of similar participants and randomly assigning each member of a pair to a different group.
41. A major problem with pair-wise matching is that subjects who do not have a match must be eliminated from the study. One way to combat loss of subjects is to match less closely. A related procedure is to rank all of the subjects, from highest to lowest, based on their scores on the control variable; the participants receiving each two adjacent scores constitute a pair.
42. Another way of controlling an extraneous variable is to compare groups that are homogeneous with respect to that variable. A similar but more satisfactory approach is to form subgroups representing all levels of the control variable.
43. If the researcher is interested not just in controlling the variable but also in seeing if the independent variable affects the dependent variable differently at different levels of the control variable, the best approach is to build the control variable right into the design.
44. Using participants as their own controls involves exposing the same group to the different treatments, one treatment at a time.
45. The analysis of covariance is a statistical method for equating randomly formed groups on one or more variables. It adjusts scores on a dependent variable for initial differences on some other variable related to the dependent variable.

Types of Group Designs

46. Selection of a given design dictates such factors as whether there will be a control group, whether subjects will be randomly assigned to groups, whether each group will be pretested, and how resulting data will be analyzed.
47. Different designs are appropriate for testing different types of hypotheses, and designs vary widely in the degree to which they control the various threats to internal and external validity. From the designs that are appropriate and feasible, you select the one that controls the most sources of internal and external invalidity.
48. There are two major classes of experimental designs: single-variable designs, which involve one independent variable (which is manipulated), and factorial designs, which involve two or more independent variables (at least one of which is manipulated).
49. Single-variable designs are classified as pre-experimental, true experimental, or quasi-experimental, depending on the control they provide for sources of internal and external invalidity. Pre-experimental designs do not do a very good job of controlling threats to validity and should be avoided. True experimental designs represent a very high degree of control and are always to be preferred. Quasi-experimental designs do not control as well as true experimental designs but do a much better job than the pre-experimental designs.
50. Factorial designs are basically elaborations of true experimental designs and permit investigation of two or more variables, individually and in interaction with each other.

Pre-Experimental Designs
51. The one-shot case study involves one group that is exposed to a treatment (X) and then posttested (O). No relevant threat to validity is controlled.
52. The one-group pretest–posttest design involves one group that is pretested (O), exposed to a treatment (X), and posttested (O). It controls several sources of invalidity not controlled by the one-shot case study, but additional factors are not controlled.
53. The static-group comparison involves at least two groups; one receives a new or unusual treatment, and both groups are posttested. Because participants are not randomly assigned to groups and there are no pretest data, it is difficult to determine just how equivalent the treatment groups are.

True Experimental Designs
54. True experimental designs control for nearly all sources of internal and external invalidity. True experimental designs have one characteristic in common that none of the other designs has: random assignment of participants to groups. Ideally, participants should be randomly selected and randomly assigned to treatments.
55. All the true designs have a control group.
56. The pretest–posttest control group design involves at least two groups, both of which are formed by random assignment. Both groups are administered a pretest of the dependent variable, one group receives a new or unusual treatment, and both groups are posttested. The combination of random assignment and the presence of a pretest and a control group serves to control for all sources of internal invalidity.

57. The only definite weakness with the pretest–posttest control group design is a possible interaction between the pretest and the treatment, which may make the results generalizable only to other pretested groups. A variation of this design seeks to more closely control extraneous variables by using random assignment of members of matched pairs to the treatment groups.

58. The posttest-only control group design is the same as the pretest–posttest control group design except there is no pretest. Participants are randomly assigned to at least two groups, exposed to the independent variable, and posttested to determine the effectiveness of the treatment. The combination of random assignment and the presence of a control group serves to control for all sources of invalidity except mortality, which is not controlled because of the absence of pretest data. A variation of this design is random assignment of matched pairs.

59. The Solomon four-group design involves random assignment of subjects to one of four groups. Two of the groups are pretested and two are not; one of the pretested groups and one of the unpretested groups receive the experimental treatment. All four groups are posttested. This design controls all threats to internal validity.

60. The best way to analyze data resulting from the Solomon four-group design is to use a 2×2 factorial analysis of variance. This procedure indicates whether there is an interaction between the treatment and the pretest.

Quasi-Experimental Designs

61. When it is not possible to randomly assign subjects to groups, quasi-experimental designs are available to the researcher. They provide adequate control of sources of invalidity.

62. The nonequivalent control group design looks very much like the pretest–posttest control group design, except that the nonequivalent control group design does not involve random assignment. The lack of random assignment raises the possibility of interactions between selection and variables such as maturation, history, and testing. Reactive effects are minimized.

63. In the nonequivalent control group design, every effort should be made to use groups that are as equivalent as possible. If differences between the groups on any major extraneous variable are identified, analysis of covariance can be used to statistically equate the groups.

64. In the time-series design, one group is repeatedly pretested, exposed to a treatment, and then repeatedly posttested. If a group scores essentially the same on a number of pretests and then significantly improves following a treatment, the researcher has more confidence in the effectiveness of the treatment than if just one pretest and one posttest were administered. History is a problem, as is pretest–treatment interaction.

65. Determining the effectiveness of the treatment in the time-series design basically involves analyzing the pattern of test scores. The multiple time-series design is a variation that involves adding a control group to the basic design. This variation eliminates all threats to internal invalidity.

66. In a counterbalanced design, all groups receive all treatments but in a different order, the number of groups equals the number of treatments, and groups are posttested after each treatment. This design is usually employed when intact groups must be used and when administration of a pretest is not possible. A weakness of this design is potential multiple-treatment interference.

Factorial Designs

67. Factorial designs involve two or more independent variables, at least one of which is manipulated by the researcher. They permit investigation of two or more variables, individually and in interaction with each other. The term *factorial* indicates that the design has several factors, each with two or more levels. The 2×2 is the simplest factorial design.

68. The purpose of a factorial design is to determine whether an interaction between the independent variables exists. If one value of the independent variable is more effective regardless of the level of the control variable, there is no interaction. If an interaction exists between the variables, different values of the independent variables are differentially effective depending on the level of the control variable. Factorial designs rarely include more than three factors.

Now go to the Companion Website at www.prenhall.com/gay to assess your understanding of chapter content with Practice Quiz, apply comprehension in Applying What You Know, broaden your knowledge about research in Web Links, and expand your research skills in Evaluating Articles, Analyzing Qualitative Data, and Research Tools and Tips.

EFFECTS OF WORD PROCESSING ON SIXTH GRADERS' HOLISTIC WRITING AND REVISIONS

GAIL F. GREJDA
Clarion University of Pennsylvania

MICHAEL J. HANNAFIN
Florida State University

ABSTRACT   The purpose of this study was to examine the effects of word processing on overall writing quality and revision patterns of sixth graders. Participants included 66 students who were randomly assigned to one of three revision treatments: paper and pencil, word processing, and a combination of the two techniques. Training in word processing was provided, and instruction was subsequently given during the 3-week study. The students were given a standard composition to revise and were also required to write and revise an original composition. Significant differences were found for both mechanical and organizational revisions in favor of the word-processing group. In addition, word-processing students tended to correct more first-draft errors and to make fewer new errors than their counterparts did. Although a similar pattern was found, no significant differences were discovered for holistic writing quality.

Interest in the potential of word processors to improve writing has grown substantially during the past decade. Various authorities have lauded the capability to increase writer productivity (Zaharias, 1983), to reduce the tediousness of recopying written work (Bean, 1983; Daiute, 1983; Moran, 1983), to increase the frequency of revising (Bridwell, Sirc, & Brooke, 1985; Daiute, 1986), and to improve both attitudes toward writing (Rodriguez, 1985) and the writing process (McKenzie, 1984; Olds, 1982). Some researchers have argued that word processors alter both individuals' writing styles and the methods used to teach writing (Bertram, Michaels, & Watson-Geges, 1985).

Yet, research findings on the effects of word processing have proved inconsistent (Fitzgerald, 1987). Some researchers have reported positive effects on writing (Daiute, 1985), whereas others have reported mixed effects (Wheeler, 1985). Although word processing seems to increase the frequency of revision, the revisions are often surface level and do little to improve the overall quality of composition (Collier, 1983; Hawisher, 1987). In some cases, word processing has actually hampered different aspects of writing (Grejda & Hannafin, in press; Perl, 1978).

However, comparatively little has been demonstrated conclusively. Attempts to study word processing have been confounded by both typing requirements and limited word-processing proficiency. Inadequate definition has also plagued word-processing

research. Many studies have isolated only mechanical attributes of revision, such as punctuation, requiring only proofreading rather than sophisticated revision skills (Collier, 1983; Dalton & Hannafin, 1987). Other research has focused only on global writing measures, with little attribution possible for observed changes in writing quality (Boone, 1985; Woodruff, Bereiter, & Scardamalia, 1981–82). Both mechanical and holistic aspects of writing are important, but they are rarely considered concurrently (cf. Humes, 1983).

Although comparatively few studies have focused on young writers, the results have been encouraging. Daiute (1986) reported that junior high school students using word processors were more likely to expand their compositions, as well as to identify and correct existing errors, than were paper-and-pencil students. Likewise, word-processing students were more likely than paper-and-pencil students were to revise their language-experience stories (Barber, 1984; Bradley, 1982). Boone (1985) reported that the compositions of fourth, fifth, and sixth graders became increasingly sophisticated through revisions focusing on both mechanics and higher level organizations. In contrast, despite improving students' attitudes, word processing has failed to improve overall compositions based upon holistic ratings of writing quality (Woodruff, Bereiter, & Scardamalia, 1981–82).

The purpose of this study was to examine the effects of word processing on the holistic writing quality and revision patterns of sixth graders. We predicted that word processing would improve both the accuracy of revisions as well as the overall holistic quality of student writing.

METHODS

Subjects

The subjects included 66 sixth graders (23 girls and 43 boys), and 3 classroom teachers. The students were enrolled in a school in a rural university community. Overall language achievement of the participating students, based upon the Language Scale of the Stanford Achievement Test, was at the 79th percentile.

Address correspondence to Gail F. Grejda, Education Department, 110 Stevens Hall, Clarion University of Pennsylvania, Clarion, PA 16214.

Preliminary Training

Prior to the study, the sixth-grade teachers and the students in word-processing groups received 1 hour of word-processing training during each of 5 days. The *Bank Street Writer* was used because of its widespread availability and popularity among elementary school teachers. The training included entering text, deleting and inserting characters, capitalizing letters, moving the cursor, centering, indenting, making corrections, moving and returning blocks of text, erasing and unerasing, saving, retrieving, and printing. In addition, the purpose and design of the study, as well as procedural information and materials required, were presented.

Revision Instruction

An hour of daily instruction on mechanical and organizational revisions was provided for 10 days of the 3-week study. The instruction reviewed previously taught revision rules commonly found in sixth-grade language books and focused on errors typical of those in the compositions of young writers.

The first 5 days included instruction on five mechanical error categories: capitalization, commas, punctuation, possessive nouns, and sentence structure. Daily lessons included rules for the error category under consideration, pertinent examples of each rule, and a paragraph containing numerous violations of the rules that were subsequently identified and revised by the students. During the next 5 days, the subjects focused on revising the following organizational errors, phrasing the main idea, adding relevant detail sentences, deleting irrelevant sentences. sequencing or ordering sentences, and, finally, applying the rhetorical devices vital to paragraph unity and coherence.

Original Writing Sample

All the students were allotted 60 min to write an original composition on a given topic. The task was to describe a planned trip itinerary to Canada, a topic based on a recently completed unit of study. The writing sample was obtained to provide a unique composition for each student, and it was subsequently used to identify and to make needed revisions in individual writing. All the students used paper and pencil to create the initial compositions.

Standard Composition

A standard composition was developed to determine each student's ability to identify and revise typical mechanical and organizational errors. The writing yielded a common metric from which revision comparisons could be made across students. The composition contained 57 mechanical errors and eight organizational writing errors. The errors, violations of rules found in typical sixth-grade language books, required the application of rules stressed during the daily lessons.

Instructional Groups

The students were assigned to one of three groups, depending on how revisions were made: exclusively with computer word processing (C-C); exclusively with paper and pencil (P-P); or a combination of the two techniques (C-P). All the treatment groups received identical revision instruction.

In the C-C group, the students used word-processing software during all phases of the study. That group examined the influence of continuous access to word processing on student editing, revising, and writing quality. The students in the P-P treatment group used paper and pencil to make all revisions on both compositions throughout the 10 days of instruction. That group approximated writing without the aid of the word processor. In the C-P treatment, the students used a word processor to revise the 10 daily lessons and paper and pencil to revise the compositions. That method examined the potential transfer of word-processing skills to non-computer writing and approximated the circumstances encountered when word processors were provided for some, but not all, of a student's writing needs.

Design and Data Analysis

In this study we used a one-way design, featuring three word-processing groups: pencil-pencil (P-P), computer-computer (C-C), and computer-pencil (C-P). Individual scores on the Stanford Achievement Test–Language Scale were used as a covariate in the analysis to adjust for potential prestudy writing differences. In addition, because of the relatively high prior achievement in the sample (only 4 students scored below the 50th percentile on the language scale) and the high correlation between writing and general language, the use of the standardized test scores as a covariate in the analysis permitted greater precision in isolating true treatment effects. The highly significant effect for the covariate, paired with the nonsignificant preliminary test for homogeneity of slopes, further supported the analysis.

A one-way multivariate analysis of covariance (MANCOVA), with the four composition subscale scores and the holistic writing rating, was run to test for treatment group effects. Analysis of covariance (ANCOVA) procedures were subsequently executed for each measure: a priori contrasts were constructed to test for differences between the C-C group and each of the other word-processing groups. The remaining scores were used to provide descriptive data related to revision strategies.

Procedures

Regularly assigned sixth-grade classroom teachers were presented an overview of the purpose and design of the study, procedural information, and required materials. The students were randomly assigned to one of the three treatment groups. The students and teachers in both word-processing groups (C-C and C-P) were then given word-processing training.

The students in each group were allotted 60 min to write their original composition. All students wrote the preliminary composition with pencil and paper. The compositions of students in the C-C group were subsequently entered electronically by a typist, because those students were required to revise the writing via word processing.

Next, instruction on revising mechanical and organizational writing error categories was provided. Each lesson included rules for the error category under consideration, pertinent examples of each rule, and a paragraph containing violations of the rules to be identified and revised by the students. After discussing the rules and examples of applications, the students revised the given paragraph, using their designated writing instrument. Upon completion, the students were given an errorless copy of the paragraph and were instructed to correct any existing errors. On subsequent days the subjects followed the same format, each day focusing on another of the mechanical and organizational error categories. During the study, the first author scheduled regular conferences with the classroom teachers to ensure compliance with current instruction topics as well as to preview upcoming lessons. In addition, the first author randomly rotated among the classes to ensure that planned activities were implemented as scheduled.

After the 10 daily lessons were completed, the students revised both the standard composition and the original composition. On the standard composition, students were allotted 60 min to revise mechanical errors in capitalization, punctuation, commas, possessive nouns, sentence structure, and organizational errors, including rephrasing the main idea, adding relevant detail sentences, deleting irrelevant sentences, sequencing sentences, and applying rhetorical devices vital to paragraph unity and coherence. None of the mechanical or organizational errors were cued in any way. The score for each measure was a percentage of the number of correct revisions to the total possible errors (57 mechanical, 8 organizational) on the standard composition.

The students were also provided 60 min to revise the mechanical and organizational errors on their original composition. The number of possible errors varied in each student's composition, so percentage correction scores were derived to account for differences in the number of mechanical and organizational errors. The score was a percentage of the correct revisions versus the total number of initial mechanical and organizational errors on the students' original composition.

Each original composition was then evaluated holistically for overall writing quality based on the procedures developed by Myers (1980) and Potkewitz (1984). Three trained composition instructors, experienced in both process writing and holistic scoring, served as raters; none of them were participants in the study. Each composition was evaluated "blind" by at least two of the raters by comparing the works to a rubric consisting of six competency levels ranging from lowest (1) to highest (6). If the two ratings were within one point of one another, the ratings were summed to yield a total rating score. If discrepancies of greater than one point were found, the third evaluator rated the composition independently, and the most discrepant rating of the three was discarded. Interrater agreement, based upon the percentage of rating pairs identical or within one point of one another, was .91. Discrepancies of more than one point in the initial ratings occurred on only 6 of the 66 compositions.

The students inadvertently introduced additional errors in their revisions, so new errors in the final compositions were also tallied. New errors, mechanical as well as organizational, were computed beyond those provided in the standard composition or generated by the students in the original composition. The errors were tallied according to the same criteria established for mistakes in the standard and original compositions.

Finally, revisions on both the standard and original compositions were classified to examine the nature of editorial revisions made by different writing groups. The instructors tallied word insertions and deletions, sentence insertions and deletions, sentences moved, sentence fragments and run-on-sentences inserted, and sentence fragments or run-on sentences corrected.

All compositions were typed, printed, coded, and randomized to prevent rater bias. In addition, that step allowed the students to work with comparably "clean" copies, and equalized the time spent revising versus recopying: To isolate specific revision skills without the confounding of either excessive typing or manual recopying, we provided the students with typed versions of their work.

RESULTS

The means for each of the subscales, adjusted for the influence of the covariate, are contained in Table 1. The one-way MANCOVA revealed a significant difference among word-processing groups, $F(2, 62) = 9.28, p < .001$. ANCOVA results, shown in Table 2, revealed a significant difference among treatment groups for all scales except for the mechanical revisions on the original composition.

Table 1.
Adjusted Percentage Means for Composition Subscales

Source	C-C	C-P	P-P
Standard composition			
Mechanical revisions	74.86	68.59	68.23
Organizational revisions	81.14	58.82	66.18
Original composition			
Mechanical revisions	57.32	42.91	45.00
Organizational revisions	63.64	48.55	42.73

Table 2.
ANCOVA Source Data for Composition Subscales

Source	df	M	F	p<
Standard composition				
Mechanical revisions				
Covariate (prior achievement)	1	7,915.55	76.11	.0001
Writing group	2	459.58	4.42	.016
Error	62	104.00		
Organizational revisions				
Covariate (prior achievement)	1	8,463.83	13.62	.0001
Writing group	2	3,353.83	5.40	.007
Error	62	621.48		
Original composition				
Mechanical revisions				
Covariate (prior achievement)	1	5,156.74	6.27	.015
Writing group	2	1,590.89	1.93	nsd
Error	62	822.93		
Organizational revisions				
Covariate (prior achievement)	1	5,027.33	7.69	.007
Writing group	2	2,818.37	4.31	.018
Error	62	653.86		

A priori contrasts for each significant difference indicated that the C-C students corrected a higher percentage of mechanical and organizational errors than the C-P or P-P groups did, on both the standard and original compositions (min. $p < .05$ in each case). No differences were found between the C-P and P-P groups for any of the subscales. In addition, although not statistically significant, the performance pattern for the mechanical revisions on original compositions was similar to the other subscales, with the C-C group performing best.

A profile of revision errors is shown in Table 3. The C-C word-processing group made fewer new mechanical and organizational errors than the other groups on both the standard and the original compositions. The C-C students also made fewer new errors on their own compositions. Paper-and-pencil and mixed-writing groups corrected a comparable percentage of organizational errors on both compositions.

Table 3.
Frequency of New Errors Introduced
During Final Revision

Revision type	C-C	C-P	P-P
Original			
Mechanical	12	20	39
Organizational	2	45	56
Standard			
Mechanical	0	7	12
Organizational	5	38	43

Table 4.
Revision Types for Original and Standard Compositions

Revision activity	C-C	C-P	P-P
Original composition			
Words inserted	167	52	31
Words deleted	13	9	17
Sentences inserted	121	47	64
Sentences deleted	9	14	3
Sentences moved	27	3	0
Sentence fragments/run-on sentences inserted	2	19	13
Sentence fragments/run-on sentences corrected	26	12	18
Standard composition			
Words inserted	9	0	0
Words deleted	0	15	23
Sentences inserted	0	1	0
Sentences deleted	59	43	38
Sentences moved	31	3	0
Sentence fragments/run-on sentences inserted	0	4	5
Sentence fragments/run-on sentences corrected	37	29	23

Revision patterns, summarized in Table 4, suggest different strategies among the three groups. On the original composition, word-processing students inserted more words and sentences, moved more sentences, and corrected more sentence fragments or run-on sentences than did students in the remaining groups. On the standard composition, word-processing students were more likely to insert words and move sentences, but less likely to delete words, than their counterparts.

Students in all groups revised the standard composition more effectively than their original compositions; that was true for both mechanical and organizational revisions. Comparatively few new mechanical and organization errors were made by the word-processing students, whereas new errors were substantially more common for the other writing groups.

Although adjusted means for holistic ratings fell in the predicted direction, there were only marginal differences in overall writing quality, $F(2, 62) = 2.31$, $p > .107$. Computer word-processing students (6.36) and the mixed-treatment group (6.27) were marginally higher than the paper-and-pencil group (5.00).

DISCUSSION

Several findings warrant further discussion. Consistent with much research on revising (Bridwell, Sirc, & Brooke, 1985; Daiute, 1986), word-processing students performed consistently better than other students did. Those students were more successful in revising existing as well as original writing, and they made more revisions to their work. In the present study, face evidence for improving editing via word processing is strong.

Yet, consistent with other researchers (Collier, 1983; Hawisher, 1987), overall quality did not improve significantly. Though word-processing groups performed marginally better than the paper-and-pencil group did, reliable differences were not detected. Despite strong evidence that mechanical and organizational revisions improved significantly, holistic writing quality was only marginally affected. Overall quality improvements may require substantially more time to develop (Riel, 1984). Word processing may, in the absence of concerted efforts to offset the tendency, inadvertently direct proportionately more attention to structural than holistic aspects of writing. Structural skills are important and yield the most visible features of composition, but they do not, by themselves, ensure improvement in the holistic quality of compositions (Flower & Hayes, 1981).

Editing is a necessary, but not sufficient, skill for effective writing (cf. Hodges, 1982; Sommers, 1980). The conceptual aspects of holistic writing, although not diminished in our study by word processing, require more than simple mechanical and even organizational changes in written products (Hairston, 1986; Humes, 1983; Kintsch & van Dijk, 1978). Yet, word processors seem to bias students toward mechanical editing. A spelling or capitalization error is substantially more apparent than an error of logic, argumentation, or internal inconsistency. Process-writing advocates promote recursive methods in the teaching of writing—methods designed to promote writer-level problem solving in their expression. Though such goals are likely attainable and supportable through well-constructed writing-via-word-processing efforts, they are less likely to be supported directly in typical word-processing software. Mechanical improvements may be necessary to overall quality, but they are clearly insufficient when emphasized exclusively.

Contrary to the findings of some researchers (Bartlett, 1982), more revisions were made and a higher proportion of initial errors were detected on the standard composition than on the original composition. That finding is not surprising because the standard composition was essentially an editing task. On the other hand, the students were more likely to embellish their own compositions by inserting words and sentences. In this study, in which we used both types of composition, different revision patterns clearly emerged for student- versus instructor-generated compositions.

In contrast to the findings of others, the students in this study focused principally on in-text revisions, and they made few new additions during revisions. Daiute (1986) noted that word-processing students appended words to their text rather than making corrections within the text. In this study, however, word-processing students made both mechanical and organizational revisions throughout the text. They also corrected more first-draft errors and made fewer new errors than did students in the other treatment groups. The emphasis on identifying and revising in-text errors rather than on adding new text during the instructional phase of the study might account for that difference.

Various authorities have expressed concern that providing writing instruction exclusively via word processors may ultimately interfere with conventional writing (Keifer & Smith, 1983). The rationale has been that students develop writing strategies that are dependent upon technological capabilities of limited accessibility. The combined word-processing and paper-and-pencil group was designed to test the transfer of revision skills developed via word processing to traditional writing tools. Consistent with previous research (Grejda & Hannafin, in press), intermittent word processing neither improved nor impeded transfer to paper-and-pencil formats.

Several other aspects of the present study are noteworthy. The initial training provided to both students and teachers, paired with control of supporting instruction, permitted increased precision in localizing those effects reasonably attributable to word processing. The short-term effects of word processing appear most pronounced for structural revisions; the long-term effects on both structural and holistic aspects remain unproved. Likewise, examining revision skills on both standard and student-generated compositions allowed us to focus on both specific editing and the constructive aspects of process writing.

Considerable work is needed to refine both research methods and instructional practices. Keyboarding, although not a major issue in our study, remains a concern. Young students can be trained nominally, but few of them actually develop proficiency. Daiute (1983) suggested that sustained word-processing training, for as much as 1 year, may be needed before sufficient technical proficiency is acquired to improve writing. In addition, the potential antagonism between the structural versus holistic approaches to word processing is troublesome. Methods designed to optimize both are needed, but the present findings suggest that one often benefits at the expense of the other.

From a research perspective, we have not generated clear-cut answers but, rather, clarifications regarding the relevant questions and needed methods of study. Neither writing nor the tools available to improve writing are likely to be advanced appreciably through studies that simplify complex processes artificially or control everyday factors unrealistically. From an academic perspective, educators must temper the enthusiasm for technologies and tools of such high-face validity with the sobering reality that a word processor "does not a writer make."

REFERENCES

Barber, B. (1984). Creating Bytes of language. *Language Arts, 59,* 472–475.

Bartlett, E. J. (1982). Learning to revise. In M. Nystrand (Ed.), *What writers know* (pp. 345–363). New York: Academic Press.

Bean, H. C. (1983). Computerized word processing as an aid to revision. *College Composition and Communication, 34,* 146–148.

Bertram, B., Michaels, S., & Watson-Geges, K. (1985). How computers can change the writing process. *Language Arts, 2,* 143–149.

Boone, R. A. (1985). *The revision processes of elementary school students who write using a word processing computer program.* Unpublished doctoral dissertation. University of Oregon, Eugene, OR.

Bradley, V. (1982). Improving students' writing with microcomputers. *Language Arts, 59,* 732–743.

Bridwell, L., Sirc, G., & Brooke, R. (1985). Revising and computing: Case studies of student writers. In S. W. Fredman (Ed.), *The acquisition of written language: Response and revision* (pp. 172–194). Norwood, NJ: Ablex.

Collier, R. M. (1983). The word processor and revision strategies. *College Composition and Communication, 34,* 149–155.

Daiute, C. (1983). The computer as stylus and audience. *College Composition and Communication, 34,* 134–145.

Daiute, C. (1985). *Writing and computers.* Reading, MA: Addison-Wesley.

Daiute, C. (1986). Physical and cognitive factors in revising: Insights from studies with computers. *Research in the Teaching of English, 20,* 141–159.

Dalton, D., & Hannafin, M. J. (1987). The effects of word processing on written composition. *Journal of Educational Research, 80,* 338–342.

Fitzgerald, J. (1987). Research on revision in writing. *Review of Educational Research, 57(4),* 481–506.

Flower, L., & Hayes, J. (1981). A cognitive process theory of writing. *College Composition and Communication, 32,* 365–387.

Grejda, G. F., & Hannafin, M. J. (in press). The influence of word processing on the revisions of fifth graders. *Computers in the Schools.*

Hairston, M. (1986). Different products, different processes: A theory about writing. *College Composition and Communication, 37,* 12.

Hawisher, G. (1987). The effects of word processing on the revision strategies of college freshmen. *Research in the Teaching of English, 21,* 145–159.

Hodges, K. (1982). A history of revision: Theory versus practice. In R. Sudol (Ed.), *Revising: New essays for teachers of writing* (pp. 24–42). Urbana, IL: National Council of Teachers of English.

Humes, A. (1983). Research on the composing process. *Review of Educational Research, 53,* 201–216.

Keifer, K., & Smith, C. (1983). Textual analysis with computers: Tests of Bell Laboratories' computer software. *Research in the Teaching of English, 17,* 201–214.

Kintsch, W., & van Dijk, T. (1978). Toward a model of text comprehension and production. *Psychological Review, 85,* 363–394.

McKenzie, J. (1984). Accordion writing: Expository composition with the word processor. *English Journal, 73,* 56–58.

Moran, C. (1983). Word processing and the teaching of writing. *English Journal, 72,* 113–115.

Myers, M. (1980). *A procedure for writing assessment and holistic scoring.* Urbana, IL: National Council of Teachers of English.

Olds, H. (1982). Word processing: How will it shape the student as writer? *Classroom Computer News, 3,* 24–26.

Perl, S. (1979). The composing process of unskilled college writers. *Research in the Teaching of English, 13*, 317–336.

Potkewitz, R. (1984). *The effect of writing instruction on the written language proficiency of fifth and sixth grade pupils in remedial reading programs.* Unpublished doctoral dissertation.

Riel, M. M. (1984). *The computer chronicles newswire: A functional learning environment for acquiring skills.* Paper developed for Laboratory of Comparative Human Cognition, San Diego, CA.

Rodrigues, D. (1985). Computers and basic writers. *College Composition and Communication, 36*, 336–339.

Sommers, N. (1980). Revision strategies of student writers and experienced adult writers. *College Composition and Communication, 31*,378–388.

Wheeler, F. (1985). "Can word processing help the writing process?" *Learning, 3*, 54–62.

Woodruff, E., Bereiter, C., & Scardamalia, M. (1981–82). On the road to computer-assisted composition. *Journal of Educational Technology Systems, 10*, 133–148.

Zaharias, J. (1983). Microcomputers in the language arts classroom: Promises and pitfalls. *Language Arts, 60*, 990–995.

Source: The Journal of Educational Research, 85, *pp. 144–149, 1992. Reprinted with the permission of the Helen Dwight Reid Educational Foundation. Published by Heldref Publications, 1319 Eighteenth St., N.W., Washington, DC 20036-1802, Copyright © 1992.*

"Single-subject experimental designs . . . are typically used to study the behavior change an individual exhibits as a result of some treatment." (p. 275)

Single-Subject Experimental Research

OBJECTIVES

After reading Chapter 10, you should be able to do the following:

1. For each of the A-B-A single-subject designs discussed in this chapter, (1) draw a diagram, (2) list the steps involved in its application, and (3) identify major problems with which it is associated.
2. Briefly describe the procedures involved in using a multiple-baseline design.
3. Briefly describe an alternating treatments design.
4. Briefly describe three types of replication involved in single-subject research.

Completing Chapter 10 should enable you to perform the following task.

TASK 6E

For a quantitative study, you have created research plan components (Tasks 2, 3a), described a sample (Task 4a), and considered appropriate measuring instruments (Task 5). If your study involves single-subject experimental research, now develop the methods section of a research report. Include a description of participants, data collection methods, and research design. (See Performance Criteria, p. 287.)

⸬ SINGLE-SUBJECT EXPERIMENTAL DESIGNS

As you learned in Chapter 1, **single-subject experimental designs** (also referred to as *single-case experimental designs*) are designs that can be applied when the sample size is one or when a number of individuals are considered as one group. These designs are typically used to study the behavior change an individual exhibits as a result of some treatment. In single-subject designs each participant serves as her or his own control, similar to participants in a time-series design. Basically, the participant is exposed to a nontreatment and a treatment phase, and performance is measured during each phase. The nontreatment condition is symbolized as A and the treatment condition is symbolized as B. For example, if we (1) observed and recorded a student's out-of-seat behavior on five occasions, (2) applied a behavior modification procedure and observed behavior on five more occasions, and (3) stopped the behavior modification procedure and observed behavior five more times, our design would be symbolized as A-B-A. Although single-subject designs have their roots in clinical psychology and psychiatry, they are useful in many educational settings, particularly those involving studies of students with disabilities.

Single-Subject Versus Group Designs

As single-subject designs have become progressively refined and capable of addressing threats to validity, they are increasingly viewed as acceptable substitutes for traditional group designs in a number of situations. Most traditional experimental research studies use group designs. This is mainly because the desired results are intended to be generalized to other groups. As an example, if we were investigating the comparative effectiveness of two approaches to teaching reading, we would be interested in learning which approach *generally* produces better reading achievement, since schools usually seek strategies that are beneficial for groups of students, not individual students. Thus, in studies like this, group comparison designs are widely used. A single-subject design would not be very practical because it would focus on single students and require multiple measurements over the course of a study. For example, it would be highly impractical to administer a reading achievement test repeatedly to the same students.

There are, however, some research questions for which traditional group designs are not appropriate. First, group comparison designs are sometimes opposed on ethical or philosophical grounds because such designs include a control group that does not receive the experimental treatment. Withholding students with a demonstrated need from a potentially beneficial program may be opposed or prohibited, as is the case with certain federally funded programs. If the treatment is potentially effective, objections may be raised when eligible participants are denied it. Second, group comparison designs are not possible in many cases because of the size of the population of interest. There may simply not be enough potential participants to permit the formulation of two equivalent groups. If, for example, the treatment is aimed at improving the social skills of children with profound emotional disturbances, the number of such children available in any one locale is probably too small to conduct comparative research. A single-subject design is clearly preferable to the formulation of two more-or-less equivalent treatment groups composed of five children each. Further, single-subject designs are most frequently applied in clinical settings where the primary emphasis is on therapeutic impact, not contribution to a research base. In such settings the overriding objective is the identification of intervention strategies that will change the behavior of a specific individual—for example, one who is engaging in self-abusive or aggressive behavior.

External Validity

A major criticism of single-subject research studies is that they suffer from low external validity; in other words, results cannot be generalized to a population of interest. Although this criticism is basically true, it is also true that the results of a study using a group design cannot be directly generalized to any individual within the group. Thus, group designs and single-subject designs each have their own generalizability problems. If your aim is to improve the functioning of an individual, a group design is not going to be appropriate.

Nonetheless, we usually are interested in generalizing the results of our research to persons other than those directly involved in the study. For single-subject designs, the key to generalizability is replication. If a researcher applies the same treatment using the same single-subject design individually to a number of participants and gets essentially the same results in every case (or even in most cases), confidence in the generalizability of the findings is increased. Different students respond similarly to the treatment. The more diverse the replications are (i.e., they feature different kinds of subjects, different behaviors, different settings), the more generalizable the results.

One important generalizability problem associated with many single-subject designs is the effect of the baseline condition—the condition before the experimental treatment is introduced—on the subsequent effects of the treatment condition. We can never be sure that the treatment effects are the same as they would have been if the treatment phase had come before the baseline phase. This problem parallels the pretest–treatment interaction problem associated with a number of the group designs.

Internal Validity

If proper controls are exercised in connection with the application of a single-subject design, the internal validity of the resulting study may be quite good.

Repeated and Reliable Measurement

In a time-series design (see Chapter 9), pretest performance is measured a number of times before the implementation of the treatment. In single-subject designs, similar multiple measures of pretest performance are referred to as **baseline measures.** By obtaining baseline measures over a period of time, sources of invalidity such as maturation are controlled in the same way that they are in the time-series design. However, unlike the time-series design, the single-subject design measures performance at various points in time while the treatment is being applied. This added dimension greatly reduces the potential threat to validity from history, a threat to internal validity in a time-series design.

One very real threat to the internal validity of most single-subject designs is instrumentation, the unreliability or inconsistency of measuring instruments. Because repeated measurement is a characteristic of all single-subject designs, it is especially important that measurements of participants' performance be as consistent as possible. Every effort should be made to obtain observer reliability by clearly defining and measuring the dependent variable. Because single-subject designs often rely on some type of observed behavior as the dependent variable, it is critical that the observation conditions (e.g., location, time of day) be standardized. If a single observer makes all the observations, intraobserver reliability should be obtained. If more than one observer makes observations, interobserver reliability should be obtained. Measurement consistency is especially crucial when moving from phase to phase. If a change in measurement procedures occurs at the same time a new phase is begun, the result can be invalid assessment of the treatment effect.

Also, the nature and conditions of the treatment should be specified in sufficient detail to permit replication. For example, one type of single-subject design has a baseline phase, a treatment phase, a return to baseline conditions (withdrawal of the treatment), and a second treatment phase. If effects at each phase are to be validly assessed, the treatment must have the same procedures each time it is introduced. Also, since the key to the generalizability of single-subject designs is replication, it is clearly a necessity for the treatment to be sufficiently standardized to permit other researchers to apply it as it was originally applied.

Baseline Stability

The length of the baseline and treatment phases can influence the internal validity of single-subject designs. A key question is, "How many measurements of behavior should be taken before treatment is introduced?" There is no single answer to this question. The purpose of baseline measurements is to provide a description of the target behavior as it naturally occurs before the treatment is applied. The baseline serves as the basis of comparison for determining the effectiveness of the treatment. If most behaviors were stable, the baseline phase would be simple to implement. But human behavior is quite variable, and the researcher must allow time for the observation of variations. For example, if a student's disruptive behavior were being measured, we would not expect that student to exhibit exactly the same number of disruptive acts in each observation period. The student would likely be more disruptive at some times than at others. Fortunately, such fluctuations usually fall within some consistent range, permitting the researcher to establish a pattern or range of student baseline performance; the establishment of a baseline pattern is referred to as achieving *baseline stability*. We might observe, for example, that the child normally exhibits 5 to 10 disruptive behaviors during a 30-minute period. These figures then become our basis of comparison for assessing the effectiveness of the treatment. If during the treatment phase the number of disruptive behaviors ranges from, say, 0 to 3, or steadily decreases until it reaches 0, and if the number of disruptive behaviors increases when treatment is withdrawn, the effectiveness of the treatment is demonstrated.

The existence of a trend can affect the number of baseline data points needed. If the baseline behavior is observed to be getting progressively worse, fewer measurements are required to establish the baseline pattern. If, on the other hand, the baseline behavior is getting progressively better, there is no point in introducing the treatment until, or unless, the behavior stabilizes. Three data points are usually considered the minimum number of measurements necessary to establish baseline stability, but as noted, more than three are often required. Normally, the length of the treatment phase and the number of measurements taken during the treatment phase should parallel the length and measurements of the baseline phase. If baseline stability is established after 10 observation periods, then the treatment phase should include 10 observation periods.

The Single-Variable Rule

An important principle of single-subject research is the **single-variable rule,** which states that only one variable at a time should be manipulated. In other words, as we move from phase to phase, only one variable should be added or withdrawn at any phase. Sometimes an attempt is made to simultaneously manipulate two variables to assess their interactive effects. This is not sound practice in single-subject designs because it prevents us from assessing adequately the effects of either variable.

Types of Single-Subject Designs

Single-subject designs are classified into three major categories: A-B-A withdrawal, multiple-baseline, and alternating treatments designs. The following sections describe these basic designs and some common variations.

A-B-A Withdrawal Designs

A-B-A withdrawal designs involve alternating phases of baseline (A) and treatment (B). There are a number of variations of the basic A-B-A withdrawal design, the least complex of which is the A-B design. Although this design is an improvement over the simple **case study,** the in-depth investigation of one unit (e.g., program), its internal validity is suspect. In the **A-B design,** baseline measurements (*O*) are repeatedly made until stability is established, the treatment (*X*) is introduced, and an appropriate number of measurements (*O*) are made during treatment implementation. If behavior improves during the treatment phase, the effectiveness of the treatment is allegedly demonstrated. The specific number of measurements involved in each phase will vary from experiment to experiment. We could symbolize this design as follows:

O   *O*   *O*   *O* | *X*   *O*   *X*   *O*   *X*   *O*   *X*   *O*

Baseline Phase | Treatment Phase

A | B

The problem with this design is that we don't know if behavior improved because of the treatment or for some other nontreatment reason. It is possible that the observed behavior change occurred as a result of some other, unknown variable or that the behavior would have improved naturally without the treatment. Using an **additive design,** a variation of A-B design that involves the addition of another phase or phases in which the experimental treatment is supplemented with another treatment, improves the researcher's ability to make such determinations. Additive designs include the A-B-A design and A-B-A-B design.

The A-B-A Design.   In **A-B-A design,** baseline measurements are repeatedly made until stability is established, treatment is introduced, a number of measurements are made, and the treatment phase is followed by a second baseline phase. By simply adding this second baseline phase to the A-B design, we get a much improved design. If the behavior is better during the treatment phase than during either baseline phase, the effectiveness of the treatment has been demonstrated. Symbolically, we can represent this design in the following way:

O   *O*   *O*   *O* | *X*   *O*   *X*   *O*   *X*   *O*   *X*   *O* | *O*   *O*   *O*   *O*

Baseline | Treatment | Baseline

Phase | Phase | Phase

A | B | A

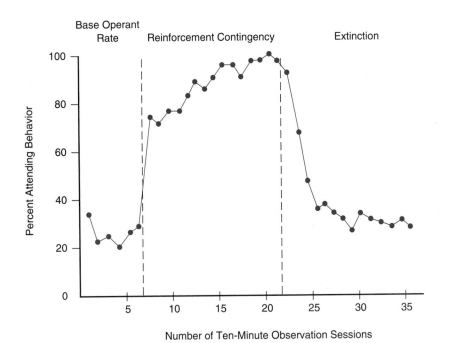

FIGURE 10.1

Percentage of attending behavior of a subject during successive observation periods in a study utilizing an A-B-A design
Source: From "The Use of Positive Reinforcement in Conditioning Attending Behavior," by H. M. Walker and N. K. Buckley, 1968, *Journal of Applied Behavior Analysis, 1*(3), p. 247. Reprinted with permission.

During the initial baseline phase of a study of attention, for example, we might observe on-task behaviors during five observation sessions (as in A-B design, the number of measurements will vary from experiment to experiment). We might then introduce the treatment—tangible reinforcement in the form of small toys for on-task behaviors—and observe on-task behaviors during five observation periods in the treatment phase. Lastly, we might stop the tangible reinforcement and observe on-task behaviors during an additional five sessions. If on-task behavior was greater during the treatment phase, we would conclude that the tangible reinforcement was the probable cause. A variation on this design is the **changing criterion design,** in which the baseline phase is followed by successive treatment phases, each of which has a more stringent criterion for acceptable (improved) behavior.

In an actual study using an A-B-A design, researchers did examine the impact of positive reinforcement on the attending behavior of an easily distracted 9-year-old boy.[1] A reinforcement program was developed for the student. Before actual data collection began, observers were trained until interrater reliability was .90 or above for 5 randomly selected attending behavior observations of 10 minutes each. Figure 10.1 shows the three stages of the design: baseline, treatment, and baseline. Each dot represents a data collection point. The reinforcement program established for the student improved his attending behaviors a great deal compared to the initial baseline. When the treatment was removed, attending behavior decreased, demonstrating the effectiveness of the reinforcement program.

It should be noted that there is some terminology confusion in the literature concerning A-B-A designs. A-B-A withdrawal designs are frequently referred to as *reversal designs,* which they are not, because treatment is generally withdrawn following baseline assessment, not reversed. You should be alert to this distinction.

---

[1] "The Use of Positive Reinforcement in Conditioning Attending Behavior," by H. M. Walker and N. K. Buckely, 1968, *Journal of Applied Behavior Analysis, 1*(3), pp. 245–250.

The internal validity of the A-B-A design is superior to that of the A-B design. With A-B designs it is possible that improvements in behavior are not due to treatment intervention. It is very unlikely, however, that behavior would coincidentally improve during the treatment phase and coincidentally deteriorate during the subsequent baseline phase, as could be demonstrated in A-B-A designs. The major problem with A-B-A design is an ethical one, since the experiment ends with the subject not receiving the treatment. Of course, if the treatment has not been shown to be effective, there is no problem. But if it has been found to be beneficial, the desirability of removing treatment is questionable.

A variation of the A-B-A design that eliminates this problem is the B-A-B design, which involves a treatment phase (B), a withdrawal phase (A), and a return to treatment phase (B). Although this design provides an experiment that ends with the subject receiving treatment, the lack of an initial baseline phase makes it very difficult to assess the effectiveness of the treatment. Some studies have involved a short baseline phase before application of the B-A-B design, but this strategy only approximates a better solution, which is application of an A-B-A-B design.

The A-B-A-B Design. In **A-B-A-B design,** baseline measurements are made until stability is established, treatment is introduced, a number of measurements are made, and the treatment phase is followed by a second baseline phase, which is followed by a second treatment phase. In other words, it is the A-B-A design with the addition of a second treatment phase. Not only does this design overcome ethical objections to the A-B-A design, it also greatly strengthens the research conclusions by demonstrating the effects of the treatment twice. If treatment effects are essentially the same during both treatment phases, the possibility that the effects are a result of extraneous variables is greatly reduced. The A-B-A-B design can be symbolized as follows:

```
O O O O | X O X O X O X | O | O O O O | X O X O X O X O
Baseline  |  Treatment        | Baseline  | Treatment
Phase     |  Phase            | Phase     | Phase
A         |  B                | A         | B
```

When application of this design is feasible, it provides very convincing evidence of treatment effectiveness.

Figure 10.2 shows a hypothetical example of the A-B-A-B design. The figure shows the summarized results of 5 days of observations in each of the four design phases. Baseline A_1 shows the student's average talking-out behavior for a 5-day period. Treatment B_1 shows the effect of a reinforcement program designed to diminish talking-out behavior. The figure shows that talking-out behavior diminished greatly with the treatment. Baseline A_2 shows that removal of the treatment led to increased talking-out behavior. The reintroduction of Treatment B_2 again led to diminished talking-out behavior. These patterns strongly suggest the efficacy of the treatment.

Multiple-Baseline Designs

Multiple-baseline designs entail the systematic addition of behaviors, subjects, or settings for intervention. These designs are used when it is not possible to withdraw a treatment and have performance return to baseline or when it would not be ethical to withdraw or reverse treatment. They are also used when a treatment can be withdrawn, but the effects of the treatment "carry over" so that a return to baseline conditions is difficult or impossible. The effects of many treatments do not disappear when a treatment is removed. In many cases, it is highly desirable for treatment effects to sustain. Reinforcement techniques, for example, are designed to produce improved behavior that will be maintained when external reinforcements are withdrawn.

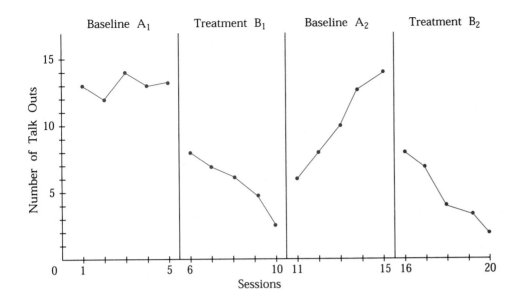

FIGURE 10.2

Talking out behavior during four 5-day observations of a student: Baseline 1, Treatment 1 (reinforcement program), Baseline 2 (no treatment), and Treatment 2 (reinforcement program)

The three basic types of multiple-baseline designs are across-behaviors, across-subjects, and across-settings designs. With a **multiple-baseline design**, instead of collecting baseline data on one specific behavior, data are collected on (1) several behaviors for one subject, (2) one behavior for several subjects, or (3) one behavior and one subject in several settings. Then, over a period of time, the treatment is systematically applied to each behavior (or subject or setting) one at a time until all behaviors (or subjects or settings) are exposed to the treatment. The "multiple" part of a multiple-baseline design refers to the study of more than one behavior, subject, or setting. For example, a study might seek to sequentially change three different behaviors using the multiple-baseline design. If measured performance improves only after a treatment is introduced, then that treatment is judged to be effective. There are, of course, variations that can be applied. We might, for example, collect data on one target behavior for several participants in several settings. In this case, performance for the group of participants in each setting would be summed or averaged, and results would be presented for the group as well as for each individual.

The multiple-baseline design can be symbolized as follows:

Behavior 1   *O O OXOXOXOXOXOXOXOXOXOXOXOXOXO*
Behavior 2   *O O O O O OXOXOXOXOXOXOXOXOXOXO*
Behavior 3   *O O O O O O O O OXOXOXOXOXOXOXO*

In this example a treatment was applied to three different behaviors—Behavior 1 first, then Behavior 2, and then Behavior 3—until all three behaviors were under treatment. If measured performance improved for each behavior only after the treatment was introduced, the treatment would be judged to be effective. We could symbolize examination of different participants or settings in the same manner. In all cases, the more behaviors, subjects, or settings involved, the more convincing the evidence is for the effectiveness of the treatment. What constitutes a sufficient minimum number of replications, however, is another issue. Although some investigators believe that four or more are necessary, three replications are generally accepted to be an adequate minimum.

When applying treatments across behaviors, it is important that the behaviors be independent of one another. If we apply treatment to Behavior 1, Behaviors 2 and 3 should remain at baseline levels. If the other behaviors change when Behavior 1 is treated, the design is not valid for assessing treatment effectiveness. When applying treatment across participants, the participants should be as similar as possible (matched on key variables such as age and gender), and the experimental setting should be as identical as possible for each participant. When applying treatment across settings, it is preferable that the settings be natural, not artificial. We might, for example, systematically apply a treatment (e.g., tangible reinforcement) during successive class periods. Or we might apply the treatment first in a clinical setting, then at school, and then at home. Sometimes it is necessary, due to the nature of the target behavior, to evaluate the treatment in a contrived, or simulation, setting. The target behavior may be an important one, but one that does not often occur naturally. For example, if we are teaching a child who is mentally challenged how to behave in various emergency situations (e.g., when facing a fire, an injury, an intruder), simulated settings may be the only feasible approach.

Figure 10.3 shows the results of a hypothetical study using a multiple-baseline design. The treatment, a program for improving social awareness, was applied to three types of behavior: (1) social behaviors, (2) help-seeking behaviors, and (3) criticism-handling behaviors. The figure shows that for each of the three types of behavior, more instances of the desired behavior occurred during the treatment period than during the baseline period, thus indicating that the treatment was effective.

Although multiple-baseline designs are generally used when there is a problem with returning to baseline conditions, they also can be used very effectively for situations in which

FIGURE 10.3

Multiple-baseline analysis of social awareness training on a student's social, help-seeking, and criticism-handling behaviors

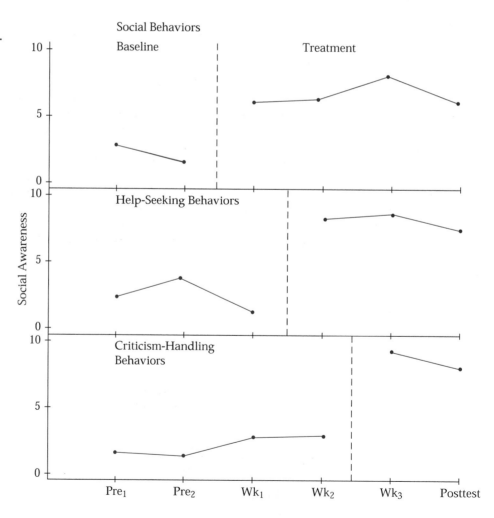

baseline conditions are recoverable. We could, for example, target talking out behavior, out-of-seat behavior, and aggressive behavior, which over time could return to baseline conditions. If we applied an A-B-A design within a multiple-baseline framework, the result could be symbolized as follows:

Talking-out behavior   A-B-A-A-A
Out-of-seat behavior   A-A-B-A-A
Aggressive behavior   A-A-A-B-A

Talking-out behavior   *O O OXOXOXO O O O O O O O O O*
Out-of-seat behavior   *O O O O O OXOXOXO O O O O O O*
Aggressive behavior   *O O O O O O O O OXOXOXO O O O*

Such a design would combine the best features of the A-B-A and the multiple-baseline designs and would provide very convincing evidence regarding treatment effects. In essence, it would represent three replications of an A-B-A experiment. Whenever baseline is recoverable and there are no carryover effects, any of the A-B-A designs can be applied within a multiple-baseline framework.

Alternating Treatments Design

The alternating treatments design is very useful in assessing the relative effectiveness of two (or more) treatments, in a single-subject context. Although the design has many names (*multiple schedule design, multi-element baseline design, multi-element manipulation design,* and *simultaneous treatment design*), there is some consensus that "alternating treatments" most accurately describes the nature of the design. The name of the design describes what it involves; specifically, the **alternating treatments design** involves the relatively rapid alternation of treatments for a single subject. The qualifier *relatively* is attached to *rapid* because alternation does not necessarily occur within fixed intervals of time. If a child with behavior problems saw a therapist who used an alternating treatment design every Tuesday, the design would require that on some Tuesdays the child would receive one treatment (e.g., verbal reinforcement), and on other Tuesdays another treatment (e.g., tangible reinforcement). The treatments (call them T_1 and T_2) would not be alternated in a regular, ordered pattern (T_1-T_2-T_1-T_2). Rather, to avoid potential validity threats, the treatments would be alternated on a random basis (e.g., T_1-T_2-T_2-T_1-T_2-T_1-T_1-T_2). Figure 10.4 illustrates this random application of two treatments. In the

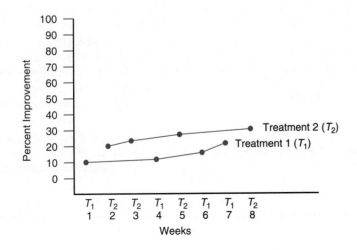

FIGURE 10.4

Hypothetical example of an alternating treatments design comparing treatments T_1 and T_2
Source: From Barlow, D. H. & Hersen, M. *Single Case Experimental Designs,* 2/e. Published by Allyn and Bacon, Boston, MA. Copyright © 1984 by Pearson Education. Reprinted by permission of the publisher.

example in the figure, the data points are consistently higher for T_2 than for T_1, so Treatment 2 appears to be more effective for this participant than Treatment 1. To determine whether Treatment 2 would also be more effective for other participants would require replication.

This design has several pluses that make it attractive to investigators. First, no withdrawal is necessary; thus, if one treatment is found to be more effective, it may be continued. Second, no baseline phase is necessary since we are usually attempting to determine which treatment is more effective, not whether a treatment is better than no treatment. Another major advantage is that a number of treatments can be studied more quickly and efficiently than with other designs. However, one potential problem with this design is multiple-treatment interference—that is, carryover effects from one treatment to the other.

Data Analysis and Interpretation

Data analysis in single-subject research typically is based on visual inspection and analysis of a graphic presentation of results. First, an evaluation is made concerning the adequacy of the design. Second, assuming a sufficiently valid design, an assessment of treatment effectiveness is made. The primary criterion of effectiveness is typically clinical significance, not statistical significance. Clinical effects that are small may not be large enough to make a sufficient difference in the behavior of a participant. As an example, suppose the participant is an 8-year-old male who exhibits dangerous, aggressive behavior toward other children. A treatment that produced a 5% reduction in such behavior may be statistically significant, but it is clearly not clinically significant. There are a number of statistical analyses available to the single-subject researcher, including t and F tests (to be discussed in Chapter 12). Whether statistical tests should be used in single-subject research is currently debated. To date, they have not been widely used in this type of research.

Replication

In Chapter 2 we described replication as a repetition of a study or retesting of its hypothesis. Replication is vital to all research, especially single-subject studies, whose initial findings are generally based on one or a small number of participants. The more results are replicated, the more confidence we can have in the procedures that produced those results. This is true for all types of research. Replication also serves to establish the generalizability of findings by providing data about participants' behaviors and settings to which results are applicable.

There are three basic types of replication of single-subject experiments: direct, systematic, and clinical. **Direct replication** is replication by the same investigator, with the same or different participants, in a specific setting (e.g., a classroom). Generalizability is promoted when replication is done with other participants who share the same problem, matched closely on relevant variables. When replication is done on a number of participants with the same problem, at the same location and same time, the process is referred to as **simultaneous replication. Systematic replication** follows direct replication and involves different investigators, behaviors, or settings. Over time, techniques are identified that are consistently effective in a variety of situations. We know, for example, that teacher attention can be a powerful factor in behavior change. At some point, enough data are amassed to permit the third stage of replication, clinical replication. **Clinical replication** involves the development of a treatment package, composed of two or more interventions that have been found to be effective individually, designed for persons with complex behavior disorders. Individuals with autism, for example, exhibit a number of characteristics, including apparent sensory deficit, mutism, and self-injurious behavior. Clinical replication would utilize research on each of these individually to develop a total program to apply to individuals with autism. Regardless of the type, replication is critically important in establishing the generalizability of single-subject research.

An example of a single-subject experimental research design appears at the end of this chapter. See if you can figure out which single-subject experimental design was used. Don't be concerned if you don't understand the statistical analysis at this stage. Focus on the problem, the procedures, and the conclusions.

SUMMARY

Single-Subject Experimental Designs

1. Single-subject experimental designs, also referred to as *single-case experimental designs,* can be applied when the sample size is one; they are typically used to study the behavior change an individual exhibits as a result of some intervention, or treatment.

2. Basically, the participant is alternately exposed to a nontreatment and a treatment condition, or phase, and performance is repeatedly measured during each phase. The nontreatment condition is symbolized as A, and the treatment condition is symbolized as B.

Single-Subject Versus Group Designs

3. At the very least, single-subject designs are considered to be valuable complements to group designs. There are two limitations of traditional group designs: (1) They are frequently opposed on ethical or philosophical grounds because by definition such designs involve a control group that does not receive the experimental treatment, and (2) application of a group comparison design is not possible in many cases because of the small sample sizes. Single-subject designs are most frequently applied in clinical settings where the primary emphasis is on therapeutic, not statistical, outcomes.

External Validity

4. Results of single-subject research cannot be generalized to the population of interest as they can with group design research. For single-subject designs, the key to generalizability is replication. A main threat to these designs is the possible effect of the baseline condition on the subsequent effects of the treatment condition.

Internal Validity

5. Single-subject designs require repeated and reliable measurements or observations. Pretest performance is measured or observed a number of times before implementation of the treatment to obtain a stable baseline. Performance is also measured at various points while the treatment is being applied. Because repeated data collection is a fundamental characteristic of all single-subject designs, it is especially important that measurement or observation of performance be standardized. Intraobserver and interobserver reliability should be estimated.

6. Also, the nature and conditions of the treatment should be specified in sufficient detail to permit replication. If its effects are to be validly assessed, the treatment must involve the same procedures each time it is introduced.

7. The purpose of the baseline measurements is to provide a description of the target behavior as it naturally occurs prior to the treatment. The baseline serves as the basis of comparison for assessing the effectiveness of the treatment. The establishment of a baseline pattern is referred to as achieving *baseline stability.*

8. Normally, the length of the treatment phase and the number of measurements taken during it should parallel the length and measurements of the baseline phase.

9. An important principle of single-subject research is that only one variable at a time should be manipulated.

Types of Single-Subject Designs

10. In the A-B design, baseline measurements are repeatedly made until stability is established, treatment is then introduced, and multiple measurements are made during treatment. If behavior improves during the treatment phase, the effectiveness of the treatment is allegedly demonstrated. This design is open to many internal and external validity threats.

11. By simply adding a second baseline phase to the A-B design, we obtain a much improved design, the A-B-A design. The internal validity of the A-B-A design is superior to that of the A-B design. It is unlikely that behavior would coincidentally improve during the treatment phase and coincidentally deteriorate during the subsequent

baseline phase. A problem with this design is the ethical concern that the experiment ends with the treatment being removed.

12. The B-A-B design involves a treatment phase (B), a withdrawal phase (A), and a return to treatment phase (B). Although the B-A-B design does yield an experiment that ends with the subject receiving treatment, the lack of an initial baseline phase makes it difficult to assess the effectiveness of treatment.

13. The A-B-A-B design is basically the A-B-A design with the addition of a second treatment phase. This design overcomes the ethical objection to the A-B-A design and greatly strengthens the conclusions of the study by demonstrating the effects of the treatment twice. When application of the A-B-A-B design is feasible, it provides very convincing evidence of treatment effectiveness. The second treatment phase can be extended beyond the termination of the actual study to examine stability of treatment.

14. Multiple-baseline designs are used when the treatment is such that it is not possible to withdraw or return it to baseline or when it would not be ethical to withdraw it or reverse it. They are also used when treatment can be withdrawn but the effects of the treatment "carry over" into other phases of the study.

15. There are three basic types of multiple-baseline designs: across-behaviors, across-subjects, and across-settings designs.

16. In a multiple-baseline design, data are collected on several behaviors for one subject, one behavior for several subject, or one behavior and one subject in several settings. Systematically, over a period of time, the treatment is applied to each behavior (or subject or setting) one at a time until all behaviors (or subjects or settings) are under treatment. If performance improves in each case only after a treatment is introduced, then the treatment is judged to be effective.

17. When applying a treatment across behaviors, it is important that the behaviors treated be independent of each other. When applying treatment across participants, they and the setting should be as similar as possible. When applying treatment across settings, it is preferable that the settings be natural, although this is not always possible.

18. Whenever baseline is recoverable and there are no carryover effects, any of the A-B-A designs can be applied within a multiple-baseline framework.

19. The alternating treatments design represents a highly valid approach to assessing the relative effectiveness of two (or more) treatments, within a single-subject context. The alternating treatments design involves the relatively rapid alternation of treatments for a single subject. To avoid potential validity threats, treatments are alternated on a random basis.

20. The alternating treatments design is attractive to investigators because no withdrawal is necessary, no baseline phase is necessary, and a number of treatments can be studied more quickly and efficiently than with other designs. One potential problem is multiple-treatment interference (carryover effects from one treatment to the other).

Data Analysis and Interpretation

21. Data analysis in single-subject research usually involves visual and graphical analysis. Given the small sample size, the primary criterion is the clinical significance of the results, rather than the statistical significance. Effects that are small, but statistically significant, may not be large enough to make a sufficient difference in the behavior of a subject. Statistical analyses may supplement visual and graphical analysis.

Replication

22. The more results are replicated, the more confidence we can have in the procedures that produced those results. Also, replication serves to set limits on the generalizability of findings.

23. There are three basic types of replication. Direct replication is replication by the same investigator, with the same or different subjects, in a specific setting (e.g., a classroom). Systematic replication follows direct replication and involves different investigators, behaviors, or settings. Clinical replication involves the development of a treatment package, composed of two or more interventions that have been found to be effective individually, designed for persons with complex behavior disorders.

 Now go to the Companion Website at **www.prenhall.com/gay** to assess your understanding of chapter content with Practice Quiz, apply comprehension in Applying What You Know, broaden your knowledge about research in Web Links, and expand your research skills in Evaluating Articles, Analyzing Qualitative Data, Analyzing Quantitative Data, and Research Tools and Tips.

PERFORMANCE CRITERIA

The description of participants should describe the population from which the sample was selected (allegedly, of course!), including its size and major characteristics.

The description of the instrument(s) should describe the purpose of the instrument (what it is intended to measure) and available validity and reliability coefficients.

The description of the design should indicate why it was selected, potential threats to validity associated with the design, and aspects of the study that are believed to have minimized their potential effects. A figure should be included illustrating how the selected design was applied in the study. For example, you might say:

> Because random assignment of participants to groups was possible, and because administration of a pretest was not advisable due to the reactive nature of the dependent variable (attitudes toward school), the posttest-only control group design was selected for this study (see Figure 1).

Group	Assignment	n	Treatment	Posttest
I	Random	25	Daily homework	So-so Attitude Scale
II	Random	25	No homework	So-so Attitude Scale

Figure 1. Experimental design.

The description of procedures should describe in detail all steps that were executed in conducting the study. The description should include (1) the manner in which the sample was selected and the groups formed, (2) how and when pretest data were collected (if applicable), (3) the ways in which the groups were different (the independent variable, or treatment), (4) aspects of the study that were the same or similar for all groups, and (5) how and when posttest data were collected. (Note: If the dependent variable was measured with a test, the specific test or tests administered should be named. If a test was administered strictly for selection-of-subjects purposes—that is, not as a pretest of the dependent variable—it too should be described.)

The example on the following pages illustrates the performance called for by Tasks 6a–e. (See Task 6 Example.) Although the example pertains to an experimental study, the components shown would be presented in a similar way for the other types of quantitative studies as well. The task in the example was prepared by the same student whose work for Tasks 2, 3a, 4a, and 5 was previously presented. You should therefore be able to see how Task 6 builds on previous tasks. Note especially how Task 3a, the method section of the research plan, has been refined and expanded. Keep in mind that Tasks 3a, 4a, and 5 will not appear in your final research report; Task 6 will. Therefore, all of the important points in those previous tasks should be included in Task 6.

Additional examples for the tasks are included in the *Student Study Guide* that accompanies this text.

1

Effect of Interactive Multimedia on the Achievement of 10th-Grade Biology Students

Method

Participants

The sample for this study was selected from the total population of 213 10th-grade students at an upper middle class all-girls Catholic high school in Miami, Florida. The population was 90% Hispanic, mainly of Cuban-American descent, 9% Caucasian non-Hispanic and 1% African-American. Sixty students were randomly selected (using a table of random numbers) and randomly assigned to two groups of 30 each.

Instrument

The biology test of the National Proficiency Survey Series (NPSS) was used as the measuring instrument. The test was designed to measure individual student performance in biology at the high school level but the publishers also recommended it as an evaluation of instructional programs. Content validity is good; items were selected from a large item bank provided by classroom teachers and curriculum experts. High school instructional materials and a national curriculum survey were extensively reviewed before objectives were written. The test objectives and those of the biology classes in the study were highly correlated. Although the standard error of measurement is not given for the biology test, the range of KR-20s for the entire battery is from .82 to .91 with a median of .86. This is satisfactory since the purpose of the test was to evaluate instructional programs not to make decisions concerning individuals. Catholic school students were included in the battery norming and its procedures were carried out in April and May of 1988 using 22,616 students in grades 9–12 from 45 high schools in 20 states.

Experimental Design

The design used in this study was the posttest-only control group design (see Figure 1). This design was selected because it provides control for most sources of invalidity and random assignment to groups was possible. A pretest was not necessary since the final science grades from June 1993 were available to check initial group equivalence and to help control mortality, a potential threat to internal validity with this design. Mortality, however, was not a problem as no students dropped from either group.

Group	Assignment	n	Treatment	Posttest
1	Random	30	IMM instruction	NPSS:B[a]
2	Random	30	Traditional instruction	NPSS:B

[a]National Proficiency Survey Series: Biology

Figure 1. Experimental design.

Procedure

Prior to the beginning of the 1993–94 school year, before classes were scheduled, 60 of the 213 10th-grade students were randomly selected and randomly assigned to two groups of 30 each, the average biology class size; each group became a biology class. One of the classes was randomly chosen to receive IMM instruction. The same teacher taught both classes.

The study was designed to last eight months beginning on the first day of class. The control group was taught using traditional methods of lecturing and open class discussions. The students worked in pairs for laboratory investigations which included the use of microscopes. The teacher's role was one of information disseminator.

The experimental classroom had 15 workstations for student use, each one consisting of a laser disc player, a video recorder, a 27-inch monitor, and a Macintosh computer with a 40 MB hard drive, 10 MB RAM, and a CD-ROM drive. The teacher's workstation incorporated a Macintosh computer with CD-ROM drive, a videodisc player, and a 27-inch monitor. The workstations were networked to the school library so students had access to online services such as Prodigy and Infotrac as well as to the card catalogue. Two laser printers were available through the network for the students' use.

In the experimental class the teacher used a videodisc correlated to the textbook. When barcodes provided in the text were scanned a section of the videodisc was activated and appeared on the monitor. The section might be a motion picture demonstrating a process or a still picture offering more detail than the text. The role of the teacher in the experimental group was that of facilitator and guide. After the teacher had introduced a new topic, the students worked in pairs at the workstations investigating topics connected to the main idea presented in the lesson. Videodiscs, CD-ROMs, and online services were all available as sources of information. The students used HyperStudio to prepare multimedia reports, which they presented to the class.

Throughout the study the same subject matter was covered and the two classes used the same text. Although the students of the experimental group paired up at the workstations, the other group worked in pairs during lab time, thus equalizing any effect from cooperative learning. The classes could not meet at the same time as they were taught by the same teacher, so they met during second and third periods. First period was not chosen as the school sometimes has a special schedule that interferes with first period. Both classes had the same homework reading assignments, which were reviewed in class the following school day. Academic objectives were the same for each class and all tests measuring achievement were identical.

During the first week of May, the biology test of the NPSS was administered to both classes to compare their achievement in biology.

EFFECTS OF FUNCTIONAL MOBILITY SKILLS TRAINING FOR YOUNG STUDENTS WITH PHYSICAL DISABILITIES

STACIE B. BARNES
KEITH W. WHINNERY
University of West Florida

ABSTRACT The Mobility Opportunities Via Education (MOVE®) Curriculum is a functional mobility curriculum for individuals with severe disabilities. This study investigated the effects of the MOVE Curriculum on the functional walking skills of five elementary-aged students with severe, multiple disabilities. The MOVE Curriculum was implemented using a multiple-baseline across subjects design. Repeated measures were taken during baseline, intervention, and maintenance phases for each participant. All students demonstrated progress in taking reciprocal steps during either intervention or maintenance. Results for each participant are discussed as well as implications and future directions for research.

Since the passage of P. L. 94-142, students served in special education programs have had the right to related services (e.g., occupational therapy and physical therapy) as needed to benefit from their educational program (Beirne-Smith, Ittenbach, & Patton, 2002). Therapists in educational settings who are typically trained under the medical model of disability traditionally have provided therapy services separate from educational goals (Craig, Haggart, & Hull, 1999; Dunn, 1989; Rainforth & York-Barr, 1997). Treatment within this traditional approach is based on the developmental model in which therapists attempt to correct specific deficits and remediate underlying processes of movement to promote normalization (Campbell, McInerney, & Cooper, 1984; Fetters, 1991). As a result, these treatment programs typically do not focus on the development of functional motor skills in natural environments because students often are viewed as *not ready* to perform such high level skills (Rainforth & York-Barr). Until recently, this traditional approach to therapy was considered acceptable in school settings because educational programming for students with disabilities also relied on a developmental model. It has been only in the past 15 to 20 years that educational programs for individuals with disabilities have begun to move away from instruction based on a developmental model to curriculum approaches emphasizing functional outcomes (Butterfield & Arthur, 1995).

Current educational practices promote the use of a *support model* that emphasizes an individual's future potential rather than an individual's limitations (Barnes, 1999). While earlier practices that focused on deficits often limited an individual's access to environments and activities (Brown et al., 1979), current practices employ a top-down approach to program planning designed to teach an individual to function more independently in his or her natural environments. Top-down program planning typically incorporates the concept of *place then train*, promoting instruction in the environments in which the skills will be used (Beirne-Smith et al., 2002). Individuals served under a support model are not excluded from activities because they lack prerequisite skills; rather they are supported to participate to their highest potential. A support model approach to programming provides a framework for identifying adult outcomes, determining current levels of functioning, and identifying supports needed to achieve the targeted outcomes.

As educational practices change, therapy approaches that stressed remediation of individual skills in isolated environments are being replaced by the practice of integrated therapy in which services are provided in natural settings where skills will be functional and performance meaningful for individual students (Rainforth & York-Barr, 1997). Integrated therapy breaks from the more traditional, multidisciplinary model where team members conduct assessments and set goals in relative isolation (Orelove & Sobsey, 1996). Parents, teachers, and therapists collaborate as a team to assess the student, write goals, and implement intervention. The team develops the IEP together by setting priorities and developing child-centered goals through consensus (Rainforth & York-Barr). In this way, all team members are aware of the IEP goals and can work cooperatively to embed them into the child's natural activities.

As the fields of physical therapy, occupational therapy, and education have begun to move away from a developmental approach toward a functional model that emphasizes potential and support, the link between special education and pediatric therapy has been strengthened (McEwen & Shelden, 1995). Recent research suggests that when therapy is integrated into the student's natural environments, treatment is just as effective as traditional therapy and that the integrated approach is more preferred by the school team (Giangreco, 1986; Harris, 1991). The benefits of providing therapy in integrated settings include (a) the availability of natural motivators (Atwater, 1991; Campbell et al., 1984), (b) repeated opportunities for practicing motor skills in meaningful situations (Campbell et al.; Fetters, 1991), and (c) increased generalization of skills across different environmental settings (Campbell et al.; Craig et al., 1999; Harris). "Although intervention has historically focused on deficient skills with the assumption that isolated skills must be learned and then eventually transferred to functional activities, we now know that for learners with severe disabilities, task-specific instruction must take place in the natural environment for retention to occur" (Shelden, 1998, p. 948).

In response to the shortcomings of traditional motor treatment approaches, the MOVE (Mobility Opportunities Via Education) Curriculum was developed to teach functional mobility skills to students with severe disabilities (Kern County Superintendent of Schools, 1999). MOVE is a top-down, activity-based curriculum designed to link educational programs and therapy by providing functional mobility practice within typical daily activities in the natural context. Individuals using the MOVE Curriculum follow a top-down approach to program planning, rather than selecting skills from a developmental hierarchy. A transdisciplinary team that includes parents, educators, and therapists works collaboratively to assess the student's skills, design an individualized program, and teach targeted skills while the student participates in school and community activities (for additional information on the MOVE Curriculum see Bidabe, Barnes, & Whinnery, 2001.)

Since the inception of the MOVE Curriculum in 1986, this seemingly successful approach has spread to a great number of classrooms, rehabilitation facilities, and homes for students with disabilities across the United States as well as throughout Europe and Asia. Although testimony from practitioners and families as well as informal studies have praised the effectiveness of MOVE, there has been no systematic research related to the effectiveness of this approach to teaching functional mobility skills. While the great number of anecdotal reports of student successes in the MOVE Curriculum should not be disregarded, there is a critical need for demonstrable data to support the efficacy of the program. Therefore, this study asked the following question: Do functional mobility skills in students with physical disabilities improve as a result of direct training using the MOVE Curriculum and will these skills be maintained over time?

METHOD

Participants

Five children with severe, multiple disabilities between the ages of 3 and 9 were selected to participate in this study. All of the children attended a public elementary school located in an urban, southeastern school district, were served in special education classes, and received occupational and physical therapy as related services. Four of the participants were served in a preschool classroom for students with severe, multiple disabilities. The remaining participant was served in a varying exceptionalities classroom for students with moderate to severe disabilities.

The following criteria were used to select participants for the study: (a) diagnosis of a severe, multiple disability including a physical impairment, (b) parental consent, (c) medical eligibility, (d) willingness of the school team to participate and to be trained in MOVE, and (e) no prior implementation of the MOVE Curriculum. Five of the 17 students served in the two classes met all the selection criteria.

The primary means of mobility for all participants was either being pushed in a wheelchair or being carried. Participant 1, Kim, was a 7-year-old female diagnosed with Down syndrome, severe mental retardation, general hypotonia in all extremities, and a seizure disorder for which she took anticonvulsant medication. Kim was able to bear her own weight in standing while

holding a stationary object and could move her feet reciprocally while being supported for weight shifting and balance. Although she demonstrated these skills on rare occasions in physical therapy, she typically refused to use them.

Participant 2, Melissa, was a 4-year-old female diagnosed with a developmental delay and cerebral palsy with hypotonia. Melissa was able to bear weight in standing while holding a stationary object and move her legs reciprocally while being supported for balance and weight shifting in physical therapy, but she also refused to use these skills.

Participant 3, Kevin, was a 3-year-old male diagnosed with cerebral palsy with hypotonia, right hemiparesis, cortical blindness, and a seizure disorder for which he took medication. Kevin was unable to bear weight in standing unless his knees, hips, and trunk were held in alignment by a standing device.

Participant 4, David, was a 9-year-old male diagnosed with spastic quadriplegic cerebral palsy and asthma for which he took medication. David had the ability to maintain hip and knee extension when supported by an adult and to tolerate fully prompted reciprocal steps when supported in a walker.

Participant 5, Caleb, was a 4-year-old male diagnosed with global developmental delays, spastic quadriplegic cerebral palsy, chronic lung disorder, and a seizure disorder for which he took medication. Additionally, Caleb had a tracheostomy that required frequent suctioning, a gastrostomy tube, and occasionally had breathing distress. He required a one-on-one nurse in attendance at all times, and his medical complications sometimes resulted in extended absences. Caleb had the ability to maintain hip and knee extension when supported by an adult and to tolerate fully prompted reciprocal steps when supported in a walker.

Research Methodology

A single-subject, multiple-baseline across subjects study was employed. The independent variable was the MOVE Curriculum that consists of six steps: (1) Testing, (2) Setting Goals, (3) Task Analysis, (4) Measuring Prompts, (5) Reducing Prompts, and (6) Teaching the Skills. The dependent variable was the number of reciprocal steps. A reciprocal step was defined as a step within a time interval of not more than 10 seconds between initial contact of one foot and initial contact of the opposite foot in a forward motion.

Setting

Mobility practice was conducted in the natural context in accordance with the principles of the MOVE Curriculum. Meaningful and relevant activities that naturally occur during the school day were selected for each participant. These activities occurred throughout the school campus.

The study was conducted over the course of one school year beginning in the third week of the fall term and lasting until the 27th week in spring. Maintenance data was collected over a 2-week period 2 years following the intervention year.

Staff Training

Two special education teachers, a physical therapist, and an occupational therapist from the selected school participated in a 2-day MOVE International Basic Provider training on the MOVE Curriculum. Basic Provider training incorporates 16 hrs of instruction on the six steps of the MOVE Curriculum including hands-on instruction in assessment, goal setting, and adaptive prompts and equipment with families and individuals with disabilities.

Materials and Equipment

The Rifton Gait Trainer (Community Playthings, 1999) was used during intervention. The Gait Trainer, also known as the Front Leaning Walker, provides support for an individual to learn to take reciprocal steps. The Gait Trainer is designed to provide total support (if needed) for individuals who are just beginning to bear weight in standing. The prompts can be removed as an individual requires less support with the long-term goal of independent walking.

PROCEDURES

Baseline

During the baseline phase, repeated measures of the number of reciprocal steps were taken twice a week until a pattern of stable performance was established. Baseline measures began by the fifth week of the school year. Due to the multiple baseline design, baseline was collected for 1 1/2 weeks for the first participant, Kim, and continued for 12 weeks for the last participant, Caleb. Each participant was given the least amount of adult assistance (i.e., one or two hands held or support at trunk) necessary for weight bearing in standing and verbal directions to walk. No assistance was provided for taking reciprocal steps. Baseline measures of reciprocal stepping were taken with adult support for all participants. Additional measurements without assistance were taken for Kim and Melissa because they had demonstrated the ability to bear weight in standing while holding a stationary object. Baseline measures occurred within the participants' normal school environments; however, no measures were taken using the Gait Trainer or within functional activities because these were considered to be part of the intervention.

Data Collection

Although practice of walking skills occurred throughout the day, measurement of the number of reciprocal steps was taken twice a week during specifically targeted activities to provide consistency of measurement. Measurement was taken at the first walking opportunity during each activity.

For the purpose of data collection, three general levels of support were used for participants according to their abilities and needs. Support was defined as (a) no outside assistance or *independent,* (b) *adult assistance* for postural control with independent weight bearing (e.g., one or two hands held or support at trunk), and (c) use of the *Gait Trainer* to provide postural control and partial weight bearing support when necessary. As students' reciprocal stepping skills increased, the level of support decreased progressively from the use of the Gait Trainer to adult assistance to no assistance as appropriate. Therefore, measurements were taken in multiple ways for each participant because it was not possible to predict changing levels of necessary support during intervention or the eventual level of independent mobility after

intervention. For all participants, data were collected concurrently at the level of support required at the beginning of intervention and at the next more independent level. In addition, measurements were taken for Melissa at all three levels of support. Although Melissa required the use of the Gait Trainer, measurements were taken for independent walking because she had previously demonstrated the ability to bear her own weight and occasionally take one or two reciprocal steps with both hands held. Because Kim began to take reciprocal steps independently during the second trial of intervention, data collection with "adult assistance" was discontinued.

Interobserver Agreement

Although the intervention was implemented by all team members, measurements were taken by the first author to increase reliability. In addition, interobserver agreement checks were made by the second author to ensure accurate measurement. For each participant, a minimum of two checks was conducted for each targeted behavior. Percentage of agreement was calculated by dividing the total number of agreements by the sum of agreements and disagreements and multiplying that number by 100 (White & Haring, 1980). Agreement for the number of reciprocal steps taken equaled 100%.

Intervention Phase

The intervention consisted of the implementation of the six steps of the MOVE Curriculum for each participant. Using the information obtained during Step 1, Testing, the team was able to identify each participant's consistent use of mobility skills and to select functional activities during Step 2. These activities were task analyzed in Step 3 in order to identify the critical mobility skills to be addressed in each activity.

Once meaningful daily activities were identified for mobility practice, the level and type of physical support needed to accomplish the activity were determined in Step 4, Measuring Prompts. A critical component of the MOVE program is to provide the necessary but minimal prompts (physical support) needed for functional mobility within an activity. This level was determined for each individual based upon assessment data collected in Step 1. Therefore, not all participants required assistance and all three levels of support.

As is advocated in Step 5 of MOVE, physical support was faded as soon as the students demonstrated an increase in skill level as indicated by the data. The reduction of prompts differed for participants according to their individual rate of progress.

During Teaching the Skills, Step 6 of MOVE, instruction of skills was embedded into typical daily activities in order to provide meaningful, intensive, and consistent practice of reciprocal stepping. An important component of this step is the identification of practice activities that are relevant and motivating to the individual to encourage active participation. From these practice opportunities, one activity per participant was selected for data collection. Data were collected twice a week.

Maintenance Phase

After a period of 2 years, maintenance measures were taken on dependent variables for 4 of the 5 participants. David had moved from the area and was unavailable. Data were collected during the participants' natural activities at the time. Some students had moved into new classrooms and many were participating in different activities than those used during the initial intervention phase.

Measurements were taken for participants at their current level of support necessary for functional walking (e.g., independent walking for Kim and Melissa, walking with adult assistance for Caleb, and walking with the use of the Gait Trainer for Kevin).

RESULTS
Data Analysis

Data were analyzed using visual inspection of the graphs including changes in means, levels, and trends as well as percentage of overlap across phases (Kazdin, 1982). Performance data for intervention and maintenance are presented in Figures 1–3.

Kim. A stable baseline with a mean and range of 0 steps was observed for walking forward independently (see Figure 1). The mean for intervention phase was 5.25 steps with a range from 0 to 14 steps. There was only a 9% overlap of data points (4 of 45 data points) from baseline with a 5.25-point increase in the mean. There was an upward trend in reciprocal steps observed in intervention phase with one notable decrease coinciding with an increase in seizure episodes.

During the maintenance phase, there was a sizable increase in the number of independent reciprocal steps recorded. All measurements during maintenance revealed that Kim was able to walk over 500 ft independently. This resulted in a 494.74-point increase in the mean number of steps taken with a 0% overlap of data points from intervention phase to the maintenance phase.

Melissa. A stable baseline with a mean and range of 0 steps was observed for walking (see Figure 1). Intervention included the use of the Gait Trainer (see Figure 3) and adult support (see Figure 2). As Melissa required less support, the Gait Trainer was discontinued (after the 37th trial). For adult support, there was a general increase in the number of steps with a mean of 30.16 with a range from 0 to 100 steps. A 38% overlap of data points (10 of 26 data points) was noted from baseline to intervention.

During the maintenance phase, measurements were taken on independent reciprocal steps since Melissa no longer required the use of the Gait Trainer or adult support. All measurements during maintenance showed that Melissa was able to walk over 500 ft independently. A 500-point increase in the mean with a 0% overlap of data points from intervention to maintenance was observed.

Kevin. For walking forward with adult support, Kevin was unable to bear weight or to take any steps during baseline or intervention (see Figure 2). Additionally, he would not accept being placed into the Gait Trainer during intervention (see Figure 3). During maintenance, however, Kevin was taking reciprocal steps

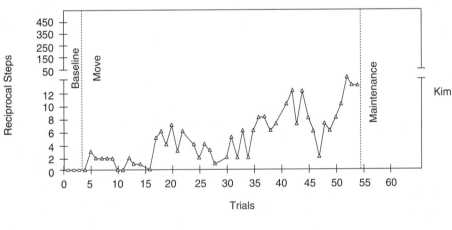

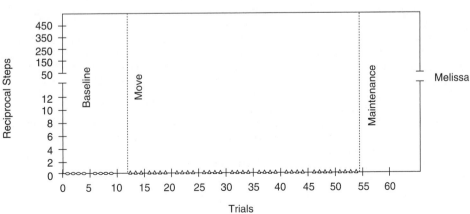

FIGURE 1. Independent walking for Kim and Melissa across baseline, intervention, and maintenance phases

FIGURE 2. Walking with adult support for Melissa (2-hand assistance), Kevin (support from behind at trunk), David (2-hand assistance), and Caleb (support from behind at trunk) across baseline, intervention, and maintenance phases

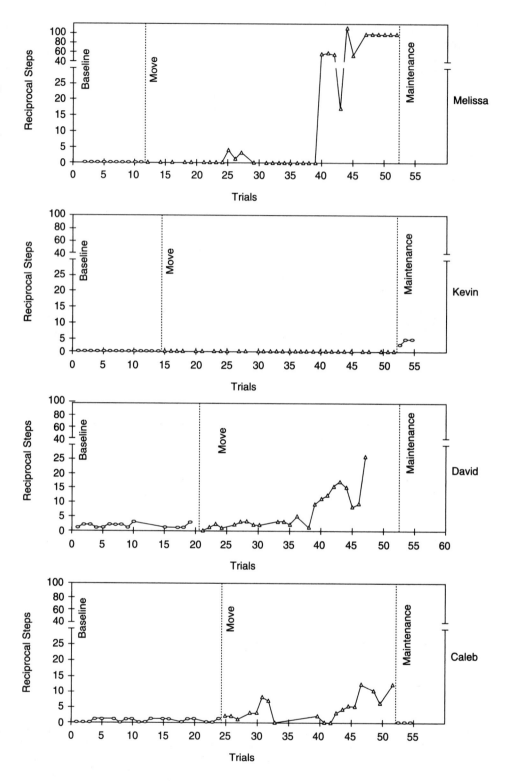

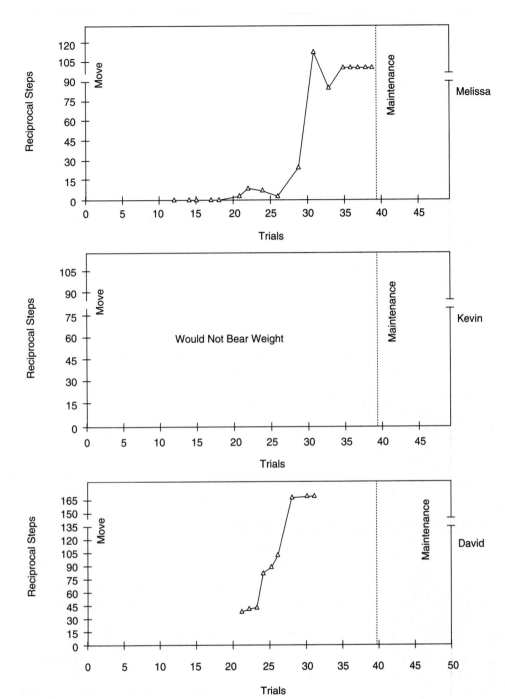

FIGURE 3. Walking with the use of the gait trainer for Melissa, Kevin, and David across baseline, intervention, and maintenance phases

both with adult support and while using the Gait Trainer. The mean for walking forward with adult support during maintenance was 3.33 steps with a range from 2 to 4 steps. This showed a slight upward trend and a mean of 3.33 steps. There was also a 0% overlap of data points (0 of 3 points) between intervention and maintenance. While using the Gait Trainer, Kevin consistently was able to take independent reciprocal steps for a minimum of 100 steps.

David. For walking forward with adult support, there was a stable baseline with a mean of 1.64 steps and a range from 1 to 3 steps (see Figure 2). An upward trend was noted during the intervention phase with a mean of 6.91 steps and a range from 0 to 26 steps. A 55% overlap of data points (12 of 22 data points) from baseline to intervention with a 5.27-point increase in the mean was observed.

Initially, measurements of reciprocal steps while walking in the Gait Trainer were taken since David was unable to walk the 70-ft distance from the bathroom to the classroom (see Figure 3). However, once David was able to consistently walk the entire distance, the measurement of distance was discontinued and the measurement of time was added (after the 30th trial). For the duration of the study, measurements of time indicated a steady decrease from 9 min 20 s to 4 min 54 s by the 53rd trial. David was unavailable during the maintenance phase due to a family move.

Caleb. For walking forward with adult support, a stable baseline with a mean of .60 steps and a range from 0 to 1 was observed (see Figure 2). The mean for the intervention phase was 4.47 steps with a range from 0 to 12 steps. However, after the 33rd trial, all walking was discontinued for 3 weeks due to medical complications. This resulted in a substantial decrease in walking skills following this period. A reintroduction of the intervention was followed by another upward trend. There was a 3.87-point increase in the mean from baseline to intervention with a 21% overlap of data points (4 of 19 data points). There was a significant decrease in skill level in the maintenance phase demonstrated by a mean of 0 steps. This represented a 4.47-point decrease from the intervention phase with a 0% overlap of data points.

DISCUSSION

The current study investigated the effects of the MOVE Curriculum on functional mobility skills (e.g., walking forward) with 5 students with severe, multiple disabilities. The results of this study provide support for the use of the MOVE Curriculum to increase functional mobility skills for students with severe disabilities. A clear functional relationship between the target behaviors and the intervention procedures was demonstrated. Four of the 5 participants showed increases in walking skills from baseline to intervention. Although the fifth participant, Kevin, did not make any gains during intervention, he did show a dramatic increase in walking during the maintenance phase.

In general, prior to intervention none of the participants was able to demonstrate functional walking skills either independently or with support. David and Caleb did demonstrate the ability to take a few steps with support during baseline, but these minimal levels did not increase their functional participation in daily activities. By the end of intervention, however, Kim was able to walk short distances independently. Melissa, David, and Caleb were able to walk with adult support to participate more fully in their selected activities. As the students gained functional walking skills, they were able to participate in other school and community activities without the use of their wheelchairs.

Although Kim demonstrated very little interest in her environment and would not attempt to take any independent steps during baseline, the addition of a motivating activity appeared to have a positive impact. Initially, Melissa resisted all attempts at walking and required the use of the Gait Trainer as well as full physical prompting to move her legs reciprocally. By the end of the intervention phase, however, she no longer required the use of the Gait Trainer and did not need to use her wheelchair during the school day. Despite Kevin's inability to take reciprocal steps during the intervention phase, the transdisciplinary team

continued to practice supported weight bearing in standing and transfers from sitting to standing with the expectation that reciprocal stepping would develop. This was found to be true when measurements were taken during maintenance.

Although David was able to take a few steps with adult support during baseline, he used the Gait Trainer to practice walking for longer distances during intervention. David's ability to walk forward with adult support also improved significantly during intervention. This new skill allowed David to walk short distances without the use of his wheelchair, allowing increased participation in crowded environments.

Caleb showed a fairly steady increase in reciprocal steps with adult support during intervention. There was a 3-week period when Caleb's nurse restricted all walking due to medical complications. After this break, Caleb experienced a temporary regression in walking skills followed by progress beyond earlier achievements.

During the maintenance phase, only 4 of the 5 participants were available. Three of the 4 participants not only maintained the gains made in walking skills, but they also continued to make improvements beyond the intervention year. The remaining participant, Caleb, experienced a significant setback in walking skills.

Kim was consistently walking over 500 ft on a variety of surfaces (e.g., sand, grass) and no longer used her wheelchair at school. Melissa was able to walk independently over 500 ft on a variety of surfaces, and her mother reported that she had greater access to the community. Kevin was consistently walking over 100 ft in the Gait Trainer and was bearing his own weight to take some steps with adult support. This was in sharp contrast to his performance during intervention when he was unable to bear his own weight. Caleb experienced numerous medical complications during the time period between intervention and maintenance. Walking skill practice was not a regular component of Caleb's education program resulting in regression in reciprocal stepping. During maintenance data collection, Caleb could bear his own weight for short periods of time, but was not strong enough to independently take reciprocal steps.

This study has limitations including a small sample size, variability of data, and difficulty in establishing a cause and effect relationship. The first issue of small sample size is characteristic of single-subject designs. The limitations of this design were reduced by the use of repeated measurements over time and multiple baselines. Additionally, the dramatic effects required of single-subject designs may be more generalizable across individuals than are larger group designs that meet relatively weaker statistical standards (Gall, Borg, & Gall, 1996; Kazdin, 1982).

A second limitation of this study is the variability of the data that makes interpretation of treatment effects difficult. The variety of influences in the natural environment and the characteristics of individuals with severe disabilities (i.e., frequent illnesses and absences, medical complexities, etc.) typically result in variations in the data. While traditional research methods consider variability to be a weakness, researchers studying the multiple factors affecting skill development advocate for the preservation of variability because it provides valuable information about behavior changes (Kamm, Thelen, & Jensen, 1990; Kratochwill & Williams, 1988).

A third limitation of this study is the difficulty in establishing a causal relationship between MOVE and increases in reciprocal stepping. In single-subject multiple-baseline designs, causal relationships can be inferred when performance changes at each point that intervention is introduced (Kazdin, 1982; Tawney & Gast, 1984). In this study some participants did not demonstrate immediate increases in skill with the introduction of the intervention. The slow rate of change of some participants also resulted in introduction of the curriculum for some students prior to significant increases of the previous participant. Although this violation of multiple-baseline design lessens the degree of experimental control, the decision was made to expose all participants to the intervention within the school year. However, a slow rate of behavior change is characteristic for the population studied (Beirne-Smith et al., 2002; Shelden, 1998). Additionally, a visual inspection of the data indicates that participants made dramatic changes in reciprocal stepping skills in either intervention or maintenance. Such dramatic changes in behavior provide more support for a causal relationship between the intervention and an increase in behavior (Kazdin; Tawney & Gast).

A second consideration related to the inference of causal relationships is the effect of external variables in relation to the intervention. In this study stable and staggered baselines helped to reduce the influence of competing variables such as maturation and historical events. Further, there were no gains in functional mobility skills for any participant until after the intervention was introduced for that individual.

The results of this preliminary study suggest that systematic mobility training programs, such as MOVE, can lead to an increase in functional mobility skills. Additional research investigating the effects of the MOVE Curriculum is warranted. Systematic direct replication should be conducted to help establish reliability and generalizability and could be replicated across at least five dimensions (e.g., subjects, behaviors, settings, procedures, and processes). In addition to replication of initial outcomes of this study, future research should investigate the criticality of specific components of the MOVE Curriculum (e.g., levels of family involvement, student-selected versus adult-selected activities, and systematic prompt reduction).

IMPLICATIONS FOR PRACTICE

This study emphasizes the importance of environmental support in the development of new skills. The importance of supports was obvious with David who was unable to walk independently, but could walk short distances with adult support and even greater distances with the use of the Gait Trainer. This discrepancy would suggest that without assistance, David would not have had the opportunity to practice walking skills. Kevin not only required postural support, but he also needed to develop weight-bearing skills before he experienced gains in walking. As muscle strength and proprioceptive awareness developed, he eventually was able to walk proficiently in the Gait Trainer. The implications of this study are significant for individuals with severe disabilities who may not have opportunities to participate in meaningful life activities without environmental support.

A second implication of this study was related to motivation. In addition to a lack of postural balance and strength, some of the participants appeared to have no interest in walking. This seemed

to be the case with Melissa who showed no signs of progress for over 2 months before making rather rapid and dramatic gains in her walking skills. The use of the Gait Trainer as well as full physical prompting allowed the school team to provide Melissa with the experience of walking to many different environments until she became actively engaged in walking. Thus, it appeared that once Melissa was motivated to walk within meaningful activities, she made dramatic increases in her functional walking abilities. Motivation was a factor with Kim's program, also. Once Kim developed walking skills, she would walk only to the table to eat or when returning to the "safety" of her classroom. As she became more excited about the freedom walking gave her, she began to generalize this skill across many environments and activities. The natural motivation associated with activity-based instruction is a key component of the MOVE Curriculum, and this study supports the importance of practice during motivating activities.

A third implication relates to the need for increased opportunities to practice new skills. For many individuals with severe disabilities, these opportunities do not always naturally occur. The results from this study support the use of practice opportunities that are both meaningful and continuous. Melissa appeared to have the potential to walk, but not the motivation. The continuous opportunities for practice seemed to be related to her increased desire to walk. With Caleb and Kevin who appeared to lack both the skill and the will to walk, increased mobility opportunities provided the consistent practice necessary for the acquisition of walking skills. When progress is not immediately apparent, as with Melissa and Kevin, educational teams must be committed to continuous meaningful practice. In both cases, the participants initially appeared to be unaffected by the intervention, but eventually made significant gains in functional walking. Regardless of whether lack of progress is due to limited skills or low motivation, continuous opportunities for practice should be a critical component of mobility training.

REFERENCES

Atwater, S. W. (1991). Should the normal motor developmental sequence be used as a theoretical model in pediatric physical therapy? In J. M. Lister (Ed.), *Contemporary management of motor control problems: Proceedings of the II Step Conference* (pp. 89–93). Alexandria, VA: The Foundation for Physical Therapy.

Barnes, S. B. (1999). The MOVE Curriculum: An application of contemporary theories of physical therapy and education. (Doctoral dissertation, University of West Florida, 1999). *Dissertation Abstracts International,* 9981950.

Beirne-Smith, M., Ittenbach, R. F., & Patton, J. R. (2002). *Mental retardation.* (5th ed.). Upper Saddle River, NJ: Prentice-Hall.

Bidabe, D. L., Barnes, S. B., & Whinnery, K. W. (2001). M.O.V.E.: Raising expectations for individuals with severe disabilities. *Physical Disabilities: Education and Related Services, 19*(2), 31–48.

Brown, L., Branson, M. B., Hamre-Nietupski, S., Pumpian, I., Certo, N., & Gruenewald, L. (1979). A strategy for developing chronological age-appropriate and functional curricular content for severely handicapped adolescents and young adults. *The Journal of Special Education, 13*(1), 81–90.

Butterfield, N., & Arthur, M. (1995). Shifting the focus: Emerging priorities in communication programming for students with a severe intellectual disability. *Education and Training in Mental Retardation and Developmental Disabilities, 30*(1), 41–50.

Campbell, P. H., McInerney, W. F., & Cooper, M. A. (1984). Therapeutic programming for students with severe handicaps. *The American Journal of Occupational Therapy, 38*(9), 594–602.

Community Playthings. (1999). *Rifton equipment* (Catalog). Rifton, NY: Community Products LLC.

Craig, S. E., Haggart, A. G., & Hull, K. M. (1999). Integrating therapies into the educational setting: Strategies for supporting children with severe disabilities. *Physical Disabilities: Education and Related Services, 17*(2), 91–109.

Dunn, W. (1989). Integrated related services for preschoolers with neurological impairments: Issues and strategies. *Remedial and Special Education, 10*(3), 31–39.

Fetters, L. (1991). Cerebral palsy: Contemporary treatment concepts. In J. M. Lister (Ed.), *Contemporary management of motor control problems: Proceedings of the II Step Conference* (pp. 219–224). Alexandria, VA: The Foundation for Physical Therapy.

Gall, M. D., Borg, W. R., & Gall, J. P. (1996). *Educational research: An introduction* (6th ed.). White Plains, NY: Longman.

Giangreco, M. F. (1986). Effects of integrated therapy: A pilot study. *Journal of The Association for Persons with Severe Handicaps, 11*(3), 205–208.

Harris, S. R. (1991). Functional abilities in context. In J. M. Lister (Ed.), *Contemporary management of motor control problems: Proceedings of the II Step Conference* (pp. 253–259). Alexandria, VA: The Foundation for Physical Therapy.

Kamm, K., Thelen, E., & Jensen, J. L. (1990). A dynamical systems approach to motor development. *Physical Therapy, 70,* 763–775.

Kazdin, A. E. (1982). *Single-case research designs.* New York: Oxford.

Kern Country Superintendent of Schools. (1999). *MOVE: Mobility Opportunities Via Education.* Bakersfield, CA: Author.

Kratochwill, T. R., & Williams, B. L. (1988). Perspectives on pitfalls and hassles in single-subject research. *Journal for The Association of Persons with Severe Handicaps, 13*(3), 147–154.

McEwen, I. R., & Shelden, M. L. (1995). Pediatric therapy in the 1990's: The demise of the educational versus medical dichotomy. *Occupational and Physical Therapy in Educational Environments, 15*(2), 33–45.

Orelove, F. P., & Sobsey, D. (1996). *Educating children with multiple disabilities: A transdisciplinary approach.* Baltimore: Paul H. Brookes.

Rainforth, B., & York-Barr, J. (1997). *Collaborative teams for students with severe disabilities: Integrating therapy and educational services.* Baltimore: Paul H. Brookes.

Shelden, M. L. (1998). Invited commentary. *Physical Therapy, 78,* 948–949.

Tawney, J. W., & Gast, D. L. (1984). *Single subject research in special education.* Columbus, OH: Merrill.

White, O. R., & Haring, N. G. (1980). *Exceptional teaching* (2nd ed.). Columbus, OH: Merrill.

"Looks bad, right?" (p. 320)

Descriptive Statistics

OBJECTIVES

After reading Chapter 11, you should be able to do the following:

1. List the steps involved in scoring standardized and self-developed tests.
2. Describe the process of coding data, and give three examples of variables that would require coding.
3. List the steps involved in constructing a frequency polygon.
4. Define or describe three measures of central tendency.
5. Define or describe three measures of variability.
6. List four characteristics of normal distributions.
7. List two characteristics of positively skewed distributions and negatively skewed distributions.
8. Define or describe two measures of relationship.
9. Define or describe four measures of relative position.
10. Generate (in other words, make up) a column of 10 numbers, each between 1 and 10. You may use any number more than once. Assume those numbers represent scores on a posttest. Using these "scores," give the formula and compute the following (showing your work): mean, standard deviation, z scores, and Pearson r (divide the column in half and make two columns of five scores each).

The goal of Chapters 11 and 12 is for you to be able to select, apply, and correctly interpret analyses appropriate for a given study. After you have read Chapter 13, you should be able to perform the following task.

TASK 7

For the same quantitative study you have been developing in Tasks 2–6, write the results section of a research report. Specifically,

1. Generate data for each of the participants in your study.

2. Summarize and describe data using descriptive statistics.
3. Statistically analyze data using inferential statistics.
4. Interpret the results in terms of your original research hypothesis.
5. Present the results of your data analyses in a summary table.

If SPSS is available to you, use it to check your work. (See Performance Criteria at the end of Chapter 13, p. 392.)

▪▪ THE WORD IS "STATISTICS," NOT "SADISTICS"

Statistics is a set of procedures for describing, synthesizing, analyzing, and interpreting quantitative data. Using statistical procedures, 1,000 scores can be represented by a single number, for example. As another example, you would not expect two groups to perform exactly the same on a posttest, even if they were essentially equal. Application of the appropriate statistic helps you to decide if the difference between two groups' scores is big enough to represent a true rather than a chance difference.

Choice of appropriate statistical techniques is determined to a great extent by your research design, hypothesis, and the kind of data that will be collected. Thus, different research focuses lead to different statistical analyses. The statistical procedures and techniques of the study should be identified and described in detail in the research plan. Data analysis is as important as any other component of research. Regardless of how well the study is conducted, inappropriate analyses can lead to inappropriate research conclusions. Note, however, the complexity of the analysis is not necessarily an indication of its "goodness" or appropriateness.

Many statistical approaches are available to a researcher. This chapter and Chapter 12 will describe and explain those commonly used in educational research. The focus is on your ability to apply and interpret these statistics, not your ability to describe their theoretical rationale and mathematical derivation. Despite what you have heard, statistics is easy. To calculate the statistics in these chapters, you need to know only how to add, subtract, multiply, and divide. That is all. No matter how gross or complex a formula is, it can be turned into an arithmetic problem when applied to your data. The arithmetic problems involve only addition, subtraction, multiplication, and division; the formulas tell you how often, and in what order, to perform those operations. Even if you haven't had a math course since junior high school, you will be able to calculate statistics. The hardest formula requires arithmetic at the sixth-grade level. In fact, you are encouraged to use a calculator! All you have to do is follow the steps we present. Trust us. You are going to be pleasantly surprised to see just how easy statistics is.

∷ PREPARING DATA FOR ANALYSIS

A research study usually produces a mass of raw data, such as the responses of participants to an achievement, ability, interest, or attitude test. Collected data must be accurately scored and systematically organized to facilitate data analysis.

Scoring Procedures

All instruments administered should be scored accurately and consistently; each participant's test results should be scored in the same way and with one criterion. When a standardized instrument is used, scoring is greatly facilitated. The test manual usually spells out the steps to follow in scoring each test, and a scoring key is usually provided. If the manual is followed conscientiously and each test is scored carefully, errors are minimized. It is usually a good idea to recheck all or at least some of the tests (say, 25% or every third test) for consistency of scoring.

Scoring self-developed instruments is more complex than scoring standardized instruments, especially if open-ended items are involved. The researcher has no manual to follow and so must develop and refine a scoring procedure. Steps for scoring each item and for arriving at a total score must be delineated and carefully followed. If other than objective-type items (such as multiple-choice questions) are to be scored, at least two people should independently score some or all of the tests as a reliability check. Planned scoring procedures should be tried out by administering the instrument to some individuals from the same or a similar population as the one from which research participants will be selected for the actual study. In this way, problems with the instrument or its scoring can be identified and corrected before the start of the study. The procedure ultimately used to score study data should be described in detail in the final research report.

Test questions that can be responded to on a standard, machine-scorable answer sheet can save a lot of time and increase the accuracy of the scoring process. If tests are to be machine scored, answer sheets should be checked carefully for stray pencil marks, and a percentage of them should be scored by hand just to make sure the key is correct and the machine is scoring properly. The fact that the tests are being scored by a machine does not relieve the researcher of the responsibility of carefully checking data before and after processing.

Tabulation and Coding Procedures

After instruments have been scored, the results are transferred to summary data sheets or, more likely, to a computer program. Tabulation involves organizing the data. Recording the scores in a systematic manner facilitates examination and analysis of the data. If analysis consists of comparing the posttest scores of two or more groups, data are generally placed in columns, one for each group, with the data arranged in ascending or descending order. If pretest scores

TABLE 11.1 Hypothetical results of a study based on a 2 × 2 factorial design			
High Aptitude		**Low Aptitude**	
Method A	**Method B**	**Method A**	**Method B**
68	55	50	60
72	60	58	66
76	65	60	67
78	70	62	68
80	72	64	69
84	74	64	69
84	74	65	70
85	75	65	70
86	75	66	71
86	76	67	71
88	76	70	72
90	76	72	75
91	78	72	76
92	82	75	77
96	87	78	79

are involved, additional columns should be formed. If analyses involve subgroup comparisons, scores should be tabulated separately for each subgroup. Table 11.1 shows the results of a study with four subgroups: two types of mathematics instruction (Methods A and B) and two levels of aptitude (a 2 × 2 factorial design). This is the common method of dealing with quantitative data.

If the data to be analyzed are categorical, tabulation usually involves counting responses. For example, a superintendent might be interested in comparing the attitude toward unions of elementary and secondary teachers. Thus, for a question such as, "Would you join a union if given the opportunity?" the superintendent would tally the number of "yes," "no," and "undecided" responses separately for elementary and secondary teachers.

When a number of different kinds of data (such as demographic information and several different test scores) are collected from each participant, both the variable names and the actual data are frequently coded. The variable "pretest reading comprehension scores," for example, may be coded as "PRC," and gender of participants may be recorded as "M" or "F" or "1" or "2." Use of a computer program for tabulating data and doing data analysis is recommended in general, but particularly if complex or multiple analyses are to be performed, or if a large number of participants are involved. In these cases, coding the data is especially important. The major advantage of using a computer program to organize and analyze data is the capacity to rearrange data by subgroups and extract information without reentering all the data.

The first step in coding data is to give each participant an ID number. If there are 50 participants, for example, number them from 01 to 50. As this example illustrates, if the highest value for a variable is two digits (e.g., 50), then all represented values must be two digits. Thus, the first participant is 01, not 1. Similarly, achievement scores that range from 75 to 132 are coded 075 to 132. The next step is to make decisions as to how nonnumerical, or categorical, data will be coded. Nominal or categorical data include variables such as gender, group membership, and college level (e.g., sophomore). Thus, if the study involves 50 participants, with two groups of 25, then group membership may be coded "1" or "2" or "experimental" or "control." Categorical data also occur in survey instruments on which participants choose from a small number of alternatives representing a wider range of values. For example, teachers might be asked the following question:

How many hours of classroom time do you spend per week in nonteaching activities?

> (a) 0–5   (b) 6–10   (c) 11–15   (d) 16–20

Responses might be coded as follows: (a) = 1, (b) = 2, (c) = 3, and (d) = 4.

Once the data have been prepared for analysis, the choice of statistical procedures to be applied is determined not only by the research hypothesis and design but also by the type of measurement scale (categorical, ordinal, interval, ratio) represented by the data.

Using a Computer

Generally the computer is a logical choice for data analysis. However, a good guideline for beginning researchers is this: Do not use the computer to perform an analysis that you have never done yourself by hand, or at least studied extensively. For example, after you have performed several analyses of variance on various sets of data, you will have the experience to understand the information produced by a computer analysis. In addition, instructions for preparing data for computer processing will make sense to you, and you will know what the resulting output should look like.

Rapid advances and the development of user-friendly computers have made it possible for researchers to perform a variety of analyses efficiently and accurately. One of the most popular statistical packages, commonly used in many colleges and universities, is the Statistical Package for the Social Sciences (SPSS). SPSS is used widely in quantitative research and is relatively easy to learn. We will demonstrate the usefulness of SPSS (version 12.0) in this chapter and the next.

:: TYPES OF DESCRIPTIVE STATISTICS

The first step in data analysis is to describe, or summarize, the data using descriptive statistics. In some studies, particularly survey ones, the entire data analysis procedure may consist solely of calculating and interpreting descriptive statistics. **Descriptive statistics** are data analysis techniques that enable a researcher to meaningfully describe many pieces of data with a small number of indices. If such indices are calculated for a sample drawn from a population, the resulting values are referred to as statistics; if they are calculated for an entire population, they are referred to as parameters. Most of the statistics used in educational research are based on data collected from well-defined samples, so most analyses deal with statistics, not parameters. Restated, a **statistic** is a numerical index that describes the behavior of a sample or samples, and a **parameter** is a numerical index that describes the behavior of a population.

The major types of descriptive statistics are measures of central tendency, measures of variability, measures of relative position, and measures of relationship, each of which will be described in a subsequent section. Before actually calculating any of these measures, it is often useful to present the data in graphic form.

Graphing Data

As discussed, data are usually recorded on summary sheets or in computers—in columns, placed in ascending order. Data in this form are easily graphed, permitting the researcher to

TABLE 11.2	Frequency distribution based on 85 hypothetical achievement test scores	
Score	**Frequency of Score**	
78	1	
79	4	
80	5	
81	7	
82	7	
83	9	
84	9	
85	12	
86	10	
87	7	
88	6	
89	3	
90	4	
91	1	
	Total: 85 students	

see what the distribution of scores looks like. The shape of the distribution may not be self-evident, especially if a large number of scores are involved, and as we shall see later, the shape of the distribution may influence the researcher's choice of certain descriptive statistics.

The most common method of graphing data is to construct a frequency polygon. The first step is to list all scores and to tabulate how many subjects received each score. If 85 tenth-grade students were administered an achievement test, the results might be as shown in Table 11.2. Once the scores are tallied, the steps are as follows:

1. Place all the scores on a horizontal axis, at equal intervals, from lowest score to highest.
2. Place the frequencies of scores at equal intervals on the vertical axis, starting with zero.
3. For each score, find the point where the score intersects with its frequency of occurrence and make a dot.
4. Connect all the dots with straight lines.

From Figure 11.1 we can see that most of the 10th graders scored at or near 85, with progressively fewer students achieving higher or lower scores. In other words, the scores appear to form a relatively normal, or bell-shaped, distribution, a concept we will discuss a little later. This knowledge would be helpful in selecting an appropriate measure of central tendency.

There are many other approaches to displaying data—for example, using bar graphs, scatter plots, pie charts (see Figure 11.1), box plots, and stem-and-leaf charts.[1] Examining a picture of the data can give some clues about which statistics are appropriate analyses.

---

[1] *Graphing Statistics and Data,* by A. Wallgren, B. Wallgren, R. Persson, U. Jorner, and J. Haaland, 1996, Thousand Oaks, CA: Sage.

FIGURE 11.1

Frequency polygon
(left) and pie chart
(right) based on 85
hypothetical
achievement test
scores

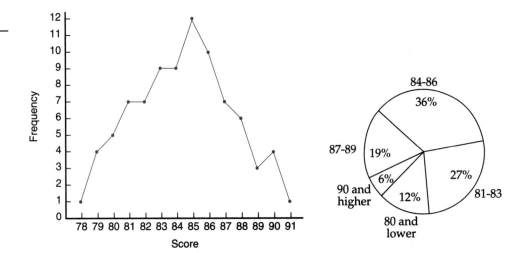

Measures of Central Tendency

Measures of central tendency are indices that represent the typical or average score among
a group of scores. They provide a convenient way of describing a set of data with a single number.[2] The number resulting from computation of a measure of central tendency represents the
average or typical score attained by a group of subjects. The three most frequently encountered
indices of central tendency are the mode, the median, and the mean. Each of these indices is
used with a different scale of measurement: the mode is appropriate for describing nominal
data, the median for describing ordinal data, and the mean for describing interval or ratio data.
Because most quantitative measurement in educational research uses an interval scale, the
mean is the most frequently used measure of central tendency.

The Mode

The **mode** is the score that is attained by more subjects than any other score. The data presented in Figure 11.1, for example, show that the group mode is 85, since more participants
(12) achieved that score than any other. The mode is not established through calculation; it is
determined by looking at a set of scores or at a graph of scores and seeing which score occurs
most frequently. There are several problems associated with the mode, and it is therefore of
limited value and seldom used. For one thing, a set of scores may have two (or more) modes,
in which case they are referred to as *bimodal*. Another problem with the mode is that it is an
unstable measure of central tendency; equal-sized samples randomly selected from the same
accessible population are likely to have different modes. However, when nominal data are being analyzed, the mode is the only appropriate measure of central tendency.

The Median

The **median** is that point, after scores are organized from low to high or high to low, above and
below which are 50% of the scores. In other words, the median is the midpoint (like the median strip on a highway). If the total number of scores is odd, the median is the middle score
(assuming the scores are arranged in order). For example, for the scores 75, 80, 82, 83, 87,
the median is 82, because it is the middle score. If the number of scores is even, the median is

---

[2] Any set of numerical data can be described using measures of central tendency. Our discussion in this text focuses
on test scores, which are frequently encountered in educational research.

the point halfway between the two middle scores. For example, for the scores 21, 23, 24, 25, 26, 30, the median is 24.5; for the scores 50, 52, 55, 57, 59, 61, the median is 56. Thus, the median is not necessarily the same as one of the scores. There is no calculation for the median except finding the midpoint when there are an even number of scores.

The median does not take into account each and every score; it focuses on the middle scores. Two quite different sets of scores may have the same median. For example, for the scores 60, 62, 65, 67, 72, the median is 65; for the scores 30, 55, 65, 72, 89, the median is also 65. As we shall see shortly, this apparent lack of precision can be advantageous at times.

The median is the appropriate measure of central tendency when the data represent an ordinal scale. For certain distributions, the median may be the most appropriate measure of central tendency even though the data represent an interval or ratio scale. Although the median appears to be a rather simple index to determine, it cannot always be arrived at by simply looking at the scores; it does not always neatly fall between two different scores. For example, determining the median for the scores 80, 82, 84, 84, 84, 88 would require application of a relatively complex formula.

The Mean

The **mean** is the arithmetic average of the scores and is the most frequently used measure of central tendency. It is calculated by adding up all of the scores and dividing that total by the number of scores. In general, the mean is the preferred measure of central tendency. It is appropriate when the data represent either an interval or ratio scale. It is more precise than the median and the mode, because if equal-sized samples are randomly selected from the same population, the means of those samples will be more similar to each other than either the medians or the modes. By the very nature of the way in which it is computed, the mean takes into account, or is based on, each and every participant's score. Because all scores count, the mean can be affected by extreme scores. Thus, in certain cases the median may actually give a more accurate estimate of the typical score.

When a group of scores contains one or more extreme scores, the median will not be the most accurate representation of the performance of the total group, but it will be the best index of typical performance. As an example, suppose you had the following IQ scores: 96, 96, 97, 99, 100, 101, 102, 104, 195. For these scores, the three measures of central tendency are

mode = 96 (most frequent score)
median = 100 (middle score)
mean = 110.6 (arithmetic average)

In this case, the median clearly best represents the typical score. The mode is too low, and the mean is higher than all of the scores except one. The mean is "pulled up" in the direction of the 195 score, whereas the median essentially ignores it.

The different pictures presented by the different measures are part of the reason for the phrase "lying with statistics." And in fact, selecting one index of central tendency over another one may present a particular point of view in a stronger light. In a labor-versus-management union dispute over salary, for example, very different estimates of typical employee salaries will be obtained depending on which index of central tendency is used. Let us say that the following are typical employee salaries in a union company: $18,000, $20,000, $20,000, $23,000, $24,000, $27,000, $68,000. For these salaries, the measures of central tendency are

mode = $20,000 (most frequent score)
median = $23,000 (middle salary)
mean = $28,571 (arithmetic average)

Both labor and management could overstate their cases, labor by using the mode and management by using the mean. The mean is higher than every salary except one, $68,000, which in all likelihood would be the salary of a company manager. Thus, in this situation the most appropriate, and most accurate, index of typical salary would be the median. In research we are not interested in "making cases" but rather in describing the data in the most accurate way. For the majority of sets of data, the mean is the appropriate measure of central tendency.

Measures of Variability

Although measures of central tendency are very useful statistics for describing a set of data, they are not sufficient. Two sets of data that are very different can have identical means or medians. As an example, consider the following sets of data:

| Set A: | 79 | 79 | 79 | 80 | 81 | 81 | 81 |
| Set B: | 50 | 60 | 70 | 80 | 90 | 100 | 110 |

The mean of both sets of scores is 80 and the median of both is 80, but Set A is very different from Set B. In Set A the scores are all very close together and clustered around the mean. In Set B the scores are much more spread out; in other words, there is much more variation or variability in Set B. To describe a situation such as this, we need **measures of variability,** indices that indicate how spread out a group of scores are. The three most frequently encountered are the range, the quartile deviation, and the standard deviation. Although the standard deviation is by far the most often used, the range is the only appropriate measure of variability for nominal data, and the quartile deviation is the appropriate index of variability for ordinal data. As with measures of central tendency, measures of variability appropriate for nominal and ordinal data may be used with interval or ratio data even though the standard deviation is generally the preferred index for such data.

The Range

The **range** is simply the difference between the highest and the lowest score and is determined by subtraction. As an example, 2 is the range for the scores 79, 79, 79, 80, 81, 81, 81; whereas 60 is the range for the scores 50, 60, 70, 80, 90, 100, 110. Thus, if the range is small, the scores are close together; if it is large, the scores are more spread out. Like the mode, the range is not a very stable measure of variability, and its chief advantage is that it gives a quick, rough estimate of variability.

The Quartile Deviation

In "research talk" the **quartile deviation** is one half of the difference between the upper quartile and the lower quartile in a distribution. Put plainly, the upper quartile is the 75th percentile, that point below which are 75% of the scores. Correspondingly, the lower quartile is the 25th percentile, that point below which are 25% of the scores. By subtracting the lower quartile from the upper quartile and then dividing the result by 2, we get a measure of variability. If the quartile deviation is small, the scores are close together; if it is large, the scores are more spread out. The quartile deviation is a more stable measure of variability than the range and is appropriate whenever the median is appropriate. Calculation of the quartile deviation involves a process very similar to that used to calculate the median, which just happens to be the second quartile or the 50th percentile.

Variance

Variance indicates the amount of spread among scores. If the variance is small, the scores are close together; if it is large, the scores are more spread out. The square root of the variance is called the **standard deviation,** and as with variance, a small standard deviation indicates that scores are close together and a large one indicates that the scores are more spread out.

Calculation of the variance is quite simple. Suppose five students took a test and received scores of 35, 25, 30, 40, and 30. The mean of these scores is—what? Right, 32. The difference of each student's score from the mean is as follows:

$$35 - 32 = 3$$
$$25 - 32 = -7$$
$$30 - 32 = -2$$
$$40 - 32 = 8$$
$$30 - 32 = -2 \text{ (Notice that the sum of the differences is 0. That's why we have to square the differences in the next step.)}$$

Squaring and then summing each difference gives $9 + 49 + 4 + 64 + 4 = 130$. Dividing the sum of the squared differences by the number of scores gives us $130/5 = 26$. This is the variance of the scores. Although seldom used by itself, the variance is commonly used to obtain the standard deviation. The standard deviation is the square root of the variance (26). Get your calculator out. The square root of 26 is 5.1, and this is the standard deviation of the five scores.

The Standard Deviation

The standard deviation, used with interval and ratio data, is by far the most frequently used index of variability. Like the mean, its central tendency counterpart, the standard deviation is the most stable measure of variability and includes every score in its calculation. In fact, the first step in calculating the standard deviation is to find out how far away each score is from the mean by subtracting the mean from each score (as we did in our example about variance). If you know the mean and the standard deviation of a set of scores, you have a pretty good picture of what the distribution looks like. If the distribution of scores is relatively normal, or bell-shaped (a concept we will have more to say about shortly), then more than 99% of the scores will fall somewhere between a score that represents the mean minus 3 standard deviations and a score that represents the mean plus 3 standard deviations. This rule will hold true for any normal distribution of scores, even though each distribution will have its own mean and its own standard deviation that are calculated based on the scores.

As an example, suppose that the mean of a set of scores ($\overline{X}$) is calculated to be 80 and the standard deviation (SD) to be 1. In this case, the mean plus 3 standard deviations is equal to $80 + 3(1) = 80 + 3 = 83$. The mean minus 3 standard deviations is equal to $80 - 3(1) = 80 - 3 = 77$. Thus, almost all the scores in the set fall between 77 and 83. This makes sense because, as we mentioned before, a small standard deviation (in this case $SD = 1$) indicates that the scores are close together, not very spread out.

As another example, suppose that a different set of scores had a mean ($\overline{X}$) calculated to be 80, but this time the standard deviation (SD) is calculated to be 4. The mean plus 3 standard deviations, $\overline{X} + 3\,SD$, is equal to $80 + 3(4) = 80 + 12 = 92$. In case you still do not see,

$$80 + 1\,SD = 80 + 4 = 84$$
$$80 + 2\,SD = 80 + 4 + 4 = 88$$
$$80 + 3\,SD = 80 + 4 + 4 + 4 = 92$$

Now, the mean minus 3 standard deviations, $\overline{X} - 3\,SD$, is equal to $80 - 3(4) = 80 - 12 = 68$. In other words,

$$80 - 1\,SD = 80 - 4 = 76$$
$$80 - 2\,SD = 80 - 4 - 4 = 72$$
$$80 - 3\,SD = 80 - 4 - 4 - 4 = 68$$

Thus, almost all the scores fall between 68 and 92. This makes sense because a larger standard deviation (in this case, $SD = 4$) indicates that the scores are more spread out. Clearly, if you know the mean and standard deviation of a set of scores, you have a pretty good idea of what the scores look like. You know the mean score and you know how spread out or variable the scores are. Using both, you can describe a set of data quite well.

The Normal Curve

The "plus and minus 3" concept is valid only when the scores are normally distributed—that is, when they form a normal, or bell-shaped, score distribution. Many, many variables—for example, height, weight, IQ scores, and achievement scores—yield a normal curve if a sufficient number of participants are measured.

If a variable is *normally distributed,* that is, forms a normal, or bell-shaped, curve, then several things are true:

1. Fifty percent of the scores are above the mean, and 50% are below the mean.
2. The mean, the median, and the mode are the same value.
3. Most scores are near the mean and the farther from the mean a score is, the fewer the number of participants who attained that score.
4. The same number, or percentage, of scores is between the mean and plus 1 standard deviation $(\overline{X} + 1\ SD)$ as is between the mean and minus 1 standard deviation $(\overline{X} - 1\ SD)$, and similarly for $\overline{X} \pm 2\ SD$ and $\overline{X} \pm 3\ SD$ (Figure 11.2).

The normal curve is illustrated in Figure 11.2. The symbol σ (the Greek letter sigma) is used to represent the standard deviation (that is, $1\ \sigma = 1\ SD$), and the mean $(\overline{X})$ is designated as 0 (zero). The vertical lines at each of the standard deviation (σ) points divide the total area under the curve; the percentage within each area is the percentage of scores that fall there. As Figure 11.2 indicates, if a set of scores forms a normal distribution, then 34.13% of scores fall between the mean and 1 standard deviation above the mean $(\overline{X} + 1\ SD)$, and another 34.13% fall between the mean and 1 standard deviation below the mean $(\overline{X} - 1\ SD)$. Each succeeding standard deviation encompasses a constant percentage of the cases. Because $\overline{X} \pm 2.58\ SD$ includes 99% of the cases, we see that $\overline{X} \pm 3\ SD$ includes almost all the scores, as pointed out previously.

Below the row of standard deviations in the figure is a row of percentages. As you move from left to right, from point to point, the cumulative percentage of scores that fall below each point is indicated. Thus, at the point that corresponds to $-3\ SD$, we see that only .1% of the scores fall below this point. At the point that corresponds to $+1\ SD$, on the other side of the curve, we see that 84.1% (rounded to 84% on the next row) of the scores fall below this point. Relatedly, the next row, percentile equivalents, also involves cumulative percentages. The figure 20 in this row, for example, indicates that 20% of the scores fall below this point. We will discuss percentiles and the remaining rows further as we proceed through this chapter, but for now, we will look at one more row. Near the bottom of the figure, under "Wechsler Scales," is a row labeled "Deviation IQs." This row tells us that the mean IQ for the Wechsler scales is 100, and the standard deviation is 15 (115 is in the column corresponding to $+1\ SD\ [+1\ \sigma]$). Since the mean is 100, 115 represents $\overline{X} + 1\ SD = 100 + 15 = 115$. An IQ of 145 represents a score 3 standard deviations above the mean (average) IQ. If your IQ is in this neighborhood, you are certainly a candidate for Mensa! An IQ of 145 corresponds to a percentile of 99.9. On the other side of the curve, we see that an IQ of 85 corresponds to a score 1 standard deviation below the mean $(\overline{X} - 1\ SD = 100 - 15 = 85)$ and to the 16th percentile. Note that the mean always corresponds to the 50th percentile. In other words, the average score is always that point above

FIGURE 11.2   Characteristics of the normal curve

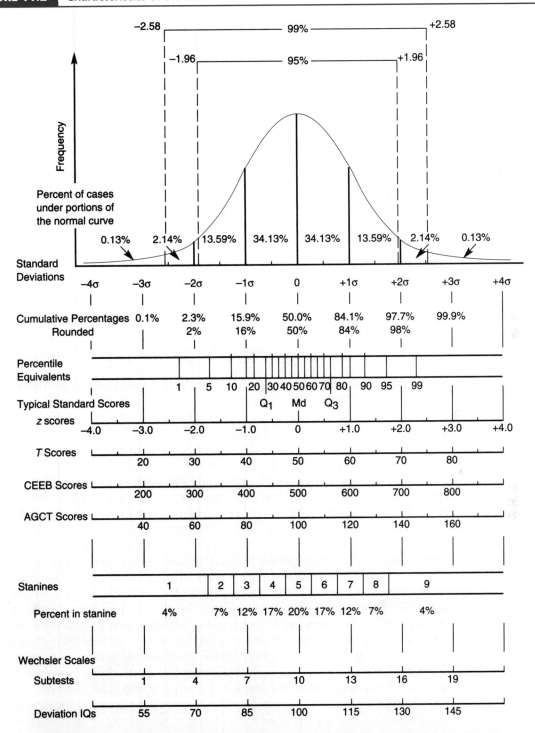

Note. This chart cannot be used to equate scores on one test to scores on another test. For example, both 600 on the CEEB and 120 on the AGCT are one standard deviation above their respective means, but they do not represent "equal" standings because the scores were obtained from different groups.

Note: Based on a figure appearing in *Test Service Bulletin* No. 48, January, 1955, of The Psychological Corporation.

which are 50% of the cases and below which are 50% of the cases. Thus, if scores are normally distributed, the following statements are true:

$$\overline{X} \pm 1.0\ SD = \text{approximately } 68\% \text{ of the scores}$$
$$\overline{X} \pm 2.0\ SD = \text{approximately } 95\% \text{ of the scores}$$
$$(1.96\ SD \text{ is exactly } 95\%)$$
$$\overline{X} \pm 2.5\ SD = \text{approximately } 99\% \text{ of the scores}$$
$$(2.58\ SD \text{ is exactly } 99\%)$$
$$\overline{X} \pm 3.0\ SD = \text{approximately } 99+\% \text{ of the scores}$$

And similarly, the following are always true:

$$\overline{X} - 3.0\ SD = \text{approximately the .1 percentile}$$
$$\overline{X} - 2.0\ SD = \text{approximately the 2nd percentile}$$
$$\overline{X} - 1.0\ SD = \text{approximately the 16th percentile}$$
$$\overline{X} = \text{the 50th percentile}$$
$$\overline{X} + 1.0\ SD = \text{approximately the 84th percentile}$$
$$\overline{X} + 2.0\ SD = \text{approximately the 98th percentile}$$
$$\overline{X} + 3.0\ SD = \text{approximately the 99th} + \text{percentile}$$

You may have noticed that the ends of the curve never touch the baseline and that there is no definite number of standard deviations that corresponds to 100%. This is because the curve allows for the existence of unexpected extremes at either end and because each additional standard deviation includes only a tiny fraction of a percent of the scores. As an example, for the Wechsler IQ test, the mean plus 5 standard deviations would be $100 + 5(15) = 100 + 75 = 175$. Surely 5 SDs would include everyone. Wrong! A very small number of persons have scored near 200, which corresponds to $+6.67\ SD$s. Thus, although $\pm 3\ SD$s includes just about everyone, the exact number of standard deviations required to include every score varies from variable to variable.

As mentioned earlier, many variables form a normal distribution, including physical measures, such as height and weight, and psychological measures, such as intelligence and aptitude. In fact, most variables measured in education form normal distributions if enough subjects are tested. Note, however, that a variable that is normally distributed in a population may not be normally distributed in smaller samples from the population. In Figure 11.2 the standard deviation is symbolized as σ, instead of SD, to indicate that the curve represents the scores of a population, not a sample; thus, σ represents a population parameter, whereas SD represents a sample-based statistic. Depending on the size and nature of a particular sample, the assumption of a normal curve may or may not be a valid one. Because research studies deal with a finite number of participants, and often not a very large number, research data only more or less approximate a normal curve. Correspondingly, all of the equivalencies (standard deviation, percentage of cases, and percentile) are also only approximations. This is an important point, since most statistics used in educational research are based on the assumption that the variable is normally distributed. If this assumption is badly violated in a given sample, then certain statistics should not be used. In general, however, the fact that most variables are normally distributed allows us to quickly determine many useful pieces of information concerning a set of data.

Skewed Distributions

When a distribution is not normal, it is said to be *skewed*. A normal distribution is symmetrical; the values of the mean, the median, and the mode are the same, and there are approximately the same number of extreme scores (very high and very low) at each end of the distribution. A **skewed distribution** is not symmetrical; the values of the mean, the median,

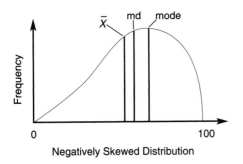
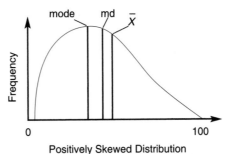

FIGURE 11.3

A positively skewed distribution and a negatively skewed distribution, each resulting from the administration of a 100-item test
Note: $\bar{X}$ = mean; md = median

and the mode are different, and there are more extreme scores at one end than the other. A **negatively skewed distribution** has extreme scores at the lower end of the distribution, and a **positively skewed distribution** has extreme scores at the higher end (Figure 11.3).

Looking at the negatively skewed distribution in Figure 11.3, we can see that most of the participants did well but a few did very poorly. Conversely, in the positively skewed distribution, most of the participants did poorly but a few did very well. In both cases, the mean is "pulled" in the direction of the extreme scores. Because the mean is affected by extreme scores (all scores are used) and the median is not (only the middle score or scores are used), the mean is always closer to the extreme scores than the median. Thus, for a negatively skewed distribution, the mean ($\bar{X}$) is always lower, or smaller, than the median (md); for a positively skewed distribution, the mean is always higher, or greater, than the median. The mode is not affected by extreme scores, so no "always" statements can be made concerning its relationship to the mean and the median in a skewed distribution. Usually, however, as Figure 11.3 indicates, in a negatively skewed distribution the mean and the median are lower, or smaller, than the mode, whereas in a positively skewed distribution the mean and the median are higher, or greater, than the mode.

To summarize:

> Negatively skewed: mean < median < mode
> Positively skewed: mean > median > mode

Because the relationship between the mean and the median is a constant, the skewness of a distribution can be determined without constructing a frequency polygon. If the mean is less than the median, the distribution is negatively skewed; if the mean and the median are the same, or very close, the distribution is symmetrical; if the mean is greater than the median, the distribution is positively skewed. The farther apart the mean and the median are, the more skewed the distribution. If the distribution is very skewed, then the assumption of normality required for many statistics is violated.

Measures of Relative Position

Measures of relative position indicate where a score is in relation to all other scores in the distribution; in other words, measures of relative position show how well an individual has performed as compared to all other individuals in the sample who have been measured on the same variable. In Chapter 5 this was called *norm-referenced scoring*. A major advantage of measures of relative position is that they make it possible to compare the performance of an individual on two or more different tests. For example, if Ziggy's score in reading is 40 and his score in math is 35, it does not follow that he did better in reading; 40 may have been the lowest score on the reading test and 35 the highest score on the math test! Measures of relative position express different scores on a common scale. The two most frequently used measures of relative position are percentile ranks and standard scores.

Percentile Ranks

A **percentile rank** indicates the percentage of scores that fall at or below a given score. If Matt Mathphobia's score of 65 corresponds to a percentile rank of 80, the 80th percentile, this means that 80 percent of the scores in the distribution are lower than 65. Matt scored higher than 80 percent of those taking the test. Conversely, if Dudley Veridull scored at the 7th percentile, this would mean that Dudley did better than, or received a higher score than, only 7% of the test takers.

Percentiles are appropriate for data representing an ordinal scale, although they are mainly computed for interval data. The median of a set of scores corresponds to the 50th percentile, which makes sense since the median is the middle point and therefore the point below which fall 50% of the scores. Percentile ranks are not used very often in research studies, but they are frequently used in the public schools to report students' test results in a form that is understandable to most audiences.

Standard Scores

Figure 11.2, "Characteristics of the Normal Curve," depicts a number of standard scores. Basically, a **standard score** is a derived score that expresses how far a given raw score is from some reference point, typically the mean, in terms of standard deviation units. A standard score is a measure of relative position that is appropriate when the test data represent an interval or ratio scale of measurement. The most commonly reported and used standard scores are z scores, T scores (or Z scores), and stanines. Standard scores allow scores from different tests to be compared on a common scale and, unlike percentiles, permit valid mathematical operations to be performed. As a result, averages can be computed. Averaging nonstandard scores on a series of tests in order to obtain an overall average score is like averaging apples and oranges and getting an "orapple." Such tests are likely to vary in level of difficulty and variability of scores. By coverting test scores to standard scores, however, we can average them and arrive at a valid final index of average performance.

The normal curve equivalencies indicated in Figure 11.2 for the various standard scores are accurate only to the degree to which the distribution is normal. Further, standard scores can be compared only if all the derived scores are based on the raw scores (number correct) of the same group. For example, a CEEB (College Entrance Examination Board) score of 700 is not equivalent to a Wechsler IQ of 130 because the tests were normed on different groups. If a set of raw scores is normally distributed, then so are the standard score equivalents. But as noted, all distributions are not normal. For example, height is normally distributed, but the measured heights of the girls in a seventh-grade gym class may not be. There is a procedure for transforming raw scores that ensures that the distribution of standard scores will be normal. Raw scores thus transformed are referred to as *normalized scores*. All resulting standard scores are normally distributed, and the normal curve equivalencies are accurate.

z Scores. A **z score** is the most basic standard score; it expresses how far a score is from the mean in terms of standard deviation units. A score that is exactly "on" the mean corresponds to a z score of 0. A score that is exactly 1 standard deviation above the mean corresponds to a z score of $+1.00$, and a z score that is exactly 2 standard deviations below the mean corresponds to a z score of -2.00. Get it? As Figure 11.2 indicates, if a set of scores is transformed into a set of z scores (each score is expressed as a z score), the new distribution has a mean of 0 and a standard deviation of 1.

The major advantage of z scores is that they allow scores from different tests or subtests to be compared. As an example, suppose Bobby Bonker's mother, a woman who is really on top of things, comes in and asks his teacher, "How is Bobby doing in the basic skills area?" If the teacher tells her that Bobby's reading score is 50 and his math score is 40, she still does not know how well Bobby is doing. In fact, she might get the false impression that he is better in reading when in fact 50 may be a very low score on the reading test and 40 may be a very good score on the math test. Now suppose Bobby's teacher also tells his mother that the average score (the mean, $\overline{X}$) received on the reading test is 60, and the average score received on the math test is 30. Aha! Now it looks as if Bobby is better in math than in reading. Further, if the standard deviation (SD) on both tests is 10, Bobby's true status becomes even more evident. Since his score in reading is exactly 1 SD below the mean ($60 - 10 = 50$), his z score is -1.00. On the other hand, his score in math is 1 SD above the mean ($30 + 10 = 40$) and his z score is $+1.00$. As shown, z scores can be translated into percentiles to show that Bobby is clearly better in math than in reading.[3]

	Raw Score	$\overline{X}$	SD	z	Percentile
Reading	50	60	10	-1.00	16th
Math	40	30	10	$+1.00$	84th

We can use Figure 11.2 to estimate percentile equivalents for given z scores, but this becomes more difficult for z scores that fall *between* the values given in the figure—for example, z scores of .63 or -1.78. A better approach is to use Table A.3 in Appendix A. For each z between -3.00, and $+3.00$, the column labeled "Area" gives the proportion of cases that are included up to that point. In other words, for any value of z, the area created to the left of the line on the curve represents the proportion of cases that falls below that z score. Thus, for $z = .00$ (the mean score), we go down the z columns until we come to .00 (p. 568), and we see that the corresponding area is .5000, representing 50% of the cases and the 50th percentile. For Bobby, we simply go down the z columns until we come to -1.00 (his z score for reading), and we see that the corresponding area under the curve is .1587. By multiplying by 100 and rounding, we see that Bobby's reading score corresponds to approximately the 16th percentile (16% of the cases fall below $z = -1.00$). Similarly, for his math score of $+1.00$, the area is .8413, or approximately the 84th percentile.

Of course, there are lots of other fun things we can do with Table A.3. If we want to know the proportion of cases in the area of the curve to the right of a given z score, for example, we simply subtract the left area value from 1.00, since the total area under the curve equals all, or 1.00 (100% of the cases). So, if we want to know the percentage of students who did better than Bobby on the reading test, we subtract .1587 from 1.00 and get .8413, or approximately 84%. Similarly, if we want to know the percentage of scores for any test that falls between $z = -1.00$ and $z = +1.00$, we subtract .1587 from .8413 and get .6826, or approximately 68%. In other words, approximately 68% (68.26% to be exact) of the scores fall between $z = -1.00$ and $z = +1.00$ (as indicated by Figure 11.2, 34.13% + 34.13% = 68.26%). Thus, we can find the percentage of cases that falls between any two z scores by subtracting their Table A.3 area values.

Also by subtraction, we can find the percentage of cases that falls between the mean ($z = .00$, area $= .5000$) and any other z score. We can also reverse the process to find, for example, the z score that corresponds to a given percentile. To become a member of Mensa, for example, you have to have an IQ at or higher than the 98th percentile. The closest area

---

[3] This analysis is based on the assumption that the same groups took the test and that the tests were normally distributed.

value in Table A.3 that reflects 98th percentile is .9803, which corresponds to $z = 2.06$. In other words, your IQ has to be approximately 2 standard deviations ($+2\ \sigma$) above average, which corresponds to an IQ of 130 (see Figure 11.2).

Of course, as mentioned previously and as Table A.3 indicates, scores are not always exactly 1 *SD* (or 2 *SD* or 3 *SD*) above or below the mean. Usually we have to apply the following formula to convert a raw score to a z score:

$$z = \frac{X - \overline{X}}{SD}, \text{ where } X \text{ is the raw score}$$

The only problem with z scores is that they involve negative numbers and decimals. It would be pretty hard to explain to Mrs. Bonker that her son was a -1.00. How do you tell a mother her son is a negative?! A simple solution is to transform z scores into *T* (or *Z*) scores. As Figure 11.2 indicates, z scores are actually the building blocks for a number of standard scores. Other standard scores represent transformations of z scores that communicate the same information in a more generally understandable form by eliminating negatives, decimals, or both.

T Scores. A *T* **score** (also called a *Z score*) is nothing more than a z score expressed in a different form; it is derived by multiplying the z score by 10 and adding 50. In other words, $T = 10z + 50$. Thus, a z score of 0 (the mean score) becomes a *T* score of 50 [$T = 10(0) + 50 = 0 + 50 = 50$]. A z score of $+1.00$ becomes a *T* score of 60 [$T = 10(1.00) + 50 = 10 + 50 = 60$], and a z score of -1.00 becomes a *T* score of 40 [$T = 10(-1.00) + 50 = -10 + 50 = 40$]. Thus, when scores are transformed to *T* scores, the new distribution has a mean of 50 and a standard deviation of 10 (see Figure 11.2). It would clearly be much easier to communicate to Mrs. Bonker that Bobby is a 40 in reading and a 60 in math and that the average score is 50 than to tell her that he is a $+1.00$ and a -1.00 and the average score is .00.

If the raw score distribution is normal, then so is the z score distribution and the *T* score distribution. If, on the other hand, the original distribution is not normal (such as when a small sample group is involved), then neither are the z and *T* score distributions. In such cases, the distribution resulting from the $10z + 50$ transformation is more accurately referred to as a *Z distribution*. However, even with a set of raw scores that are not normally distributed, we can produce a set of normalized *Z* scores. In either case, we can use the normal curve equivalencies to convert such scores into corresponding percentiles, or vice versa. As Figure 11.2 indicates, for example, a *T* of 50 is equal to a percentile of 50%. Similarly, a *T* of 30 corresponds to the 2nd percentile, and a *T* of 60 corresponds to the 84th percentile. The same is true for the other standard score transformations illustrated in Figure 11.2. The CEEB distribution is formed by multiplying *T* scores by 10 to eliminate decimals; it is calculated directly using $\text{CEEB} = 100z + 500$. The AGCT (Army General Classification Test) distribution is formed by multiplying *T* scores by 2 and is formed directly using $\text{AGCT} = 20z + 100$. In both cases, given values can be converted to percentiles (and vice versa) using normal curve equivalencies. Thus, a CEEB score of 400 corresponds to the 16th percentile, and an AGCT score of 140 corresponds to the 98th percentile.

Stanines. **Stanines** are standard scores that divide a distribution into nine parts. Stanine (short for "standard nine") equivalencies are derived using the formula $2z + 5$ and rounding resulting values to the nearest whole number. Stanines 2 through 8 each represent $\frac{1}{2}$ *SD* of the distribution; Stanines 1 and 9 include the remainder. In other words, Stanine 5 includes $\frac{1}{2}$ *SD* around the mean ($\overline{X}$); it equals $\overline{X} \pm \frac{1}{4}$ *SD*. Stanine 6 goes from $+\frac{1}{4}$ *SD* to $+\frac{3}{4}$ *SD* ($\frac{1}{4}$ *SD* + $\frac{1}{2}$ *SD* = $\frac{3}{4}$ *SD*, and so forth. Stanine 1 includes any score that is less than $-1\frac{3}{4}$ *SD* (-1.75 *SD*) below the mean, and Stanine 9 includes any score that is greater than $+1\frac{3}{4}$ *SD* ($+1.75$ *SD*) above the mean. As Figure 11.2 indicates (see the "Percent in stanine" row directly beneath the stanines), Stanine 5 includes 20% of the scores, Stanines 4 and 6 each contain 17%, Stanines 3 and 7 each contain 12%, Stanines 2 and 8 each contain 7%, and Stanines 1 and 9 each contain 4% of the scores (percentages approximate). Thus, if a student was at the 7th stanine, her percentile would be approximately $4 + 7 + 12 + 17 + 20 + 17 + 12 = 89$th percentile.

Like percentiles, stanines are very frequently reported in norms tables for standardized tests. They are very popular with school systems because they are so easy to understand and to explain to others. They are not as exact as other standard scores but are useful for a variety of purposes. They are frequently used as a basis for ability grouping and are also used as a criterion for selecting students for special programs. A remediation program, for example, may select students who scored in the first and second stanine on a standardized reading test.

Use Figure 11.2 and Appendix A, Table A.3, to answer the following questions:

1. What percentile corresponds to a z score of $+2.00$?
2. What z score corresponds to a percentile of $-.20$?
3. Approximately what percentile corresponds to a stanine of 3?
4. What range of z scores encompasses 95% of the area in a normal curve?
5. What is the relationship of the mean, median, and mode in the normal distribution?

Measures of Relationship

Measures of relationship indicate the degree to which two sets of scores are related. Remember correlation? Correlational research, the examination of the relationships between variables, was discussed in detail in Chapter 7. You will recall that correlational research involves collecting data to determine whether and to what degree a relationship—not a causal relationship, just a relationship—exists between two or more quantifiable variables. Degree of relationship is expressed as a correlation coefficient, which is computed using two sets of scores from a single group of participants. The correlation coefficient provides an estimate of just how related two variables are. If two variables are highly related, a correlation coefficient near $+1.00$ or -1.00 will be obtained; if two variables are not related, a coefficient near .00 will be obtained. A number of different methods can be used to compute a correlation coefficient; which one is appropriate depends on the scale of measurement represented by the data. The two most frequently used correlational analyses are the rank difference correlation coefficient, usually referred to as the Spearman rho, and the product moment correlation coefficient, usually referred to as the Pearson r; these were introduced in Chapter 7. See Table 7.2 for other correlational approaches, including the phi coefficient, biserial, and intraclass correlations, among others.

The Spearman Rho

The Spearman rho coefficient is used to correlate ranked data. The Spearman rho is thus appropriate when the data represent an ordinal scale (although it may be used with interval data) and is used when the median and quartile deviation are used. If only one of the variables to be correlated is ranked, the other variable to be correlated must also be expressed in terms of ranks. Thus, if intelligence were to be correlated with class rank, students' intelligence scores would have to be translated into ranks. If more than one participant received the same score, then the corresponding ranks would be averaged. So, for example, two participants with the same highest score would each be assigned Rank 1.5, the average of Rank 1 and Rank 2. The next highest score would be assigned Rank 3. Similarly, the 24th and 25th highest scores, if identical, would each be assigned the rank 24.5. Like most other correlation coefficients, the Spearman rho produces a coefficient somewhere between -1.00 and $+1.00$. If, for example, a group of participants achieved identical ranks on both variables, the coefficient would be $+1.00$.

The Pearson r

The Pearson *r* correlation coefficient is the most appropriate measure when the variables to be correlated are expressed as either interval or ratio data. Like the mean and the standard deviation, the Pearson *r* takes into account each and every score in both distributions; it is also the most stable measure of correlation. In education, most of the measures represent interval scales, so the Pearson *r* is the coefficient most frequently used for determining relationship. An assumption associated with the application of the Pearson *r* is that the relationship between the variables being correlated is a linear one. If this is not the case, the Pearson *r* will not yield a valid indication of relationship. If there is any question concerning the linearity of the relationship, the two sets of data should be plotted as previously shown in Figure 7.1.

:: CALCULATION FOR INTERVAL DATA

Because most educational data are represented in interval scales, we will calculate the measures of central tendency, variability, relationship, and relative position that are appropriate for interval data. Several alternate formulas are available for computing each of these measures; in each case, however, we will use the easiest, raw score formula. At first glance, some of the formulas may look scary, but they are really easy. The only reason they look hard is because they involve symbols with which you may be unfamiliar. As promised, however, each formula transforms "magically" into an arithmetic problem; all you have to do is substitute the correct numbers for the correct symbols.

The statistics described in this chapter (e.g., measures of central tendency, measures of relationship, and so on), as well as other statistics, are used to analyze various types of quantitative data. The remainder of this chapter and Chapter 12 will focus on quantitative data analysis. We will demonstrate two approaches to data analysis: analysis conducted manually, using step-by-step procedures and analysis by computer.

Although computer-based data analysis can be more efficient, it is important to work through data analyses for yourself to obtain a basic understanding of the research results. Once you are familiar with the step-by-step examples, you should also carry out analyses by computer.

For our computer analysis, we will use the SPSS student version 12.0 for Windows. SPSS is the most commonly used quantitative desktop computer analysis application. Please bear in mind that this is not a statistics course; our purpose is not to teach you how to use SPSS, but rather to illustrate how to use it to perform your quantitative data analysis. We will not examine all the analyses available in SPSS, but we will look at many of the basic ones commonly used in quantitative research. You will be able to compare the two approaches to data analysis and see how each can be used to produce the same results. (Note that the step-by-step and SPSS analyses do produce slightly different results because the step-by-step analyses are worked out to two decimal places and the SPSS analyses are worked out variously to up to five decimal places. These differences do not significantly affect the results.)

Symbols

Before we start calculating, let's get acquainted with a few basic statistical symbols. First, X (without a bar) is usually used to symbolize a score. If you see a column of numbers with an X at the top, you know that the column represents a set of scores. If there are two sets of scores, they may be labeled X_1 and X_2 or X and Y—it does not matter which.

Another symbol used frequently is the Greek capital letter sigma, Σ, which is used to indicate addition. The symbol Σ means "the sum of," or "add them all up." Thus, ΣX means "add up all the Xs," and ΣY means "add up all the Ys." Isn't this easy? Now, if any symbol has a bar over it, such as $\overline{X}$, that indicates the mean, or arithmetic average, of the scores. Thus, $\overline{X}$ refers to the mean of the X scores, and $\overline{Y}$ refers to the mean of the Y scores.

A capital N refers to the number of participants; $N = 20$ means that there are 20 participants (N is for number; makes sense, doesn't it?). If one analysis involves several groups, the number of participants in each group is indicated with a lowercase letter n and a subscript indicating the group. If there are three groups, and the first group has 15 participants, the second group has 18, and the third group has 20, this is symbolized as $n_1 = 15$, $n_2 = 18$, and $n_3 = 20$. The total number of subjects is represented as $N = 53$ (15 + 18 + 20 = 53).

Finally, you must get straight the difference between ΣX^2 and $(\Sigma X)^2$; they do not mean the same thing. Different formulas may include one or the other or both expressions, and interpreting each correctly is crucial if a formula is to work as intended. Now let us look at ΣX^2. What does it tell you? The Σ tells you that you are supposed to add something up. What you are supposed to add up are X^2s. What do you suppose X^2 means? Right. It means the square of the score; if $X = 4$, then $X^2 = 4^2 = 4 \times 4 = 16$. Thus, ΣX^2 says to square each score and then add up all the squares. Now let us look at $(\Sigma X)^2$. Since whatever is in the parentheses is always done first, the first thing we do is ΣX. You already know what that means—it means "add up all the scores." And then what? Right. You add up all the scores, and *then* you square the total. As an example,

X	X^2
1	1
2	4
3	9
4	16
5	25
$\Sigma X = 15$	$\Sigma X^2 = 55$
$(\Sigma X)^2 = 225$	

As you can see, there is a big difference between $(\Sigma X)^2$ and ΣX^2, so watch out! To summarize, symbols commonly used in statistical formulas are as follows:

X = any score
Σ = the sum of; add them up
ΣX = the sum of all the scores
$\overline{X}$ = the mean, or arithmetic average, of the scores
N = total number of subjects
n = number of subjects in a particular group
ΣX^2 = the sum of the squares; square each score and add up all the squares
$(\Sigma X)^2$ = the square of the sum; add up the scores and square the sum, or total

Approaching each statistic in an orderly fashion will make your work much easier. A suggested procedure is as follows:

1. Make the columns required by the formula (e.g., X, X^2), as in the preceding example, and find the sum of each column.
2. Label the sum of each column; in the example the label for the sum of the X column is ΣX, and the label for the sum of the X^2 column is ΣX^2.
3. Write the formula.
4. Write the arithmetic equivalent of the formula [e.g., $(\Sigma X)^2 = (15)^2$].
5. Solve the arithmetic problem [e.g., $(15)^2 = 225$].

The Mean

Although sample sizes of 5 are hardly ever considered to be acceptable, we will use this number of participants for illustration purposes. Our calculations will be based on the scores of 5 participants so that you can concentrate on how the calculation is being done and will not get lost in the numbers. For the same reason, we will use other small numbers. Now, assume we have the following scores for some old friends of ours, and we want to compute the mean, or arithmetic average.

	X
Iggie	1
Hermie	2
Fifi	3
Teenie	4
Tiny	5

Remember that a column labeled X means "here come the scores!"

The formula for the mean is $\overline{X} = \dfrac{\Sigma X}{N}$

You are now looking at a statistic. Looks bad, right? Let us first see what it really says. It reads, "the mean $\overline{X}$ is equal to the sum of the scores (ΣX) divided by the number of subjects: (N)." So, in order to find $\overline{X}$, we need ΣX and N.

$$
\begin{array}{c}
X \\
1 \\
2 \\
3 \\
4 \\
\underline{5} \\
\Sigma X = 15
\end{array}
$$

Clearly, $\Sigma X = 1 + 2 + 3 + 4 + 5 = 15$
$N = 5$ (There are 5 subjects, right?)

Now we have everything we need to find the mean, and all we have to do is substitute the correct number for each symbol.

$$\overline{X} = \frac{\Sigma X}{N} = \frac{15}{5}$$

Now what do we have? Right! An arithmetic problem. A hard arithmetic problem? No! An elementary school arithmetic problem? Yes! And all we did was to substitute each symbol with the appropriate number. Thus,

$$\overline{X} = \frac{\Sigma X}{N} = \frac{15}{5} = 3, \text{ or } 3.00$$

The mean is equal to 3.00. If you look at the scores, you can see that 3 is clearly the average score. Traditionally, statistical results are given with two decimal places, so our "official" answer is 3.00.

Was that hard? Certainly not! And guess what—you just learned how to do a statistic! Are they all going to be that easy? Of course!

The Standard Deviation

Earlier we explained that the standard deviation is the square root of the variance, which is based on the distance of each score from the mean. To calculate the standard deviation (SD), however, we do not have to calculate variance scores; we can use a raw score formula that gives the same answer with less grief. Now, before you look at the formula, remember that no matter how bad it looks, it is going to turn into an easy arithmetic problem. Ready?

$$SD = \sqrt{\frac{SS}{N-1}}, \text{ where } SS = \Sigma X^2 = \frac{(\Sigma X)^2}{N}$$

or

$$SD = \sqrt{\frac{\Sigma X^2 - \frac{(\Sigma X)^2}{N}}{N-1}}$$

In other words, the *SD* is equal to the square root of the sum of squares (*SS*) divided by $N - 1$.

If the standard deviation of a *population* is being calculated, the formula is exactly the same, except we divide the sum of squares by N, instead of $N - 1$. The reason is that a sample standard deviation is considered to be a biased estimate of the population standard deviation. When we select a sample, especially a small sample, the probability is that participants will come from the middle of the distribution and that extreme scores will not be represented. Thus, the range of sample scores will be smaller than the population range, as will be the sample standard deviation. As the sample size increases, so do the chances of getting extreme scores; thus, the smaller the sample, the more important it is to correct for the downward bias. By dividing by $N - 1$ instead of N, we make the denominator (bottom part!) smaller, and thus $\frac{SS}{N-1}$ is larger, closer to the population *SD* than $\frac{SS}{N}$. For example, if $SS = 18$ and $N = 10$, then

$$\frac{SS}{N-1} = \frac{18}{9} = 2.00 \quad \text{and} \quad \frac{SS}{N} = \frac{18}{10} = 1.80$$

Now just relax and look at each piece of the formula; you already know what each piece means. Starting with the easy one, N refers to what? Right—the number of subjects. How about (ΣX)? Right—the sum of the scores. And $(\Sigma X)^2$? Right—the square of the sum of the scores. That leaves ΣX^2, which means the sum of what? Fantastic. The sum of the squares. OK, let's use the same scores we used to calculate the mean. The first thing we need to do is to square each score and then add those squares up. While we are at it, we can also go ahead and add up all the scores.

	X	X²	
Iggie	1	1	
Hermie	2	4	$\Sigma X = 15$
Fifi	3	9	$\Sigma X^2 = 55$
Teenie	4	16	$N = 5$
Tiny	5	25	$N - 1 = 4$
	$\Sigma X = 15$	$\Sigma X^2 = 55$	

Do we have everything we need? Yes. Does the formula ask for anything else? No. We are in business. Substituting each symbol with its numerical equivalent, we get

$$SS = \Sigma X^2 - \frac{(\Sigma X)^2}{N} = 55 - \frac{(15)^2}{5}$$

Now what do we have? A statistic? No! An arithmetic problem? Yes! A hard arithmetic problem? No! It is harder than $\frac{15}{5}$ but it is not hard. If we just do what the formula tells us to do, we will have no problem at all. The first thing it tells us to do is to square 15:

$$SS = \Sigma X^2 - \frac{(\Sigma X)^2}{N} = 55 - \frac{(15)^2}{5} = 55 - \frac{225}{5}$$

So far so good. The next thing the formula tells us to do is divide 225 by 5, which equals 45. It is looking a lot better; now it is really an easy arithmetic problem. Next, we subtract 45 from 55 and get a sum of squares (SS) equal to 10.00. Mere child's play.

Think you can figure out the next step? Terrific! Now that we have SS, we simply substitute it into the SD formula as follows:

$$SD = \sqrt{\frac{SS}{N-1}} = \sqrt{\frac{10}{4}} = \sqrt{2.5}$$

To find the square root of 2.5, simply enter 2.5 into your calculator and hit the square root button ($\sqrt{\ }$); the square root of 2.5 is 1.58. Substituting in our square root, we have

$$SD = \sqrt{2.5} = 1.58$$

The standard deviation is 1.58. If we had calculated the standard deviation for the IQ distribution shown in Figure 11.2, what would we have gotten? Right, 15. Now you know how to compute two useful descriptive statistics.

Standard Scores

Your brain has earned a rest, and the formula for a z score is a piece of cake:

$$z = \frac{X - \bar{X}}{SD}$$

To convert scores to z scores, we simply apply that formula to each score. We have already computed the mean and the standard deviation for the following scores:

	X	
Iggie	1	
Hermie	2	$\bar{X} = 3$
Fifi	3	
Teenie	4	$SD = 1.58$
Tiny	5	

Let's see how Iggie's z score works out:

$$\text{Iggie } z = \frac{X - \bar{X}}{SD} = \frac{1 - 3}{1.58} = \frac{-2}{1.58} = -1.26$$

Our computations tell us that Iggie's standard score is 1.26 standard deviations below average. In case you have forgotten, if the signs are the same (two positives or two negatives), the answer in a multiplication or division problem is a positive number; if the signs are different, the answer is a negative number, as in Iggie's case.

For the rest of our friends, the results are

$$\text{Hermie } z = \frac{X - \overline{X}}{SD} = \frac{-1}{1.58} = -.63$$

$$\text{Fifi } z = \frac{X - \overline{X}}{SD} = \frac{0}{1.58} = .00$$

$$\text{Teenie } z = \frac{X - \overline{X}}{SD} = \frac{1}{1.58} = +.63$$

$$\text{Tiny } z = \frac{X - \overline{X}}{SD} = \frac{2}{1.58} = +1.26$$

Notice that Fifi's score is the same as the mean score. Her z score is .00, meaning that her score is no distance from the mean (it's on the mean). Iggie's and Hermie's scores are below the mean, so their z scores are negative. Teenie and Tiny scored above the mean, and their z scores are positive. If we want to eliminate the negatives, we can convert each z score to a Z score. Remember how? Multiplying each z score by 10 and adding 50 gives $Z = 10z + 50$. If we apply the z score formula, we get

$$
\begin{aligned}
\text{Iggie } Z = 10z + 50 &= 10(-1.26) + 50 \\
&= -12.6 + 50 \\
&= 50 - 12.6 \\
&= 37.40 \\
\text{Hermie } Z = 10z + 50 &= 10(-.63) + 50 \\
&= -6.3 + 50 \\
&= 50 - 6.3 \\
&= 43.70 \\
\text{Fifi } Z = 10z + 50 &= 10(.00) + 50 \\
&= .00 + 50 \\
&= 50 + .00 \\
&= 50.00 \\
\text{Teenie } Z = 10z + 50 &= 10(.63) + 50 \\
&= 6.3 + 50 \\
&= 50 + 6.3 \\
&= 56.30 \\
\text{Tiny } Z = 10z + 50 &= 10(1.26) + 50 \\
&= 12.6 + 50 \\
&= 50 + 12.6 \\
&= 62.60
\end{aligned}
$$

Note the analyses produced by these three common statistics: the mean is 3; the standard deviation is 1.58; and standard scores are -1.26, $-.63$, .00, .63., and 1.26. Now we will illustrate the use of SPSS to obtain the same statistics. In this chapter and the next, we will show you both the analyses generated by the step-by-step approach and the SPSS approach.

Obtaining Descriptive Statistics With SPSS 12.0

When the data set is large, it is often easier to input the scores into a spreadsheet and generate the statistics you want using a computer program such as SPSS. Figure 11.4 shows the same five scores for our friends as we just discussed. This time they have been entered into the SPSS spreadsheet.

To generate the descriptive statistics you want, you simply click on *Analyze* and choose *Descriptive Statistics* from the pulldown menu, as shown in Figure 11.5. In the Descriptive Statistics menu, choose the *Descriptives . . .* option.

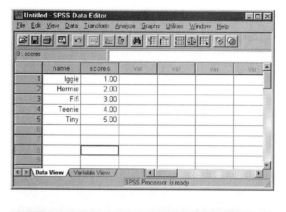

FIGURE 11.4

Spreadsheet with data entered

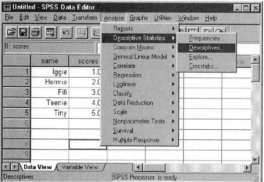

FIGURE 11.5

SPSS menu options for descriptive statistics

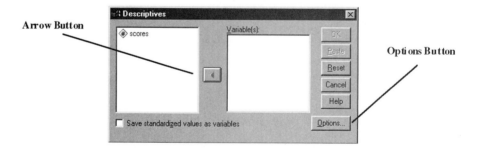

FIGURE 11.6

Descriptive statistics window

Analyze
Descriptive Statistics
Descriptives . . .

Now, SPSS shows you the window displayed in Figure 11.6, where you are able to choose the variables you wish to generate statistics on and where you select the statistics you would like generated.

All variables appropriate for computing statistics are listed in the left section of the window. Notice that the variable containing the name of our friends is not included in the list because statistics cannot be computed on names of people. The first thing you need to do is click on each needed variable in the left section of the window and move it to the right section of the window by using the arrow button in the center of the window.

Now you can choose the statistics you want to generate. To make your selections, click on the *Options . . .* button at the bottom right corner of the Descriptives window. In the Options window shown in Figure 11.7, you just click on the buttons to the left of the statistics

FIGURE 11.7

Descriptive statistics Options window

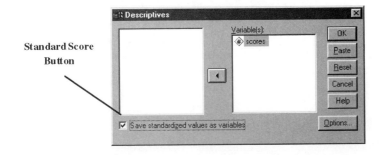

Standard Score Button

Descriptive Statistics

	N	Sum	Mean	Std. Deviation
SCORES	5	15.00	3.0000	1.5811
Valid N (listwise)	5			

FIGURE 11.9

Descriptive statistics output

you would like to see generated. Keep in mind that the window lists statistics that you may not need or want; choose only those you think you will need. Once your selections are made, click on the *Continue* button in the upper right corner of the window.

Back at the Descriptives window, you will notice a button in the bottom left corner with a label that reads "Save standardized values as variables" (Figure 11.8). By clicking on this button, the z scores will be saved for each score in the data set in another variable labeled "z scores."

Once you click the *OK* button to generate the statistics, the new variable containing the z scores will be visible in your data set.

Figure 11.9 shows the output SPSS generates containing the statistics. The first column lists the variable used to generate the statistics; in this case, it is the variable labeled "scores." Just below the name is the row label "Valid N (listwise)," which means the number of cases that had actual values or scores in the data set. This number will be the number of scores used in generating the statistics you selected. The second column in the output lists the number of cases in the data set. The second number in this column is the "Valid N"—as you can see, we have five cases with scores. The third column shows the sum of scores; our sum is 15.00, which is consistent with the earlier computations. The third and fourth columns show the mean and standard deviation for the scores. Compare these numbers with those found earlier.

Now, looking at the spreadsheet shown in Figure 11.10, with the names and scores for our friends, you can see that z scores for all of the people have been added to the list of variables.

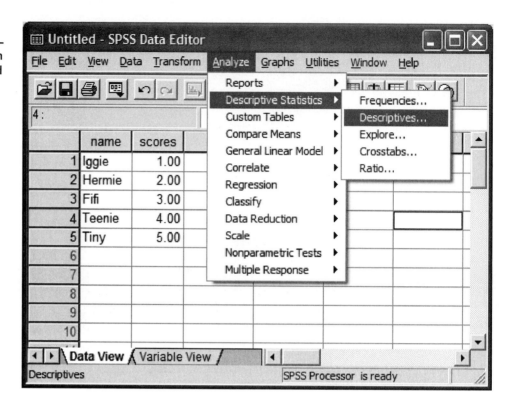

Congratulations! The step-by-step analysis and the SPSS analysis give the same results, although the SPSS analysis reports results to five decimal places, and the step-by-step analysis reports to only two (our step-by-step results were −1.26, −.63, .00, .63, and 1.26).

The Pearson *r*

Now that your brain is rested, you are ready for the Pearson *r*. The formula for the Pearson *r* looks very, very complicated, but it is not (have we lied to you so far?). It looks tough because it has a lot of pieces, but each piece is quite simple to calculate. To calculate correlations including a Pearson *r*, we need two sets of scores. Let us assume we have the following sets of scores for two variables for our old friends:

	X	*Y*
Iggie	1	2
Hermie	2	3
Fifi	3	4
Teenie	4	3
Tiny	5	5

The question is, "Are these two variables related?" Positively? Negatively? Not at all?

To answer those questions, we apply the formula for the Pearson *r* to the data. Here goes!

$$r = \frac{\sum XY - \dfrac{(\sum X)(\sum Y)}{N}}{\sqrt{\left[\sum X^2 - \dfrac{(\sum X)^2}{N}\right]\left[\sum Y^2 - \dfrac{(\sum Y)^2}{N}\right]}}$$

If you look closely, you will see that you already know how to calculate all of the pieces of the formula except one. You should have no problem with ΣX, ΣY, ΣX^2, or ΣY^2. And even though there are 10 scores, there are only 5 subjects, so $N = 5$. What is left? The only new expression in the formula is ΣXY. What could that mean? Well, you know that it is the sum of something, namely the XYs, whatever they are. An XY is just what you would guess it is— the product of an X score and its corresponding Y score. Thus, Iggie's XY score is $1 \times 2 = 2$, and Teenie's XY score is $4 \times 3 = 12$. OK, let's get all the pieces we need:

	X	Y	X^2	Y^2	XY
Iggie	1	2	1	4	2
Hermie	2	3	4	9	6
Fifi	3	4	9	16	12
Teenie	4	3	16	9	12
Tiny	5	5	25	25	25
	15	17	55	63	57
	ΣX	ΣY	ΣX^2	ΣY^2	ΣXY

Now guess what we are going to do. Right! We are going to turn that horrible-looking statistic into a horrible-looking arithmetic problem! Just kidding. It will really be an easy arithmetic problem if we do it one step at a time.

$$r = \frac{\Sigma XY - \frac{(\Sigma X)(\Sigma Y)}{N}}{\sqrt{\left[\Sigma X^2 - \frac{(\Sigma X)^2}{N}\right]\left[\Sigma Y^2 - \frac{(\Sigma Y)^2}{N}\right]}} = \frac{57 - \frac{(15)(17)}{5}}{\sqrt{\left[55 - \frac{(15)^2}{5}\right]\left[63 - \frac{(17)^2}{5}\right]}}$$

It still does not look good, but you have to admit it looks better! Let us start with the numerator (the top part). The first thing the formula tells you to do is multiply 15 by 17, which gets you

$$= \frac{57 - \frac{(255)}{5}}{\sqrt{\left[55 - \frac{(15)^2}{5}\right]\left[63 - \frac{(17)^2}{5}\right]}}$$

The next step is to divide 255 by 5, giving you

$$= \frac{57 - 51}{\sqrt{\left[55 - \frac{(15)^2}{5}\right]\left[63 - \frac{(17)^2}{5}\right]}}$$

The next step is a real snap. All you have to do is subtract 51 from 57 to produce

$$= \frac{6}{\sqrt{\left[55 - \frac{(15)^2}{5}\right]\left[63 - \frac{(17)^2}{5}\right]}}$$

So much for the numerator. Was that hard? No! *Au contraire,* it was very easy. Right? Right.

Now for the denominator (the bottom part). If you think hard, you will realize that you have seen part of the denominator before. Hint: It was not in connection with the mean. Let's go through it step by step, just in case you did not really understand what we were doing the last time. The first thing the formula says to do is to square 15. That gives

$$= \frac{6}{\sqrt{\left[55 - \frac{225}{5}\right]\left[63 - \frac{(17)^2}{5}\right]}}$$

Now we divide 225 by 5 and insert the answer, 45, into the equation:

$$= \frac{6}{\sqrt{\left[55 - 45\right]\left[63 - \frac{(17)^2}{5}\right]}}$$

Can you figure out the next step? Good. We subtract 45 from 55 to get

$$= \frac{6}{\sqrt{\left[10\right]\left[63 - \frac{(17)^2}{5}\right]}}$$

It is looking a lot better, isn't it? OK, now we need to square 17; $17 \times 17 = 289$.

$$= \frac{6}{\sqrt{\left[10\right]\left[63 - \frac{289}{5}\right]}}$$

Next, we divide 289 by 5, which results in 57.8 (sorry, life doesn't always come out even):

$$= \frac{6}{\sqrt{\left[10\right]\left[63 - 57.8\right]}}$$

We are getting there. Now we subtract 57.8 from 63. Do not let the decimals scare you:

$$= \frac{6}{\sqrt{\left[10\right]\left[63 - 57.8\right]}} = \frac{6}{\sqrt{\left[10\right]\left[5.2\right]}}$$

Can you figure out what to do next? If you can, you are smarter than you thought. Next, we multiply 10 by 5.2:

$$= \frac{6}{\sqrt{\left[10\right]\left[5.2\right]}} = \frac{6}{\sqrt{52}}$$

Next, we find the square root of 52:

$$= \frac{6}{\sqrt{52}} = \frac{6}{\sqrt{7.2}}$$

Almost done. All we have to do is divide 6 by 7.2:

$$= \frac{6}{\sqrt{7.2}} = .83$$

Thus, the Pearson r correlation coefficient is .83. Well done!

Is .83 good? Does it represent a true relationship? Is .83 significantly different from .00? If you recall the related discussion in Chapter 7, you know that a correlation coefficient of .83 indicates a high positive relationship between the variables. To determine whether .83 represents a true relationship, we need to consult a table. Table A.2 in Appendix A will tell us how large our correlation needs to be to be significant, that is, different from zero, given the number of participants we have and the level of significance at which we are working. The number of participants affects the degrees of freedom, which for the Pearson r are always computed by the formula $N - 2$. Thus, for our example, degrees of freedom (df) = $N - 2 = 5 - 2 = 3$. If we select .05 as our level of significance (P), we are now ready to use Table A.2. (Degrees of freedom and level of significance are among the coming attractions of Chapter 12.) Reading down the column labeled .05 to the line that corresponds with a df value of 3 (first column), you will find the coefficient .8783. This number rounds to .88.

Now we compare our Pearson r coefficient to the table value. Is .83 greater than .88? No, .83 is not greater than or equal to .88. Therefore, our coefficient does not indicate a true relationship between variables X and Y. Even though the correlation looks big, it is not big enough, given that we have only five subjects. We are not absolutely positive that there is no relationship (remember measurement error), but the odds are against it. Note that if we had had just one more participant ($N = 6$), our df would have been 4 ($N - 2 = 6 - 2 = 4$) and Table A.2 would have indicated a significant relationship (.83 is greater than the table value .81). Note, too, that the same table is used for both positive and negative correlations. If our Pearson r had been $-.83$ rather than $+.83$, we would have ignored the negative sign when comparing our number to the coefficient in the table. The table tells us how large r must be to indicate a true relationship. The direction of the relationship is not important.

Do not forget, however, that even if a correlation coefficient is statistically significant, it does not imply a causal relationship nor does it necessarily mean that the coefficient has any practical significance. Whether the coefficient is useful depends on the use to which it will be put; a coefficient to be used in a prediction study needs to be much higher than a coefficient to be used in a relationship study.

Obtaining the Pearson r Using SPSS 12.0

The procedures for obtaining the Pearson r correlation coefficient in SPSS are similar to those used to generate the mean and standard deviation. First, find *Analyze* at the top of the SPSS Data Editor window. Choose *Correlate* from the pulldown menu, and a submenu will appear. Now choose the *Bivariate . . .* option. This will give you the correlation between two sets of scores (between two variables). Figure 11.11 shows the menu options to choose. In summary, the options are as follows:

Analyze
Correlate
Bivariate . . .

Once you have followed this procedure, you will get the Bivariate Correlations window shown in Figure 11.12. This is where you will select the variables you wish to correlate. The upper left side of the window contains a list of variables that may be correlated. Here, you can see the variables for the first and the second set of scores for our friends. With the cursor, highlight one variable at a time and move it to the Variables section of the window using the arrow button in the middle of the window.

After choosing the variables you wish to correlate, make sure you are asking for the Pearson correlation. To do this, find the section of the window labeled "Correlation Coefficients" and select the *Pearson* check box shown in Figure 11.13.

Click on the *OK* button in the upper right corner to run your analysis. You should get output that looks like that shown in Figure 11.14.

Figure 11.14 shows a 2 × 2 matrix with four cells. The cells contain the correlation coefficients between the variables. Two variables are shown across the top, and two are shown down the left side; they are the same sets of variables. In the column labeled "scores," the first cell is the correlation with the variable "scores." Note that the Pearson correlation is equal to one. Since this is the correlation of the variable "scores" with itself, it makes sense that there

FIGURE 11.11

SPSS menu options
for correlations

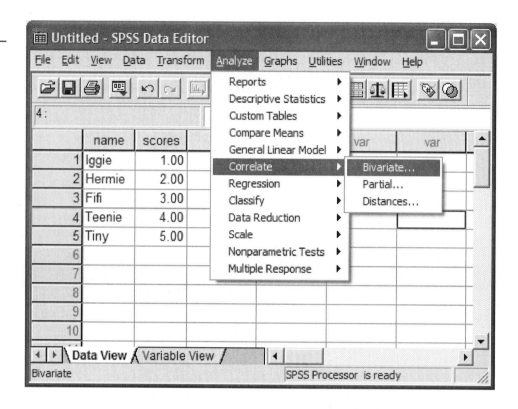

FIGURE 11.12

Bivariate Correlations
window

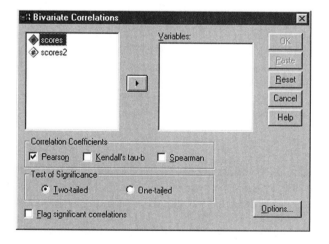

would be a perfect correlation. This is also the case in the second cell of the second column of the 2×2 matrix, where the variable "scores2" is correlated with itself. This set of perfect correlations is called the *diagonal* of the matrix.

The other two cells in the matrix are called the *off-diagonal* cells. These cells show the Pearson correlation of one variable with the other. Because there are only two variables in this analysis, both off-diagonal boxes represent the same information. As you can see, the Pearson correlation coefficient represented in the bottom cell in the first column is the same as that computed earlier; that is, the Pearson r equals 0.83 (.832 rounded off).

Congratulations!

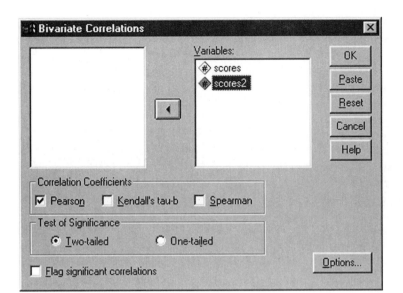

FIGURE 11.13

Correlation coefficient
options

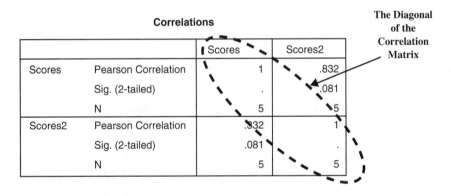

The Diagonal
of the
Correlation
Matrix

FIGURE 11.14

Correlation output

Correlations

		Scores	Scores2
Scores	Pearson Correlation	1	.832
	Sig. (2-tailed)	.	.081
	N	5	5
Scores2	Pearson Correlation	.832	1
	Sig. (2-tailed)	.081	.
	N	5	5

Postscript

Almost always in a research study, descriptive statistics such as the mean and standard deviation are computed separately for each group in the study. A correlation coefficient is usually computed only in a correlational study (unless it is used to compute the reliability of an instrument used in a causal–comparative or experimental study). Standard scores are rarely used in research studies. However, to test our hypothesis, we almost always need more than descriptive statistics; we need the application of one or more inferential statistics to test hypotheses and determine the significance of results. We discuss inferential statistics in the next chapter.

SUMMARY

Preparing Data for Analysis

1. All instruments administered should be scored accurately and consistently, using the same procedures and criteria.

2. A standardized instrument comes with a test manual that usually spells out the steps to be followed in scoring and includes a scoring key.

3. Scoring self-developed instruments is more complex than scoring standardized instruments, especially if

open-ended items are involved. Steps for scoring each item and for arriving at a total score must be delineated and carefully followed. If open-ended items are to be scored, at least two people should independently score the tests as a reliability check. Tentative scoring procedures should always be tried out beforehand by administering the instrument to individuals similar to but not among the study participants.

4. After instruments have been scored, the results are transferred to summary data sheets or, more commonly, to a computer program. If planned analyses involve subgroup comparisons, scores should be tabulated for each subgroup.

5. The more complex the data are, the more useful computer record keeping and analysis can be.

6. Computer programs can facilitate data analysis and should be used when possible. However, a good guideline is that you should not use the computer to perform an analysis that you have never done yourself by hand, or at least studied extensively.

Types of Descriptive Statistics

7. The first step in data analysis is to describe, or summarize, the data using descriptive statistics, which permit you to meaningfully describe many, many scores with a small number of indices.

8. The values calculated for a sample drawn from a population are referred to as *statistics*. The values calculated for an entire population are referred to as *parameters*.

Graphing Data

9. The shape of the distribution may not be self-evident, especially if a large number of scores are involved. The most common method of graphing research data is to construct a frequency polygon. Data can also be displayed in bar graphs, scatter plots, pie charts, and the stem-and-leaf charts.

Measures of Central Tendency

10. Measures of central tendency are indices that represent the typical or average score among a group of scores. They are a convenient way of describing a set of data with a single number.

11. Each index of central tendency is appropriate for a different scale of measurement; the mode is appropriate for nominal data, the median for ordinal data, and the mean for interval or ratio data.

12. The mode is the score that is attained by more subjects than any other score. It is determined by looking at a set of scores or at a graph of scores and seeing which score occurs most frequently. A set of scores may have two (or more) modes. When nominal data are involved, however, the mode is the only appropriate measure of central tendency.

13. The median is that point in a distribution above and below which fall 50% of the scores; in other words, the median is the midpoint. The median does not take into account each and every score; it ignores, for example, extremely high scores and extremely low scores.

14. The mean is the arithmetic average of the scores and is the most frequently used measure of central tendency. The mean takes into account, or includes, each and every score in its computation. It is a more precise, stable index than both the median and the mode except in situations in which there are extreme scores, making the median the best index of typical performance.

Measures of Variability

15. Two sets of data that are very different can have identical means or medians, thus creating a need for measures of variability, indices that indicate how spread out a group of scores are.

16. Although the standard deviation is used with interval and ratio data and is the most commonly used measure of variation, the range is the only appropriate measure of variability for nominal data, and the quartile deviation is the appropriate index of variability for ordinal data.

17. The range is simply the difference between the highest and lowest score in a distribution and is determined by subtraction. It is not a very stable measure of variability, but its chief advantage is that it gives a quick, rough estimate of variability.

18. The quartile deviation is one half of the difference between the upper quartile (the 75th percentile) and lower quartile (the 25th percentile) in a distribution. The quartile deviation is a more stable measure of variability than the range and is appropriate whenever the median is appropriate.

19. Like the mean, the standard deviation is the most stable measure of variability and takes into account each and every score. If you know the mean and the standard deviation of a set of scores, you have a pretty good picture of the distribution.

20. If the score distribution is relatively normal, then more than 99% of the scores will fall between a score that represents the mean minus 3 standard deviations and a score that represents the mean plus 3 standard deviations.

The Normal Curve

21. Many variables do yield a normal, bell-shaped curve if a sufficient number of subjects are measured.
22. If a variable is normally distributed, then several things are true. First, 50% of the scores are above the mean, and 50% of the scores are below the mean. Second, the mean, the median, and the mode are the same. Third, most scores are near the mean, and the farther from the mean a score is, the fewer the number of subjects who attained that score. Fourth, the same number, or percentage, of scores is between the mean and plus 1 standard deviation ($\overline{X} + 1\,SD$) as is between the mean and minus 1 standard deviation ($\overline{X} - 1\,SD$), and similarly for $\overline{X} \pm 2\,SD$ and $\overline{X} \pm 3\,SD$.
23. If scores are normally distributed, the following are true statements:

$\overline{X} \pm 1.0\,SD$ = approximately 68% of the scores
$\overline{X} \pm 2.0\,SD$ = approximately 95% of the scores
    (1.96 SD is exactly 95%)
$\overline{X} \pm 2.5\,SD$ = approximately 99% of the scores
    (2.58 SD is exactly 99%)
$\overline{X} \pm 3.0\,SD$ = approximately 99+% of the scores
And similarly, the following are always true:

$\overline{X} - 3.0\,SD$ = approximately the .1 percentile
$\overline{X} - 2.0\,SD$ = approximately the 2nd percentile
$\overline{X} - 1.0\,SD$ = approximately the 16th percentile
   $\overline{X}$ = the 50th percentile
$\overline{X} + 1.0\,SD$ = approximately the 84th percentile
$\overline{X} + 2.0\,SD$ = approximately the 98th percentile
$\overline{X} + 3.0\,SD$ = approximately the 99th+ percentile

24. Because research studies deal with a finite number of subjects, and often a not very large number, research data only more or less approximate a normal curve.

Skewed Distributions

25. When a distribution is not normal, it is said to be *skewed,* and the values of the mean, the median, and the mode are different.
26. In a skewed distribution, there are more extreme scores at one end than the other. If the extreme scores are at the lower end of the distribution, the distribution is said to be *negatively skewed;* if the extreme scores are at the upper, or higher, end of

the distribution, the distribution is said to be *positively skewed.* In both cases, the mean is "pulled" in the direction of the extreme scores.
27. For a negatively skewed distribution, the mean ($\overline{X}$) is always lower, or smaller, than the median (md); for a positively skewed distribution, the mean is always higher, or greater, than the median.

Measures of Relative Position

28. Measures of relative position indicate where a score is in relation to all other scores in the distribution. They make it possible to compare the performance of an individual on two or more different tests.
29. A percentile rank indicates the percentage of scores that fall at or below a given score. Percentiles are appropriate for data representing an ordinal scale, although they are frequently computed for interval data. The median of a set of scores corresponds to the 50th percentile.
30. A standard score is a measure of relative position that is appropriate when the data represent an interval or ratio scale. A z score expresses how far a score is from the mean in terms of standard deviation units. If a set of scores is transformed into a set of z scores, the new distribution has a mean of 0 and a standard deviation of 1. The z score allows scores from different tests to be compared.
31. A table of normal curve areas corresponding to various z scores can be used to determine the proportion (and percentage) of cases that fall below a given z score, above a given z score, and between any two z scores.
32. A problem with z scores is that they can involve negative numbers and decimals. A simple solution is to transform z scores into z scores by multiplying the z score by 10 and adding 50.
33. Stanines are standard scores that divide a distribution into nine parts.

Measures of Relationship

34. Degree of relationship is expressed as a correlation coefficient, which is computed from two sets of scores from a single group of participants. If two variables are highly related, a correlation coefficient near +1.00 or −1.00 will be obtained; if two variables are not related, a coefficient near .00 will be obtained.
35. The Spearman rho is the appropriate measure of correlation when the variables are expressed as ranks instead of scores. It is appropriate when the

data represent an ordinal scale (although it may be used with interval data) and is used when the median and quartile deviation are used.

36. The Spearman rho is interpreted in the same way as the Pearson r and produces a coefficient somewhere between -1.00 and $+1.00$. When more than one subject receives the same score, the corresponding ranks are averaged.

37. The Pearson r is the most appropriate measure of correlation when the sets of data to be correlated represent either interval or ratio scales, as is true with most educational measures. An assumption associated with the application of the Pearson r is that the relationship between the variables being correlated is a linear one.

Calculation for Interval Data

Symbols

38. Symbols commonly used in statistical formulas are as follows:

X = any score
Σ = the sum of; add them up
ΣX = the sum of all the scores
$\overline{X}$ = the mean, or arithmetic average, of the scores
N = total number of subjects
n = number of subjects in a particular group
ΣX^2 = the sum of the squares; square each score and add up all the squares
$(\Sigma X)^2$ = the square of the sum; add up the scores and square the sum, or total

The Mean

39. The formula for the mean is $\overline{X} = \dfrac{\Sigma X}{N}$.

The Standard Deviation

40. The formula for the standard deviation is

$$SD = \sqrt{\frac{SS}{N-1}}, \text{ where } SS = \Sigma X^2 - \frac{(\Sigma X)^2}{N}$$

Standard Scores

41. The formula for a z score is $z = \dfrac{X - \overline{X}}{SD}$.

The formula for a Z score is $Z = 10z + 50$.

The Pearson r

42. The formula for the Pearson r is

$$r = \frac{\Sigma xy - \dfrac{(\Sigma X)(\Sigma Y)}{N}}{\sqrt{\left[\Sigma X^2 - \dfrac{(\Sigma X)^2}{N}\right]\left[\Sigma Y^2 - \dfrac{(\Sigma Y)^2}{N}\right]}}$$

43. The formula for degrees of freedom for the Pearson r is $N - 2$.

Companion Website

Now go to the Companion Website at **www.prenhall.com/gay** to assess your understanding of chapter content with Practice Quiz, apply comprehension in Applying What You Know, broaden your knowledge about research in Web Links, and expand your research skills in Evaluating Articles, Analyzing Qualitative Data, Analyzing Quantitative Data, and Research Tools and Tips.

"Inferential statistics allow researchers to generalize to a population of individuals based on information obtained from a limited number of research participants." (p. 337)

Inferential Statistics

OBJECTIVES

After reading Chapter 12, you should be able to do the following:

1. Explain the concept of standard error.
2. Describe how sample size affects standard error.
3. Describe the null hypothesis.
4. State the purpose of a test of significance.
5. Describe Type I and Type II errors.
6. Describe the concept of significance level (probability level).
7. Describe one-tailed and two-tailed tests.
8. Explain the difference between parametric tests and nonparametric tests.
9. State the purpose, and explain the strategy, of the *t* test.
10. Describe independent and nonindependent samples.
11. State the purpose and appropriate use of the *t* test for independent samples.
12. State the purpose and appropriate use of the *t* test for nonindependent samples.
13. Describe one major problem associated with analyzing gain or difference scores.
14. State the purpose of the simple analysis of variance.
15. State the purpose of multiple comparision procedures.
16. State the purpose of a factorial analysis of variance.
17. State the purpose of analysis of covariance.
18. State two uses of multiple regression.
19. State the purpose of chi square.
20. Generate three columns of five one-digit numbers ("scores") and compute each of the following statistics (give the formula and show your work):
    a. *t* test for independent samples
    b. *t* test for nonindependent samples
    c. simple analysis of variance for three groups
    d. the Scheffé test
    e. chi square (Sum the numbers in each column and treat them as if they were the total number of people responding "yes," "no," and "undecided," respectively, in a survey.)

State whether each result is statistically significant at $\alpha = .05$, and interpret each result.

▓ CONCEPTS UNDERLYING INFERENTIAL STATISTICS

Inferential statistics deal with, of all things, inferences. Inferences about what? Inferences about populations based on the results of samples. Inferential statistics allow researchers to generalize to a population of individuals based on information obtained from a limited number of research participants. Most educational research studies deal with samples from larger populations. Recall that the appropriateness of the various sampling techniques discussed in Chapter 4 is based on their effectiveness in producing representative samples. Representative samples of what? Right, of the populations they are drawn from. The more representative a sample is, the more generalizable its results will be to the population from which the sample was selected. Results that are representative only of that particular sample are of very limited research use. Consequently, random samples are preferred.

To summarize, then, **inferential statistics** are data analysis techniques for determining how likely it is that results obtained from a sample or samples are the same results that would have been obtained for the entire population. As mentioned in Chapter 11, sample values, such as the mean, are referred to as *statistics*. The corresponding values in the population are referred to as *parameters*. Thus, if a mean is based on a sample, it is a statistic; if it is based on an entire population, it is a parameter. Inferential statistics are used to make inferences about parameters, based on the statistics from a sample. If a difference between means is found for two groups at the end of a study, the question of interest is whether a similar difference exists in the population from which the samples were selected. That is, can the results of the study be generalized to the larger population? It could be that no real difference exists in the population and that the difference found for the samples was a chance one (remember sampling error?).

And now we get to the heart of inferential statistics, the concept of "how likely is it?" If your study indicates a difference between two sample means (say $\overline{X}_1 = 35$ and $\overline{X}_2 = 43$) how likely is it that this difference is a real one in the population? What kind of process can you use to determine whether the difference between $\overline{X}_1$ and $\overline{X}_2$ is a real, significant one rather than one attributable to sampling error? It is important to understand that using samples to make inferences about populations produces only probability statements about the populations. The degree to which the results of a sample can be generalized to a population is expressed in terms of probabilities; analyses do not "prove" that results are true or false. There are many concepts underlying the application of inferential statistics that must be discussed before describing and illustrating types of these statistics. We look at those concepts in the following sections.

Standard Error

Inferences about populations are based on information from samples. The chances of any sample being exactly identical to its population are virtually nil, however. Even when random samples are used, we cannot expect that the sample characteristics will be exactly the same as those of the population. For example, if we randomly select a number of samples from the same population and compute the mean for each, it is very likely that the means will be somewhat different from one another and that none of the means will be identical to the population mean. This expected random, or chance, variation among the means is referred to as *sampling error*. Recall that in Chapter 4 we noted that unlike sampling bias, sampling error is not the researcher's fault. Sampling error just happens and is as inevitable as taxes and educational research courses! Thus, if a difference is found between two sample means, the important question is whether the difference is a true or significant one or just the result of sampling error.

A useful characteristic of sampling errors is that they are usually normally distributed. As discussed in Chapter 11, sampling errors vary in size (small errors versus large errors), and these errors tend to form a normal, bell-shaped curve. Thus, if a large number of samples of the same size are randomly selected from a population, we know that all the samples will not be the same but that the means of all these samples should form a normal distribution around the population mean. Further, the mean of all these sample means will yield a good estimate of the population mean.[1] Most of the sample means will be close to the population mean, and the number of means that are considerably different from the population mean will decrease as the size of the difference increases. In other words, very few means will be much higher or much lower than the population mean. An example may help to clarify this concept.

Let's suppose that we do not know the population mean IQ for the Stanford-Binet, Form L-M. To determine the population mean, we decide to randomly select 100 samples of the same size from the possible Stanford-Binet scores (the population of scores). We get the following 100 means:

---

[1] To find the mean of the sample means, simply sum the sample means and divide by the number of means, as long as each sample is the same size.

64	82	87	94	98	100	104	108	114	121
67	83	88	95	98	101	104	109	115	122
68	83	88	96	98	101	105	109	116	123
70	84	89	96	98	101	105	110	116	124
71	84	90	96	98	102	105	110	117	125
72	84	90	97	99	102	106	111	117	127
74	84	91	97	99	102	106	111	118	130
75	85	92	97	99	103	107	112	119	131
75	86	93	97	100	103	107	112	119	136
78	86	94	97	100	103	108	113	120	142

If we compute the mean of these sample means, we get 10,038/100 = 100.38, which is a darn good estimate of the population mean, which for this test is 100. Further, if you check the scores, you will discover that 71% of the scores fall between 84 and 116. The standard deviation for the Stanford-Binet is 16, so these scores are ±1 *SD* from the mean. Ninety-six percent of the scores fall between 69 and 132, or ±2 *SD* from the mean. As it turns out, our distribution approximates a normal curve quite well. The percentage of cases falling within each successive standard deviation is very close to the percentage depicted in Figure 11.2 (Chapter 11) as characteristic of the normal curve (71% as compared to 68%, and 96% as compared to 95%). The concept illustrated by this example is a comforting one. It tells us, in essence, that most of the sample means we obtain will be close to the population mean and only a few will be very far away. In other words, once in a while, just by chance, we will get a sample that is quite different from the population, but not very often.

As with any normal distribution, a distribution of sample means has not only its own mean (the mean of the means) but also its own standard deviation (the difference of each sample mean from the mean of the means). The standard deviation of the sample means is usually called the standard error of the mean. The word *error* indicates that the various sample means making up the distribution contain some error in their estimate of the population mean. The **standard error of the mean** $(SE_{\bar{X}})$ tells us by how much we would expect our sample means to differ if we used other samples from the same population. According to the normal curve percentages (Figure 11.2), we can say that approximately 68% of the sample means will fall between plus and minus 1 standard error of the mean (remember, the standard error of the mean is a standard deviation), 95% will fall between plus and minus 2 standard errors, and 99+% will fall between plus and minus 3 standard errors. In other words, if the mean is 60, and the standard error of the mean is 10, we can expect 68% of the sample means to be between 50 and 70 (60 ± 10), 95% of the sample means to fall between 40 and 80 [60 ± 2(10)], and 99% of the sample means to fall between 30 and 90 [60 ± 3(10)]. Thus, in this example it is very likely that a sample mean might be 65, but a sample mean of 98 is highly unlikely, because 99% of sample means fall between 30 and 90. Thus, given a number of large, randomly selected samples, we can quite accurately estimate population parameters by computing the mean and standard deviation of the sample means. The smaller the standard error, the more accurate the sample means as estimators of the population mean.

It is not necessary to select a large number of samples from a population to estimate the standard error, however. The standard error of the mean can be estimated from the standard deviation of a single sample using this formula:

$$(SE_{\bar{X}}) = \frac{SD}{\sqrt{N-1}}$$

where

$SE_{\bar{X}}$ = the standard error of the mean
SD = the standard deviation for a sample
N = the sample size

Thus, if the *SD* of a sample is 12 and the sample size is 100,

$$SE_{\bar{X}} = \frac{12}{\sqrt{100-1}} = \frac{12}{\sqrt{99}} = \frac{12}{9.95} = 1.21$$

Using this estimate of the $SE_{\bar{X}}$, the sample mean, $\bar{X}$, and the normal curve, we can estimate probable limits within which the population mean falls. These limits are referred to as *confidence limits*. Thus, if a sample $\bar{X}$ is 80 and the $SE_{\bar{X}}$ is 1.00, the population mean falls between 79 and 81 ($\bar{X} \pm 1\ SE_{\bar{X}}$), approximately 68% of the time, the population mean falls between 78 and 82 ($\bar{X} \pm 2\ SE_{\bar{X}}$) approximately 95% of the time, and the population mean falls between 77 and 83 ($\bar{X} \pm 3\ SE_{\bar{X}}$) approximately 99+% of the time. In other words, the probability of the population mean being less than 78 or greater than 82 is only 5/100, or 5% (± 2 *SD*), and the probability of the population mean being less than 77 or higher than 83 is only 1/100, or 1% (± 3 *SD*). Note that as our degree of confidence increases, the limits get farther apart. This makes sense because we are 100% confident that the population mean is somewhere between our sample mean plus infinity and minus infinity!

You have probably realized by now that the smaller the standard error of the mean, the better, since a smaller standard error indicates less sampling error. The major factor affecting the standard error of the mean is sample size. As the size of the sample increases, the standard error of the mean decreases. This makes sense because if we used the whole population, there would be no sampling error at all. A large sample is more likely to represent a population than a small sample. This discussion should help you to understand why samples should be as large as possible; smaller samples include more error than larger samples. Another factor affecting the standard error of the mean is the size of the population standard deviation. If it is large, members of the population are very spread out on the variable of interest, and sample means will also be very spread out. Although researchers have no control over the size of the population standard deviation, they can control sample size to some extent. Thus, researchers should make every effort to acquire as many participants as possible so that inferences about the population of interest will be as error free as possible.

Our discussion thus far has been in reference to the standard error of a *mean*. However, estimates of standard error can also be computed for other statistics, such as measures of variability, relationship, and relative position. Further, an estimate of standard error can also be calculated for the difference between two or more means. At the conclusion of an experimental study, we may have data on two sample means, the experimental and the control groups. To determine if the difference between those two means represents a true population difference, we need an estimate of the standard error of the difference between the two means. Differences between two sample means are normally distributed around the mean difference in the population. Most differences will be close to the true difference, but a few will be way off. To determine whether a difference found between sample means probably represents a true difference or a chance difference (due to sampling error), tests of significance are applied to the data. Many tests of significance are based on an estimate of standard error and typically test a null hypothesis, the subject of the next section.

The Null Hypothesis

Hypothesis testing is a process of decision making about the results of a study. If the experimental group's mean is 35 and the control group's mean is 27, the researcher has to make a decision about whether the difference between the two means represents a real, significant difference in the treatments or simply sampling error. A *true* or *real* difference is one caused by the treatment (the independent variable) and not by chance. In other words, an observed difference is either caused by the treatment, as stated in the research hypothesis, or is the result of chance, random sampling error. The chance explanation for the difference is called the null hypothesis. As noted in Chapter 2, the null hypothesis states that there is no true difference or relationship between parameters in the populations and that any difference or relationship found for the samples is the result of sampling error. For example, a null hypothesis might state

> There is no significant difference between the mean reading comprehension of first-grade students who receive whole language reading instruction and first-grade students who receive basal reading instruction.

This hypothesis says that there really is not any difference between the two methods and if you find one in your study, it is not a true difference, but a chance difference resulting from sampling error.

The null hypothesis for a study is usually (although not necessarily) different from the research hypothesis. The research hypothesis typically states that one method is expected to be more effective than another, wheras the null hypothesis states that there is no difference between the methods. Why have both? Good question! It is difficult to explain simply, but essentially the reason is that rejection of a null hypothesis is more conclusive support for a positive research hypothesis. In other words, if the results of your study support your research hypothesis, you have only one piece of evidence based on one sample in one situation. If you also reject a null hypothesis, your case is stronger. As an analogy, suppose you hypothesize that all research textbooks contain a chapter on sampling. If you examine a research textbook and it does contain a sampling chapter, you have not proven your hypothesis, because you have found only one piece of evidence to support your hypothesis. There may always be a book somewhere that does not contain a chapter on sampling. If, on the other hand, the textbook you examine does not contain a chapter on sampling, your hypothesis is disproven. You can never prove your hypothesis, only disprove it. Thus, 1 book is enough to disprove your hypothesis, but 1,000 books are not enough to prove it. Hypothesis testing is a process of disproving or rejecting, and the null hypothesis is best suited for this purpose.

In a research study, the test of significance selected to determine whether a difference between means is a true difference provides a test of the null hypothesis. As a result, the null hypothesis is either rejected as being probably false, or not rejected as being probably true. Notice the word *probably*. You can never know with total certainty that you are making the correct decision; what you can do is estimate the probability of being wrong. After you make the decision to reject or not reject the null hypothesis, you make an inference back to your research hypothesis. Suppose your research hypothesis states that A is better than B. If you reject the null hypothesis (that there is no difference between A and B), and if the mean for A is greater than the mean for B, then you may conclude that your research hypothesis was supported—not proven! If you do not reject the null hypothesis (A is not different from B), then you conclude that your research hypothesis was not supported.

To test a null hypothesis requires both a test of significance and a selected probability level that indicates how much risk you are willing to take that the decision you make is wrong.

Tests of Significance

At the end of an experimental research study, the researcher typically has two or more group means. These means are very likely to be at least a little different. The researcher must then decide whether the means are significantly different, different enough to conclude that they represent a true difference. In other words, the researcher must make the decision whether to reject the null hypothesis. The researcher does not make this decision based on his own best guess. Instead, the researcher selects and applies an appropriate **test of significance,** a statistical test used to determine whether or not there is a significant difference between or among two or more means at a selected probability level. If the difference is too large to be attributed to chance, the researcher rejects the null hypothesis because he infers that a real difference exists between A and B. If the difference is not large enough, he does not reject the null hypothesis because he infers that no difference exists between A and B.

The test of significance is usually carried out using a preselected *probability level,* or *level of significance,* that serves as a criterion to determine whether to reject or fail to reject the null hypothesis. The usual preselected probability level is either 5 out of 100 or 1 out of 100 chances that the observed difference did not occur by chance. If the probability of the difference between two means is likely to occur less than 5 times in 100 (or 1 time in 100), the difference is very unlikely to have occurred by chance, sampling error. Thus, there is a high (but not perfect) probability that the difference between the means did not occur by chance. Thus, the most likely explanation for the difference is that the two treatments were differentially effective. That is, there was a real difference between the means. Obviously, if we can say we would expect such a difference by chance only 1 time in 100, we are more confident in our decision than if we say we would expect such a chance difference 5 times in 100. How confident we are depends upon the probability level at which we perform our test of significance.

A number of different statistical tests of significance can be applied in research studies. Factors such as the scale of measurement represented by the data (e.g., nominal, ordinal, etc.), method of participant selection, number of groups being compared, and number of independent variables determine which test of significance should be used in a given study. Shortly, we will discuss and calculate several frequently used tests of significance—the *t* test, analysis of variance, and chi square.

Decision Making: Levels of Significance and Type I and Type II Errors

Based on a test of significance, the researcher will either reject or not reject the null hypothesis as a probable explanation for results. In other words, the researcher will make the decision that the difference between the means is, or is not, too large to attribute it to chance. As noted, because we are dealing with probability, not certainty, the researcher never knows for sure whether she is correct. There are four possibilities that can occur when testing the null hypothesis. If the null hypothesis is really true (there is no difference) and the researcher agrees that it is true (does not reject it), the researcher has made a correct decision. Similarly, if the null hypothesis is false (there really is a difference) and the researcher rejects it (says there is a difference), she also makes the correct decision. But what if the null hypothesis is true (there really is no difference) and the researcher rejects the null hypothesis and says there is a difference? The researcher makes an incorrect decision. Similarly, if the null hypothesis is false, (there really is a significant difference between the means) but the researcher concludes that the null hypothesis is true and does not reject it, the researcher also makes an incorrect decision. The four possibilities, again, are as follows:

1. The null hypothesis is true (A = B), and the researcher concludes that it is true. Correct!
2. The null hypothesis is false (A ≠ B), and the researcher concludes that it is false. Correct!
3. The null hypothesis is true (A = B), and the researcher concludes that it is false. Oops!
4. The null hypothesis is false (A ≠ B), and the researcher concludes that it is true. Ooops?

The two wrong decisions (oops and ooops) have "official" names. If the researcher rejects a null hypothesis that is really true (possibility 3), the researcher makes a **Type I error.** If the researcher fails to reject a null hypothesis that is really false (possibility 4), the researcher makes a **Type II error.** Figure 12.1 illustrates the four possible outcomes of decision making.

When the researcher makes the decision to reject or not reject the null hypothesis, she does so with a given probability of being correct. The level of significance, or probability level, selected determines how large the difference between the means must be to be declared sig-

The true status of the null
hypothesis. It is really

FIGURE 12.1

The four possible
outcomes of decision
making concerning
rejection of the null
hypothesis

		True (should not be rejected)	False (should be rejected)
The researcher's decision. The researcher concludes that the null hypothesis is	True (does not reject)	Correct Decision	Type II Error
	False (rejects)	Type I Error	Correct Decision

nificantly different. As noted, the most commonly used probability level (*alpha*, symbolized as α) is the α = .05 level. Some studies use α = .01, and occasionally an exploratory study will use α = .10.

The probability level selected determines the probability of committing a Type I error—that is, of rejecting a null hypothesis that is really true. Thus, if you select α = .05, you have a 5% probability of making a Type I error, whereas if you select α = .01, you have only a 1% probability of committing a Type I error. The less chance of being wrong you are willing to take, the greater the difference between the means must be. To understand this idea a little better, take a look at the six possible outcomes presented here. For each outcome, decide whether you think the means are significantly different. The means are the final performances on a 100-item test for two groups of 20 subjects each:

	Group A	Group B
1.	70.0	70.4
2.	70.0	71.0
3.	70.0	72.0
4.	70.0	75.0
5.	70.0	80.0
6.	70.0	90.0

How about outcome 1? Is 70.0 likely to be significantly different from 70.4? Probably not; such a difference could easily occur by chance. How about outcome 2, 70.0 versus 71.0 (a difference of 1.0)? Probably not significantly different. How about outcome 6, 70.0 versus 90.0 (a difference of 20.0)? That difference probably is significant. How about 5, 70.0 versus 80.0? Probably a significant difference. How about 4, 70.0 versus 75.0? Hmm . . . Is a 5-point difference a big enough difference for significance? It's a tough call. In general, large differences probably indicate a true difference, whereas small differences do not. Where is that magic point? When does a difference stop being too small and become "big enough" to be significant? The answer to these questions depends on the probability level, or significance level, at which you perform your selected test of significance. The smaller your probability level, the larger the difference must be. In the preceding example, if you were working at α = .05, then a difference of 5 (say, 70.0 versus 75.0) might be significant. If, on the other hand, you were working at α = .01 (a smaller chance of being wrong), a difference of at least 10 might be needed to reach significance. Got the idea?

Thus, if you are working at α = .05 and, as a result of your test of significance, reject the null hypothesis, you are saying that there is a real difference between the means. You are saying in essence that you do not believe the null hypothesis (no difference) is true because the chances are only 5 out of 100 (.05) that a difference as large (or larger) as the one you have found would occur solely by chance. In other words, there is a 95% chance that the difference

FIGURE 12.2

Regions of rejection
for α = .05 and
α = .01

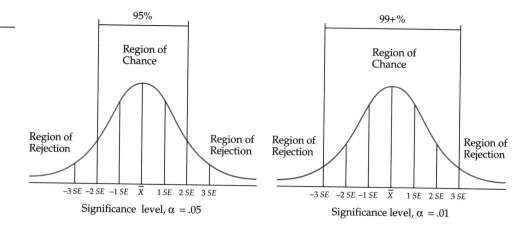

resulted from the independent variable, not random error. Similarly, if you are working at α = .01 and reject the null hypothesis, you are saying that a difference as large as the one you have found would be expected to occur by chance only once for every 100 studies—it is highly unlikely to occur by chance. In essence, we are saying that any differences between ±2 *SD* will be considered as chance differences at the .05 level, and any differences between ±3 *SD* will be considered chance differences at the .01 level. Thus, real or significant differences fall outside ±2 *SD* (.05) or ±3 *SD* (.01). Figure 12.2 illustrates the regions of significance and nonsignificance on the normal curve.

So why not set α at .000000001 and hardly ever be wrong? Good question; glad you asked it. If you select α to be very, very small, you definitely decrease your chances of committing a Type I error; you will hardly ever reject a true null hypothesis. But guess what happens to your chances of committing a Type II error? Right. As you decrease the probability of committing a Type I error, you increase the probability of committing a Type II error—that is, of not rejecting a null hypothesis when you should (another Catch-22!). For example, you might conduct a study for which a mean difference of 9.5 represents a true difference. If you set α at .0001, however, you might require a mean difference of 20.0 to reach significance. If the difference actually found was 11.0, you would not reject the null hypothesis (11.0 is less than 20.0), although there really is a difference (11.0 is greater than 9.5). How do you decide which level to work at, and when do you decide?

The choice of a probability level, α, is made before execution of the study. The researcher considers the relative seriousness of committing a Type I versus a Type II error and selects α accordingly. The researcher must compare the consequences of making the two possible wrong decisions. As an example, suppose you are a teacher and one day your principal comes up to you and says this: "I understand you have research training and I want you to do a study for me. I'm considering implementing the Whoopee-Do Reading method in the school next year. This program is very costly, and if it is implemented, we will have to spend a great deal of money on materials and in-service training. I don't want to do that unless it really works. I want you to conduct a pilot study this year with several groups and then tell me if the Whoopee-Do program really results in better reading achievement. You have my complete support in setting up the groups the way you want to and in implementing the study."

For this study, which would be more serious, a Type I error or a Type II error? Suppose you conclude that the groups are significantly different, that the Whoopee-Do program really works. But suppose it really does not. You will have made a Type I error. In this case, the principal is going to be very upset if a big investment is made based on your decision and at the end of a year's period there is no difference in achievement. On the other hand, suppose you conclude that the groups are not significantly different, that the Whoopee-Do program does not really make a difference. Suppose it really does. You will have made a Type II error. In this case, what will happen? Nothing. You will tell the principal the program does not work, you will be thanked for the input, the program will not be implemented, and life will go on as usual. Therefore, for this situation, which would you rather commit, a Type I error or a Type II error? Obviously, a Type II error. You want to be very sure you do not commit a Type I error. Therefore, you would select a very small probability level, perhaps $\alpha = .01$ or even $\alpha = .001$. You want to be pretty darn sure there is a real difference before you say there is.

As another example, suppose you are going to conduct an exploratory study to investigate the effectiveness of a new counseling technique. If you conclude that it is more effective (does make a difference), further research will be conducted. If you conclude that it does not make a difference, the new technique will be labeled as "not very promising." Now, which would be more serious, a Type I error or a Type II error? If you mistakenly conclude there is a difference (Type I error), no real harm will be done and the only real consequence will be that further research will probably disconfirm your finding. If, on the other hand, you incorrectly conclude that the technique makes no difference (Type II error), a technique may be prematurely abandoned; with a little refinement, this new technique might make a real difference. In this study, you would probably rather commit a Type I error than a Type II error. Therefore, you might select an a level as high as .10.

For most studies, $\alpha = .05$ is a reasonable probability level. The consequences of committing a Type I error are usually not too serious. However, a no-no in selecting a probability level is to first compute a test of significance to see "how significant it is" and then select a probability level. If the results just happen to be significant at $\alpha = .01$, you do not say "Oh goodie!" and report that the t was significant at the .01 level. Most of the time, you must put your cards on the table *before* you play the game, by stating a probability level for the significance test before data analysis. Some researchers, however, do not state a probability level before the study, preferring to report the exact probability level of the significance test at the end. This approach lets the reader of the study judge whether the results are "significant" for their purpose or use. We recommend that you stick to stating your α value at the start of your study.

A common misconception is that rejecting a null hypothesis means you have "proven" your research hypothesis. As stated earlier, however, rejection or lack of rejection of a null hypothesis supports or does not support a research hypothesis. It does not prove it. If you reject a null hypothesis and conclude that the groups are really different, it does not necessarily mean that they are different for the reason you hypothesized. They may be different for some other reason. On the other hand, if you fail to reject the null hypothesis, it does not necessarily mean that your research hypothesis is wrong. Perhaps the study did not represent a fair test of your hypothesis. To use a former example, if you were investigating cooperative learning and the cooperative learning group and the control group each received its respective treatment for one day only, you probably would not find any differences between the groups. This would not mean that cooperative learning is not effective. If your study were conducted over a 6-month period, it might very well make a difference.

Two-Tailed and One-Tailed Tests

Tests of significance can be either one-tailed or two-tailed. When we talk about "tails," we are referring to the extreme ends of the bell-shaped curve that illustrates a normal distribution; values at the left end are extremely low, and those at the right end are extremely high. The null hypothesis states that there is no difference between the groups ($A = B$), and a *two-tailed test* allows for the possibility that a difference may occur in either direction: either group mean may be higher than the other ($A > B$ or $B > A$). A *one-tailed test* assumes that a difference can occur in only one direction. The null hypothesis states that one group is not better than another, and the one-tailed test assumes that if a difference occurs it will be in favor of that particular group $(A > B)$.

As an example, consider the following research hypothesis:

> Kindergarten children who receive a midmorning snack exhibit better behavior during the hour before lunch than kindergarten students who do not receive a midmorning snack.

For this research hypothesis, the null hypothesis would state,

> There is no difference between the behavior during the hour before lunch of kindergarten students who receive a midmorning snack and kindergarten students who do not receive a midmorning snack.

A two-tailed test of significance would allow for the possibility that either the group that received a snack or the group that did not might exhibit better behavior. For a one-tailed test, the null hypothesis might state,

> Kindergarten children who receive a midmorning snack do not exhibit better behavior during the hour before lunch than kindergarten children who do not receive a midmorning snack.

In this case, the assumption would be that if a difference were found between the groups, it would be in favor of the group that received the snack. In other words, the researcher would consider it highly unlikely that not receiving a snack could result in better behavior than receiving one (although it could if the children were fed super sugar-coated chocolate twinkos!).

Tests of significance are almost always two-tailed. To select a one-tailed test of significance, the researcher has to be pretty darn sure that a difference will occur in only one direction, and this is not very often the case. When appropriate, a one-tailed test has one major advantage: The score difference required for significance is smaller than for a two-tailed test. In other words, it is "easier" to obtain a significant difference. It is difficult to explain simply why this is so, but it has to do with probability level (α). Suppose you are computing a test of significance at $\alpha = .05$. If your test is two-tailed, you are allowing for the possibility of a positive result or a negative result in your test of significance—a positive t or negative t in a t test, for example. In other words, you are allowing that the mean of the first group may be higher than the mean of the second group $(\overline{X}_1 - \overline{X}_2 = \text{a positive number})$ or that the mean of the second group may be higher than the mean of the first group $(\overline{X}_1 - \overline{X}_2 = \text{a negative number})$. Thus, our significance level, say .05, has to be divided into two halves (.025 and .025) to cover both possible outcomes ($\overline{X}_1 - \overline{X}_2$ is positive and $\overline{X}_1 - \overline{X}_2$ is negative). For a one-tailed test, the entire significance level, say .05, is concentrated on only one side of the normal curve. Because .025 has a smaller probability of committing a Type I error than .05, a larger result (e.g., t value) is required. The preceding explanation applies to any α value and to other tests of significance besides the t test. Although the explanation just given is definitely not the most scientific explanation of two-tailed and one-tailed tests, it should give you some conceptual understanding. The darkened areas of Figure 12.3 compare the significance areas of a one- and two-tailed test at $\alpha = .05$. These are called *regions of rejection* because results that occur in these areas lead to a rejection of the null hypothesis.

Degrees of Freedom

After you have determined whether your significance test will be two-tailed or one-tailed, selected a probability level, and computed a test of significance, you must consult the appropri-

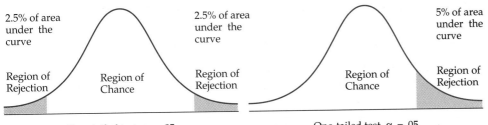

ate table to determine the significance of your results. (Most statistical computer programs provide information about the significance of the results computed in their output.) As you no doubt recall from our discussion of the significance of a correlation coefficient in Chapter 11, the appropriate table is usually entered at the intersection of your probability level and your degrees of freedom (df). Degrees of freedom are dependent on the number of participants and the number of groups. Recall that for the correlation coefficient, r, the appropriate degrees of freedom were determined by the formula $N - 2$ (number of participants minus 2). An illustration may help explain the concept of degrees of freedom. Suppose I ask you to name any five numbers. You agree and say "1, 2, 3, 4, 5." In this case, N is equal to 5; you had 5 choices or 5 degrees of freedom to select the numbers. Now suppose I tell you to name five numbers and you say "1, 2, 3, 4 . . . ," and I say "Wait! The mean of the five numbers you choose must be 4." Now you have no choice—your last number must be 10 because $1 + 2 + 3 + 4 + 10 = 20$, and 20 divided by 5 is 4. You lost one degree of freedom because of the restriction (lack of freedom) that the mean must be 4. In other words, instead of having $N = 5$ degrees of freedom, you only had $N = 4$ ($5 - 1$) degrees of freedom. Got the idea?

Each test of significance has its own formula for determining degrees of freedom. For the product moment correlation coefficient, Pearson r, the formula is $N = 2$. The number 2 is a constant, requiring that degrees of freedom for r are always determined by subtracting 2 from N, the number of participants. Each of the inferential statistics we are about to discuss also has its own formula for degrees of freedom.

::: TESTS OF SIGNIFICANCE: TYPES

Different tests of significance are appropriate for different types of data. It is important that the researcher select the appropriate test, since an incorrect test can lead to incorrect conclusions. The first decision in selecting an appropriate test of significance is whether a parametric or nonparametric test must be selected. Parametric tests are usually more powerful and generally preferrable. "More powerful" in this case means more likely to reject a null hypothesis that is false; in other words, use of the test makes the researcher less likely to commit a Type II error—not rejecting a null hypothesis that should be rejected.

A **parametric test**, however, is a test of significance that requires certain assumptions to be met in order for it to be valid. One of the major assumptions underlying use of parametric tests is that the variable measured is normally distributed in the population (or at least that the form of the distribution is known). Many variables studied in education are normally distributed, so this assumption is often met. A second major assumption is that the data represent an interval or ratio scale of measurement. Again, because most measures used in education represent or are assumed to represent interval data, this assumption is usually met. In fact, this is one major advantage of using an interval scale—it permits the use of a parametric test. A third assumption is that the selection of participants is independent. In other words, the selection of one subject in no way affects selection of any other subject. Recall that random sampling is sampling in which every member of the population has an equal and independent chance to be selected for the sample. Thus, if randomization is used in participant selection, the assumption of independence is met. Another assumption is that the variances of the population comparison groups are equal (or at least that the ratio of the variances is known). Remember, the variance of a group of scores is nothing more than the standard deviation squared.

With the exception of independence, some violation of one or more of these assumptions usually does not make too much difference in the statistical significance of the results. However, if one or more assumptions are greatly violated—for example, if the distribution is extremely skewed—parametric statistics should not be used. In such cases, a nonparametric test, which makes no assumptions about the shape of the distribution, should be used. A **nonparametric test** is a test of significance appropriate when the data represent an ordinal or nominal scale, when a parametric assumption has been greatly violated, or when the nature of the distribution is not known.

If the data represent an interval or ratio scale, a parametric test should be used unless one of the assumptions is greatly violated. As mentioned, parametric tests are more powerful. It is more difficult with a nonparametric test to reject a null hypothesis at a given level of significance; usually, a larger sample size is needed to reach the same level of significance as in a parametric test. Another advantage of parametric statistics is that they permit tests of a number of hypotheses that cannot be tested with a nonparametric test—many parametric statistics have no counterpart among nonparametric statistics. Because parametric statistics seem to be relatively hardy, doing their job even with moderate assumption violation, they will usually be selected for analysis of research data.

In the following sections, we examine both parametric and nonparametric statistics. Although we cannot discuss each and every statistical test available to the researcher, we will describe a number of useful, commonly used statistics. We will also calculate some of the more frequently used statistics.

The *t* Test

The **t test** is used to determine whether two means are significantly different at a selected probability level. In determining significance, the *t* test makes adjustments for the fact that the distribution of scores for small samples becomes increasingly different from the normal distribution as sample sizes become increasingly smaller. For example, distributions for smaller samples tend to be higher at the mean and at the two ends of the distribution. Because of this, the *t* values required to reject a null hypothesis are higher for small samples. As the size of the samples becomes larger, the score distribution approaches normality. Table A.4 in Appendix A shows the values needed to reject the null hypothesis for different sample sizes (indicated by the degrees of freedom column on the extreme left). As the number of participants increases (df), the value needed to reject the null hypothesis becomes smaller. As previously discussed, Table A.4 also shows that as the probability, or significance, level becomes smaller (.10, .05, .01, .001), it takes a larger value to reject the null hypothesis.

The strategy of the *t* test is to compare the *actual* mean difference observed $(\overline{X}_1 - \overline{X}_2)$ with the difference *expected* by chance. The *t* test involves forming the ratio of these two values. In other words, the numerator for a *t* test is the difference between the sample means $\overline{X}_1$ and $\overline{X}_2$, and the denominator is the chance difference that would be expected if the null hypothesis were true. Thus, the denominator is the standard error of the difference between the means. The denominator, or error term, is a function of both sample size and group variance. Smaller sample sizes and greater variation within groups are associated with greater random differences between groups. To explain it one more way, even if the null hypothesis is true, you do not expect two sample means to be identical; there is going to be some chance variation. The *t* test determines whether the observed difference is sufficiently larger than a difference that would be expected solely by chance. After the numerator is divided by the denominator, the resulting t value is compared to the appropriate t table value (for the appropriate probability level and degrees of freedom). If the t value is equal to or greater than the table value, then the null hypothesis is rejected. There are two different types of t tests, the t test for independent samples and the t test for nonindependent samples.

Calculating the t Test for Independent Samples

Independent samples are two samples that are randomly formed without any type of matching. The members of one sample are not related to members of the other sample in any systematic way other than that they are selected from the same population. If two groups are randomly formed, the expectation is that at the beginning of a study they are essentially the same with respect to performance on the dependent variable. Therefore, if they are also essentially the same at the end of the study (their means are close), the null hypothesis is probably true. If, on the other hand, their means are not close at the end of the study, the null hypothesis is probably false and should be rejected. The key word is *essentially.* We do not expect the means to be identical at the end of the study—they are bound to be somewhat different. The question of interest, of course, is whether they are significantly different. The **t test for independent samples** is a parametric test of significance used to determine whether, at a selected probability level, a significant difference exists between the means of two independent samples.

Suppose we have the following sets of posttest scores for two randomly formed groups. (Recognize that samples of five participants in each group are not considered acceptable but will be used here for simplicity and clarity.)

Posttest Scores

Group 1	Group 2
3	2
4	3
5	3
6	3
7	4

Are these two sets of scores significantly different? They are different, but are they *significantly* different? The appropriate test of significance to use in order to answer this question is the t test for independent samples. The formula is

$$t = \frac{\overline{X}_1 - \overline{X}_2}{\sqrt{\left(\frac{SS_1 + SS_2}{n_1 + n_2 - 2}\right)\left(\frac{1}{n_1} + \frac{1}{n_2}\right)}}$$

Does it look bad? Is it? What will it turn into? (The answers are: Yes! No! An arithmetic problem.) If you look at the formula, you will see that you are already familiar with each of the pieces. The numerator is simply the difference between the two means $\overline{X}_1$ and $\overline{X}_2$. Each n refers to the number of subjects in one of the groups; thus, $n_1 = 5$ and $n_2 = 5$. What about SS_1 and SS_2? How do we find them? Right! We calculate each SS in the same way as we did for the standard deviation. Thus,

$$SS_1 = \Sigma X_1^2 - \frac{(\Sigma X_1)^2}{n_1} \text{ and } SS_2 = \Sigma X_2^2 - \frac{(\Sigma X_2)^2}{n_2}$$

Remember? OK, now let's find each piece.

First, let's label the scores for Group 1 as X_1 and the scores for Group 2 as X_2 and label the squares for each group as X_1^2 and X_2^2. We can then calculate the sums, means, and sums of squares:

X_1	X_1^2	X_2	X_2^2
3	9	2	4
4	16	3	9
5	25	3	9
6	36	3	9
7	49	4	6
$\Sigma X_1 = 25$	$\Sigma X_1^2 = 135$	$\Sigma X_2 = 15$	$\Sigma X_2^2 = 47$
$\overline{X}_1 = \dfrac{25}{5} = 5$		$\overline{X}_2 = \dfrac{15}{5} = 3$	

Next, we need SS for each group:

$$SS_1 = \Sigma X_1^2 - \frac{(\Sigma X_1)^2}{n_1} \qquad SS_2 = \Sigma X_2^2 - \frac{(\Sigma X_2)^2}{n_2}$$

$$= 135 - \frac{(25)^2}{5} \qquad = 47 - \frac{(15)^2}{5}$$

$$= 135 - 125 \qquad\qquad = 47 - 45$$

$$= 10 \qquad\qquad\qquad = 2$$

Now we have everything we need, and all we have to do is substitute the correct number for each symbol in the formula:

$$t = \frac{\overline{X}_1 - \overline{X}_2}{\sqrt{\left(\dfrac{SS_1 + SS_2}{n_1 + n_2 - 2}\right)\left(\dfrac{1}{n_1} + \dfrac{1}{n_2}\right)}} = \frac{5 - 3}{\sqrt{\left(\dfrac{10 + 2}{5 + 5 - 2}\right)\left(\dfrac{1}{5} + \dfrac{1}{5}\right)}}$$

Now, if we just do what the formula tells us to do, we will have no problem at all. The first thing it says to do is to subtract 3 from 5:

$$= \frac{2}{\sqrt{\left(\dfrac{10 + 2}{5 + 5 - 2}\right)\left(\dfrac{1}{5} + \dfrac{1}{5}\right)}}$$

So far so good. Now let's add $10 + 2$ and $5 + 5 - 2$, and then add $\frac{1}{5} + \frac{1}{5}$ (the same number is on the bottom, so just add the top, $1 + 1$). What do we have? Right:

$$= \frac{2}{\sqrt{\left(\dfrac{12}{8}\right)\left(\dfrac{2}{5}\right)}}$$

Before we go any further, this would be a good time to convert those fractions to decimals. To convert a fraction to a decimal, you simply divide the numerator by the denominator. If you are using a calculator, you enter the top number (e.g., 12) first, hit the ÷ key, and then enter the bottom number (e.g., 8). Thus, $\frac{12}{8} = 1.5$ and $\frac{2}{5} = .4$.

After substituting the decimals for the fractions, we have

$$t = \frac{2}{\sqrt{\left(\dfrac{12}{8}\right)\left(\dfrac{2}{5}\right)}} = \frac{2}{\sqrt{(1.5)(.4)}}$$

the parentheses indicate multiplication, so next we multiply 1.5 by .4 and get

$$t = \frac{2}{\sqrt{(1.5)(.4)}} = \frac{2}{\sqrt{.60}}$$

Now we have to find the square root of .60 (get your calculator out). It's .774. Substituting .774 for the square root and dividing gives us

$$t = \frac{2}{\sqrt{.60}} = \frac{2}{.774} = 2.58$$

Therefore, $t = 2.58$.

Assuming we selected $\alpha = .05$, the only thing we need before we go to the t table is the appropriate degrees of freedom. For the t test for independent samples, the formula for degrees of freedom is $n_1 + n_2 - 2$. For our example, $df = n_1 + n_2 - 2 = 5 + 5 - 2 = 8$. Therefore, $t = 2.58$, $\alpha = .05$, $df = 8$.

Now go to Table A.4 in Appendix A. The p values in the table are the probabilities associated with various α levels. In our case, we are really asking the following question: Given $\alpha = .05$ and $df = 8$, what is the probability of getting $t \geq 2.58$ if there really is no difference? OK, now find the p value in the table that corresponds to a probability level of .05 and 8 degrees of freedom. The .05 probability column and the $df = 8$ row intersect at 2.306. The value 2.306, or 2.31, is the t value required for rejection of the null hypothesis with $\alpha = .05$ and $df = 8$. Is our t value 2.58 greater than 2.31? Yes; therefore, we reject the null hypothesis. Are the means different? Yes. Are they significantly different? Yes. Was that hard? Of course not. Congratulations! As a beginning researcher, you will find it useful to look up p values a few times, but after that, you can rely on your statistical packages to automatically provide them.

Note that the table value, 2.306, or 2.31, is the value required to reject the null hypothesis given α equal to .05. If, instead of $t = 2.58$, we got $t = 2.31$, then our probability of committing a Type I error would be exactly .05. But because our value, $t = 2.58$, is greater than the table value, 2.31, our probability of committing a Type I error is less—that is, $p < .05$. In other words, the t value we found is more than what we needed, so our chances of being wrong are less.

Suppose we found a t value of 2.29. What would we conclude? We would conclude that there is no significant difference between the groups, because 2.29 is less than 2.31. We could express this conclusion by stating $p > .05$; in other words, because our value is less than required for $\alpha = .05$, our probability of committing a Type I error is greater. Usually, however, if results are not significant, the researcher uses the abbreviation N.S. to (not significant) when reporting results. How about if we concluded that our t was almost significant or "approached" significance? Boooo! A t test is not *almost* significant or *really* significant; it is or it is not significant. Period! You will *not* see research reports that say, "The rats almost made it," or "Gosh, that really approached significance!"

What if we selected $\alpha = .01$? Table A.4 indicates that 3.355, or 3.36, is the t value required for rejection of the null hypothesis with $\alpha = .01$ and $df = 8$. Is our value $2.58 > 3.36$? No; therefore, we would not reject the null hypothesis at the .01 level. Are the means different? Yes. Are they significantly different? For $\alpha = .05$ the answer is yes, but for $\alpha = .01$ the answer is no. Thus, we see that the smaller the risk we are willing to take of committing a Type I error, the larger our t value has to be.

What if our t value had been -2.58? (Table A.4 has no negative values). We would have done exactly what we did; we would have compared the p value in the table to 2.58 (no negative). The only thing that determines whether the t is positive or negative is the order of the means; the denominator is always positive. In our example, we had a mean difference of $5 - 3$, or 2. If we had reversed the means, we would have had $3 - 5$, or -2. As long as we know which mean goes with which group, the order is unimportant. The only thing that matters is the size of the difference. So, if you do not like negative numbers, put the larger mean

FIGURE 12.4

SPSS menu options for independent samples *t* test

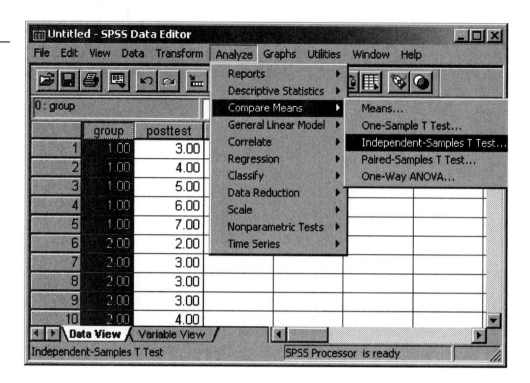

first. Remember, the table is two-tailed; it is prepared to deal with a difference in favor of either group. Direction does make a difference in one-tailed tests. Are we having fun yet?

We will now carry out an analysis using SPSS 12.0, parallel to the one just conducted.

Calculating the t Test for Independent Samples Using SPSS 12.0

As you saw in the previous section, the *t* test for independent samples is used when you want to compare the scores for two groups. In the previous example, we used the *t* test to determine whether the students in Group 1 did better or worse than the students in Group 2 on a posttest.

To perform the test in SPSS, first click on *Analyze* and choose *Compare Means* from the pulldown menu. A submenu appears, as shown in Figure 12.4. From this submenu choose *Independent-Samples T Test*. . . . In summary, the options are as follows:

Analyze
Compare Means
Independent Samples T Test . . .

Once you have done this, you will get the Independent-Samples T Test window, shown in Figure 12.5.

Next, move the variable that you are interested in testing into the Test Variable(s) section. In the case of our example, we are interested in whether different groups scored the same on the posttest, so we move the variable *posttest* into the Test Variable(s) section. Now we need to specify which groups' test scores we want compared. We do this in the Grouping Variable section. Because we are interested in comparing the scores for two groups of students, our grouping variable is *group*. After specifying the grouping variable, we must define the groups. In the case of this example, there are only two groups, but in the future there may be more, so SPSS has a place for you to specify the groups to be compared. To do this, click on the *Define Groups* button, shown in Figure 12.6.

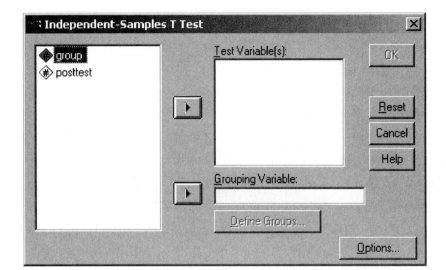

FIGURE 12.5

Independent-Samples
T Test window

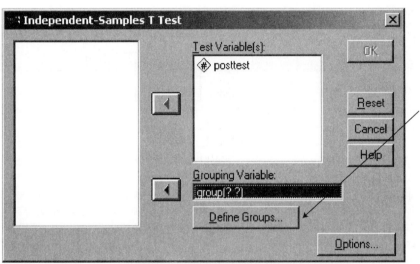

FIGURE 12.6

Independent-Samples
T Test window with
Define Groups button

Define Groups
Button

FIGURE 12.7

Define Groups
window

In the Define Groups window, shown in Figure 12.7, you will see a place for two groups to be specified. Since the groups in our data set are specified as Group 1 and Group 2, you type the number 1 (for Group 1) in the section labeled "Group 1" and the number 2 in the section labeled "Group 2."

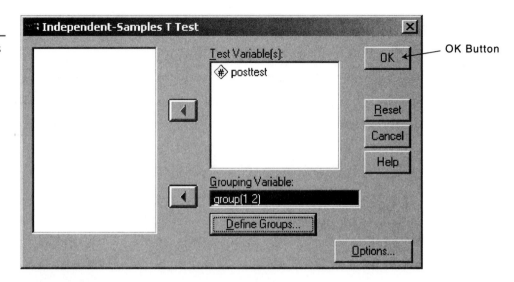

FIGURE 12.8

Independent-Samples
T Test window with
OK button

TABLE 12.1 Independent samples output

Group Statistics

	GROUP	N	Mean	Std. Deviation	Std. Error Mean
POSTTEST	1.00	5	5.0000	1.5811	.7071
	2.00	5	3.0000	.7071	.3162

You are now ready to run your analysis. Click *Continue* to return to the Independent-Samples T Test window. Click on the *OK* button, shown in Figure 12.8.

When you run your analysis, you will get two tables in your output. The first table is the "Group Statistics" table, shown in Table 12.1. This table shows you each group's sample size (represented in the "N" column), as well as the mean test score for each group, the standard deviation, and the standard error of the mean.

Table 12.2 shows the results of the independent means *t* test. The table includes many statistics for which you didn't ask. The first set of statistics comes under the heading "Levene's Test for Equality of Variances." This test checks to see if the variances of the two groups in the analysis are equal. If they are not, then SPSS makes an adjustment to the remainder of the statistics to account for this difference. When the observed probability value of the Levene's test (shown in "Sig." column) is greater than .05, you use the top row of *t* test statistics. When the observed probability value is less than .05 for the Levene's test, you use the bottom row of *t* test statistics. In Table 12.2 you can see that the observed probability value for the Levene's test is greater than .05 (sig. = .624), so we can use the top row of *t* test statistics.

Once you know which set of *t* statistics to use, you can find the observed *t* statistic value and its corresponding probability value. In Table 12.2 the observed *t* statistic is 2.582 and its observed probability value is .111. So there is a statistically significant difference between the average scores of the students in Group 1 and Group 2.

Calculating the t Test for Nonindependent Samples

The *t* test for nonindependent samples is used to compare groups that are formed by some type of matching or to compare a single group's performance on a pre- and posttest or on two different treatments. In nonindependent samples, the members of one group are systematically

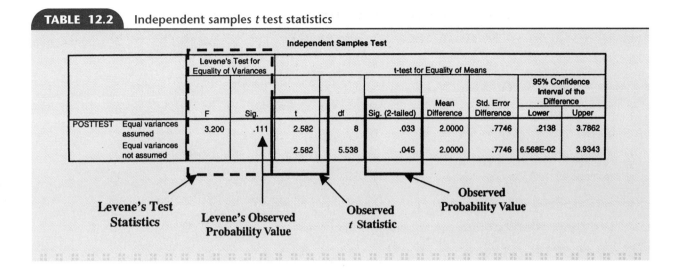

| TABLE 12.2 | Independent samples *t* test statistics |

Independent Samples Test

		Levene's Test for Equality of Variances		t-test for Equality of Means							
										95% Confidence Interval of the Difference	
		F	Sig.	t	df	Sig. (2-tailed)	Mean Difference	Std. Error Difference	Lower	Upper
POSTTEST	Equal variances assumed	3.200	.111	2.582	8	.033	2.0000	.7746	.2138	3.7862
	Equal variances not assumed			2.582	5.538	.045	2.0000	.7746	6.568E-02	3.9343

Levene's Test Statistics

Levene's Observed Probability Value

Observed t Statistic

Observed Probability Value

related to the members of a second group (especially if it is the same group at two different times). If samples are nonindependent, scores on the dependent variable are expected to be correlated with each other and a special *t* test for correlated, or nonindependent, means is used. The error term of the *t* test tends to be smaller, and there is therefore a higher probability that the null hypothesis will be rejected. Thus, the ***t* test for nonindependent samples** is used to determine whether, at a selected probability level, a significant difference exists between the means of two matched, or nonindependent, samples (or between the means for one sample at two different times).

Assume we have the following sets of scores for two matched groups (or pretest and posttest scores for a single group).

X_1	X_2
2	4
3	5
4	4
5	7
6	10

Are these two sets of scores significantly different? They are different, but are they significantly different? The appropriate test of significance to use to answer this question is the *t* test for nonindependent samples. The formula is

$$t = \frac{\overline{D}}{\sqrt{\frac{\Sigma D^2 - \frac{(\Sigma D)^2}{N}}{N(N - 1)}}}$$

Except for the *D*s, the formula should look very familiar. If the *D*s were *X*s, you would know exactly what to do. Whatever *D*s are, we are going to find their mean, $\overline{D}$, add up their squares, ΣD^2, and square their sum $(\Sigma D)^2$. What do you suppose *D* could possibly stand for? Right! The *D* stands for *difference*. The difference between what? Yes, *D* is the difference between the matched pairs of scores. Thus, each *D* equals $X_2 - X_1$. For our data, the first pair of scores is 2 and 4 and *D* = +2. OK, find the *D*s for each pair of scores. While you're at it, you might as well get the squares, the sums, and the mean. The mean of the Ds is found the same way as any other mean, by adding up the Ds and dividing by the number of Ds. Here are the results:

X_1	X_2	D	D^2
2	4	+2	4
3	5	+2	4
4	4	0	0
5	7	+2	4
6	10	+4	16
		$\Sigma D = 10$	$\Sigma D^2 = 28$

$$\overline{D} = \frac{\Sigma D}{N} = \frac{10}{5} = 2$$

Now we have everything we need, and all we have to do is substitute the numbers for the corresponding symbols in the formula:

$$t = \frac{\overline{D}}{\sqrt{\dfrac{\Sigma D^2 - \frac{(\Sigma D)^2}{N}}{N(N-1)}}} \qquad \frac{2}{\sqrt{\dfrac{28 - \frac{(10)^2}{5}}{5(5-1)}}}$$

We have another easy arithmetic problem. Now that you are a pro at this, we can solve this arithmetic problem rather quickly.

$$t = \frac{2}{\sqrt{\dfrac{28 - \frac{(10)^2}{5}}{5(5-1)}}} \qquad 10^2 = 100$$

$$= \frac{2}{\sqrt{\dfrac{28 - \frac{100}{5}}{5(5-1)}}} \qquad \frac{100}{5} = 20$$

$$= \frac{2}{\sqrt{\dfrac{28 - 20}{5(5-1)}}} \qquad 28 - 20 = 8$$

$$= \frac{2}{\sqrt{\dfrac{8}{5(5-1)}}} \qquad (5-1) = 4$$

$$= \frac{2}{\sqrt{\dfrac{8}{5(4)}}} \qquad 5(4) = 20$$

$$= \frac{2}{\sqrt{\dfrac{8}{20}}} \qquad \frac{8}{20} = \frac{4}{10}$$

$$= \frac{2}{\sqrt{.4}} \qquad \sqrt{.4} = .63$$

$$= \frac{2}{.63}$$

$$t = 3.17$$

Thus, $t = 3.17$. Assuming $\alpha = .05$, the only thing we need before we go to the t table is the appropriate degrees of freedom. For the t test for nonindependent samples, the formula for degrees of freedom is $N - 1$, where N is the number of *pairs* minus 1. For our example, $N - 1 = 5 - 1 = 4$. Therefore, $t = 3.17$, $\alpha = .05$, $df = 4$.

Now go to Table A.4 again. Notice that the t table does not know whether our t is for independent or nonindependent samples. For $\alpha = .05$ and $df = 4$, the table value for t required for rejection of the null hypothesis is 2.776, or 2.78. Is our value $3.17 > 2.78$? Yes; therefore, we reject the null hypothesis. Are the groups different? Yes. Are they significantly different? Yes.

Calculating the t Test for Nonindependent Samples Using SPSS 12.0

Once again, you will be choosing *Analyze* in the SPSS Data Editor window. To find the nonindependent or dependent samples t test, scroll down the Analyze menu and select the *Compare Means* option. From the submenu choose the option called *Paired-Samples T Test. . . .* This difference in designation may seem a bit confusing. One way to think of it is that you are comparing two sets of scores for the same group of people. So the relationship between the sets of scores is dependent upon the group of people. In this case, you are comparing a "pair" of scores for a particular group. In summary, the options are as follows:

Analyze
Compare Means
Paired-Samples T Test . . .

The menu options are shown in Figure 12.9.

Notice that the Paired-Samples T Test window (Figure 12.10) looks similar to the windows of previous analyses. On the left is the list of variables that may be included in the analysis. For the paired-samples t test, you must choose two variables to be compared and move them to the right section labeled "Paired Variables." Once you have selected the variables to be included in the analysis, the Current Selections section of the window shows you which pair of variables are being compared.

Now click the *OK* button to run the analysis.

FIGURE 12.9   SPSS menu options for dependent (paired) samples *t* test

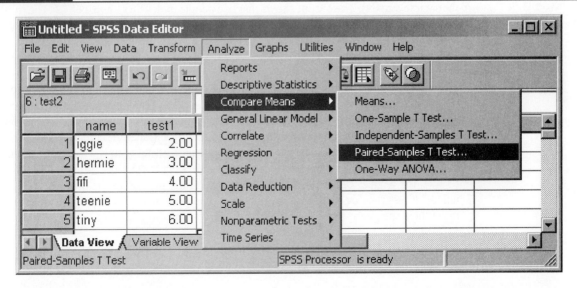

FIGURE 12.10 Paired-Samples T Test window

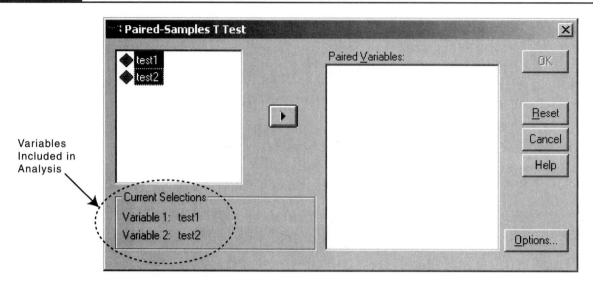

Variables Included in Analysis

TABLE 12.3 Dependent samples output

Paired Samples Statistics

		Mean	N	Std. Deviation	Std. Error Mean
Pair 1	TEST1	4.0000	5	1.5811	.7071
	TEST2	6.0000	5	2.5495	1.1402

The first section of the output is displayed in Table 12.3. For each of the paired variables, the output shows several statistics that are necessary for the *t* test statistic to be computed. First, the average score, or the mean, for each variable is shown. For TEST1 the mean score is 4, and for TEST2 the mean score is 6. The next number shown is the number of cases, or the sample size (N). The output shows that five people took TEST1 and TEST2. The third statistic shown is the standard deviation for each set of test scores. This is used to compute the final statistic shown in the table, the standard error of the mean scores.

Table 12.4 shows the statistics for your *t* test. When using the step-by-step procedures, you needed to calculate the *t* statistic, find the degrees of freedom, and look up the critical value of *t* in a table. When using SPSS, the program generates the statistic, degrees of freedom, and the *p* value (probability value) for making the decision about the test. The first box in the table shows you which variables are being compared. The next four boxes show you the difference between the mean scores, the standard deviation, the standard error of "the difference between the mean scores," and the confidence interval within which you can be 95% confident the real "difference between mean scores" falls. The last three boxes show the *t* value, the degrees of freedom, and the *p* value. If the *p* value in the box labeled "Sig. (2-tailed)" is less than or equal to $\alpha = .05$, then there is a statistically significant difference between how the group scored on TEST1 and how it scored on TEST2.

Why is the *t* value negative instead of positive? This is because SPSS automatically subtracts the second mean score (in this case, the larger score) in the list from the first. If the group had done better on the first test than the second (if the mean scores had been reversed), then

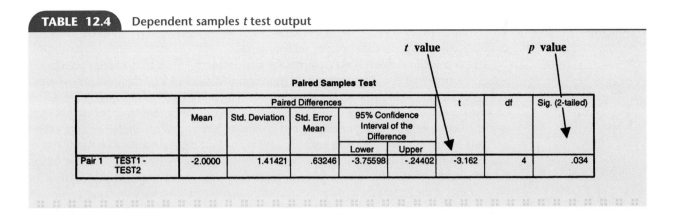

TABLE 12.4 Dependent samples *t* test output

t value

p value

Paired Samples Test

	Paired Differences					t	df	Sig. (2-tailed)
	Mean	Std. Deviation	Std. Error Mean	95% Confidence Interval of the Difference				
				Lower	Upper			
Pair 1 TEST1 - TEST2	-2.0000	1.41421	.63246	-3.75598	-.24402	-3.162	4	.034

the difference would have been positive, generating a positive test statistic. This is OK, because the significance level set *a priori* (before the fact), $\alpha = .05$, is specified for a two-tailed test.

Analysis of Gain or Difference Scores

Many researchers think that a viable way to analyze data from two groups who are pretested, treated, and posttested is to (1) subtract each participant's pretest score from his or her posttest score (resulting in a gain, or difference, score), (2) compute the mean gain or difference for each group, and (3) calculate a *t* value for the difference between the two average mean differences. This approach has two main problems. First, every participant does not have the same opportunity to gain. A participant who scores very low on a pretest has a large opportunity to gain, but a participant who scores very high has only a small opportunity to improve (referred to as the *ceiling effect*). Who has improved, or gained, more—a participant who goes from 20 to 70 (a gain of 50) or a participant who goes from 85 to 100 (a gain of only 15 but perhaps a perfect score)? Second, gain or difference scores are less reliable than analysis of posttest scores alone.

The appropriate analysis for two pretest–posttest groups depends on the performance of the two groups on the pretest. For example, if both groups are essentially the same on the pretest and neither group has been previously exposed to the treatment planned for it, then posttest scores are best compared using a *t* test. If, on the other hand, there is a difference between the groups on the pretest, the preferred approach is the analysis of covariance. You may recall, from our discussion in Chapter 9, that analysis of covariance adjusts posttest scores for initial differences on some variable (in this case the pretest) related to performance on the dependent variable. To determine whether analysis of covariance is necessary, calculate a *t* test on the two pretest means. If the two pretest means are significantly different, use the analysis of covariance. If not, a simple *t* test can be computed on the posttest means.

Simple Analysis of Variance

Simple, or *one-way,* **analysis of variance (ANOVA)** is a parametric test of significance used to determine whether a significant difference exists between two or more means at a selected probability level. Thus, for a study involving three groups, ANOVA is the appropriate analysis technique. Like two posttest means in the *t* test, three (or more) posttest means in ANOVA are very unlikely to be identical, so the key question is whether the differences among the means represent true, significant differences or chance differences due to sampling error. To answer this question, ANOVA is used and an **F ratio** is computed. You may be wondering why you cannot just compute a bunch of *t* tests, one for each pair of means. Aside from some statistical problems concerning distortion of your probability level, it is more convenient to perform one ANOVA than several t tests. For example, to analyze four means, six separate t tests would be required $(\overline{X}_1 - \overline{X}_2, \overline{X}_1 - \overline{X}_3, \overline{X}_1 - \overline{X}_4, \overline{X}_2 - \overline{X}_3, \overline{X}_2 - \overline{X}_4, \overline{X}_3 - \overline{X}_4)$. ANOVA is much more efficient and keeps the error rate under control.

The concept underlying ANOVA is that the total variation, or variance, of scores can be divided into two sources—variance between groups (variance caused by the treatment groups) and variance within groups (error variance). A ratio is formed—the F ratio—with group differences as the numerator (variance between groups) and error in the denominator (variance within groups). It is assumed that randomly formed groups of participants are chosen and are essentially the same at the beginning of a study on a measure of the dependent variable. At the end of the study, the researcher determines whether the *between* groups (or treatment) variance differs from the *within* groups (or error) variance by more than what would be expected by chance. In other words, if the treatment variance is sufficiently larger than the error variance, a significant F ratio results; the null hypothesis is rejected, and it is concluded that the treatment had a significant effect on the dependent variable. If, on the other hand, the treatment variance and error variance do not differ by more than what would be expected by chance, the resulting F ratio is not significant, and the null hypothesis is not rejected. The greater the difference, the larger the F ratio. To determine whether the F ratio is significant, an F table is entered at the place corresponding to the selected probability level and the appropriate degrees of freedom. The degrees of freedom for the F ratio are a function of the number of groups and the number of participants.

Calculating Simple Analysis of Variance (ANOVA)

Suppose we have the following set of posttest scores for three randomly selected groups.

X_1	X_2	X_3
1	2	4
2	3	4
2	4	4
2	5	5
3	6	7

We ask the inevitable question: Are these sets of data significantly different? The appropriate test of significance to answer this question is the simple, or one-way, analysis of variance (ANOVA). Recall that the total variation, or variance, is a combination of *between* (treatment) variance and *within* (error) variance. In other words:

total sum of squares = between sum of squares + within sum of squares

or

$$SS_{total} = SS_{between} + SS_{within}$$

To compute an ANOVA we need each term, *but,* because $C = A + B$, or $C(SS_{total}) = A(SS_{between}) + B(SS_{within})$, we can compute only two terms and then easily get the third. We might as well begin by calculating the two easiest terms, SS_{total} and $SS_{between}$. Once we have these, we can get SS_{within} by subtraction; SS_{within} will equal $SS_{total} - SS_{between}$ ($B = C - A$). The formula for SS_{total} is as follows:

$$SS_{total} = \Sigma X^2 - \frac{(\Sigma X)^2}{N}$$

How easy can you get? First, we need ΣX^2. You know how to get that; all we have to do is square every score in all three groups and add up the squares. For the second term, all we have to do is add up *all* the scores $(X_1 + X_2 + X_3)$, square the total, and divide by $N(n_1 + n_2 + n_3)$. Note that if an X or N refers to a particular group, it is subscripted (X_1, X_2, X_3 and n_1, n_2, n_3). If an X or N is not subscripted, it refers to the total for all the groups.

Now let's look at the formula for $SS_{between}$:

$$SS_{between} = \frac{(\Sigma X_1)^2}{n_1} + \frac{(\Sigma X_2)^2}{n_2} + \frac{(\Sigma X_3)^2}{n_3} - \frac{(\Sigma X)^2}{N}$$

This formula has more pieces, but each piece is easy. For the first three terms, all we have to do is add up all the scores in each group, square the total for each group, and divide by the number of scores in each group. We will have calculated the fourth term, $(\Sigma X)^2/N$, when we figure out SS_{total}. So, what do we need? We need the sum of scores for each group, the total of all the scores, and the sum of all the squares. That should be easy; let's do it:

X_1	X_1^2	X_2	X_2^2	X_3	X_3^2
1	1	2	4	4	16
2	4	3	9	4	16
2	4	4	16	4	16
2	4	5	25	5	25
3	9	6	36	7	49
$10 \ \Sigma X_1$	$22 \ \Sigma X_1^2$	$20 \ \Sigma X_2$	$90 \ \Sigma X_2^2$	$24 \ \Sigma X_3$	$122 \ \Sigma X_3^2$

$$\Sigma X = \Sigma X_1 + \Sigma X_2 + \Sigma X_3 = 10 + 20 + 24 = 54$$
$$\Sigma X^2 = \Sigma X_1^2 + \Sigma X_2^2 + \Sigma X_3^2 = 22 + 90 + 122 = 234$$
$$N = n_1 + n_2 + n_3 = 5 + 5 + 5 = 15$$

Now we are ready to do SS_{total}:

$$SS_{total} = \Sigma X^2 - \frac{(\Sigma X)^2}{N}$$
$$= 234 - \frac{(54)^2}{15}$$
$$= 234 - \frac{2916}{15} \quad (54^2 = 2916)$$
$$= 234 - 194.4 \ (2916 \div 15 = 194.4)$$
$$= 39.6$$

That was easy. Now let's do $SS_{between}$:[2]

$$SS_{between} = \frac{(\Sigma X_1)^2}{n_1} + \frac{(\Sigma X_2)^2}{n_2} + \frac{(\Sigma X_3)^2}{n_3} - \frac{(\Sigma X)^2}{N}$$ (We already computed the last term, remember?)

$$= \frac{(10)^2}{5} + \frac{(20)^2}{5} + \frac{(24)^2}{5} - 194.4$$ $10^2 = 100, 20^2 = 400, 24^2 = 576$

$$= \frac{100}{5} + \frac{400}{5} + \frac{576}{5} - 194.4$$ $\frac{100}{5} = 20, \frac{400}{5} = 80, \frac{576}{5} = 115.2$

$$= 20 + 80 + 115.2 - 194.4$$ $20 + 80 + 115.2 = 215.2$

$$= 215.2 - 194.4$$
$$= 20.8$$

---

[2] For more than three groups, the ANOVA procedure is exactly the same except that $SS_{between}$ has one extra term for each additional group. For example, for four groups

$$SS_{between} = \frac{(\Sigma X_1)^2}{n_1} + \frac{(\Sigma X_2)^2}{n_2} + \frac{(\Sigma X_3)^2}{n_3} + \frac{(\Sigma X_4)^2}{n_4} - \frac{(\Sigma X)^2}{N}$$

Now how are we going to get SS_{within}? Right. We subtract $SS_{between}$ from SS_{total}:

$$SS_{within} = SS_{total} - SS_{between}$$
$$= 39.6 - 20.8$$
$$= 18.8$$

Now we have everything we need to begin! Seriously, we have all the pieces but we are not quite there yet. Let us fill in a summary table with what we have and you will see what is missing:

Source of Variation	Sum of Squares	df	Mean Square	F
Between	20.8	$(K - 1)$		
Within	18.8	$(N - K)$		
Total	39.6	$(N - 1)$		

The first thing you probably noticed is that each term has its own formula for degrees of freedom. The formula for the *between* term is $K - 1$, where K is the number of treatment groups; thus, the degrees of freedom are $K - 1 = 3 - 1 = 2$. The formula for the *within* term is $N - K$, where N is the total sample size and K is still the number of treatment groups; thus, degrees of freedom for the *within* term $N - K = 15 - 3 = 12$. We do not need degrees of freedom, but for the *total* term $df = N - 1 = 15 - 1 = 14$. Now what about mean squares? Mean squares are found by dividing each sum of squares by its appropriate degrees of freedom. Here we represent mean squares as *MS*, using the subscript B for *between* and W for *within*. Thus, we have the equation,

$$mean\ square = \frac{sum\ of\ squares}{degrees\ of\ freedom}$$

or

$$MS = \frac{SS}{df}$$

For *between*, MS_B, we get

$$MS_B = \frac{SS_B}{df}$$
$$= \frac{20.8}{2}$$
$$= 10.40$$

For *within*, MS_W, we get

$$MS_W = \frac{SS_W}{df}$$
$$= \frac{18.8}{12}$$
$$= 1.57$$

Now all we need is our *F* ratio. The *F* ratio is a ratio of MS_B and MS_W:

$$F = \frac{MS_B}{MS_W}$$

Therefore, for our example:

$$F = \frac{MS_B}{MS_W}$$
$$= \frac{10.40}{1.57}$$
$$= 6.62$$

Filling in the rest of our summary table, we have

Source of Variation	Sum of Squares	df	Mean Square	F
Between	20.8	$(K - 1) = 2$	10.40	6.62
Within	18.8	$(N - K) = 12$	1.57	
Total	39.6	$(N - 1) = 14$		

Note that we simply divided across ($20.8 \div 2 = 10.40$ and $18.8 \div 12 = 1.57$) and then down ($10.40 = 1.57 = 6.62$). Thus, $F = 6.62$ with 2 and 12 degrees of freedom.

Assuming $\alpha = .05$, we are now ready to go to our F table, Table A.5 in Appendix A. Across the top of the table is the label n_1. It tells us that the degrees of freedom running horizontally across the table are for the *between* term. In our case, we find 2. Find it? On the extreme left-hand side of the table, the label n_2 tells us that the degrees of freedom listed vertically are for the *within* term. In our case, we find 12. Find it? Good. Now, at the intersection of the 2 column and the 12 row, we find 3.88, the value of F required for statistical significance (required in order to reject the null hypothesis) if $\alpha = .05$. The question is whether our F value, 6.62, is greater than 3.88. Obviously it is. Therefore, we reject the null hypothesis and conclude that there is a significant difference among the group means. Note that because two separate degrees of freedom, 2 and 12, are involved, a separate table is required for each α level. Thus, the .05 α table is on one page, and the .01 α table is on another.

Whew! That was long, but you made it, didn't you?

Multiple Comparisons

If the F ratio is determined to be nonsignificant, the party is over. But what if it is significant? What do you really know if the F ratio is rejected? All you know is that there is at least one significant difference somewhere among the means, but you do not know where that difference is. You do not know which means are significantly different from which other means. It might be, for example, that three of the four means tested are equal but all greater than a fourth mean; $\overline{X}_1 = \overline{X}_2 = \overline{X}_3$, and each is greater than $\overline{X}_4$. Or it might be that $\overline{X}_1 = \overline{X}_2$ and $\overline{X}_3 = \overline{X}_4$ ($\overline{X}_1$ and $\overline{X}_2$ are each greater than $\overline{X}_3$ and $\overline{X}_4$). Or it might be that $\overline{X}_1$ is greater than $\overline{X}_2, \overline{X}_3$, and $\overline{X}_4$.

When the F ratio is significant and more than two means are involved, procedures called **multiple comparisons** are used to determine which means are significantly different from which other means. A number of different multiple comparison techniques are available to the researcher. In essence, they involve calculation of a special form of the t test. This special t adjusts for the fact that many tests are being executed. When many significant tests are performed, the probability level, α, tends to increase, because doing a large number of significance tests makes it more likely that significant differences will be obtained. Thus, the chance of finding a significant difference is increased but so is the chance of committing a Type I error. The comparisons of the means to be made should generally be decided on before the study is conducted, not after, and should be based on research hypotheses. Such comparisons, as discussed previously, are called *a priori* (before the fact), or planned, comparisons. Often, however, it is not possible to state a priori tests. In these cases, we can use *a posteriori* (after the fact), or post hoc, comparisons. In either case, multiple comparisons should not be a "fishing expedition" in which the researcher looks for any difference she can find.

Of the many multiple comparison techniques available, the Scheffé test is one of the most widely used. It is an a posteriori test. The **Scheffé test** is appropriate for making any and all possible comparisons involving a set of means. The calculations are quite simple, and sample sizes do not have to be equal, as is the case with some multiple comparison techniques. The Scheffé test is very conservative, which is good news and bad news. The good news is that the probability of committing a Type I error for any comparison of means is the least likely. The bad news is that it is entirely possible, given the comparisons selected for investigation, to find no significant differences even though the F for the analysis of variance was significant. In general, however, the flexibility of the Scheffé test and its ease of application make it useful for a variety of situations. Other common multiple comparison tests are Tukey's HSD test and Duncan's multiple range test. Here we discuss the Scheffé test.

Calculating Scheffé Multiple Comparisons

We will use the results of the preceding ANOVA example to examine multiple comparisons. In the ANOVA example, the only thing the F ratio told us was that there was at least one significant difference somewhere among the three means. To find out where, we will apply the Scheffé test. The Scheffé test involves calculation of an F ratio for each mean comparison of interest. As you study the following formula, you will notice that we already have almost all of the information we need to apply the Scheffé test:

$$F = \frac{(\overline{X}_1 - \overline{X}_2)^2}{MS_W\left(\dfrac{1}{n_1} + \dfrac{1}{n_2}\right)(K-1)} \quad \text{with } df = (K-1), (N-K)$$

Where in the world do we get MS_W? Correct! MS_W is the MS_W from the analysis of variance, which is 1.57. The degrees of freedom are also from the ANOVA, 2 and 12. Of course, the preceding formula is for the comparison of $\overline{X}_1$ and $\overline{X}_2$. To compare any other two means, we simply change the $\overline{X}$s and the ns. So before applying the Scheffé test, the only thing we have to calculate is the mean for each group.

Looking back at our ANOVA example, the sums for each group of five scores were 10, 20, and 24, respectively, and so the three $\overline{X}$s are 2.00, 4.00, and 4.80. Applying the Scheffé test to $\overline{X}_1$ and $\overline{X}_2$, we get

$$F = \frac{(\overline{X}_1 - \overline{X}_2)^2}{MS_W\left(\dfrac{1}{n_1} + \dfrac{1}{n_2}\right)(K-1)} = \frac{(2.00 - 4.00)^2}{1.57\left(\dfrac{1}{5} + \dfrac{1}{5}\right)2}$$

$$= \frac{(-2.00)^2}{1.57\left(\dfrac{2}{5}\right)2}$$

$$= \frac{4}{1.57(.4)2}$$

$$= \frac{4}{1.57(.8)}$$

$$= \frac{4}{1.256}$$

$$= 3.18$$

Because the value of F required for significance is 3.88 is $\alpha = .05$ and $df = 2$ and 12, and because $3.18 < 3.88$, we conclude that no significant difference exists between $\overline{X}_1$ and $\overline{X}_2$. Calculate the Scheffé test for $\overline{X}_1$ and $\overline{X}_3$ and for $\overline{X}_2$ and $\overline{X}_3$ yourself, and determine whether significant differences exist between these two sets of means. You should get the following results:

Scheffé Tests

Group 1 vs. Group 2	3.18	Fail to reject
Group 1 vs. Group 3	6.24	Reject
Group 2 vs. Group 3	0.51	Fail to reject

The Scheffé test can also be used to compare combinations of means. Suppose, for example, that Group 1 was a control group and we wanted to compare the mean of Group 1 to the mean of Groups 2 and 3 combined. First, we would have to combine the means for Groups 2 and 3 as follows:

$$\overline{X}_{2+3} = \frac{n_2 \overline{X}_2 + n_3 \overline{X}_3}{n_2 + n_3} = \frac{5(4.00) + 5(4.80)}{5 + 5}$$

$$= \frac{20.00 + 24.00}{10}$$

$$= \frac{44.00}{10}$$

$$= 4.40$$

Of course, since $n_2 = n_3$, we could have simply replaced n_3 with n_2 and averaged the means as follows:

$$\overline{X}_{2+3} = \frac{n_2 \overline{X}_2 + n_2 \overline{X}_3}{n_2 + n_2}$$

$$\overline{X}_{2+3} = \frac{n_2 (\overline{X}_2 + \overline{X}_3)}{n_2 (1 + 1)}$$

$$\overline{X}_{2+3} = \frac{\overline{X}_2 + \overline{X}_3}{2} = \frac{4.00 + 4.80}{2} = \frac{8.80}{2} = 4.40$$

Next, we calculate the F ratio using $\overline{X}_1 = 2.00$ and the combined mean $\overline{X}_{2+3} = 4.40$:

$$F = \frac{(\overline{X}_1 - \overline{X}_{2+3})^2}{MS_W \left(\frac{1}{n_1} + \frac{1}{n_2 + n_3}\right)(K - 1)} = \frac{(2.00 - 4.40)^2}{1.57 \left(\frac{1}{5} + \frac{1}{10}\right) 2}$$

$$= \frac{(-2.4)^2}{1.57(.2 + .1)2}$$

$$= \frac{5.76}{1.57(.3)2}$$

$$= \frac{5.76}{.94}$$

$$= 6.13$$

Because $6.13 > 3.88$, we conclude that there is a significant difference between $\overline{X}_1$ and $\overline{X}_{2+3}$. In other words, the experimental groups performed significantly better than the control group.

Calculating Post Hoc Multiple Comparison Tests Using SPSS 12.0

We can also use SPSS to run multiple comparison tests to determine which means are significantly different from other means. Begin by clicking on the *Post Hoc . . .* button in the One-Way ANOVA window, shown in Figure 12.11.

The Post Hoc Multiple Comparisons window is shown in Figure 12.12. To specify the multiple comparison technique, simply select the check box to the left of the named test. Once you have specified the post hoc tests you wish to have performed, click on the *Continue* button to continue with your analysis.

FIGURE 12.11

One-Way ANOVA
window with Post Hoc
button

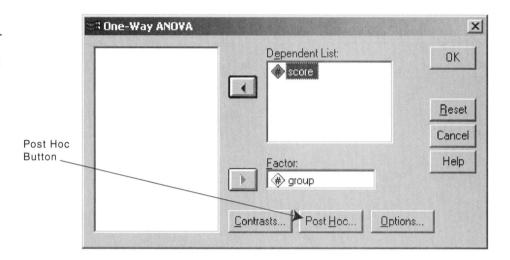

FIGURE 12.12

Post Hoc Multiple
Comparisons window

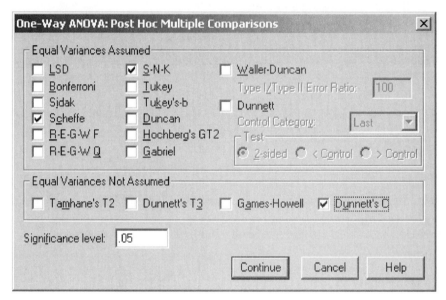

Once you have run your analysis, SPSS produces a series of tables to help you make sense of your analysis. The first table, shown in Table 12.5, is the overall ANOVA solution displaying the observed *F* statistic and the associated probability value. Here one can see that because the probability value associated with the *F* statistic is less than .05, a statistically significant relationship has been found. It is important to note that SPSS rounds the probability value and displays only three decimal places, so in Table 12.5 the probability value listed, .011, may not be the exact result. (Likewise, if an analysis shows .000 as the probability value, the result may actually be .00025, for instance—not zero.)

If you specified a priori contrasts, as in the preceding example, then the next table SPSS generates is the contrast coefficients table. This table displays the contrast coefficients you specified and the corresponding variable value labels. The table enables you to check to make sure you specified the coefficients properly.

When you specify that you want a multiple comparison post hoc test run as part of your analysis, SPSS provides a summary table for each type of test that you select. Table 12.6 shows a summary table for the Scheffé multiple comparison tests comparing the average test score of each group with all other groups. Each row of the table corresponds to the group of interest being

TABLE 12.5 Overall ANOVA solution

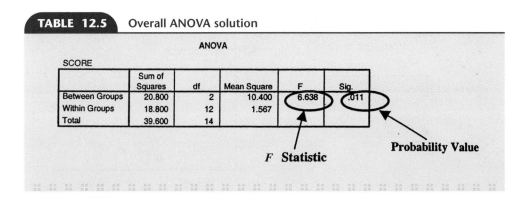

ANOVA

SCORE

	Sum of Squares	df	Mean Square	F	Sig.
Between Groups	20.800	2	10.400	6.638	.011
Within Groups	18.800	12	1.567		
Total	39.600	14			

F Statistic

Probability Value

TABLE 12.6 SPSS summary table for Scheffé multiple comparison test

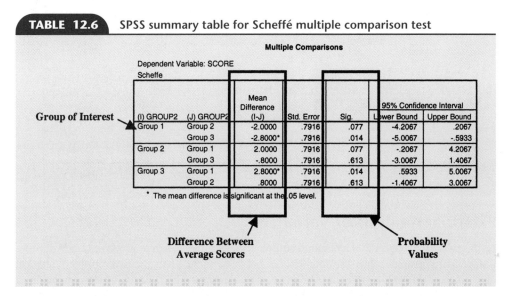

Multiple Comparisons

Dependent Variable: SCORE
Scheffe

(I) GROUP2	(J) GROUP2	Mean Difference (I-J)	Std. Error	Sig.	95% Confidence Interval Lower Bound	95% Confidence Interval Upper Bound
Group 1	Group 2	-2.0000	.7916	.077	-4.2067	.2067
	Group 3	-2.8000*	.7916	.014	-5.0067	-.5933
Group 2	Group 1	2.0000	.7916	.077	-.2067	4.2067
	Group 3	-.8000	.7916	.613	-3.0067	1.4067
Group 3	Group 1	2.8000*	.7916	.014	.5933	5.0067
	Group 2	.8000	.7916	.613	-1.4067	3.0067

* The mean difference is significant at the .05 level.

Group of Interest

Difference Between Average Scores

Probability Values

compared to the others. The difference between the average scores is shown along with the standard error of the difference and a probability value for the test. If the probability value is less than .05, then a statistically significant difference exists between the scores of the two groups.

Looking at Table 12.6, you can compare the results to those shown in the "Scheffé Tests" table on page 364. Notice that the first group of interest is Group 1. This is the group that will be compared to Group 2 and then to Group 3. In the calculation preceding the table on page 364, in which we tested the difference between the average for Group 1 and Group 2, you can see that the difference between the means is −2.00. This is the same value found in the first row of the "Mean Difference" column in Table 12.6. To tell if the difference is statistically significant, we look in the significance, or "Sig.," column. It shows an observed probability value of .077, which is larger than .05. Hence, we fail to reject the null hypothesis. The "Scheffé Tests" table on page 364 indicates that we came to the same conclusion—to fail to reject the null hypothesis—in our step-by-step test for Group 1 versus Group 2. Likewise, our conclusions also match those in the SPSS output (Table 12.6) for Group 1 versus Group 3 and Group 2 versus Group 3.

The results in SPSS are consistent with step-by-step calculated tests; they are just formatted differently. The SPSS output does not include the *F* scores found in the step-by-step calculations. Rather, it gives significance levels (probability values) associated with the test's three groups.

Illustration of
interaction and no
interaction in a 2 × 2
factorial experiment

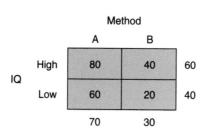

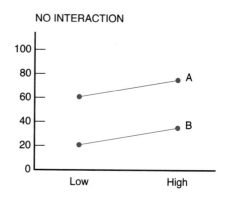

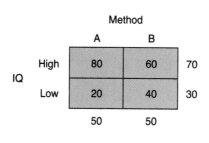

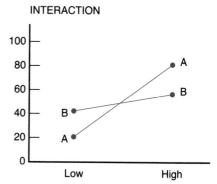

Factorial Analysis of Variance

As discussed in Chapter 8, if a research study uses a factorial design to investigate two or more
independent variables and the interactions between them, then the appropriate statistical
analysis is a factorial, or multifactor, analysis of variance. The factorial analysis provides a
separate F ratio for each independent variable and for each interaction. For example, analysis of the 2 × 2 factorial presented in Figure 12.13 would yield three F ratios—one for the independent variable (Method), one for the control independent variable (IQ), and one for the
interaction between Method and IQ. For the "No Interaction" example in Figure 12.13, the F
for Method would probably be significant since Method A appears to be significantly more effective than Method B (70 versus 30). The F for IQ is also likely to be significant since high-
IQ participants appear to have performed significantly better than low-IQ participants (60
versus 40). The F for the interaction between Method and IQ would not be significant, given
that Method A is more effective than Method B for both IQ groups (80 > 40, 60 > 20).

On the other hand, for the "Interaction" example, the F for Method would not be significant
since, overall, Method A is equally as effective as Method B (50 for A and 50 for B). The F for IQ
probably would be significant since high-IQ participants have performed significantly better than
low-IQ subjects (70 versus 30). The F for the interaction between Method and IQ, however, would
probably be significant, given that the methods appear to be differentially effective depending on
the IQ level. That is, Method A is better for high-IQ subjects (80 versus 60), and Method B is better for low-IQ subjects (20 versus 40). Another way of looking at it is to see that for the "No Interaction" example, (80 + 20) = (60 + 40); for the "Interaction" example, (80 + 40) ≠ (20 + 60).

A factorial analysis of variance is not as difficult to calculate as you may think. If no more
than two variables are involved and you have access to a calculator, it can be performed without too much difficulty. Most statistics texts outline the procedure to be followed. If more than
two variables are involved, it is usually better to use a computer if possible.

Analysis of Covariance

Analysis of covariance (ANCOVA) is used in two major ways, as a technique for controlling extraneous variables and as a means of increasing the power of a statistical test. ANCOVA is a form of ANOVA and is a statistical, rather than an experimental, method that (as you learned in Chapter 8) can be used to equate groups on one or more variables. Use of ANCOVA is basically equivalent to matching groups on the variable or variables to be controlled. Essentially, ANCOVA adjusts posttest scores for initial differences on a variable and compares the adjusted scores; groups are equalized with respect to the control variable and then compared. It's sort of like handicapping in bowling; in an attempt to equalize teams, high scorers are given little or no handicap, low scorers are given big handicaps, and so forth. Any variable that is correlated with the dependent variable can be controlled for using covariance. Examples of variables commonly controlled using ANCOVA are pretest performance, IQ, readiness, and aptitude. By using covariance, we are attempting to reduce variation in posttest scores that is attributable to another variable. Ideally, we would like all posttest variance to be attributable to the treatment conditions.

ANCOVA is a control technique used in both causal–comparative studies in which already-formed, but not necessarily equal, groups are involved and in experimental studies in which either existing groups or randomly formed groups are involved. Remember, randomization does not guarantee that groups will be equated on all variables. Unfortunately, the situation for which ANCOVA is least appropriate is the situation for which it is most often used. Use of ANCOVA assumes that participants have been randomly assigned to treatment groups. Thus, it is best used in true experimental designs. If existing, or intact, groups are not randomly selected but are assigned to treatment groups randomly, ANCOVA may still be used, but results must be interpreted with caution. If covariance is used with existing groups and nonmanipulated independent variables, as in causal–comparative studies, the results are likely to be misleading at best. There are other assumptions associated with the use of ANCOVA. Violation of these assumptions is not as serious, however, if participants have been randomly assigned to treatment groups.

A second, not previously discussed, function of ANCOVA is that it increases the power of a statistical test by reducing within-group (error) variance. **Power** refers to the ability of a significance test to reject a null hypothesis that is false—in other words, to avoid a Type II error by making the correct decision to reject the null hypothesis. Although increasing sample size also increases power, researchers are often limited to samples of a given size because of financial and practical reasons. Because ANCOVA can reduce random sampling error by "equating" different groups, it increases the power of the significance test. The power-increasing function of ANCOVA is directly related to the degree of randomization involved in formation of the groups. The results of ANCOVA are least likely to be valid when groups have not been randomly selected and assigned. As pointed out earlier, the procedure for applying ANCOVA is lengthy and quite complex and hardly ever hand calculated. Almost all researchers use computer programs for reasons of accuracy and sanity!

Multiple Regression

A combination of variables usually results in a more accurate prediction than any single variable. A prediction equation that includes more than one predictor is referred to as a *multiple regression equation*. As noted in Chapter 7, multiple regression equation uses variables that are known to individually predict (correlate with) the criterion to make a more accurate prediction. Thus, for example, we might use high school GPA, Scholastic Aptitude Test (SAT) scores, and rank in graduating class to predict college GPA at the end of the first semester of college. Use of multiple regression is increasing, primarily because of its versatility and precision. It can be used with data representing any scale of measurement and can be used to analyze the results of experimental and causal–comparative, as well as correlational, studies. Further, it determines not only whether variables are related but also the degree to which they are related.

To see how multiple regression works, we will use the example about college GPA. The first step in multiple regression is to identify the variable that best predicts the criterion—that is, the variable most highly correlated with it. Past performance is generally the best predictor of future performance, so high school GPA would probably be the best predictor. The next step is to identify a second variable that will most improve the prediction. Usually this is a variable that is related to the criterion (college GPA) but uncorrelated with other predictors. In our case, the question would be, "Do we get a more accurate prediction using high school GPA and SAT scores or using high school GPA and rank in graduating class?" The results of multiple regression would give us the answer to that question and would also tell us by how much the prediction was improved. In our case, the answer might be high school GPA and SAT scores. That would leave rank in graduating class as the last variable, and the results of multiple regression would tell us by how much our prediction would be improved if we included it. Considering that our three predictors would most probably all be correlated with each other to some degree as well as to the criterion, it might be that rank in graduating class adds very little to the accuracy of a prediction based on high school GPA and SAT scores. A study involving more than three variables works exactly the same way; at each step it is determined which variable adds the most to the prediction and how much it adds. (See Chapter 7 for another example of multiple regression.)

The sign, positive or negative, of the relationship between a predictor and the criterion has nothing to do with how good a predictor it is. Recall that $r = -1.00$ represents a relationship just as strong as $r = +1.00$; the only difference is the nature of the relationship. It should also be noted that the number of predictor variables is related to the sample size; the larger the number of variables, the larger the sample size needs to be. Large sample sizes increase the probability that the prediction equation will generalize to groups beyond those involved in creating the initial equation.

With increasing frequency, multiple regression is being used as an alternative to the various analysis of variance techniques. When this is the case, the dependent variable, or posttest scores, becomes the criterion variable, and the predictors include group membership (e.g., experimental versus control) and any other appropriate variables, such as pretest scores. The results indicate not only whether group membership is significantly related to posttest performance but also the magnitude of the relationship. For analyses such as these, the researcher typically specifies the order in which variables are to be checked. For ANCOVA, with pretest scores as the covariate, for example, the researcher specifies that pretest scores be entered into the equation first; it can then be determined whether group membership significantly improves the equation.

Chi Square

Chi square, symbolized as X^2, is a nonparametric test of significance appropriate when the data are in the form of frequency counts or percentages and proportions that can be converted to frequencies. Two or more mutually exclusive categories are required. Thus, chi square is appropriate when the data are a nominal scale and fall into either true categories (e.g., male vs. female) or artificial categories (e.g., tall vs. short). A **true category** is one in which persons or objects naturally fall, independently of any research study, whereas an **artificial category** is one that is operationally defined by a researcher. A chi square test compares the proportions actually observed in a study to the expected proportions to see if they are significantly different. Expected proportions are usually the frequencies that would be expected if the groups were equal, although occasionally they also may be based on past data. The chi square value increases as the difference between observed and expected frequencies increases. Whether the chi square is significant is determined by consulting a chi square table.

One-Dimensional Chi Square

The chi square can be used to compare frequencies occurring in different categories or groups. As an example, suppose you stopped 90 shoppers in a supermarket and asked them to taste three unlabeled different brands of peanut butter (X, Y, Z) and to tell you which one tasted best. Suppose that 40 of the 90 shoppers chose Brand X, 30 chose Brand Y, and 20 chose Brand Z. If the null hypothesis were true—if there were no difference in taste among the three brands—we would expect an equal number of shoppers (30) to select each brand. We can present our data in what is called a *contingency table,* as shown:

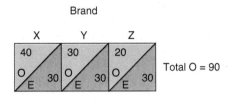

where

O = observed frequencies

E = expected frequencies

To determine whether the observed frequencies (40, 30, 20) are significantly different from the expected frequencies (30, 30, 30), you could carry out a chi square test. If you find that the chi square is significant, you would reject the null hypothesis and conclude that the brands do taste different.

As another example, you might wish to investigate whether college sophomores prefer to study alone or with others. Tabulation, based on a random sample of 100 sophomores, might reveal that 45 prefer to study alone and 55 prefer to study with others. The null hypothesis of no preference would suggest a 50–50 split. The corresponding contingency table would look like this:

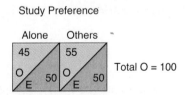

To determine whether the groups are significantly different, you would compare the observed frequencies (45, 55) with the expected frequencies (50, 50) using a chi square test of significance.

Two-Dimensional Chi Square

The chi square may also be used when frequencies are categorized along more than one dimension. A two-dimensional chi square is a sort of factorial chi square. In the study sequence example, you might select a stratified sample, comprising 50 males and 50 females. Responses could then be classified by study preference and by gender, a two-way classification that would allow you to see whether study preference is related to gender. The corresponding contingency table would be set up as follows:

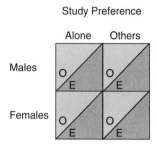

Although 2 × 2 applications are quite common, contingency tables may be based on any number of categories, for example, 2 × 3, 3 × 3, 2 × 4, and so forth. When a two-way classification is used, calculation of expected frequencies is a little more complex, but not difficult.

Calculating Chi Square

A one-dimensional chi square (X^2) is the easiest statistic of all. In our peanut butter example, we asked 90 people to indicate which brand they thought tasted best; 40 picked Brand X, 30 picked Brand Y, and 20 picked Brand Z. If there were no difference among the brands, we would expect the same number of people to choose each brand: 30, 30, 30. Therefore, we have the following table:

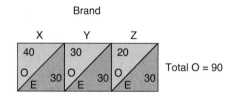

where

O = observed frequencies

E = expected frequencies

To determine whether the observed frequencies are significantly different from the expected frequencies, we apply the following formula:

$$x^2 = \Sigma \left[\frac{(fo - fe)^2}{fe} \right]$$

Now that is some sum sign! All this formula says, however, is that for each cell, or category (X, Y, and Z) we subtract the expected frequency (fe) from the observed frequency (fo), square the difference $(fo - fe)^2$, and then divide by the expected frequency, fe. The big Σ says that after we perform these steps for each term, we add up the resulting values. Thus, substituting our table values into the formula, we get

$$\chi^2 = \frac{\overset{X}{\overset{fo \quad fe}{(40 - 30)^2}}}{30} + \frac{\overset{Y}{\overset{fo \quad fe}{(30 - 30)^2}}}{30} + \frac{\overset{Z}{\overset{fo \quad fe}{(20 - 30)^2}}}{30}$$

$$= \frac{(10)^2}{\underset{fe}{30}} + \frac{(0)^2}{\underset{fe}{30}} + \frac{(-10)^2}{\underset{fe}{30}}$$

$$= \frac{100}{30} + 0 + \frac{100}{30}$$

$$= 3.333 + 0 + 3.333$$

$$= 6.67$$

Thus, $X_2 = 6.67$. The degrees of freedom for a one-dimensional chi square are determined by the formula $(C - 1)$, where C equals the number of columns, in our case 3. Thus, $df = C - 1 = 3 - 1 = 2$. Therefore, we have $X^2 = 6.67$, $\alpha = .05$, $df = 2$. To determine whether the differences between observed and expected frequencies are significant, we compare our chi square value to the appropriate value in Table A.6 in Appendix A. Run the index finger of your right hand across the top until you find $\alpha = .05$. Now run the index finger of your left hand down the extreme left-hand column and find $df = 2$. Run your left hand across and your right hand down and they will intersect at 5.991, or 5.99. Is our value of $6.67 > 5.99$? Yes. Therefore, we reject the null hypothesis. There is a significant difference between observed and expected proportions; the brands of peanut butter compared do taste different! Suppose we selected $\alpha = .01$. The chi square value required for significance would be 9.210, or 9.21. Is our value of $6.67 > 9.21$? No. Therefore, we would not reject the null hypothesis, and we would conclude that there is no significant difference between observed and expected proportions; the three brands of peanut butter taste the same. Thus, once again you can see that selection of a probability level is important; different conclusions may very well be drawn with different probability levels.

Now let's look at our study preference example. We asked 100 college sophomores whether they preferred to study alone or with others; 45 said alone and 55 said with others. Under a null hypothesis of no preference, we would expect a 50–50 split.

Therefore, we have the following table:

Study Preference

Alone   Others

| 45 | 55 |

O / 50 O / 50   Total O = 100
/ E   / E

Applying the chi square formula, we get

$$\chi^2 = \frac{(45 - 50)^2}{50} + \frac{(55 - 50)^2}{50}$$

$$= \frac{(-5)^2}{50} + \frac{(5)^2}{50}$$

$$= \frac{25}{50} + \frac{25}{50}$$

$$= .50 + .50$$

$$\chi^2 = 1.00$$

Since degrees of freedom are $C - 1$, we have $2 - 1$, or 1. Thus $X^2 = 1.00$, $\alpha = .05$, $df = 1$. Table A.6 indicates that for $\alpha = .05$ and $df = 1$, the required value is 3.841, or 3.84. Is our value of $1.00 > 3.84$? No. Therefore, we do not reject the null hypothesis. There is not a significant difference between observed and expected proportions; sophomores do not prefer to study alone or with others.

Now suppose we wanted to know if study preference is related to the gender of the students. Our 2×2 contingency table might look like this:

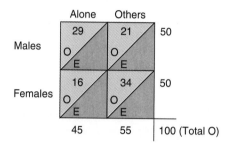

To find the expected frequency for a particular cell, or category, we multiply the corresponding row total by the corresponding column total and divide by the overall total. This isn't as bad as it sounds, honest. So, for males who prefer to study alone, the observed frequency is 29. To find the expected frequency, we multiply the total for the "males" row (50) by the total for the "Alone" column (45) and divide by the overall total (100):

$$\text{males (alone)} = \frac{50 \times 45}{100} = \frac{2250}{100} = 22.5$$

Similarly, for the other cells, we get

$$\text{males (others)} = \frac{50 \times 55}{100} = \frac{2750}{100} = 27.5$$

$$\text{females (alone)} = \frac{50 \times 45}{100} = \frac{2250}{100} = 22.5$$

$$\text{females (others)} = \frac{50 \times 50}{100} = \frac{2750}{100} = 27.5$$

Now we can fill in the expected frequencies in our table, as follows:

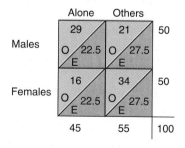

Chi square is calculated in the same way as for the other examples, except now we have four terms:

$$\chi^2 = \frac{(29 - 22.5)^2}{22.5} + \frac{(21 - 27.5)^2}{27.5} + \frac{(16 - 22.5)^2}{22.5} + \frac{(34 - 27.5)^2}{27.5}$$

$$= \frac{(6.5)^2}{22.5} + \frac{(-6.5)^2}{27.5} + \frac{(-6.5)^2}{22.5} + \frac{(6.5)^2}{27.5}$$

$$= \frac{42.25}{22.5} + \frac{42.25}{27.5} + \frac{42.25}{22.5} + \frac{42.25}{27.5}$$

$$= 1.88 \quad + \quad 1.54 \quad + \quad 1.88 \quad + \quad 1.54$$

$$\chi^2 = 6.84$$

The degrees of freedom for a two-dimensional chi square are determined by the following formula:

$$df = (R - 1)(C - 1)$$

where

R = the number of rows in the contingency table

C = the number of columns in the contingency table

Since we have two rows and two columns,

$$df = (R - 1)(C - 1) = (2 - 1)(2 - 1) = 1 \times 1 = 1$$

Therefore, we have $\chi^2 = 6.84$, $\alpha = .05$, $df = 1$. The value in Table A.6 for $\alpha = .05$ and $df = 1$ is 3.841, or 3.84. Is our value of 6.84 > 3.84? Yes. Therefore, we conclude that gender is related to study preference. For larger contingency tables (e.g., a 3 × 2), expected frequencies and chi square are calculated in the same way. The only difference is that the number of terms increases; for a 3 × 2, for example, the number of terms is six (3 × 2 = 6).

Calculating Chi Square Using SPSS 12.0

To specify the chi square statistic for a given table of data, you go to the Descriptive Statistics submenu by clicking on *Analyze*. Within this submenu, choose the *Crosstabs . . .* option. (A chi square statistic is a nonparametric statistic, so it is listed under the descriptive statistics.) Figure 12.14 shows the menu options in SPSS. This is one of the few analysis options in SPSS that does not have a menu option named after the statistic of interest. In summary, the menu options are as follows:

Analyze
Descriptive Statistics
Crosstabs . . .

Once in the *Crosstabs* window, you need to specify the variables to go in the rows and columns of the table, as shown in Figure 12.15. Doing this will construct the table used to calculate the chi square statistic, but if you want the statistic computed by SPSS, click on the *Statistics . . .* button. Figure 12.16 shows the *Statistics* window where you specify that you want a chi square statistic by selecting the check box to the left of the statistic name. Click on the *Continue* button to return to the Crosstabs window to continue your analysis.

Additionally, you may wish to display the expected frequencies in each cell. To do this, return to the Crosstabs window and click on the *Cells . . .* button, shown in Figure 12.15.

The first table SPSS generates is the cross-tabulation table (Table 12.7). This table shows the observed values for each of the cells.

The observed frequency for men preferring to study alone is 29 and the expected frequency is 22.5. Table 12.8 shows the computed chi square statistic generated using the values shown in Table 12.7. The observed chi square is 6.82 with a corresponding probability value equal to .009.

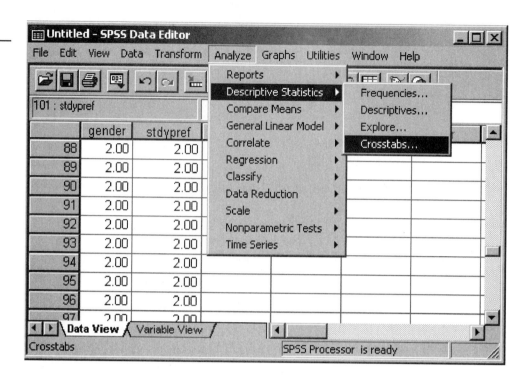

FIGURE 12.15   SPSS Crosstabs window with Cells button

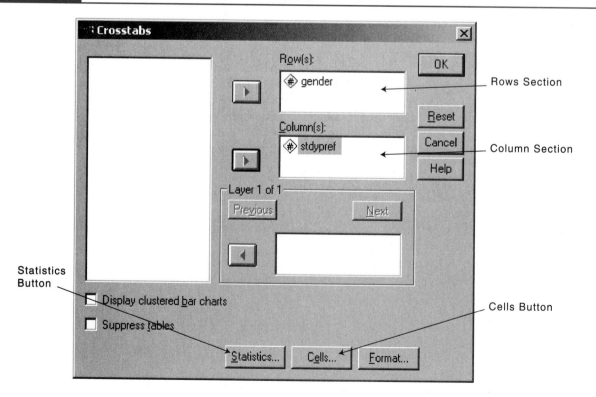

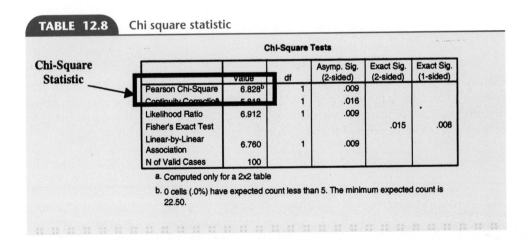

FIGURE 12.16

SPSS Crosstabs: Statistics window

Chi-Square Statistic Button

Continue Button

TABLE 12.7 SPSS cross-tabulation table

Observed and Expected Frequency for Males Who Like to Study Alone

GENDER * STDYPREF Crosstabulation

			STDYPREF		
			Alone	Others	Total
GENDER	males	Count	29	21	50
		Expected Count	22.5	27.5	50.0
	females	Count	16	34	50
		Expected Count	22.5	27.5	50.0
Total		Count	45	55	100
		Expected Count	45.0	55.0	100.0

TABLE 12.8 Chi square statistic

Chi-Square Statistic

Chi-Square Tests

	Value	df	Asymp. Sig. (2-sided)	Exact Sig. (2-sided)	Exact Sig. (1-sided)
Pearson Chi-Square	6.828[b]	1	.009		
Continuity Correction	5.818	1	.016		
Likelihood Ratio	6.912	1	.009		
Fisher's Exact Test				.015	.008
Linear-by-Linear Association	6.760	1	.009		
N of Valid Cases	100				

a. Computed only for a 2x2 table

b. 0 cells (.0%) have expected count less than 5. The minimum expected count is 22.50.

Types of Parametric and Nonparametric Statistical Tests

There are too many parametric and nonparametric statistical methods to describe in detail here. Table 12.9 provides an overview of some of the more commonly used tests. The table is best used by first identifying the levels of measurement your study is dealing with. Then

TABLE 12.9	Commonly used parametric and nonparametric significance tests

Name of Test	Test Statistic	df	Parametric (P) Nonparametric (NP)	Purpose	Var. 1 Independent	Var. 2 Dependent
t test for independent samples	t	$n_1 + n_2 - 2$	P	Test difference between means of two independent groups	Nominal	Interval or ratio
t test for dependent samples	t	$N - 1$	P	Test difference between means of two dependent groups	Nominal	Interval or ratio
Analysis of variance	F	SS_B = groups − 1; SS_w = participants − groups − 1	P	Test the difference among three or more independent groups	Nominal	Interval or ratio
Pearson product correlation	r	$N - 2$	P	Test whether a correlation is different from zero (a relationship exists)	Interval or ratio	Interval or ratio
Chi square test	χ^2	rows − 1 times column − 1	NP	Test the difference in proportions in two or more groups	Nominal	Nominal
Median test	χ^2	rows − 1 times column − 1	NP	Test the difference of the medians of two independent groups	Nominal	Ordinal
Mann–Whitney U test	U	$N - 1$	NP	Test the difference of the medians of two independent groups	Nominal	Ordinal
Wilcoxon signed rank test	Z	$N - 2$	NP	Test the difference in the ranks of two related groups	Nominal	Ordinal
Kruskal–Wallis test	H	groups − 1	NP	Test the difference in the ranks of three or more independent groups	Nominal	Ordinal
Freidman test	χ	groups − 1	NP	Test the difference in the ranks of three or more dependent groups	Nominal	Ordinal
Spearman rho	ρ	$N - 2$	NP	Test whether a correlation is different from zero	Ordinal	Ordinal

examine the purpose statements that fit your levels of measurement, and select the one that comes closest to the purpose of your significance test. This should narrow selection. Other information in the table will help in carrying out your significance test. If you have not used or been exposed to the selected test, you should find out more about it before using it.

SUMMARY

Concepts Underlying Inferential Statistics

1. Inferential statistics deal with inferences about populations based on the behavior of samples. Inferential statistics are concerned with determining how likely it is that results based on a sample or samples are the same results that would have been obtained for the entire population.

2. Values calculated from samples, such as the mean, are referred to as *statistics*. The corresponding population values are referred to as *parameters*.

3. The question that guides inferential statistics is whether expected differences are real, significant ones or only the result of sampling errors.

4. Inferences concerning populations provide only probability statements; the researcher is never

perfectly certain when making an inference about a population.

Standard Error

5. Expected, chance variation among the means is referred to as *sampling error*. Sampling errors are normally distributed.

6. If a sufficiently large number of equal-sized large samples are randomly selected from a population, all samples will not have the same mean on the variable measured, but the means of those samples will be normally distributed around the population mean. The mean of all the sample means will yield a good estimate of the population mean.

7. A distribution of sample means not only has its own mean but also its own standard deviation. The standard deviation of the sample means (the standard deviation of sampling errors) is usually referred to as the *standard error of the mean* $(SE_{\bar{X}})$.

8. In a normal curve, approximately 68% of the sample means will fall between plus and minus one standard error of the mean, 95% will fall between plus and minus two standard errors, and 99+% will fall between plus and minus three standard errors.

9. In most cases, we do not know the mean or standard deviation of the population, so we estimate the standard error by dividing the standard deviation of the sample by the square root of the sample size minus one.

10. The smaller the standard error of the mean, the less sampling error. As the size of the sample increases, the standard error of the mean decreases. The researcher should make every effort to acquire as large a sample as possible.

11. A standard error can also be calculated for other measures of central tendency, as well as for measures of variability, relationship, and relative position. Further, a standard error can also be determined for the difference between means.

The Null Hypothesis

12. When we talk about the real or significant difference between two sample means, we mean that the difference was caused by the treatment (the independent variable), not by chance.

13. The null hypothesis says that there is no true difference or relationship between parameters in the populations and that any differences or relationship found for the samples is the result of sampling error.

14. Rejection of a null hypothesis provides more conclusive support for a positive research hypothesis. The test of significance selected to determine whether a difference between means is a true one provides a test of the null hypothesis. The null hypothesis is either rejected, as being probably false, or not rejected, as being probably true.

15. To test a null hypothesis, we need a statistical test of significance, and we need to select a probability level that indicates how much risk we are willing to take that our decision to reject or not reject the null hypothesis, is wrong. After we make the decision, we make an inference back to our research hypothesis.

Tests of Significance

16. A test of significance helps us to decide whether we can reject the null hypothesis and infer that the difference is a true one, not a chance one resulting from sampling error. A test of significance is made at a preselected probability level that allows us to state that we have rejected the null hypothesis because we would expect to find a difference as large as we have found by chance only 5 times out of every 100 studies, or only 1 time in every 100 studies, or whatever.

17. There are a number of different tests of significance. Factors such as the scale of measurement represented by the data, method of subject selection, the number of groups, and the number of independent variables determine which test of significance should be selected for a given experiment.

Decision Making: Levels of Significance and Type I and Type II Errors

18. There are four possibilities that can result from testing the null hypothesis. If the null hypothesis is really true, and the researcher agrees that it is true (does not reject it), the researcher makes the correct decision. Similarly, if the null hypothesis is false, and the researcher rejects it (says there is a difference), the researcher also makes the correct decision. But if the null hypothesis is true, there really is no difference, and the researcher rejects the hypothesis and says there is a difference, the researcher makes an incorrect decision, referred to as a *Type I error*. Similarly, if the null hypothesis is false, there really is a significant difference between the means, but the researcher concludes that the null hypothesis is true and does not reject it, the

researcher also makes an incorrect decision, referred to as a *Type II error.*

19. If the decision is made to reject the null hypothesis, the means are concluded to be significantly different, too different to be the result of chance error. If the null hypothesis is not rejected, the means are determined to be not significantly different. The selected level of significance, or probability, determines how large the difference between the means must be to be declared significantly different. The most commonly used probability levels (symbolized as α) are the .05 and the .01 levels.

20. The probability level selected determines the probability of committing a Type I error, that is, of rejecting a null hypothesis that is really true. The smaller the probability level is, the larger the mean difference must be to be a significant difference.

21. As the probability of committing a Type I error decreases, the probability of committing a Type II error—that is, of not rejecting a null hypothesis when you should—increases.

22. The choice of a probability level, α, should be made before execution of the study. Rejection of a null hypothesis, or lack of rejection, only supports or does not support a research hypothesis; it does not "prove" it.

Two-Tailed and One-Tailed Tests

23. Tests of significance are usually two-tailed. The null hypothesis states that there is no difference between groups ($A = B$) and a two-tailed test allows for the possibility that a difference may occur in either direction. That is, either group mean may be higher than the other ($A > B$ or $B > A$).

24. A one-tailed test assumes that a difference can occur in only one direction; the null hypothesis states that one group is not better than another, and the one-tailed test assumes that if a difference occurs it will be in favor of that particular group ($A > B$). To select a one-tailed test of significance, the researcher has to be quite sure that a difference can occur in only one direction.

25. If strong evidence exists for a one-tailed test, the level of the test of significance required for significance is smaller. In other words, it is "easier" to find a significant difference.

Degrees of Freedom

26. Inferential statistics are dependent on degrees of freedom to test hypothesis. Each test of significance

has its own formula for determining degrees of freedom. Degrees of freedom are a function of such factors as the number of subjects and the number of groups. The intersection of the probability level and the degrees of freedom, *df,* determine the level needed to reject the null hypothesis.

Tests of Significance: Types

27. Different tests of significance are appropriate for different sets of data. The first decision in selecting an appropriate test of significance is whether a parametric test may be used or whether a nonparametric test must be selected.

28. Parametric tests are more powerful and are generally to be preferred. "More powerful" means more likely to result in rejection of a null hypothesis that is false; in other words, the researcher is less likely to commit a Type II error (not rejecting a null hypothesis that should be rejected).

29. Parametric tests require that certain assumptions be met for them to be valid. One of the major assumptions underlying use of parametric tests is that the variable measured is normally distributed in the population. A second major assumption is that the data represent an interval or ratio scale of measurement. A third assumption is that participants are randomly selected for the study. Another assumption is that the variances of the population comparison groups are equal (or at least that the ratio of the variances is known).

30. With the exception of independence, some violation of one or more of these assumptions usually does not make too much difference in the decision made concerning the statistical significance of the results.

31. If one or more of the parametric assumptions are greatly violated, a nonparametric test should be used. Nonparametric tests make no assumptions about the shape of the distribution. Nonparametric tests are used when the data represent an ordinal or nominal scale, when a parametric assumption has been greatly violated, or when the nature of the distribution is not known. If the data represent an interval or ratio scale, a parametric test should be used unless another of the assumptions is greatly violated.

The *t* Test

32. The *t* test is used to determine whether two means are significantly different at a selected probability

level. For a given sample size, the t indicates how often a difference as large or larger $(\overline{X}_1 - \overline{X}_2)$ would be found when there is no true population difference.

33. The t test makes adjustments for the fact that the distribution of scores for small samples becomes increasingly different from a normal distribution as sample sizes become increasingly smaller.

34. For a given significance level, the values of t required to reject a null hypothesis are progressively higher as sample sizes become smaller; as the sample size becomes larger, the t value required to reject the null hypothesis becomes smaller.

35. The t test compares the observed mean difference $(\overline{X}_1 - \overline{X}_2)$ to the difference expected by chance. The t test forms a ratio of these two values. The numerator for a t test is the difference between the sample means $\overline{X}_1$ and $\overline{X}_2$, and the denominator is the chance difference that would be expected if the null hypothesis were true—the standard error of the difference between the means.

36. The t ratio determines whether the observed difference is sufficiently larger than a difference that would be expected by chance. After the numerator is divided by the denominator, the resulting t value is compared to the appropriate t table value (depending on the probability level and the degrees of freedom); if the calculated t value is equal to or greater than the table value, then the null hypothesis is rejected.

37. There are two different types of t tests: the t test for independent samples and the t test for nonindependent samples. Independent samples are samples that are randomly formed. If two groups are randomly formed, the expectation is that they are essentially the same at the beginning of a study with respect to performance on the dependent variable. Therefore, if they are essentially the same at the end of the study, the null hypothesis is probably true; if they are different at the end of the study, the null hypothesis is probably false (that is, the treatment probably makes a difference).

38. A nonindependent sample is a sample formed by some type of matching or a single sample being pre- and posttested. In nonindependent samples, the members of one group are systematically related to the members of a second group, especially if it is the same group at two different times. If samples are nonindependent, scores on the dependent variable are expected to be correlated and a special t for correlated, or nonindependent, means must be used.

Analysis of Gain or Difference Scores

39. A number of problems are associated with the use of gain or difference scores. The major one is lack of equal opportunity to grow. Every participant does not have the same room to gain. If two groups are essentially the same on a protest, their posttest scores can be directly compared using a t test. If a t test between the groups shows a difference on the pretests, the preferred posttest analysis is analysis of covariance.

Simple Analysis of Variance

40. Simple, or one-way, analysis of variance (ANOVA) is used to determine whether a significant difference exists between two or more means at a selected probability level.

41. In ANOVA, the total variation, or variance, of scores is attributed to two sources—variance between groups (variance caused by the treatment) and variance within groups (error variance). As with the t test, a ratio is formed (the F ratio) with group differences as the numerator (variance between groups) and an error term as the denominator (variance within groups). We determine whether the *between* groups (treatment) variance differs from the *within* groups (error) variance by more than what would be expected by chance.

42. The degrees of freedom for the F ratio are a function of the number of groups and the number of subjects.

Multiple Comparisons

43. Multiple comparison procedures are used following ANOVA to determine which means are significantly different from which other means. A special t test that adjusts for the fact that many tests are being executed is used because when many tests are performed, the probability level tends to increase, thus increasing the likelihood of finding a spurious significant result.

44. The mean comparisons to be examined should be decided on before, not after, the study is conducted.

45. Of the many multiple comparison techniques available, a commonly used one is the Scheffé test, which is a very conservative test. The calculations for the Scheffé test are quite simple, and sample sizes do not have to be equal.

Factorial Analysis of Variance

46. If a research study is based on a factorial design and investigates two or more independent variables and

the interactions between them, the appropriate statistical analysis is a factorial, or multifactor, analysis of variance. This analysis yields a separate F ratio for each independent variable and one for each interaction.

Analysis of Covariance

47. Analysis of covariance (ANCOVA) is used as a technique for controlling extraneous variables and as a means of increasing power, the statistical ability to reject a false null hypothesis. ANCOVA increases the power of a statistical test by reducing within-group (error) variance.

48. ANCOVA is a form of ANOVA and is a method that can be used to equate groups on one or more variables. Essentially, ANCOVA adjusts posttest scores for initial differences on some variable (such as pretest performance or IQ) and compares adjusted scores.

49. ANCOVA is based on the assumption that participants have been randomly assigned to treatment groups. It is therefore best used in conjunction with true experimental designs. If existing, or intact, groups are involved but treatments are assigned to groups randomly, ANCOVA may still be used but results must be interpreted with caution.

Multiple Regression

50. A multiple regression equation uses variables that are known to individually predict (correlate with) the criterion to make a more accurate prediction about a criterion variable.

51. Use of multiple regression is increasing, primarily because of its versatility and precision. It can be used with data representing any scale of measurement and can be used to analyze the results of experimental and causal–comparative, as well as correlational, studies. It determines not only whether variables are related but also the degree to which they are related.

52. The first step in multiple regression is to identify the variable that best predicts (is most highly correlated with) the criterion. Variables are added to the multiple regression equation based on their likelihood of being correlated with the criterion and of being not highly correlated with the other predictor variables.

53. With increasing frequency, multiple regression is being used as an alternative to the various analysis of variance techniques. When this is the case, the dependent variable, or posttest scores, becomes the criterion variable, and the predictors include group membership (e.g., experimental versus control) and any other appropriate variables, such as pretest scores.

Chi Square

54. Chi square, symbolized as X^2, is a nonparametric test of significance appropriate when the data are in the form of frequency counts occurring in two or more mutually exclusive categories. Chi square is appropriate when the data represent a nominal scale, and the categories may be true categories (e.g., male versus female) or artificial categories (e.g., tall versus short).

55. Expected frequencies are usually the frequencies that would be expected if the groups were equal.

56. One-dimensional chi square is used to compare frequencies occurring in different categories so that the chi square is comparing groups with respect to the frequency of occurrence of different events. Data are presented in a contingency table.

57. Two-dimensional chi square is used when frequencies are categorized along more than one dimension. It is a sort of factorial chi square. Although 2×2 applications are quite common, contingency tables may be based on any number of categories, such as 2×3, 3×3, or 2×4.

Now go to the Companion Website at **www.prenhall.com/gay** to assess your understanding of chapter content with Practice Quiz, apply comprehension in Applying What You Know, broaden your knowledge about research in Web Links, and expand your research skills in Evaluating Articles, Analyzing Qualitative Data, Analyzing Quantitative Data, and Research Tools and Tips.

"Whether you do your analyses by hand, calculator, or computer, all data should be thoroughly checked and stored in an organized manner." (p. 385)

Postanalysis Considerations

OBJECTIVES

After reading Chapter 13, you should be able to do the following:

1. List guidelines to be followed in verifying and storing quantitative data.
2. Explain how a rejected null hypothesis relates to a research hypothesis.
3. Explain how a null hypothesis that is not rejected relates to a research hypothesis.
4. Identify the major use of significant unhypothesized relationships.
5. Explain the factors that influence the interpretation of research results, including statistical, methodological, and significance.
6. Understand the role of power in significance testing.
7. Describe replication.

▓ VERIFYING AND STORING DATA

After you have completed the analyses necessary to describe your data and test your hypothesis, you do not say, "Thank goodness, I'm done!" and happily throw away all your data and your worksheets. Whether you do your analyses by hand, calculator, or computer, all data should be thoroughly checked and stored in an organized manner.

Verification and Data Checking

Verification involves double-checking the data, organizing it, and evaluating the research conclusion. Original data—as much of it as possible—should be rechecked, and the coded data should be compared to the initial uncoded data to make sure coding was done properly. Data kept in a computer file should be printed and examined.

When analyses are done by hand or with a calculator, both the accuracy of computations and the reasonableness of the results should be checked. You undoubtedly noticed that in the previous chapters we applied each analysis step by step. This was probably helpful to some readers and annoying to others. Math superstar types seem to derive great satisfaction from doing several steps in a row "in their heads" and listing the results, instead of separately recording the result of each step. This may save time in the short run, but not necessarily in the long run. If you end up with a result that just does not look right, it is a lot easier to spot an error if every step is in front of you. Computer analyses rarely show each step, only the final result. This is a disadvantage of computer analyses, especially if the researcher is not familiar with the procedures being used.

A very frustrated student once came to one of the authors, quite upset and with a very sad tale about being up all night, rechecking his work over and over and over, and still getting a negative sum of squares in his ANOVA. He was at the point where he could easily have been convinced that the square of a number can be negative! An inspection of his work revealed quickly that the problem was not in his execution of the ANOVA, but in the numbers he was using to do the ANOVA. Early in the game he had added ΣX_1, ΣX_2, and ΣX_3 and obtained a number much, much larger than their actual sum. From that point on, he was doomed. The moral of the story is that if you have checked the steps of analysis or a set of figures several times and they still seem incorrect, do not check them 50 more times. Look elsewhere! For example, make sure you are using the correct formula or make sure you have used the correct numbers. The anecdote also illustrates that the research results should make sense. If your scores range from 20 to 94 and you get a standard deviation of 1.20, you have probably made a mistake somewhere, because 1.20 is not a reasonable value with such a large range. Similarly, if your means are 24.20 and 26.10 and you get a *t* ratio of 44.82, you had better recheck your data and analysis.

When analyses are done by computer, the output must be checked very carefully. Some people are under the mistaken impression that if a result was produced by a computer, it is automatically correct. Remember the human error factor: People make mistakes inputting data and selecting analyses from the choices provided. Computer analyses are generally accurate *if the data have been correctly entered into the program*. One way to check for accurate entry of data is to examine the reasonableness of the results. Don't succumb to a "blind faith" view of the computer, and don't use the computer to perform analyses that you yourself do not understand. Computer programs have almost made data analysis too easy. A person with little or no knowledge of analysis of covariance, for example, can, by following directions, have a computer perform the analysis. Such a person, however, could not possibly know the nuances of interpretation and whether the results make sense. You may now be beginning to understand the wisdom of our earlier advice to never use the computer to apply a method that you have not previously done by hand at least one time. Also, although you can usually be pretty safe in assuming that the computer will accurately execute each analysis, it is a good idea to spot-check. The computer does only what it has been programmed to do, and programming errors do occur. Thus, if the computer gives you six *F* ratios, calculate at least one yourself. If it matches the one the computer produced, the rest are probably also correct.

Storage

Once you are convinced that your work is accurate, you will need to label, organize, and file your data in a safe place. You may need the information again. Sometimes an additional analysis is desired either by the original researcher, an advisor, or another researcher who wishes to analyze the data using a different statistical technique. Also, data from one study may be reused in a later study. Therefore, you should label all data with as many identification labels as possible. Such labels might include the dates of the study, the nature of each treatment group, and whether data are pretest data, posttest data, or data for a control variable. Store your paperwork in a safe place, not in your junk drawer, wet basement, or rental storage unit two states away. Data stored on a computer must also be safeguarded. Keep one set of data on your hard drive but also keep a copy on a labeled disk or CD-ROM as a backup.

:: INTERPRETING QUANTITATIVE RESEARCH RESULTS

The product of a test of significance is a number, a value that is or is not statistically significant. What the number actually means requires interpretation by the researcher. The results of statistical analyses need to be interpreted in terms of the purpose of the study and the original research hypothesis, and with respect to other studies that have been conducted in the same area of research.

Hypothesized Results

In your research report, you must discuss whether the results support the research hypothesis. Are the results in agreement with other findings? Why or why not? Minimally, this means that you will state, for example, that hypotheses one and two were supported and that hypothesis three was not. The supported hypotheses are relatively simple to deal with; unsupported hypotheses require some explanation regarding possible reasons. There may have been validity or reliability problems in your study, for example. Similarly, if your results are not in agreement with other research findings, possible reasons for the discrepancy should be discussed. There may have been validity problems in your study, or you may have discovered a relationship previously not uncovered.

Remember, if you reject a null hypothesis (there is a difference), your research hypothesis may be supported, but it is not proven. One study does not prove anything. It represents one instance in which the research hypothesis was supported (and the null hypothesis was rejected). A supported research hypothesis does not necessarily mean that your treatment would "work" with different populations, different materials, and different dependent variables. As an example, if token reinforcement is found to be effective in improving the behavior of first graders, this does not mean that token reinforcement will necessarily be effective in reducing referrals to the principal at the high school level. In discussing your results, do not overgeneralize.

If you do not reject the null hypothesis (there is no difference), so that your research hypothesis (there is a difference) is not supported, do not feel bad and apologize for your results. A common reaction for some researchers in this situation is to be very disappointed; after all, "I didn't find a significant difference." In the first place, failure to reject a null hypothesis does not necessarily mean that your research hypothesis is false. But more importantly, even if significance is not attained, it is just as important to know what does not work as what does. The researcher's task is to carry out a well-designed, well-analyzed study. It is the researcher's responsibility to provide a fair and valid examination of the study hypotheses. It is not the researcher's task to reject the null hypothesis or produce statistically significant results. If researchers knew the results of their study beforehand, there would be no need for research.

If problems occurred within your study, you should of course describe them in detail. For example, if your study encountered high participant mortality, or if intact groups were compared instead of randomly selected ones, this should be reported. There are many problems or threats to validity that can arise in a study that are not the researcher's fault. You should report these when describing your research results. But do not rationalize. If your study was well planned and well conducted, and no unforeseen mishaps occurred, do not try to come up with some reason why your study did not "come out right." It may very well have "come out right"; remember, the null hypothesis might be true only for this particular study.

Unhypothesized Results

Results that are not hypothesized but appear during a study should be interpreted with great care. Often, during a study, an apparent relationship will be noticed that was not hypothesized. For example, you might notice that the experimental group appears to require fewer examples than the control group to learn new math concepts—an unhypothesized relationship. In such a circumstance, do not go and change your original hypothesis to conform to this new apparent finding, and don't add the unhypothesized finding as a new hypothesis. Hypotheses should be formulated a priori—before the study—on the basis of deductions from theory, experience, or both. A true test of a hypothesis comes from its ability to explain and predict what *will* happen, not *what* is happening. You can, however, collect and analyze data on these unforeseen relationships and present your results as such. A later study, conducted by yourself or another investigator, can be specifically designed to test a hypothesis related to the findings. Do not fall into the trap, however, of searching frantically for something that might be significant if your study does not appear to be going as hypothesized. Fishing expeditions in experimental studies are just as bad as fishing expeditions in correlational studies.

Statistical and Methodological Issues

Inferential statistics allow researchers to make inferences about a population based on a sample. For inferences and conclusions about a target population to be valid and legitimate, two factors must apply: the sample must be representative, and the assumptions of the statistical test must be met. When randomization is not possible, as is often the case in educational research, researchers choose their samples by matching or selecting intact groups. The lack of randomized samples, however, can introduce bias into a study and limit its usefulness. Similarly, the statistical procedures used to analyze data rely on certain assumptions. For example, most parametric statistics assume an underlying normal distribution and that each participant's scores are independent of any other participant's scores. If these assumptions are not met, the statistics are less valid and research generalizations are weakened.

A number of methodological practices can lead to invalid or inaccurate research results. Three such practices are ignoring measurement error, low statistical power, and performing multiple comparisons. Most statistical models assume error-free measurement, particularly of the independent variables. However, as discussed in Chapter 5, measurements are seldom error free. Large amounts of measurement error hamper the ability to find statistically significant research results. Recall that in parametric significance tests, the denominator is a measure of error. Thus, the larger the denominator, the larger the numerator must be to attain significance.

Statistical power refers to the ability of a significance test to avoid a Type II error—that is, to correctly reject the null hypothesis. If an analysis has little statistical power, the researcher is likely to overlook or miss the outcome she is seeking. The analysis does not reveal a significant difference that would have been evident if the statistical power had been greater. The power of a significance test depends on four interrelated factors: (1) the sample size, (2) the significance level selected, (3) the directionality of the significance test, and (4) the effect size, which indicates degree of the departure from the null hypothesis. The greater the departure from the null hypothesis, the greater the effect size. As the sample size, significance level, and effect size increase, so does the power of the significance test. For example, power increases automatically with an increase in sample size. Thus, virtually any difference can be made significant if the sample is large enough. However, it is difficult to interpret the practical meaning of small but significant results obtained primarily by using a very large sample. In addition, the higher the level of significance at which the null hypothesis will be rejected, the more powerful the test. Increasing the significance level, say, from .05 to .10, increases power by making it easier to reject the null hypothesis. Further, if a one-tailed test is justified, it will increase the power to reject the null hypothesis (reduce the chance of a Type II error).

Although researchers are likely to know the significance level of a study and its sample size, they are not likely to know the effect size. Without all three pieces of information, the power of the statistical test cannot be determined. Thus, three strategies are used to estimate the effect size.[1] First, the effect sizes of studies of the same phenomenon can be found and used as guidelines for the likely effect size in the proposed study. Second, a cutoff score below which an effect size is judged unimportant may be used to estimate effect size. For example, a researcher might decide that if a new treatment did not have an effect size of .40 or higher, it would not be worth pursuing. Thus, an effect size of .40 would be chosen. Third, conventional, generally agreed-on definitions of small, medium, and large effect sizes can be chosen. For example, for *t* tests, an effect size of .20 is considered small, .50 is considered medium, and .80 is considered high. Upon choosing desired effect size (say, .50) and a *t* test significance level (say, .05), the researcher can consult a table that shows the total number of participants needed in each group in the study (in this case, 30).

---

[1] *Applied Multiple Regression/Correlation Analysis for the Behavioral Sciences*, by J. Cohen and P. Cohen, 1975, Hillsdale, NJ: Lawrence Erlbaum Associates.

Normally, a researcher examines the power of a study before beginning it in order to determine whether the power will be sufficient. If the examination shows that the power is insufficient, the researcher can revise the study to increase power, usually by increasing the sample size or significance level.

Another statistical issue is the use of multiple comparison techniques, such as the Scheffé, to test the significance of a large number of means. This practice can lead to erroneous interpretations. Simply put, the more significance tests one carries out in a study, the more likely that false rejections of the null hypotheses (Type I errors) will occur. Suppose, for example, that a researcher did 100 significance tests at the .05 level. Suppose also that there really were no significance differences among all the 100 tests. However, given the .05 level, how many of the tests are likely to be significant? How about at least 5? Remember, we deal in probabilities, not certainties, and at the .05 level we leave 5% for error. In simple terms, a large number of multiple comparisons enhances the likelihood of Type I errors.

Statistical Versus Practical Significance

The difference between statistical significance and practical significance is often unclear to those who deal with statistical results. The fact that results are statistically significant does not automatically mean that they are of any educational value—that is, that they have practical significance. Results that are statistically significant are unlikely to have occurred by chance (they are likely to occur by chance only a small percentage of the time, say, 5%). Thus, the observed statistical relationship or difference is probably a *real* one, but not necessarily an *important* one. Significance in the statistical sense is, as noted in the previous section, largely a function of sample size, significance level, and a valid research design. For example, very large samples can result in statistically significant relationships or differences but have no real practical use to anybody. As the sample size increases, the error term (denominator) tends to decrease and thus increases the r or t ratio so that very large samples with very small correlations or mean differences may become significant. A mean difference of two points might be statistically significant but probably not worth the effort of revising a curriculum.

Thus, in a way, the smaller sample sizes typically used in educational research studies actually have a redeeming feature. Given that smaller sample sizes mean less power, and given that a greater mean difference is probably required for rejection of the null hypothesis, typical education sample sizes are probably more practically significant than if much larger samples were involved. Of course, lack of statistical power due to small sample sizes may keep researchers from finding some important relationships. In any event, you should always take care in interpreting results. The fact that Method A is significantly more effective than Method B statistically does not mean that the whole world should immediately adopt Method A! Always consider the practical significance of statistically significant differences.

Another concern in interpreting the results of research is the difference between research precision and research accuracy. *Precision* refers to how narrowly an estimate is specified. *Accuracy* refers to how close an estimate is to the true value. Estimates can be precise but not accurate. Often a computer user or a zealous calculator user will report data to the 6th or 10th decimal place—for example, 25.046093 or 7.28403749. Such precision is not useful. What is important is the accuracy of the calculated estimates, not the number of digits used to state it. Accuracy is more important in interpreting research outcomes than precision.

In sum, a number of considerations go into interpreting the results of research, including methodological and statistical factors as well as concerns over the difference between statistical and practical significance.

Replication of Results

Perhaps the strongest support for a research hypothesis comes from replication—from doing a study again and producing the same or similar results. The second (third, etc.) study may be a repetition of the original study, using the same or different subjects, or it may represent an alternative approach to testing the same hypothesis. Repeating the study with the same subjects is feasible only in certain types of research, such as single-subject designs. Repeating the study with different subjects in the same or different settings increases the generalizability of the findings.

The need for replication is especially great when an unusual or new relationship is found, or when the results have practical significance so that the treatment investigated might really make a difference. Interpretation and discussion of a replicated finding will invariably be less tentative than a first-time-ever finding, and rightly so. The significance of a relationship may also be enhanced if it is replicated in a more natural setting. A highly controlled study, for example, might find that Method A is more effective than Method B in a laboratory-like environment. Interpreting and discussing the results in terms of practical significance and implications for classroom practice would have to be done with caution. If the same results could then be obtained in a classroom situation, however, the researcher could be less tentative concerning their generalizability.

SUMMARY

Verifying and Storing Data

1. Whether you do your analyses by hand, calculator, or computer, all data should be thoroughly checked and stored in an organized manner.
2. Verification involves double-checking the data and evaluating the research results. Coded data should be compared with uncoded data to make sure all data were coded properly.
3. When analyses are done by hand, or with a calculator, both the accuracy of the computations and the reasonableness of the results need to be checked. When analyses are done by computer, the key concern is inputing the data correctly.
4. All of the data should be carefully labeled with as many identification labels as possible, such as the dates of the study, the nature of each treatment group, and whether data are pretest data, posttest data, or data for a control variable. Data stored on a computer hard drive should be copied onto a disk or CD-ROM and kept as a backup.

Interpreting Quantitative Research Results

5. The results of statistical analyses need to be interpreted in terms of the purpose of the study and the original research hypothesis, and with respect to other studies that have been conducted in the same area of research.
6. The researcher must discuss both whether the results support the research hypothesis and whether the results are in agreement with other findings. The researcher should explain why the results do or do not do these things.
7. A supported research hypothesis does not necessarily mean that your treatment would "work" with different populations, different materials, and different dependent variables.
8. Failure to reject a null hypothesis does not necessarily mean that your research hypothesis is false, but even if it is, it is just as important to know what does not work as what does work.
9. Unhypothesized results should be interpreted with great care and should be kept and analyzed separately from the hypotheses stated before the start of the study.
10. Unhypothesized findings may form the basis for a later study.
11. Statistical and methodological issues influence the interpretation of research results. When statistical requirements such as random selection and normal distributions are not met, research generalizations are weakened. Methodological factors such as ignoring measurement error, performing multiple comparisons, and using small samples can lead to inaccurate or invalid research results.
12. Statistical power is the ability of a significance test to avoid a Type II error by correctly rejecting the null hypothesis. Four factors influence power: sample size, significance level, direction of the significance test, and the effect size. A table can be

consulted to determine how many participants are required to attain a certain power level given the significance level and desired effect size.

13. The fact that results are statistically significant does not automatically mean that they are of any educational value. With very large samples, a very small mean difference may yield a significant t. A mean difference of two points might be statistically significant but probably not worth the effort of revising a curriculum.

14. Replication is the repetition of a study or retesting of its hypothesis. The need for replication is especially great when an unusual or new relationship is found in a study or when the results have practical significance.

Now go to the Companion Website at www.prenhall.com/gay to assess your understanding of chapter content with Practice Quiz, apply comprehension in Applying What You Know, broaden your knowledge about research in Web Links, and expand your research skills in Evaluating Articles, Analyzing Qualitative Data, Analyzing Quantitative Data, and Research Tools and Tips.

PERFORMANCE CRITERIA

Task 7 should look like the results section of a research report. The data that you generate (scores you make up for each subject) should make sense. If your dependent variable is IQ, for example, do not generate scores such as 2, 11, and 15; generate scores such as 84, 110, and 120. Got it? Unlike in a real study, you can make your study turn out any way you want!

Depending on the scale of measurement represented by your data, select and compute the appropriate descriptive statistics.

Depending on the scale of measurement represented by your data, your research hypothesis, and your research design, select and compute the appropriate test of significance. Determine the statistical significance of your results for a selected probability level. Present your results in a summary table, and relate how the significance or nonsignificance of your results supports or does not support your original research hypothesis. For example, you might say the following:

> Computation of a *t* test for independent samples ($\alpha = .05$) indicated that the group that received weekly reviews retained significantly more than the group that received daily reviews (see Table 1). Therefore, the original hypothesis that "ninth-grade algebra students who receive a weekly review will retain significantly more algebraic concepts than ninth-grade algebra students who receive a daily review" was supported.

An example of the table referred to (Table 1) appears at the bottom of this page.

An example that illustrates the performance called by for Task 7 appears on the following pages. (See Task 7 Example.) Note that the scores are based on the administration of the test described in the Task 5 example. Note also that the student used a formula used in meta-analysis (described briefly in Chapter 2) to calculate effect size (ES). The basic formula is

$$ES = \frac{\overline{X}_e - \overline{X}_c}{SD_c}$$

where

$\overline{X}_e$ = the mean (average) score for the experimental group

$\overline{X}_c$ = the mean (average) score for the control group

SD_c = the standard deviation (variability) of the scores for the control group

Although your actual calculations should not be part of Task 7, they should be attached to it. We have attached the step-by-step calculations for the Task 7 example. You may also perform your calculations using SPSS 12.0 and attach these computations as well.

Additional examples of the tasks are included in the *Student Study Guide* that accompanies this text.

Table 1

Means, standard deviations, and *t* for the daily-review and weekly-review grops on the delayed retention test

	Review Group		
	Daily	Weekly	*t*
M	44.82	52.68	2.56*
SD	5.12	6.00	

Note. Maximum score score = 65.

$df = 38, p < .05.$

⁝⁝ TASK 7 Example

1

Effect of Interactive Multimedia on the Achievement of 10th-Grade Biology Students

Results

Prior to the beginning of the study, after the 60 students were randomly selected and assigned to experimental and control groups, final science grades from the previous school year were obtained from school records in order to check initial group equivalence. Examination of the means and a t test for independent samples ($\alpha = .05$) indicated essentially no difference between the groups (see Table 1). A t test for independent samples was used because the groups were randomly formed and the data were interval.

Table 1

Means, Standard Deviation, and t Tests for the Experimental and Control Groups

Score	Group		t
	IMM instruction[a]	Traditional instruction[a]	
Prior Grades			
M	87.47	87.63	−0.08*
SD	8.19	8.05	
Posttest NPSS:B			
M	32.27	26.70	4.22**
SD	4.45	5.69	

Note. Maximum score for prior grades = 100. Maximum score for posttest = 40.

[a]$n = 30$.

*$p > .05$.   **$p < .05$.

At the completion of the eight-month study, during the first week in May, scores on the NPSS:B were compared, also using a t test for independent samples. As Table 1 indicates, scores of the experimental and control groups were significantly different. In fact, the experimental group scored approximately one standard deviation higher than the control group ($ES = .98$). Therefore, the original hypothesis that "10th-grade biology students whose teachers use IMM as part of their instructional technique will exhibit significantly higher achievement than 10th-grade biology students whose teachers do not use IMM" was supported.

PRIOR GRADES

S	EXPERIMENTAL			CONTROL	
	X_1	X_1^2		X_2	X_2^2
1	72	5184		71	5041
2	74	5476		75	5625
3	76	5776		75	5625
4	76	5776		77	5929
5	77	5929		78	6084
6	78	6084		78	6084
7	78	6084		79	6241
8	79	6241		80	6400
9	80	6400		81	6561
10	84	7056		83	6889
11	85	7225		85	7225
12	87	7569		88	7744
13	87	7569		88	7744
14	88	7744		89	7921
15	89	7921		89	7921
16	89	7921		89	7921
17	90	8100		90	8100
18	91	8281		91	8281
19	92	8464		92	8464
20	93	8649		92	8464
21	93	8649		93	8649
22	93	8649		94	8836
23	94	8836		94	8836
24	95	9025		95	9025
25	95	9025		96	9216
26	97	9409		96	9216
27	97	9409		97	9409
28	98	9604		97	9409
29	98	9604		98	9604
30	99	9801		99	9801
	2624	231,460		2629	232,265
	ΣX_1	ΣX_1^2		ΣX_2	ΣX_2^2

$$\overline{X_1} = \frac{\Sigma X_1}{n_1} = \frac{2624}{30} = 87.47 \qquad \overline{X_2} = \frac{\Sigma X_2}{n_2} = \frac{2629}{30} = 87.63$$

$$SD_1 = \sqrt{\frac{SS_1}{n_1 - 1}} \qquad\qquad SD_2 = \sqrt{\frac{SS_2}{n_2 - 1}}$$

$$SS_1 = \sum X_1^2 - \frac{\left(\sum X_1\right)^2}{n_1} \qquad SS_2 = \sum X_2^2 - \frac{\left(\sum X_2\right)^2}{n_2}$$

$$= 231{,}460 - \frac{(2624)^2}{30} \qquad\qquad = 232{,}265 - \frac{(2629)^2}{30}$$

$$= 231{,}460 - \frac{6885376}{30} \qquad\qquad = 232{,}265 - \frac{6911641}{30}$$

$$= 231{,}460 - 229{,}512.53 \qquad\qquad = 232{,}265 - 230388.03$$

$$SS_1 = 1947.47 \qquad\qquad\qquad SS_2 = 1876.97$$

$$SD_1 = \sqrt{\frac{1947.47}{29}} \qquad\qquad SD_2 = \sqrt{\frac{1876.97}{29}}$$

$$= \sqrt{67.154} \qquad\qquad\qquad = \sqrt{64.72}$$

$$SD_1 = 8.19 \qquad\qquad\qquad SD_2 = 8.05$$

$$t = \frac{\bar{X}_1 - \bar{X}_2}{\sqrt{\left(\frac{SS_1 + SS_2}{n_1 + n_2 - 2}\right)\left(\frac{1}{n_1} + \frac{1}{n_2}\right)}} \qquad = \frac{87.47 - 87.63}{\sqrt{\left(\frac{1947.47 + 1876.97}{30 + 30 - 2}\right)\left(\frac{1}{30} + \frac{1}{30}\right)}}$$

$$= \frac{-0.16}{\sqrt{\left(\frac{3824.44}{58}\right)\left(\frac{1}{15}\right)}}$$

Note: the t table does not have $\underline{df} = 58$. To be conservative I used $\underline{df} = 40$. For $\underline{df} = 40$ the table value is 2.021

$$= \frac{-0.16}{\sqrt{(65.9386)(.0667)}}$$

$$= \frac{-0.16}{\sqrt{4.398}}$$

$$= \frac{-0.16}{2.097}$$

$$t = -.08 \qquad df = 58 \qquad p < .05$$

POSTTEST   NATIONAL PROFICIENCY SURVEY SERIES: BIOLOGY

S	EXPERIMENTAL		CONTROL	
	X_1	X_1^2	X_2	X_2^2
1	20	400	15	225
2	24	576	16	256
3	26	676	18	324
4	27	729	20	400
5	28	784	21	441
6	29	841	22	484
7	29	841	22	484
8	29	841	23	529
9	30	900	24	576
10	31	961	24	576
11	31	961	25	625
12	31	961	25	625
13	32	1024	25	625
14	32	1024	26	676
15	33	1089	26	676
16	33	1089	27	729
17	33	1089	27	729
18	34	1156	28	784
19	34	1156	29	841
20	35	1225	29	841
21	35	1225	30	900
22	35	1225	30	900
23	36	1296	31	961
24	36	1296	31	961
25	36	1296	32	1024
26	37	1369	33	1089
27	37	1369	34	1156
28	38	1444	35	1225
29	38	1444	36	1296
30	39	1521	37	1369
	968	31808	801	22327
	ΣX_1	ΣX_1^2	ΣX_2	ΣX_2^2

$$\overline{X}_1 = \frac{\Sigma x_1}{n_1} = \frac{968}{30} = 32.27 \qquad \overline{X}_2 = \frac{\Sigma x_2}{n_2} = \frac{801}{30} = 26.70$$

$$SD_1 = \sqrt{\frac{SS_1}{n_1 - 1}} \qquad\qquad SD_2 = \sqrt{\frac{SS_2}{n_2 - 1}}$$

$$SS_1 = \sum x_1^2 - \frac{\left(\sum x_1\right)^2}{n_1} \qquad\qquad SS_2 = \sum x_2^2 - \frac{\left(\sum x_2\right)^2}{n_2}$$

$$= 31808 - \frac{(968)^2}{30} \qquad\qquad = 22327 - \frac{(801)^2}{30}$$

$$= 31808 - \frac{937024}{30} \qquad\qquad = 22327 - \frac{641601}{30}$$

$$= 31808 - 31234.13 \qquad\qquad = 22327 - 21386.70$$

$$SS_1 = 573.87 \qquad\qquad SS_2 = 940.30$$

$$SD_1 = \sqrt{\frac{573.87}{29}} \qquad\qquad SD_2 = \sqrt{\frac{940.30}{29}}$$

$$= \sqrt{19.789} \qquad\qquad = \sqrt{32.424}$$

$$SD_1 = 4.45 \qquad\qquad SD_2 = 5.69$$

$$t = \frac{\bar{x}_1 - \bar{x}_2}{\sqrt{\left(\frac{SS_1 + SS_2}{n_1 + n_2 - 2}\right)\left(\frac{1}{n_1} + \frac{1}{n_2}\right)}} \qquad = \frac{32.27 - 26.70}{\sqrt{\left(\frac{573.87 + 940.30}{30 + 30 - 2}\right)\left(\frac{1}{30} + \frac{1}{30}\right)}}$$

$$= \frac{5.57}{\sqrt{\left(\frac{1514.17}{58}\right)\left(\frac{1}{15}\right)}}$$

$$= \frac{5.57}{\sqrt{(26.1064)(.0667)}}$$

$$= \frac{5.57}{\sqrt{1.7404}}$$

$$= \frac{5.57}{1.3192}$$

$$t = 4.22 \qquad df = 58 \qquad p < .05$$

"Qualitative researchers spend a great deal of time with participants and are immersed in the research setting. The detailed recording of the processes occurring in the natural setting provides the basis for understanding the setting, the participants, and their interactions." (p. 402)

Overview of Qualitative Research

OBJECTIVES

After reading Chapter 14, you should be able to do the following:

1. State the definition and purpose of qualitative research.
2. Describe the six steps in the qualitative research process.
3. Identify different qualitative research approaches.
4. Describe the characteristics of qualitative research.
5. State the definition of validity in qualitative research.
6. Describe strategies to address the trustworthiness (validity) of qualitative research.
7. Describe strategies to address the replicability (reliability) of qualitative research.
8. Describe the relationship between validity and reliability in qualitative research.
9. Describe the role of ethics in qualitative research.

The goal of Chapters 14 through 18 is for you to be able to develop a qualitative research study: develop a qualitative topic, identify data collection and analysis procedures, and consider other important qualitative research issues (e.g., getting started). Completing these chapters should enable you to complete the following task.

TASK 8

Apply the six steps of qualitative research to develop a plan for your own qualitative research study. (See Performance Criteria at the end of Chapter 18, p. 483).

QUALITATIVE RESEARCH: DEFINITION AND PURPOSE

Simplistically put, **qualitative research** is the collection, analysis, and interpretation of comprehensive narrative and visual data in order to gain insights into a particular phenomenon of interest. The purposes of qualitative research are broad in scope and center around promoting a deep and holistic or complex *understanding* of a particular phenomenon, such as an environment, a process, or even a belief.

The term *qualitative research* is used not so much because it accurately describes a unique strategy of inquiry, but rather because it conveniently differentiates it from what we refer to as quantitative research. Descriptive, correlational, causal–comparative, experimental research, and single-subject research (discussed in Chapters 6–10) are all considered forms of quantitative research because they all primarily involve the collection and analysis of *numerical* data (e.g., test scores). Qualitative research, on the other hand, involves mostly nonnumerical data, such as extensive notes taken at a research site, interview data, videotape and audiotape recordings, and other nonnumerical artifacts.

Qualitative research differs from quantitative research in two key ways: (1) Qualitative research often involves the simultaneous collection of a wealth of narrative and visual data over an extended period of time, and (2) as much as is possible, data collection occurs in a naturalistic setting. In other words, qualitative researchers try to study phenomena where they naturally occur. This is not the case with quantitative studies, where the research is conducted in researcher-controlled environments under researcher-controlled conditions and where the activities of data collection, analysis, and writing are separate, discrete activities. Because qualitative researchers strive to study things in their naturalistic settings, qualitative research is sometimes referred to as *naturalistic research, naturalistic inquiry,* or *field-oriented research.*

These two characteristics of qualitative research, the simultaneous study of many aspects of a phenomenon and the attempt to study things as they exist naturally, help in part to explain the recent growing enthusiasm for qualitative research in education. Some researchers and educators feel that certain kinds of educational problems and questions do not lend themselves well to quantitative methods, which use principally numerical analysis and try to control variables in what are very complex environments. As qualitative researchers point out, findings should be derived from research conducted in real-world settings in order to have relevance to real-world settings.

:: THE QUALITATIVE RESEARCH PROCESS

In Chapter 1 we presented four general, conceptual research steps. In this chapter we expand the steps to six to help you delineate your tasks. Both quantitative researchers and qualitative researchers follow the six basic steps; however, as we shall see in subsequent chapters, the application of the steps differs. For example, the research procedures in quantitative research are often more rigid than those in qualitative research. Similarly, although both quantitative and qualitative researchers collect data, the nature of the data differs. Figure 14.1 compares the

FIGURE 14.1

Characteristics of quantitative and qualitative research
Source: Educational Research: Planning, Conducting, and Evaluating by Creswell, John W., © 2002. Adapted by permission of Pearson Education, Inc., Upper Saddle River, NJ.

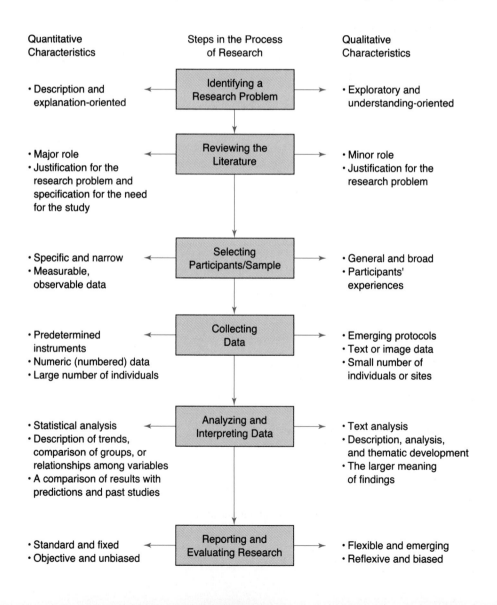

Quantitative Characteristics	Steps in the Process of Research	Qualitative Characteristics
• Description and explanation-oriented	**Identifying a Research Problem**	• Exploratory and understanding-oriented
• Major role • Justification for the research problem and specification for the need for the study	**Reviewing the Literature**	• Minor role • Justification for the research problem
• Specific and narrow • Measurable, observable data	**Selecting Participants/Sample**	• General and broad • Participants' experiences
• Predetermined instruments • Numeric (numbered) data • Large number of individuals	**Collecting Data**	• Emerging protocols • Text or image data • Small number of individuals or sites
• Statistical analysis • Description of trends, comparison of groups, or relationships among variables • A comparison of results with predictions and past studies	**Analyzing and Interpreting Data**	• Text analysis • Description, analysis, and thematic development • The larger meaning of findings
• Standard and fixed • Objective and unbiased	**Reporting and Evaluating Research**	• Flexible and emerging • Reflexive and biased

six steps of qualitative and quantitative research and lists traits that characterize each approach at every step.

For the most part, the methods used to conduct varied types of qualitative research (for example, ethnographic research, narrative research, and case study) are similar. Because of these commonalities, we will focus on general methods used to identify research topics, review related literature, select participants, collect data, analyze and interpret data, and report and evaluate the research results:

1. *Identifying a research topic.* The researcher identifies a topic or study of interest to research. Often the initial topic is narrowed to be more manageable.
2. *Reviewing the literature.* The researcher examines existing research to identify useful information and strategies for carrying out the study.
3. *Selecting participants.* The researcher must select participants to provide data collection. Participants are purposefully selected (i.e., not randomly selected) and are usually fewer in number than in quantitative samples.
4. *Collecting data.* The researcher collects data from participants. Qualitative data tend to be gathered from interviews, observations, and artifacts.
5. *Analyzing and interpreting data.* The researcher analyzes the themes and results of the collected data and provides interpretations of the data.
6. *Reporting and evaluating the research.* The researcher summarizes and integrates the qualitative data in narrative and visual form.

:: QUALITATIVE RESEARCH APPROACHES

Table 14.1 provides a brief description of some of the most commonly utilized qualitative research approaches. Examining the table shows that the primary difference among the

TABLE 14.1	Common qualitative research approaches
Approach	**Key Question**
case study	What are the characteristics of this particular entity, phenomenon, or person?
ethnography	What are the cultural patterns and perspectives of this group in its natural setting?
ethology	How do the origins, characteristics, and culture of different societies compare to one another?
ethnomethodology	How do people make sense of their everyday activities in order to behave in socially accepted ways?
grounded theory	How is an inductively derived theory about a phenomenon grounded in the data in a particular setting?
phenomenology	What is the experience of an activity or concept from these particular participants' perspective?
symbolic interaction	How do people construct meanings and shared perspectives by interacting with others?
historical research	How does one systematically collect and evaluate data to understand and interpret past events?

Source: M. Q. Patton, *Qualitative Evaluation and Research Methods,* copyright © 1990, by Sage Publications, Inc. Adapted by permission of Sage Publications, Inc.

approaches is in the particulars of the social context examined and the participants selected. For example, some qualitative researchers focus on the exploration of phenomenon that occur within a bounded system (e.g., a person, event, program, life cycle) (case study); some focus in depth on a group's cultural patterns and perspectives to understand participants' behavior and their context (ethnography); some examine how multiple cultures compare to one another (ethology); some examine people's understanding of their daily activities (ethnomethodology); some derive theory using multiple steps of data collection and interpretation that link actions of participants to general social science theories or work inductively to arrive at a theory that explains a particular phenomenon (grounded theory); some ask what is the meaning of this experience for these participants (phenomenology); some look for common understandings that have emerged to give meaning to participants' interactions (symbolic interaction); some seek to understand the past by studying documents, relics, and interviews (historical research); and some describe the lives of individuals (narrative). Overall, a collective, generic name for these qualitative approaches is **interpretive research.**[1]

As mentioned in Chapter 1, in this text we focus on two qualitative approaches: narrative research (Chapter 16) and ethnographic research (Chapter 17).

:: CHARACTERISTICS OF QUALITATIVE RESEARCH

The central focus of qualitative research is to provide an understanding of a social setting or activity as viewed from the perspective of the research participants. In addition to involving the collection of narrative and visual data over a period of time in a natural, nonmanipulated setting, qualitative studies share several other characteristics.

Qualitative researchers spend a great deal of time with participants and are immersed in the research setting. The detailed recording of the processes occurring in the natural setting provides the basis for understanding the setting, the participants, and their interactions. Without this immersion, the search for understanding would elude the qualitative researcher.

The focus of qualitative research is on individual, person-to-person interactions. The researcher strives to describe the meaning of the findings from the perspective of the research participants. To achieve this focus, the researcher gathers data directly from the participants.

Qualitative researchers avoid making premature decisions or assumptions about the study and remain open to alternative explanations. They typically wait until they are in the research context before making tentative decisions based on initial data analysis.

Qualitative data are analyzed inductively. The qualitative researcher does not impose an organizing structure or make assumptions about the relationships among the data before collecting evidence. Rather, the researcher focuses on discovery and understanding, which requires flexibility in the research design. As the data are analyzed, the researcher seeks to find patterns, relationships, or common themes among the data. The more data collected, the stronger the foundation for the inductive analysis.

Qualitative research reports include clear and detailed descriptions of the study that include the voices of the participants. The report also includes a description of the role of the researcher and her or his biases or preferences concerning the research topic or research processes. Qualitative researchers must also remain vigilant to their responsibility to obtain ongoing informed consent from participants and to ensure their ethical treatment.

---

[1] For a discussion, see *Qualitative Evaluation and Research Methods* (3rd ed.), by M. Q. Patton, 2002, Thousand Oaks, CA: Sage.

:: VALIDITY AND RELIABILITY IN QUALITATIVE RESEARCH

Validity in Qualitative Research

In qualitative research, **validity** is the degree to which the qualitative data we collect accurately gauge what we are trying to measure. As you can see, the definition is essentially the same as that given in the discussion of quantitative research in Chapter 5—that is, the degree to which a test measures what it is intended to measure. For example, teachers will ask, "Are the results of this standardized test really valid?" Or teachers will comment, "My students did poorly on the history test I gave them, but I'm not sure it's an accurate representation of what they really know." Both of these scenarios raise issues about the validity of the data, that is, whether or not the data measures what it claims to measure. Historically, validity has been linked to numerically based quantitative research. However, as qualitative research became more popular in the late 1970s and early 1980s, qualitative researchers felt pressure to begin to justify and defend the accuracy and credibility of their studies. Two common terms used to describe validity in qualitative research are *trustworthiness* and *understanding*.

Qualitative researchers can establish the **trustworthiness** of their research by addressing the credibility, transferability, dependability, and confirmability of their studies and findings.[2] First, a researcher must take into account all the complexities in the study being conducted and address problems that are not easily explained (*credibility*). The researcher should also include descriptive, context-relevant statements so the consumer can identify with the setting (*transferability*). Remember, qualitative researchers believe that everything they study is context-bound and do *not* seek to develop "truth" statements that can be generalized to larger groups of people. Therefore, qualitative researchers should include as much detail as possible so others can see the setting for themselves. Another issue the researcher needs to address is the stability of the data collected (*dependability*). Finally, the researcher should address the neutrality and objectivity of the data (*confirmability*).

According to Maxwell,[3] researchers can contribute to the trustworthiness of their research, and to the understanding of it, by addressing descriptive validity, interpretive validity, theoretical validity, generalizability, and evaluative validity. **Descriptive validity** refers to the factual accuracy of the account. Qualitative researchers must ensure that they are not distorting or making up anything they see or hear. For example, if the research study contains quotations from participants, the researcher must make sure that they are accurate. **Interpretive validity** refers to the meaning attributed to the behaviors or words of the participants being studied (the "participants' perspective"). The researcher must accurately interpret the participants' words or actions. For example, a participant might say something fully intended as a joke; if the researcher takes the participant seriously and presents the statement as such in the study, the participant will not be accurately portrayed. **Theoretical validity** refers to the ability of the research report to explain the phenomenon being studied in relation to a theory. For example, a narrative account about educational change processes in schools and the role of gender and power in these processes should help the reader of the account understand the theoretical construct involved and apply the theory to other aspects of the school community. **Evaluative validity** has to do with whether the researcher was objective enough to report the data in as unbiased a way as possible, instead of making judgments and evaluations of the data. No account is immune to questions of whether the qualitative researcher

---

[2] "Criteria for Assessing the Trustworthiness of Naturalistic Inquiries," by E. G. Guba, 1981, *Educational Communication and Technology Journal, 29,* pp. 75–91.
[3] "Understanding and Validity in Qualitative Research," by J. A. Maxwell, 1992, *Harvard Educational Review, 62*(3), pp. 279–300.

TABLE 14.2	Maxwell's criteria for validity of qualitative research
Criteria	**Definition**
Descriptive validity	Factual accuracy.
Interpretive validity	Concern for the participant's perspective.
Theoretical validity	The ability of the research report to explain the phenomenon that has been studied and described.
Generalizability	*Internal generalizability:* Generalizability within the community that has been studied.
	External generalizability: Generalizability to settings that were not studied by the researcher.
Evaluative validity	Whether the researcher was able to present the data without being evaluative or judgmental.

Source: From "Understanding and Validity in Qualitative Research," by J. A. Maxwell, 1992, *Harvard Educational Review,* *62*(3), pp. 279–300. Adapted with permission.

was focusing on being evaluative instead of being concerned with describing and understanding the phenomenon being studied. We discuss generalizability later in the chapter. Table 14.2 shows Maxwell's criteria for validity of qualitative research.

Strategies for Ensuring the Validity of Qualitative Research

When conducting qualitative research, you can facilitate the trustworthiness and understanding of your research findings by using a number of strategies. The followed strategies were adapted from Guba's classic discussion in "Criteria for Assessing the Trustworthiness of Naturalistic Inquiries":[4]

- *Do prolonged participation at the study site* to overcome distortions produced by the presence of researchers and to provide yourself with the opportunity to test biases and perceptions.
- *Do persistent observation* to identify pervasive qualities as well as atypical characteristics.
- *Do peer debriefing* to provide yourself with the opportunity to test your growing insights through interactions with other professionals. For example, most of us will be able to identify a critical friend, colleague, or significant other who would be willing and able to help us reflect on our research by listening, prompting, and recording our insights throughout the process.
- *Collect documents, films, videotapes, audio recordings, artifacts, and other "raw" or "slice-of-life" data items.*
- *Do member checks* to test the overall report with the study's participants before sharing it in final form.
- *Establish structural corroboration or coherence* to ensure that there are no internal conflicts or contradictions.
- *Establish referential adequacy*—that is, check that analyses and interpretations accurately reflect the documents, recordings, films, and other primary sources of data collected as part of the study.
- *Collect detailed descriptive data* that will permit comparison of a given context (classroom/school) to other possible contexts to which transfer might be contemplated.
- *Develop detailed descriptions of the context* to make judgments about fittingness with other contexts possible.

---

[4] "Criteria for Assessing the Trustworthiness," Guba, 1981.

TABLE 14.3	Guba's criteria for validity of qualitative research	
Criteria	**Definition**	**Strategies**
Credibility	The researcher's ability to take into account all of the complexities that present themselves in a study and to deal with patterns that are not easily explained.	Do prolonged participation at study site. Do persistent observation. Do peer debriefing. Practice triangulation. Collect "slice-of-life" data items. Do member checks. Establish structural corroboration or coherence. Establish referential adequacy.
Transferability	The researcher's belief that everything is context-bound.	Collect detailed descriptive data. Develop detailed descriptions of the context.
Dependability	The stability of the data.	Overlap methods. Establish an "audit trail."
Confirmability	The neutrality or objectivity of the data collected.	Practice triangulation. Practice reflexivity.

Source: From "Criteria for Assessing the Trustworthiness of Naturalistic Inquiries," by E. G. Guba, 1981, *Educational Communication and Technology Journal, 29*(1), pp. 75–91. Adapted with permission.

■ *Establish an "audit trail."* This process makes it possible for an external "auditor" (maybe a critical friend, principal, or graduate student) to examine the processes of data collection, analysis, and interpretation. This audit trail may take the form of a written description of each process and may include access to original field notes, artifacts, videotapes, photographs, archival data, and so on.

■ *Practice triangulation.* **Triangulation** is the process of using multiple methods, data collection strategies, and data sources to obtain a more complete picture of what is being studied and to cross-check information. The strength of qualitative research lies in collecting information in many ways, rather than relying solely on one, and often two or more methods can be used in such a way that the weakness of one is compensated by the strength of another. For example, interviews with students may be used to contribute to our understanding of what we observed happening in a lesson.

■ *Practice reflexivity.* Intentionally reveal underlying assumptions or biases that may cause you to formulate a set of questions or present findings in a particular way. One technique for doing this is to keep a journal in which you record your reflections and musings on a regular basis.

Table 14.3 lists Guba's criteria for establishing the validity of qualitative research.

In addition to the strategies just listed, criteria developed by Wolcott[5] provide qualitative researchers with practical options for making sure their research is trustworthy, robust, and contributes to an understanding of the phenomenon under investigation. The strategies described in the following paragraphs have been adapted from Wolcott.

[5] *Transforming Qualitative Data: Description, Analysis, and Interpretation,* by H. F. Wolcott, 1994, Thousand Oaks, CA: Sage.

Talk little, listen a lot. As qualitative researchers conducting interviews, asking questions, or engaging children, parents, and colleagues in discussions about the problem being studied, we ought to carefully monitor the ratio of listening to talking. For example, interviewing children can be difficult work—our best thought-out questions elicit painfully brief replies, and we are left wondering what to do next. Those of us who are teachers are in the business of talking for a living, so it comes quite naturally to us to jump in with our own answer for the child. The trustworthiness of our inquiries will be enhanced if we can bite our tongues, think of some other probing questions, and wait patiently for the respondents to respond.

Record observations accurately. It is nearly impossible to record all observations while conducting research in a setting. It is important, however, that you record observations as soon as possible to accurately capture the essence of what took place. Audio and video recordings can assist with our efforts to record accurately, but there will still be many occasions when, as participant observers, we have to rely on our field notes, journals, or memories.

Begin writing early. Make time to write down your reflections in journals. The act of writing down your recollections of an observation will show you what blanks need to be filled in—for example, what questions need to be asked the next day or what should be the focus of your observations.

Let readers "see" for themselves. Include primary data in any narrative account to let the readers of your accounts (colleagues, principals, university professors) see the data for themselves. This may mean using charts, graphs, photographs, film—whatever you have collected. In so doing, you will draw the recipient of your work into the research process. *Showing* can be more persuasive than *telling*.

Report fully. In our quest to find neat answers and solutions to our problems, it is often easy to avoid keeping track of discrepant events and data. Just when we think we know the answer, some pieces of data come along to shatter the illusion of having neatly resolved the problem! We do not need to be fearful of discrepant data. After all, it is all grist for the research mill, and although we do not need to report everything, it is helpful to keep track of the discrepant data and to seek further explanation to understand what is happening in the setting.

Be candid. As a qualitative researcher, you should be candid about your work and should explicitly state in the research report any biases you may have about the inquiry you have undertaken. You also should spell out instances where judgments have been made, for it is easy to slip into a narrative that seeks to validate one's own position. Being candid may also provide an opportunity to be explicit about events that occurred during the study and that may have affected the outcomes.

Seek feedback. It is always a good idea to seek feedback from colleagues (and perhaps even students, parents, volunteers, and administrators) on your written study. Other readers will raise questions about things that you as the writer may have taken for granted. If readers raise questions about the accuracy of the account, you will have the opportunity to go back to the research setting and get the story right (or at least, not all wrong).

Write accurately. Examine the language you use in your written account to make sure you are communicating clearly. In addition to having others give you feedback, it is a good idea to read the account aloud to yourself to look for contradictions in the text. The accuracy of the account is critical to the validity of the study.

Figure 14.2 summarizes Wolcott's strategies for ensuring the validity of qualitative action research.[6]

---

[6] For further discussion of these points and a discussion of "When It Really Matters, Does Validity Really Matter?" see *Transforming Qualitative Data* (pp. 348–370), Wolcott, 1994.

```
_____  Talk a little, listen a lot.
_____  Record accurately.
_____  Begin writing early.
_____  Let readers "see" for themselves.
_____  Report fully.
_____  Be candid.
_____  Seek feedback.
_____  Write accurately.
```

FIGURE 14.2

Wolcott's strategies for ensuring the validity of action research
Source: From *Transforming Qualitative Data: Description, Analysis, and Interpretation* (pp. 348–370), by H. F. Wolcott, 1994, Thousand Oaks, CA: Sage. Copyright 1994 by Sage Publications. Adapted with permission.

Reliability in Qualitative Research

Reliability is the degree to which our study data consistently measure whatever they measure. Although the term *reliability* is usually used to refer to instruments and tests in quantitative research, qualitative researchers can also consider reliability in their studies. Instead of evaluating a test or an instrument for its reliability, qualitative researchers consider the reliability of the techniques they are using to gather data. For example, as qualitative researchers examine the results of their inquiry, they should consider whether the data would be consistently collected if the same techniques were utilized over time.

Reliability, however, is not the same thing as validity. Remember, a valid test that measures what it purports to measure will do so consistently over time. A reliable test may consistently measure the wrong thing!

Generalizability

Historically, research in education has concerned itself with **generalizability,** a term that refers to the applicability of findings to settings and contexts different from the one in which they were obtained. That is, based on the behavior of a small group (sample) of individuals, researchers try to explain the behavior of a larger group (population) of people. This view of generalizability, however, is not directly applicable to qualitative research.

The goal of qualitative research is to understand *what is happening* and *why.* Therefore, qualitative researchers are less concerned than quantitative researchers about the generalizability of their research. Qualitative researchers are not seeking to define ultimate truths, or solutions to problems that can transferred from a unique setting (sample) to a broader population. Qualitative researchers challenge the quantitative researcher's view that the only credible research is that which can be generalized to a larger population. The power of qualitative research is not in its generalizability although there may be some applicability and transferability of the findings from one qualitative study to a similar setting. It is in the *relevance* of the findings to the researcher or the audience of the research.

:: DOING THE RIGHT THING: THE ROLE OF ETHICS IN QUALITATIVE RESEARCH

The role of ethics in qualitative research can be considered in terms of how we treat the individuals with whom we interact in research settings. The very nature of the qualitative research enterprise provides the potential for conflict and harm. It is critical to the success of qualitative research efforts that everyone involved has a clear understanding of the intimate and open-ended nature of the research process and that participants are not "wronged" in the name of research. For this reason, it is important to think about ethical dilemmas *before* they occur. Considering the ethics of qualitative research before commencing the work is one way to ensure that you will be prepared to respond in an ethical, caring manner if difficult situations arise.

Qualitative research is intimate because there is little distance between researchers and their study participants. Qualitative research is open-ended because the direction of the research often unfolds during the course of the study. This significantly complicates the ability of qualitative researchers to obtain participants' "fully informed consent" to participate in the research process. As we discussed in Chapter 3, informed consent is central to research ethics. It is the principle that seeks to ensure that all human subjects retain autonomy and the ability to judge for themselves what risks are worth taking for the purpose of furthering scientific knowledge.

Ethical Guideposts

The following common sense ethical guideposts, adapted from Smith,[7] may help qualitative researchers respond appropriately when faced with ethical decisions before, during, and after a qualitative research inquiry.

Researchers should have an ethical perspective that is very close to their personal ethical position. This may seem like a statement of the obvious except for the caveat that as qualitative researchers we may find ourselves in situations that are foreign to us. For example, suppose that in a collaborative action research project focused on the effects of a new math problem-solving curriculum on student achievement and attitude, teachers are asked to administer a student attitude survey. The surveys are then analyzed by a team of teacher researchers representing different grades in the school. During the analysis it becomes clear that students in one of the groups are very unhappy with their math instruction and have supported their assertions with negative comments about the teacher. What will you do with the data? Should they be shared in an unedited form with the teacher? Who stands to be hurt in the process? What potential good can come from sharing the data? What assurances of confidentiality were given to the participants before collecting the data?

This scenario is not meant to scare you away from doing qualitative research. It is meant to illustrate the unexpected outcomes that occasionally face qualitative researchers. Smith's guidepost is an important one. You will potentially avoid such awkward situations if you clarify your own ethical perspectives at the outset. A values clarification activity that can be undertaken individually or collectively may be helpful. The point is this: Be prepared to respond in a manner that is comfortable and natural for you.

As you begin to clarify your personal, ethical perspective, it is worthwhile to reflect on how you would want to be treated as a participant in a research study. How would you feel if you were deceived by the researchers? What action would you take? How can you prevent research participants from feeling exploited? Again, there are no simple answers to these ethical questions.

Informed consent should take the form of a dialogue that mutually shapes the research and the results. Be clear about whether you need to seek permission from participants in the study. This may be determined by discussing the research project with a school administrator or central office person who can describe instances that require written permission (you must also check the requirements of your university's Institutional Review Board). For example, if you are collecting photographs or videotapes as data and intend to use these artifacts in a public forum, such as a presentation at a conference, make sure that you know whether written permission is necessary.

Similarly, consider how confidentiality impacts informed consent. Confidentiality is important for protecting research informants from stress, embarrassment, or unwanted publicity as well as for protecting participants from themselves should they reveal something to a researcher that could be used against them by others interested in the outcomes of the research.

---

[7] "Ethics in Qualitative Field Research," by L. M. Smith, 1990, in *Qualitative Inquiry in Education: The Continuing Debate,* by E. W. Eisner and A. P. Peshkin (Eds.), New York: Teachers College Press.

_____ Develop an ethical perspective that is close to your personal, ethical position.

_____ Seek research participants' informed consent.

_____ Determine the broader social principles that affect your ethical stance.

_____ Consider confidentiality to avoid harm.

_____ There is no room for deception!

FIGURE 14.3

Checklist: Ethical guidelines for teacher researchers
Source: Mills, Geofrey, *Action Research: A Guide for the Teacher Researcher,* 2nd Edition, © 2003. Adapted by permission of Pearson Education, Inc., Upper Saddle River, NJ.

Confidentiality usually involves the use of codes or pseudonyms to conceal identities. However, in some qualitative research efforts, simply assigning pseudonyms is not enough. For example, a team of researchers responsible for a schoolwide research effort will likely be made privy to the intimate details of teachers' classrooms. It will be the researchers' challenge to protect the teachers from stress, embarrassment, or unwanted publicity that may come from sharing the findings.

Researchers should be able to identify broader social principles that are an integral part of who they are as researchers and as contributing members of the communities in which they live. These broader social principles should dictate your ethical stance. For example, democratic processes, social justice, equality, and emancipation may be the principles that guide your ethical behavior in a given situation.

Qualitative researchers are morally bound to conduct their research in a manner that minimizes potential harm to those involved in the study. A broader view of this concept suggests that qualitative researchers need to convey with confidence to research participants that they will not suffer harm as the result of their involvement in the research effort.

Even though an action may bring about good results, it is not ethical unless that action also conforms to ethical standards such as honesty and justice. From this perspective, acting ethically may be viewed in terms of "doing unto others as you would have them do unto you"! For example, it would clearly be unethical to deceive participants in a research study or to simply treat them as research pawns—a means to an end.

The qualitative researcher must remain attentive to the relationships between the researcher and the participants—a relationship that is determined by "roles, status, language, and cultural norms."[8] The lesson for qualitative researchers who are proponents of this perspective is to pay attention to the research processes of giving information, reciprocity, and collaboration and to be sensitive to how these processes are viewed by other participants in the research. Again, this perspective forces us to confront the socially responsive characteristics of our research efforts as being democratic, equitable, liberating, and life enhancing.

The purpose of this discussion on ethics in qualitative research has been to prepare you to think about a whole range of issues that face any researcher. Carefully consider how you will respond when confronted with difficult questions from colleagues, parents, students, and administrators. Taking time to clarify your values and ethical perspectives will help you respond in a professional, personal, and caring fashion.

As you embark on your qualitative research journey, remember that, in matters of ethics, there are few absolutes. Working through issues related to confidentiality, anonymity, informed consent, and rational judgment will ensure that you avoid potentially difficult situations that may arise in implementing your qualitative research effort. (See Figure 14.3 for a summary of ethical guidelines for qualitative researchers.)

---

[8] "In Search of Ethical Guidance: Constructing a Basis for Dialogue," by D. J. Flinders, 1992, *Qualitative Studies in Education, 5*(2), p. 108.

SUMMARY

Qualitative Research: Definition and Purpose

1. Qualitative research is the collection, analysis, and interpretation of comprehensive narrative and visual data in order to gain insights into a particular phenomenon of interest.
2. The purposes of qualitative research are to promote a deep and holistic understanding of a particular phenomenon, such as an environment, a process, or even a belief.
3. Qualitative research often involves the simultaneous collection of a wealth of narrative and visual data over an extended period of time and in a naturalistic setting.

The Qualitative Research Process

4. Identifying a research topic: The researcher identifies a topic or study of interest to research. Often the initial topic is narrowed to be more manageable.
5. Reviewing the literature: The researcher examines existing research to identify useful information and strategies for carrying out the study.
6. Selecting participants: The researcher must select participants to provide data collection. Participants are purposefully selected (i.e., not randomly selected) and are usually fewer in number than in quantitative samples.
7. Collecting data: The researcher collects data from participants. Qualitative data tend to be gathered from interviews, observations, and artifacts.
8. Analyzing and interpreting data: The researcher analyzes the themes and results of the collected data and provides interpretations of the data.
9. Reporting and evaluating the research: The researcher summarizes and integrates the qualitative data in narrative and visual form.

Qualitative Research Approaches

10. The primary difference among qualitative research approaches is in the particulars of the social context examined and the participants selected.
11. Common qualitative research approaches include case study, ethnography, ethology, ethnomethodology, grounded theory, phenomenology, symbolic interaction, historical research, and narrative research.

Characteristics of Qualitative Research

12. Researchers spend a great deal of time with participants and are immersed in the research setting.
13. The focus of qualitative research is on individual, person-to-person interactions.
14. Qualitative researchers avoid making premature decisions or assumptions about the study and remain open to alternative explanations.
15. Qualitative data are analyzed inductively. The qualitative researcher does not impose an organizing structure or make assumptions about the relationships among the data before collecting evidence.
16. Qualitative research reports include clear and detailed descriptions of the study that include the voices of the participants.
17. Qualitative researchers must remain vigilant to their responsibility to obtain informed consent from participants and to ensure their ethical treatment.

Validity and Reliability in Qualitative Research

Validity in Qualitative Research

18. Validity (trustworthiness and understanding) is the degree to which the qualitative data we collect accurately gauge what we are trying to measure.
19. The trustworthiness of qualitative research can be established by addressing the following characteristics of study findings: credibility, transferability, dependability, and confirmability.
20. According to Maxwell, researchers can contribute to the trustworthiness of their research, and to the understanding of it, by addressing descriptive validity, interpretive validity, theoretical validity, and evaluative validity.
21. Wolcott suggests the following strategies for ensuring the validity of qualitative research: Talk a little, listen a lot; record observations accurately; begin writing early; let readers "see" for themselves; report fully; be candid; seek feedback; and write accurately.

Reliability in Qualitative Research

22. Reliability is the degree to which study data consistently measure whatever they measure.
23. Validity and reliability are not the same. A valid test that measures what it purports to measure will do so consistently over time. A reliable test may consistently measure the wrong thing!

Generalizability

24. The goal of qualitative is to understand what is happening and why. Therefore, qualitative researchers do not need to worry about the generalizability of data because they are not seeking ultimate truths. The power of qualitative research is in the relevance of the findings to the researcher or the audience of the research, not in its generalizability.

Doing the Right Thing: The Role of Ethics in Qualitative Research

25. The role of ethics in qualitative research can be considered in terms of how researchers treat the individuals with whom they interact in research settings.
26. It is important to think about ethical dilemmas before they occur.
27. Qualitative research is intimate because there is little distance between researchers and study participants.
28. Informed consent is central to research ethics. It is the principle that seeks to ensure that all human subjects retain autonomy and the ability to judge for themselves what risks are worth taking for the purpose of furthering scientific knowledge.

Ethical Guideposts

29. Researchers should have an ethical perspective that is very close to their personal ethical position.
30. Informed consent should take the form of a dialogue that mutually shapes the research and the results.
31. Researchers should be able to identify broader social principles that are an integral part of who they are as researchers and as contributing members of the communities in which they live.
32. Qualitative researchers are morally bound to conduct their research in a manner that minimizes potential harm to those involved in the study.
33. Even though an action may bring about good results, it is not ethical unless that action also conforms to ethical standards such as honesty and justice.
34. The qualitative researcher must remain attentive to the relationships between the researcher and the participants—a relationship that is determined by "roles, status, language, and cultural norms."

Now go to the Companion Website at **www.prenhall.com/gay** to assess your understanding of chapter content with Practice Quiz, apply comprehension in Applying What You Know, broaden your knowledge about research in Web Links, and expand your research skills in Evaluating Articles, Analyzing Qualitative Data, Analyzing Quantitative Data, and Research Tools and Tips.

"There is no one recipe that tells how to proceed with data collection efforts. Rather, the researcher must determine what data will contribute to his understanding and resolution of a given problem and collect the appropriate and accessible data for that problem." (p. 413)

Qualitative Data Collection

OBJECTIVES

After reading Chapter 15, you should be able to do the following:

1. Define and state the purpose of qualitative data collection.
2. Identify the sources of qualitative data collection.
3. Identify specific qualitative data collection techniques and how they can be used in a qualitative study.
4. Describe the differences between unstructured and structured interviews.
5. Identify the threats to quality of observations and interviews in qualitative research.

QUALITATIVE DATA COLLECTION: DEFINITION AND PURPOSE

After obtaining entry into a setting and selecting participants, the qualitative researcher is ready to begin data collection, also commonly called *fieldwork*. **Fieldwork** involves spending considerable time in the setting under study, immersing oneself in this setting, and collecting as much relevant information as possible as unobtrusively as possible. Qualitative researchers collect descriptive—narrative and visual—nonnumerical data in order to gain insights into the phenomena of interest. Because the data that are collected should contribute to the understanding of the phenomenon studied, data collection is largely determined by the nature of the problem. There is no one recipe that tells how to proceed with data collection efforts. Rather, the researcher must determine what data will contribute to his understanding and resolution of a given problem and collect the appropriate and accessible data for that problem.

TYPES OF DATA COLLECTION SOURCES

Observations, interviews, questionnaires, phone calls, personal and official documents, photographs, recordings, drawings, journals, e-mail messages and responses, and informal conversations are all sources of qualitative data. Bear in mind that many sources are acceptable to use in data collection as long as the collection approach is ethical, feasible, and contributes to an understanding of the phenomenon under study. The most commonly used sources, however, are observations and interviews. Each of these data types shares one common aspect: The researcher is the primary data collection instrument.

DATA COLLECTION TECHNIQUES

The typical qualitative study involves a number of different data collection strategies, and although all options are open, some strategies are used more often than others. The three primary data collection techniques we will discuss in this chapter are observing, interviewing, and examining records.

Observing

In observation, qualitative researchers obtain data by simply watching the participants. The emphasis during observation is on understanding the natural environment as lived by participants, without altering or manipulating it. For certain research questions, observation is the most appropriate and effective data collection approach. If you ask teachers how they handle discipline in their classrooms, for example, you run the risk of collecting biased information. By actually observing the classes, you will obtain much more objective information that can be "checked" against the self-reports of the research participants. There are two common types of observation: participant and nonparticipant observation.

Participant Observation

In **participant observation,** the observer actually becomes a part of, a participant in, the situation being observed. In other words, the researcher participates in the situation while observing and collecting data on the activities, people, and physical aspects. A benefit of participant observation is that it allows the researcher to gain insights and develop relationships with participants that would not be possible if the researcher observed but did not participate. There are varying degrees of participant observation; a researcher can be an *active participant observer;* a *privileged, active observer;* or a *passive observer.* We will discuss these varying degrees of observation in detail in Chapter 17.

Although participant observation can provide valuable insights, it has drawbacks. The researcher may lose objectivity and become emotionally involved with participants, for instance, or may simply have difficulty participating and collecting data at the same time. In cases where the group under study is tight-knit and closely organized, participation may be difficult for both the researcher and the group. Before adopting the role of a participant observer, the researcher must decide how capable she will be at simultaneously participating in the situation and gathering the desired data. If it is not feasible for the researcher to be a full participant observer in the group being studied, it is best to be a nonparticipant observer.

Nonparticipant Observation

Nonparticipant observation, also called *external observation,* is observation in which the observer is not directly involved in the situation being observed. In other words, the researcher observes and records behaviors but does not interact or participate in the life of the setting being studied. Nonparticipant observers are less intrusive and less likely to become emotionally involved with participants than participant observers. On the other hand, nonparticipant observers may have more difficulty obtaining information on participants' opinions, attitudes, and emotional states.

Nevertheless, there are a number of reasons for a researcher to choose nonparticipant observation. First, the researcher may not have the background or needed expertise to meaningfully act as a true participant. Also, as already mentioned, the group being observed might be too closely organized for the researcher to easily fit in. For example, it might be awkward for a middle-aged researcher to be a true participant in a group of fifth graders. In these cases, nonparticipant observation would be the best way to observe the research setting.

Whether you are a participant or nonparticipant observer, you will need a method to document your observations. Field notes are the best way to collect and document what you observe.

Field Notes

Qualitative research materials gathered, recorded, and compiled (usually on-site) during the course of a study are known as **field notes.** Field notes describe, as accurately as possible and as comprehensively as possible, all relevant aspects of the situation observed. They contain two basic types of information: (1) descriptive information that directly records what the observer has specifically seen or heard on-site through the course of the study and (2) reflective information that captures the researcher's personal reactions to observations, the researcher's experiences, and the researcher's thoughts during an observation session.

Because field notes are the data that will be analyzed to provide the description and understanding of the research setting and participants, they should be as extensive, clear, and detailed as possible. For example, don't simply write, "The class was happy." Instead, describe the activities of the students, the looks on their faces, their interactions with each other, the teachers' activities, and other observations that led you to think the class was happy. It is a good rule of thumb to avoid such words as *good, happy, useful,* and the like, and replace them with words describing what was actually seen or heard. Figure 15.1 illustrates both the descriptive and the reflective aspects of field notes. As you read Figure 15.1, notice the clarity and level of detail in the researcher's notes as he describes the physical setting, the actions of the students, and the interactions that took place. Each O.C. (observer's comments) entry represents a reflection that the researcher had while writing the descriptive field notes. They represent a more personal and subjective aspect of the field notes and should be distinguished from the descriptive material in the notes themselves. In the O.C. entries, you can probably identify times when the researcher wanted to note something unusual, something that had recurred, something that had to be explored, and the like.

Field notes can be taken in the actual setting or recorded as soon as possible after leaving the setting. However, because of the need for clarity and detail, whenever possible notes should be made in the field, during the observation, while fresh in the mind of the researcher. The longer the interval between observing and writing field notes, the more likely that there will be some distortion from the original observation. To aid in taking field notes in the setting, it is often useful to have a protocol, or list of issues, to guide observation. Protocols provide the researcher with a focus during the observation and also provide a common framework for field notes, making it easier to organize and categorize data across various sets of notes. A simple protocol for observation might include these topics:

- Who is being observed? How many people are involved, who are they, and what individual roles and mannerisms are evident?
- What is going on? What is the nature of the conversation? What are people saying or doing?
- What is the physical setting like? How are people seated, and where? How do the participants interact with each other?
- What is the status or roles of people; who leads, who follows, who is decisive, who is not? What is the tone of the session? What beliefs, attitudes, values, and so on, seem to emerge?
- How did the meeting end? Was the group divided, united, upset, bored, or relieved?
- What activities or interactions seemed unusual or significant?
- What was the observer doing during the session? What was the observer's level of participation in the observation (participant observer, nonparticipant observer, etc.)?

Certainly different studies with different participants in different settings would have alternative protocol questions. The aim here is not to be exhaustive, but to encourage you to develop and refine some form of protocol that will guide you in answering the overarching question, "What is going on here?" Figure 15.2 illustrates a simple protocol.

A protocol is an important tool for recording information from observation sessions. The following guidelines should also help you in successfully recording information and organizing field notes:

- Start slowly. Do not assume you know what you're looking for until you "experience" the setting and participants for a while.
- Try to enter the field with no preconceptions. Try to recognize and dismiss your own assumptions and biases and remain open to what you see; try to see things through the participants' perspectives.
- Write up your field notes as soon as possible. When you're done, list the main ideas or themes you've observed and recorded. Don't discuss your observation until the field notes are written; discussion may alter your initial perspective.
- List the date, site, time, and topic on every set of field notes. Leave wide margins to write in your impressions next to sections of the descriptive field notes. The wide margins also

FIGURE 15.1   Section of fieldnotes

March 24, 1980
Joe McCloud
11:00 a.m. to 12:30 p.m.
Westwood High
6th Set of Notes

THE FOURTH-PERIOD CLASS IN MARGE'S ROOM

I arrived at Westwood High at five minutes to eleven, the time Marge told me her fourth period started. I was dressed as usual: sport shirt, chino pants, and a Woolrich parka. The fourth period is the only time during the day when all the students who are in the "neurologically impaired/learning disability" program, better known as "Marge's program," come together. During the other periods, certain students in the program, two or three or four at most, come to her room for help with the work they are getting in other regular high school classes.

It was a warm, fortyish, promise of a spring day. There was a police patrol wagon, the kind that has benches in the back that are used for large busts, parked in the back of the big parking lot that is in front of the school. No one was sitting in it and I never heard its reason for being there. In the circular drive in front of the school was parked a United States Army car. It had insignias on the side and was a khaki color. As I walked from my car, a balding fortyish man in an Army uniform came out of the building and went to the car and sat down. Four boys and a girl also walked out of the school. All were white. They had on old dungarees and colored stenciled t-shirts with spring jackets over them. One of the boys, the tallest of the four, called out, "oink, oink, oink." This was done as he sighted the police vehicle in the back.

O.C.: This was strange to me in that I didn't think that the kids were into "the police as pigs." Somehow I associated that with another time, the early 1970s. I'm going to have to come to grips with the assumptions I have about high school due to my own experience. Sometimes I feel like Westwood is entirely different from my high school and yet this police car incident reminded me of mine.

Classes were changing when I walked down the halls. As usual there was the boy with girl standing here and there by the lockers. There were three couples that I saw. There was the occasional shout. There were no teachers outside the doors.

O.C.: The halls generally seem to be relatively unsupervised during class changes.

Two black girls I remember walking down the hall together. They were tall and thin and had their hair elaborately braided with beads all through them. I stopped by the office to tell Mr. Talbor's (the principal) secretary that I was in the building. She gave me a warm smile.

O.C.: I feel quite comfortable in the school now. Somehow I feel like I belong. As I walk down the halls some teachers say hello. I have been going out of my way to say hello to kids that I pass. Twice I've been in a stare-down with kids passing in the hall. Saying, "How ya' doin'?" seems to disarm them.

I walked into Marge's class and she was standing in front of the room with more people than I had ever seen in the room save for her homeroom which is right after second period. She looked like she was talking to the class or was just about to start. She was dressed as she had been on my other visits—clean, neat, well-dressed but casual. Today she had on a striped blazer, a white blouse and dark slacks. She looked up at me, smiled, and said: "Oh, I have a lot more people here now than the last time."

O.C.: This was in reference to my other visits during other periods where there are only a few students. She seems self-conscious about having such a small group of students to be responsible for. Perhaps she compares herself with the regular teachers who have classes of thirty or so.

There were two women in their late twenties sitting in the room. There was only one chair left. Marge said to me something like: "We have two visitors from the central office today. One is a vocational counselor and the other is a physical therapist," but I don't remember if those were the words. I felt embarrassed coming in late. I sat down in the only chair available next to one of the women from the central office. They had on skirts and carried their pocketbooks, much more dressed up than the teachers I've seen. They sat there and observed.

FIGURE 15.1 (continued)

Below is the seating arrangement of the class today:

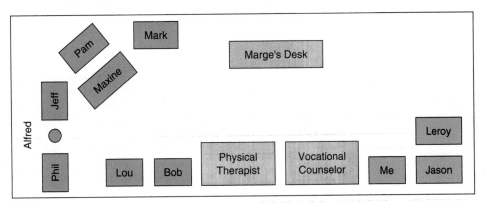

Alfred (Mr. Armstrong, the teacher's aide) walked around but when he stood in one place it was over by Phil and Jeff. Marge walked about near her desk during her talk which she started by saying to the class: "Now remember, to-morrow is a fieldtrip to the Rollway Company. We all meet in the usual place, by the bus, in front of the main entrance at 8:30. Mrs. Sharp wanted me to tell you that the tour of Rollway is not specifically for you. It's not like the trip to G.M. They took you to places where you were likely to be able to get jobs. Here, it's just a general tour that everybody goes on. Many of the jobs that you will see are not for you. Some are just for people with engineering degrees. You'd better wear comfortable shoes because you may be walking for two or three hours." Maxine and Mark said: "Ooh," in protest to the walking.

She paused and said in a demanding voice: "OK, any questions? You are all going to be there. (Pause) I want you to take a blank card and write down some questions so you have things to ask at the plant." She began passing out cards and at this point Jason, who was sitting next to me, made a tutting sound of disgust and said: "We got to do this?" Marge said: "I know this is too easy for you, Jason." This was said in a sarcastic way but not like a strong put-down.

O.C.: It was like sarcasm between two people who know each other well. Marge has known many of these kids for a few years. I have to explore the implications of that for her relations with them.

Marge continued: "OK, what are some of the questions you are going to ask?" Jason yelled out "Insurance," and Marge said: "I was asking Maxine not Jason." This was said matter of factly without anger toward Jason. Maxine said: "Hours—the hours you work, the wages." Somebody else yelled out: "Benefits." Marge wrote these things on the board. She got to Phil who was sitting there next to Jeff. I believe she skipped Jeff. Mr. Armstrong was standing right next to Phil. She said: "Have you got one?" Phil said: "I can't think of one." She said: "Honestly Phil. Wake up." Then she went to Joe, the white boy. Joe and Jeff are the only white boys I've seen in the program. The two girls are white. He said: "I can't think of any." She got to Jason and asked him if he could think of anything else. He said: "Yeah, you could ask 'em how many of the products they made each year." Marge said: "Yes, you could ask about production. How about Leroy, do you have any ideas, Leroy?" He said: "No." Mr. Armstrong was standing over in the corner and saying to Phil in a low voice: "Now you know what kinds of questions you ask when you go for a job?" Phil said: "Training, what kind of training do you have to have?" Marge said: "Oh yes, that's right, training." Jason said out loud but not yelling: "How much schooling you need to get it." Marge kept listing them.

O.C.: Marge was quite animated. If I hadn't seen her like this before I would think she was putting on a show for the people from central office.

FIGURE 15.2

Sample of observation protocol

```
Setting:
Individual Observed:
Observation #: (first observation, second, etc.)
Observer Involvement:

Date/Time:
Place:
Duration of Observation (indicate start/end times):
```

| **Descriptive Notes** | **Reflective Notes** |
| (Detailed, chronological notes about what the observer sees, hears; what occurred; the physical setting) | (Concurrent notes about the observer's thoughts, personal reactions, experiences) |

provide space for doing initial coding and analysis. Write on only one side of a page. This will save you much photocopying when the time comes to "cut and paste" the field notes into different categories. Draw diagrams of the site.

■ In writing field notes, first list key words related to your observation, then outline what you saw and heard. Then, using the key words and outline, write your detailed field notes.

■ Keep the descriptive and reflective sections of field notes separate (although collected together). Focus on writing detailed descriptive field notes.

■ Write down your hunches, questions, and insights after each observation. Use memos.

■ Number the lines or paragraphs of your field notes. This will help you find particular sections when needed.

■ Enter your field notes into a computer program for future examination and data analysis.

(For further discussion of field notes, refer to Chapter 17.)

Interviewing

Interviewing is the second major data collection technique. As you may remember from Chapter 6, an **interview** is a purposeful interaction in which one person is trying to obtain information from another. Interviews permit researchers to obtain important data they cannot acquire from observation alone, although pairing observation and interviewing provides a valuable way to gather complementary data. Observational data can suggest questions that can be asked in subsequent interviews with the participants in the study. For example, observation cannot provide information about past events, or the way things used to be before Mr. Hardnosed became principal, or why Ms. Haddit has had it and is considering transferring to another school. Information about these events cannot be observed; they must be obtained from peoples' own words. Interviewers can explore and probe participants' responses to gather more in-depth data about their experiences and feelings. They can examine attitudes, interests, feelings, concerns, and values more easily than they can through observation.

Interviews are distinguished by their degree of structure and formality. Some are **structured interviews,** with a specified set of questions to be asked, whereas others are **unstructured interviews,** with questions prompted by the flow of the interview. Semistructured interviews combine both structured and unstructured approaches. Interviews may be formal and planned (we'll meet Tuesday at 1:00 to discuss your perceptions) or informal and unplanned (I'm glad I caught you in the corridor; I've been meaning to ask you . . .).

In addition to their structure and formality, interviews also vary in a number of other ways. For example, interviews may range in length from a few minutes to a few hours. They may consist of a one-time session or multiple sessions conducted over time with the same participant. In addition, participants may be interviewed individually or in groups.

Unstructured Interview

The unstructured interview is little more than a casual conversation that allows the qualitative researcher to inquire into something that has presented itself as an opportunity to learn about what is going on at the research setting. The point of informal interviews is not to get answers to predetermined questions, but rather to find out where the participants are coming from and what they have experienced. Often informal interviews are used further in the study to obtain more complex or personal information. Agar[1] suggests that researchers have a ready set of questions to ask participants by guiding the conversation around *who, what, where, when, why,* and *how.* Using these prompts, researchers will never be at a loss for a question to add to their understanding of what is happening in the research setting.

Structured Interview

Qualitative researchers may also want to consider formally interviewing research participants as part of their data collection efforts. In a formal, structured interview, the researcher has a specified set of questions that elicits specific information from the respondents. Using a structured interview format allows the qualitative researcher to ask all of the participants the same series of questions. A major challenge in constructing any interview, however, is to phrase questions in such a way that they elicit the information you really want. Although this may seem obvious, qualitative researchers often feel compelled by tradition to ask a lengthy set of questions, many of which stray from their focus. When planning interviews, consider the following options for ensuring the quality of your structured interviews:

- *Pilot questions on a similar group of respondents.* Try your questions out on a group of people who share similar characteristics with your research participants to see if the questions make sense. The participants' feedback will quickly confirm, or challenge, the assumptions (for example, about appropriate language) you have made while writing your questions. Using the feedback from this group, revise the questions before interviewing your participants.
- *Use questions that vary from convergent to divergent.* Use both open-ended and closed questions in a structured interview. For example, a closed (convergent) question allows for a brief response such as yes or no. Alternatively, an open-ended (divergent) question allows for a detailed response and elaboration on questions in ways you may not have anticipated. The information gathered through open-ended questions may be more difficult to make sense of, but it does allow the researcher to obtain important information that might otherwise be considered "outlying" or discrepant.

Guidelines for Interviewing

Although the concept of an interview seems straightforward, it can be a complex and difficult undertaking when the gender, culture, and life experiences of the interviewer and participant

---

[1] *The Professional Stranger: An Informal Introduction to Ethnography,* by M. H. Agar, 1980, Orlando, FL: Academic Press.

are quite different. There can be issues of who "controls" the interview, the accuracy of responses provided, and the extent to which the language of the interviewee and the researcher are similar enough to permit meaningful inferences about the topic under study. For these reasons, a researcher must always take the time to enter the research setting unobtrusively and build support and trust with participants before initiating an interview. A trusting relationship is essential if participants are to answers questions—particularly those on sensitive issues—with candor. In addition, the following actions can help improve communication and facilitate the collection of interview data:

- Listen more, talk less. Listening is the most important part of interviewing.
- Follow up on what participants say, and ask questions when you don't understand.
- Avoid leading questions; ask open-ended questions.
- Don't interrupt. Learn how to wait.
- Keep participants focused and ask for concrete details.
- Tolerate silence. It means the participant is thinking.
- Don't be judgmental about participants' views or beliefs; keep a neutral demeanor. Your purpose is to learn about others' perspectives, whether you agree with them or not.
- Don't debate with participants over their responses. You are a recorder, not a debater.

Collecting Data From Interviews

Interviewers have three basic choices for collecting their data: taking notes during the interview, writing notes after the interview, and audio- or videotaping the interview. Although all these approaches can be used in a study, certain ones are better suited than others. For example, taking notes during the interview can be distracting and can alter the flow of the session. Writing notes after the interview is better than trying to write during the interview; however, it can be difficult to remember the contents of the interview. Thus, the data collection method of choice is audio- or videotape recording, which provides a verbatim account of the session. Also, tapes provide researchers with the original data for use at any time. Although a few participants may balk at being recorded, most participants will not, especially if you promise them confidentiality. Make sure that the recording machine is in good working order (new batteries, too) before entering the interview setting.

To work most productively, it is useful to transcribe the tape recordings. This is a time-consuming task, especially for long interviews. Transcribing one 60-minute tape may take 4 or 5 more hours. If you choose to do the transcribing instead of hiring someone to transcribe (a costly alternative), it would help to use short interview sessions, if feasible. When transcribing, write the date, subject discussed, and participant (using a coded name) on the transcript. Number all pages. Make sure a different indicator is given and used to identify the various persons speaking on the tape.

The transcripts are the field notes for interview data. They should be reviewed against the tape for accuracy. Interview transcripts are voluminous and usually have to be reduced to focus on the data pertinent to the study. Sometimes this is difficult to do. During data analysis the transcript will be read and important sections labeled to indicate their importance. This process of culling the transcripts will be described in the next chapter.

Questionnaires

A third way to collect data from individual research participants is by using a questionnaire. As noted in Chapter 6, a **questionnaire** is a written collection of self-report questions to be answered by a selected group of research participants. The major difference between an interview and a questionnaire is that the participant will write out the responses on the form provided. Questionnaires allow the researcher to collect large amounts of data in a relatively short amount of time. Although face-to-face interviews are an opportunity for the researcher to intimately know how each respondent feels about a particular issue, interviewing is very time-consuming. A compromise is to use a questionnaire (when appropriate) and to conduct follow-up interviews with research participants who have provided written feedback that warrants further investigation.

Since a solid data collection instrument will help ensure useful responses, you should consider the following guidelines for developing and presenting questionnaires:

- *Carefully proofread questionnaires before sending them out.* Nothing will turn respondents off quicker than receiving a questionnaire that is littered with errors.
- *Avoid a sloppy presentation.* Make the survey attractive, and consider using BIG print if necessary.
- *Avoid a lengthy questionnaire.* Piloting the instrument will give you a realistic sense of how long it will take your respondents to complete the task. Remember, no matter how much respondents want to help you, a questionnaire that's too long will find its way into the "circular file" instead of back into your hands.
- *Do not ask unnecessary questions.* Asking unnecessary questions is akin to teachers developing tests that don't match what was taught. Students are stumped, and teachers learn little about the effectiveness of their lessons. Likewise, as researchers, we often feel compelled to ask a great deal of trivial information on a questionnaire. Participants become frustrated, and we collect information that is tangential to our stated purpose.
- *Use structured items with a variety of possible responses.* Indicate what you mean by *often* and *frequently* and how they differ from each other. Otherwise, your respondents will interpret the meaning of the terms in quite different ways.
- *Whenever possible, allow for an "Other Comments" section.* An "Other Comments" section provides respondents with an opportunity to respond openly to your questions and to raise new questions. These comments provide you with an excellent source of discrepant data ("I hadn't expected someone to say that!") and an opportunity to follow up with an informal interview to elicit more information from the respondent as your time, energy, and inquisitiveness allow.
- *Decide whether you want respondents to put their names on the questionnaires or whether you will use a number to keep track of who has responded.* You should assure respondents that their confidentiality will be protected throughout the process. However, you can protect respondents while also keeping track of who has responded and deciding whether they have made comments that you feel warrant a follow-up conversation. If you do so, you must communicate to respondents that they will not suffer any negative consequences for anything they might share with you so they will feel comfortable supplying honest and forthright answers.

Examining Records

This third primary data collection technique is examining records. Qualitative researchers examine various types of records or documents, including archival documents, journals, maps, videotapes, audiotapes and artifacts. Many of these data sources are naturally occurring in educational settings and require only that the researcher locate them within the research setting.

Archival Documents

Like classrooms, schools are repositories for all sorts of records—student records, standardized test scores, retention rates, minutes of meetings (faculty, PTA, school board), newspaper clippings about significant events in the community, and so on. With permission, the qualitative researcher can use these sources of data to gain valuable historical insights, identify potential trends, and explain how things got to be the way they are. Often, clerical assistants, school aides, and student teachers are happy to help with uncovering archival information and organizing it in a way that is most useful to the classroom teacher if they believe that it is contributing to the collective understanding of a pressing educational issue.

Journals

Daily journals kept by research participants are a valuable data source. Students' journals can provide teachers with a window into the students' world and their daily classroom experiences. This can have meaning for and impact future teaching practices. Daily journals kept by teachers give their accounts of what is happening in the classroom and provide a glimpse of the school from another perspective. Regardless of your specific research questions, you should encourage journaling by research participants as a way to keep track of their perceptions of what is going on in the research setting.

Maps

Qualitative researchers working in schools often find class maps and school maps useful for a number of reasons. They provide contextual insights for people who have not visited the school, and they provide the qualitative researcher with a reflective tool—a way of rethinking the way things are in schools and classrooms. For example, why are the computers in the classroom placed in a bank along one wall, and what are the effects of individual student computer time on other seatwork activities? A map can also record traffic flow in a classroom as well as teacher movement during instruction. The school map may also prove useful for teams of qualitative researchers concerned about the movement and interactions of different grade levels of students and any problems that emerge from the traffic flow. For qualitative researchers, context is everything! Figure 15.3 shows an example of a classroom map.

FIGURE 15.3

Classroom map example
Source: Mills, Geoffrey, *Action Research: A Guide for the Teacher Researcher,* 2nd Edition, © 2003. Reprinted by permission of Pearson Education, Inc., Upper Saddle River, NJ.

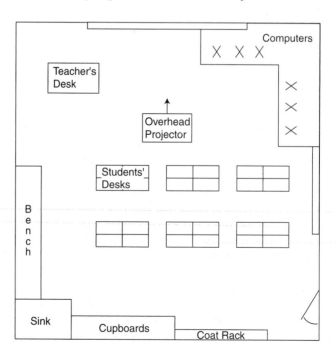

Videotape and Audiotape

Videotapes and audiotapes provide qualitative researchers with another valuable, if not somewhat obtrusive, data source. Of course, there are downsides to these techniques. For example, their presence in a classroom may elicit the usual "funny faces" and bizarre comments that we normally associate with the presence of such technology in a classroom for the first time. One way of moving ahead with these efforts is to introduce them into a classroom early in a research project and provide the illusion that the "camera is running" when, in fact, no film is in the camera. The use of audiotape and videotape also raises the serious issue of time allotment. Watching and listening to tapes and then recording observations takes an enormous amount of time. This is perhaps the number one challenge for researchers using these data sources.

Artifacts

Schools and classrooms are rich sources of what we might call *artifacts*—written or visual sources of data that contribute to our understanding of what is happening in classrooms and schools. The category of artifacts can include almost everything else that we haven't already discussed. For example, there has been a trend in schools to move toward "authentic assessment" techniques, including the use of student portfolios. A *portfolio* is a presentation of work that captures an individual student's work samples over time and the relative growth of that work. Portfolios, although difficult to quantify, provide the teacher with valuable outcome data that gets at the heart of the qualitatively different samples of work. Such artifacts are a valuable data source that qualitative researchers may use as a starting point for conversation with research participants.

:: THREATS TO THE QUALITY OF OBSERVATIONS AND INTERVIEWS

Two main threats to the validity of observation and interview studies are observer bias and observer effect. For example, the situation may be "seen" differently than it would have been through the eyes of a different researcher (observer bias) or may be a somewhat different situation than it would have been if the researcher were not present (observer effect). Although these problems are not unique to qualitative research, they are potentially more serious because of the more intimate involvement of researcher and participants.

Observer Bias

Observer bias occurs when the observer does not observe objectively and accurately, thus producing invalid observations. Each researcher brings to a setting a highly individual background, set of experiences, and perspectives, which in turn affect not only what and how she observes but also her personal reflections and interpretations of the situation. Relatedly, the qualitative researcher runs the risk of identifying with one or more participants or being judgmental towards others. This results in somewhat distorted observations. For example, after attending a number of faculty meetings, a researcher might tend to identify with the teachers, and observations of principal–teacher interactions would be affected by this role identification.

Qualitative researchers must walk a fine line in their attempt to be both involved and objective, particularly during participant observation. Experienced qualitative researchers are aware of the challenge and use a number of strategies to minimize the effect of bias on the results of their research. First, researchers try to minimize the effects of their personal biases on their findings by conscientiously recording (in field notes) their thoughts and feelings about what they observe. Triangulation, the use of multiple data collection strategies and sources, provides an additional, powerful safeguard. It is not likely that data derived from different sources and data collection strategies will all be biased in the same, unnoticed way. Working with several researchers and comparing everyone's observations helps reduce bias for the same reason. It is unlikely that data provided by several researchers will be so consistently biased that the bias will be undetected. Of course, detecting bias and eliminating it are not the same thing. Qualitative researchers do not claim that they can eliminate all bias. Instead, they recognize bias as a part of the research process and use the strategies discussed to reduce it.

Observer Effect

Whereas observer bias refers to a researcher's faulty interpretations of a situation, observer effect refers to changes in the situation caused by the researcher's presence. Specifically, **observer effect** is the phenomenon whereby persons being observed behave atypically simply because they are being observed, thus producing invalid observations. Would you behave exactly the same as you normally would on a given day if you knew you were being observed? Probably not. Although this problem is by no means unique to qualitative research, it is potentially more serious since the researcher is trying to study how people naturally behave in their settings.

A major strategy employed by researchers to reduce observer effect is to be as unassuming and nonthreatening as possible as they gradually increase their participation. Initially, persons in the observational setting may be highly conscious of the researcher's presence. However, the effect of the researcher's presence on the participants' behavior typically decreases over time. For example, at the first faculty meeting attended by the observer, behavior may be somewhat artificial (more formal or more cordial); but by the tenth faculty meeting, people will tend to be their usual selves. It also helps if the exact nature of the researcher's inquiry is not described in any more detail than is ethically or legally necessary. The fact that persons being observed may initially behave differently is bad enough; focusing on their behavior change is worse! For example, it would probably be sufficient if the "official" reason given for the researcher's presence were "to observe high school faculty meetings," rather than "to observe principal–teacher interactions." As with bias, qualitative researchers are well aware that they cannot totally eliminate observer effects. They do, however, make every effort to recognize, minimize, record, and report them.

Armed with the qualitative data collection techniques that will help you understand what is going on at your research setting, and your research questions, you are now ready to "enter the field" and start collecting data. This can be a scary proposition for new researchers. What follows are suggestions to help smooth your entry into your first qualitative research setting!

:: GETTING STARTED

Having obtained entry into a setting and having selected participants, the qualitative researcher is ready to begin data collection, or fieldwork. Regardless of how much you read, think about, and discuss fieldwork, you will not really know what it is like until you actually live it. Living an experience for the first time always means uncertainty in a new role— uncertainty about how to act and interact with others. Qualitative research, by its very nature, is a very intimate and open-ended activity. It is common to feel nervous as you learn the ropes, try to establish rapport with participants, and get a feel for the setting. Bogdan and Biklen[2] suggest a number of cautions to make the initial days of entry into the setting less painful:

- Do not take what happens in the field personally.
- Set up your first visit so that someone is there to introduce you to the participants.

---

[2] *Qualitative Research in Education*, by R. C. Bogdan and S. K. Biklen (3rd ed., pp. 79–81), 1998, Needham Heights, MA: Allyn & Bacon.

- Don't try to accomplish too much in the first few days. Make your initial visit for observation short. You will have to take field notes after each data collection encounter, so start with brief data collection episodes to ease into the process of writing field notes.
- Be relatively passive. Ask general, nonspecific, noncontroversial questions that allow participants to reply without being forced to provide answers they might find uncomfortable discussing with a relative "stranger." Ease your way into the context; don't storm in. The intent is for the participants to gradually become comfortable with you, and you with them. Then you can gradually increase your degree of involvement.
- Be friendly and polite. Answer questions participants and others ask, but try not to say too much about the specifics of your presence and purpose, so that you do not influence the participants.

In short, it is critical that you establish your "OKness" with the research participants with whom you will be working. Regardless of how well thought-out your study is, if your interpersonal skills are lacking, it will be difficult to develop the trust you will need to be accepted into the setting.

SUMMARY

Qualitative Data Collection: Definition and Purpose

1. Qualitative data collection, or fieldwork, involves spending considerable time in the setting under study, immersing oneself in this setting, and collecting as much relevant information as possible as unobtrusively as possible. Descriptive—narrative and visual—nonnumerical data are collected in order to gain insights into the phenomena of interest.
2. The decision about what data is collected is largely determined by the nature of the problem.

Types of Data Collection Sources

3. The qualitative research literature emphasizes the following data collection techniques and sources: observations, interviews, questionnaires, phone calls, personal and official documents, photographs, recordings, drawings, journals, e-mail messages and responses, and informal conversations.
4. In qualitative research the researcher is the primary data collection instrument.

Data Collection Techniques

5. The three primary data collection techniques in qualitative research are observing, interviewing, and examining records.

Observing

Participant Observation

6. A researcher who becomes a part of, a participant in, the situation being observed is called a *participant observer*.
7. Participant observation can be done to varying degrees; a researcher can be an active participant observer; a privileged, active observer; or a passive observer.

Nonparticipant Observation

8. In nonparticipant observation the observer observes but does not participate in the situation being studied.

Field Notes

9. Field notes are the record of what the observer has specifically seen or heard. In addition to these literal descriptions, field notes contain personal reactions, or what the observer has experienced and thought about during an observation session.

Interviewing

10. An interview is a purposeful interaction in which one person is trying to obtain information from another.
11. Pairing observation and interviewing provides a valuable way to gather complementary data.

12. The *unstructured interview* is little more than a casual conversation that allows the qualitative researcher to inquire into something that has presented itself as an opportunity to learn about what is going on at the research setting.
13. Using a *structured interview* format allows the qualitative researcher to ask all of the participants the same series of questions.
14. When planning interviews, consider the following options for ensuring the quality of your structured interviews:
    a. Pilot questions on a similar group of respondents.
    b. Use questions that vary from convergent to divergent.
15. Guidelines for interviewing include the following:
    a. Listen more, talk less.
    b. Follow up on what participants say, and ask questions when you don't understand.
    c. Avoid leading questions; ask open-ended questions.
    d. Don't interrupt. Learn how to wait.
    e. Keep participants focused and ask for concrete details.
    f. Tolerate silence. It means the participant is thinking.
    g. Don't be judgmental about participants' views or beliefs.
    h. Don't debate with participants over their responses.
16. Interviewers have three basic choices for collecting their data: taking notes during the interview, writing notes after the interview, and audio or videotaping the interview.

Questionnaires

17. The major difference between a structured interview schedule and a questionnaire is that the participant will write out the responses on the form provided.
18. Consider the following guidelines for developing and presenting questionnaires:
    a. Carefully proofread questionnaires before sending them out.
    b. Avoid a sloppy presentation.
    c. Avoid a lengthy questionnaire.
    d. Do not ask unnecessary questions.
    e. Use structured items with a variety of possible responses.

    f. Whenever possible, allow for an "Other Comments" section.
    g. Decide whether you want respondents to put their names on the questionnaires or whether you will use a number to keep track of who has responded.

Examining Records

19. Qualitative researchers can gain valuable information from examining various types of records or documents found in educational environments. These include archival documents, journals, maps, videotapes, audiotapes, and artifacts.

Threats to the Quality of Observations and Interviews

20. Two main threats to the validity of observation and interview studies are observer bias and observer effect.

Observer Bias

21. Observer bias occurs when the observer does not observe objectively and accurately, thus producing invalid observations.
22. It is generally accepted in qualitative research that researchers should use triangulation and should not rely on any single source of data, interview, observation, or instrument.

Observer Effect

23. Observer effect is the phenomenon whereby persons being observed behave atypically simply because they are being observed. Qualitative researchers should avoid drawing attention to the fact that study participants are under observation.

Getting Started

24. Do not take what happens in the field personally.
25. Set up your first visit so to the research setting that someone is there to introduce you to the participants.
26. During the first few days in the setting, don't try to accomplish too much, be relatively passive, and be friendly and polite.

Now go to the Companion Website at **www.prenhall.com/gay** to assess your understanding of chapter content with Practice Quiz, apply comprehension in Applying What You Know, broaden your knowledge about research in Web Links, and expand your research skills in Evaluating Articles, Analyzing Qualitative Data, Analyzing Quantitative Data, and Research Tools and Tips.

"... if you are a person who does not interact well with others, narrative research is probably not for you!" (p. 434)

Narrative Research

OBJECTIVES

After reading Chapter 16, you should be able to do the following:

1. Briefly state the definition and purpose of narrative research.
2. Describe the narrative research process.
3. Describe the different types of narrative research.
4. Describe the key characteristics of narrative research designs.
5. Describe narrative research techniques.

▓ NARRATIVE RESEARCH: DEFINITION AND PURPOSE

As you first learned in Chapter 1, **narrative research** is the study of how different humans experience the world around them, and it uses a methodology that allows people to tell the stories of their "storied lives."[1] Narrative researchers collect data about people's lives and collaboratively construct a narrative (written account) about the individual's experiences and the *meanings* they attribute to the experiences.

Narrative research has a long history in such diverse disciplines as literature, history, art, film, theology, philosophy, psychology, anthropology, sociology, sociolinguistics, and education, and as such does not fit neatly into any single scholarly field. Within the field of education, a number of recent trends have influenced the development of narrative research:

■ The increased emphasis in the past 15 years on teacher reflection, teacher research, action research, and self-study

■ The increased emphasis on teacher knowledge—for example, what teachers know, how they think, how they develop professionally, and how they make decisions in the classroom
■ The increased emphasis on empowering teacher voices in the educational research process through collaborative educational research efforts

These trends in education have resulted in a changing landscape of educational research and the promotion of "scientifically based research" practices to address social, cultural, and economic issues.

We live (and perhaps teach or work in schools in some other capacity) in a time when we are being challenged by educational issues such as adolescent drug use, cultural differences in diverse urban school settings, and the achievement gap that separates children raised in poverty from children who are less economically disadvantaged. There are no "silver bullets" to solve these (and many other) issues that have come to the forefront of political and educational policy in the late 20th and early 21st centuries. By using narrative research in education, we attempt to *increase understanding* of central issues related to teaching and learning through the telling, and retelling, of teachers' stories. Narrative research provides educational researchers with an opportunity to validate the practitioner's voice in these important political and educational debates.

Having a hard time visualizing what "narrative" and "research" in the same sentence really mean? Let's look at an example:

> Hilda, a teacher at High High School, has students coming to her class who appear "distracted" (which is perhaps teacher code for under the influence of drugs). As an educational researcher, you decide that it would be helpful to know more about how Hilda deals with this significant educational issue and what she does in order to work with the distracted, drug-using adolescents in her classroom. You think of this

---

[1] "Stories and Experience and Narrative Inquiry," by F. M. Connelly and D. J. Clandinin, 1990, *Educational Research, 19*(5), p. 2.

research question: "What have been Hilda's experiences in confronting and dealing with a student who has a drug problem?" To study this question, you plan to interview Hilda and listen to stories about her experiences working with one particular distracted student. You will talk to the student, the student's parents, other teachers, administrators, and counselors, all of whom are stakeholders in the student's educational experience. You also want to know about Hilda's life and any significant events that have impacted her ability to work effectively with adolescent drug users. Perhaps Hilda holds economic, social, cultural, or religious beliefs and values that affect her ability to deal with the drug culture in her school.

From the information you collect in interviews, you will slowly construct a story of Hilda's work with the troubled student. You will then share (retell) the story and, with Hilda's help, shape the final report of the narrative research. This final report will be Hilda's story of working with a student who is troubled by drug use, and it will contribute to our understanding of what it takes, on the part of a teacher, to work with adolescent drug users in our schools.

Starting to make sense yet? Narrative research allows the researcher to share the storied lives of teachers in the hope of providing insights and understandings about challenging educational issues as well as enriching the lives of those teachers. Narrative research can contribute to our understanding of the complex world of the classroom and the nuances of the educational enterprise that exist between teachers and students. It simply is not always possible, nor desirable, to reduce our understanding of teaching and learning to numbers.

:: THE NARRATIVE RESEARCH PROCESS

The first thing that a researcher interested in a narrative study must do is to decide if he has the time, access, experience, personal style, and commitment to undertake this particular style of on-site research. Once the decision is made, he can begin thinking about and planning the study. A plan for a narrative study contains the same general components as those outlined in Figure 3.4, in Chapter 3 (you may wish to revisit that figure now). In this section we describe some basic steps in the narrative research process. Each study will have unique requirements, and the steps are meant simply as guideposts (you should notice a parallel between the steps and the outline for writing a qualitative research proposal in Chapter 3). To illustrate how the steps work, we will build on the example of our teacher, Hilda.

1. Identify the purpose of the research study, and identify a phenomenon to explore.

    The purpose of the study at High High School is to describe Hilda's experiences in confronting and dealing with a student who has a drug problem. The specific phenomenon that will be explored is that of adolescent drug use in high school.

2. Select an individual to learn about the phenomenon.

    Hilda, a teacher at High High School, has volunteered to work collaboratively with the researcher (you) on the research.

3. Pose initial narrative research questions.

    What have been Hilda's experiences in confronting and dealing with a student who has a drug problem? What life experiences influenced the way Hilda approached the problem?

4. Describe the researcher's role (entry to the research site, reciprocity, and ethics).

    The researcher will collaboratively obtain permission to conduct the research in Hilda's school. In addition to permission from an Institutional Review Board (IRB), the researcher and Hilda will likely need to complete a signed informed consent form and any other permission required by the school or school district.

5. Describe data collection methods, paying particular attention to interviewing.

   The researcher will utilize a variety of **narrative research data collection techniques**, including interviewing and examining written and nonwritten sources of data.

6. Describe appropriate strategies for the analysis and interpretation of data.

   The researcher and Hilda will collaboratively participate in restorying the narrative and then validating the final written account. (*Restorying*—a writing process that involves synthesizing story elements—is described further later in the chapter.)

7. Collaborate with the research participant to construct the narrative and to validate the accuracy of the story.
8. Complete the writing of the narrative account.

The narrative research process is a highly personal, intimate approach to educational research that demands a high degree of caring and sensitivity on the part of the researcher. Although negotiating entry to the research setting is usually considered an ethical matter with assurances of confidentiality and anonymity, in narrative research it is necessary to think about this negotiation in terms of a shared narrative. That is, narrative research necessitates a relationship between the researcher and the participant more akin to a close friendship, where trust is a critical attribute. However, this friendship quality is not easily attained in an educational research setting (let alone in our lives in general). It is not uncommon for teachers, for example, to be cynical about *any* educational research, let alone a style of research whose success relies on a friendship between the researcher and participant. Imagine how you would feel if approached by one of your educational research classmates (or colleagues at school) with a proposition such as this one: "I heard you talking about the difficulty you were having teaching kids who come to school stoned and wondered how you would feel about me spending a lot of time talking to you about it. Maybe by working on the problem together, we can gain a greater understanding of the issues involved." Think about the kind of person you would trust to undertake this kind of research in your workplace; for your narrative study to succeed, you would need to become that person.

As Connelly and Clandinin and Clandinin and Connelly[2] have suggested, it is important that the relationship between researcher and participant be a mutually constructed one that is *caring, respectful,* and characterized by an *equality of voice.* As will become evident in this process, storytelling, not only on the part of the participant but also the researcher, and restorying of the narrative account, are critical to the success of the research effort. If the researcher is unable to let go of the control that is typical in many styles of educational research, the narrative research process is less likely to succeed. The educational researcher using a narrative research methodology must be prepared to follow the lead of the research participant and, in the immortal words of Star Trek, go where "no man (or woman) has gone before!" In a very real sense, narrative research is a pioneering effort that takes a skilled researcher committed to living an individual's story and working in tandem with that individual.

Equality of voice is especially critical in the researcher–participant relationship because the participant (in all likelihood a teacher) must feel empowered to tell her story. Throughout the research process, the researcher must leave any judgmental baggage at home. The first

---

[2] "Stories," Connelly and Clandinin, 1990, pp. 2–14; *Narrative Inquiry: Experience and Story in Qualitative Research,* by D. J. Clandinin and F. M. Connelly, 2000, San Francisco: Jossey-Bass.

hint of criticism, or "ivory tower" superiority, will be a nail in the research coffin. The researcher's intent must be clear: to empower the participant to tell her story and to be collaborative and respectful in the process. The researcher should listen to the participant's story before contributing his own perspective—even if asked. That is, it is important that the narrative researcher not become his own best informant! Being a patient listener provides the researcher with an opportunity to validate the participant's voice and allows the participant to gain authority during the telling of her story. After all, it is the participant's story we are trying to tell.

:: TYPES OF NARRATIVE RESEARCH

Like other types of qualitative research (for example, ethnographic research), narrative research may take a variety of forms. Some of these forms are listed in Figure 16.1.

How a particular narrative research approach is categorized depends on five characteristics: who authored the account (the researcher or the participant, which is the same person in an autobiography), the scope of the narrative (an entire life or an episode in a life), who provides the "story" (for example, teachers or students), the kind of theoretical/conceptual framework that has influenced the study (for example, critical or feminist theory), and finally, whether or not all of these elements are included in the one narrative.[3] The nuances that distinguish the different forms of narrative research listed in Figure 16.1 are embedded in the disciplines in which they originated. If one specific style of narrative research piques your interest, you would do well to focus on the discipline-based literature to guide your research efforts.[4]

:: KEY CHARACTERISTICS OF NARRATIVE RESEARCH

Narrative research can be characterized by the following elements:[5]

- Narrative research focuses on the experiences of individuals.
- Narrative research is concerned with the chronology of individuals' experiences.
- Narrative research focuses on the construction of life stories based on data collected through interviews.
- Narrative research uses restorying as a technique for constructing the narrative account.
- Narrative research incorporates context and place in the story.
- Narrative research is a collaborative approach that involves the researcher and the participants in the negotiation of the final text.
- The construction of a narrative always involves responding to the question, "And then what happened?"

In narrative research, data are collected primarily through interviews and written exchanges. The narrative research process is similar to the construction of a biography in that the educational researcher does not have direct access to observational data but must rely on primary (the participant's recollections) and secondary (oftentimes written documents by the

---

[3] *Educational Research: Planning, Conducting, and Evaluating Quantitative and Qualitative Research* (2nd ed.) by J. W. Creswell, 2005, Upper Saddle River, NJ: Merrill/Prentice Hall.
[4] For examples of how narrative research has been applied to a wide range of contexts (e.g., school-based violence, Holocaust survivors, undocumented immigrant families, and other challenging social problems), consider reading *Narrative Analysis: Studying the Development of Individuals in Society,* by C. Dauite and C. Lightfoot (Eds.), 2004, Thousand Oaks, CA: Sage.
[5] Elements of narrative research were adapted from those in *Educational Research,* Creswell, 2005, and "Narrative Analysis," by C. K. Riessman, 2002, in *The Qualitative Researcher's Companion,* by A. M. Huberman and M. B. Miles, Thousand Oaks, CA: Sage.

- Autobiographies
- Biographies
- Life writing
- Personal accounts
- Personal narratives
- Narrative interviews

- Personal documents
- Documents of life
- Life stories and life histories
- Oral histories
- Ethnohistories
- Ethnobiographies

- Autoethnographies
- Ethnopsychologies
- Person-centered ethnographies
- Popular memories
- Latin American *testimonios*
- Polish memoirs

FIGURE 16.1

Examples of types of narrative research forms
Sources: Creswell, John W., *Educational Research: Planning, Conducting, and Evaluating Quantitative and Qualitative Research,* 2nd Edition, © 2005. Reprinted by permission of Pearson Education, Inc., Upper Saddle River, NJ. Information from "The New Narrative Research in Education," by K. Casey, 1995/1996, *Review of Research in Education, 21,* pp. 211–253.

participant) data sources. As mentioned previously, narrative research places considerable emphasis on the collaborative construction of the written account—the narrative text. Although researchers using other styles of on-site research may share accounts with research participants as a way to test the trustworthiness of those accounts, they place little emphasis on the restoring process that is quite unique to narrative research.

:: NARRATIVE RESEARCH TECHNIQUES

Empirical data is central to narrative research in spite of the inevitable interpretation that occurs during the data collection process (for example, during the telling and restorying activities). As in any form of interpretive research, the interpretation alone does not make for fiction as an outcome of the process. However, like researchers using other on-site research approaches, the narrative researcher must be prepared to use multiple data sources to counteract challenges that narratives could be written without ever leaving home. Accordingly, Clandinin and Connelly[6] recommend that data be in the form of field notes on shared research experiences. These experiences occur as the researcher collects data through journal and letter writing and documents such as lesson plans and class newsletters.

The immensity of the writing task for the narrative researcher becomes clear if you consider what is involved—for both the researcher and the participant—in "living the story." The main challenge involves the participants' abilities to live their lives while telling their stories in words and explaining themselves to one another. Picture yourself as Hilda, the teacher focused on coping with adolescent drug users in her classroom. As the research participant (Hilda), could you imagine yourself fully engaged in the living the daily life of a classroom teacher while at the same time relaying the story of your daily events and the meaning of your actions to a researcher? You would be having a kind of out-of-body experience in which you had to look down on yourself from above while living your life at the same time. As Connelly and Clandinin remind us, "A person is, at once, engaged in living, telling, retelling, and reliving stories."[7] Now imagine yourself as the researcher who is faced with the task of recording and communicating Hilda's story. It is no wonder that the researcher and the research participant must establish a high degree of trust and respect akin to the kind of relationship we all expect in a close friendship.

As with other styles of on-site research, narrative research relies on the triangulation of data in order to address issues of trustworthiness (see Chapter 14 for a more detailed discussion of validity, or trustworthiness, in qualitative research). As noted earlier, the data collection techniques used in narrative research are sometimes criticized as leading to fictitious, romanticized versions of life in schools. Researchers can best counter this criticism by ensuring the use of multiple data sources as well as the collaborative negotiation of the written narrative account.

---

[6] *Narrative Inquiry,* Clandinin and Connelly, 2000.
[7] "Stories," Connelly and Clandinin, 1990, p. 4.

In the following sections, we will focus on some of the data collection techniques some-what unique to narrative research (storytelling, letter writing, autobiographical and biographical writing, and other narrative sources) and refer you to Chapters 15 and 17 for detailed explanations of field notes, journals, and interviews. In writing about personal experience methods, Clandinin and Connelly have described these data collection techniques as "field texts"[8] that are focused on capturing the essence of collaboratively created artifacts of the field experience of the researcher and the participant. You have probably realized by now that if you are a person who does not interact well with others, narrative research is probably not for you!

Restorying

A characteristic of narrative research that distinguishes it from other on-site research approaches is the technique of restorying the stories that individuals tell about their life experiences. According to Creswell, **restorying** is "the process in which the researcher gathers stories, analyzes them for key elements of the story (e.g., time, place, plot, and scene), and then rewrites the story to place it in a chronological sequence."[9] Oftentimes when individuals share with researchers stories about their experiences, they do so without attention to the "real time" order of events. When prompted by the researcher, participants may share graphic details of a particular event, but in all likelihood, they will share the story in a somewhat random sequence as events surface in memory. This should not be a shocking revelation for any of us who have ever been asked, "Tell me what you did on your summer vacation." Invariably, our recollections are far from chronological or built around key themes—such as our favorite activity, place, or acquaintances! With each interview, the researcher records these recollections, amassing many pages of notes, or "raw data." Although the notes contain many interesting stories and details, they do not constitute a narrative account of the participant's experiences. The researcher must go through the process of restorying.

There are three stages in the restorying process:[10]

1. The researcher conducts the interview and transcribes the audiotape in order to obtain the raw data from the interview. This process involves noting not just the spoken words but also the nuances of the interview—for example, humor, laughter, anger, and so on.
2. The researcher retranscribes the raw data based on the key elements that are identified in the story. For example, in an interview, Hilda (our teacher at High High School) would describe how she copes with students who come to class under the influence of drugs. From her comments we might identify certain themes, such as seeking assistance from a school nurse or counselor and establishing individual educational plans and contracts.
3. The researcher organizes the story into a chronological sequence with attention to the setting, characters, actions, problems, and resolutions. For example, Hilda's story would be set in the context of her classroom with the adolescents who use drugs (characters) and would be focused on the actions of the students (their off-task behavior and other relevant classroom behavior), the problems caused by the actions (other students distracted, teacher time focused on a few students, etc.), and any resolutions to the problems that Hilda employed (seeking assistance from outside the classroom, establishing learning contracts with students, etc.).

---

[8] "Personal Experience Methods," by D. J. Clandinin and F. M. Connelly, 1994, in *Handbook of Qualitative Research* (p. 419), by N. K. Denzin and Y. S. Lincoln (Eds.), Thousand Oaks, CA: Sage.
[9] *Educational Research* (p. 480), Creswell, 2005.
[10] Ibid.

After these stages are completed, the participant would be asked to collaborate with the researcher to write the final restoried narrative of the individual's experiences. This collaboration is critical to ensure that there is no gap between the "narrative told and narrative reported."[11] One of the tests of the trustworthiness of the narrative account is the participant's validation of the restoried account as being representative of the individual's lived experiences as relayed in the interviews.

The goal of the educational researcher working with Hilda would be to collaboratively construct a narrative that describes her experiences working with adolescent drug users, as well as the meaning these experiences had for Hilda, in an effort to increase our collective understanding of how a teacher confronts and deals with adolescent drug users in the classroom.

Narrative Analysis and the Analysis of Narrative

It is important for us to briefly distinguish between *narrative analysis* and the *analysis of narrative*. Polkinghorne[12] presents narrative analysis and analysis of narrative as two primary kinds of narrative research for researchers to consider as they develop their narratives.

In **narrative analysis** the researcher collects descriptions of events through interviews and observations and synthesizes them *into* narratives or stories (similar to the process of restorying). In this type of narrative research, the story is the outcome of the research and an attempt by the researcher to answer how and why a particular outcome came about. The second type of narrative research, **analysis of narrative,** is a process in which the researcher collects stories as data and analyzes them to produce a description of themes that applies to all of the stories captured in the narratives. Using this approach, the researcher develops a statement of themes as general knowledge about a collection of stories, but in so doing, underemphasizes the unique aspects of each story.

Given this distinction, it is on narrative analysis that this chapter focuses its discussion. That is, we are describing the development of a narrative or story that focuses on particular knowledge about how or why an outcome occurred, rather than the development of a collection of stories and the search for themes to develop general knowledge about the collection of stories.

Oral History

One method for creating field texts is to have participants share an oral history. An oral history may be obtained by the researcher during a structured interview schedule with predetermined questions (and hence with the researcher's agenda clearly stated) or through an open-ended approach where the researcher asks the participant to tell his own story in his own way. In constructing an oral history, a researcher might ask the participant to create a timeline (or *chronicle*) that is divided into segments of significant events or memories. An oral history of a teacher working with adolescents who use drugs, for example, might include a timeline from the beginning of the year (or previous years if there has been a long-term relationship) that indicates when significant events related to the drug use occurred. There may be times when students were suspended from school because they violated a zero tolerance policy on drug use or times when students were arrested for drug possession. The timeline would be a helpful tool for the narrative researcher attempting to make sense of the importance of these events in the teacher's overall story. The teacher would also be asked to expand

---

[11] Ibid., p. 483.
[12] "Narrative Analysis in Qualitative Research," by D. E. Polkinghorne, 1995, in *Life History and Narrative* (pp. 5–23), by J. A. Hatch and R. Wisniewski (Eds.), London: Falmer Press.

on these significant events and to write a description in an *annal*. Together, the chronicle and annal of the teacher's experiences provide the narrative researcher with a powerful descriptive tool.

Photographs, Memory Boxes, and Other Artifacts

Teachers have a proclivity for being "pack rats." The materials they squirrel away, apart from the obvious curriculum materials, often include cards from former students, newspaper clippings, yearbooks, photographs, and audio- and videotapes of student performances. Oftentimes these artifacts adorn a teacher's desk and bulletin board as badges of honor. The narrative researcher can use these artifacts as prompts to elicit details about the teacher's life in school and how they might relate to the specific phenomenon under investigation. For example, the teacher may share thank-you cards from students who, due to the teacher's intervention, were able to kick a drug habit.

Storytelling

There are many opportunities in narrative research to engage participants in storytelling. Teachers, by nature, are master storytellers, and many will happily share stories about their experiences in school as "competent narrators of their lives."[13] The manner in which narrative researchers engage participants in storytelling sessions will have a large impact on the nature of the story. That is, making storytelling a routine part of the narrative research process will provide researchers with many opportunities to add to their understanding of a "day in the life" of a teacher who is focused on finding a resolution to a challenging educational problem. Oftentimes these stories will be shared at times when a tape recorder is not handy, and the researcher will have to rely on her ability to accurately record field notes and verbatim accounts as necessary. (For a complete discussion of field notes, see Chapter 14.) These stories are critical in providing insights into teachers' work and explanations of their actions.

Letter Writing

Another way to engage participants in writing about their lived experiences, and to engage the narrative researcher and participant in a dialogue, is through letter writing. Because of the widespread availability of e-mail, this kind of dialogue can be easily initiated and maintained. By providing the narrative researcher with valuable insights into the evolving, tentative interpretations that the participant may be considering, the dialogue serves as a working chronicle of the participant's thinking about issues related to the research phenomenon. The commitment of thought to text helps both the researcher and the participant. Further, if each e-mail includes previous messages, the narrative researcher and the participant can then reflect on the evolution of the themes by reading the increasing record of the narrative dialogue.

Autobiographical and Biographical Writing

One of the keys to narrative research is the researcher's ability to engage the research participant in writing activities. Although this skill may also be important in other research endeavors, it is especially useful for a researcher trying to accurately capture the lived experiences of the research participant—through the eyes of that participant. Engaging a participant in constructing, or collaboratively constructing, a life history through autobio-

---

[13] *The Active Interview* (p. 29), by J. A. Holstein and J. F. Gubrium, 1995, Thousand Oaks, CA: Sage.

graphical or biographical writing has the potential to broaden the narrative researcher's understandings about past events and experiences that have impacted the participant's experiences with the phenomenon under investigation. Perhaps Hilda, for example, has had other professional or personal experiences with adolescent drug users that would contribute to an understanding of how she operates in her current educational environment. Autobiographical or biographical writing about Hilda's life could bring these experiences to light. Again, the use of e-mail could provide a wonderful electronic record of the emerging narrative.

Other Narrative Data Sources

There are many other narrative data sources that a researcher can access that will contribute to the construction of the written narrative. For example, documents such as lesson plans, parent newsletters, and personal philosophy statements are readily available to the narrative researcher. These sources provide a window into a world of classrooms that is not easily accessible to outsiders.

:: WRITING THE NARRATIVE

The final step in the narrative research process is the writing of the narrative. Many of the data collection techniques used in narrative research result in products—such as e-mail letters and a participant's biography—that have the potential of finding their way into the final written account. Given the collaborative nature of narrative research, from the beginning until the end, the negotiation of the final narrative account should be relatively easy to achieve. However, it is worth remembering that our goal in conducting narrative research has been to "learn about the general from the particular."[14] As such, we should be modest in the claims we make for the collaboratively constructed written narrative that is the final product of our research efforts.

SUMMARY

Narrative Research: Definition and Purpose

1. Narrative research is the description of the lives of individuals, the collection of individual's experience stories, and a discussion of the meaning of those experiences for the individual.
2. Narrative research is the study of the way humans experience the world.
3. Narrative research is an attempt to increase understanding of central issues related to teaching and learning through the telling, and retelling, of teachers' stories.

The Narrative Research Process

4. The following steps can serve as guideposts in the narrative research process:

a. Identify the purpose of the research study, and identify a phenomenon to explore.
b. Select an individual to learn about the phenomenon.
c. Pose initial narrative research questions.
d. Describe the researcher's role (entry to the research site, reciprocity, and ethics).
e. Describe data collection methods, paying particular attention to active interviewing.
f. Describe appropriate strategies for the analysis and interpretation of data.
g. Collaborate with the research participant to construct the narrative and to validate the accuracy of the story.
h. Complete the writing of the narrative account

---

[14] "Narrative Analysis," Riessman, 2002, p. 262.

5. The relationship between researcher and participant must be a mutually constructed one that is caring, respectful, and characterized by an equality of voice.
6. Participants in narrative research must feel empowered to tell their stories.

Types of Narrative Research

7. Narrative research may take a variety of forms.
8. How a narrative research approach is characterized depends on five factors: who authored the account, the scope of the narrative, the kind of theoretical/conceptual framework that has influenced the study, and whether or not all of these elements are included in the one narrative.

Key Characteristics of Narrative Research

9. Narrative research focuses on the experiences of individuals.
10. Narrative research is concerned with the chronology of individuals' experiences.
11. Narrative research focuses on the construction of life stories based on data collected through interviews.

12. Narrative research uses restorying as a technique for constructing the narrative account.
13. Narrative research incorporates context and place in the story.
14. Narrative research is a collaborative approach that involves the researcher and the participants in the negotiation of the final text.
15. The construction of a narrative always involves responding to the question, "And then what happened?"

Narrative Research Techniques

16. Narrative researchers employ a number of unique data collection techniques, including restorying; oral history; examination of photographs, memory boxes, and other artifacts; storytelling; letter writing; and autobiographical and biographical writing.
17. Restorying is the process of gathering stories, analyzing them for key elements, and the rewriting of the story to place events in a chronological sequence.

Now go to the Companion Website at **www.prenhall.com/gay** to assess your understanding of chapter content with Practice Quiz, apply comprehension in Applying What You Know, broaden your knowledge about research in Web Links, and expand your research skills in Evaluating Articles, Analyzing Qualitative Data, Analyzing Quantitative Data, and Research Tools and Tips.

"Ethnographic research is the study of the cultural patterns and perspectives of participants in their natural setting." (p. 441)

Ethnographic Research

OBJECTIVES

After reading Chapter 17, you should be able to do the following:

1. Briefly define and state the purpose of ethnographic research.
2. Describe the ethnographic research process.
3. Identify and describe the different types of ethnographic research.
4. Describe the key characteristics of ethnographic designs.
5. Describe ethnographic research techniques.

❖ ETHNOGRAPHIC RESEARCH: DEFINITION AND PURPOSE

As you learned in Chapter 1, **ethnographic research** (also called *ethnography*) is the study of the cultural patterns and perspectives of participants in their natural setting. Ethnographers engage in a long-term study of a particular phenomenon in an attempt to situate understandings about the phenomenon into a meaningful context. Ethnographic fieldwork, which has its origins in cultural anthropology, most commonly involves intensive participant observation. By participating in varying degrees in the research setting, the researcher attempts to discern patterns and regularities of human behavior in social activity. Ethnographic research embraces the application of multiple data collection techniques and demands prolonged time in the research setting. It also requires the researcher to appreciate the tension caused by bringing together contrasting and perhaps incompatible perspectives, all in the spirit of describing and understanding what is actually going on in a specific context. The goal of ethnographic research is to describe, analyze, and inter-pret the culture of a group, over time, in terms of the group's shared beliefs, behaviors, and language.

A construct that is central to the understanding of ethnography and ethnographic research is culture. **Culture** is the set of attitudes, values, concepts, beliefs, and practices shared by members of a group. As you begin to think about your own ethnographic research studies, keep the concept of culture in your mind as an organizing principle for your work. It is tempting to talk in generalities about the "culture of the school" or the "culture of adolescent drug users." However, in qualitative research, statements about culture are bold assertions that can be made about a group only after the group has been studied over an extended period of time. Use of the word *cultural* can help you clarify, in more concrete terms, what it is that you are attempting to describe in the ethnographic research setting. Wolcott[1] suggests thinking in terms of three broad conceptual areas that focus on tangible behaviors: cultural orientation (where the people being studied are situated in terms of physical space and activities), cultural know-how (how a group goes about its daily activities), and cultural beliefs (why a group does what it does). This strategy will help the ethnographic researcher to identify the actual phenomena that are at the heart of ethnographic research enterprise and, in so doing, "capture the culture" of the group.

Having a hard time picturing what an ethnographic research study might look like? Imagine that you have been asked by a teacher (Hilda) working at a secondary school (High High School) to help her and her colleagues look into adolescent drug use at the school. So, you ask yourself, "What kind of research approach is appropriate to investigate this problem?" Could you structure an

---

[1] *Ethnography: A Way of Seeing*, by H. F. Wolcott, 1999, Walnut Creek, CA: AltaMira Press.

experiment to look at the impact of a particular treatment on the outcome of reducing drug use? But what treatment would you choose? What do you really know about the drug culture of this school community? Would students really be willing to be assigned to a control group and an experimental group? Perhaps your head hurts just thinking about all of these issues.

As we think about so-called social problems such as "adolescent drug use in high schools," it becomes clear that we probably know very little about what is really going on in the drug culture that exists right under our noses. Indeed, although there are scientifically based approaches and school policies (such as zero tolerance policies) that attempt to address the problem of adolescent drug use, we may be surprised to learn that a universal panacea for adolescent drug use in our schools probably does not exist. We may do well to think about an ethnographic study of adolescent drug use in order to better *understand* how to address the problem.

A unique type of understanding can be gained by implementing a research approach that focuses on everyday, taken-for-granted behaviors (such as adolescent drug use). Our aim in ethnographic research is not to "prove" that a particular intervention (drug treatment) "solves" a particular "problem" (adolescent drug use), but rather to understand "what's going on" in a particular setting (schools for example). It should be clear that the goal of an ethnographic study is quite different from the goals of descriptive, correlational, causal–comparative, and experimental studies and that the methodology we use dictates the kind of research we will want to conduct.

:: THE ETHNOGRAPHIC RESEARCH PROCESS

As with narrative research, an individual interested in conducting an ethnographic study must first decide if he has the time, access, experience, personal style, and commitment to undertake this style of research. A plan for an ethnographic study contains the same general components as those outlined in Figure 3.4, in Chapter 3. In this section we describe some basic steps that can serve as guideposts in the process of conducting an ethnographic study (you will notice the parallel between these steps and the outline for writing a qualitative research proposal):

1. Identify the purpose of the research study.
2. Frame the study as a larger theoretical, policy, or practical problem.
3. Pose initial ethnographic research questions.
4. Describe the overall approach and rationale for the study.
5. Describe the site and sample selection.
6. Describe the researcher's role (entry to the research site, reciprocity, and ethics).
7. Describe data collection methods.
8. Describe appropriate strategies for the analysis and interpretation of data.
9. Write the ethnographic account.

In discussing the steps, we will use the example of an ethnographic study on adolescent drug use in a secondary school (High High School).

From the start, we need to be clear about the purpose of the research. For the scenario chosen, you might identify the following purpose:

> **The purpose of this study is to understand the social, cultural, and economic influences affecting the use of drugs at High High School.**

OK, not a bad start, right? How about framing the study as a larger theoretical, policy, or practical problem? Given a national preoccupation with the "war on drugs," it will not be difficult to frame the importance of this study in terms of a larger societal, cultural, and economic study on adolescent drug use, whether it occurs in school or outside of school.

What about some initial ethnographic research questions? Oftentimes, beginning researchers are challenged by what they will ask when they arrive at the research setting. Guided by the overriding goal of describing "what's going on here," you could enter the research site with this initial research question in mind: "How do teachers describe the effects of students' drug use on the classroom/academic setting?" Such a question naturally suggests other questions that you would want to ask of teachers and administrators:

- "How do you know that students in your class are using drugs?"
- "What are the school policies on drug use, drug possession, and intoxication in school?"
- "What social services exist to help students deal with drug-related problems?"

As mentioned previously, as a qualitative researcher, you would ease into the research setting and refrain from asking questions until after you had done some initial observation of the setting and participants. The questions just listed would be good ones to start with. If you followed up by prompting the participant to tell *who, what, where, when,* or *how* or to "Tell me a little bit more about that," you would never be at a loss for questions to ask in your study.

What is the overall approach and rationale for the study? You might express it as follows:

> The overall approach for this study of adolescent drug use in secondary schools will be ethnographic. The rationale for the study is based on society's need to understand how teachers cope with adolescent drug users in their classrooms and the social, cultural, and economic influences affecting the widespread use of drugs at High High School.

How will you decide on the site for your study and your sample selection? In this case, you have been invited by a teacher, Hilda, to participate in a collaborative ethnographic research study that she hopes will ultimately contribute to her (and perhaps others') understanding of adolescent drug use in high schools. Having negotiated your entry to the research setting, your next step would be to establish rapport with your collaborators in the research process—the "key informants," "subjects," or "active participants." There are a number of ways you could identify participants (other than Hilda). For example, school counselors, teachers, administrators, community law enforcement officers, and so on, would probably be able to provide names of likely drug users or students who have a history of drug use. A good starting point would be to establish a trusting relationship with one or more of these students and then, after explaining the purpose of your study, ask for volunteers who would be willing to be observed. For minor-age students, you would need to obtain approval from parents for the students to participate in the study. You would also want to assure students and parents that students' identities would be kept confidential. After receiving consent, you could begin your work as a "participant observer." Does this mean we are suggesting that you participate in the illegal use of drugs? Of course not. As you will see in a later section, "Participant Observation," we are suggesting that you participate in the social and cultural setting you'd be attempting to understand and explain.

How about the researcher's role? It is likely that your role, as researcher in this study, would need to be carefully negotiated in terms of entry to the school setting and the ethical dilemmas that would likely be faced. In this study in particular, issues of confidentiality and anonymity would be crucial, especially if illegal behavior were observed. You would also need to consider what you would do if you observed unhealthy behavior, such as cigarette smoking, which, although legal, is a violation of school policy. The very intimate nature of ethnographic research makes the possibility of facing an ethical dilemma omnipresent, but that doesn't mean we should shy away from doing it! Chapter 14 has more to say about the role of ethics in qualitative research.

What data collection techniques will be used? Your primary data collection techniques would be participant observation, field notes, interviews, and the examination of artifacts such as school policy documents and attendance records.

What strategies will be used to analyze and interpret the data? You would analyze your field notes for themes emerging from the data that might help you increase understanding of "what is going on" at High High School.

What will the ethnographic account look like? In all likelihood, your ethnographic account would be a narrative that captured the social, cultural, and economic themes that emerged from the study. The account would include a description of the limitations of the study and recommendations for what you would do differently next time. The story of adolescent drug use at High High School would also acknowledge the incomplete nature of the story given; qualitative researchers craft an "end" to a story while knowing full well that the story continues beyond their involvement.

It should be noted that one of the challenges for time-strapped educational researchers wishing to do any type of ethnographic research is the length of time in the field, usually a "full cycle" (a calendar year), and the length of the written account. If you are a graduate student, conducting ethnographic research could lengthen your graduate program and add cost to your education. Or you may be fortunate enough to be working and studying at the same time. Researchers in all circumstances need to consider whether or not they have the time to spend in the field before making the decision to undertake an ethnographic research study.

:: TYPES OF ETHNOGRAPHIC RESEARCH

There are a number of different types of ethnographic research. Figure 17.1 is a comprehensive list of the types of ethnographies you are likely to encounter in your studies or likely to produce as a result of your fieldwork.

Although examples of all of these types of ethnography can be found in educational research, the three most common are the critical ethnography, the realist ethnography, and the ethnographic case study. What distinguishes these types of research from one another is the *product* (the written account) itself, the **ethnography.** However, the researcher's *intent* in conducting the research is an equally important distinguishing feature. A **critical ethnography**

FIGURE 17.1   Types of ethnographies

- Realist ethnography—an objective, scientifically written ethnography
- Confessional ethnography—a report of the ethnographer's fieldwork experiences
- Life history—a study of one individual situated within the cultural context of his or her life
- Autoethnography—a reflective self-examination by an individual set within his or her cultural context
- Microethnography—a study focused on a specific aspect of a cultural group and setting
- Ethnographic case study—a case analysis of a person, event, activity, or process set within a cultural perspective

- Critical ethnography—a study of the shared patterns of a marginalized group with the aim of advocacy
- Feminist ethnography—a study of women and the cultural practices that serve to disempower and oppress them
- Postmodern ethnography—an ethnography written to challenge the problems in our society that have emerged from a modern emphasis on progress and marginalizing individuals
- Ethnographic novels—a fictional work focused on cultural aspects of a group

Sources: Creswell, John W., *Educational Research: Planning, Conducting, and Evaluating Quantitative and Qualitative Research,* 2nd Edition, © 2005. Reprinted by permission of Pearson Education, Inc., Upper Saddle River, NJ. Information from *Interpretive Ethnology: Ethnology Practices for the 21st Century,* by N. K. Denzin, 1997, Thousand Oaks, CA: Sage; *Ethnography and Qualitative Design in Educational Research* (2nd ed.), by M. D. LeCompte, J. Preissle, and R. Tesch, 1993, San Diego, CA: Academic Press; and *Tales of the Field: On Writing Ethnography,* by J. Van Maanen, 1988, Chicago: University of Chicago Press.

is a highly politicized form of ethnography written by a researcher in order to advocate against inequalities and domination of particular groups that exist in society (including schools). The researcher's intent is to advocate "for the emancipation of groups marginalized in our society."[2] These ethnographies typically address issues of power, authority, emancipation, oppression, and inequity—to name a few. Realist ethnographies are most commonly used by cultural and educational anthropologists who study the culture of schools. A **realist ethnography** is written with an objective style and uses common categories for cultural description, analysis, and interpretation; such categories include "family life, work life, social networks, and status systems."[3] Case studies, as a type of ethnographic research design, are less likely to focus on cultural themes. Instead, an **ethnographic case study** focuses on describing the activities of a specific group and the shared patterns of behavior it develops over time. It is important that beginning ethnographic researchers recognize the different ways in which they can focus their research to distinguish it as a particular type of ethnography. The literature provides numerous examples of ethnographic research that can serve as models of particular designs and that illustrate for enquiring minds what the final written accounts look like.

KEY CHARACTERISTICS OF ETHNOGRAPHIC RESEARCH

There is a pretty good chance that you have already read an ethnographic account but may not have recognized it as such. Ethnographic research possesses the following characteristics:[4]

- It is carried out in a natural setting, not a laboratory.
- It involves intimate, face-to-face interaction with participants.
- It presents an accurate reflection of participants' perspectives and behaviors.
- It uses inductive, interactive, and repetitious collection of "unstructured" data and analytic strategies to build local cultural theories.
- Data is primarily collected through fieldwork experiences.
- It typically uses multiple methods for data collection, including conducting interviews and observations, and reviewing documents, artifacts, and visual materials.
- It frames all human behavior and belief within a sociopolitical and historical context.
- It uses the concept of culture as a lens through which to interpret results.
- It places an emphasis on exploring the nature of particular social phenomena, rather than setting out to test hypotheses about them.
- It investigates a small number of cases, perhaps just one case, in detail.
- It uses data analysis procedures that involve the explicit interpretation of the meanings and functions of human actions. Interpretations occur within the context or group setting and are presented through the description of themes.
- It requires that researchers be reflective about their impact on the research site and the cultural group.
- It offers interpretations of people's actions and behaviors that must be uncovered through an investigation of what people actually do and their reasons for doing it.

---

[2] *Educational Research: Planning, Conducting, and Evaluating Quantitative and Qualitative Research* (2nd ed., p. 441), by J. W. Creswell, 2005, Upper Saddle River, NJ: Merrill/Prentice Hall.
[3] Ibid., p. 438.
[4] Characteristics were adapted from those in "Ethnography and Participant Observation," by P. Atkinson and M. Hammersley, 1994, in *Handbook of Qualitative Research* (pp. 249–261), by N. K. Denzin and Y. S. Lincoln (Eds.), Thousand Oaks, CA: Sage, *Educational Research: Planning, Conducting, and Evaluating Quantitative and Qualitative Research* (2nd ed) by J. W. Creswell, 2005, Upper Saddle River, NJ: Merrill/Prentice Hall; *Conceptualizing Qualitative Inquiry: Mindwork for Fieldwork in Education and the Social Sciences*, by T. H. Schram, 2003, Upper Saddle River, NJ: Merrill/Prentice Hall; and *Ethnographer's Toolkit: Vol. 1. Designing and Conducting Ethnographic Research*, by J. J. Schensul and M. D. LeCompte (Eds.), 1999, Walnut Creek, CA: AltaMira Press.

- It offers a representation of a person's life and behavior that is neither the researcher's nor the person's. Instead, it is built upon points of understanding and misunderstanding that occur between researcher and participant.
- It cannot provide an exhaustive, absolute description of anything. Rather, ethnographic descriptions are necessarily partial, bound by what can be handled within a certain time, under specific circumstances, and from a particular perspective.

These characteristics will help you recognize ethnographic research studies as well as help you determine if this approach to educational research feels like a good fit for your individual personality and the problems you wish to investigate.

⠿ ETHNOGRAPHIC RESEARCH TECHNIQUES

In Chapter 15 we described in some detail the qualitative data collection techniques that are used to varying degrees in all types of qualitative research (observing, interviewing, and examining records). Like other qualitative researchers, an ethnographic researcher collects descriptive narrative and visual data. As mentioned, the researcher is engaging in an activity in order to answer the question, "What is going on here?" It is not a mysterious quest but is quite simply an effort to collect data that increases our understanding of the phenomenon under investigation.

Wolcott, however, reminds us that "the most noteworthy thing about ethnographic research techniques is their lack of noteworthiness."[5] Although the techniques may not be noteworthy, they are systematic and rigorous and over an extended period of time allow the researcher to describe, analyze, and interpret the social setting under investigation.

In the following sections, we will focus on participant observation and field notes as the primary data collection techniques used in ethnographic research. Before doing so, we must examine the concept of triangulation of data, an important aspect of any ethnographic study.

Triangulation

It is generally accepted in qualitative research circles that researchers should not rely on any single source of data, whether it be an interview, observation, or survey instrument. Therefore, the strength of qualitative research lies in its multi-instrument approach, or triangulation. Triangulation is the use of multiple methods, data collection strategies, and data sources to get a more complete picture of what is being studied and to cross-check information. As you may recall from Chapter 14, triangulation is a primary way that qualitative researchers ensure the trustworthiness (validity) of their data. In ethnographic research the researcher is *the* research instrument who, in collecting data, utilizes a variety of techniques over an extended period of time, "ferreting out varying perspectives on complex issues and events."[6] It is important that researchers apply the principle of triangulation throughout their ethnographic research data collection efforts.

Participant Observation

A researcher who is a genuine participant in the activity being studied is called a *participant observer.* Participant observation is undertaken with at least two purposes in mind:[7]

- To *observe* the activities, people, and physical aspects of a situation
- To *engage in* activities that are appropriate to a given situation and that provide useful information

---

[5] "Ethnographic Research in Education" by H. F. Wolcott, 1988, in *Complementary Methods for Research in Education* (p. 191), by R. M. Jaegar (Ed.), Washington, DC: American Educational Research Association.
[6] Ibid., p. 192.
[7] *Participant Observation,* by J. Spradley, 1980, New York: Holt, Rinehart & Winston.

The participant observer is fully immersed in the research setting in order to get close to those studied as a way of understanding what their experiences and activities mean to them. This immersion provides a window through which the researcher can see how participants in the study lead their lives as they carry out their daily activities. It also provides an opportunity for the researcher to determine what is meaningful to participants, and why.

Participant observation can be done to varying degrees, depending on the situation being observed and the opportunities presented. A participant observer can be an *active participant observer;* a *privileged, active observer;* or a *passive observer.*[8] Depending on the nature of the problem, ethnographic researchers have many opportunities to actively participate and observe as they work. However, the tendency with observing is to try to see it all! A good rule of thumb is to try to do less—better. As you embark on some degree of participant observation, do not be overwhelmed. It is not humanly possible to take in everything that you experience. Be content with furthering your understanding of "what is going on here" through *manageable* observations. Avoid trying to do too much, and you will be happier with the outcomes.

Active Participant Observer

Ethnographic researchers, by virtue of the problems they choose to investigate, are likely to have opportunities to be active participant observers. For example, when doing educational research, researchers often negotiate roles as teacher's aides, student teachers, or even substitute teachers in order to gain access to schools and classrooms (the research settings). When actively engaged in teaching, teachers naturally observe the outcomes of their teaching. Each time they teach, they monitor the effects of their teaching and adjust their instruction accordingly. Teacher researchers who are observing their own teaching practices, however, may become so fully immersed in what they are doing that they don't record their observations in a systematic way during the school day. Such recording is a necessary part of being an active participant observer (see the discussion on field notes to follow).

Privileged, Active Observer

Ethnographic researchers may also have opportunities to observe in a more privileged, active role. For example, a researcher may observe children in classrooms during a time when there is no other expectation of participating in the instructional setting as "the teacher." During these times, the researcher can work as a "teacher's aide" and at the same time can withdraw, stand back, and watch what is happening during a teaching episode. As an active observer, the ethnographer can move in and out of the role of teacher's aide and observer.

Passive Observer

Ethnographic researchers may be passive observers in schools. When a researcher takes on the role of passive observer, she assumes no responsibilities in the classroom setting—she focuses on her data collection. A researcher may spend her time in the setting as a passive observer only, or she may enter the setting as a privileged, active observer and then, on occasion, choose to act as a passive observer by making explicit to the students and a teaching colleague that the "visitor" is present only to "see what's going on around here."

---

[8] *Anthropological Research: The Structure of Inquiry,* by P. J. Pelto and G. H. Pelto, 1978, Cambridge, MA: Cambridge University Press; *Participant Observation,* Spradley, 1980; "Differing Styles of On-Site Research, or 'If It Isn't Ethnography, What Is It?'" by H. F. Wolcott, 1982, *Review Journal of Philosophy and Social Science, 7,* pp. 154–169; and "Ethnographic Research in Education," by H. F. Wolcott, 1997, in *Complementary Methods for Research in Education* (2nd ed.) (pp. 325–398), Washington, DC: American Educational Research Association.

According to Wolcott, success as a participant observer depends on the personal characteristics of the researcher, as evidenced by "what is going on in the researcher's mind"[9] and the conduct of the researcher in the field. While in the research setting, you need to conduct yourself in a manner that will allow you to build rapport with research participants; otherwise, there will be little to learn from the field-based experience. Everyday courtesy and common sense will go a long way in helping you establish your OKness in the field. When was the last time you were approached by someone (maybe a telemarketer or pollster) and asked for a "few minutes of your time" (which of course turned into many minutes of your time!)? Was the person pleasant, patient, and genuinely interested in what you had to say? Or was the person pushy, inconsiderate, and relatively uninterested in what you had to say? Were you tempted to hang up or walk away? When you work as a researcher, you need to be accepted into the research setting as an OK person who can be trusted. Wolcott offers guidelines in the following areas of social behavior to encourage researchers to think about how they carry themselves in the participant observation experience, such as:

Gaining entry and maintaining rapport. During the very early stages of the ethnographic research process, you will need to negotiate your entry into the research setting. In educational research you will most likely make arrangements with key players in the setting, such as teachers, principals, and superintendents. You will need to clearly describe to these educators what it is that you are planning to do, what kinds of time constraints will be placed on them, what the "value added" will be for the educational process, and other important details. Furthermore, you will need to maintain a good working rapport with the folks in the setting. Be considerate of others and thoughtful about how you are being perceived. If in doubt, ask for feedback from a highly trusted person at the research setting.

Reciprocity. Reciprocity in the ethnographic study of education can take many forms. As the researcher, you may be asked by teachers to assist with classroom tasks. Because of your connection to a university, you may be asked to provide some kind of curriculum resource or access to teaching materials. You may even be asked to pay for informants' time for interviews if such activities require time beyond informants' "contract hours"—although it is best if you clear up this matter during your initial request for access to the setting. Unless you have a large, funded research study, it is unlikely that you will be in a position to pay teachers for their time. Reciprocity for educational ethnographic researchers more commonly takes the form of a willingness to share personal information and professional courtesy. Folks who are going to spend considerable time with you will want to know something about who you are as a person. They may also look to you as an "educational expert"—after all, you are probably working at the university on an "advanced" degree, so you must know something about teaching and learning! As you negotiate your degree of participation in the setting, you will want to set your boundaries about what you are willing and able (qualified) to do.

A tolerance for ambiguity. Fieldwork does not always (or perhaps ever) proceed at the speed or intensity we might like it to. We may enter the field with a naive view that something exciting and directly related to what we are investigating will be occurring at every moment. The reality is, there will be many times when you find yourself frustrated with living the life of an ethnographic researcher. Rather than offering perfect examples of this or that type of behavior, most of the episodes you observe are likely to be ambiguous in meaning. You must learn patience unless you are already blessed with this trait.

Personal determination coupled with faith in oneself. Wolcott offers ethnographic researchers this valuable advice: "Self-doubt must be held in check so that you can go about your business of conducting research, even when you may not be sure what that entails."[10] At some

---

[9] *The Art of Fieldwork* (p. 90), by H. F. Wolcott, 1995, Walnut Creek, CA: AltaMira Press.
[10] Ibid., p. 94.

time during your fieldwork, you may experience what is commonly termed "culture shock"—that is, you will encounter an unexpected set of events that challenges everything you assumed about your research setting and participants. Sound exciting? Frightening? If you find yourself in this kind of situation, concentrate on simply writing down what you are seeing, hearing, experiencing, and feeling. You will inevitably make sense of it over time. Have faith in what you are doing, and hang in there!

Letting go of control. Similar to our ability to tolerate ambiguity is the important trait of being able to let go of control. Fieldwork can be challenging and stressful, especially when our future academic lives (theses, dissertations, contracts, grades, etc.) rest on the outcome of our work. In all likelihood, we have entered the field with an approved research plan and feel "in control" of the situation. However, ethnographic researchers must be prepared to relinquish control of the research timeline and agenda to take advantage of the emergent nature of the ethnographic research process. For example, you should be prepared to abandon your plans to talk to a participant at a certain time and place. Unanticipated events will occur, and you need to be willing to go with the flow! As we have all heard, wonderful things can happen when you let go of control!

Field Notes

As you learned previously, field notes are gathered, recorded, and compiled on-site during the course of a study. For an ethnographic researcher, field notes provide a record of the researcher's understandings of the lives, people, and events that are the focus of the research. In all likelihood, you will embark on a research journey that thrusts you into an educational setting, and you will spend considerable time and energy trying to understand what is going on. A critical component of this research journey will be the data you collect as a "trained observer." You will need a way to capture your experiences in a way that will enable you to eventually craft a narrative of what is going on. Your primary tool for doing this is your field notes. Emerson and colleagues provide several insights into the use and nature of field notes in ethnographic research:

> (1) What is observed and ultimately treated as "data" or "findings" is inseparable from the observational process. (2) In writing fieldnotes, the field researcher should give special attention to the indigenous meanings and concerns of the people studied. (3) Contemporaneously written fieldnotes are an essential grounding and resource for writing broader, more coherent accounts of others' lives and concerns. (4) Such fieldnotes should detail the social and interactional processes that make up people's everyday lives and activities.[11]

In the past the craft of recording field notes was learned in a constructivist graduate school environment. This is our kind way of saying that students learned how to write field notes through folklore and on-the-job training. There was little in the literature to help them prepare for entering the research setting with trusty notebook and pencil in hand! The literature now has some helpful guidelines that suggest ways to record field notes and the process to use to move from writing scribbles on a table napkin to writing cohesive narratives that can ultimately find their way into the ethnographic research account.

So, what do you write down in these field notes? Well, it depends on what you are looking for! We can offer only limited guidance to help quell your concerns about the how-to of writing field notes. But first let us start with an example of how *not* to do field notes!

During his studies at the University of Oregon, one of the authors (Geoff Mills) took a class on "Ethnographic Research in Education" and was required to conduct a beginning ethnography of something that was "culturally different" for him. As an Australian studying

---

[11] *Writing Ethnographic Fieldnotes* (p. 11), by R. M. Emerson, R. I. Fretz, and L. L. Shaw, Chicago, IL: University of Chicago Press.

in the United States, Geoff had a number of opportunities to study a culturally different phenomenon while at the same time having fun with the project. He chose to study a sorority. As part of this study, he participated in one of the regular ceremonies that was part of the sorority members' lives: a formal dinner held each Monday night at which members were required to wear dresses and male guests were expected to wear a jacket and tie.

During the course of the dinner, Geoff frequently excused himself to visit the restroom, stopping along the way to take out his notebook so he could record quotes and reconstruct events as they were happening—trying to capture in great detail all that he was observing. Of course, the irony in this strategy was that he was missing a great deal of the dinner by removing himself from the setting. The ridiculousness of the situation became evident when a dinner host asked him if he was feeling well or if the meal was to his satisfaction. After all, why did he keep leaving the dinner table?! The message for ethnographic researchers who use field notes as part of their data collection efforts is clear: You cannot physically record everything that is happening during an observation, nor should you try to.

There are some general guidelines you can follow in making observations and recording field notes that should help you combat the naivety exhibited by Geoff in the preceding example. As noted in Chapter 15, you should write up your field notes as soon as possible after the observational episode. You will find that you rely heavily on the mental notes, or "headnotes," that you have made during the day, and you should record your thoughts while fresh in mind.

Depending on the setting you are researching, and the degree of participation you are engaged in, the detail you record in your field notes will vary considerably. You may find by the end of the day that you have a pocket full of scrap paper with jottings from the day to augment your more detailed notes. Sometimes these jottings will capture keywords and phrases without a whole lot more to explain them. It is a good habit to let research participants know that you will be scribbling things down in your notepad; soon, they will become accustomed to this and it will not cause a distraction. Your jottings will serve as a mnemonic device to help you reconstruct the day's events. In short, when combined with your headnotes, these jottings can be a crucial aid in reconstructing and writing up your observations.

Your jottings and expanded field notes are for your own use, so you needn't worry about editorial concerns or journalistic conventions. There will not be a professor poised with red pen in hand to grade your field notes. They are not intended to be polished text. Your goal in recording field notes should be on description, not analysis and interpretation. It is helpful to think of field notes as a way to capture a slice of life while acknowledging that all descriptions are selective because they have been written by a researcher trying to capture it all. Once you accept that the purpose is to describe, and that through your descriptions will come understandings, you can easily focus on the task of creating field notes without being constrained about concerns for style and audience. (The processes for coding field notes, to aid in organization, are described in Chapter 15.)

Sometimes beginning researchers are troubled by how to begin writing up their field notes for the day. A simple approach is to trace what you did during the day and to write up the notes in chronological order. That is, start at the beginning and finish at the end of the day!

You should avoid the temptation to recreate the dialogue. Use quotation marks only when the words were taken down at the time of the observation. Anything else should be paraphrased. Although a tape recorder is appropriate for structured ethnographic interviews, in your day-to-day observations you should stick with the convention of recording the quote on the spot or paraphrasing after the event.

Whether taken in the actual setting or recorded as soon as possible after leaving the setting, field notes describe as accurately as possible and as comprehensively as possible all relevant aspects of the situation observed. As described in Chapter 15, they include what was actually observed *and* the observer's reactions to the same. What was actually observed represents the who, what, where, and when portion of the field notes. To appreciate the enormity of the task, imagine yourself trying to describe, in writing, in excruciating detail, even one of your current research class meetings. What was the physical setting like? What did it look like? Who was present? What did they look like? How did they act? What about your instructor? How did he or she look and act? What was said? What interactions took place? The task appears even more awesome when you consider that descriptions must be very specific and must represent what was actually seen (or heard), not your interpretation of what was seen. Patton gives several good examples that clearly illustrate the difference between "vague and overgeneralized notes" and "detailed and concrete notes." One of them is presented below:

> *Vague and over generalized notes:* The next student who came in to take the test was very poorly dressed.
>
> *Detailed and concrete notes:* The next student who came into the room was wearing clothes quite different from the three students who'd been in previously. The three previous students looked like they'd been groomed before they came to the test. Their hair was combed, their clothes were clean and pressed, the colors of their clothes matched, and their clothes were in good condition. This new student had on pants that were soiled with a hole or tear in one knee and a threadbare seat. The flannel shirt was wrinkled with one tail tucked into the pants and the other tail hanging out. Hair was disheveled and the boy's hands looked like he'd been playing in the engine of a car.[12]

Clearly, the detailed notes are superior to the vague notes. What constitutes being "very poorly dressed" may well vary from observer to observer (as those who read the tabloids know), but the detailed description speaks for itself, and anyone who reads it will have a similar mental picture of what the boy looked like.

In addition to literal descriptions, the observer also records personal reactions in *reflective field notes.* These notes include interpretations, and other subjective thoughts and feelings, but they are clearly differentiated from the more objective, strictly descriptive, field notes; typically they are identified with a special code (e.g., *PC* for personal comment or *OC* for observer's comments—see Figure 15.1). In these notes the observer is free to express any thoughts regarding how things are going, where things are going, and what might be concluded. Reflective field notes might include statements such as the following:

PC I have the feeling that tension among faculty members has been growing for some time.

PC I think Mr. Haddit has been egging on other faculty members.

PC I'm finding it hard to be objective because Mr. Hardnozed is rather abrasive.

PC I think the transition would have been smoother if key faculty members had been informed and involved in the process.

Such insights add a significant dimension to the observations and thus contribute to producing a "rich" description, the objective of ethnographic research.

Observing and Recording Everything You Possibly Can

If going into an observation you knew exactly what you wanted to observe, you would probably have no reason to go. Engaging in an effort to "record everything" will quickly attune you to what is of most interest to you. During these observational periods, you can start with a broad sweep of the setting and gradually narrow your focus as you get a clearer sense of what is most pressing. You can also decide on your strategies for recording observations. You might record verbatim conversations, make maps and illustrations, take photographs, make videotape or audiotape recordings, or even write furiously in the fashion of a principal or university

---

[12] *Qualitative Evaluation and Research Methods* (2nd ed., pp. 240–241), by M. Q. Patton, 1990, Newbury Park, CA: Sage.

professor undertaking an evaluation! Recording observations is a very idiosyncratic activity, but you should follow one rule: Don't run off to the restroom every 5 minutes—you *will* miss something! Do try to maintain a running record of what is happening in a format that will be most helpful for you.

For example, in his ethnographic research study of a school district attempting multiple change efforts,[13] Geoff Mills attended the district's teacher in-service day. The following are some of his field notes from this observation:

8:30 AM

An announcement is made over the public address system requesting that teachers move into the auditorium and take a seat in preparation for the in-service. As the teachers file into the auditorium, the pop song "The Greatest Love of All" is played.

8:41 AM

The Assistant Superintendent welcomes the teachers to the in-service with the conviction that it is also the "best district with the best teachers." The brief welcome is then followed by the Pledge of Allegiance and the introduction of the new Assistant Superintendent.

8:45 AM

The Assistant Superintendent introduces the Superintendent as "the Superintendent who cares about kids, cares about teachers, and cares about this district."

The next hour of the in-service was focused on the introduction of new teachers to the district (there were 60 new appointments) and the presentation of information about at-risk children becoming a new focus for the district.

10:00 AM

The Superintendent returns to the lyrics of "The Greatest Love of All" and suggests that the message from the song may be suitable as the district's charge: "Everyone is searching for a hero. People need someone to look up to. I never found anyone who fulfilled my needs. . . ." The Superintendent compels the teachers to be the heroes for their students and wishes them a successful school year before closing the in-service.

As you can see from this abbreviated example, there is nothing mystical about field notes. They serve as a record of what a researcher attended to during the course of an observation and help guide subsequent observations and interviews. This was the beginning of Geoff's yearlong fieldwork in the McKenzie School District, and this initial observation helped him to frame questions that guided his efforts to understand how central office personnel, principals, and teachers manage and cope with multiple innovations.

Observing and Looking for Nothing in Particular

While working in the field, you should try to see routines in new ways. If you can, try to look with "new eyes" and approach the scene as if you were an outsider. Wolcott offers helpful advice for teachers conducting observations in classrooms that are so familiar that everything seems ordinary and routine:

> Aware of being familiar with classroom routines, an experienced observer might initiate a new set of observations with the strategy that in yet another classroom one simply assumes "business as usual" . . . The observer sets a sort or radar, scanning constantly for whatever it is that those in the setting are doing to keep the system operating smoothly.[14]

[13] *Managing and Coping With Multiple Educational Change: A Case Study and Analysis*, by G. E. Mills, 1988, unpublished doctoral dissertation, University of Oregon, Eugene.
[14] *Transforming Qualitative Data: Description, Analysis, and Interpretation* (p. 162), by H. F. Wolcott, 1994, Thousand Oaks, CA: Sage.

Looking for "Bumps" or Paradoxes

You should consider the environment you are observing as if it were "flat," with nothing in particular standing out to you. This strategy gives you an opportunity to look for the "bumps" in the setting. In ethnographic research studies focused in classrooms, these bumps might be unexpected student responses to a new curriculum or teaching strategy or an unexpected response to a new classroom management plan, seating arrangement, monitoring strategy, or innovation.

For example, a teacher concerned with gender inequity in the classroom might notice that one or two boys seem to be controlling the classroom. Upon noticing this bump, he keeps a tally of the number of times students command his attention by answering or asking questions, and it becomes painfully evident that one or two boys are regularly the focus of attention during a lesson.

In addition to looking for bumps, ethnographic researchers should also look for contradictions or paradoxes in their classrooms. Like a bump, a paradox will often stand out in an obvious way to the researcher who has taken the time to stand back and look at what is happening in the classroom. Teacher researchers using ethnographic techniques often comment on the unintended consequences of a particular teaching strategy or a curriculum change that has become evident only when they have had an opportunity to observe the results of their actions. These consequences often present themselves in the form of a paradox—a contradiction in terms. For example, one teacher researcher had recently incorporated manipulatives (tiles, blocks, etc.) into her math instruction in a primary classroom. After observing her students, she commented: "I thought that the use of manipulatives in teaching mathematics would also lead to increased cooperation in group work. Instead, what I saw were my kids fighting over who got to use what and not wanting to share."

Figure 17.2, which represents an adaptation of Patton's "Top 10" guidelines, provides a useful summary of our discussion of fieldwork and field notes.

In this chapter we have described the complex business of ethnographic research and presented it as an alternative to quantitative research techniques—should the chosen problem be suitably studied by an ethnographic research approach. It is not intended as an "easy

---

1. Be descriptive in taking fieldnotes.

2. Gather a variety of information from different perspectives.

3. Cross-validate and triangulate by gathering different kinds of data (e.g., observations, documents, interviews) and by using multiple methods.

4. Use quotations; represent people in their own terms. Capture their experiences in their own words.

5. Select "key informants" wisely and use them carefully. Draw on the wisdom of their informed perspectives, but keep in mind that their perspectives are limited.

6. Be aware of and sensitive to different stages of fieldwork.
   a) Build trust and rapport at the beginning. Remember that the observer is also being observed.
   b) Stay alert and disciplined during the more routine, middle phase of fieldwork.
   c) Focus on pulling together a useful synthesis as fieldwork draws to a close.

7. Be disciplined and conscientious in taking fieldnotes at all stages of fieldwork.

8. Be as involved as possible in experiencing the situation as fully as possible while maintaining an analytical perspective grounded in the purpose of the fieldwork.

9. Clearly separate description from interpretation and judgment.

10. Include in your fieldnotes and report your own experiences, thoughts, and feelings.

FIGURE 17.2

Summary guidelines for fieldwork and fieldnotes
Source: From M. Q. Patton, *Qualitative Evaluation and Research Methods,* pp. 272–273, copyright © 1990 by Sage Publications, Inc. Adapted by permission of Sage Publications, Inc.

out" for graduate students who are math phobic! If you undertake this intimate and open-ended form of research, you will be faced with a set of personal (and perhaps interpersonal) challenges that may make that statistics class look like small potatoes. You may also find yourself engaged in a meaning-making activity that belies description and that redefines your life as an educational researcher.

An example of ethnographic research appears at the end of this chapter.

SUMMARY

Ethnographic Research: Definition and Purpose

1. Ethnographic research is the study of the cultural patterns and perspectives of participants in their natural setting.

2. Ethnography produces a picture of a "way of life" of some identifiable group of people using a process (primarily participant observation) that enables the researcher to discern patterns of behavior in human social activity.

3. The culture of any group is the set of attitudes, values, concepts, beliefs, and practices that an ethnographer has found could be attributed successfully to the members of that society.

The Ethnographic Research Process

4. Several steps can serve as guideposts in conducting ethnographic research:
   a. Identify the purpose of the research study.
   b. Frame the study as a larger theoretical, policy, or practical problem.
   c. Pose initial ethnographic research questions.
   d. Describe the overall approach and rationale for the study.
   e. Describe the site and sample selection.
   f. Describe the researcher's role (entry to the research site, reciprocity, and ethics).
   g. Describe data collection methods.
   h. Describe appropriate strategies for the analysis and interpretation of data.
   i. Write the ethnographic account.

Types of Ethnographic Research

5. A critical ethnography is a highly politicized form of ethnography written by a researcher in order to advocate against inequalities and domination of particular groups that exist in society.

6. A realist ethnography is form of ethnography written with an objective style and using common categories (e.g., "family life") for cultural description, analysis, and interpretation.

7. An ethnographic case study is a form of ethnography that focuses on describing the activities of a specific group and the shared patterns of behavior it develops over time.

Key Characteristics of Ethnographic Research

8. Ethnographic research is carried out in a natural setting, not a laboratory.

9. It involves intimate, face-to-face interaction with participants.

10. It presents an accurate reflection of participants' perspectives and behaviors.

11. It uses inductive, interactive, and repetitious collection of "unstructured" data and analytic strategies to build local cultural theories.

12. Data is primarily collected through fieldwork experiences.

13. It typically uses multiple methods for data collection, including conducting interviews and observations, and reviewing documents, artifacts, and visual materials.

14. It frames all human behavior and belief within a sociopolitical and historical context.

15. It uses the concept of culture as a lens through which to interpret results.

16. It places an emphasis on exploring the nature of particular social phenomena, rather than setting out to test hypotheses about them.

17. It investigates a small number of cases, perhaps just one case, in detail.

18. It uses data analysis procedures that involve the explicit interpretation of the meanings and functions of human actions. Interpretations occur within the context or group setting and are presented through the description of themes.

19. It requires that researchers be reflective about their impact on the research site and the cultural group.

20. It offers interpretations of people's actions and behaviors that must be uncovered through an

investigation of what people actually do and their reasons for doing it.

21. It offers a representation of a person's life and behavior that is neither the researcher's nor the person's. Instead, it is built upon points of understanding and misunderstanding that occur between researcher and participant.

22. It cannot provide an exhaustive, absolute description of anything. Rather, ethnographic descriptions are necessary partial, bound by what can be handled within a certain time, under specific circumstances, and from a particular perspective.

Ethnographic Research Techniques

23. Participant observation is undertaken with two purposes in mind: to observe the activities, people, and physical aspects of a situation and to engage in activities that are appropriate to a given situation and that provide useful information.

24. Participant observation can be done to varying degrees, depending on the situation being observed and opportunities presented. A participant observer can be an active participant observer; a privileged, active observer; or a passive observer.

25. Participant observation is characterized by the following social behaviors: gaining entry and maintaining rapport, reciprocity, a tolerance for ambiguity, and personal determination coupled with faith in oneself.

26. Field notes are the written records of participant observers.

27. Field notes are characterized by headnotes and jottings that are written up at the end of a day's observation.

28. Field notes should be written up as soon as possible after completion of the observation.

29. In addition to providing literal descriptions, the observer also records personal reactions, generally referred to as reflective field notes.

Now go to the Companion Website at **www.prenhall.com/gay** to assess your understanding of chapter content with Practice Quiz, apply comprehension in Applying What You Know, broaden your knowledge about research in Web Links, and expand your research skills in Evaluating Articles, Analyzing Qualitative Data, Analyzing Quantitative Data, and Research Tools and Tips.

Many Roles, Many Faces: Researching School–Community Relations in a Heterogeneous American Urban Community

R. TIMOTHY SIEBER

In 1972 I embarked on fifteen months of field research[1] in Chestnut Heights, a polyethnic and multi-social-class New York City community, and in its three elementary schools.[2] At the time, I was unaware that the complexities of this field situation would severely put to the test the traditional anthropological methods— participant observation and interviewing—with which I had chosen to approach the research. In this chapter I examine my fieldwork experiences in this heterogeneous community and its schools, emphasizing the implications that the cultural complexities of the field situation had for problems of entry, rapport building, data collection, and analysis. My account is intended as a case illustration of the variety of problems, particularly in rapport building, that are likely to fall to the lot of participant observers researching complex urban communities and their relations with the formal institutions that serve them. Despite the many field difficulties that will be enumerated, I contend that traditional anthropological field methods are adequate to the task of investigating complex urban situations.

THE RESEARCH PROBLEM

The aim of my research in Chestnut Heights was twofold: (1) to examine the elementary-school classroom as a setting for child socialization in bureaucratic behavior; and (2) to investigate the implications of such school-based socialization for the formation of social-class and ethnic subcultures in community life. My interest in the first of these problems was chiefly generated by the work of Leacock (1969) and Dreeben (1968), whose studies of school-based enculturation had emphasized children's role socializations in the domain of formal organizational behavior. My graduate training, strong in British social anthropology, predisposed me to focus investigation on classroom social organization as the basic situational milieu for the child's organizational role socialization. Previous research suggested the guiding hypothesis of my study: that the organizational role socialization of the school pupil constitutes early preparation for his or her future role behavior as employee, client, consumer, and citizen in large-scale formal organizations of the American polity and economy.

In addition to documenting the content of the norms, values, and general expectations maintained by the school staff for pupil conduct, I was interested in investigating the means by which such expectations are communicated to children in the school. Durkheim's pedagogical writings (1956, 1966), as well as my own previous exploratory field research, suggested the school disciplinary process as the central vehicle for the transmission to pupils of school expectations for their behavior. In my focus on classroom social organization, I therefore sought to give special attention to its disciplinary and social-control dimensions.

As regards the second of my research problems, Eddy (1965), Leacock (1969), Rist (1970), and Gintis and Bowles (1972–1973)

had reported significant patterned variations in the nature of the pupil role socializations received by children of different class and ethnic groups in American society and had suggested that such variations contribute to the intergenerational reproduction of class and ethnic subcultures in American life. My desire to complete a comparative case study of the pupil role socializations experienced by a social-class and ethnically diverse sample of school pupils led to my choice of Chestnut Heights as a research site.

Chestnut Heights is a New York City community whose population exhibits great diversity both ethnically and in social class. As well as having a culturally heterogeneous population, the community is served by three quite different elementary schools – one public, one Catholic, and one Episcopal. The heterogeneity of the community and its schools permitted the comparative study of pupil role socializations I desired. Another contributing factor in my choice of Chestnut Heights as field site was my familiarity with it, acquired during two years of residence there while a graduate student and a previous brief period of field research in an adjacent neighborhood.

THE RESEARCH SETTING

The Community

Chestnut Heights is a quiet, medium-density residential community of 9,000 people located in New York City. Its twenty-one square blocks of tree-lined streets and attached four-story townhouses are naturally bounded on three sides by an expressway and two wide commercial thoroughfares. It is outstanding for its cultural heterogeneity: Over forty ethnic groups are represented in a population that residents call "polyglot" or "Heinz variety." Marked differences in economic standing are also present among the residents; they range from the relief-receiving poor to the well-to-do upper middle class. In residents' cognitive maps of the community, in marriage and intermarriage patterns, in community political cleavages, and in social interaction, however, three broad categorical groupings subsume all other identities. These groupings are the Oldtimers, the Brownstoners, and the Spanish.

Oldtimers. This group includes the area's longest-term residents, the European-derived Catholic ethnic groups that comprise 70 percent of the local population. Dominant among them are the third-generation Italians[3] and smaller populations of third-generation Syrians and fifth-generation and longer resident Irish. Terming themselves "working people," Oldtimers characteristically engage in local small business; work as skilled or semi-skilled workers in maritime shipping, manufacturing, and construction; or hold lower-level civil service or other white-collar positions.

Brownstoners. These newcomers to the area since 1960 comprise 15 percent of the local population. They are predominantly

Anglo-Saxon, Protestant, young, and cosmopolitan. As professional people, most have migrated to New York City for career reasons and work in the city's downtown business district in law, publishing, architecture, finance, advertising, public relations, or the arts. The term "Brownstoner" derives from "brownstone," the name given the community's modal dwelling type, the attached four-story nineteenth-century townhouse. These young professionals came to be closely identified with the low-cost townhouses they purchased and avidly rehabilitated. Not all Brownstoners are homeowners, however; many tenants have followed in the wake of the homeowners. My own residence in the neighborhood occurred as part of the continuing in-migration of this grouping.

Spanish (Hispanos). The third major group is the Hispanics, a diverse group of people who have migrated to the area since the 1950s. Whereas Oldtimers and Brownstoners live residentially interspersed throughout Chestnut Heights, the Hispanics are residentially segregated on its fringes. Puerto Ricans predominate, making up more than 80 percent of the Hispanics, although substantial minorities of Cubans, Dominicans, and Colombians are also present. Although approximately 40 percent receive public assistance, most Hispanics consider themselves to be working people. They are generally more marginally employed than Oldtimer working people, however. Many work as low-paid factory operatives in a variety of local seasonal industries, especially garment work, or as lower-echelon service workers in restaurants, health institutions, and janitorial services. The most well-to-do, largely Cubans and Colombians, own small businesses or work in lower-echelon white-collar employment as bank tellers, store clerks, or clerical workers. Occupational designations are not important in Hispanic references to themselves, however. The most important designation is that relating to language and culture – that they are Spanish, or *Hispanos.* They contrast their group with the "Americans," whom they see to include both Oldtimers and Brownstoners.

The Community's Three Elementary Schools

Chestnut Heights is served by three elementary schools located in the community: PS 4, a public school; the Wright School, a private Episcopal day school; and St. Michaels School, a Catholic parish school. In this heterogeneous community, where clear group boundaries are evident in most spheres of social life, children are recruited into the schools and their component classrooms in such a way that these group boundaries are preserved in the social organization of elementary education.

PS 4. The public school is the largest of the elementary schools, with 782 pupils. At 59 percent of the enrollment, Hispanic children predominate in the school. Ninety-seven percent of Hispanic children are Puerto Rican. The remaining 41 percent of the school enrollment is evenly split between children of Oldtimers and Brownstoners. Even though the school draws its enrollment from the immediate neighborhood, it lacks close integration with the local community. The school is an organ of city and state government, from which it receives its funding, and is subordinate to extensive, higher district- and system-wide levels of administration. Its staff members are recruited from outside the neighborhood as well. Fewer than a quarter (23 percent) of its teaching and administrative staff of

forty-three persons are members of ethnic groups resident in Chestnut Heights, and only four (9 percent) of the staff reside locally. Informal, nonschool interaction between staff and community residents rarely occurs. The staff also maintain highly negative views of the neighborhood and its residents. The nonlocal control and staffing and the school's heterogeneous enrollment preclude its identification with any of the community's groups in the way that St. Michaels and the Wright School are thought of as belonging, respectively, to the Oldtimers and the Brownstoners.

The Wright School. This school, an Episcopal private day school, is the smallest of the three schools with an enrollment of seventy-two. The school is highly autonomous in its operations, as it has only nominal ties to a diocesan school system that provides few services and little supervision for the school. Its funding is purely local, through endowment income and tuition receipts. The school's operations reflect its progressive educational philosophy, termed by staff as "modified open classroom." The Wright School has close ties to the Brownstoner segment of the community. Forty-three percent of its pupils are from local Brownstoner families; most of the remaining enrollment is of West Indian children from other neighborhoods. All but one member of the adult staff of twelve are locally resident Brownstoners. The school and the attached church premises also serve as the prime location for Brownstoner civic association meetings and other social functions, such as the yearly arts-and-crafts sale and the annual spring house tour reception.

St. Michaels School. While St. Michaels is part of a large but loose diocesan school system, the school is largely locally controlled and autonomous in formulating educational policies. Moreover, its autonomy is enhanced because the school is financed entirely through local parish sources. The school has close ties to the Oldtimers, most of whom send their children there. A large minority of the enrollment (35 percent) is composed of Hispanic children, primarily from the more upwardly mobile and better-off national groups, such as the Cubans and Colombians. Ninety-four percent of St. Michaels' sixteen teaching staff members are members of Oldtimer ethnic groups, and 87 percent reside locally.

Most Oldtimer voluntary associational life in the community is done under the rubric of the local parish, and within the parish the school serves as the physical and symbolic focus of nearly all this associational life. The building and grounds are used for an extensive array of activities, numbering in the hundreds over a year's time, from the at least monthly dinners, dances, and gambling events sponsored by various associations to the regular monthly meetings of the nearly twenty parish organizations (such as the Mission Guild, the Home-School Association, the Parish Council, the Women's Society, and so forth). Two-thirds of the school's budget is financed through the proceeds generated by the many activities sponsored by these organizations.

RESEARCH METHODS AND PROCEDURES

In studying Chestnut Heights and its schools I decided to rely primarily on participant observation, supplemented wherever possible with in-depth and other interviewing of informants. A major factor in my decision to use traditional methods was the desire to compensate for my choice of a nonconventional, familiar American site by using methods that maximized face-to-face encounters and social immersion in the study community. I had been taught that it was only through such immersion and deep personal encounter that one experienced the fieldwork rite of passage. A traditional methodological stance was also consistent with my training and, it seemed, with my aim to complete basic anthropological research on my chosen problem. I put participant observation and interviewing to different uses however, in my investigations of school life and of community affairs.

School Research

My research in the three study schools was concentrated on a sample of eight classrooms chosen from the first and fifth grades in each school. My general procedures were the same in each of the classrooms. For the most part, I operated as a silent observer, usually sitting at the back of the classroom taking running notes on selected areas of classroom behavior. In each class I periodically sought and received teacher permission to sit more toward the middle of the room, amongst the children, so as to record closer observations of some forms of pupil behavior. In keeping with the expressed desires of school personnel, however, I attempted to keep a low profile in the classrooms. While being an adult gave me freedoms not permitted pupils—for example, I could leave the room or school for any purpose and at my own discretion—I tried to observe the general classroom standards of behavior established for pupils.

My attention in the classrooms focused on two main areas: (1) social organization—classroom roles, formal and informal subgroups, ritual and routine behavior, and the activity schedule; and (2) school discipline, including all teacher statements evaluating behavior and accompanying sanctions of behavior, sanction-eliciting forms of pupil behavior, and any noticeable results from teacher application of sanctions. My general practice was to stay with the class through the entire day, coming to the school in the morning, lining up with the children in the schoolyard, following them to the classroom and through the day's schedule, and so forth.

I also sought opportunities for informal interaction and conversation with the school staffs. Most days I took several short breaks from the classroom to visit the teachers' lounge or its equivalent in each school. I also ate lunch each day in the schools with the teachers in their staff dining areas. My conversations with teachers in these informal settings provided a rich source of information on their perceptions of a wide variety of school matters. These settings also gave me the opportunity of speaking with most of the teachers in each school and allowed me informally to interview the study teachers about events I had observed in their classrooms. These informal interviews supplemented more formal ones with the study teachers.

I also spent a considerable amount of time, largely after regular school hours, attending school-wide, as opposed to classroom, events and affairs—staff meetings, teacher union meetings, parent–teacher conferences, special assemblies, parent association meetings, school holiday pageants, fund-raising events, and so forth. These settings permitted gathering of information through observation and interview on school social organization, particularly intrastaff relations, school educational goals, policies, and philosophies, and school–community rela-

tions. Such contextual data were indispensable to proper analysis of classroom organization and behavior.

Research on Community Life

My research on community affairs centered on delineating significant group boundaries and patterns of intergroup relations in Chestnut Heights. I sought information on these topics as an aid to explaining differential patterns of pupil recruitment to the three local schools and the differing character of school-community relations in each case. Another purpose of the community research was to provide a context for interpreting the class and ethnic implications of observed variations in pupil role socialization in the schools.

Through my earlier research in the area, I had become aware of the considerable local political ferment in Chestnut Heights. This active political life was a reflection of the substantial population changes in the area resulting from the in-migrations of Brownstoners and Hispanics. It seemed that many expressions of group identities, boundaries, and alignments would be evident through study of community political activity.

Each of the community's three major groupings has its own maze of voluntary associations, whose activities give expression to the groupings' respective public concerns, cultural outlooks, and visions for the community's future. Most of these associations take an active role in community politics by attempting to advance their grouping's usually conflicting interests in a wide variety of local political struggles, including but not limited to contests for local elective offices. When I began my research, the balance of power in community politics had been moving for several years toward increasing Brownstoner ascendancy. On many issues of concern to the community, such as the desirability of preservation over new housing development, each of the groupings had its own position, responding to its own values and perceived needs.

Quasi-governmental and governmental boards and commissions—including the 97th Police Precinct Community Council, the District 41 Community School Board, and the District 33 Planning Board—also held regular public meetings and a number of special open hearings on issues of local concern, such as the proposal for modernizing and expanding the local waterfront containerport, and the proposal for constructing a new high school, in which site location was the issue. Such hearings and meetings were often raucous affairs, with speakers and segments of the audience from the range of community groupings articulating and debating differing viewpoints. Similar articulation of local issues and expressions of group alignments and cleavages were also evident in the more than a dozen local candidates' nights held in connection with local electoral political contests.

Throughout the fifteen months of my research, the majority of evenings each week was spent in attending meetings and other functions of the community's various voluntary associations, ranging from the Brownstoner-controlled Chestnut Heights Association and the Burkham Court Improvement Association, to Oldtimer groups such as the St. Michaels Golden Age Society and the LaBella Democratic Club, to Hispanic associations such as the Anti-Poverty Program-linked LaLucha League and the St. Michaels Cursillo devotional association. Excluding the governmental boards, over the course of my research I attended at least one meeting or other function of over 110 different voluntary associations.

Little of this associational activity had direct bearing on the community's schools. I did, however, give special attention to the somewhat separate sphere of education-related associational and political activity that flourished within the arena of the public-school system's community school district, an administrative unit encompassing twenty-four elementary and junior high schools in a geographical area much larger than Chestnut Heights. It was fortunate also that the biannual Community School Board election took place during my research. The three-month election campaign spawned dozens of special meetings, candidates' nights, and debates on local educational issues; it reactivated a series of local parent, community, and teacher interest groups and drew many other local associations into supporting candidates for election and articulating their perceptions of the schools and educational issues.

Generally, before first attending some function of any local association, I would approach its formal leader for an interview focusing on Chestnut Heights intergroup relations and during the interview seek permission to attend a meeting. I was never denied such permission. The meetings and other functions of these associations represented important phenomena for study in themselves, but they also afforded opportunities for informal interaction with and interviewing of participants, for renewing previous acquaintances, and for making new ones. Contacts made with participants during these affairs often led to arrangements for interviewing them at a future date in their homes.

My focus on intergroup relations led beyond investigating the political and associational to the employment of other research methods. I completed a great deal of observation and interviewing of a more general nature—in the shops and on the stoops and streets of the area—on such matters as shopping patterns, neighboring interactions, children's play patterns, interethnic face-to-face relations, and the history and character of the community. Largely through contacts made in voluntary associational meetings, I also conducted a series of more formal interviews, at their homes, with an ethnically and class stratified sample of thirty residents on the subjects of ethnic classifications and education. I also conducted some archival research at the local historical society on the history of population shifts in the area and in two of the local churches on interethnic marriage patterns as reflected in their marriage records. Although I did not employ any formal survey methods, for some purposes I found more impersonal approaches to residents both possible and effective in this urban community. To engage quick, unself-conscious answers on the location of community boundaries, for example, I posed as a lost stranger and systematically stopped strangers on the street with inquiries on this subject.

GAINING ENTRY AND BUILDING RAPPORT: A MULTIFACETED PROCESS

In seeking to undertake research in Chestnut Heights and its schools, I discovered that each segment of the diverse study population required a somewhat different avenue of approach. The quality of the rapport I was able to achieve and maintain with each segment was variable as well. The teaching staffs of the schools perceived my activities differently, in keeping with the constraints afforded by school social structural characteristics and the varying quality of school–community relations in each setting. Perceptions of me by community residents were similarly variable.

In taking into account my complement of statuses as young, male, single, middle-class, student, WASP, community resident, and, last but not least, researcher, each segment of the research community tended to interpret my status and activities in terms that were familiar to them. On the basis of these interpretations, each group made its assessment of the potential benefits and dangers that my activities implied for them and cooperated with me in a fashion consistent with this assessment. As a consequence, the community presented a quite variable profile of situations calling for differing strategies of entry, rapport building, and even data collection. My concurrent study of the different groupings and institutions, as well, precipitated boundary and loyalty conflicts whose management required some special adaptations on my part. I begin discussion of these matters with treatment of my experiences in the schools, reserving until later the consideration of my experiences in researching community life outside the schools.

Research at PS 4: The Stranger Within

Gaining entry to PS 4 was a bureaucratically cumbersome process that consumed a full year. Fortunately, I had anticipated the delays and had begun the process a year before I planned to start my observations there. The Bureau of Educational Research of the Board of Education of the City of New York has ultimate authority over all research, external and in-house, that takes place in the city school system. Following standard procedure, I submitted a proposal, personal information, and letters of university sponsorship to them for their preliminary screening and approval. This preliminary approval was to take six months, and occurred only after my initial materials had been lost in their office and then resubmitted.

It was then necessary for me to approach PS 4's principal to gain her written approval of my project. This approval was easily granted, although I later learned that the teaching staff had not been informed of my impending presence until some months later when I first began to appear at their classroom doors with the principal. With the principal's authorization in hand, I then was required to secure the approval of the community district superintendent, to whom more materials were submitted. It was a quirk of fate that led to a relatively painless securing of his permission. The community superintendent was at that point in time in a lame duck position; because he had been terminated in favor of his deputy he was due to leave office in a matter of weeks. In a conference I had with him and his designated successor, the latter pressed him to have my request presented to the community school board for public discussion and debate. This would have no doubt led to considerable delay, if not to other difficulties. The deputy's request provoked the superintendent, in dramatic display of his flagging authority, to sign my authorization without further word and summarily to dismiss me. A final submission of the principal's and the superintendent's authorizations to the Bureau of Educational Research yielded, some months later and after telephone promptings, my final approval from them.

Once inside PS 4 I entered into successive study of four of its classrooms over a ten-week period. The resulting extended observations of the study classrooms permitted me to gain a relatively intimate knowledge with their day-to-day operations.

Because of my classroom and other school activities, the staff became habituated to my presence in the school. Although I did come to enjoy cordial relations with most of the staff, particularly with the study teachers, my growing familiarity with classroom life did not result in an increasing acceptance by the staff. Instead, the amount and natural quality of the information I was gathering on their classrooms rendered me a dangerous threat to the boundaries of their authority. This is because my other research activities placed me in frequent association with people who are normally excluded from the knowledge I came to possess.

Warren (1973, 1975), Dreeben (1973), and others have written of the closed, sanctuary-like character of classroom life for most teachers, who work largely in isolation from and out of view of other adults, ideally guided in their actions by internalized professional norms of conduct. Indeed, I was not in the school long before I realized that my role as classroom observer afforded me more detailed information of life in the study classrooms than was available to any other outside category of person, whether administrator or parent or teacher or pupil from another class.

As an observer I was also able to witness the ways in which these other categories of people are restricted in their access to information on normal behavior in the classroom. Except for custodians and older pupils,[4] classes observe special patterns of behavior when visitors make their infrequent appearances in the room. Teachers and pupils alike exhibit tension, and pupils exhibit a learned set of responses in the form of increased behavioral caution, restraint, and formality that contrasts with their usual style of action. Teachers normally prod pupils into this style of behavior with such comments as, "Children, we have a visitor in the room!" or, "Boys and girls, while Miss Fox is visiting show her how nice you can be!" Such caution was especially observed during visits from school administrators, either during their usual momentary visits at the doorway or during more extended observations. These more formal observations of teachers' classroom performances are conducted annually by school administrators for purposes of personnel evaluation. The annual fifteen- to thirty-minute observations provide the occasion for the most sustained administrative presence in any given classroom.

Contending With Staff Fears of Evaluation

Several factors led teachers to view me as an evaluator potentially serving the interests of local and even higher-level school-system administrators. I was conducting lengthy, silent observations, and, like the administrators during their evaluations, from the rear of the room. Also, the teaching staff had not been consulted by the principal when she granted me permission to study their classrooms. Relations in general between PS 4's teaching staff and its triple-tiered administrative hierarchy were also, I learned at the school, characteristically strained and impersonal. The teachers' propensity to view me as an evaluator was also compounded by my contacts with supraschool levels of administration. I had received research permission from the district and central offices and, as part of my information-gathering activities, regularly visited the district office, where I had encountered the principal and some of the staff. For this reason, to my chagrin, in my first week at the school I was introduced several times as "the man from the district office."

Finally, my educational status as doctoral candidate led many teachers to assume that, like most doctoral candidates in education, I was completing an evaluation of their classroom or their teaching, in spite of the different descriptions I gave them of my research interests. The field services division of the school of education at my university had, in fact, conducted several official evaluations of school programs in the local district. Most teachers knew little of the nature of anthropological research and its potential contributions to education, and there seemed never to be adequate time for full explanations. Also, in the highly bureaucratic public-school system, the importance of all higher educational advancement is generally reckoned in terms of the attendant increased salary increments and promotional opportunities that accrue. I discovered that the teachers, not unexpectedly, were highly conscious of educational credentials and tended to equate doctoral study with aspirations for promotion to the supervisory ranks.

For these reasons, regardless of the number and extent of my explanations that I was interested in the basic features of schoolroom life, there was the continual desire of staff to believe that I aimed to judge their classroom behavior and teaching performance on the basis of their traditional professional norms. Throughout the period of my research in the school, there existed a residual staff suspicion of me because of this perceived vulnerability to my supposed professional judgments. Teachers, for example, regularly apologized to me for the academic performance deficiencies of their pupils—that they were not yet doing complex sentences or long division, and so forth. Similarly, when I arrived at their classes to begin observations, several teachers unfavorably compared their teaching to idealized and unrealistic conceptions they maintained of the performance of colleagues I had previously visited.

Other remarks of teachers acknowledged their awareness of my unusual access to information on the intimacies of life in some classes. Their perceived vulnerability, for example, was often expressed in joking. In my presence one teacher quipped to another who was about to receive my visit that "You haven't got a thing to worry about—only three people have lost their jobs so far!" Knowing of my interest in pupil peer relations, teachers frequently drew laughter in the lunchroom by warning their colleagues to watch their behavior, since I might be studying their peer groups too. Also, as compared with the staffs of the two non-public schools, the staff at PS 4 showed resistance to granting me anything resembling fictive teacher status. My general curiosity about the school and my resulting attendance at all types of school functions, including staff meetings, were not rebuffed, but they were not positively welcomed. Staff members indicated in nervous remarks that it would be more appropriate were I to restrict my study to children's activities. I was also never invited to informal staff gatherings away from the school, as I was in the private schools.

I attempted to allay the teachers' fears first by unobtrusively noting that my observational data were confidential and second by demonstrating this fact in my behavior, by disclosing as few of my impressions as possible when queried by other staff. I believe neither response did much to reduce the teachers' suspicions. To some extent I was able more successfully to mitigate these suspicions of me as a dangerous evaluator by taking on classroom duties that are usually associated with the more subordinate student role.

Such duties entailed helping to carry and lift heavy objects, assisting in the various forms of classroom clean-ups, making minor repairs to equipment such as phonographs, and so forth. At teachers' requests, I also frequently assisted children with various kinds of schoolwork, for example, going around the room to check answers or to help on certain simple cognitive operations. On many occasions I was asked to spend time assisting individual children by reading with them. At other times I was commissioned to lead small groups in recitation (reading out loud) or in math and spelling exercises with the use of flash cards.

This avenue of response was not without its problems, however. Although I did not feel I could refuse occasional requests to watch over the class when the teacher momentarily left the room, some teachers were less than pleased that for ethical reasons I eschewed any disciplinary role toward the children. Performance of other classroom duties, nevertheless, aided in the establishment of rapport with the study teachers by allowing me to reciprocate their cooperation with my research and by permitting expressions of deference that countered their fear of me as a dangerous evaluator.

Adapting to School Organizational Boundaries

In spite of, or perhaps because of, their fears of professional evaluations I might make of their performance, and the vague sanction given my efforts by higher administrative authorities, the PS 4 staff accepted my presence in their school as legitimate. In their assessment of this legitimacy, it was clear that my residence and research in the neighborhood were, at best, irrelevant factors. While all the teachers knew that my research carried beyond the school, my neighborhood activities appeared to be of little interest to them. Never, for example, did they ask what I had learned of the neighborhood.

I quickly learned that the teachers' lack of interest masked their fear of the threat to the boundaries of their authority that my simultaneous school and community activities posed for them. Again, their suspicion was that my outside contacts would lead me to divulge normally secret, damaging information to people who could then use it against them; in this case, the outsiders were parents and community activists. The few times that I mentioned in the school any item of information, however innocuous, showing personal familiarity with parents or community leaders resulted in looks of apprehension, raised eyebrows, noticeable tension, and momentary cooling of relations. For a few teachers, the mere fact of my residence in the community represented grounds for suspicion. My obvious membership in the Brownstoner category must also have been a factor in generating this suspicion.

It was necessary, in consequence, for me to be discreet while in the school about the existence of my contacts per se with parents as individuals and with community groups aligned with parents' interests. While I thus resolved not to discuss my neighborhood activities inside the school, I should add that there was no necessity for these activities to be conducted under stealth in order to be concealed from the teachers. The school staff, who resided elsewhere, were never present in the community when I worked there. This made it quite possible for me to adapt to the situation by keeping my outside life separate from my school life, much as the teachers themselves did.

The Private Schools: St. Michaels and the Wright School

Gaining entry to the private schools, St. Michaels and the Wright School, was a direct and uncomplicated matter. At St. Michaels,

with an introduction from a community leader, I met with the principal to explain my research. After two days, during which time she checked that teachers in the requested grades were willing to entertain my presence, she granted oral approval. At the Wright School, the principal's permission was forthcoming within an hour of my meeting her. After we discussed my research plans, she had me wait in her office while she consulted with the first- and fifth-grade teachers whose classes I wished to study, and then she granted permission.

Both St. Michaels and the Wright School are neighborhood schools in the way that no big-city public school can ever be: They are both locally controlled and financed, and they have next to no administrative subordinance to higher-level structures. Additionally, the schools' respective teaching staffs reside in the community, for the most part, and share common ethnic and social-class orientations with the families they serve. School personnel and pupil families view each other in a much more positive and less suspicious way than is the case in the public school. Parents at both private schools are more knowledgeable and supportive of existing school practices as well. The cultural discontinuities between school and community, in sum, are not so great as in the public-school situation.

Both schools, being less bureaucratized, exhibit more collegiality in staff relations, show less concern with protecting their boundaries from outside interference, and are more permeable to community influences. The fluidity of school boundaries is evident in the many important supportive roles that parents, particularly at St. Michaels, play in the day-to-day operations of the schools—staffing the library, assisting in the school office, patrolling the halls, and substituting for absent teachers in emergencies. More than a few of the teachers, in turn, are parents or former parents of children in the schools. At St. Michaels, some are former pupils as well, and as community residents most teachers participate in the Brownstoner or Oldtimer associational activity that is centered around the schools.

In contrast with the situation at PS 4, where my simultaneous involvement in school and community affairs caused boundary conflicts and necessitated special adaptations on both fronts, at the private schools my simultaneous school and community activities positively reinforced one another in enhancing the rapport I was able to develop with informants in both settings. My entry into the private schools was eased by the fact of my previous ongoing participation in Brownstoner and Oldtimer community activities, where I had demonstrated my interest in and concern for the community and had become known to teachers in both schools. Even before I approached the schools for research permission, their staffs had had opportunities to observe and judge me.

Inside the private schools, my research procedures were the same as in the public school, yet the relative informality and flexibility of the institutions and their greater permeability to outsiders led the teaching staffs to define my activities in a more accommodating and favorable fashion. Where in the public school I was considered as a stranger, in both private school I was quickly assimilated into the schools as an honorary member of their faculties. I was careful to keep my observations and interviews confidential, of course, but the staffs expressed no anxiety over school or classroom secrets that I could disclose to outsiders or administrators.

Treated and referred to by staff and parents alike as "Tim, the teacher," I was routinely invited to official and unofficial staff functions and honored with the staffs at their respective school testimonial dinners held for them by parents at the end of the school year. In addition, two months after completing my research at St. Michaels, the school lived up to the role assignment it had given me and asked if I might substitute teach for a week in one of my previous study classrooms.

Situational Constraints, Rapport, and Research Methodology: A Comparison of Classroom and Community

In all the schools I was restricted to a considerable degree to the role of silent, relatively passive observer. This was especially true of my activities in the classroom. There are many reasons that contributed to this restriction. As formal organizations, schools represent tightly bounded and articulated social systems. Institutional status roles are few in number, and in the interests of rational attainment of formal goals, they are carefully circumscribed by rules. Maintenance of procedure, order, and schedule are the predominant concerns of those in authority.

For the researcher the consequence is little maneuverability for role negotiation or action. The press of classroom and school routine allows researchers little latitude for accommodating their own agendas, which are fundamentally extraneous to institutional operations. In the classroom, for example, spontaneous interaction with participants is next to impossible. It is rarely possible to interview teacher or pupil participants to an event, such as a violent dispute, either during or immediately after it, when actors' accounts would be most fresh and accessible. Instead, hours can intervene before the schedule permits a few brief questions of actors, if it does so at all. Additionally, because participants' behavior is largely of a ritual or routine nature, there are few occasions for nondisruptive informal interaction with them. I found that variations in the degree of my acceptance by the school staffs did not alter these situational constraints peculiar to the classroom. Whether in PS 4 or private-school classrooms, my status as an outsider was always evident.

Because of the constraints against participation, my ethnographic accounts of classroom life are from an observer's viewpoint far more than from the viewpoint of a participant. The restrictions I encountered appear to be fairly typical in anthropological investigations of school life (Khleif 1974; Wolcott 1975d). Khleif has pointed out that as compared with the normal anthropological field situation the school setting "lacks. . . avenues for participation" by the fieldworker, that studying schools is an "essentially observer's, not a participant's function," and that the anthropologist finally "remains more of a stranger than a friend" (Khleif 1974:391).

As compared with my school activities, the greater diversity of research methods used in the community reflects the greater scale, complexity, and social heterogeneity of the community as a domain of inquiry requiring more diverse methods of approach. Also true, however, is that the more loosely structured domain of Chestnut Heights community life permitted such methodological flexibility on my part. Community life offers many opportunities for striking more of a balance between ob-servation and participation and consequently presents greater possibilities for conversations and interviews with actors.

My residence in the community, in particular, was indispensable in granting legitimacy to my presence there and in opening up many avenues for participation in its life. With considerable naturalness, for example, my residence there allowed me to shop for all my personal goods and services locally, seek my medical and dental care there, participate in the activities of my own block association, register to vote, be canvassed by political workers, be invited to political meetings of various kinds, take two adult-education courses at local churches, and utilize other community facilities such as the bank, post office, and bars. After my research had gotten under way and my local relationships broadened because of it, I engaged in mutual visiting and entertaining with neighbors and other informants, attended their weddings and other special occasions, celebrated religious and secular holidays with them, and exchanged cards, food, and other gifts at Christmas.

My local residence also legitimated my presence at the many community functions I attended. Residents, who knew I was conducting a study of the neighborhood, nevertheless complimented me for my regular attendance at these affairs. None of the community functions, except block parties, were attended by more than a small minority of residents. My presence at them was seen by many as indicating my active involvement and my concern and interest in the community. In more than one organization, because of my dedicated record of attending meetings, and in spite of the fact that I had played no active roles in them, I was even offered positions of leadership.

A great many of the association affairs I attended were benefits and fund raisers of various kinds. These included boxing matches sponsored by the local Longshoremen's Union Scholarship Fund, bake and plant sales held by the PS 4 Parents Association, the Chestnut Heights Association's annual art show and sale, and its community house tour, the testimonial dinner sponsored by the LaBella Democratic Club for its leader, LaLucha's Puerto Rican Discovery Day Street Fair, and the St. Michaels Parish Council's special Hawaiian night and "St. Paddy's" dinner dances. My attendance at these affairs demonstrated my moral and material support for the sponsoring organizations and their constituencies.

The participation roles that were possible permitted my engagement in many forms of reciprocity with local residents. These ranged from those intrinsic to unfettered informal conversation and face-to-face interaction to those with a more material basis, such as the dispensing of Halloween candy, patronage of local businesses, or financial contributions to community organizations and causes. All contributed to sustaining interaction with residents, allowing for mutual demonstrations of good will, and defusing suspicions on both sides. In consequence, I was permitted great flexibility and latitude in actively negotiating my role with different individuals and organizations and was able to gain greater access to actors' perspectives than I was in the school setting. These aspects of my community relationships, as I have noted, increased my acceptance by the private-school staffs, facilitated easier access to information on schoolwide affairs, and made my private-school research less tension ridden, although they did not influence the quality of the classroom data I was able to obtain.

Problems in Managing Diversity: Loyalty Conflicts and the Maintenance of Confidence

To some extent my ability to maintain rapport with so many separate groups was enhanced by the structural boundaries and political cleavages dividing them. I learned to adapt my speech usages, language choice (English or, occasionally, Spanish), topics of conversation, and interaction style to the group I was currently dealing with. Because the different groups so rarely came into personal contact with one another, I was largely able to keep my relationships with them distinct from one another. In attending events in the Hispanic blocks, for example, I hardly ever encountered anyone from among the Brownstoners or the Oldtimers. Similarly, Oldtimer and Brownstoner gatherings, whether formal or informal, were typically group homogeneous. Although each group maintained extensive stereotypes of the others, each was fundamentally ignorant of the others' ways and lived its own life largely in isolation from the others. Similar boundary maintenance, as I have noted, insulated public-school staff from community residents. My research in this heterogeneous community and its schools constituted, in some respects, several separate but concurrent fieldwork experiences.

Many boundary and loyalty conflicts were, nonetheless, unavoidable. Demands, some more subtle than others, were made for me to demonstrate loyalty by performing services to show gratitude for aid and confidences extended me. Had I been studying a single group or institution I would have been more easily able, ethically and politically, to respond to these demands. Because many of the requests would have entailed public actions implicitly or explicitly counter to the interests of other groups in the community, I had to decline or otherwise evade most of them. Some of these loyalty and boundary problems arose from role conflicts generated by simultaneous school and community research, and others arose from simultaneous research on different community social groupings.

Not surprisingly, most of the difficult requests came from the Brownstoners. Because of my cultural similarities to them, Brownstoners tended to assume, inaccurately, that I shared their judgments and general outlook on the community and its groups. They expected that I would not hesitate to lend whatever skills or information I possessed to serve their interests in community affairs. For example, with the explicitly stated aim of improving the Wright School's image and enrollments, I was asked by the local Brownstoner-controlled weekly newspaper to write articles favorably comparing the school to the others in the community. In another case, the primary Brownstoner civic association, the Chestnut Heights Association, which had few if any ties to the local Catholic parish of St. Michaels, wished its cooperation in their efforts to "improve the neighborhood." Aware of my acquaintance with parish figures, the association's leadership pressed me to serve as their St. Michaels liaison.

The PS 4 teachers were realistic in their fears that my outside contacts with parents would subject me to pressures to divulge confidential information of their classroom performance. The staff saw the middle-class Brownstoner parents as pushy, interfering, and condescending. Brownstoner parents, who enjoyed a measure of influence over school affairs through their control of the Parents Association, did in fact attempt to extract information from me on teachers' classroom performances. They hoped to use this information in their political efforts, as individuals and through the Parents Association, to change school practices and, in some cases, personnel. My own ties to the school were not threatening to the Brownstoners, who assumed that I shared their own negative stereotypes regarding the teachers, who they thought of as provincial in outlook and manners, lacking in social sophistication, and lower in social standing than themselves. With the Brownstoners it became necessary for me to protect the confidentiality of my classroom observations by scrupulously refraining from reporting them, even though this did dampen rapport with some parents who resented my terse, vague responses to their questions. As one parent remarked to me, "You sure don't let out much, do you?"

Whereas Brownstoner parents sought to use me in their efforts to intervene in PS 4 affairs, and my school research enhanced my status with them, my school connections were a hindrance to the development of rapport with Puerto Rican parents. The Puerto Rican parents view themselves and are viewed by the school as socially subordinate to the teachers and as linguistically inept in dealing with the school authorities. Each party considers the other to be culturally inept in their dealings together. The Puerto Rican parents had little familiarity with the nature of graduate research and interpreted my presence at the school to mean that I was a functionary of the school system, despite my many attempts to explain otherwise. As an "American" who was not too dissimilar in appearance and manner from the school staff, and as one who had access to their children's classrooms, most Puerto Rican parents assumed I was in a position to judge their children's school performance and to influence their fortunes there. I found interviews with the parents, in their homes or elsewhere, to be punctuated by displays of deference and by their insistent seeking of my reassurance that their children were well behaved in school. No substantive information on school practices was forthcoming from them. I learned to approach Hispanics whenever I could by referring not to my PS 4 connections but rather to my status as a university student. This was not entirely successful, however. My strategy of approaching the group through its voluntary associations, most of which had dealings with the school, made it difficult for me to shed the label of "the man from the school."

I learned a great deal from the more politically active Puerto Rican parents, such as those associated with the local antipoverty organization's Education Action agency. Their comments in interviews invariably centered, perhaps again in response to my imputed school status, on their extensive criticisms of the school's methods of handling and categorizing their children and on the Brownstoner parents' insensitivities to them in Parents Association activities. Interviews and other interaction with Hispanics unconnected to the school similarly gravitated to the unjust treatment they believed they were accorded by Brownstoner civic and political organizations. Never, however, did the Hispanics—whether parents, community leaders, or other residents—ask more than sympathy of me.

Oldtimers did not fully assimilate my explanations of my research and were wont to categorize me in more familiar ways, as "that college boy" or as an aspiring schoolteacher "working on his master's." Many of the St. Michaels parents, of course, knew me as Tim the teacher. In retrospect, I can only conclude that they saw my specific research activities as rather benign in nature and as having little to offer them one way or another. In any case, any advantages that they could gain from my research data were overshadowed by my more immediately useful moral support of and involvement in their financially beleaguered parish school. Being vaguely associated with the school staff enhanced their acceptance of me, as teachers are viewed as dedicated and underpaid professionals whose work constitutes a sacrifice for the good of the community and its children. The only problem requests from Oldtimers were for my labor in Democratic Party political work in support of candidates for elective office opposing Brownstoner-supported candidates.

In such a heterogeneous research site, with so many different and competing interests, it was clear from the outset that no single group's perspective could offer a complete, unbiased account of the community. Questions of objectivity aside, it is clear that the plurality of viewpoints in the community provided a constant check against any one of them gaining ascendancy in my analysis. Curiously, this was particularly true in the case of the Brownstoners, the grouping whose cultural outlook I shared more than any other in my private life. My relationships with Oldtimers, Hispanics, and school personnel assisted in giving me a more detached and comparative perspective on the Brownstoners' roles in the community and toward me as a researcher. Perhaps not unexpectedly, I found it necessary to develop an especially critical and questioning frame of mind in my dealings with the group I most resembled.

CONCLUSIONS: IS PARTICIPANT OBSERVATION VIABLE AS A CORE METHODOLOGICAL TECHNIQUE?

Because participant observation is tailored to the study of informal, face-to-face behavior, many anthropologists have questioned the technique's utility to research in complex urban settings. Some have pointed out the limitations of participant observation's characteristic ground-level underview for an understanding of urban form and organization (Fox 1977:19–20, 157ff.) The greater degrees of scale and complexity and the higher levels of sociocultural integration demonstrated in urban settings can severely tax the utility of a methodological technique refined in the study of clearly bounded, small-scale cultural units (Weaver and White 1972). Similar objections have been made regarding the technique's weakness in producing significant insights into formal organizations and the cultural roles they play in complex societies. Steward noted that ethnographic research "could deal only with. . . culturally-prescribed institutional behavior" and believed that in factories and other national institutions such as schools, "this behavior would represent only a very incomplete portion. . . of the larger cultural functions of the institution itself" (1955:63, his emphasis).

It would appear, however, that so long as thoughtful adaptations are made to the exigencies of the newer urban research settings, participant observation can continue to serve as the core methodological technique in anthropological research. Wolf (1966) and Weaver and White (1972), among others, have contended that the task of contemporary urban anthropology is to elucidate the often neglected linkages between face-to-face behavior and "large-scale sociopolitical phenomena and issues" (Weaver and White 1972:117). This end does not require the abandonment of traditional ethnographic methods, Weaver and

White suggest, but rather their continued employment, in a "strategy of working from the bottom up, drawing on intensive analysis to find the threads by which the sociocultural determinants of action within situational constraints influence these larger phenomena" (Weaver and White 1972:117).

My own research has led me to argue elsewhere (Sieber 1978) that such analytic linkages as these observers call for are facilitated when research focuses on informal face-to-face behavior occurring in schools and similar public institutions. This is because schools and kindred ideological institutions serve their "larger cultural functions," in Steward's terms, by carrying out "people work" (Goffman 1961)—by inculcating new forms of social relations, values, and skills in their clients (Sieber 1979). The primary vehicle for such "people work" is the naturally occurring, face-to-face informal interaction among teachers and pupils in the classroom, a phenomenon highly amenable to study by participant observation.

In Chestnut Heights, through supplementary participant observation research on community social differentiation, it was possible to suggest linkages between these observable school processes, the New York City occupational structure, and local patterns of class and ethnic differentiation. Such analytic linkages were possible because, in facilitating pupils' socialization in modes of behavior appropriate to formally organized work settings, the schools' social processes contribute to the orderly future recruitment of the community's young people into adult occupational roles. Comparative school analysis, as well, indicated that the differing pupil role socializations afforded by the schools consolidate local group identities and boundaries by offering children the socialization variant fitting them to assume the characteristic adult work roles of their particular group (Sieber 1978).

My Chestnut Heights research leads me to believe that, in participant observation in complex urban settings, problems of rapport and situation management more than equal any analytic problems that may arise from deficits in collectable field data. In the case of my own research, data generated through participant observation have lent themselves to forms of computer-assisted quantitative analysis, as well as more conventional qualitative forms of analysis. In any case, other methods (such as interviewing and archival research) are available as complements to participant observation to ensure that the collected data are adequate for analytic purposes.

The sheer complexity of many urban communities, however, with their cultural heterogeneity and conflict and their welter of structural boundaries, can approach practical unmanageability for the solitary participant observer. The necessity of regularly crossing social boundaries untraversed by locals can bring social and psychological tensions to the research process. Such tensions, moreover, are especially likely to fall to the lot of participant observers heeding Nader's (1974) advice to "study up," particularly if study focuses on the relations of large-scale organizations with their publics, as my own experience with public education indicates. The researcher must adapt to different settings that require differing balances of participation and observation. He or she must learn to play many roles and to present many faces.

Yet it is precisely these features of cultural heterogeneity, social complexity, role differentiation, and multiple levels of integration that, anthropological theory has long noted, characterize the urban scene in complex societies. My own research experience suggests that there are benefits to be gained from encountering these features directly in the research process, rather than attempting to circumvent them, if indeed it is possible to do so. Participant observation in complex urban settings affords the researcher personal social experience and thereby enhances analytical appreciation of cultural complexity. The regularly occurring discontinuities in one's own research behavior can serve to alert the researcher to the patterning of such complexity. The encountered structural discontinuities, cleavages, and boundaries also provide a necessary temper to the tendency of participant observation research to overemphasize cultural uniformity and consensus in study populations.

The practical problems and social tensions that participant observation generates for the researcher are not, in any case, new or unusual in anthropological research. Similar experiences have been reported by others, as in Henry's study of political attitudes among Trinidadian workers and management in a political situation that had become highly polarized during her research (F. Henry 1966, 1969). Powdermaker (1966) acknowledged similar problems in describing her 1930s research on race relations in a southern American town. Such problems as I experienced in using participant observation in Chestnut Heights do not appear to be different in kind from those encountered by other researchers in complex settings, whether the settings are modernizing or industrial, rural or urban, here or abroad.

The traditional anthropological search for homogeneous groups and communities, for which the method of participant observation was developed and is still most applicable, will no doubt continue to lead many researchers to a more manageable focus on well-bounded cultural isolates or on organizations and higher-status groups as if they were self-enclosed entities. Dividing responsibility for different sociocultural groups and institutions among different fieldworkers in "team research" (e.g. Price 1972) is another promising option in the handling of culturally diverse situations, one that allows the individual researcher to avoid boundary and loyalty conflicts. To achieve closer analytic linkages between informal face-to-face behavior and higher-level structures and cultural processes, however, most researchers will have to confront the kinds of social tensions I experienced in Chestnut Heights. My own experience indicates, in balance, that accommodation to the tensions is both possible and profitable for the participant observer.

NOTES

1. I thank Nicholas S. Hopkins and Susan Reverby for their valuable comments on earlier versions of this paper. The reported research was carried out under support of P.H.S. Grant No. 17216 from the Center for Urban Ethnography.

2. "Chestnut Heights" is a pseudonym, as are all other proper names in the chapter, except for the designation of New York City.

3. As a shorthand, and in keeping with local usage, I eliminate hyphenated forms (e.g., Irish-American) in discussing the community's groups.

4. "Extra-good behavior" was expected to be demonstrated toward visiting pupils from lower grades, so as to set a good example for them.

REFERENCES

Dreeban, Robert (1968) *On What Is Learned in School*. Reading, Mass.: Addison-Wesley.

Dreeban, Robert (1973) "The school as a workplace." In Robert M. W. Travers (ed.). *Second Handbook of Research on Teaching*. Chicago: Rand-McNally, pp. 450–473.

Durkheim, Emile (1956) *Education and Sociology*. Trans. and ed. S. D. Fox. New York: Free Press.

Durkheim, Emile (1966) *Moral Education*. E. K. Wilson and H. Shnurer (ed.). New York: Free Press.

Eddy, Elizabeth M. (1965) *Walk the White Line: A Profile of Urban Education*. New York: Anchor.

Fox, Richard A. (1977) *Urban Anthropology: Cities in Their Cultural Settings*. Englewood Cliffs, N.J.: Prentice-Hall.

Gintis, Herbert, and Samuel Bowles (1972–1973) "IQ in the United States class structure." Parts 1 and 2. *Social Policy* 3:65–97.

Goffman, Erving (1959) *The Presentation of Self in Everyday Life*. Garden City, N.Y.: Doubleday.

Goffman, Erving (1961) *Asylums: Essays on the Social Situations of Mental Patients and Other Inmates*. New York: Anchor.

Henry, Frances (1966) "The role of the fieldworker in an explosive political situation." *Current Anthropology* 7:552–559.

Henry, Frances (1969) "Stress and strategy in three field situations." In F. Henry and S. Saberwal (eds.). *Stress and Strategy in Fieldwork*. New York: Holt, pp. 35–46.

Khleif, Bud B. (1974) "Issues in anthropological fieldwork in schools." In George D. Spindler (ed.). *Education and Cultural Process: Toward an Anthropology of Education*. New York: Holt, pp. 389–398.

Leacock, Eleanor B. (1969) *Teaching and Learning in City Schools*. New York: Basic Books.

Nader, Laura (1974) "Up the anthropologist—perspectives gained from studying up." In Dell Hymes (ed.). *Reinventing Anthropology*. New York: Random House, Vintage Books, pp. 284–311.

Powdermaker, Hortense (1966) *Stranger and Friend: The Way of an Anthropologist*. New York: Norton.

Price, John A. (1972) "Reno, Nevada: The city as a unit of study." *Urban Anthropology* 1:14–28.

Rist, Ray C. (1970) "Student social class and teacher expectations: The self-fulfilling prophecy in ghetto education." *Harvard Educational Review* 40:411–451.

Sieber, R. Timothy (1978) "Schooling, socialization and group boundaries: A study of informal social relations in the public domain." *Urban Anthropology* 7:67–98.

Sieber, R. Timothy (1979) "Schoolroom, pupils and rules: The role of informality in bureaucratic socialization." *Human Organization* 39:273–282.

Steward, Julian H. (1955) "The concept and method of cultural ecology." In Julian H. Steward (ed.). *The Theory of Culture Change*. Urbana: University of Illinois Press.

Warren, Richard L. (1973) "The classroom as a sanctuary for teachers: Discontinuities in social control." *American Anthropologist* 75:280–291.

Warren, Richard L. (1975) "Context and isolation: The teaching experience in an elementary school." *Human Organization* 34:139–148.

Weaver, Thomas, and D. White (1972) "Anthropological approaches to urban and complex society." In Thomas Weaver and D. White (eds.). *The Anthropology of Urban Environments*. Washington, D.C.: Society for Applied Anthropology, monograph no. 11, pp. 109–125.

Wolcott, Harry F. (1975d) "Introduction." In Harry F. Wolcott (ed.). *Ethnographic Approaches to Research in Education: A Bibliography on Method*. Athens, Ga.: University of Georgia, Anthropology Curriculum Project.

Wolf, Eric R. (1966) "Kinship, friendship and patron–client relations in complex societies." In Michael Banton (ed.). *The Social Anthropology of Complex Societies*. London: Tavistock, pp. 1–22.

Source: "Many Roles, Many Faces: Researching School–Community Relations in a Heterogeneous American Urban Community," by R. T. Sieber, 1981, in Anthropologists at Home in North America: Methods and Issues in the Study of One's Own Society (pp. 202–220), by D. A. Messerschmidt, New York: Cambridge University Press. Copyright © 1981 by Cambridge University Press. Reprinted with the permission of Cambridge University Press.

" . . . the thinker, imaginer, and hypothesizer—that is, the qualitative researcher—is the
data analyzer . . . " (p. 470)

Qualitative Research: Data Analysis and Interpretation

OBJECTIVES

After reading Chapter 18, you should be able to do the following:

1. Describe the purpose of qualitative research data analysis.
2. Identify the cautions to avoid premature analysis and action in qualitative research.
3. State approaches to qualitative data analysis.
4. Describe processes involved in analyzing and interpreting data.
5. Distinguish between data analysis and data interpretation.
6. Describe strategies for data analysis.
7. Describe strategies for data interpretation.

⁙ DATA ANALYSIS AND INTERPRETATION: DEFINITION AND PURPOSE

Analyzing qualitative data is a formidable task for all qualitative researchers, especially those just starting their qualitative careers. These novice researchers follow the urgings of mentors who emphasize the need to collect rich data that reveal the perspectives and understandings of the research participants. After weeks (months, years) of data collection using a variety of qualitative data collection techniques (observations, interviews, surveys, and the like), they find themselves sitting in their living rooms surrounded by boxes of data in all shapes and forms! This less-than-romantic image of qualitative researchers is a common one. Having immersed themselves in the systematic study of a significant problem, qualitative researchers are confronted with the somewhat daunting task of engaging in analysis that will accurately represent the mountains of descriptive data. There is no easy way to do this work: It is difficult, time-consuming, and challenging. And yet it is potentially the most important step in the research process as we try to understand what we have learned through our investigations.

Data analysis is an attempt by the researcher to summarize collected data in a dependable and accurate manner. It is the presentation of the findings of the study in a manner that has an air of undeniability. Given the narrative, descriptive, and nonnumerical nature of the data that are collected in a qualitative study, it is not possible to "number crunch" and quickly reduce the data to a manageable form, as in quantitative studies. Qualitative data analysis requires the researcher to be patient and reflective in a process that strives to make sense of multiple data sources, including field notes from observations and interviews, questionnaires, maps, pictures, and even audiotape transcripts and videotape observations. On the other hand, **data interpretation** is an attempt by the researcher to find meaning in the data and to answer the "So what?" question in terms of the implications of the study's findings. Put simply, analysis involves summarizing what's in the data, whereas interpretation involves making sense of—finding meaning in—that data.

Data analysis and interpretation are critical stages in the research process that require the researcher to both know and understand the data. When analyzing and interpreting qualitative data, challenge yourself to explore every possible angle and try to find patterns and seek out new understandings among the data. The techniques outlined in this chapter will serve as guideposts and prompts to move you through your analysis and interpretation as efficiently as possible.

▪▪ DATA ANALYSIS DURING DATA COLLECTION

Data analysis in qualitative research is not left until all data are collected, as is the case with quantitative research. The qualitative researcher begins data analysis from the initial interaction with participants and continues that interaction and analysis throughout the entire study. To avoid collecting data that are not important or that come in a form that cannot be understood, the researcher must think about "How am I going to make sense of this data?" before conducting the study. During the study, the researcher tries to progressively narrow, and focus in on, the key aspects of the participants' perspectives. Thus, the qualitative researcher goes through a series of steps and iterations: gathering data, examining data, comparing prior data to newer data, writing up field notes before going back to the research site, and making plans to gather new data. Data collection and analysis continually interact, so that the researcher's emerging hunches or thoughts become the focus for the next data collection period.

While gathering data, the researcher reviews and asks questions about it: "Why do participants act as they do?" "What does this focus mean?" "What else do I want to know about that participant's attitude?" "What new ideas have emerged in this round of data collection?" "Is this a new concept, or is it the same as a previous one?" and so forth. This ongoing process—almost a protracted discussion with oneself—leads to the collection of new important data and the elimination of other data.

Anderson and colleagues suggest that qualitative researchers answer two questions to guide their work and reflections:

1. Is your research question still answerable and worth answering?
2. Are your data collection techniques catching the kind of data you wanted and filtering out the data that you don't?[1]

Consciously "pausing" during the research process will allow you to reflect on what you are attending to and what you are leaving out. Such a reflective stance will continue to guide your data collection efforts (in process) as well as to allow for early "hunches" about what you are seeing so far.

Although ongoing analysis and reflection is a natural part of the qualitative research process, it is important to avoid premature actions based on early analysis and interpretation of data. Researchers engaged in their first systematic study tend to zealously collect, analyze, and interpret data in a rapid-fire fashion. Their efforts can go awry if they become their own best informants and jump to hasty conclusions and impulsive actions. The qualitative research process takes time; researchers must be wary of the lure of quick-fix strategies and patient enough to avoid the pitfalls of stating research outcomes on the basis of premature analysis.

▪▪ DATA ANALYSIS AFTER DATA COLLECTION

After the data have been collected, the romance of fieldwork is over and the researcher must concentrate solely on the task of data analysis. The researcher must fully examine each piece of information and, building upon those insights and hunches gained during data collection, attempt to make sense of the data as a whole. Qualitative data analysis is based on induction: The researcher starts with a large set of issues and data and seeks to progressively narrow them into small and important groups of key data. There are no predefined variables to focus analysis, as there are in quantitative research. The qualitative researcher constructs meaning by identifying patterns and themes that emerge during the data analysis.

---

[1] *Studying Your Own School: An Educator's Guide to Qualitative Practitioner Research* (p. 155), by G. L. Anderson, K. Herr, and A. S. Nihlen, 1994, Thousand Oaks, CA: Corwin Press.

A problem that faces virtually all qualitative researchers is the lack of agreed-on approaches for analyzing qualitative data. There are some guidelines and general strategies for analysis but few specific rules for their application. Thus, once data are collected, the qualitative researcher undertakes a multistage process of organizing, categorizing, synthesizing, analyzing, and writing about the data. In most cases, the researcher will cycle through the stages more than once, in a continual effort to narrow and make sense of what is in the data. The length of data analysis is difficult to state. It depends mainly on the nature of the study, the amount of data to be analyzed, and the analytic and synthesizing abilities of the researcher.

Remember, there is no substitute for taking time to fully immerse yourself in your data. You should bury yourself in what you have. Read and reread, listen and relisten, watch and rewatch. Get to know intimately what you have collected. Struggle with the nuances and caveats, the subtleties, the persuasive, the incomplete. Avoid premature judgment. These are lofty goals, but they are at the heart of what we are trying to achieve in qualitative data analysis and data interpretation.

:: STEPS IN ANALYZING QUALITATIVE RESEARCH DATA

If data are to be thoroughly analyzed, they must be organized. Ideally, the researcher will have carefully managed notes, records, and artifacts as they were collected. As we mentioned when discussing the qualitative research plan in Chapter 3, the importance of attention to detail in managing data becomes all too clear when it is time to write up the research! Nevertheless, some additional organization at the end of the data collection stage is usually necessary. Figure 18.1 lists some ways to "tidy up" your data, ensure their completeness, and make them easier to study. Once the data are organized, the analysis can begin in earnest.

One way to proceed with the analysis is to follow three iterative, or repeating, steps: reading/memoing, describing what is going on in the setting, and classifying research data. The process focuses on (1) becoming familiar with the data and identifying potential themes in it (reading/memoing); (2) examining the data in depth to provide detailed descriptions of the setting, participants, and activity (describing); and (3) categorizing and coding pieces of data and grouping them into themes (classifying).

Note that the interrelationships among these steps are not necessarily linear. At the start of data analysis, the logical sequence of activities is from reading/memoing, to description, to classifying, and finally to interpretation. However, as the researcher begins to internalize and reflect on the data, the initial ordered sequence may lose its structure and become more flexible. If you've ever been driving home pondering some issue or problem and out of the blue had a sudden flash of understanding that provides a solution, you have a sense of how qualitative data analysis takes place. Once you are *into* the data, it is not the three steps that lead to understanding; it is your ability to think, imagine, create, intuit, and analyze that guides

---

FIGURE 18.1

Data organizing activities

- Write dates (month, day, year) on all notes.
- Sequence all notes with labels (e.g., 6th set of notes).
- Label notes according to type (such as observer's notes, memo to self, transcript from interview).
- Make two photocopies of all notes (field notes, transcripts, etc.) and retain original copies.
- Organize computer files into folders according to data type and stages of analysis.
- Make backup copies of all files.
- Read through data and make sure all information is complete and legible before proceeding to analysis and interpretation.
- Begin to note themes and patterns that emerge.

the data analysis. Knowing the steps is not enough; the thinker, imaginer, and hypothesizer—that is, the qualitative researcher—is the data analyzer, and the quality of the research analysis will depend heavily on the intellectual qualities of the researcher. Let us be very clear about the process being discussed. It is a process of digesting the contents of qualitative data and finding related threads in it. You will not meaningfully accomplish these tasks with one or two or more readings of your collected data. To make the kinds of connections needed to analyze and interpret qualitative data, you must know your data—really know it, in your head, not just on paper. The process can be tedious, time-consuming, and repetitious; however, the steps can help you understand, describe, and classify qualitative data.

Reading/Memoing

As your first analytical step, you will read and write memos about all field notes, transcripts, and observer comments to get an initial sense of the data. To begin, find a quiet place and plan on spending a few hours at a time reading through the data. Krathwohl wisely points out that "the first time you sit down to read your data is the only time you come to that particular set fresh."[2] It is important that you write notes in the margins or underline sections or issues that seem important to you so that you will have a record of your initial thoughts and sense of the data. Later, when you are deeper into the analysis, you may find that many of these early impressions are not useful; however, you may also find that some initial impressions do hold up throughout. In addition to recording initial impressions from the data, at this stage of analysis you should also begin the search for recurring themes or common threads.

Describing

The next step, describing, involves developing thorough and comprehensive descriptions of the participants, the setting, and the phenomenon studied in order to convey the rich complexity of the research. The descriptions are based on your collected observations, interview data, field notes, and artifacts. The aim of this step is to provide a narrative picture of the setting and events that take place in it, so you will have an understanding of the context in which the study is taking place. Attention to the research context is a common and important theme in qualitative research, because the context influences participants' actions and understandings. Meaning is influenced by context; without a thorough description of the context, actions, and interactions of participants, analysis (and therefore, interpretation) is hampered.

An important concern of qualitative researchers is portraying the views of the research participants. It is crucial that you describe thoroughly how participants define situations and explain their actions. Also, your descriptions should make note of how interactions and social relations among the participants may have changed during the course of the study. The descriptions of the research context, meanings, and social relations can be presented in a number of forms. For example, you can describe events in chronological order, create a composite of a typical "day in the life" of a participant in the setting, focus on key contextual episodes, or illuminate different perspectives of the participants.

Classifying

Qualitative data analysis is basically a process of breaking down data into smaller units, determining their import, and putting the pertinent units together in a more general, analytical

---

[2] *Methods of Educational and Social Science Research: An Integrated Approach,* by D. R. Krathwohl (2nd ed., p. 309), 1998, New York: Longman.

form. The typical way qualitative data are broken down is through the process of classifying or *coding* (discussed shortly) and categorizing pieces of data and grouping them into themes. A *category* is a classification of ideas or concepts. When concepts in the data are examined and compared to one another and connections are made, categories are formed. Categories are used to organize similar concepts into distinct groups.

For example, consider a researcher who is conducting a qualitative study on characteristics of fifth-grade students' study methods. Suppose the researcher had collected 20 sets of field notes (describing observations) or 20 transcripts of interviews. The researcher's task is to read through all the notes or transcripts and categorize the meanings or understandings that emerge from the data. Without data that are classified and grouped, a researcher has no reasonable way to analyze qualitative studies. The categories provide the basis for structuring the analysis and interpretation. However, the categories identified by one researcher would not necessarily be the same as those identified by another researcher, even if they analyzed the same data. There is no one single "correct" way to organize and analyze the data. There are many reasons why different researchers would not produce the same categories from the same data. Some of these reasons are researcher biases, personal interests, style, and interpretive focus.

:: DATA ANALYSIS STRATEGIES

In this section we will describe strategies that are used to analyze qualitative data: identifying themes; coding surveys, interviews and questionnaires; asking key questions; doing an organizational review; concept mapping, analyzing antecedents and consequences; displaying findings; and stating what is missing. Each is important in identifying research categories and patterns.

Identifying Themes.   Another way to begin analyzing data is to consider the big picture and start to list "themes" that you have seen emerge in your literature review and in the data collection. Are there patterns that emerge, such as events that keep repeating themselves, key phrases that participants use to describe their feelings, or survey responses that seem to "match" one another? Making a note of these themes can be helpful during the first reading of the data (as part of memoing). In subsequent readings of the data, additional themes may emerge.

Coding Qualitative Data.   One of the most frequent data analysis activities undertaken by qualitative researchers is **coding,** the process of categorically marking or referencing units of text (e.g., words, sentences, paragraphs, and quotations) with codes and labels as a way to indicate patterns and meaning.

As you analyze and code your data, you will want to reduce that data to a manageable form. One way to proceed when working with field notes, transcripts of taped interviews, pictures, maps, charts, and so on is to record important data on index cards, which are manageable and allow for sorting. As you read and reread through your data (possibly now reduced to your cards), you can compile your data in categories or themes. Although there is nothing magical about the process of coding, it does take time and a willingness to check that the mountains of descriptive data have been analyzed in an accurate and reliable way. The way in which you code your data, in fact, will play a large role in determining the nature of the results. If, for example, you approach your data with preconceived categories and assumptions, you will likely begin analyzing your data by coding text units according to what you expect to find. Conceptually, you are beginning to construct a web of relationships that may or may not appear as you thought they would. If, on the other hand, you approach your data with questions you hope your research will illuminate, but no clear sense as to what the findings might be, you will likely start to build themes as you read through your data.

To get an idea of the process of coding, imagine that you are organizing a deck of playing cards, but you don't know the meaning of any of the cards' symbols. Each card in the deck contains data, and the order of the cards is random. As you initially scan the cards, you have an intuitive sense that the data on some of the cards looks similar to other cards. You finish carefully looking at all of the cards and reshuffle the deck. Again you look through the deck, but this time you group together the cards (data) that look alike. You end up with 13 collections of four cards that have some trait in common (the number or face value of the card). Again, you reshuffle the cards. This time as you start to sort through the cards, you notice a different theme (the suit of the card) and end up with four piles of 13 cards. Puzzling. Not to be thwarted in your efforts, you again reshuffle the deck and attempt to settle on an organizing theme. You group together cards (data) that have sufficient common characteristics that you feel confident that your analysis of the data is undeniably accurate. But there is just one problem: What do you do with the Joker that found its way into the pack?! And what about that wildcard?! Where did they come from, and where do they fit?! Just when you thought you had it all worked out, in crept something that challenges the themes you have used to organize and represent the data you have collected. The shuffling and sorting continues.

A few common sense guidelines may make this somewhat overwhelming activity of coding mountains of data more manageable:

1. Gather photocopies of your original data.
2. Read through all of the data, and attach working labels to blocks of text. These labels should have meaning for you; they should be a kind of shorthand that will serve as reference points when you return to the text later in the process.
3. Literally cut and paste the blocks of text onto index cards so that you now have the data in a manageable form. (Shuffling cards is much easier than sorting through reams of paper.) Use some kind of numbering system so that you can track the block of text back to the original context in which it appeared. For example, marking the data and time (1/26 10:15) can help you locate the text in the journal or field notes from which it was excerpted. Remember: Context is important and you will want to check that you have correctly labeled the text you are trying to funnel into a category with similar text.
4. Start to group together cards that have the same or similar labels on them.
5. Revisit each pile of cards, and see if in fact the label still fits or whether similar labels actually warrant their own category. This process is not dissimilar to brainstorming and seeking categories that will encapsulate similar thoughts and ideas.

Asking Key Questions.   Another strategy used in data analysis involves asking key questions. According to Stringer, working through a series of questions can enable qualitative researchers to "extend their understanding of the problems and contexts"[3] they have investigated. Such questions might include the following: Who is centrally involved? Who has resources? Which ones? What major activities, events, or issues are relevant to the problem? How do acts, activities, and events happen? When does this problem occur? Although not all of these questions will be applicable to any single situation, they may provide a starting point for qualitative researchers who are engaged individually or collectively in analysis.

Doing an Organizational Review.   Almost any educational problem is influenced in some way by the spoken and unspoken rules of organizations: state education departments, school districts, individual schools, teacher unions, and so on. Even in a qualitative study

---

[3] *Action Research: A Handbook for Practitioners* (p. 87), by E. T. Stringer, 1996, Thousand Oaks, CA: Sage.

where the emphasis is on the personal story of a single individual or the intimate workings of a small group, it is sometimes helpful to step back and take a look at the larger setting. Stringer[4] suggests that researchers consider undertaking an organizational review that focuses on the following features of the organization: vision and mission, goals and objectives, structure of the organization, operation, and problems, issues, and concerns. As Stringer notes: "As participants work through these issues, they will extend their understanding of the organization and aspects of its operation that are relevant to their problems, issues, and concerns."[5] A review of a school, for example, with these features in mind, may provide insight into the data you have collected.

Concept Mapping. As discussed previously, the qualitative researcher often works collaboratively with participants in a study, and that collaboration can extend to the data analysis process. To better visualize the major influences that have affected the study, Stringer[6] suggests that the researcher have participants create concept maps. What are the perspectives of the students, parents, teachers, and administrators involved in the study? For example, the concept map in Figure 18.2 shows a research participant's ideas about which factors influenced the success of his school absenteeism policy. Concept mapping gives participants an opportunity to display their analyses of the problem and helps the researcher to determine consistencies and inconsistencies that may exist between the disparate groups.

Analyzing Antecedents and Consequences. The process of mapping antecedents (causes) and consequences (effects) is another strategy to help qualitative researchers identify the major elements of their analysis, according to Stringer.[7] Using this framework provides a visual representation of the causal relationships that the qualitative researcher now believes exists. It is also helpful to revisit the causal relationships uncovered in your review of literature to determine challenges and support for your analysis and interpretations.

Displaying Findings. It is important to try to summarize the information you have collected in an appropriate and meaningful format that you can share with interested colleagues. To do this, it is helpful to "think display" as you consider how to convey your findings to colleagues. You might use matrixes, charts, concept maps, graphs, and figures—whatever works as a practical way to encapsulate the findings of your study. These visual displays of data serve an important function for qualitative researchers who wish to share findings and celebrate their insights in a public forum (such as a research conference). Putting your data into a visual format might also help you "see" new aspects of your data!

Stating What's Missing. Finally, as part of your full reporting, you should flag for the consumers of your research the pieces of the puzzle that are still missing and identify the questions for which you have not been able to provide answers. Often we find ourselves wanting and needing to provide answers, to move beyond our data with unwarranted assertions that may, in some cases, ultimately lead to embarrassing questions about what we actually did! In keeping with the theme of avoiding premature judgment (arriving at answers to problems without systematic inquiry), the data analysis strategy of stating what's missing allows you to hint at what might or should be done next in your quest to better understand the findings of your study.

---

[4] Ibid., p. 90.
[5] Ibid., pp. 90–91.
[6] *Action Research* (p. 91), Stringer, 1996.
[7] Ibid., p. 96.

FIGURE 18.2

Concept map of the factors affecting absenteeism
Source: Mills, Geoffrey, *Action Research: A Guide for the Teacher Researcher,* 2nd Edition, © 2003. Reprinted by permission of Pearson Education, Inc., Upper Saddle River, NJ.

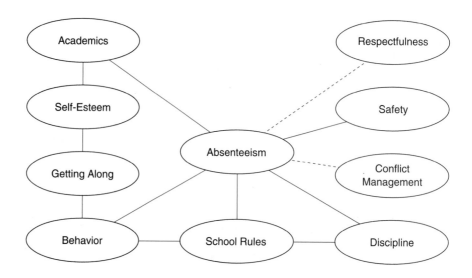

:: QUALITATIVE DATA ANALYSIS: AN EXAMPLE

The example that follows is intended to provide a sense of qualitative analysis. A true qualitative study would entail more data analysis than shown here. However, the basic ideas represent the process a qualitative researcher would undertake when analyzing data throughout a study.

Here is some basic information about the study:

- *Topics under study:* Concerns of parents regarding their first child's entering kindergarten; a kindergarten teacher's interactions with students and families.
- *Participants:* Four parents, three female and one male, representing four families; first child in each of the families (the children attend the same school); kindergarten teacher.
- *Data collection:* Observations and interviews with students, parents, and kindergarten teacher.

Data analysis would proceed as follows:

1. From the field notes of your classroom observations, you begin to list some common items or topics that you noticed. You recorded in your notes that during classroom instruction the teacher was using books, videos, and handouts. You also noted that at times, instruction was directed toward individual students, sometimes toward the whole class, and sometimes toward students who were working together in small groups.

2. From your interviews with the teacher, you realize that she gave you information about how she communicated with families about the children. You note that she talked about how she indirectly communicates through grading and report cards and how her lesson plans and tests were related to her overall assessment of the students' work. She also mentioned that she talked about report cards directly with families during conferences. Other ways that she communicated with families about their children were through progress reports and phone calls.

3. From your initial analysis, you decide how to group the individual items or topics together into categories that show how the items or topics are related. For example, as shown in Figure 18.3, you could group books, videos, and handouts under a category

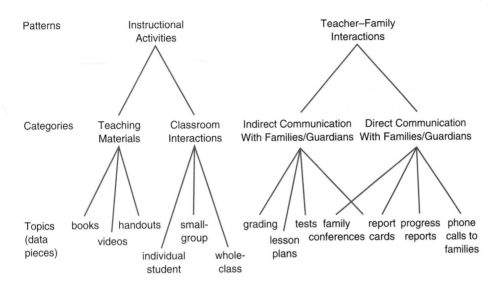

FIGURE 18.3

Diagram of category levels and organization

called "Teaching Materials." You could group together the ways in which the instruction was carried out—individual, small-group, and whole-class—and label this category as "Classroom Interactions." Using information from the interviews, you could construct the category "Indirect Communication With Families/Guardians" to include grading, lesson plans, tests, and report cards. A category of "Direct Communication With Families/Guardians" could include family conferences, report cards, progress reports, and phone calls to families. Notice that report cards appears in both the indirect and direct communication categories.

4. You organize your four categories into patterns. A pattern is made up of two or more categories. For example, the categories of "Teaching Materials" and "Classroom Interactions" indicate a pattern of "Instructional Activities." The categories of "Indirect Communication" and "Direct Communication" fit together under a pattern of "Teacher–Family Interactions."

You then decide whether you need to collect further data by interviewing students and parents about their experiences of interacting with the teacher to confirm your categories and patterns.

:: USING COMPUTER SOFTWARE TO ASSIST WITH DATA ANALYSIS

Increasingly, computer software is being developed to assist with the analysis of qualitative data. The key word in this sentence is *assist*. This software will not do the analysis for you! It is important for novice qualitative researchers to remember that computers alone do not analyze or even code data. They are designed only to help expedite these operations when researchers are working with large bodies of text and other kinds of data. The process of coding, retrieving, and subsequently mulling over and making sense of data remains a laborious process completely controlled by researchers. Even if a computer is used, researchers still must go through the process of creating codes and labels and keying these into the computer as they read through their interviews, field notes, and audio- and videotapes. Computers are merely handy and extremely fast labeling and retrieval tools. Researchers also must remember that they alone can tell or program the computer to retrieve and sort data in specific ways; the machines do not do these tasks automatically. Although computers can enhance and broaden qualitative research analysis, if you are not connected in some way with a research university it is unlikely that you will have access to the software and the expertise of someone to teach you how to use it.

To help you with your decision about whether or not to proceed with locating and learning a qualitative data analysis software package, consider the following as some of the factors that might affect the decision:[8]

- Are you analyzing large amounts (for example, more than 500 pages of field notes and transcripts?)
- Are you adequately trained in the use of the programs and in using computers in general?
- Do you have the resources to purchase a program, or do you know someone who has the program?
- Do you need to be able to capture specific quotes from a large data base?

Four of the more common and popular qualitative analysis software packages are NVivo 2.0, The Ethnograph, HyperRESEARCH, and NUD*IST 6.

- NVivo is designed for qualitative researchers who need to work complex data (especially multimedia data). More information on NVivo can be found on the QSR International Web site at http://www.qsr-ecommerce.com/us/acatalog/ and the DataSense site at http://www.datasense.org.
- The Ethnograph is a program designed to help qualitative researchers work with text files (in any format) and search for, and code, segments of interest to the researcher. More information about The Ethnograph can be found on the Qualis Research Web site at http://www.qualisresearch.com/.
- HyperRESEARCH is a more advanced software program that allows the qualitative researcher to work with text, graphics, audio, and video sources, and to code and retrieve data. More information about HyperRESEARCH can be found on the ResearchWare Web site at http://www.researchware.com.
- NUD*IST 6 (N6), the latest version of the original NUD*IST, is a powerful program for teams of qualitative researchers working with large amounts of data. More information about N6 can be found on the QSR International Web site at http://www.qsr-ecommerce.com/us/acatalog/ and the DataSense site at http://www.datasense.org.

Let's look more closely at one of these programs, N6, to see how it can help with your data analysis efforts.

The QSR NUD*IST (nonnumerical unstructured data index searching and theorizing) series, including N6, provides qualitative researchers with a system for storing, coding, and searching large amounts of word processed data, such as field notes, interview transcripts, and open-ended survey responses. Table 18.1 lists various data analysis elements, their manual tasks (writing objectives), and corresponding procedures that may be carried out or made easier by using NUD*IST.

Once the text is coded, N6 allows you to pose questions that involve the retrieval of one or more categories of responses. The computer program collates the coded "text units," but again it is the qualitative researcher who must construct meaning from the search results, to

---

[8] List items adapted from *Educational Research: Planning, Conducting, and Evaluating Quantitative and Qualitative Research* (2nd ed., p. 234), by J. W. Creswell, 2005, Upper Saddle River, NJ: Merrill/Prentice Hall.

TABLE **18.1**	Data analysis elements, writing objectives, and NUD-IST procedures	
Data Analysis Element	**Writing Objective**	**NUD*IST Procedure**
Create a template for analysis	Develop a visual of data analysis plan	Create a tree of steps in analysis into which data segments are placed
Create headings in the manuscript for major themes	Create four or five major themes in the study in words of participants	Create a node for each heading and put text that applies into the node
Title the manuscript	Create a title in words of the participants—to make report realistic, to catch attention of readers	Create a node based on short phrases found in the text; create alternative titles in this node as they appear in analyzing the texts
Include quotes in the manuscript	Identify good quotes that provide sound evidence for the themes, description, interpretation, and so forth	Create a general node and place all good quotes in that node; create a node for quotes under each theme or category of information
Phrase study in words of participants	Locate commonly used words or phrases and develop them into themes	Use word search procedure, string or pattern search, and place contents into a node; spread text around the word (or phrase) to capture the context of the word (or phrase)
Create a comparison table	Compare categories of information	Use matrix feature of program
Show levels of abstraction in the analysis	Present a visual of the categories in the analysis	Present the "tree" diagram
Discuss metaphors	Find text in which metaphors are presented and group into categories	Set up one node for metaphors with children of different types of metaphors; place text in nodes by types of metaphors

Source: From J. Creswell, *Qualitative Inquiry and Research Design: Choosing Among Five Traditions*, p. 162, copyright © 1998 by Sage Publications, Inc. Reprinted by permission of Sage Publications, Inc.

look for patterns and contradictions, and to decide how best to proceed with the analysis. It is at this point that qualitative researchers often rethink their initial preconceptions or research questions and may even decide to revise or recode their data. It is also at this point that you may be glad your massive amount of data is stored, manipulatable, and responsive to new lines of questioning.

As an illustration of a researcher's thought processes while coding and recoding data, let's consider a study by William Greene on the ethnic identity among adolescents in Hawaii.[9] The study involved transcripts of 40 interviews and close to 400 pages of text. Each of the interview transcripts was initially coded by thematic categories. If a student's response related to more than one category, all related categories were coded with the corresponding portion of the response. For instance, this was common when the question asked for students' perceptions of ethnic relations within their school; sometimes aspects of several categories would be evoked simultaneously. In such cases, relevant passages were coded for all categories referenced.

[9] "Ethnic Identity and the Sociocultural Playing Field: Choices Made by Ethnically Mixed Adolescents in Hawaii," by W. L. Green, 2002, in *Research on Sociocultural Influences on Motivation and Learning: Vol. 2. Sociocultural Influences on Motivation and Learning* (pp. 23–56), by D. M. McInerney and S. Van Etten (Series Eds.), Greenwich, CT: Information Age.

The initial categories of this study were family, peers, schoolwide/communitywide generalizations, ethnic self-identity, values, personal changes, intergroup relationships, ethnic group status, perceptions of ethnic groups, mixed ethnicities, differential treatment, and future plans. Initial categories evolved and new categories emerged as the transcripts were read and coded. In this process of changing and re-coding data during analysis, the researcher continually built upon and extended theoretical notions about the findings. An example of this occurred in coding for references to personal values. It became evident that comments frequently clustered in various subcategories: education, family, religion, social, ethnic, and maxims. Two weeks after the initial reading and coding was completed, the researcher read each transcript a second time, verifying the consistency of the initial coding and updating codes to reflect expanded or consolidated categories. Coding in more specific subcategories permitted a finer degree of analysis within the database.

In addition to the categorical coding, demographic coding allowed for comparisons across various subgroups of students interviewed. Demographic variables included the following: grade, gender, school, ethnic mix, birthplace, years of residence in urban or rural communities, and household (both parents, one parent, or other). For example, all of the coded statements about ethnic self-awareness were divided into subcategories by school, age, gender, ethnic mix, and years of Hawaii residence. Similarities and differences among subcategories were the basis for identifying patterns.[10]

As this example illustrates, the use of computer software will not do the data analysis for you, but it will help retrieve categories from a large amount of narrative (text) data. There will still be many decisions that you need to make about how to code your data. You will also want to revisit your data and verify that the computer "got it right"! (This is akin to estimating the outcome of a math problem for which a calculator has been used. Does the outcome make sense?)

:: DATA INTERPRETATION

Because the goal of data interpretation is to find the meaning of the data, it is based heavily on the connections, common aspects, and linkages among the data, especially the identified categories and patterns. One cannot classify data into categories without thinking about the meaning of the categories. To aid interpretation, it is important to make explicit what the conceptual bases or understandings of the categories are and what makes one category different from another. Interpretation requires more conceptual and integrative thinking than data analysis, because interpretation involves identifying and abstracting important understandings from the detail and complexity of the data.

The implicit issue in data interpretation is the answer to these four questions:

What is important in the data?
Why is it important?
What can be learned from it?
So what?

The researcher's task, then, is to determine how one identifies what is important, why it is important, and what it indicates about the participants and context studied. The process for answering these four questions is to a large extent idiosyncratic. Interpretation is personal. There are no hard and fast rules for how to go about the task of interpreting the meaning of data. As in most qualitative studies, it depends on the perspective and interpretive abilities of the researcher.

---

[10] Ibid.

You may wonder, why bother with interpretation, especially since interpretation involves taking risks and making educated guesses that might be off base? Wolcott[11] argues for the importance of interpretation because as qualitative researchers, our interpretations matter to the lives of those being studied. In addition, the process of interpretation is important because it can challenge qualitative researchers' taken-for-granted assumptions and beliefs about the educational processes they have investigated.

The techniques for data interpretation that follow are adapted from those in Wolcott and in Stringer.[12]

Extend the analysis. One technique that is low on the data interpretation risk scale is to simply extend the analysis of your data by raising questions about the study, noting implications that *might* be drawn without actually drawing them. As Wolcott suggests, "This is a strategy for *pointing* the way rather than *leading* the way"[13] (italics added).

Connect findings with personal experience. Qualitative research is very personal business, so it makes sense to personalize our interpretations. For example, you may present your findings with the prelude, "Based on my experiences in conducting this study, this is what I make of it all." Remember, you know your study better than anyone else. You have been there for every twist and turn along the way, trying to make sense of discrepant events just when you thought you "had it right." Share your interpretations based on your intimate knowledge and understandings of the research setting.

Seek the advice of "critical" friends. If you have difficulty focusing an interpretive lens on your work, rely on your trusted colleagues to offer insights that you may have missed because of your closeness to the work. Offer your accounts to colleagues with the request that they share with you their possible interpretations. Similarly, you may ask your informants (students, parents, teachers, and administrators) for their insights. But beware! The more opinions you seek, the more you will receive, and often these suggestions will come with the expectation that you accept the advice! Over time you will develop reciprocity with a cadre of trusted, like-minded colleagues who will selflessly fulfill the role of critical friend. Take the time to build these relationships and reap the rewards they offer.

Contextualize findings in the literature. Uncovering external sources as part of the review of related literature is a powerful way for qualitative researchers to provide support for the study's findings. Making these connections also provides qualitative researchers with a way to share with colleagues the existing knowledge base on a research problem and to acknowledge the unique contribution the qualitative researcher has made to our understanding of the topic studied.

Turn to theory. Theory serves a number of important roles for qualitative researchers. First, theory provides a way for qualitative researchers to link their work to broader issues of the day. Second, theory allows the researcher to search for increasing levels of abstraction and to move beyond a purely descriptive account. Levels of abstraction allow us to communicate the essence of our descriptive work to colleagues at research meetings. Lastly, theory can provide a rationale or sense of meaning to the work we do.

Know when to say "when"! Finally, if you don't feel comfortable with offering an interpretation, don't do it. Be satisfied with suggesting what needs to be done next and use that as a starting point for the next research cycle. Restate the problem as you now see it, and explain how you think you will fine-tune your efforts as you strive to increase your understanding of the phenomenon you have investigated. As Wolcott cautions, "don't detract from what you have accomplished by tacking on a wimpy interpretation."[14]

---

[11] *Transforming Qualitative Data: Description, Analysis, and Interpretation,* by H. F. Wolcott, 1994, Thousand Oaks, CA: Sage.
[12] Ibid., pp. 39–46; *Action Research* (p. 87–96), Stringer, 1996.
[13] *Transforming Qualitative Data* (p. 40), Wolcott, 1994.
[14] Ibid., p. 41.

All researchers, and qualitative researchers in particular, must face the prospect of not being able to report in their analysis all of the data they have collected. This is a difficult reality for any researcher, but more so for qualitative researchers because of the time and effort it typically takes them to obtain and understand their data. Rarely is every piece of data used in the report of a study. Remember, the task of interpreting data is to identify the important themes or meanings in the data, not necessarily *every* theme.

A final piece of advice regarding data interpretation is to share your interpretations wisely. At some time we have all been exposed to what are variously called "fads," "the pendulum swing," the "bandwagon," and so on. As such, many of us may hesitate to embrace anything new or different that comes our way in schools, calming ourselves with the mantra "This, too, shall pass!" If we as researchers attempt to use our qualitative research findings only as a soapbox from which we simply have sought findings to confirm our beliefs and values, then we risk being alienated by our colleagues. Avoid being evangelical about your interpretations, connect them closely to your data and analysis, and share your newfound understandings with colleagues in an appropriate manner.

:: ENSURING CREDIBILITY IN YOUR STUDY

Throughout this chapter we have emphasized the centrality of the researcher as the integrator and interpreter of data. You might infer that this emphasis means that researchers have carte blanche when analyzing and interpreting data; that is, they can rely strictly on their personal feelings or preferences. This is definitely not the case. If qualitative research were based solely on producing unsubstantiated opinions, ignoring data that did not confirm the researcher's expectations, and failing to examine biases of research participants, it would be of little value. Thus, although data analysis and interpretations are heavily determined by the researcher, there are criteria that researchers should respect and respond to in conducting their own studies. For example, Dey identifies six questions intended to help researchers check the quality of their data:[15]

- Are the data based on one's own observation, or is it hearsay?
- Is there corroboration by others of one's observation?
- In what circumstances was an observation made or reported?
- How reliable are those providing the data?
- What motivations might have influenced a participant's report?
- What biases might have influenced how an observation was made or reported?

Qualitative researchers who attend to these guidelines for conducting credible data analysis and data interpretation are rewarded with a trustworthy research report that will withstand the scrutiny of the research community.

SUMMARY

Data Analysis and Interpretation: Definition and Purpose

1. Data analysis is an attempt by the qualitative researcher to summarize collected data in a dependable and accurate manner. It is the presentation of the findings of the study in a manner that has an air of undeniability.

2. Data interpretation is an attempt by the researcher to find meaning in the data and to answer the "So what?" question in terms of the implications of the study's findings.

---

[15] *Qualitative Data Analysis* (p. 224), by I. Dey, 1993, New York: Routledge.

Data Analysis During Data Collection

3. A great deal of data analysis occurs before data collection is complete. Researchers think about and make hunches about what they see and hear during data collection.
4. An important step in the ongoing analysis of qualitative data is to reflect on data collection efforts by answering two questions:
   a. Is your research question still answerable and worth answering?
   b. Are your data collection techniques catching the kind of data you wanted and filtering out the data that you don't?
5. Although ongoing analysis and reflection is a natural part of the qualitative research process, it is important to avoid premature actions based on early analysis and interpretation of data.

Data Analysis After Data Collection

6. Once fieldwork has been completed, the researcher must concentrate solely on the multistage process of organizing, categorizing, synthesizing, analyzing, and writing about the data. During the process, the researcher works to progressively narrow a large set of issues and data into small and important groups of key data.
7. The length of data analysis is difficult to state. It depends mainly on the nature of the study, the amount of data to be analyzed, and the analytic and synthetic abilities of the researcher.

Steps in Analyzing Qualitative Research Data

8. There is no single, agreed-on approach for analyzing qualitative data. Once data are organized, one approach is to follow three iterative steps: reading/memoing, describing what is going on in the setting, and classifying research data.
9. Qualitative data analysis is a cyclical, iterative process of reviewing data for common topics or themes. The researcher has the key role, and the quality of the analysis will depend heavily on his or her intellectual qualities.
10. Reading/memoing is the process of writing notes in the field note margins and underlining sections or issues that seem important during the initial reading of narrative data.
11. Describing involves developing thorough and comprehensive descriptions of the participants, the setting, and the phenomenon studied in order to convey the rich complexity of the research.

12. Classifying small pieces of data into more general categories is the qualitative researcher's way to make sense and find connections among the data. Field notes and transcripts are broken down into small pieces of data, and these pieces are integrated into categories and often to more general patterns.

Data Analysis Strategies

13. Identifying themes is a strategy that relies on the identification of ideas that have emerged from the review of literature and in the data collection.
14. Coding is the process of categorically marking units of text with codes or labels as a way to indicate patterns and meaning in data. It involves the reduction of narrative data to a manageable form to allow sorting to occur.
15. Asking key questions is a strategy that involves the researcher asking questions of the data such as "Who is centrally involved?" "What major activities, events, or issues are relevant to the problem?" and so on.
16. Doing an organizational review is a strategy for helping the researcher understand the school or other organization as the larger setting. A review should focus on the following features of an organization: vision and mission, goals and objectives, structure of the organization, operation, and problems, issues and concerns.
17. Concept mapping is a strategy that allows the qualitative researcher to visualize the major influences that have affected the study and to create a visual display that allows for the identification of consistencies and inconsistencies that may exist between disparate groups.
18. Analyzing antecedents and consequences is a strategy that allows the researcher to map the antecedents (causes) and consequences (effects) that have emerged throughout the study.
19. Displaying findings is a strategy for using matrixes, charts, concept maps, graphs and figures to encapsulate the findings of a study.
20. Stating what's missing is a strategy that encourages the researcher to reflect on the pieces of the puzzle that are still missing at the conclusion of the study and to identify any questions for which answers have not been provided.

Using Computer Software to Assist with Data Analysis

21. Many computer programs are available to aid in analyzing qualitative data.

22. It is important for novice qualitative researchers to remember that computers alone do not analyze or code data.

23. N6, a version of NUD*IST, is one popular qualitative analysis software package used by researchers.

Data Interpretation

24. Data interpretation is based heavily on the connections, common aspects, and linkages among the data pieces, categories, and patterns. Interpretation cannot be meaningfully accomplished unless the researcher knows the data in great detail.

25. The aim of interpretation is to answer four questions: What is important in the data? Why is it important? What can be learned from it? So what?

26. Extending the analysis is a data interpretation strategy in which the researcher simply extends the data analysis by raising questions about the study, noting implications that might be drawn without actually drawing them. This is a strategy for pointing the way rather than leading the way.

27. Connecting findings with personal experience is a strategy that encourages the researcher to personalize interpretations based on intimate knowledge and understanding of the research setting.

28. Seeking the advice of "critical" friends is a strategy that involves inviting a trusted colleague to offer insights on the research that may have been missed due the researcher's closeness to the study.

29. Contextualizing the findings of the study in the related literature is a strategy that uses the review of related literature to provide support for the study's findings and encourages the researcher to link to "external authority."

30. Turning to theory is a strategy that encourages researchers to link their findings to broader issues of the day and, in so doing, to search for increasing levels of abstraction and to move beyond a purely descriptive account.

31. Knowing when to say "when" is a strategy that encourages the researcher to refrain from offering an interpretation rather than offer a wimpy interpretation.

32. As a qualitative researcher, you should share your interpretations wisely and avoid being evangelical about your interpretations. Provide a clear link between data collection, analysis, and interpretation.

Now go to the Companion Website at **www.prenhall.com/gay** to assess your understanding of chapter content with Practice Quiz, apply comprehension in Applying What You Know, broaden your knowledge about research in Web Links, and expand your research skills in Evaluating Articles, Analyzing Qualitative Data, Analyzing Quantitative Data, and Research Tools and Tips.

PERFORMANCE CRITERIA

TASK 8

The qualitative research topic or problem should be open ended and exploratory in nature. Your qualitative research questions should be worded to illuminate an issue and provide understanding of a topic, not answer specific questions. You should mention the type of research approach you will use—for instance, you should note whether it is a case study, a grounded theory study, an ethnography, or a narrative study. The reason you chose this topic, or the nature of its importance, should be mentioned.

Qualitative studies may include literature citations in the introduction of a study to provide background information for the reader and to build a case for the need for the study. Literature relevant to the research topic should be presented in your example, and citations should follow APA style (i.e., Smith, 2002). Despite the fact that your study may not require a literature review until data collection begins, cite some related texts anyway to get practice weaving the literature into the plan.

The description of participants should include the number of participants, how they were selected, and major characteristics (for example, occupation). Participants are ideally interviewed or observed in their natural setting to keep the interview or observation as authentic as possible. The description of the setting should be included.

Data collection methods should be described, and there may be more than one data collection method in a study. Qualitative data are descriptive; they are collected as words. Data may be in the form of interview notes and transcripts, observation field notes, and the like. The researcher will be immersed in the data and participate in data collection. Instruments may be video cameras, audio tape recorders, notepads, researcher-created observation records, and so forth. The description of instruments should also describe their validity and reliability.

An example that illustrates the performance called for by Task 8 appears on the following pages. (See Task 8 Example.) The task example is representative of the level of understanding you should have after studying Chapters 14–18. When the researcher created her plan, she still needed to choose her core participants, carry out data collection and data analysis, and write the final study. She constructed her plan taking into consideration the six steps in the research process. Note that not all plans or proposals require a results section.

Additional examples of the tasks are included in the *Student Study Guide* that accompanies this text.

1

Research Plan for: How Do Teachers Grade Student Essays?

The Research Aim

The purpose of this study was to examine the ways that freshman and sophomore high school English teachers grade their students' essays. I chose this topic to study because students in my school complain that their essays are graded unfairly. For example, one student said, "Teachers give the same scores for essays of different length." Other comments I hear include, "Teachers don't provide enough information about the number of examples they want included in an essay" and "Teachers don't give enough information about features they want included in essays so I can never match what they expect." I wanted to understand how teachers actually grade student essays. I also wanted to find out what criteria teachers use and whether they explain their essay grading criteria to their students, or whether the students' complaints are legitimate.

At the beginning of my exploration, my topic was stated generally, but through my initial investigations, it has narrowed a bit. Because qualitative research involves recurring study and examination, the topic may narrow some more. My approach is to carry out an ethnographic study. The research context is participants' classrooms.

Literature Review

An initial concern was the decision of whether to obtain and study existing literature, and if so, at what point in the study. For this study, I have consulted two assessment books frequently read by teachers in teacher education programs, Nitko (2001) and Linn and Gronlund (2000), to find out what sort of training teachers receive in scoring essays. Having some understanding of the following will help me to recognize scoring practices in the teachers I plan to interview: forms and uses of essay questions, their advantages and limitations, how essay questions should be constructed to measure the attainment of learning outcomes, and essay question scoring criteria. Later in the study, I may find a need to examine additional literature, but for now, this has been sufficient.

Choosing Participants

I identified teachers in freshman and sophomore English classes in an urban high school as participants for the study. The high school is the context for the ethnographic setting of the study. I contacted the school principal initially to propose the study and receive her approval before proceeding and contacting potential participants. She was cordial, and asked for more information about the role that the teachers and students would have. We discussed her concerns and she consented. She indicated that she would send informed consent forms to the parents involved in the study. All but two of the students' parents agreed to let their children participate. There was no indication why the parents declined the request.

The principal of the school also provided me with copies of the school's Human Subject Review Form to give to the teachers to sign when I explained their part in the study to them. I contacted the freshman and sophomore English teachers in the school, and described the project to them as an exploratory study about how teachers plan lessons and assess their students. I also told them, and the principal concurred, that each teacher participant would be identified by a number rather than by a name in the final written study. Only I would know the identities of the teachers. I thought this would allow the teachers to be more open when providing data. All but three teachers agreed to become participants in the study. Two of these teachers asked for more information about what would be asked of them. One of the two teachers agreed to participate after more discussion, but the remaining two teachers still opted not to participate. I thought this final number, 8 teacher participants, was a good sample for the study. The principal has been a helpful gatekeeper and interested observer. In general, the school personnel are supportive.

I will identify approximately 10 students to participate in the study and provide comments about essay items and graded essays. I suspect that this number will decrease once data collection begins and I determine which participants can provide the most helpful comments.

As the research data are collected, I will note the comments of the teachers, not only to obtain their comments on grading essays, but also to identify the most articulate and conceptual teachers to focus on during data collection. Ultimately, I will have a smaller number of core participants than I began with.

Data Collection

The teachers will be studied in their own context, in each teacher's own classroom. If this is not possible, data collection will take place somewhere else in the school. Ethnographic data collection relies heavily on asking questions, interviewing, and observing participants. Each of these methods will be applied over a period of 12 weeks. I plan to collect data in the form of completed and graded student essays from the teachers. I expect to collect approximately 7 to 9 essays per teacher over the 12 weeks. I think this will be sufficient to capture and integrate the data.

I have arranged to receive a copy of each essay exam or assignment. The purpose of this form of data collection is to assess the characteristics of the essay items. I plan to examine the essay items to evaluate whether students understand what is expected of them in this type of performance assessment. I will also look at samples of the teachers' essay items that will be critiqued by students. Again, the names of the students will be confidential.

I also plan to informally interview teachers and ask questions such as "Tell me how you grade your essays and why," "What do you consider to be the best feature of your essay grading?" "What do you consider to be the weakest feature of your essay grading?" Similar questions will be asked of the students in informal interviews.

During the 12-week period, I plan to hold several focus groups, one with teachers, and one with students, in which grading is discussed. The focus groups will be audiotaped and then transcribed. Finally, I will employ observation to obtain data. I will observe teachers grading student essays, question them about why they assign the grade they do, note the time it takes them to grade the items, and so forth. If written feedback is provided for the graded essays, I will collect a copy as data, for later analysis. I will also follow these graded essays and ask the students whether they feel the essay items are fairly graded. Therefore, my data will include student artifacts, audiotapes, field notes and memos from informal questioning and interviews, and field notes from observations.

Data Analysis

As data are collected from the participants, I will examine and reexamine the data in search of themes and integration in the data to arrive at a number of themes. I anticipate that analyzing and synthesizing the data will take approximately three to four weeks, eight hours a day, after data collection ends. Triangulation among asking questions, observing, interviewing, and analyzing essays will help to integrate the analysis.

Results

The final step will be to describe the procedures and interpretation in a written format for others to examine and critique. Before writing up the study, it will be important to spend time thinking about the data analysis and interpret what the data reveal. I hope to be able to express a contribution or insight that emerges from this study.

"Researchers creatively combine the elements of methods in any way that makes the best sense for the study they want to do." (p. 489)

Mixed Methods Research: Integrating Qualitative and Quantitative Methods

OBJECTIVES

After reading Chapter 19, you should be able to do the following:

1. Define mixed methods research.
2. Distinguish between three types of mixed methods research designs.
3. Illustrate mixed methods research designs with a diagram that captures the priority and sequencing of data collection techniques.
4. Describe strategies for conducting mixed methods data analysis.
5. Use questions to help evaluate a mixed methods study.

✷ INTRODUCTION TO MIXED METHODS

Now that you have gotten a flavor for qualitative research, and before we proceed much further, you need to be aware of something: You can mix quantitative and qualitative methods in a single study! Now, before you close your book in frustration, or decide right now would be a good time for a nap, stay with us for the next few pages for an introduction to mixed methods research. Your study may be better off if you know how to integrate both qualitative and quantitative aspects.

In Chapter 1 we introduced qualitative and quantitative research methods, and we have mentioned occasionally since then the possibilities of mixing them. Recall some of the characteristics of each approach:

1. Quantitative research methods are characterized by a deductive approach; qualitative methods are characterized by an inductive approach.
2. Quantitative researchers are concerned with objective reality that is "out there" to be discovered;

qualitative researchers focus on interpreting their participants' perspectives.
3. Quantitative researchers focus on establishing cause–effect relationships; qualitative researchers focus on describing and understanding relationships.
4. Quantitative researchers identify hypotheses to test; qualitative researchers work with a guiding hypothesis and allow a specific focus to emerge as a study progresses.
5. Quantitative researchers select participants as randomly as possible; qualitative researchers purposefully select research participants based on their articulateness and experience in the research setting.

These distinctions do not completely define quantitative and qualitative approaches, but they do highlight important differences. As Krathwohl notes, "Research, however, is a creative act; don't confine your thinking to specific approaches. Researchers creatively combine the elements of methods in any way that makes the best sense for the study they want to do. Their own limits are their own imagination and the necessity of presenting their findings convincingly. The research question to be answered really determines the method."[1] With this in mind, and a clear idea about the research question you wish to investigate, it may be appropriate for you to consider using a mixed methods approach to study your phenomenon of choice. For example, you may be interested (and concerned) about students' attitudes towards, and use of, birth control measures. You might decide to collect quantitative and qualitative data. First, you might survey college freshmen and then conduct follow-up interviews with students to increase your understanding of

---

[1] *Methods of Educational and Social Science Research: An Integrated Approach,* by D. R. Krathwohl (2nd ed., p. 27), 1998, Reading, MA: Addison-Wesley.

the survey results. For the first quantitative phase, your research question might be "What factors affect college freshmen's attitudes toward, and use of, appropriate birth control measures?" In the follow-up qualitative phase (perhaps conducted at the student health center in collaboration with a health professional), your research question might be "When students mention alcohol as an 'influencing factor' with respect to their use of birth control, what do they mean?" In this hypothetical study, you would collect quantitative survey data in the first phase, and then follow up with qualitative interview data in the second phase. This mixed methods study would provide you with a breadth (survey results) and depth (interview data) of understanding not possible using either a quantitative or qualitative design by itself.

:: MIXED METHODS RESEARCH: DEFINITION AND PURPOSE

Mixed methods research designs combine quantitative and qualitative approaches by essentially mixing both quantitative and qualitative data in a single study. The purpose of mixed methods research is to build on the synergy and strength that exists between quantitative and qualitative research methods in order to understand a phenomenon more fully than is possible using either quantitative or qualitative methods alone. Although this approach to research may appear a "no-brainer" (of course we want a complete understanding of any phenomenon worthy of investigation!), it requires a thorough understanding of both quantitative and qualitative research. In fact, there are few researchers who possess all of the knowledge and skills to master the full range of research techniques encompassed in quantitative and qualitative research approaches. Similarly, researchers who undertake a mixed methods study must have the considerable time and resources needed to implement such a comprehensive approach to research.

In spite of these potential limitations, mixed methods can be used to build on the findings of a qualitative study by pursuing a quantitative phase of the research, or vice versa. Alternatively, you may find yourself working in a graduate program that is less receptive to qualitative research than quantitative research, but you may be genuinely interested in incorporating a qualitative component into the study. A mixed methods approach will enable you to achieve this goal.

The same issues in the general debate over qualitative versus quantitative paradigms arise in discussions of mixed methods evaluation. For example, qualitative researchers who are philosophically opposed to quantitative methods argue that these methods have taught us very little about how and why programs work. However, both sides can benefit from collaboration. Quantitative studies are good at establishing *what,* but qualitative studies help us to understand *how* a program succeeds or fails.

:: TYPES OF MIXED METHODS RESEARCH DESIGNS

There are three common types of mixed methods research designs: the QUAL–quan model, the QUAN–qual model, and the QUAN–QUAL model. In the names of the models, our use of uppercase and lowercase letters follows the conventions presented by Creswell:[2] The method in uppercase letters is weighted more heavily than that in lowercase, and when both methods are in uppercase, they are in balance. The methods are described in the following sections.

---

[2] *Educational Research: Planning, Conducting, and Evaluating Quantitative and Qualitative Research* (2nd ed.), by J. W. Creswell, 2005, Upper Saddle River, NJ: Merrill/Prentice Hall.

The QUAL–Quan Model.   In the **QUAL–quan model,** also known as the *exploratory mixed methods design,* qualitative data are collected first and are more heavily weighted than quantitative data. A qualitative study (or phase in a study) comes first and is typically an "exploratory" study in which observation and open-ended interviews with individuals or groups are conducted and concepts and potential hypotheses are identified. In a second study or phase, variables are identified from concepts derived from the qualitative analysis and hypotheses are tested with quantitative techniques. The QUAL–quan approach is useful for researchers who obtain results from multi-item scales to measure phenomena. The validity of the qualitative results can be enhanced by quantitative results obtained from the second study or phase.

The QUAN–Qual Model.   In the **QUAN–qual model,** also known as the *explanatory mixed methods design,* quantitative data are collected first and are more heavily weighted than qualitative data. In the first study or phase, the researcher formulates a hypothesis, collects quantitative data, and conducts data analysis. The findings of the quantitative study determine the type of data collected in a second, qualitative study or phase. This study or phase is comprised of qualitative data collection, analysis, and interpretation. The researcher can then use the qualitative analysis and interpretation to help explain or elaborate on the quantitative results.

The QUAN–QUAL Model.   In the third type of mixed methods design, the **QUAN–QUAL model,** also known as the *triangulation mixed methods design,* quantitative and qualitative data are equally weighted and are collected concurrently throughout the same study—the data are not collected in separate studies or distinct phases, as in the other two methods. One method may be dominant over the other (QUAN–qual or QUAL–quan), or the two methods may be given equal weight throughout. When quantitative methods are dominant (QUAN–qual), for example, researchers might enliven their quantitative findings by collecting and writing case vignettes. When qualitative methods are dominant (QUAL–quan), qualitative researchers might decide to include survey, census, and Likert-scale data along with narrative data. The fully integrated QUAN–QUAL approach is the most challenging type of mixed methods research.

Figure 19.1 provides a visual representation of the three types of mixed methods designs.

As can be seen from this overview of mixed methods designs, the basic differences among the designs relate to the following:

- *The **priority** given to either qualitative or quantitative data collection.* The researcher has three choices about the priority given to qualitative and quantitative data; qualitative and

I. Triangulation Mixed Methods Designs

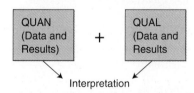

III. Exploratory Mixed Designs

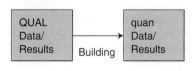

II. Explanatory Mixed Methods Designs

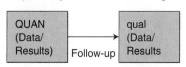

Legend:
Box = data collection and results
Uppercase letters/lowercase letters = major emphasis, minor emphasis
Arrow = sequence + = concurrent or simultaneous

FIGURE 19.1

Types of mixed methods designs
Source: Creswell, John W., *Educational Research: Planning, Conducting, and Evaluating Quantitative and Qualitative Research,* 2nd Edition, © 2005. Reprinted by permission of Pearson Education, Inc., Upper Saddle River, NJ.

quantitative data are of equal weight, quantitative data are of greater weight than qualitative data, or qualitative data are of greater weight than quantitative data.

■ *The sequence of collecting qualitative or quantitative data.* The researcher can't collect quantitative and qualitative data simultaneously. Quantitative data are collected first, followed by qualitative data; qualitative data are collected first, followed by quantitative data; or, in a QUAN–QUAL approach both types of data are collected during the same time period.

■ *The data analysis techniques used to either combine the analyses of data or keep the two types of data separate.* As we have discussed throughout this text, one of the most difficult aspects of any research endeavor is the analysis of data. This problem is showcased when we attempt to analyze quantitative and qualitative data sources concurrently or in sequence and attempt to find points of intersection as well as discrepancies. Creswell[3] provides a comprehensive overview of mixed methods design data analysis and interpretation procedures in Table 19.1. This table is particularly helpful for the novice mixed methods researcher because it provides a series of strategies for beginning the data analysis process for both quantitative and qualitative data. Many of the suggestions in the table build on the information in the quantitative and qualitative analysis and interpretation chapters in this text and therefore should be familiar to you.

:: CHARACTERISTICS OF MIXED METHODS DESIGNS

As a consumer of educational research, you may sometimes be baffled by how best to classify the type of research that was used in a particular study, especially if the researcher is not kind enough to make it explicit! The following characteristics will help you identify a study as a mixed methods design:

1. The study title includes such terms as *quantitative* and *qualitative, mixed methods, integrated, triangular,* or other terms that suggest a mixture of methods.
2. Both qualitative and quantitative methods are used in the study.
3. The researcher describes the kinds of mixed methods applied.
4. The data collection section describes the kinds of data that are collected, and it is possible to determine whether narrative, numerical, or both kinds of data were collected.
5. The purpose statement or the research questions indicate the type(s) of method(s) used.
6. Questions are stated and described for both quantitative and qualitative approaches.
7. The researcher indicates the preference given to qualitative or quantitative data collection techniques.
8. The researcher indicates the sequence of in which qualitative, quantitative, or both types of data were collected. Knowing the sequence will enable you to determine the type of mixed methods research—that is, QUAN–qual, QUAL–quan, or QUAN–QUAL—used by the researcher.
9. The researcher describes how data were analyzed using both quantitative and qualitative strategies.
10. The writing is balanced in terms of qualitative and quantitative approaches.

Table 19.2 illustrates the interaction of qualitative methods with quantitative designs. Table 19.3 shows the interaction of quantitative methods with qualitative designs. These tables illustrate the varied strategies available for linking qualitative and quantitative methods in the same research study.

---

[3] Ibid.

TABLE 19.1	Type of mixed methods designs and data analysis/interpretation procedures
Type of Mixed Methods Designs	**Examples of Analytic and Interpretive Procedures**
Triangulation (QUAN and QUAL data collected simultaneously)	• *Quantifying qualitative data:* Qualitative data are coded, codes are assigned numbers, and the number of times codes appear are recorded as numeric data. Quantitative data are descriptively analyzed for frequency of occurrence. The two data sets are compared. • *Qualifying quantitative data:* Quantitative data from questionnaires are factor analyzed. These factors then become themes that are compared with themes analyzed from qualitative data. • *Comparing results:* The results from qualitative data collection are directly compared with results from quantitative data collection. Statistical trends are supported by qualitative themes or vice versa. • *Consolidating data:* Qualitative data and quantitative data are combined to form new variables. Original quantitative variables are compared with qualitative themes to form new quantitative variables. (Caracelli & Greene, 1993)
Explanatory (QUAN followed by qual)	• *Following up on outliers or extreme cases:* Gather quantitative data and identify outlier or residual cases. Collect qualitative data to explore the characteristics of these cases. (Caracelli & Greene, 1993) • *Explaining results:* Conduct a quantitative survey to identify how two or more groups compare on a variable. Follow up with qualitative interviews to explore the reasons why these differences were found. • *Using a typology:* Conduct a quantitative survey and develop factors through a factor analysis. Use these factors as a typology to identify themes in qualitative data, such as observations or interviews. (Caracelli & Greene, 1993) • *Examining multilevels:* Conduct a survey at the student level. Gather qualitative data through interviews at the class level. Survey the entire school at the school level. Collect qualitative data at the district level. Information from each level builds to the next level. (Tashakkori & Teddlie, 1998)
Exploratory (QUAL followed by quan)	• *Locating an instrument:* Collect qualitative data and identify themes. Use these themes as a basis for locating instruments that use parallel concepts to the qualitative themes. • *Developing an instrument:* Obtain themes and specific statements from individuals that support the themes. In the next phase, use these themes and statements to create scales and items as a questionnaire. Alternatively, look for existing instruments that can be modified to fit the themes and statements found in the qualitative exploratory phase of the study. After developing the instrument, test it out with a sample of a population. • *Forming categorical data:* Site-level characteristics (e.g., different ethnic groups) gathered in an ethnography in the first phase of a study become a categorical variable in a second phase correlational or regression study. (Caracelli & Greene, 1993) • *Using extreme qualitative cases:* Qualitative data cases that are extreme in a comparative analysis are followed in a second phase by quantitative surveys. (Caracelli & Greene, 1993).

Source: Creswell, John W., *Educational Research: Planning, Conducting, and Evaluating Quantitative and Qualitative Research,* 2nd Edition, © 2005. Reprinted by permission of Pearson Education, Inc., Upper Saddle River, NJ. Cited data and information from "Data Analysis Strategies for Mixed-Methods Evaluation Designs," by V. J. Daracelli and J. C. Greene, 1993, *Educational Evaluation and Policy Analysis, 15*(2), pp. 195–207; and *Mixed Methodology: Combining Qualitative and Quantitative Approaches,* by A. Tashakkori and C. Teddlie, 1998, Thousand Oaks, CA: Sage.

Figure 19.2, p. 496, is an example of an abstract for a combined qualitative and quantitative research study. The abstract provides an overview of how combined quantitative and qualitative research can work together to broaden educational research from a single to a multiple perspective.

TABLE 19.2	The interaction of qualitative research methods with quantitative research designs
Quantitative Design Type	**Role of Ethnography in Quantitative Research Designs**
Cross-sectional research: Population and sample surveys	*Preparation for survey* — Identification of the problem and context — Identification of the range of responses — Identification of target population, characteristics, locations, and possible barriers to survey research *Complementary data* — Identification and exploration of social subgroups, explaining patterned variation in survey results
Experiments	*Preparation* — Identification of elements of the experiment — Identification of constraints in the field — Pilot testing for acceptability and feasibility — Developing and validating measures of change *Process* — Finding differences in implementation — Documenting content of intervention for comparison with outcome measures
Controlled field studies/ quasi-experiments	*Preparation* — Identification of elements of the treatment — Identification of potential differences among treatment and control groups — Identification of constraints to experimentation in the field — Pilot testing for acceptability and feasibility — Developing and validating measures of change *Process* — Finding differences in implementation — Documenting content of intervention for comparison with outcome measures

Source: From *Ethnographer's Toolkit: Vol. 1. Designing and Conducting Ethnographic Research* (p. 93), by M. D. LeCompte and J. J. Schensul, 1999, Lanham, MD: AltaMira/Roman & Littlefield. Reprinted with permission.

:: EVALUATING A MIXED METHODS STUDY

Now that you have a general understanding of the types of mixed methods research designs and the strategies you can use to conduct a mixed methods analysis, you will be able to use the following questions to help you evaluate a mixed methods study:[4]

---

[4] Questions adapted from *Educational Research* (p. 524), Creswell.

TABLE 19.3	The interaction of quantitative methods with qualitative research designs
Qualitative Research Designs	**Role of Quantitative Research in Relation to Ethnography**
Case studies/ethnographies	— Survey to confirm and validate ethnographically defined patterns
	— "Case-control" matched sample to identify factors associated with presence/absence of element (e.g., disease, school performance, etc.)
Ethnographies	— Survey to confirm and validate ethnographically defined patterns
	— "Case-control" matched sample to identify factors associated with presence/absence of element (e.g., disease, school performance, etc.)
	— Time series design (repeated observations of the same units over time) to define change more accurately
Narratives	— Survey to demonstrate presence of patterns revealed by narratives, using language and concepts of respondents
Compressed or rapid ethnographic assessments or focused ethnography	— Brief cross-sectional surveys with small samples
	— Brief pre-post surveys and panel designs for assessing intervention
Action research	— Action research makes use of both qualitative and quantitative design features to accomplish the purpose designated by the problem and the partnership

Source: From *Ethnographer's Toolkit: Vol. 1. Designing and Conducting Ethnographic Research* (p. 94), by M. D. LeCompte and J. J. Schensul, 1999, Lanham, MD: AltaMira/Roman & Littlefield. Reprinted with permission.

■ Does the study use at least one quantitative and one qualitative data research method?
■ Does the study include a rationale for using a mixed methods research design?
■ Does the study include a classification of the type of mixed methods research design?
■ Does the study describe the priority given to quantitative and qualitative data collection and the sequence of their use?
■ Was the study feasible given the amount of data to be collected and concomitant issues of resources, time, and expertise?
■ Does the study include both quantitative and qualitative research questions?
■ Does the study clearly identify qualitative and quantitative data collection techniques?
■ Does the study use appropriate data analysis techniques for the type of mixed methods design?

   Armed with answers to these questions, you will be prepared to evaluate a mixed methods study that you encounter during a review of related literature as well as evaluate a design you may be considering for your own mixed methods research. Given the complexity of planning and conducting a mixed methods study, a novice researcher interested in this type of research would be well advised to team up with a colleague who possesses a skill set (in either qualitative or quantitative research) that complements his or her own.

FIGURE 19.2   Abstract of a mixed methods study

AUTHOR	Holbrook, Allyson; Bourke, Sid; Owen, John M.; McKenzie, Phil; Ainley, John
TITLE	Mapping Educational Research and Exploring Research Impact: A Holistic, Multi-Method Approach.
PUB DATE	2000
NOTE	31P.; Paper presented at the Annual Meeting of the American Educational Research Association (New Orleans, LA, April 24–26, 2000). "Mapping Educational Research and Its Impact on Schools" was one of three studies of the "Impact of Educational Research" commissioned and funded by the Australian Federal Dept. of Education, Training, and Youth Affairs in 1999 (Minister: The Honorable Dr. David Kemp, MP).
PUB TYPE	Reports—Research (143)—Speeches/Meeting Papers (150)
EDRS PRICE	MFOI/PCO2 Plus Postage.
DESCRIPTORS	Administrator Attitudes; Databases; Educational Administration; Educational Policy; *Educational Research; Elementary Secondary Education; Foreign Countries; *Graduate Students; Higher Education; *Principals; *Research Utilization; *Teacher Attitudes; Theory Practice Relationship
IDENTIFIERS	*Australia
ABSTRACT	This paper discusses the main analytical techniques used in "Mapping Educational Research and Its Impact on Schools." The study considered the impact of the outcomes of educational research on the practice of teaching and learning in Australian schools and on educational policy and administration. Mixed methods were used, beginning with a review of the literature and the exploration of the Australian Education Index (AEI) educational research database. Documents were collected from faculties of education in Australia, and questionnaires about the use of educational literature were developed for postgraduate students ($n = 1{,}267$), school principals ($n = 73$), and representatives of 72 professional associations. Interviews were then conducted with seven policymakers and selected respondents to the postgraduate student questionnaires. The study indicates that it is possible to use an existing database to monitor educational research in Australia. A clear majority of all three groups surveyed provided evidence of the awareness, acceptance, and valuing of educational research in Australia. Interviews with policymakers also showed the use of educational research in policy formation. The multiple perspectives of this study give a picture of the links between research and its use in schools and departments of education in Australia. An appendix summarizes the database descriptors from the database investigation. (Contains 3 tables, 3 figures, and 34 references.) (SLD)

Note that the title indicates that the research involves both qualitative and quantitative methods.

The topic states that the study "considered the impact"—not "determined the impact"—giving the abstract a distinct qualitative flavor.

Note that the study used both questionnaires (quantitative) and interviews (qualitative) to collect data. It is common in mixed-method studies to combine these two data-collection methods.

Source: ERIC Document Reproduction Service No. ED 441 850.

SUMMARY

Mixed Methods Research: Definition and Purpose

1. Mixed methods research is a style of research that uses procedures for conducting research that are typically applied in both quantitative and qualitative studies in order to more fully understand a research problem.

2. The purpose of mixed methods research is to build on the synergy and strength that exists between quantitative and qualitative research methods in order to more fully understand a given research phenomena.

Types of Mixed Methods Research Designs

3. In the QUAL–quan model (also known as the *exploratory mixed methods design*), a qualitative study (or phase in a study) comes first and is typically an "exploratory" study in which observation and open-ended interviews with individuals or groups are

conducted and concepts and potential hypotheses are identified.

4. In the QUAN–qual model (also known as the *explanatory mixed methods design*) a quantitative study is followed by a qualitative study. It is the findings of the quantitative study that determine the type of data collected in the qualitative study.

5. The third type of mixed methods design, QUAN–QUAL (also known as the *triangulation mixed methods design*), integrates qualitative and quantitative methods, and gives equal weight to both types of data, throughout the same study.

6. The differences among the mixed methods designs relate to (1) the priority given to either qualitative or quantitative data collection, (2) the sequence in which either qualitative or quantitative data are collected, and (3) the data analysis techniques used.

Characteristics of Mixed Methods Designs

7. The following are some of the characteristics that can be used to identify a study as a mixed methods design:

   a. The study title includes such terms as *quantitative* and *qualitative, mixed methods, integrated, triangular,* or other terms that suggest a mixture of methods.

   b. The data collection section describes the kinds of data that are collected, and it is possible to determine whether narrative, numerical, or both kinds of data were collected.

   c. The purpose statement or the research questions indicate the type(s) of method(s) used.

   d. The researcher indicates the preference given to qualitative or quantitative data collection techniques.

   e. The researcher indicates the sequence in which qualitative, quantitative, or both types of data were collected. Knowing the sequence will enable the reader to determine the type of mixed methods research—that is, QUAN–qual, QUAL–quan, or QUAN–QUAL—used by the researcher.

   f. The researcher describes how data were analyzed using both quantitative and qualitative strategies.

Evaluating a Mixed Methods Study

8. A mixed methods study can be evaluated by answering questions related to the use of at least one qualitative and one quantitative research method, the rationale for using a mixed methods research design, the priority and sequence given to qualitative and quantitative data collection, the use of qualitative and quantitative research questions and matching data collection techniques, and the use of appropriate data analysis techniques for mixed methods designs.

Now go to the Companion Website at **www.prenhall.com/gay** to assess your understanding of chapter content with Practice Quiz, apply comprehension in Applying What You Know, broaden your knowledge about research in Web Links, and expand your research skills in Evaluating Articles, Analyzing Qualitative Data, Analyzing Quantitative Data, and Research Tools and Tips.

"Quite often, individual teachers seek to study aspects of their classroom that are unique to them and their students." (p. 503)

Action Research

OBJECTIVES

After reading Chapter 20, you should be able to do the following:

1. State a definition of action research.
2. Describe the purposes of action research.
3. Describe the processes of action research.
4. Identify the four basic steps in conducting action research.
5. Describe the key characteristics of action research.
6. Identify common data collection sources and strategies used to carry out action research in schools.

TASK 9

Develop a design for an action research study to answer a school-based research question. (See Performance Criteria, p. 510.)

▓ ACTION RESEARCH: DEFINITION AND PURPOSE

As you may recall from Chapter 1, **action research** in education is any systematic inquiry conducted by teachers, principals, school counselors, or other stakeholders in the teaching–learning environment, to gather information about the ways in which their particular schools operate, the teachers teach, and the students learn. This information is gathered with the goals of gaining insight, developing reflective practice, effecting positive changes in the school environment (and on educational practices in general), and improving student outcomes and the lives of those involved.

The purpose of action research is to provide teacher researchers with a method for solving everyday problems in schools, in order to improve both student learning and teacher effectiveness. Action research is research done *by* teachers, *for* themselves; it is not imposed on them by someone else. Action research is largely about developing the *professional disposition* of teachers, that is, encouraging teachers to be continuous learners—in their classrooms and of their practice. In conducting research in their own classrooms and schools, teachers have the opportunity to model for students not only the skills needed for effective learning but also curiosity and an excitement about gaining new knowledge.

Action research is also about incorporating into a teacher's daily routine a *reflective stance*—a willingness to look critically at one's own teaching so that it can be improved or enhanced. Action research significantly contributes to the professional stance that teachers adopt because it encourages them to examine the dynamics of their classrooms, ponder the actions and interactions of students, validate and challenge existing practices, and take risks in the process. When teachers gain new understandings about both their own and their students' behaviors through action research, they are empowered to do the following:[1]

- Make informed decisions about what to change and what not to change
- Link prior knowledge to new information
- Learn from experience (even failures)
- Ask questions and systematically find answers

This goal of teachers to be professional problem solvers who are committed to improving both their own practice and student outcomes provides a powerful reason to practice action research.

---

[1] "Teacher as Researcher: A Synonym for Professionalism," by V. Fueyo and M. A. Koorland, 1997, *Journal of Teacher Education, 48,* pp. 336–344.

:: THE ACTION RESEARCH PROCESS

The basic steps in the action research process are (1) identifying an area of focus, (2) data collection, (3) data analysis and interpretation, and (4) action planning. This four-step process has been termed the **Dialectic Action Research Spiral**[2] and is illustrated in Figure 20.1. It provides teacher researchers with a practical guide and illustrates how to proceed with inquiries. It is a model for research done by teachers and for teachers and students, not research done *on* them, and as such is a dynamic and responsive model that can be adapted to different contexts and purposes. It was designed to provide teacher researchers with "provocative and constructive ways" of thinking about their work.[3]

For example, a high school teacher confronted with the challenges of teaching "unmotivated" students critically reflects on her teaching practices to determine which specific strategies are most effective in improving student outcomes. Teaching students who are unmotivated and apathetic can be a difficult challenge for any teacher to overcome. This example illustrates the power of action research to empower the teacher to try different teaching strategies and to systematically collect student outcome data (e.g., test scores, student attitudes, and on-task behavior) to help determine which teaching strategy works best for the unmotivated students in her classroom.

:: TYPES OF ACTION RESEARCH

In this section we will briefly review the two main types of action research: critical (or theory-based) action research and practical action research.

Critical Action Research

Critical action research is action research in which the goal is liberating individuals through knowledge gathering; for this reason, it is also known as *emancipatory action research*. Critical action research is so named because it is based on a body of critical theory, *not* because this type of action research is critical, as in "faultfinding" or "important," although it may certainly be both!

The values of critical action research dictate that all educational research should not only be socially responsive but should also exhibit the following characteristics:[4]

1. Democratic—enabling participation of people
2. Equitable—acknowledging people's equality of worth
3. Liberating—providing freedom from oppressive, debilitating conditions
4. Enhancing—enabling the expression of people's full human potential

Although this critical theory-based approach has been criticized by some for lack of practical feasibility,[5] it is nonetheless important to consider because this perspective provides a helpful heuristic, or problem-solving approach, for teachers who are committed to investigate

---

[2] *Action Research: A Guide for the Teacher Researcher* (2nd ed.), by G. E. Mills, 2003, Upper Saddle River, NJ: Merrill/Prentice Hall.

[3] *Kwakiutl Village and School* (p. 137), by H. F. Wolcott, 1989.

[4] "Socially Responsive Educational Research: Linking Theory and Practice," by E. T. Stringer, 1993, in *Theory and Concepts in Qualitative Research: Perspectives From the Field* (p. 148), by D. Flinders and G. E. Mills, New York: Teachers College Press.

[5] "On the Teacher as Researcher," by M. Hammersley, 1993, *Educational Action Research, 1,* pp. 425–441.

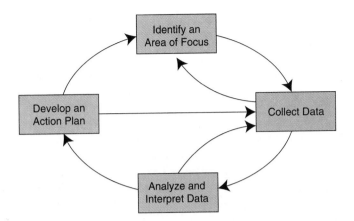

FIGURE 20.1

The Dialectic Action Research Spiral
Source: Mills, Geoffrey, *Action Research: A Guide for the Teacher Researcher,* 2nd Edition, © 2003. Reprinted by permission of Pearson Education, Inc., Upper Saddle River, NJ.

TABLE 20.1	Components of a critical perspective of action research
Key Concept	**Example**
Action research is participatory and democratic.	You have identified an area in your teaching that you believe can be improved (based on data from your students). You decide to investigate the impact of your intervention and to monitor if it makes a difference.
Action research is socially responsive and takes place in context.	You are concerned that minority children (for example ESL [English as a Second Language] students) in your classroom are not being presented with curriculum and teaching strategies that are culturally sensitive. You decide to learn more about how best to teach ESL children and to implement some of these strategies.
Action research helps teacher researchers examine the everyday, taken-for-granted ways in which they carry out professional practice.	You have adopted a new mathematics problem-solving curriculum and decide to monitor its impact on student performance on open-ended problem-solving questions and students' attitudes toward mathematics in general.
Knowledge gained through action research can liberate students, teachers, and administrators and enhance learning, teaching, and policy making.	Your school has a high incidence of student absenteeism in spite of a newly adopted district-wide policy on absenteeism. You investigate the perceptions of colleagues, children, and parents toward absenteeism to more fully understand why the existing policy is not having the desired outcome. Based on what you learn, you implement a new policy and systematically monitor its impact on absenteeism levels and students' attitudes toward school.

Source: Mills, Geoffrey, *Action Research: A Guide for the Teacher Researcher,* 2nd Edition, © 2003. Reprinted by permission of Pearson Education, Inc., Upper Saddle River, NJ.

through action research the taken-for-granted relationships and practices in their professional lives. Table 20.1 summarizes the most important components of a critical perspective of action research.

Practical Action Research

As compared to critical action research, **practical action research** emphasizes more of a "how-to" approach to the processes of action research and has a less philosophical bent. It assumes, to some degree, that individual teachers or teams of teachers are autonomous and can determine the nature of the investigation to be undertaken. It also assumes that teacher researchers

TABLE 20.2	Components of a practical perspective of action research

Key Concept	Example
Teacher researchers have decision-making authority.	Your school has adopted a school-based decision-making approach that provides teachers with the authority to make decisions that most directly impact teaching and learning. Given this decision-making authority, you decide as part of your continued professional development to investigate the effectiveness of a newly adopted science curriculum on students' process skills and attitudes.
Teacher researchers are committed to continued professional development and school improvement.	Based on the results of statewide assessment tests and classroom observations, the teachers and principal at your school determine that reading comprehension skills are weak. Collaboratively, the staff determines the focus for a school improvement effort and identifies the necessary professional development that will be offered to change the ways teachers teach reading.
Teacher researchers want to reflect on their practices.	You are a successful classroom teacher who regularly reflects on your daily teaching and what areas could be improved. You believe that part of being a professional teacher is the willingness to continually examine your teaching effectiveness.
Teacher researchers will use a systematic approach for reflecting on their practice.	Given a schoolwide reading comprehension focus, you have decided to monitor the effectiveness of a new reading curriculum and teaching strategies by videotaping a reading lesson (once per month), administering reading comprehension "probes" (once per week), interviewing children in your classroom (once per term), and administering statewide assessment tests (at the end of the school year).
Teacher researchers will choose an area of focus, determine data collection techniques, analyze and interpret data, and develop action plans.	To continue the example above, you have focused on the effectiveness of a new reading curriculum and teaching strategies. You have decided to collect data using videotapes of lessons, regular "probes," interviews, and statewide assessment tests. During the year you try to interpret the data you are collecting and decide what these data suggest about the effectiveness of the new curriculum and teaching strategies. When all of the data have been collected and analyzed, you decide what action needs to be taken to refine, improve, or maintain the reading comprehension curriculum and teaching strategies.

Source: Mills, Geoffrey, *Action Research: A Guide for the Teacher Researcher,* 2nd Edition, © 2003. Reprinted by permission of Pearson Education, Inc., Upper Saddle River, NJ.

are committed to continued professional development and school improvement and that they want to systematically reflect on their practices. Finally, the practical action research perspective assumes that as decision makers, teacher researchers will choose their own areas of focus, determine their data collection techniques, analyze and interpret their data, and develop action plans based on their findings. These beliefs are summarized in Table 20.2.

:: LEVELS OF ACTION RESEARCH

Educational action research can be undertaken at three levels: the individual teacher level; the single school or department level, in which small teacher groups or teams conduct the research; or the schoolwide level. It is important to note that teachers rarely carry out action research involving multiple schools because of the organizational complexity and the uniqueness of the many settings or schools.

It also is likely that in a single school, action research is carried out by groups of teachers, rather than an individual teacher, who all seek to understand and improve a common issue. For example, a group of high school math teachers might wish to work together to implement a promising "hands-on" math strategy for students who are lagging in math performance and then determine its impact on student math performance. Similarly, shared goals are surely voiced by teachers in other content areas as well. This does not imply that teachers never collaborate across subject areas, just that it is more common and interesting for teachers to focus their action research in their own disciplines. As another example, elementary teachers might form a small group and design a study to answer questions about such varied strategies as inclusion of special education students, inquiry-based learning, or literary clubs, which cross content area and grade lines. Or some teachers might be involved in collaborative or participatory research by working with university-based researchers in their classrooms. For example, teachers may study their own research questions along with similar or related questions that the university researcher has.

In schoolwide action research, the majority of the school community identifies a problem and conducts research together with a common, focused goal in mind. For example, a schoolwide emphasis on reading is a common goal of many elementary schools. Or counselors, teachers, and administrators may band together in a middle school and try strategies to integrate cliques or other groups of students to create a more cooperative environment.

Although a group of teachers working together is more common, individual teachers can conduct action research to improve their understanding and practice in their own classrooms. Quite often, individual teachers seek to study aspects of their classrooms that are unique to them and their students. As an example of carrying out action research individually, a teacher may gather information by observing students to better understand their interests or behaviors in a particular subject area. Alternatively, the teacher may select or construct simple instruments or tests to collect student information pertaining to the issue or topic under study. Individual teacher action research can be a useful tool for solving educational problems in one's own setting.

:: KEY CHARACTERISTICS OF ACTION RESEARCH

The key characteristics of action research can be derived from the research studies of the connections between research and practice and the apparent failure of educational research to affect teaching. This research has provided the following insights:[6]

- Teachers do not find research persuasive or authoritative.
- Research has not been relevant to practice and has not addressed teachers' questions.
- Findings from research have not been expressed in ways that are comprehensible to teachers.
- The education system itself is unable to change, or conversely, it is inherently unstable and susceptible to fads.

Given these insights, action research exhibits five characteristics, each discussed next.

Action Research Is Persuasive and Authoritative

Research done by teachers for teachers involves collecting persuasive data. Because teachers are invested in the legitimacy of the data collection, they identify data sources that provide persuasive insights into the impact of an intervention on student outcomes. Similarly, the findings

---

[6] "The Connection Between Research and Practice," by M. M. Kennedy, 1997, *Educational Researcher, 26*(7), pp. 4–12.

of action research and the recommended actions are authoritative for teacher researchers. In doing action research, teacher researchers have developed solutions to their own problems. The teachers—not outside "experts"—are the authorities on what works in their classrooms. It is persuasive and authoritative, is relevant, is accessible, challenges the intractability of reform of the education system, and is not a fad.

Action Research Is Relevant

The relevance of research published in journals to the real world of teachers is perhaps the most common concern raised by teachers when asked about the practical applications of educational research. Either the problems investigated by researchers are not the problems teachers really have, or the schools or classrooms in which the research was conducted are not even close to the teachers' own school environments. In reviewing two decades of research on schools and teaching, however, Kennedy cites the seminal works of Jackson's (1968) *Life in Classrooms* and Lortie's (1975) *Schoolteacher* as ways to illustrate the relevance of the findings of these studies.[7] These findings were that classroom life was characterized by crowds, power, praise, and uncertainty:[8]

- *Crowds.* Students are always grouped with 20 or 30 others, which means that they must wait in line, wait to be called on, and wait for help.
- *Power.* Teachers control most actions and events and decide what the group will do.
- *Praise.* Teachers also give and withhold praise so that students know which students are favored by the teacher.
- *Uncertainty.* The presence of 20 to 30 children in a single classroom means there are 20 to 30 possibilities for an interruption in one's work.

Kennedy goes on to argue that one of the aims of educational research is to increase certainty by creating *predictability* within the classroom. An outcome of action research is that it satisfies the desire that all teachers have to increase the predictability of what happens in their classrooms—in particular, to increase the likelihood that a given curriculum, instructional strategy, or use of technology will positively affect student outcomes. In other words, the results of action research are relevant to the work of individual teacher researchers.

Action Research Is Accessible

Kennedy also hypothesizes that the apparent lack of connection between research and practice is due to teachers' poor access to research findings. She contends that research does not affect teaching because it does not address teachers' prior beliefs and values, and even if teachers were informed of the results of studies, most would be unlikely to change their practices. Herein lies the beauty, power, and potential of action research to positively affect practice. As an action researcher, you challenge your taken-for-granted assumptions about teaching and learning. Your research findings are meaningful to you because *you* have identified the area of focus. *You* have been willing to challenge the conventional craft culture. In short, *your* willingness to reflect on and change your thinking about your teaching has led you to become a successful and productive member of the professional community.

---

[7] Ibid., p. 6; *Life in Classrooms,* by P. W. Jackson, 1968, New York: Holt, Rinehart & Winston; *Schoolteacher: A Sociological Study,* by D. C. Lortie, 1975, Chicago: University of Chicago Press.
[8] "The Connection Between Research and Practice," Kennedy, 1997.

Action Research Challenges the Intractability of Reform of the Educational System

The final hypothesis offered by Kennedy is that the lack of connection between research and practice can be attributed to the education system itself, not the research. The educational system has been characterized as follows:[9]

- A system for which there is a lack of agreed-on goals and guiding principles
- A system that has no central authority to settle disputes
- A system that is continually bombarded with new fads and fancies
- A system that provides limited evidence to support or refute any particular idea
- A system that encourages reforms that are running at cross-purposes to each other
- A system that gives teachers (in the United States) less time than those in most other countries to develop curricula and daily lessons

Given this characterization, it is little wonder that the more things change, the more they stay the same! Reform is difficult to direct or control—it is *intractable*. Action research gives teacher researchers the opportunity to embrace a problem-solving philosophy and practice as an integral part of the culture of their schools and their professional disposition and to challenge the intractability of educational reform by making action research a part of the system.

Action Research Is Not a Fad

Action research is decidedly not a fad for one simple reason: *Good teachers have always systematically looked at the effects of their teaching on student learning.* They may not have called this practice action research, and they may not have thought their reflection was formal enough to be labeled *research,* but it was action research!

:: ACTION RESEARCH TECHNIQUES

Action research techniques can be viewed in terms of the Dialectic Action Research Spiral presented in this chapter: identifying an area of focus, collecting data, analyzing and interpreting data, and action planning. In this section we will discuss specific action research techniques related to this model.

Identifying an Area of Focus

Finding an area of focus can be hard work for teacher researchers who, confronted with many "problems" in their classrooms and schools, are not sure which one to choose! It is critical in the early stages of the action research process that the researcher take time to identify a meaningful, engaging question or problem to investigate. One technique that can help in identifying an area of focus is to ensure that the following criteria are satisfied:

- The area of focus should involve teaching and learning and should focus on your own practice.
- The area of focus is something within your locus of control.
- The area of focus is something you feel passionate about.
- The area of focus is something you would like to change or improve.

---

[9] "The Connection Between Research and Practice," Kennedy, 1997.

The next important step in the action research process is *reconnaissance*, or preliminary information gathering. More specifically, reconnaissance is taking time to reflect on your own beliefs and to understand the nature and context of your general idea. Doing reconnaissance involves gaining insight into your area of focus through self-reflection, descriptive activities, and explanatory activities.

Gaining Insight Through Self-Reflection

You can begin reconnaissance by exploring your own understandings of the following:[10]

- The *theories* that impact your practice
- The *educational values* you hold
- How your work in schools fits into the *larger context* of schooling and society
- The *historical contexts* of your *school* and *schooling* and how things got to be the way they are
- The *historical contexts* of how you came to believe what it is that you believe about *teaching* and *learning*

Suppose that your general idea for your action research inquiry is the question, "How can I improve the integration and transfer of problem-solving skills in mathematics?" Your exploration of the topics just listed might include the following observations:

- In my reading of the subject, I have been influenced by Van de Walle's (1994)[11] *theory* about teaching and learning mathematics developmentally. In particular, the goal of mathematics is *relational understanding,* which is the connection between *conceptual* and *procedural knowledge* in mathematics. This theory of mathematics directly affects the ways I think about teaching mathematics to my children.
- I hold the *educational value* that children ought to be able to transfer problem-solving skills to other areas of mathematics as well to life outside of school. That is, I am committed to relevancy of curricula.
- I believe that mathematical problem solving, and problem solving in general, fits the *larger context* of schooling and society by providing children with critical lifelong learning skills that can be transferred to all aspects of their life.
- The *historical context* of mathematics teaching suggests a rote method of memorizing facts and algorithms. Although this approach to teaching mathematics worked for me (as a child and young teacher), it no longer suffices as a teaching method today.
- The *historical context* of how I came to believe in the importance of changing how I teach mathematics to children has grown out of my own frustration with knowing what to do to solve a problem, but not knowing *why* I need to use a particular approach or algorithm.
- Given this self-reflection on an area of focus related to the integration and transfer of problem-solving skills in mathematics, I can now better understand the problem before I implement an intervention that addresses my concern for how to best teach a *relevant* problem-solving curriculum.

Gaining Insight Through Descriptive Activities

To continue in the reconnaissance process, you should try to describe as fully as possible the situation you want to change or improve by focusing on *who, what, where,* and *when.* Grappling with these questions to clarify the focus area for your action research efforts will keep you from moving ahead with an investigation that was too murky to begin with. For example, in this stage, you might answer these questions:

---

[10] *The Action Research Reader* (3rd ed.), by S. Kemmis and R. McTaggart (Eds.), 1988, Geelong, Victoria, Australia: Deakin University Press.
[11] *Elementary School Mathematics: Teaching Developmentally,* by J. A. Van de Walle, 1994, New York: Longman.

- What evidence do I have that this (the problem-solving skills of math students) is a problem?
- Which students are not able to transfer problem-solving skills to other mathematics tasks?
- How is problem solving presently taught?
- How often is problem solving taught?
- What is the ratio of time spent teaching problem solving to time spent teaching other mathematics skills?

Gaining Insight Through Explanatory Activities

Once you've adequately described the situation you intend to investigate, you can try to explain it. Focus on the *why*. Can you account for the critical factors that have an impact on the general idea? In essence, this is the step in which you develop a hypothesis stating the expected relationships between variables in your study.

In this case, you might hypothesize that students are struggling with the transfer of problem-solving skills to other mathematics tasks because they are not getting enough practice, because they lack fundamental basic math skills, or because the use of math manipulatives has been missing or not used to its full potential. Given these possible explanations for why children have not been successfully transferring problem-solving skills to other areas of mathematics, you might develop the following hypotheses:

- There is a relationship between the use of a mathematics curriculum that emphasizes the children's ability to know *what* to do and *why* to do it and children's abilities to transfer problem-solving skills.
- There is a relationship between the use of a mathematics curriculum that emphasizes the use of manipulatives (to help children create meaning) and children's abilities to transfer problem-solving skills.

These reconnaissance activities (self-reflection, description, and explanation) help teacher researchers clarify what they already know about the proposed focus of the study; what they believe to be true about the relationships of the factors, variables, and contexts that make up their work environment; and what they believe can improve the situation.

Collecting, Analyzing, and Interpreting Data

The decision about what data are collected for an action research study is largely determined by the nature of the problem. Teacher researchers must determine what data will contribute to their understanding and resolution of a given problem. Hence, data collection associated with action research is largely an idiosyncratic approach fueled by the desire to understand one's practice and to collect data that are appropriate and accessible.

It is interesting to note that the literature on action research supports the assertion that qualitative data collection methods (discussed in Chapter 15) are more appropriately applied to action research problems than are quantitative methods and designs. In part, this can be attributed to the fact that teachers (and administrators) do not routinely assign children on a random basis, or assign children within a class to an experimental or control group in order to receive a "treatment."

Action researchers do not—and should not—avoid numerical data, however. Clearly, there are many quantitative data sources that are readily available for collection by teacher researchers. For example, standardized test scores are an increasingly important accountability measure used to justify state and federal funding of academic programs. For the most part, the kinds of numerical data collected as part of an action research study will be appropriately analyzed through the use of descriptive statistics for measures of central tendency (mean, mode, median) and variability (standard deviation). (See Chapter 11 for a comprehensive discussion of descriptive statistics.) Our advice here is simple: Count what counts! If it makes sense to tally and count events, categories, occurrences, test scores, and the like, use an appropriate descriptive statistic. However, do not feel compelled to include elaborate statistical measures simply to add to a perceived sense of rigor or credibility to your inquiry.

Action Planning

One of the final tasks of an action researcher is to share research findings with others, in both formal and informal settings. Results can be shared with other teachers, both in the researcher's school or in other schools. As an action researcher, you may share information verbally, in presentations and conversations, and also may write about your results. Writing can lead to further analysis, improved interpretation, and deeper understanding of the problem—as well as how to act on your findings. Writing also creates a permanent record of the research that others may use. Fellow teachers, administrators, other researchers, and current or potential funders for your program may be in a position to benefit from your results.

As the name suggests, action research is action oriented, and it is directed toward both understanding and improving practice. Thus, the last step in the research process is deciding what steps, if any, need to be taken to alter or improve practice.

There are many techniques that can be used to implement action research results in schools. For example, study results can be used in the classroom, school, or district to improve instruction, procedures, and outcomes of education, and aid teacher understanding of instruction and applications. Often, action research leads to new questions to examine, thus forging new forms of understanding and deeper insights in practice. It is the practical nature of action research that fosters much of the teacher-based improvement in schools.

SUMMARY

Action Research: Definition and Purpose

1. Action research in education is any systematic inquiry conducted by teacher researchers, principals, school counselors, or other stakeholders in the teaching–learning environment, to gather information about the ways in which their particular schools operate, the teachers teach, and the students learn.

2. The purpose of action research is to provide teacher researchers with a method for solving everyday problems in schools, in order to improve both student learning and teacher effectiveness.

3. Action research is research done by teachers, for themselves; it is not imposed on them by someone else.

4. Educational change that enhances the lives of children is a main goal of action research.

5. Action research is largely about developing the professional disposition of teachers, that is, encouraging teachers to be continuous learners—in their classrooms and of their practice.

6. Action research is about incorporating into a teacher's daily routine a reflective stance—a willingness to look critically at one's own teaching so that it can improved or enhanced.

The Action Research Process

7. The action research process includes identifying an area of focus, data collection, data analysis and interpretation, and action planning.

8. This four-step action research process has been termed the Dialectic Action Research Spiral.

Types of Action Research

9. There are two main types of action research: critical action research and practical action research.

10. Critical action research is action research in which the goal is liberating individuals through knowledge gathering; for this reason, it is also known as *emancipatory action research*.

11. Critical action research is so named because it is based on a body of critical theory, not because this type of action research is critical, as in "faultfinding."

12. Practical action research emphasizes the "how-to" approach to the processes of action research and has

a less philosophical bent than critical action research. It assumes that individual teachers and teams of teachers are autonomous and can determine the nature of the investigation to be undertaken.

13. Education action research can be undertaken at three levels: the individual teacher level; the single school or department level, in which small teacher groups or teams conduct the research; or the schoolwide level.

Key Characteristics of Action Research

14. Action research is persuasive and authoritative.
15. Action research is relevant.
16. Action research is accessible.
17. Action research challenges the intractability of reform of the educational system.
18. Action research is not a fad.

Action Research Techniques

19. Action research techniques can be viewed in terms of the Dialectic Action Research Spiral.
20. Identifying an area of focus should satisfy the following criteria:
    a. The area of focus should involve teaching and learning and should focus on your practice.
    b. The area of focus is something within your locus of control.
    c. The area of focus is something you feel passionate about.
    d. The area of focus is something you would like to change or improve.
21. Insight into an area of focus can also be gained through self-reflection, descriptive activities, and explanatory activities.
22. Data collection techniques used in action research are largely determined by the nature of the area of focus.
23. The literature on action research suggests that qualitative data collection techniques are more appropriately applied to action research problems than are quantitative methods and designs.
24. The use of qualitative data collection techniques in action research can be attributed to the fact that teachers do not routinely assign children on a random basis to an experimental or control group to receive a treatment.
25. As the name suggests, action research is action oriented. It is critical that action researchers follow through with their action plans to ensure that "lessons learned" are implemented in the classroom or school setting.

Companion
Website

Now go to the Companion Website at **www.prenhall.com/gay** to assess your understanding of chapter content with Practice Quiz, apply comprehension in Applying What You Know, broaden your knowledge about research in Web Links, and expand your research skills in Evaluating Articles, Analyzing Qualitative Data, Analyzing Quantitative Data, and Research Tools and Tips.

PERFORMANCE CRITERIA AND EXAMPLES

Your task is to design an action research study to answer a school-based question. Use the following steps to create the components of your written plan:

1. Write an area-of-focus statement.
2. Define the variables.
3. Develop research questions.
4. Describe the intervention or innovation.
5. Describe the membership of the action research group.
6. Describe negotiations that need to be undertaken.
7. Develop a timeline.
8. Develop a statement of resources.
9. Develop data collection ideas.

Write an Area-of-Focus Statement

An area of focus identifies the purpose of your study. To start, write a statement that completes the following sentence: "The purpose of this study is to. . . . " For example:

> The purpose of this study is to describe the effects of an integrated problem-solving mathematics curriculum on student transfer of problem-solving skills and the retention of basic math facts and functions.

> The purpose of this study is to describe the impact of bringing audience members into an interactive relationship with teen theater productions on participants' abilities to identify issues and incorporate solutions to similar problems in their own lives.

The purpose of this study is to describe the effects of student-led conferences on parent and student satisfaction with the conferencing process.

Define the Variables

As part of the area-of-focus statement construction process, write definitions of what you will focus on in the study. These definitions should accurately represent what the factors, contexts, and variables *mean to you*. A variable is a characteristic of your study that is subject to change. That is, it might be the way you are going to change how you teach, the curriculum you use, and student outcomes. Definitions may also emerge from the literature, but it is important that you are committed to whatever you are defining and communicate that to others. In the preceding examples, the researchers would define what they mean by "an integrated problem-solving mathematics curriculum," "transfer of problem-solving skills," "the retention of basic math facts and functions," "interactive relationship with teen theater productions," "student-led conferences," and "parent and student satisfaction with the conferencing process." If you are clear about what you are examining, it will be easy to determine how you will know it when you see it! That is, your data collection ideas will flow more freely, and there will be no confusion when you communicate with your action research collaborators about your purpose.

Develop Research Questions

Develop questions that breathe life into the area-of-focus statement and help provide a focus for your data collection plan. These questions will also help you validate that you have a workable way to proceed with your investigation. For example:

> What is the effect on student performance on open-ended problem-solving tests of incorporating math manipulatives into problem-solving activities?

In what ways do students transfer problem-solving skills to other areas of mathematics?

How do students incorporate problem-solving skills into other curriculum areas?

How do students transfer problem-solving skills to their life outside of school?

Describe the Intervention or Innovation

Describe what you are going to do to improve the situation you have described. For example, you might say, "I will implement a standards-based integrated problem-solving mathematics curriculum," "I will include audience improvisation as part of the teen theater performances I direct," or "I will incorporate student participation in student-parent-teacher conferences." You need only to provide a simple statement about what you will do in your classroom or school to address the teaching–learning issue you have identified.

Describe the Membership of the Action Research Group

Describe the membership of your action research group, and discuss why its members are important. Will you be working with a site council team? A parent group? If so, what will be the roles and responsibilities of the group's participants? For example:

> I will be working with seven other high school math teachers who are all members of the math department. Although we all have different teaching responsibilities within the department, as a group we have decided on problem solving as an area of focus for the department. Each of us will be responsible for implementing curriculum and teaching strategies that reflect the new emphasis on problem solving and for collecting the kinds of data that we decide will help us monitor the effects of our teaching. The department chair will be responsible for keeping the principal informed about our work and securing any necessary resources we need to complete the research. The chair will also write a description of our work to be included in the school newsletter (sent home to all parents), thus informing children and parents of our focus for the year.

Describe Negotiations That Need to Be Undertaken

Describe any negotiations that you will have to undertake with others before implementing your plan. Do you need permission from an administrator? parents? students? colleagues? It's important that you control the focus of the study and that you undertake the process of negotiation to head off any potential obstacles to implementation of the action plan. It's very frustrating to get immersed in the action research process only to have the project quashed by uncooperative colleagues or administrators.

Develop a Timeline

In developing a timeline, you will need to decide who will be doing *what, when.* Although not part of a timeline in the strictest sense, you can also include information on *where* and *how* your inquiry will take place, which will help you in this stage of your planning. For example:

> *Phase 1 (August–October).* Identify area of focus, review related literature, develop research questions, do reconnaissance.

> *Phase 2 (November–December).* Collect initial data. Analyze videotapes of lessons, do first interviews with children, administer first problem-solving probe.

> *Phase 3 (January–May).* Modify curriculum and instruction as necessary. Continue ongoing data collection. Schedule two team meetings to discuss early analysis of data.

Phase 4 (May–June). Review statewide assessment test data, and complete analysis of all data. Develop presentation for faculty. Schedule team meeting to discuss and plan action based on the findings of the study. Assign tasks to be completed prior to year two of the study.

Develop a Statement of Resources

Briefly describe what resources you will need to enact your plan. This is akin to listing materials in a lesson plan—there is nothing worse than starting to teach and finding you don't have all the materials you need to achieve your objectives. For example, to participate in the study of math problem-solving skills, the team determines that it will need teacher release time for project planning, reviewing related literature, and other tasks; funds to purchase classroom sets of manipulatives; and a small budget for copying and printing curriculum materials. After all, there is no sense developing a study that investigates the impact of a new math problem-solving curriculum if you don't have the financial resources to purchase the curriculum.

Develop Data Collection Ideas

Give a preliminary statement of the kinds of data that you think will provide evidence for your reflections on the general idea you are investigating. For example, brainstorm the kind of intuitive, naturally occurring data that you find in your classroom or school, such as test scores, attendance records, portfolios, and anecdotal records. As you learn more about other types of data that can be collected, this list will grow, but in the early stages think about what you already have easy access to and then be prepared to supplement it with interviews, surveys, questionnaires, videotapes, audiotapes, maps, photos, and observations as the area of focus dictates.

The tasks just described can be undertaken whether you are working individually, in a small group, or as part of a schoolwide action research effort. The resolution of these issues early in the action research process will ensure that you do not waste valuable time backtracking (or even apologizing) once you are well down the action research path.

"The research report should be written in a clear, simple, straightforward style and reflect scholarship."
(p. 517)

Preparing a Research Report

OBJECTIVES

After reading Chapter 21, you should be able to do the following:

1. Identify and briefly describe the major sections of a research report.
2. List general rules for writing and preparing a research report.

People conduct research for a variety of reasons. The motivation for doing a research project may be no more than that such a project is a degree requirement, or it may come from a strong desire to contribute to educational theory or practice. Whatever the reason for their execution, most research studies culminate with the production of a research report. Unlike a research plan or proposal, which focuses on what will be done, a research report describes what has happened in the study and what results were obtained. All research reports strive to communicate as clearly as possible the purpose, procedures, and findings of the study. A well-written report describes a study in enough detail to permit replication by another researcher.

You have already written many of the components of a research report through your work in Tasks 2 through 9. In this chapter you will learn how to integrate all your previous efforts to produce a complete report.

The goal of Chapter 21 is for you, having conducted a study, to be able to produce a complete report. Completing Chapter 21 enable you to perform the following task.

TASK 10

Building upon previous tasks, prepare a research report that follows the general format for a thesis or dissertation. (See Performance Criteria, p. 527.)

GENERAL GUIDELINES

If this chapter were written even a few years ago, it would have focused almost exclusively on writing research reports for quantitative studies. In recent years, however, the number of reports on qualitative research has grown steadily. As noted in previous chapters, the purposes and conduct of quantitative studies differ in important ways from the purposes and conduct of qualitative studies. In this chapter we emphasize the general issues and practices associated with writing a research report. It is important that you understand that all research reports address similar topics—for example, all contain a description of the topic or problem studied, a review of literature, a description of procedures, and a description of results. However, as seen in earlier chapters, qualitative and quantitative studies address these topics in somewhat different ways and give them different emphases. You are encouraged to examine and compare the reports reprinted at the end of Chapters 6, 7, 8, 9, and 17 to see their differences. Further, when you are actually writing your report, you should look through journals pertinent to your study to view the sections, level of detail, and types of results commonly reported. This is the best way to determine the appropriate format for your report.

While you are conducting your study, you can profitably use spare time to begin revising or refining the introduction and method sections of your report. After all the data are analyzed, you can begin to write the report's final sections. The major guideline for all stages of writing is to make an outline. The chances of your report being presented in an organized, logical manner are greatly increased if you think the sequence through before you actually write anything. Formulating an outline greatly facilitates this "thinking through." To review briefly, developing an outline involves identifying and ordering major topics and then differentiating each major heading into logical subheadings. The time spent working on an outline is well worth it, since it is much easier to reorganize an outline that is not quite right than to reorganize a document written in paragraph form. Of course, this does not mean that your first report draft will be your last. Two or three revisions of each section might be needed. Remember, writing inevitably uncovers issues or activities that must be rethought. Each time you read a section, you will see ways to improve its organization or clarity. Also, others who review your report will see areas in need of rethinking or rewording that you have not noticed.

Getting Started: Overcoming Writing Obstacles

Writing is nothing more than putting thought to paper, yet many writers hold irrational beliefs about the task or even insist on rituals that must be completed if writing sessions are to be successful. In an informal survey of friends and colleagues, one suggested that writing can occur only between the hours of 7:00 AM and 12:00 PM; another that writing can be done only in longhand, using a blue pen and white legal pad; and yet another that the house must be clean before writing can start.

   Getting started—clean house or messy—is a problem for many of us. There is no easy way around the pragmatic issue of time: Writing takes time, and we never have enough time to do all that we have to do, professionally and personally. The best advice we can offer is to make writing part of your professional life and responsibility. A study is not over until the report has been completed, and the time you will need for writing should be included in the time schedule you create when planning your research (see Task 3a Example, p. 95). As pointed out in Chapter 3, however, some call research a process designed to take 3 to 6 months longer than the researcher thinks it will. Other tasks pile up, and the writing gets pushed aside. When this happens, you must capture the minutes and hours where they fall—before and after school, on professional development days, in preparation periods, and at times when meetings and conferences are cancelled. We know of no other way, besides attacking personal and family time, to get our writing done. In the short term, our loved ones will put up with the "I need to stay home and get this writing (could also be grading, lesson planning, studying, and so on) done. You go ahead and enjoy the movie, dinner, picnic, hike, river rafting, skiing (we could all fill in the blank based on our lives as students and teachers)."

   However you make it happen, there will come a time when you sit down in front of a keyboard, or with a blank pad of paper, and start the task of writing up your research. We can picture you now—pencil in hand, keyboard at the ready—poised to pen the story of your research! Go to that place for a while. Get ready to write!

   In the spirit of sharing tips for successful writing, let us start with some tips in Figure 21.1 for what *not to do* once you finally get settled down to work. It's not hard to see how activities such as those listed can eat up precious writing time. You may wish to write down your own avoidance list and stick it next to wherever it is that you write. Check it occasionally, but get the behaviors out of your system.

   What follows is a list of more helpful writing tips.

Tips to Succeed at Writing

- Look for progress, not perfection.
- Write whatever comes to mind. Then go back and hunt for what you are really trying to say—it's there.
- Have you ever thought to yourself: I wish I had done that differently? With writing, you can do it differently; editing your own work is a delight. Write boldly and then say it again—better.

- Think about all the things at school that I need to do before tomorrow.
- Scan my desk to see if someone has left me a note about a meeting, sports practice, birthday party that I need to go to **NOW**.
- Check my voicemail.
- Check my e-mail.
- Check my checkbook to see if it is balanced.
- Call my wife/child/colleague/friend/enemy to see what they are doing.
- Walk down the hallway to see if I can find someone to talk to.
- Dream about winning the lottery.
- Make an appointment to see my dentist.

FIGURE 21.1

Geoff's tips for being able to avoid writing
Source: Mills, Geoffrey, *Action Research: A Guide for the Teacher Researcher,* 2nd Edition, © 2003. Reprinted by permission of Pearson Education, Inc., Upper Saddle River, NJ.

- Writing is an exercise in learning about your own work. Writing, then editing, then rewriting, then editing again, clarifies thoughts into a coherent package.
- Editing: Even a gem needs to be mined roughly, cut ruthlessly, then buffed.
- Nobody knows your work better than you do. You'll be surprised how much better you know it when you've discussed it with your computer a few times.
- Write without consideration for grammar, syntax, or punctuation. Just write. Sometimes editing is an avoidance technique.
- Write at the same time every day, at a time when you know you won't be disturbed.
- Write up your research as though you're sending an e-mail to a friend. Pretend your friend needs it explained simply.

Fortunately, once you begin writing, it becomes easier to continue writing. When you're working productively and staying on task, catch yourself being good! You might even think of a little reward system (if you are somewhat extrinsically motivated, that is). After dedicating himself to some writing time, one of your authors (Geoff again) treats himself to a run, time with family or friends, or something sweet (you know, some sugar to help with the fatigue!).

▒ GENERAL RULES FOR WRITING

Probably the foremost rule of research report writing is that the writer should try to relate aspects of the study in a manner that accurately reflects what was done and what was found. Although the style of reporting may vary for quantitative and qualitative studies, the focus in all instances should be on providing accurate description for the reader. For example, in quantitative reports personal pronouns such as *I* and *we* are usually avoided, and the passive voice is used. In contrast, in qualitative reports the researcher often adopts a more personal tone, uses active voice, and shares the words of the participants. Such stylistic differences do not alter the need for accurate reporting.

The research report should be written in a clear, simple, straightforward style and reflect scholarship. You do not have to be boring, just concise. In other words, convey what you wish to convey, do it in an efficient way, avoid jargon, and use simple language. For example, instead of saying, "The population comprised all students who matriculated for the fall semester at Egghead University," it would be better to say, "The population was all students enrolled for the fall semester at Egghead University." Obviously the report should contain correct spelling, grammatical construction, and punctuation. Your computer probably has a spelling and grammar checker. Use it. Or consult a dictionary. It is also a good idea to have someone you know, someone who is perhaps stronger in these areas, review your manuscript and indicate errors.

Although different style manuals emphasize different rules of writing, there are several common to most manuals. Use of abbreviations and contractions, for instance, is generally discouraged in formal writing. For example, instead of "the American Psychological Assn.," you would write "the American Psychological Association." Instead of *shouldn't,* write *should not.* Exceptions to the abbreviation rule include commonly used and understood abbreviations (such as IQ and GPA) and abbreviations defined by the researcher to promote clarity, simplify presentation, or reduce repetition. If the same sequence of words is going to be used repeatedly, the researcher will often define an abbreviation in parentheses when first using the sequence and thereafter use only the abbreviation. Authors of cited references are usually referred to in the main body of the report by last name only; first names, initials, and titles are not given. Instead of saying, "Professor Dudley Q. McStrudle (2002) concluded . . . ," you normally would say "McStrudle (2002) concluded. . . ." These guidelines hold only for the main body of the report. Tables, figures, footnotes, and references may include abbreviations; footnotes and references usually give at least the author's initials. Most style manuals address the treatment of numbers as well. One convention is to always spell out a number that comes at the start of a sentence ("Six schools were contacted . . . "). There are many guidelines about the use of words versus numerals within a discussion, but one common convention is to use words if the number is nine or less ("a total of five lists . . . ") and to use Arabic numerals if the number is greater than nine ("a total of 500 questionnaires was sent").

The final report should be proofread carefully at least twice. Reading the report silently to yourself will usually be sufficient to identify major errors. If you have a willing listener, however, reading the manuscript out loud often helps you to identify grammatical or constructional errors. Sometimes sentences do not make nearly as much sense when you hear them as when you write them; also, your listener will frequently be helpful in bringing to your attention sections that are unclear. Reading the report backwards, last sentence first, will also help you to identify poorly constructed or unclear sentences. Preparing a research report is greatly facilitated by computer word processing, which commonly provides features such as automatic page numbering and heading centering; the ability to rearrange words, sentences, and paragraphs; and spellchecking.

:: FORMAT AND STYLE

Format refers to the general pattern of organization and arrangement of the report. The number and types of headings and subheadings to be included in the report are determined by the format used. Style refers to the rules of grammar, spelling, capitalization, and punctuation followed in preparing the report. Formats may vary in terms of specific headings included, and research reports generally follow a format that parallels the steps involved in conducting a study. For example, although one format may call for a discussion section and another format may require a summary or conclusions and a recommendations section (or both), all formats require a section in which the results of the study are discussed and interpreted. All research reports also include a condensed description of the study, whether it be a summary of a dissertation or an abstract of a journal article.

Most colleges, universities, and professional journals require the use of a specific style, either a style they have developed or that in a published style manual. Check with your advisor about the style used in your institution. Do this before you begin writing, since rearranging a format after the fact is tedious and time-consuming. One manual that is increasingly being required as a guide for those writing theses and dissertations is the *Publication Manual of the American Psychological Association,* also called the APA manual (currently in its fifth edition). If you are not bound by any particular format and style system, we recommend that you acquire and study a copy of the APA manual. It is also very helpful to study several reports that have been written using APA style, if that is what your institution uses. For example, look at existing dissertations (especially those directed by your advisor) to get an idea of

FIGURE 21.2 Some APA guidelines for preparing your paper

5

Results

Prior to the beginning of the study, after the 60 students were randomly selected and assigned to experimental and control groups, final science grades from the previous school year were obtained from school records in order to check initial group equivalence. Examination of the means and a t test for independent samples ($\alpha = .05$) indicated essentially no difference between the groups (see Table 1). A t test for independent samples was used because the groups were randomly formed and the data were interval.

Table 1

Means, Standard Deviation, and t Tests for the Experimental and Control Groups

Score	Group		t
	IMM instruction[a]	Traditional instruction[a]	
Prior Grades			
M	87.47	87.63	−0.08*
SD	8.19	8.05	
Posttest NPSS:B			
M	32.27	26.70	4.22**
SD	4.45	5.69	

Note. Maximum score for prior grades = 100. Maximum score for posttest = 40.

[a]$n = 30$.

*$p > .05$. **$p < .05$.

At the completion of the eight-month study, during the first week in May, scores on the NPSS:B were compared, also using a t test for independent samples. As Table 1 indicates, scores of the experimental and control groups were significantly different. In fact, the experimental group scored approximately one standard deviation higher than the control group (ES = .98). Therefore, the original hypothesis that "10th-grade biology students whose teachers use IMM as part of their instructional technique will exhibit significantly higher achievement than 10th-grade biology students whose teachers do not use IMM" was supported.

1. Page numbers go in the top right-hand corner, flush with the right margin and between the top of the page and the first line.

2. First level headings are centered, written in upper- and lowercase, and NOT underlined.

3. All text should be double spaced.

4. All statistical values should be italicized (e.g., $p < .05$).

5. Margins should always be uniform all around (1 inch is the minimum).

Source: Format information from *Publication Manual of the American Psychological Association* (5th ed., pp. 283–320), by the American Psychological Association, Washington, DC: Author.

format and what is expected. (An institution may, in fact, be using a combination of its own and APA styles and formats.) Figure 21.2 illustrates some of the basic APA guidelines using a page from the Task 10 example that appears at the end of this chapter.

⁚⁚ SECTIONS OF THESES AND DISSERTATIONS

Although specifics will vary considerably, most research reports prepared for a degree requirement follow the same general format. Figure 21.3 presents an outline of the typical contents of such a report. As the figure indicates, theses and dissertations include a set of fairly

FIGURE 21.3

Common components
of a research report
submitted for a
degree requirement

PRELIMINARY PAGES

Title Page	List of Tables and Figures
Acknowledgments Page	Abstract
Table of Contents	

MAIN BODY OF THE REPORT

Introduction	Instruments
Statement of the Problem	Design
Review of Related Literature	Procedure
Statement of the Hypothesis	Results
Significance of the Study	Discussion (Conclusions and Recommendations)
Method	References (Bibliography)
Participants	

APPENDIXES

standard preliminary pages, components that directly parallel the research process, and supplementary information, which is included in appendixes. A report on a quantitative study and that for a qualitative study would have similar contents except that the method section in the qualitative study's report would emphasize the description and selection of the research site, the sampling approach, and the process of data collection.

Preliminary Pages

The preliminary pages contain the title page, acknowlegments page, table of contents, list of tables and figures, and abstract.

The title should communicate what the study is about. Recall when you reviewed the literature and made initial decisions about the relevance of a source based on its title. A well-constructed title makes it fairly easy for the reader to determine the nature of the topic; a vaguely worded one confuses the reader, who then must search through the body of the report to get more information. After you write your title, apply the communication test: Would you know what the study was about if you read the title in an index? Ask friends or colleagues to describe what they understand from your title.

Most theses and dissertations include an acknowledgments page. This page permits the writer to express appreciation to persons who have contributed significantly to the completion of the report. Notice the word *significant.* You cannot (and should not!) mention everyone who had anything to do with the study or the report. It is acceptable to thank your advisor for her or his guidance and assistance; it is not acceptable to thank your third-grade teacher for giving you confidence in your ability. (Remember the Academy Awards!)

The table of contents is basically an outline of your report that indicates the page on which each major section (or chapter) and subsection begins. The list of tables and figures, which is presented on a separate page, gives the number and title of each table and figure and the page on which it can be found.

Many colleges and universities require an abstract, and others require a summary, but the current trend is in favor of abstracts. The content of abstracts and summaries is identical, only the positioning differs: An abstract precedes the main body of the report, and a summary follows the discussion section. Abstracts often must be limited to a given number of words, usually between 100 and 500. Many institutions require abstracts to be no more than 350 words, which is the maximum allowed by Dissertation Abstracts International, a repository of dissertation abstracts. The APA sets a limit of 120 words for publication in its journals. Because the abstract of a report is often the only part read, it should briefly describe the most important aspects of the study, including the topic investigated, the type of participants and instruments involved, the data collection procedures, and the major results and conclusions. For example, a 100-word abstract for a study investigating the effect of a writing-oriented curriculum on the reading comprehension of fourth-grade students might read as follows:

> The purpose of this study was to determine the effect of a curriculum that emphasized writing on the reading comprehension of fourth-grade students who were reading at least one level below grade level. Using a posttest-only control group design and the t test for independent samples, it was found that after 8 months the students ($n = 20$) who participated in a curriculum that emphasized writing achieved significantly higher scores on the reading comprehension subtest of the Stanford Achievement Test, Primary Level 3 (grades 3.5–4.9) than the students ($n = 20$) who did not [t (38) = 4.83, $p < .05$]. It was concluded that the curriculum emphasizing writing was more effective in promoting reading comprehension.

The Main Body

The body of the report contains information about the topic studied, literature reviewed, hypotheses (if any) posited, participants, instruments, procedures, results, and discussion.

The introduction section includes a description of the research problem or topic, a review of related literature, a statement of hypotheses or issues, and a definition of uncommon or important terms. A well-written statement of a problem or topic generally indicates the variables examined in the study. The statement of the problem or topic should be accompanied by a presentation of its background, including a justification for the study in terms of its significance; that is, why should anyone care about this study?

The review of related literature indicates what is known about the problem or topic. Its function is to educate the reader about the area that was studied. The review of related literature is not a series of abstracts or annotations but rather a summary and analysis of the relationships and differences among relevant studies and reports. The review should flow in such a way that the least related references are discussed first and the most related references are discussed last, just before the statement of the hypothesis. The review should conclude with a brief summary of the literature and its implications.

A good hypothesis for a quantitative study clearly states the expected relationship (or difference) between two variables and defines those variables in operational, measurable terms. The hypothesis (or hypotheses) logically follows the review of related literature and is based on the implications of previous research. A well-developed hypothesis is testable—that is, it can be confirmed or disconfirmed. The qualitative researcher is unlikely to state hypotheses as focused as those of a quantitative researcher, but may have and express some hunches about what the study may show. The introduction section also includes definitions of terms used in the study that do not have a commonly understood meaning.

Method

The method section includes a description of participants, instruments, design, procedure, assumptions, and limitations. A qualitative study may also include a detailed description of the site studied and the nature and length of interactions with the participants. The description of participants includes information about how they were selected and, mainly for quantitative researchers, the population they represent. A description of the sample should indicate its size and major characteristics of members such as age, grade level, ability level, and socioeconomic status. A good description of the sample enables readers of the report to determine how similar study participants are to participants the readers are concerned with.

Data collection procedures should be described fully, be they tests, questionnaires, interviews, or observations. The description should indicate the purpose of the procedure, its application, and its validity and reliability. If a procedure has been developed by the researcher, the description needs to be more detailed and should also state the manner in which it was developed, its pretesting, revisions, steps involved in scoring, and guidelines for interpretation. A copy of the instrument, accompanying scoring keys, and other pertinent data related to a newly developed test are generally placed as appendixes to the thesis or dissertation proper.

The description of the design is especially important in an experimental study. In other types of research, the description of the design may be combined with procedure. In an experimental study, the description of the basic design (or variation of a basic design) applied in the study should include a rationale for selection and a discussion of sources of invalidity associated with the design, including why these threats may have been minimized in the study being reported.

The procedure section should describe the steps followed in conducting the study, in chronological order, in sufficient detail to permit the study to be replicated by another researcher. It should be clear exactly how participants were assigned to groups, treatments, or the conditions under which qualitative participants were observed or interviewed. In essence, a step-by-step description of what went on during the study should be provided. In many cases, qualitative researchers will have more complex and detailed procedural descriptions than quantitative researchers.

The results section describes the statistical techniques or the inferential interpretations that were applied to the data and the results of these analyses. For each hypothesis, the statistical test of significance selected and applied to the data is described, followed by a statement indicating whether the hypothesis was supported or not supported. Tables and figures are used to present findings in summary or graph form and add clarity to the presentation. Tables present numerical data in rows and columns and usually include descriptive statistics, such as means and standard deviations, and the results of tests of significance, such as t tests and F ratios. Good tables and figures are uncluttered and self-explanatory; it is better to use two tables (or figures) than one that is crowded. They should stand alone, that is, be interpretable without the aid of related textual material. Tables and figures follow their related textual discussion and are referred to by number, not name or location. In other words, the text should say "see Table 1," not "see the table with the means" or "see the table on the next page." Examine the variety of tables and figures throughout this text to get a perspective on how data can be presented.

Qualitative research reporting tends to be based mainly on descriptions and quotations that support or illustrate the study results. Charts and diagrams showing the relationships among identified topics, categories, and patterns are also useful in presenting the results of a study. The logic and description of the interpretations linked to qualitative charts and diagrams are important aspects of qualitative research reporting.

All research reports have a section that discusses and interprets the results, draws conclusions and states implications, and makes recommendations. Interpretation of results may be presented in a separate section titled "Discussion," or it may be included in the same section as the other analysis of results items. What this section (or sections) is called is unimportant; what is important is how well it is constructed. Each result should be discussed in terms of its relation to the topic studied and its agreement or disagreement with previous results obtained by other researchers in other studies. Two common errors are to confuse results and conclusions and to overgeneralize results. A result is the outcome of a test of significance or a qualitative analysis; the corresponding conclusion is that the original hypothesis or topic was or was not supported by the data. In qualitative reports the conclusion may simply be a summarizing description of what was observed. Researchers *overgeneralize* when they state conclusions that are not warranted by the results. For example, if a group of first graders receiving personalized instruction were found to achieve significantly higher on a test of reading comprehension than a group receiving traditional instruction, it would be an overgeneralization to conclude that personalized instruction is a superior method of instruction for elementary students. Similarly, if a qualitative study about teacher burnout consisted of four interviewees, it would be an overgeneralization to infer that all teachers felt the same about burnout.

The report should also discuss the theoretical and practical implications of the findings and make recommendations for future research or future action. In this portion of the report, the researcher is permitted more freedom in expressing opinions that are not necessarily direct outcomes of data analysis. The researcher is free to discuss any possible revisions or additions to existing theory and to encourage studies designed to test hypotheses suggested by the results. The researcher may also discuss implications of the findings for educational practice and suggest studies designed to replicate the study in other settings, with other participants, and in other curricular areas, in order to increase the generalizability of the findings. The researcher may also suggest next-step studies designed to investigate another dimension of the problem investigated. For example, a study finding type of feedback to be a factor in retention might suggest that amount of feedback may also be a factor and recommend further research in that area.

The reference, or bibliography, section of the report lists all the sources, alphabetically by authors' last names, that were directly used in writing the report. Every source cited in the paper must be included in the references, and every entry listed in the references must appear in the paper; in other words, the sources in the paper and the sources in the references must correspond exactly. If APA style is being used, secondary sources are not included in the reference list. In-text citations of secondary sources should indicate the primary source from which they were taken; the primary source should be included in the references. For example, in the text you might say, "Nerdfais (cited in Snurd, 1995) found that yellow chalk. . . . " The Snurd source would be listed in the references. Note that no year would be given for the Nerdfais study. For thesis and dissertation studies, if sources were consulted that were not directly cited in the main body of the report, these may be included in an appendix. The style manual being followed will determine the form each reference must take. The researcher can save time by writing each reference in the proper form initially, while conducting the review of literature. Table 21.1 shows APA formats for common references in theses or dissertations.

Appendixes are usually necessary in thesis and dissertation reports to provide information and data that are pertinent to the study but are either too lengthy or not important enough to be included in the main body of the report. Appendixes commonly contain materials especially developed for the study (such as tests, questionnaires, and cover letters), raw data, and data analysis sheets.

TABLE 21.1	APA reference formats
Type of Reference	**Reference Format**

The following are examples of many of the types of references you may need to include in your research paper. These examples follow the APA style guidelines set forth in the fifth edition of the *Publication Manual of the American Psychological Association.*

Book	Bandura, A. J. (1977). *Social learning theory.* Englewood Cliffs, NJ: Prentice Hall.
Book, Edited	Gibbs, J. T., & Huang, L. N. (Eds.). (1991). *Children of color: Psychological interventions with minority youth.* San Francisco: Jossey-Bass.
Book, Chapter	O'Neil, J. M., & Egan, J. (1992). Men's and women's gender role journeys: Metaphor for healing, transition, and transformation. In B. R. Wainrib (Ed.), *Gender issues across the life cycle* (pp. 107–123). New York: Springer.
Book Review	Schatz, B. R. (2000). Learning by text or context? [Review of the book *The social life of information*]. *Science, 290,* 1304.
Journal Article	Klimoski, R., & Palmer, S. (1993). The ADA and the hiring process in organizations. *Consulting Psychology Journal: Practice and Research, 45*(2), 10–36.
Electronic Sources, Retrieval Information	Eid, M., & Langeheine, R. (1999). The measurement of consistency and occasion specificity with latent class models: A new model and its application to the measurement of affect. *Psychological Methods, 4,* 100–116. Retrieved November 19, 2000, from the PsycARTICLES database.
Abstract	Nakazato, K., Shimonaka, Y., & Homma, A. (1992). Cognitive functions of centenarians: The Tokyo Metropolitan Centenarian Study. *Japanese Journal of Developmental Psychology, 3,* 9–16. Abstract obtained from *PsycSCAN: Neuropsychology,* 1993, *2,* Abstract No. 604.
ERIC Reference	Mead, J. V. (1992). *Looking at old photographs: Investigating the teacher tales that novice teachers bring with them* (Report No. NCRTL-RR-92-4). East Lansing, MI: National Center for Research on Teacher Learning. (ERIC Document Reproduction Service No. ED346082)
Dissertation (unpublished)	Wilfley, D. E. (1989). *Interpersonal analyses of bulimia: Normal-weight and obese.* Unpublished doctoral dissertation, University of Missouri, Columbia.

Source: All examples from *Publication Manual of the American Psychological Association,* (5th ed., pp. 215–281) by the American Psychological Association, 2001, Washington, DC: Author. Copyright © 2001 by the American Psychological Association. Reprinted with permission. Neither the original nor this reproduction may be republished or distributed in any form or by any means or stored in a database or retrieval system, without the prior written permission of the publisher.

SUMMARY

General Guidelines

1. A major facilitator for writing a research report is making an outline. Developing an outline involves identifying and ordering major topics and then differentiating each major heading into logical subheadings.

2. Make writing part of your professional life and responsibility.

General Rules for Writing

3. Probably the foremost rule of research report writing is to relate aspects of the study in a manner that accurately reflects what was done and what was found.

4. Although quantitative and qualitative research approaches differ in many ways, similar topics are covered in their research reports. The emphases within the general topics, however, vary depending on which of the two approaches is being reported.

5. The research report should be written in a clear, simple, straightforward style, and correct spelling, grammar, and punctuation are expected.

6. Authors of cited references are usually referred to by last name only in the main body of the report.

7. If the first word of a sentence is a number, or if the number is nine or less, numbers are usually

expressed as words. Otherwise, numbers are generally expressed as Arabic numerals.

8. Carefully proofread the final report.

Format and Style

9. Most research reports consistently follow a selected system for format and style. Format refers to the general pattern of organization and arrangement of the report. Style refers to the rules of grammar, spelling, capitalization, and punctuation followed in preparing the report.

10. Most colleges and universities require the use of a specific style, either their own or that in a published style manual. It is helpful to study several reports that have been written in the required style.

Sections of Theses and Dissertations

11. The title of the report should describe the purpose of the study as clearly as possible.

12. The acknowledgments page allows the writer to express appreciation to persons who have contributed significantly to the completion of the report.

13. The table of contents is basically an outline of the report that indicates the page on which each major section (or chapter) and subsection begins. The list of tables and figures, presented on a separate page, gives the number and title of each table and figure and the page on which it can be found.

14. Most colleges and universities require an abstract or summary of the study. The number of pages for each will be specified and will usually range from 100 to 500 words. The abstract should describe the most important aspects of the study, including the problem investigated, the type of participants and instruments, the design, the procedures, and the major results and conclusions.

15. The introduction section is the first section of the main body of the report and includes a well-written description of the problem, a review of related literature, a statement of the hypothesis, and definition of terms.

16. The review of related literature describes and analyzes previous research related to the topic under study.

17. A good hypothesis in a quantitative study states as clearly and concisely as possible the expected relationship (or difference) between two variables and defines those variables in operational, measurable terms.

18. The introduction also includes definitions of terms used in the study that do not have a commonly understood meaning.

19. The method section includes a description of participants, instruments, design, procedure, assumptions, and limitations.

20. The description of participants in a quantitative study includes a definition and description of the population from which the sample was selected and may describe the method used in selecting the participants. The description of participants in a qualitative study will include descriptions of the way participants were selected, why they were selected, and a detailed description of the context in which they function.

21. The description of each instrument should relate the function of the instrument in the study (for example, selection of participants or a measure of the dependent variable), what the instrument is intended to measure, and data related to validity and reliability.

22. The procedure section should describe each step followed in conducting the study, in chronological order, in sufficient detail to permit the study to be replicated by another researcher.

23. The results section describes the statistical techniques or qualitative interpretations that were applied to the data and the results of these analyses. Information about the process applied during data analysis should be provided.

24. Tables and figures are used to present findings in summary or graph form and add clarity to the presentation. Good tables and figures are uncluttered and self-explanatory; it is better to use two tables (or figures) than one that is crowded. Tables and figures follow their related textual discussion and are referred to by number, not name or location.

25. Each research finding or result should be discussed in terms of its relation to the topic studied and its agreement or disagreement with previous results obtained by other researchers in other studies.

26. Overgeneralization occurs when researchers state conclusions that are not warranted by the results; it should be avoided.

27. The researcher should discuss the theoretical and practical implications of the findings and make recommendations for future research or future action.

28. The reference, or bibliography, section of the report lists all the sources, alphabetically by authors' last names, that were directly used in writing the report. Every source cited in the paper must be included in

the reference list, and every entry listed in the reference list must appear in the paper.

29. The required style manual will guide the format of various types of references.

30. Appendixes include information and data that are pertinent to the study but are either too lengthy or not important enough to be included in the main body of the report—for example, tests, questionnaires, cover letters, raw data, and data analysis sheets.

Now go to the Companion Website at **www.prenhall.com/gay** to assess your understanding of chapter content with Practice Quiz, apply comprehension in Applying What You Know, broaden your knowledge about research in Web Links, and expand your research skills in Evaluating Articles, Analyzing Qualitative Data, Analyzing Quantitative Data, and Research Tools and Tips.

PERFORMANCE CRITERIA

Your research report should include all the components listed in Figure 21.3, with the possible exceptions of an acknowledgments page and appendixes. For those of you who have worked on quantitative studies, development of Task 10 basically involves combining Tasks 2, 6, and 7, writing a discussion section, and preparing the appropriate preliminary pages (including an abstract) and references. In other words, you have already written most of Task 10. Those of you who have worked on qualitative studies should be able to build upon the information you developed for your research plans as you write the report.

An example that illustrates the performance called for by Task 10 appears on the following pages. (See Task 10 example.) This example represents the synthesis of the previously presented tasks related to the effects of interactive multimedia on biology achievement. To the degree possible with a student paper, this example follows the guidelines of the *Publication Manual of the American Psychological Association*.

Additional examples for the tasks are included in the *Student Study Guide* that accompanies this text.

Effect of Interactive Multimedia on the Achievement
of 10th-Grade Biology Students
Sara Jane Calderin
Florida International University

Submitted in partial fulfillment of

the requirements for EDF 5481

April, 1994

Table of Contents

List of Tables and Figures

Abstract

The purpose of this study was to investigate the effect of interactive multimedia on the achievement of 10th-grade biology students. Using a posttest-only control group design and a *t* test for independent samples, it was found that after approximately 8 months the students ($n = 30$) who were instructed using interactive multimedia achieved significantly higher scores on the biology test of the National Proficiency Survey Series than did the students ($n = 30$) whose instruction did not include interactive multimedia, $t(58) = 4.22, p < .05$. It was concluded that the interactive multimedia instruction was effective in raising the achievement level of the participating students.

Introduction

One of the major concerns of educators and parents alike is the decline in student achievement. An area of particular concern is science education, where the higher-level thinking skills and problem solving techniques so necessary for success in our technological society need to be developed (Smith & Westhoff, 1992).

Research is constantly providing new proven methods for educators to use, and technology has developed many kinds of tools ideally suited to the classroom. One such tool is interactive multimedia (IMM). IMM provides teachers with an extensive amount of data in a number of different formats including text, sound, and video. This makes it possible to appeal to all the different learning styles of the students and to offer a variety of material for students to analyze (Howson & Davis, 1992).

When teachers use IMM, students become highly motivated, which results in improved class attendance and more completed assignments (O'Connor, 1993). In addition, students also become actively involved in their own learning, encouraging comprehension rather than mere memorization of facts (Kneedler, 1993; Reeves, 1992).

Statement of the Problem

The purpose of this study was to investigate the effect of IMM on the achievement of 10th-grade biology students. IMM was defined as "a computerized database that allows users to access information in multiple forms, including text, graphics, video and audio" (Reeves, 1992, p. 47).

Review of Related Literature

Due to modern technology, such as videotapes and videodiscs, students receive more information from visual sources than they do from the written word (Helms & Helms, 1992), and yet in school the majority of information is still transmitted through textbooks. While textbooks cover a wide range of topics superficially, IMM can provide in-depth information on essential topics in a format that students find interesting (Kneedler, 1993). Smith and Westhoff (1992) note that when student interest is sparked, curiosity levels are increased and students are motivated to ask questions. The interactive nature of multimedia allows students to seek out their own answers, and by so doing they become owners of the concept involved. Ownership translates into comprehension (Howson & Davis, 1992).

Many science concepts are learned through observation of experiments. By using IMM, students can participate in a variety of experiments which are either too expensive, too lengthy, or too dangerous to carry out in the school laboratory (Howson & Davis, 1992; Leonard, 1989; Louie, Sweat, Gresham, & Smith, 1991). While observing experiments students can discuss what is happening and ask questions. At the touch of a button teachers are able to replay any part of the proceedings, and they also have random access to related information which can be used to illustrate completely the answer to the question (Howson & Davis, 1992). By answering students' questions in this detailed way, the content becomes more relevant to the needs of the students (Smith & Westhoff, 1992). When knowledge is relevant students are able to use it to solve problems and in so doing develop higher-level thinking skills (Helms & Helms, 1992; Sherwood, Kinzer, Bransford, & Franks, 1987).

A major challenge of science education is to provide students with large amounts of information that will encourage them to be analytical (Howson & Davis, 1992; Sherwood et al., 1987). IMM offers electronic access to extensive information allowing students to organize, evaluate, and use it in the solution of problems (Smith & Wilson, 1993). When information is introduced as an aid to problem solving it becomes a tool with which to solve other problems, rather than a series of solitary, disconnected facts (Sherwood et al., 1987).

Although critics complain that IMM is entertainment and students do not learn from it (Corcoran, 1989), research has shown that student learning does improve when IMM is used in the classroom (Sherwood et al., 1987; Sherwood & Others, 1990). A 1987 study by Sherwood et al., for example, showed that seventh- and eighth-grade science students receiving instruction enhanced with IMM had better retention of that information, and O'Connor (1993) found that the use of IMM in high school mathematics and science increased the focus on students' problem solving and critical thinking skills.

Statement of the Hypothesis

The quality and quantity of software available for science classes has dramatically improved during the past decade. Although some research has been carried out on the effects of IMM on student achievement in science, due to promising updates in the technology involved, further study is warranted. Therefore, it was hypothesized that 10th-grade biology students whose teachers use IMM as part of their instructional technique will exhibit significantly higher achievement than 10th-grade biology students whose teachers do not use IMM.

Method

Participants

The sample for this study was selected from the total population of 213 10th-grade students at an upper middle class all-girls Catholic high school in Miami, Florida. The population was 90% Hispanic, mainly of Cuban-American descent. Sixty students were randomly selected (using a table of random numbers) and randomly assigned to two groups of 30 each.

Instrument

The biology test of the National Proficiency Survey Series (NPSS) was used as the measuring instrument. The test was designed to measure individual student performance in biology at the high school level but the publishers also recommended it as an evaluation of instructional programs. Content validity is good; items were selected from a large item bank provided by classroom teachers and curriculum experts. High school instructional materials and a national curriculum survey were extensively reviewed before objectives were written. The test objectives and those of the biology classes in the study were highly correlated. Although the standard error of measurement is not given for the biology test, the range of KR-20s for the entire battery is from .82 to .91 with a median of .86. This is satisfactory since the purpose of the test was to evaluate instructional programs, not to make decisions concerning individuals. Catholic school students were included in the battery norming procedures, which were carried out in April and May of 1988 using 22,616 students in grades 9–12 from 45 high schools in 20 states.

Experimental Design

The design used in this study was the posttest-only control group design (see Figure 1). This design was selected because it provides control for most sources of invalidity and random assignment to groups was possible. A pretest was not necessary since the final science grades from June 1993 were available to check initial group equivalence and to help control mortality, a potential threat to internal validity with this design. Mortality, however, was not a problem as no students dropped from either group.

Figure 1. Experimental design.

Group	Assignment	n	Treatment	Posttest
1	Random	30	IMM instruction	NPSS:B[a]
2	Random	30	Traditional instruction	NPSS:B

[a]National Proficiency Survey Series: Biology

Procedure

Prior to the beginning of the 1993–1994 school year, before classes were scheduled, 60 of the 213 10th-grade students were randomly selected and randomly assigned to two groups of 30 each, the average biology class size; each group became a biology class. One of the classes was randomly chosen to receive IMM instruction. The same teacher taught both classes.

The study was designed to last eight months beginning on the first day of class. The control group was taught using traditional methods of lecturing and open class discussions. The students worked in pairs for laboratory investigations, which included the use of microscopes. The teacher's role was one of information disseminator.

The experimental classroom had 15 workstations for student use, each one consisting of a laserdisc player, a video recorder, a 27-inch monitor, and a Macintosh computer with a 40 MB hard drive, 128 MB RAM, and a CD-ROM drive. The teacher's workstation incorporated a Macintosh computer with CD-ROM drive, a videodisc player, and a 27-inch monitor. The workstations were networked to the school library so students had access to online services such as Prodigy and Infotrac as well as to the card catalogue. Two laser printers were available through the network for the students' use.

In the experimental class the teacher used a videodisc correlated to the textbook. When barcodes provided in the text were scanned, a section of the videodisc was activated and appeared on the monitor. The section might be a motion picture demonstrating a process or a still picture offering more detail than the text. The role of the teacher in the experimental group was that of facilitator and guide. After the teacher had introduced a new topic, the students worked in pairs at the workstations investigating topics connected to the main idea presented in the lesson. Videodiscs, CD-ROMs, and online services were all available as sources of information. The students used HyperStudio to prepare multimedia reports, which they presented to the class.

Throughout the study the same subject matter was covered and the two classes used the same text. Although the students of the experimental group paired up at the workstations, the other group worked in pairs during lab time, thus equalizing any effect from cooperative learning. The classes could not meet at the same time as they were taught by the same teacher, so they met during second and third periods. First period was not chosen as the school sometimes has a special schedule which interferes with first period. Both classes had the same homework reading assignments, which were reviewed in class the following school day. Academic objectives were the same for each class and all tests measuring achievement were identical.

During the first week of May, the biology test of the NPSS was administered to both classes to compare their achievement in biology.

Results

Prior to the beginning of the study, after the 60 students were randomly selected and assigned to experimental and control groups, final science grades from the previous school year were obtained from school records in order to check initial group equivalence. Examination of the means and a t test for independent samples ($\alpha = .05$) indicated essentially no difference between the groups (see Table 1). A t test for independent samples was used because the groups were randomly formed and the data were interval.

Table 1

Means, Standard Deviation, and t Tests for the Experimental and Control Groups

Score	Group		t
	IMM instruction[a]	Traditional instruction[a]	
Prior Grades			
M	87.47	87.63	$- 0.08^*$
SD	8.19	8.05	
Posttest NPSS:B			
M	32.27	26.70	4.22^{**}
SD	4.45	5.69	

Note. Maximum score for prior grades = 100. Maximum score for posttest = 40.

[a]$n = 30$.

$^*p > .05.$ $^{**}p < .05.$

At the completion of the eight-month study, during the first week in May, scores on the NPSS:B were compared, also using a t test for independent samples. As Table 1 indicates, scores of the experimental and control groups were significantly different. In fact, the experimental group scored approximately one standard deviation higher than the control group (ES = .98). Therefore, the original hypothesis that "10th-grade biology students whose teachers use IMM as part of their instructional technique will exhibit significantly higher achievement than 10th-grade biology students whose teachers do not use IMM" was supported.

Discussion

The results of this study support the original hypothesis: 10th-grade biology students whose teachers used IMM as part of their instructional technique did exhibit significantly higher achievement than 10th-grade biology students whose teachers did not use IMM. The IMM students' scores were 5.57 points (13.93%) higher than those of the other group. Also, it was informally observed that the IMM instructed students were eager to discover information on their own and to carry on the learning process outside scheduled class hours.

Results cannot be generalized to all classrooms because the study took place in an all-girls Catholic high school with the majority of the students having an Hispanic background. However, the results were consistent with research on IMM in general, and in particular with the findings of Sherwood et al. (1987) and O'Connor (1993) concerning the improvement of student achievement.

IMM appears to be a viable educational tool with applications in a variety of subject areas and with both cognitive and psychological benefits for students. While further research is needed, especially using other software and in other subject areas, the suggested benefits to students' learning offered by IMM warrant that teachers should be cognizant of this instructional method. In this technological age it is important that education take advantage of available tools which increase student motivation and improve academic achievement.

References

Corcoran, E. (1989, July). Show and tell: Hypermedia turns information into a multisensory event. *Scientific American, 261,* 72, 74.

Helms, C. W., & Helms, D. R. (1992, June). *Multimedia in education* (Report No. IR-016-090). Proceedings of the 25th Summer Conference of the Association of Small Computer Users in Education. North Myrtle Beach, SC. (ERIC Document Reproduction Service No. ED 357 732)

Howson, B. A., & Davis, H. (1992). Enhancing comprehension with videodiscs. *Media and Methods, 28*(3), 12–14.

Kneedler, P. E. (1993). California adopts multimedia science program. *Technological Horizons in Education Journal, 20*(7), 73–76.

Lehmann, I. J. (1990). Review of National Proficiency Survey Series. In J. J. Kramer & J. C. Conoley (Eds.), *The eleventh mental measurements yearbook* (pp. 595–599). Lincoln: University of Nebraska, Buros Institute of Mental Measurement.

Leonard, W. H. (1989). A comparison of student reaction to biology instruction by interactive videodisc or conventional laboratory. *Journal of Research in Science Teaching, 26,* 95–104.

Louie, R., Sweat, S., Gresham, R., & Smith, L. (1991). Interactive video: Disseminating vital science and math information. *Media and Methods, 27*(5), 22–23.

O'Connor, J. E. (1993, April). *Evaluating the effects of collaborative efforts to improve mathematics and science curricula* (Report No. TM-019-862). Paper presented at the Annual Meeting of the American Educational Research Association, Atlanta, GA. (ERIC Document Reproduction Service No. ED 357 083)

Reeves, T. C. (1992). Evaluating interactive multimedia. *Educational Technology, 32*(5), 47–52.

Sherwood, R. D., Kinzer, C. K., Bransford, J. D., & Franks, J. J. (1987). Some benefits of creating macro-contexts for science instruction: Initial findings. *Journal of Research in Science Teaching, 24,* 417–435.

Sherwood, R. D., & Others. (1990, April). *An evaluative study of level one videodisc based chemistry program* (Report No. SE-051-513). Paper presented at a Poster Session at the 63rd Annual Meeting of the National Association for Research in Science Teaching, Atlanta, GA. (ERIC Document Reproduction Service No. ED 320 772)

Smith, E. E., & Westhoff, G. M. (1992). The Taliesin project: Multidisciplinary education and multimedia. *Educational Technology, 32,* 15–23.

Smith, M. K., & Wilson, C. (1993, March). *Integration of student learning strategies via technology* (Report No. IR-016-035). Proceedings of the Fourth Annual Conference of Technology and Teacher Education. San Diego, CA. (ERIC Document Reproduction Service No. ED 355 937)

"A researcher critically evaluates each reference and does not consider poorly executed research."
(p. 541)

Evaluating a Research Report

OBJECTIVES

After reading Chapter 22, you should be able to do the following:

1. For each of the major sections and subsections of a research report, list at least three questions that should be asked in determining its adequacy.

2. For each of the following types of research, list at least three questions that should be asked in determining the adequacy of a study representing that type.
   a. Descriptive research
   b. Correlational research
   c. Causal–comparative research
   d. Experimental research
   e. Single-subject research
   f. Narrative research
   g. Ethnographic research
   h. Mixed methods research
   i. Action research

Knowing how to conduct research and produce a research report are valuable skills, but as a professional you should also know how to consume and evaluate research. Anyone who reads a newspaper, listens to the radio, or watches television is a consumer of research. Many people uncritically accept and act on medical and health findings, for example, because they are presented by someone in a white lab coat or because they are labeled "research." Very few people question the procedures utilized or the generalizability of the findings. On the other hand, you have a responsibility to be informed concerning the latest findings in your professional area and to be able to differentiate "good" from "poor" research when investigating a topic to study. A researcher critically evaluates each reference and does not consider poorly executed research. Decisions made on the basis of poor research are likely to be poor decisions. To competently evaluate a research study, you must have knowledge of each of

the components of the research process. Your work in previous chapters has given you that knowledge. In this chapter you will learn criteria on which evaluate a research report.

The goal of Chapter 22 is for you to be able to analyze and evaluate research reports. Completing Chapter 22 should enable you to perform the following task.

TASK 11

Given a reprint of a research report and an evaluation form, evaluate the components of the report. (See Performance Criteria, p. 550.)

:: GENERAL EVALUATION CRITERIA

Many research studies have flaws of various kinds. Just because a study is published does not necessarily mean that it is a good study or that it is reported adequately. The most common flaw is lack of validity and reliability information about data-gathering procedures such as tests, observations, questionnaires, and interviews. Other common flaws include weaknesses in the research design, inappropriate or biased selection of participants, failure to state limitations in the research, and a general lack of description about the study. These common problems in studies reinforce the importance of being a competent consumer of research reports; they also highlight common pitfalls to avoid in your own research.

At your current level of expertise, you may not be able to evaluate every component of every study. For example, you would not be able to determine whether the appropriate degrees of freedom were used in the calculation of an analysis of covariance. There are, however, a number of basic errors or weaknesses you should be able to detect in research studies. You should, for example, be able to identify the sources of invalidity associated with a study based on a one-group pretest–posttest design. You should also be able to detect obvious indications of experimenter bias that may have affected qualitative or quantitative research results. For example, a statement in a research report that "the purpose of this study was to prove. . . " should alert you to a probable bias effect.

As you read a research report, either as a consumer of research keeping up with the latest findings in your professional area or as a producer of research reviewing literature related to a defined problem, you should ask a number of questions about the adequacy of a study and its components. The answers to some of these questions are more critical than the answers to others. An inadequate title is not a critical flaw; an inadequate research plan is. Some questions are difficult to answer if the study is not directly in your area of expertise. If your area of specialization is reading, for example, you are probably not in a position to judge the adequacy of a review of literature related to anxiety effects on learning. And, admittedly, the answers to some questions are more subjective than objective. Whether a good design was used is pretty clear and objective; most quantitative researchers would agree that the randomized posttest-only control group design is a good design. Whether the most appropriate design was used, given the problem under study, often involves a degree of subjective judgment. For example, the need for inclusion of a pretest might be a debatable point depending on the study and its design. However, despite the lack of complete agreement in some areas, evaluation of a research report is a worthwhile and important activity. Major problems and shortcomings are usually readily identifiable, and by considering a number of questions, you can formulate an overall impression of the quality of the study. In the sections that follow, we list for your consideration evaluative questions about a number of research strategies and areas. This list is by no means exhaustive, and as you read it, you may very well think of additional questions to ask. You will also note that not every criterion applies equally to both quantitative and qualitative research studies.

Introduction

Problem

- Is there a statement of the problem? Does the problem indicate a particular focus of study?
- Is the problem "researchable"; that is, can it be investigated through collecting and analyzing data?
- Is background information on the problem presented?
- Is the educational significance of the problem discussed?
- Does the problem statement indicate the variables of interest and the specific relationship between those variables that were investigated?
- When necessary, are variables directly or operationally defined?
- Did the researcher have the knowledge and skill to carry out the research?

Review of Related Literature

- Is the review comprehensive?
- Are all cited references relevant to the problem under investigation?
- Are most of the sources primary (i.e., are there only a few or no secondary sources)?
- Have the references been analyzed and critiqued and the results of various studies compared and contrasted? That is, is the review more than a series of abstracts or annotations?
- Is the relevancy of each reference explained?
- Is the review well organized? Does it logically flow in such a way that the references least related to the problem are discussed first and those most related are discussed last? Does it educate the reader about the problem or topic?

- Does the review conclude with a summary and interpretation of the literature and its implications for the problem investigated?
- Do the implications discussed form an empirical or theoretical rationale for the hypotheses that follow?
- Are references cited completely and accurately?

Hypotheses

- Are specific research questions listed or specific hypotheses stated?
- Does each hypothesis state an expected relationship or difference?
- If necessary, are variables directly or operationally defined?
- Is each hypothesis testable?

Method

Participants

- Are the size and major characteristics of the population studied described?
- Are the accessible and target populations described?
- If a sample was selected, is the method of selecting the sample clearly described?
- Does the method of sample selection suggest any limitations or biases in the sample? For example, was stratified sampling used to obtain sample subgroups?
- Are the size and major characteristics of the sample described?
- If the study is quantitative, does the sample size meet the suggested guidelines for the minimum sample size appropriate for the method of research represented?

Instruments

- Do instruments and their administration meet guidelines for protecting human subjects? Were needed permissions obtained?
- Is the rationale given for the selection of the instruments (or measurements) used?
- Are the purpose, content, validity, and reliability of each instrument described?
- Are the instruments appropriate for measuring the intended variables?
- Does the researcher have the needed skills or experience to construct or administer an instrument?
- Is evidence presented to indicate that the instruments are appropriate for the intended sample? For example, is the reading level of an instrument suitable for sample participants?
- If appropriate, are subtest reliabilities given?
- If an instrument was developed specifically for the study, are the procedures involved in its development and validation described?
- If an instrument was developed specifically for the study, are administration, scoring or tabulating, and interpretation procedures fully described?
- Was the correct type of instrument used for data collection (or, for example, was a norm-referenced instrument used when a criterion-referenced one was more suitable)?

Design and Procedure

- Are the design and procedures appropriate for examining the research question or testing the hypotheses of the study?
- Are the procedures described in sufficient detail to permit replication by another researcher?
- Do procedures logically relate to one another?
- Were instruments and procedures applied correctly?

- If a pilot study was conducted, are its execution and results described as well as its effect on the subsequent study?
- Are control procedures described?
- Does the researcher discuss or account for any potentially confounding variable that he or she was unable to control?

Results

- Are appropriate descriptive statistics presented?
- Was the probability level at which the results of the tests of significance were evaluated specified in advance of the data analyses? Was every hypothesis tested?
- If parametric tests were used, is there evidence that the researcher avoided violating the required assumptions for parametric tests?
- Are the described tests of significance appropriate, given the hypotheses and design of the study?
- Was the inductive logic used to produce results in a qualitative study made explicit?
- Are the tests of significance interpreted using the appropriate degrees of freedom?
- Are the results clearly described?
- Are the tables and figures (if any) well organized and easy to understand?
- Are the data in each table and figure described in the text?

Discussion (Conclusions and Recommendations)

- Is each result discussed in terms of the original hypothesis or topic to which it relates?
- Is each result discussed in terms of its agreement or disagreement with previous results obtained by other researchers in other studies?
- Are generalizations consistent with the results?
- Are the possible effects of uncontrolled variables on the results discussed?
- Are theoretical and practical implications of the findings discussed?
- Are recommendations for future action made?
- Are the suggestions for future action based on practical significance or on statistical significance only (i.e., has the author avoided confusing practical and statistical significance)?

Abstract or Summary

- Is the problem restated?
- Are the number and type of subjects and instruments described?
- Is the design used identified?
- Are procedures described?
- Are the major results and conclusions restated?

:: TYPE-SPECIFIC EVALUATION CRITERIA

In addition to general criteria that can be applied to almost any study, there are additional questions you should ask depending on the type of research represented by the study. In other words, some concerns are specific to qualitatively oriented research (narrative, ethnographic), quantitatively oriented research (descriptive, correlational, causal–comparative, experimental, and single-subject design), mixed methods research, and action research.

Both quantitative and qualitative criteria may be applied by varying degrees to mixed methods research depending on the emphasis placed on quantitative and qualitative research methods.

Descriptive Research

Questionnaire Studies

- Are questionnaire validation procedures described?
- Was the questionnaire pretested?
- Are pilot study procedures and results described?
- Are directions to questionnaire respondents clear?
- Does each item in the questionnaire relate to one of the objectives of the study?
- Does each questionnaire item deal with a single concept?
- When necessary, is a point of reference given for questionnaire items?
- Are leading questions avoided in the questionnaire?
- Are there sufficient alternatives for each questionnaire item?
- Does the cover letter explain the purpose and importance of the study and give the potential respondent a good reason for cooperating?
- If appropriate, is confidentiality or anonymity of responses assured in the cover letter?
- What is the percentage of returns, and how does it affect the study results?
- Are follow-up activities to increase returns described?
- If the response rate was low, was any attempt made to determine any major differences between respondents and nonrespondents?
- Are data analyzed in groups or clusters rather than in a series of many single-variable analyses?

Correlational Research

Relationship Studies

- Were variables carefully selected (i.e., was a shotgun approach avoided)?
- Is the rationale for variable selection described?
- Are conclusions and recommendations based on values of correlation coefficients corrected for attenuation or restriction in range?
- Do the conclusions avoid suggesting causal relationships between the variables investigated?

Prediction Studies

- Is a rationale given for selection of predictor variables?
- Is the criterion variable well defined?
- Was the resulting prediction equation validated with at least one other group?

Causal–Comparative Research

- Are the characteristics or experiences that differentiate the groups (the independent variable) clearly defined or described?
- Are critical extraneous variables identified?
- Were any control procedures applied to equate the groups on extraneous variables?
- Are causal relationships found discussed with due caution?
- Are plausible alternative hypotheses discussed?

Experimental Research

- Was an appropriate experimental design selected?
- Is a rationale for design selection given?
- Are sources of invalidity associated with the design identified and discussed?
- Is the method of group formation described?
- Was the experimental group formed in the same way as the control group?
- Were groups randomly formed and the use of existing groups avoided?
- Were treatments randomly assigned to groups?
- Were critical extraneous variables identified?
- Were any control procedures applied to equate groups on extraneous variables?
- Were possible reactive arrangements (e.g., the Hawthorne effect) controlled for?
- Are tables clear and pertinent to the research results?
- Are the results generalized to the appropriate group?

Single-Subject Research

- Are the data time constrained?
- Was a baseline established before moving into the intervention phase?
- Was condition or phase length sufficient to represent the behavior within the phase?
- Is the design appropriate to the question being asked?
- If a multiple baseline design was used, were conditions met to move across baselines?
- If a withdrawal design was used, are limitations to this design addressed?
- Did the researcher manipulate only one variable at a time?
- Is the study replicable?

Qualitative Research (In General)

- Does the topic studied describe a general sense of the study focus?
- Does the researcher state a "guiding hypothesis" for the investigation?
- Is the application of the qualitative method chosen described in detail?
- Is the context of the qualitative study described in detail?
- Is the purposive sampling procedure described and related to the study focus?
- Is each data collection strategy described?
- Is the researcher's role stated (e.g., nonparticipant observer, participant observer, interviewer, etc.)?
- Is the research site and the researcher's entry into it described?
- Were the data collection strategies used appropriately, given the purpose of the study?
- Were strategies used to strengthen the validity and reliability of the data (e.g., triangulation)?
- Is there a description of how any unexpected ethical issues were handled?
- Are strategies used to minimize observer bias and observer effect described?
- Are the researcher's reactions and notes differentiated from descriptive field notes?
- Are data coding strategies described and examples of coded data given?
- Is the inductive logic applied to the data to produce results stated in detail?
- Are conclusions supported by data (e.g., are direct quotations from participants used to illustrate points made)?

Interview Studies

- Were the interview procedures pretested?
- Are pilot study procedures and results described?
- Does each item in the interview guide relate to a specific objective of the study?

- When necessary, is a point of reference given in the guide for interview items?
- Are leading questions avoided in the interview guide?
- Is the language and complexity of the questions appropriate for the participants?
- Does the interview guide indicate the type and amount of prompting and probing that was permitted?
- Are the qualifications and special training of the interviewers described?
- Is the method used to record responses described?
- Did the researcher use the most reliable, unbiased method of recording responses that could have been used?
- Does the researcher specify how the responses to semistructured and unstructured items were quantified and analyzed?

Narrative Research

- Does the researcher provide a rationale for the use of narrative research to study the chosen phenomenon?
- Is there a rationale for the choice of individual to study the chosen phenomenon?
- Does the researcher describe data collection methods and give particular attention to interviewing?
- Does the researcher describe appropriate strategies for analysis and interpretation (e.g., restorying)?

Ethnographic Research

- Does the written account (the ethnography) capture the social, cultural, and economic themes that emerged from the study?
- Did the researcher spend a "full cycle" in the field studying the phenomenon?

Mixed Methods

- Did the study use at least one quantitative and one qualitative data research method?
- Is a rationale for using a mixed methods research design provided?
- Is the type of mixed methods research design stated?
- Is the priority given to quantitative and qualitative data collection and the sequence of their use described?
- Was the study feasible given the amount of data to be collected and concomitant issues of resources, time, and expertise?
- Did the study investigate both quantitative and qualitative research questions?
- Are qualitative and quantitative data collection techniques clearly identified?
- Are the data analysis techniques appropriate for the type of mixed methods design?

Action Research

- Does the area of focus involve teaching and learning in the researcher's own practice?
- Does the researcher state questions that were answerable given the researcher's expertise, time, and resources?
- Was the area of focus within the researcher's locus of control?
- Is the area of focus something the researcher was passionate about?
- Is the area of focus something the researcher wanted to change or improve upon?
- Does the researcher provide an action plan detailing the impact of the research findings on practice?

Evaluating Validity and Reliability in Qualitative Studies[1]

Threats to Internal Validity

- Did the researcher effectively deal with problems of history and maturation by documenting historical changes over time?
- Did the researcher effectively deal with problems of mortality by using a sample large enough to minimize the effects of attrition?
- Was the researcher in the field long enough to effectively minimize observer effects?
- Did the researcher take the time to become familiar and comfortable with participants?
- Were interview questions pretested?
- Were efforts made to ensure intraobserver agreement by training interview teams in coding procedures?
- Were efforts made to cross-check results by conducting interviews with multiple groups?
- Did the researcher interview key informants to verify field observations?
- Were participants demographically screened to ensure that they were representative of the larger population?
- Was data collected using different media (audio- and videotape, etc.) to facilitate cross-validation?
- Were participants allowed to evaluate research results before publication?
- Is sufficient data presented to support findings and conclusions?
- Were dependent and independent variables repeatedly tested to validate results?

Threats to External Validity

- Were constructs defined in a way that has meaning outside the study's setting?
- Were both new and adapted instruments pretested to ensure that they were appropriate for the study?
- Does the researcher fully describe participants' relevant characteristics, such as socioeconomic structure, gender makeup, level of urbanization and/or acculturation, and pertinent social and cultural history?
- Are researcher interaction effects addressed by fully documenting the researcher's activities in the setting?
- Were all observations and interviews conducted in a variety of fully described settings and with multiple trained observers?

Reliability

- Is the researcher's relationship with the group and setting fully described?
- Is all field documentation comprehensive, fully cross-referenced and annotated, and rigorously detailed?
- Were observations and interviews documented using multiple means (written notes and recordings, for example)?
- Was the interviewer's training documented, and is it described?
- Was the construction, planning, and testing of all instruments documented, and are they described?
- Are key informants fully described, including information on groups they represent and their community status?
- Are sampling techniques fully documented as being sufficient for the study?

---

[1] The questions in this section were adapted from *Ethnographer's Toolkit: Vol. 2. Essential Ethnographic Methods: Observations, Interviews, and Questionnaires* (pp. 278–289), by S. L. Schensul, J. J. Schensul, and M. D. LeCompte, 1999, Lanham, MD: AltaMira/Rowman & Littlefield.

SUMMARY

General Evaluation Criteria

1. There are a number of basic errors or weaknesses that even a beginning researcher should be able to detect in a research study.
2. You should be able to detect obvious indications of experimenter bias that may have affected the results.
3. As you read a research report, either as a consumer of research keeping up with the latest findings in your professional area or as a producer of research reviewing literature related to a defined problem, you should ask a number of questions concerning the adequacy of execution of the various components.
4. The answers to some of these questions are more critical than the answers to others.
5. Major problems and shortcomings are usually readily identifiable, and by considering a number of questions, you can formulate an overall impression of the quality of the study.

Introduction

6. Problem: See page 542.
7. Review of related literature: See pages 542–543.
8. Hypotheses: See page 543.

Method

9. Participants: See page 543.
10. Instruments: See page 543.
11. Design and procedure: See page 543–544.

Results

12. See page 544.

Discussion (Conclusions and Recommendations)

13. See page 544.

Abstract or Summary

14. See page 544.

Type-Specific Evaluation Criteria

15. In addition to general criteria that can be applied to almost any study, there are additional questions that

should be asked depending on the type of research represented by the study.

Descriptive Research

16. Questionnaire studies: See page 545.

Correlational Research

17. Relationship studies: See page 545.
18. Prediction studies: See page 545.

Causal–Comparative Research

19. See page 545.

Experimental Research

20. See page 546.

Single-Subject Design Research

21. See page 546.

Qualitative Research (In General)

22. See page 546.
23. Interview studies: See pages 546–547.

Narrative Research

24. See page 547.

Ethnographic Research

25. See page 547.

Mixed Methods Research

26. See page 547.

Action Research

27. See page 547.

Evaluating Validity and Reliability in Qualitative Studies

28. See page 548.

Now go to the Companion Website at **www.prenhall.com/gay** to assess your understanding of chapter content with Practice Quiz, apply comprehension in Applying What You Know, broaden your knowledge about research in Web Links, and expand your research skills in Evaluating Articles, Analyzing Qualitative Data, Analyzing Quantitative Data, and Research Tools and Tips.

PERFORMANCE CRITERIA

The research report to be evaluated appears on the following pages. (See Task 11 Example.) Immediately following is the form you should use in evaluating the report. (See Self-Test for Task 11.) A write-on version of the form appears in the *Student Study Guide* that accompanies this text. Answer each question by writing one of the following on the line in the "Code" column:

Y = Yes
N = No
NA = Question not applicable (e.g., a pilot study was not done)
?/X = Cannot tell from information given or, given your current level of expertise, you
      are not in a position to make a judgment

In addition (and where possible), indicate where you found the answer to the question in the report. For example, if asked if a hypothesis is stated in the report, and the answer is yes, you would write "paragraph 7, sentences 6 and 7" as the location of the information. Write the information in the margin next to the question.

Additional examples for the tasks are included in the *Student Study Guide* that accompanies this text. Suggested responses for the Self-Test for Task 11 appear in Appendix C.

EFFECTS OF USING AN INSTRUCTIONAL GAME ON MOTIVATION AND PERFORMANCE

JAMES D. KLEIN
Arizona State University

ERIC FREITAG
Arizona State University

ABSTRACT   Although many educators theorize that instructional games are effective for providing students with motivating practice, research on instructional gaming is inconclusive. The purpose of this study was to determine the effect on motivation and performance of using an instructional game. The effect of using a supplemental reading on motivation and performance was also examined. We randomly assigned 75 undergraduates to one of two treatments after they had attended a lecture on the information-processing model of learning. The subjects in one treatment group used an instructional board game to practice the material presented in the lecture, while those in the other group practiced using a traditional worksheet. Results indicated that using the instructional game significantly affected the four motivational components of attention, relevance, confidence, and satisfaction. The instructional game did not influence performance. The results also suggested that the subjects who reported completion of a supplemental reading had significantly better performance and confidence than did the subjects who reported that they had not completed the reading. Implications for the design of practice are discussed.

Providing students with an opportunity to practice newly acquired skills and knowledge is an important component in designing an instructional strategy. Although many instructional design theories include recommendations for designing practice activities, Salisbury, Richards, and Klein (1986) have emphasized that most of the theories fail to address how to design practice that is motivational.

Some educators have theorized that instructional games are effective for providing motivating practice of newly acquired skills and information. They have argued that instructional games are motivational because they generate enthusiasm, excitement, and enjoyment, and because they require students to be actively involved in learning (Coleman, 1968; Ernest, 1986; Rakes & Kutzman, 1982; Wesson, Wilson, & Mandlebaum, 1988). Other scholars have theorized that instructional games decrease student motivation. Those authors have suggested that the motivational aspects of instructional games are limited to those who win, and that losing an instructional game produces a failure syndrome and reduces self-esteem (Allington & Strange, 1977; Andrews & Thorpe, 1977).

Whereas theorists have argued about the motivational aspects of instructional games, researchers have investigated the effect of using games on student motivation. Some researchers have reported that the use of instructional gaming increases student interests, satisfaction, and continuing motivation (DeVries & Edwards, 1973; Sleet, 1985; Straus, 1986). In addition, investigators have reported that instructional games influence school attendance. Allen and Main (1976) found that including instructional gaming in a mathematics curriculum helped to reduce the rate of absenteeism of students in inner-city schools. Studies by Raia (1966) and Boseman and Schellenberger (1974) indicated that including games in a college business course has a positive affect on course attendance but not on expressed interest and satisfaction. Others have reported that playing a game does not influence student satisfaction or attitude toward school (DeVries & Slavin, 1978).

In addition to the possible motivational benefits of games, many educators have theorized that games are effective for increasing student performance. They have argued that instructional games make practice more effective because students become active participants in the learning process (Ernest, 1986; Rakes & Kutzman, 1982; Wesson et al., 1988). Others have suggested that games foster incorrect responding and inefficiently use instructional time; also, the rate of practice in a game cannot compare with that of a flashcard drill or reading a connected text (Allington & Strange, 1977; Andrews & Thorpe, 1977).

Researchers have attempted to answer whether instructional games are an effective method for learning. Some investigators have reported that instructional games are effective for assisting students to acquire, practice, and transfer mathematical concepts and problem-solving abilities (Bright, 1980; Bright, Harvey, & Wheeler, 1979; DeVries & Slavin, 1978; Dienes, 1962; Rogers & Miller, 1984). Others have reported that using an instructional game to practice mathematics skills assists slow learners but not more able students (Friedlander, 1977). Research on the use of instructional games in college business courses has produced inconclusive or nonsignificant findings in many studies (Boseman & Schellenberger, 1974; Greenlaw & Wyman, 1973; Raia, 1966), whereas instructional games have positively influenced learning in actual business training settings (Jacobs & Baum, 1987; Pierfy, 1977). Even advocates of instructional gaming are unsure whether games teach intellectual content and skills (Boocock, 1968).

Address correspondence to James D. Klein, Learning and Instruction, College of Education, Arizona State University, Tempe, AZ 85287-0611.

There are several explanations for the inconsistent findings from research concerning the effect of instructional games on motivation and learning. A few authors (Reiser & Gerlach, 1977; Remus, 1981; Stone, 1982) have suggested that much of the research on instructional gaming has been conducted using flawed experimental designs and methods. Another explanation is that many studies on instructional gaming have not investigated the integration of games in an instructional system. Gaming advocates have suggested that games should be used with other instructional methods such as lecture and textbooks (Clayton & Rosenbloom, 1968). A third explanation is that researchers examining the effect of instructional gaming on motivation have not adequately defined and operationalized the variable of motivation. After an extensive review of instructional gaming, Wolfe (1985) indicated, "No rigorous research has examined a game's motivational power, [or] what types of students are motivated by games" (p. 279).

Our purpose in this article is to describe the results of a study conducted to determine the effects on student motivation and performance of using an instructional game as practice. Because the study was designed to integrate the game into an instructional system, we also attempted to determine how using a supplemental reading affects student motivation and performance. Motivation was defined using the ARCS model of motivation (Keller, 1987a). The model suggests that motivation in an instructional setting consists of four conditions: attention, relevance, confidence, and satisfaction. According to Keller (1987a), all four conditions must be met for students to become and remain motivated. We hypothesized that students using an instructional game to practice newly acquired information would indicate that the method enhanced their attention, relevance, confidence, and satisfaction. We also believed that students who reported that they had completed a supplemental reading would perform better on a posttest than would those who reported that they did not complete the reading.

METHOD

Subjects

Our subjects were 75 undergraduate education majors enrolled in a required course in educational psychology at a large southwestern university. Although students in this class were required to participate in one research study during the semester, participation in this particular study was not mandatory.

Materials

Materials used in this study were an instructional game and a worksheet (both designed to provide practice of information and concepts presented in a lecture), the textbook *Essentials of Learning for Instruction* by Gagne & Driscoll (1988), the Instructional Materials Motivation Scale (Keller, 1987b), and a measure of performance.

The term *game* has various meanings, and several characteristics are important to understand the construct of game. In general, most games include a model or representation of reality, a set of rules that describe how to proceed, a specified outcome, and a group of players who act individually or collectively as a team (Atkinson, 1977; Coleman, 1968; Fletcher, 1971; Shubik, 1975,

1989). Games usually require active participation by players and can include elements of competition and cooperation (Orbach, 1979; Shubik, 1989). Games used for instructional purposes should be based on specific educational objectives and provide immediate feedback to participants (Atkinson, 1977; Jacobs & Baum, 1987; Orbach, 1979).

The instructional game used in this study included the elements listed above. We developed the game to provide students with practice on objectives from a unit on the information-processing model of learning. The instructional game consisted of a board that graphically represented the information-processing model, a direction card that explained the rules of the game, and a set of 25 game cards. Each game card had a practice question about the information-processing model of learning on the front and feedback with knowledge of correct results on the back. The rules were developed to encourage cooperation, competition, and active participation. The rules specified that team members should discuss each question among themselves before providing an answer. Teams were also told that they would be playing against another team.

We also developed the worksheet to provide subjects with practice on the information-processing model of learning. The worksheet was four pages in length and included the same 25 questions that appeared on the game cards. After subjects completed a set of five questions, the worksheet instructed subjects to turn to the last page for feedback.

We used the Instructional Materials Motivation Scale (IMMS) developed by Keller (1987b), to measure student perception of the motivational characteristics of the instructional materials. The IMMS includes four subscales to measure the degree to which subjects believe that a set of instructional materials address the motivational components of attention, relevance, confidence, and satisfaction. Keller reported that Cronbach's alpha reliability of the instrument is .89 for attention, .81 for relevance, .90 for confidence, .92 for satisfaction, and .96 for overall motivation.

A 15-item constructed response posttest was used to measure student performance. We developed the items on this posttest to determine subject mastery of the information-processing model. The Kuder-Richardson internal consistency reliability of this measure was .77.

Procedures

All of the subjects attended a 50-min lecture on the information-processing model of learning and were told afterward to read chapter 2 in the textbook, *Essentials of Learning for Instruction,* by Gagne & Driscoll (1988). Two days later, the subjects were randomly assigned to one of two treatment groups. The subjects in both groups were given 30 min to practice the information presented in the lecture and assigned reading by using either the instructional game or the worksheet.

One group of subjects used the instructional game to practice the information-processing model. Those subjects were randomly placed in groups of 8 to 10 and formed into two teams of players. Each group received the game materials described above, and the experimenter read the game rules aloud. Subjects in this group played the game for 30 min. The other group of subjects used the worksheet to practice the same items. The latter group worked individually for 30 min to complete the worksheet. The subjects were told to review incorrect items if time permitted.

Upon completion of the practice activity, all the subjects completed the Instructional Materials Motivation Scale and then took the posttest. The subjects also were asked if they had attended the lecture on the information-processing model and if they had completed the assigned reading from the textbook. Completion of the activities took approximately 15 min.

RESULTS

Motivation

We used a multivariate analysis of variance (MANOVA) to test for an overall difference between groups on the motivation scales. Stevens (1986) indicated that MANOVA should be used when several dependent variables are correlated and share a common conceptual meaning. An alpha level of .05 was set for the MANOVA tests. The analyses were followed by univariate analyses on each of the four IMMS subscales. To account for the possibility of inflated statistical error, we set the alpha at .0125 for the univariate analyses, using the Bonferroni method (Stevens, 1986). To determine the size of the treatment effect for each variable, we calculated effect-size estimates expressed as a function of the overall standard deviation (Cohen, 1969).

Results indicated that using the instructional game to practice information had a significant effect on motivation. A significant MANOVA effect, $F(4, 64) = 6.57$, $p < .001$, was found for the treatment on the motivation measures. Univariate analyses revealed that subjects who played the game rated this method of practice as motivational in the four areas of attention, $F(1, 67) = 21.91$, $p < .001$; relevance, $F(1, 67) = 15.05$, $p < .001$; confidence, $F(1, 67) = 16.80$, $p < .001$; and satisfaction, $F(1, 67) = 24.71$, $p < .001$. Effect-size estimates for each motivation variable were .61 for attention, .91 for relevance, 1.01 for confidence, and 1.23 for satisfaction. Cohen (1969) indicated that an effect size of .80 should be considered large for most statistical tests in psychological research. Table 1 includes a summary of means and standard deviations on each motivation subscale for the game and the nongame groups.

Results also suggested that subject self-report about completion of the reading assignment was significantly related to motivation. A significant MANOVA effect $F(4, 64) = 2.94$, $p < .05$, was found for

this variable on the motivation measures. Follow-up univariate analyses revealed that the motivational area of confidence was significantly related to completion of reading assignment, $F(1, 67) = 6.52$, $p < .0125$. Attention, relevance, and satisfaction were not significantly related to self-reported completion of reading assignment. In addition, a test of the interaction between self-reported completion of reading assignment and the treatment was not statistically significant, $F(4, 64) = 0.97$, $p > .05$.

Performance

We measured performance using a 15-item constructed response posttest. Analysis of variance (ANOVA) was used to test for differences between groups on the performance measure. An alpha level of .05 was set for all statistical tests.

Analysis of the posttest data revealed that self-reported completion of assigned reading was significantly related to performance, $F(2, 71) = 14.87$, $p < .001$. Subjects who indicated that they had read the assigned text ($n = 40$) performed significantly better on the posttest than those who indicated that they did not complete the reading ($n = 35$). The mean performance score of subjects who reported reading the text was 11.25 ($SD = 3.07$), whereas the mean performance score for those who reported that they did not read the text was 8.45 ($SD = 3.22$).

No statistically significant difference was found on the performance measure when the treatment groups were compared. The mean performance score for subjects using the game was 10.49 ($SD = 3.20$), and the mean performance score for those in the nongame group was 9.39 ($SD = 3.61$). In addition, a test of the interaction between the treatment and self-reported completion of reading assignment was not statistically significant, $F(2, 71) = 0.14$, $p > .05$.

DISCUSSION

The major purpose of this study was to determine the effect of using an instructional game on student motivation and performance. The results of the study suggest that using an instructional game as a method of delivering practice did enhance the motivation of students in the four areas of attention, relevance, confidence, and satisfaction. However, the results show that using the instructional game to practice information did not contribute to enhanced performance when compared with a traditional method of practice. There are several possible explanations for the results found in this study.

Table 1.
Means and Standard Deviations on Attention (A), Relevance (R), Confidence (C), Satisfaction (S),
and Performance (P) Measures, by Treatment Group

Group	A	R	C	S	P
Game	4.22	3.71	4.06	3.88	10.49
($n = 37$)	(0.58)	(0.58)	(0.57)	(0.86)	(3.20)
Nongame	3.77	3.13	3.31	2.72	9.39
($n = 38$)	(0.89)	(0.69)	(0.90)	(1.02)	(3.60)

Note. Maximum scores = 5.00 for A, R, C, S and 15.00 for P.

In keeping with established ideas of the characteristics of a game, we used a game board that provided students with a visual representation of the information-processing model of learning and required players to be active participants. Keller (1987a) indicated that visual representations and active participation are two strategies that can increase student attention in an instructional setting. Furthermore, use of the game may have contributed to the results found for attention, because of a novelty effect. Some researchers have reported that student motivation and interest fluctuate and decrease as the novelty effect of a game wears off (Dill, 1961; Greenlaw & Wyman, 1973), whereas others have reported that interest tends to persist over time in gaming settings (Dill & Doppelt, 1963). Although novelty may be a reason for increased attention in this study, instructional designers who are concerned with providing motivating practice to students should consider that explanation as positive. Motivation and attention can be increased when variability and novelty are used in the classroom (Brophy, 1987; Keller, 1983).

The results found in this study for the motivational factor of relevance are consistent with the theories proposed by gaming advocates. Both Abt (1968) and Rogers and Miller (1984) argued that students will not question the relevance of educational content when it is presented via an instructional game. In addition, instruction can be made relevant to students by designing materials that are responsive to their needs (Keller, 1983). Orbach (1979) indicated that games are excellent methods to motivate students with a high need for achievement, because a game can include an element of competition. Orbach (1979) also theorized that games can motivate students with a high need for affiliation when the game requires interaction among individuals and teams. The instructional game used in this study included a moderate level of competition and required students to interact cooperatively through the team approach.

The instructional game used in this study also provided circumstances for student-directed learning. As a motivational strategy, researchers have linked student-centered learning with increased confidence (Keller & Dodge, 1982). The finding that the game increased student confidence is consistent with theorists who have suggested that games can influence student efficacy (Abt, 1968) and with researchers who reported that students rate the task of gaming as less difficult than other instructional techniques (DeVries & Edwards, 1973).

The positive finding for satisfaction is also consistent with theory and research. Some scholars have indicated that instructional games contribute to motivation because they provide intrinsic reward and enjoyment (Coleman, 1968; Ernest, 1986; Rakes & Kutzman, 1982). Researchers have reported that instructional games lead to increases in student satisfaction (DeVries & Edwards, 1973; Strauss, 1986). The results of this study support theorists and researchers who have suggested that students enjoy the gaming approach in instruction.

Although our results did suggest that the instructional game had an effect on student motivation, the game used in this study did not have a significant impact on student performance. However, subjects who reported completing an assigned reading performed significantly better and had more confidence about their performance than those who reported that they did not complete the reading. The results may have occurred because of the nature of the reading.

Even though all the students were provided with necessary concepts and information in a lecture, the textbook, *Essentials of Learning for Instruction* (Gagne & Driscoll, 1988), provided readers with practice and feedback in addition to supplementing the lecture. The additional practice and feedback more than likely influenced both the performance and confidence of those who completed the assigned reading.

The findings of this study have some implications for the design of practice. Although many instructional design theorists have indicated that students should be provided with an opportunity to practice newly acquired skills and knowledge, most fail to address how to design practice that is motivational (Salisbury, Richards, & Klein, 1985). The results of this study suggest that instructional designers can provide students with a motivating practice alternative that is as effective as more traditional methods of practice by including a game into instruction. Although using the game to practice did not have an effect on immediate performance in this short-term study, motivating practice alternatives can possibly influence long-term performance because of increased student contact with materials that they find motivational. Future research should investigate the impact of gaming on long-term performance.

The current study also suggests that instructional designers should include reading assignments that provide additional practice in their instruction. The use of those types of readings will not only increase student performance, but also will lead to increases in student confidence about that performance.

As in our study, future research should integrate instructional games into a system to determine if the method has an impact on educational outcomes. Besides using a game as practice, research could be conducted to examine the effect of using a game to present other instructional events, such as stimulating recall of prior knowledge or as a review of learning. Researchers of instructional gaming should continue to investigate the effect of using a game on student motivation and should be specific in their operational definition of motivation. Implementation of our suggestions will assist us in determining how to design practice that is both effective and motivational.

REFERENCES

Abt, C. C. (1968). Games for learning. In S. S. Boocock & E. O. Schild (Eds.), *Simulation games in learning* (pp. 65–84). Beverly Hills, CA: Sage.

Allen, L. E., & Main, D. B. (1976). The effect of instructional gaming on absenteeism: The first step. *Journal for Research in Mathematics Education, 7*(2), 113–128.

Allington, R. L., & Strange, M. (1977). The problem with reading games. *The Reading Teacher, 31,* 272–274.

Andrews, M., & Thorpe, H. W. (1977). A critical analysis of instructional games. *Reading Improvement, 14,* 74–76.

Atkinson, F. D. (1977). Designing simulation/gaming activities: A systems approach. *Educational Technology, 17*(2), 38–43.

Boocock, S. S. (1968). From luxury item to learning tool: An overview of the theoretical literature on games. In S. S. Boocock and E. O. Schild (Eds.), *Simulation games in learning* (pp. 53–64). Beverly Hills, CA: Sage.

Boseman, F. G., & Schellenberger, R. E. (1974). Business gaming: An empirical appraisal. *Simulation & Games, 5,* 383–401.

Bright, G. W. (1980). Game moves as they relate to strategy and knowledge. *Journal of Experimental Education, 48,* 204–209.

Bright, G. W., Harvey, J. G., & Wheeler, M. M. (1979). Using games to retrain skills with basic multiplication facts. *Journal for Research in Mathematics Education, 10,* 103–110.

Brophy, J. (1987). Synthesis of research on strategies for motivating students to learn. *Educational Leadership, 45*(2), 40–48.

Clayton, M., & Rosenbloom, R. (1968). Goals and designs. In S. S. Boocock & E. O. Schild (Eds.), *Simulation games in learning* (pp. 85–92). Beverly Hills, CA: Sage.

Cohen, J. (1969). *Statistical power analysis for the behavioral sciences.* New York: Academic Press.

Coleman, J. S. (1968). Social processes and social simulation games. In S. S. Boocock & E. O. Schild (Eds.), *Simulation games in learning* (pp. 29–51). Beverly Hills, CA: Sage.

Dienes, Z. P. (1962). *An experimental study of mathematics learning.* New York: Hutchinson.

DeVries, D. L., & Edwards, K. L. (1973). Learning games and student teams: Their effects on classroom process. *American Educational Research Journal, 10,* 307–318.

DeVries, D. L., & Slavin, R. E. (1978). Teams-games-tournaments (TGT): Review of ten classroom experiments. *Journal of Research and Development in Education, 12,* 28–37.

Dill, W. R. (1961). The educational effects of management games. In W. R. Dill (Ed.), *Proceeding of the Conference on Business Games as Teaching Devices* (pp. 61–72). New Orleans, LA: Tulane University.

Dill, W. R., & Doppelt, N. (1963). The acquisition of experience in a complex management game. *Management Science, 10,* 30–46.

Ernest, P. (1986). Games: A rationale for their use in the teaching of mathematics in school. *Mathematics in School,* 2–5.

Fletcher, J. L. (1971). The effectiveness of simulation games as learning environments. *Simulation and Games, 2,* 259–286.

Friedlander, A. (1977). The Steeplechase. *Mathematics Teaching, 80,* 37–39.

Gagne, R. M., & Driscoll, M. P. (1988). *Essentials of learning for instruction* (2nd ed.). Englewood Cliffs, NJ: Prentice Hall.

Greenlaw, P. S., & Wyman, F. P. (1973). The teaching effectiveness of games in collegiate business courses. *Simulation & Games, 4,* 259–294.

Jacobs, R. L., & Baum, M. (1987). Simulation and games in training and development. *Simulation & Games, 18,* 385–394.

Keller, J. M. (1983). Motivational design of instruction. In C. M. Reigeluth (Ed.), *Instructional-design theories and models: An overview of their current status* (pp. 386–434). Hillsdale, NJ: Lawrence-Erlbaum.

Keller, J. M. (1987a). Development and use of the ARCS model of instructional design. *Journal of Instructional Development, 10*(3), 2–10.

Keller, J. M. (1987b). *Instructional materials motivation scale (IMMS).* Unpublished manuscript. Florida State University, Tallahassee, FL.

Keller, J. M., & Dodge, B. (1982). *The ARCS model: Motivational strategies for instruction.* Unpublished manuscript. Syracuse University, Syracuse, NY.

Orbach, E. (1979). Simulation games and motivation for learning: A theoretical framework. *Simulation & Games, 10,* 3–40.

Pierfy, D. (1977). Comparative simulation game research: Stumbling blocks and stepping stones. *Simulation & Games, 8,* 255–269.

Raia, A. P. (1966). A study of the educational value of management games. *Journal of Business, 39,* 339–352.

Rakes, T. A., & Kutzman, S. K. (1982). The selection and use of reading games and activities. *Reading Horizons,* 67–70.

Reiser, R. A., & Gerlach, V. S. (1977). Research on simulation games in education: A critical analysis. *Educational Technology, 17*(12), 13–18.

Remus, W. E. (1981). Experimental designs for analyzing data on games. *Simulation & Games, 12,* 3–14.

Rogers, P. J., & Miller, J. V. (1984). Playway mathematics: Theory, practice, and some results. *Educational Research, 26,* 200–207.

Salisbury, D. F., Richards, B. F., & Klein, J. D. (1986). Prescriptions for the design of practice activities for learning. *Journal of Instructional Development, 8*(4), 9–19.

Shubik, M. (1975). *The uses and methods of gaming.* New York: Elsevier.

Shubik, M. (1989). Gaming: Theory and practice, past and future. *Simulation & Games, 20,* 184–189.

Sleet, D. A. (1985). Application of a gaming strategy to improve nutrition education. *Simulation & Games, 16,* 63–70.

Stevens, J. (1986). *Applied multivariate statistics for the social sciences.* Hillsdale, NJ: Lawrence Erlbaum.

Stone, E. F. (1982). *Research design issues in studies assessing the effects of management education.* Paper presented at the National Academy of Management Conference, New York.

Straus, R. A. (1986). Simple games for teaching sociological perspectives. *Teaching Sociology, 14,* 119–128.

Wesson, C., Wilson, R., & Mandlebaum, L. H. (1988). Learning games for active student responding. *Teaching Exceptional Children,* 12–14.

Wolfe, J. (1985). The teaching effectiveness of games in collegiate business courses. *Simulation & Games, 16,* 251–288.

SELF-TEST FOR TASK 11

Y = Yes
N = No
NA = Not applicable
?/X = Can't tell/Don't know

General Evaluation

Introduction

Code

Problem

Is there a statement of the problem? _____

Is the problem "researchable"; that is, can it be investigated through the collection and analysis of data? _____

Is background information on the problem presented? _____

Is the educational significance of the problem discussed? _____

Does the problem statement indicate the variables of interest and the specific relationship between those variables that were investigated? _____

When necessary, are variables directly or operationally defined? _____

Did the researcher have the knowledge and skill to carry out the research? _____

Review of Related Literature

Is the review comprehensive? _____

Are all cited references relevant to the problem under investigation? _____

Are most of the sources primary (i.e., are there only a few or no secondary sources)? _____

Have the references been critically analyzed and the results of various studies compared and contrasted (i.e., is the review more than a series of abstracts or annotations)? _____

Is the relevancy of each reference explained? _____

Is the review well organized? Does it logically flow in such a way that the references least related to the problem are discussed first and those most related are discussed last? _____

Does the review conclude with a summary and interpretation of the literature and its implications for the problem investigated? _____

Do the implications discussed form an empirical or theoretical rationale for the hypotheses that follow?   _____

Are references cited completely and accurately?   _____

Hypotheses

Are specific research questions listed or specific hypotheses stated?   _____

Does each hypothesis state an expected relationship or difference?   _____

If necessary, are variables directly or operationally defined?   _____

Is each hypothesis testable?   _____

Method

Participants

Are the size and major characteristics of the population studied described?   _____

Are the accessible and target populations described?   _____

If a sample was selected, is the method of selecting the sample clearly described?   _____

Does the method of sample selection suggest any limitations or biases in the sample? For example, was stratified sampling used to obtain sample subgroups?   _____

Are the size and major characteristics of the sample described?   _____

Does the sample size meet the suggested guidelines for the minimum sample size appropriate for the method of research represented?   _____

Instruments

Do instruments and their administration meet guidelines for protecting participants? Were needed permissions obtained?   _____

Is a rationale given for the selection of the instruments (or measurements) used?   _____

Are the purpose, content, validity, and reliability of each instrument described?   _____

Are the instruments appropriate for measuring the intended variables?   _____

Does the researcher have the needed skills or experience to construct or administer an instrument?   _____

Is evidence presented that indicates that the instruments are appropriate for the intended sample? For example, is the reading level of an instrument suitable for sample participants?   _____

If appropriate, are subtest reliabilities given?   _____

If an instrument was developed specifically for the study, are the procedures involved in its development and validation described?   _____

If an instrument was developed specifically for the study, are administration, scoring or tabulating, and interpretation procedures fully described?   _____

Was the correct type of instrument used for data collection (or, for
example, was a norm-referenced instrument used when a criterion-
referenced one was more suitable)?   _____

Design and Procedure

Are the design and procedures appropriate for answering the questions
or testing the hypotheses of the study?   _____

Are procedures described in sufficient detail to permit replication
by another researcher?   _____

Do procedures logically relate to one another?   _____

Were instruments and procedures applied correctly?   _____

If a pilot study was conducted, are its execution and results described,
as well as its effect on the subsequent study?   _____

Are control procedures described?   _____

Does the researcher discuss or account for any potentially confounding
variables that he or she was unable to control?   _____

Results

Are appropriate descriptive statistics presented?   _____

Was the probability level, α, at which the results of the tests of
significance were evaluated, specified in advance of data analyses?   _____

If parametric tests were used, is there evidence that the researcher
avoided violating the required assumptions for parametric tests?   _____

Are the described tests of significance appropriate, given the hypotheses
and design of the study?   _____

Was the inductive logic used to produce results in a qualitative
study made explicit?   _____

Are the tests of significance interpreted using the appropriate degrees
of freedom?   _____

Are the results clearly presented?   _____

Are the tables and figures (if any) well organized and easy to understand?   _____

Are the data in each table and figure described in the text?   _____

Discussion (Conclusions and Recommendations)

Is each result discussed in terms of the original hypothesis or topic
to which it relates?   _____

Is each result discussed in terms of its agreement or disagreement
with previous results obtained by other researchers in other studies?   _____

Are generalizations consistent with the results?   _____

Are the possible effects of uncontrolled variables on the results
discussed?   _____

Are theoretical and practical implications of the findings discussed?   _____

Are recommendations for future action made?   _____

Are the suggestions for future action based on practical significance
or on statistical significance only (i.e., has the author avoided confusing
practical and statistical significance)?   _____

Abstract or Summary

Is the problem restated?   _____

Are the number and type of participants and instruments described?   _____

Is the design used identified?   _____

Are procedures described?   _____

Are the major results and conclusions restated?   _____

Type-Specific Evaluation Criteria

Identify and diagram the experimental design used in this study:

Was an appropriate experimental design selected?   _____

Is a rationale for design selection given?   _____

Are sources of invalidity associated with the design identified and
discussed?   _____

Is the method of group formation described?   _____

Was the experimental group formed in the same way as the control group?_____

Were groups randomly formed and the use of existing groups avoided?   _____

Were treatments randomly assigned to groups?   _____

Were critical extraneous variables identified?   _____

Were any control procedures applied to equate groups on extraneous
variables?   _____

Were possible reactive arrangements (e.g., the Hawthorne effect)
controlled for?   _____

Are tables clear and pertinent to the research results?   _____

Are the results generalized to the appropriate group?   _____

Appendix A

Reference Tables

TABLE A.1   Ten thousand random numbers

	00–04	05–09	10–14	15–19	20–24	25–29	30–34	35–39	40–44	45–49
00	54463	22662	65905	70639	79365	67382	29085	69831	47058	08186
01	15389	85205	18850	39226	42249	90669	96325	23248	60933	26927
02	85941	40756	82414	02015	13858	78030	16269	65978	01385	15345
03	61149	69440	11268	88218	58925	03638	52862	62733	33451	77455
04	05219	81619	81619	10651	67079	92511	59888	72095	83463	75577
05	41417	98326	87719	92294	46614	50948	64886	20002	97365	30976
06	28357	94070	20652	35774	16249	75019	21145	15217	47286	76305
07	17783	00015	10806	83091	91530	36466	39981	62481	49177	75779
08	40950	84820	29881	85966	62800	70326	84740	62660	77379	90279
09	82995	64157	66164	41180	10089	41757	78258	96488	88629	37231
10	96754	17676	55659	44105	47361	34833	86679	23930	53249	27083
11	34357	88040	53364	71726	45690	66334	60332	22554	90600	71113
12	06318	37403	49927	57715	50423	67372	63116	48888	21505	80182
13	62111	52820	07243	79931	89292	84767	85693	73947	22278	11551
14	47534	09243	67879	00544	23410	12740	02540	54440	32949	13491
15	98614	75993	84460	62846	59844	14922	49730	73443	48167	34770
16	24856	03648	44898	09351	98795	18644	39765	71058	90368	44104
17	96887	12479	80621	66223	86085	78285	02432	53342	42846	94771
18	90801	21472	42815	77408	37390	76766	52615	32141	30268	18106
19	55165	77312	83666	36028	28420	70219	81369	41943	47366	41067
20	75884	12952	84318	95108	72305	64620	91318	89872	45375	85436
21	16777	37116	58550	42958	21460	43910	01175	87894	81378	10620
22	46230	43877	80207	88877	89380	32992	91380	03164	98656	59337
23	42902	66892	46134	01432	94710	23474	20523	60137	60609	13119
24	81007	00333	39693	28039	10154	95425	39220	19774	31782	49037
25	68089	01122	51111	72373	06902	74373	96199	97017	41273	21546
26	20411	67081	89950	16944	93054	87687	96693	87236	77054	33848
27	58212	13160	06468	15718	82627	76999	05999	58680	96739	63700
28	70577	42866	24969	61210	76046	67699	42054	12696	93758	03283
29	94522	74358	71659	62038	79643	79169	44741	05437	39038	13163
30	42626	86819	85651	88678	17401	03252	99547	32404	17918	62880
31	16051	33763	57194	16752	54450	19031	58580	47629	54132	60631
32	08244	27647	33851	44705	94211	46716	11738	55784	95374	72655
33	59497	04392	09419	89964	51211	04894	72882	17805	21896	83864
34	97155	13428	40293	09985	58434	01412	69124	82171	59058	82859
35	98409	66162	95763	47420	20792	61527	20441	39435	11859	41567
36	45476	84882	65109	96597	25930	66790	65706	61203	53634	22557
37	89300	69700	50741	30329	11658	23166	05400	66669	48708	03887
38	50051	95137	91631	66315	91428	12275	24816	68091	71710	33258
39	31753	85178	31310	89642	98364	02306	24617	09609	83942	22716
40	79152	53829	77250	20190	56535	18760	69942	77448	33278	48805
41	44560	38750	83635	56540	64900	42912	13953	79149	18710	68618
42	68328	83378	63369	71381	39564	05615	42451	64559	97501	65747
43	46939	38689	58625	08342	30459	85863	20781	09284	26333	91777
44	83544	86141	15707	96256	23068	13782	08467	89469	93842	55349
45	91621	00881	04900	54224	46177	55309	17852	27491	89415	23466
46	91896	67126	04151	03795	59077	11848	12630	98375	53068	60142
47	55751	62515	22108	80830	02263	29303	37204	96926	30506	09808
48	85156	87689	95493	88842	00664	55017	55539	17771	69448	87530
49	07521	56898	12236	60277	39102	62315	12239	07105	11844	01117

Source: Reprinted by permission from *Statistical Methods* by George W. Snedecor and William G. Cochran, sixth edition © 1967 by Iowa State University Press, pp. 543–46.

TABLE A.1   *Continued*

	50–54	55–59	60–64	65–69	70–74	75–79	80–84	85–89	90–94	95–99
00	59391	58030	52098	82718	87024	82848	04190	96574	90464	29065
01	99567	76364	77204	04615	27062	96621	43918	01896	83991	51141
02	10363	97518	51400	25670	98342	61891	27101	37855	06235	33316
03	96859	19558	64432	16706	99612	59798	32803	67708	15297	28612
04	11258	24591	36863	55368	31721	94335	34936	02566	80972	08188
05	95068	88628	35911	14530	33020	80428	33936	31855	34334	64865
06	54463	47237	73800	91017	36239	71824	83671	39892	60518	37092
07	16874	62677	57412	13215	31389	62233	80827	73917	82802	84420
08	92494	63157	76593	91316	03505	72389	96363	52887	01087	66091
09	15669	56689	35682	40844	53256	81872	35213	09840	34471	74441
10	99116	75486	84989	23476	52967	67104	39495	39100	17217	74073
11	15696	10703	65178	90637	63110	17622	53988	71087	84148	11670
12	97720	15369	51269	69620	03388	13699	33423	67453	43269	56720
13	11666	13841	71681	98000	35979	39719	81899	07449	47985	46967
14	71628	73130	78783	75691	41632	09847	61547	18707	85489	69944
15	40501	51089	99943	91843	41995	88931	73631	69361	05375	15417
16	22518	55576	98215	82068	10798	86211	36584	67466	69373	40054
17	75112	30485	62173	02132	14878	92879	22281	16783	86352	00077
18	80327	02671	98191	84342	90813	49268	94551	15496	20168	09271
19	60251	45548	02146	05597	48228	81366	34598	72856	66762	17002
20	57430	82270	10421	00540	43648	75888	66049	21511	47676	33444
21	73528	39559	34434	88586	54086	71693	43132	14414	79949	85193
22	25991	65959	70769	64721	86413	33475	42740	06175	82758	66248
23	78388	16638	09134	59980	63806	48472	39318	35434	24057	74739
24	12477	09965	96657	57994	59439	76330	24596	77515	09577	91871
25	83266	32883	42451	15579	38155	29793	40914	65990	16255	17777
26	76970	80876	10237	39515	79152	74798	39357	09054	73579	92359
27	37074	65198	44785	68624	98336	84481	97610	78735	46703	98265
28	83712	06514	30101	78295	54656	85417	43189	60048	72781	72606
29	20287	56862	69727	94443	64936	08366	27227	05158	50326	59566
30	74261	32592	86538	27041	65172	85532	07571	80609	39285	65340
31	64081	49863	08478	96001	18888	14810	70545	89755	59064	07210
32	05617	75818	47750	67814	29575	10526	66192	44464	27058	40467
33	26793	74951	95466	74307	13330	42664	85515	20632	05497	33625
34	65988	72850	48737	54719	52056	01596	03845	35067	03134	70322
35	27366	42271	44300	73399	21105	03280	73457	43093	05192	48657
36	56760	10909	98147	34736	33863	95256	12731	66598	50771	83665
37	72880	43338	93643	58904	59543	23943	11231	83268	65938	81581
38	77888	38100	03062	58103	47961	83841	25878	23746	55903	44115
39	28440	07819	21580	51459	47971	29882	13990	29226	23608	15873
40	63525	94441	77033	12147	51054	49955	58312	76923	96071	05813
41	47606	93410	16359	89033	89696	47231	64498	31776	05383	39902
42	52669	45030	96279	14709	52372	87832	02735	50803	72744	88208
43	16738	60159	07425	62369	07515	82721	37875	71153	21315	00132
44	59348	11695	45751	15865	74739	05572	32688	20271	65128	14551
45	12900	71775	29845	60774	94924	21810	38636	33717	67598	82521
46	75086	23537	49939	33595	13484	97588	28617	17979	70749	35234
47	99495	51534	29181	09993	38190	42553	68922	52125	91077	40197
48	26075	31671	45386	36583	93459	48599	52022	41330	60651	91321
49	13636	93596	23377	51133	95126	61496	42474	45141	46660	42338

TABLE A.1   *Continued*

	00–04	05–09	10–14	15–19	20–24	25–29	30–34	35–39	40–44	45–49
50	64249	63664	39652	40646	97306	31741	07294	84149	46797	82487
51	26538	44249	04050	48174	65570	44072	40192	51153	11397	58212
52	05845	00512	78630	55328	18116	69296	91705	86224	29503	57071
53	74897	68373	67359	51014	33510	83048	17056	72506	82949	54600
54	20872	54570	35017	88132	25730	22626	86723	91691	13191	77212
55	31432	96156	89177	75541	81355	24480	77243	76690	42507	84362
56	66890	61505	01240	00660	05873	13568	76082	79172	57913	93448
57	41894	57790	79970	33106	86904	48119	52503	24130	72824	21627
58	11303	87118	81471	52936	08555	28420	49416	44448	04269	27029
59	54374	57325	16947	45356	78371	10563	97191	53798	12693	27928
60	64852	34421	61046	90849	13966	39810	42699	21753	76192	10508
61	16309	20384	09491	91588	97720	89846	30376	76970	23063	35894
62	42587	37065	24526	72602	57589	98131	37292	05967	26002	51945
63	40177	98590	97161	41682	84533	67588	62036	49967	01990	72308
64	82309	76128	93965	26743	24141	04838	40254	26065	07938	76236
65	79788	68243	59732	04257	27084	14743	17520	94501	55811	76099
66	40538	79000	89559	25026	42274	23489	34502	75508	06059	86682
67	64016	73598	18609	73150	62463	33102	45205	87440	96767	67042
68	49767	12691	17903	93871	99721	79109	09425	26904	07419	76013
69	76974	55108	29795	08404	82684	00497	51126	79935	57450	55671
70	23854	08480	85983	96025	50117	64610	99425	62291	86943	21541
71	68973	70551	25098	78033	98573	79848	31778	29555	61446	23037
72	36444	93600	65350	14971	25325	00427	52073	64280	18847	24768
73	03003	87800	07391	11594	21196	00781	32550	57158	58887	73041
74	17540	26188	36647	78386	04558	61463	57842	90382	77019	24210
75	38916	55809	47982	41968	69760	79422	80154	91486	19180	15100
76	64288	19843	69122	42502	48508	28820	59933	72998	99942	10515
77	86809	51564	38040	39418	49915	19000	58050	16899	79952	57849
78	99800	99566	14742	05028	30033	94889	55381	23656	75787	59223
79	92345	31890	95712	08279	91794	94068	49337	88674	35355	12267
80	90363	65162	32245	82279	79256	80834	06088	99462	56705	06118
81	64437	32242	48431	04835	39070	59702	31508	60935	22390	52246
82	91714	53662	28373	34333	55791	74758	51144	18827	10704	76803
83	20902	17646	31391	31459	33315	03444	55743	74701	58851	27427
84	12217	86007	70371	52281	14510	76094	96579	54853	78339	20839
85	45177	02863	42307	53571	22532	74921	17735	42201	80540	54721
86	28325	90814	08804	52746	47913	54577	47525	77705	95330	21866
87	29019	28776	56116	54791	64604	08815	46049	71186	34650	14994
88	84979	81353	56219	67062	26146	82567	33122	14124	46240	92973
89	50371	26347	48513	63915	11158	25563	91915	18431	92978	11591
90	53422	06825	69711	67950	64716	18003	49581	45378	99878	61130
91	67453	35651	89316	41620	32048	70225	47597	33137	31443	51445
92	07294	85353	74819	23445	68237	07202	99515	62282	53809	26685
93	79544	00302	45338	16015	66613	88968	14595	63836	77716	79596
94	64144	85442	82060	46471	24162	39500	87351	36637	42833	71875
95	90919	11883	58318	00042	52402	28210	34075	33272	00840	73268
96	06670	57353	86275	92276	77591	46924	60839	55437	03183	13191
97	36634	93976	52062	83678	41256	60948	18685	48992	19462	96062
98	75101	72891	85745	67106	26010	62107	60885	37503	55461	71213
99	05112	71222	72654	51583	05228	62056	57390	42746	39272	96659

TABLE A.1 *Continued*

	50–54	55–59	60–64	65–69	70–74	75–79	80–84	85–89	90–94	95–99
50	32847	31282	03345	89593	69214	70381	78285	20054	91018	16742
51	16916	00041	30236	55023	14253	76582	12092	86533	92426	37655
52	66176	34037	21005	27137	03193	48970	64625	22394	39622	79085
53	46299	13335	12180	16861	38043	59292	62675	63631	37020	78195
54	22847	47839	45385	23289	47526	54098	45683	55849	51575	64689
55	41851	54160	92320	69936	34803	92479	33399	71160	64777	83378
56	28444	59497	91586	95917	68553	28639	06455	34174	11130	91994
57	47520	62378	98855	83174	13088	16561	68559	26679	06238	51254
58	34978	63271	13142	82681	05271	08822	06490	44984	49307	61617
59	37404	80416	69035	92980	49486	74378	75610	74976	70056	15478
60	32400	65482	52099	53676	74648	94148	65095	69597	52771	71551
61	89262	86332	51718	70663	11623	29834	79820	73002	84886	03591
62	86866	09127	98021	03871	27789	58444	44832	36505	40672	30180
63	90814	14833	08759	74645	05046	94056	99094	65091	32663	73040
64	19192	82756	20553	58446	55376	88914	75096	26119	83898	43816
65	77585	52593	56612	95766	10019	29531	73064	20953	53523	58136
66	23757	16364	05096	03192	62386	45389	85332	18877	55710	96459
67	45989	96257	23850	26216	23309	21526	07425	50254	19455	29315
68	92970	94243	07316	41467	64837	52406	25225	51553	31220	14032
69	74346	59596	40088	98176	17896	86900	20249	77753	19099	48885
70	87646	41309	27636	45153	29988	94770	07255	70908	05340	99751
71	50099	71038	45146	06146	55211	99429	43169	66259	99786	59180
72	10127	46900	64984	75348	04115	33624	68774	60013	35515	62556
73	67995	81977	18984	64091	02785	27762	42529	97144	80407	64524
74	26304	80217	84934	82657	69291	35397	98714	35104	08187	48109
75	81994	41070	56642	64091	31229	02595	13513	45148	78722	30144
76	59337	34662	79631	89403	65212	09975	06118	86197	58208	16162
77	51228	10937	62396	81460	47331	91403	95007	06047	16846	64809
78	31089	37995	29577	07828	42272	54016	21950	86192	99046	84864
79	38207	97938	93459	75174	79460	55436	57206	87644	21296	43393
80	88666	31142	09474	89712	63153	62333	42212	06140	42594	43671
81	53365	56134	67582	92557	89520	33452	05134	70628	27612	33738
82	89807	74530	38004	90102	11693	90257	05500	79920	62700	43325
83	18682	81038	85662	90915	91631	22223	91588	80774	07716	12548
84	63571	32579	63942	25371	09234	94592	98475	76884	37635	33608
85	68927	56492	67799	95398	77642	54913	91583	08421	81450	76229
86	56401	63186	39389	88798	31356	89235	97036	32341	33292	73757
87	24333	95603	02359	72942	46287	95382	08452	62862	97869	71775
88	17025	84202	95199	62272	06366	16175	97577	99304	41587	03686
89	02804	08253	52133	20224	68034	50865	57868	22343	55111	03607
90	08298	03879	20995	19850	73090	13191	18963	82244	78479	99121
91	59883	01785	82403	96062	03785	03488	12970	64896	38336	30030
92	46982	06682	62864	91837	74021	89094	39952	64158	79614	78235
93	31121	47266	07661	02051	67599	24471	69843	83696	71402	76287
94	97867	56641	63416	17577	30161	87320	37752	73276	48969	41915
95	57364	86746	08415	14621	49430	22311	15836	72492	49372	44103
96	09559	26263	69511	28064	75999	44540	13337	10918	79846	54809
97	53873	55571	00608	42661	91332	63956	74087	59008	47493	99581
98	35531	19162	86406	05299	77511	24311	57257	22826	77555	05941
99	28229	88629	25695	94932	30721	16197	78742	34974	97528	45447

TABLE A.2   Values of the correlation coefficient for different levels of significance

p

df	.10	.05	.01	.001
1	.98769	.99692	.99988	.99999
2	.90000	.95000	.99000	.99900
3	.8054	.8783	.95873	.99116
4	.7293	.8114	.91720	.97406
5	.6694	.7545	.8745	.95074
6	.6215	.7067	.8343	.92493
7	.5822	.6664	.7977	.8982
8	.5494	.6319	.7646	.8721
9	.5214	.6021	.7348	.8471
10	.4973	.5760	.7079	.8233
11	.4762	.5529	.6835	.8010
12	.4575	.5324	.6614	.7800
13	.4409	.5139	.6411	.7603
14	.4259	.4973	.6226	.7420
15	.4124	.4821	.6055	.7246
16	.4000	.4683	.5897	.7084
17	.3887	.4555	.5751	.6932
18	.3783	.4438	.5614	.6787
19	.3687	.4329	.5487	.6652
20	.3598	.4227	.5368	.6524
25	.3233	.3809	.4869	.5974
30	.2960	.3494	.4487	.5541
35	.2746	.3246	.4182	.5189
40	.2573	.3044	.3932	.4896
45	.2428	.2875	.3721	.4648
50	.2306	.2732	.3541	.4433
60	.2108	.2500	.3248	.4078
70	.1954	.2319	.3017	.3799
80	.1829	.2172	.2830	.3568
90	.1726	.2050	.2673	.3375
100	.1638	.1946	.2540	.3211

Source: From R. A. Fisher and F. Yates, *Statistical Tables for Biological, Agricultural and Medical Research* (6th ed.), Pearson Education Limited, copyright © 1974 Longman Group Ltd. Reprinted with permission of Pearson Education Limited.

> **TABLE A.3**   Standard normal curve areas

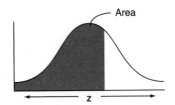

Area

z

z	Area	z	Area	z	Area	z	Area
−3.00	.0013						
−2.99	.0014	−2.64	.0041	−2.29	.0110	−1.94	.0262
−2.98	.0014	−2.63	.0043	−2.28	.0113	−1.93	.0268
−2.97	.0015	−2.62	.0044	−2.27	.0116	−1.92	.0274
−2.96	.0015	−2.61	.0045	−2.26	.0119	−1.91	.0281
−2.95	.0016	−2.60	.0047	−2.25	.0122	−1.90	.0287
−2.94	.0016	−2.59	.0048	−2.24	.0125	−1.89	.0294
−2.93	.0017	−2.58	.0049	−2.23	.0129	−1.88	.0301
−2.92	.0018	−2.57	.0051	−2.22	.0132	−1.87	.0307
−2.91	.0018	−2.56	.0052	−2.21	.0136	−1.86	.0314
−2.90	.0019	−2.55	.0054	−2.20	.0139	−1.85	.0322
−2.89	.0019	−2.54	.0055	−2.19	.0143	−1.84	.0329
−2.88	.0020	−2.53	.0057	−2.18	.0146	−1.83	.0336
−2.87	.0021	−2.52	.0059	−2.17	.0150	−1.82	.0344
−2.86	.0021	−2.51	.0060	−2.16	.0154	−1.81	.0351
−2.85	.0022	−2.50	.0062	−2.15	.0158	−1.80	.0359
−2.84	.0023	−2.49	.0064	−2.14	.0162	−1.79	.0367
−2.83	.0023	−2.48	.0066	−2.13	.0166	−1.78	.0375
−2.82	.0024	−2.47	.0068	−2.12	.0170	−1.77	.0384
−2.81	.0025	−2.46	.0069	−2.11	.0174	−1.76	.0392
−2.80	.0026	−2.45	.0071	−2.10	.0179	−1.75	.0401
−2.79	.0026	−2.44	.0073	−2.09	.0183	−1.74	.0409
−2.78	.0027	−2.43	.0075	−2.08	.0188	−1.73	.0418
−2.77	.0028	−2.42	.0078	−2.07	.0192	−1.72	.0427
−2.76	.0029	−2.41	.0080	−2.06	.0197	−1.71	.0436
−2.75	.0030	−2.40	.0082	−2.05	.0202	−1.70	.0446
−2.74	.0031	−2.39	.0084	−2.04	.0207	−1.69	.0455
−2.73	.0032	−2.38	.0087	−2.03	.0212	−1.68	.0465
−2.72	.0033	−2.37	.0089	−2.02	.0217	−1.67	.0475
−2.71	.0034	−2.36	.0091	−2.01	.0222	−1.66	.0485
−2.70	.0035	−2.35	.0094	−2.00	.0228	−1.65	.0495
−2.69	.0036	−2.34	.0096	−1.99	.0233	−1.64	.0505
−2.68	.0037	−2.33	.0099	−1.98	.0239	−1.63	.0516
−2.67	.0038	−2.32	.0102	−1.97	.0244	−1.62	.0526
−2.66	.0039	−2.31	.0104	−1.96	.0250	−1.61	.0537
−2.65	.0040	−2.30	.0107	−1.95	.0256	−1.60	.0548

TABLE A.3   *Continued*

z	Area	z	Area	z	Area	z	Area
−1.59	.0559	−1.19	.1170	−0.79	.2148	−0.39	.3483
−1.58	.0571	−1.18	.1190	−0.78	.2177	−0.38	.3520
−1.57	.0582	−1.17	.1210	−0.77	.2206	−0.37	.3557
−1.56	.0594	−1.16	.1230	−0.76	.2236	−0.36	.3594
−1.55	.0606	−1.15	.1251	−0.75	.2266	−0.35	.3632
−1.54	.0618	−1.14	.1271	−0.74	.2296	−0.34	.3669
−1.53	.0630	−1.13	.1292	−0.73	.2327	−0.33	.3707
−1.52	.0643	−1.12	.1314	−0.72	.2358	−0.32	.3745
−1.51	.0655	−1.11	.1335	−0.71	.2389	−0.31	.3783
−1.50	.0668	−1.10	.1357	−0.70	.2420	−0.30	.3821
−1.49	.0681	−1.09	.1379	−0.69	.2451	−0.29	.3859
−1.48	.0694	−1.08	.1401	−0.68	.2483	−0.28	.3897
−1.47	.0708	−1.07	.1423	−0.67	.2514	−0.27	.3936
−1.46	.0721	−1.06	.1446	−0.66	.2546	−0.26	.3974
−1.45	.0735	−1.05	.1469	−0.65	.2578	−0.25	.4013
−1.44	.0749	−1.04	.1492	−0.64	.2611	−0.24	.4052
−1.43	.0764	−1.03	.1515	−0.63	.2643	−0.23	.4090
−1.42	.0778	−1.02	.1539	−0.62	.2676	−0.22	.4129
−1.41	.0793	−1.01	.1562	−0.61	.2709	−0.21	.4168
−1.40	.0808	−1.00	.1587	−0.60	.2743	−0.20	.4207
−1.39	.0823	−0.99	.1611	−0.59	.2776	−0.19	.4247
−1.38	.0838	−0.98	.1635	−0.58	.2810	−0.18	.4286
−1.37	.0853	−0.97	.1660	−0.57	.2843	−0.17	.4325
−1.36	.0869	−0.96	.1685	−0.56	.2877	−0.16	.4364
−1.35	.0885	−0.95	.1711	−0.55	.2912	−0.15	.4404
−1.34	.0901	−0.94	.1736	−0.54	.2946	−0.14	.4443
−1.33	.0918	−0.93	.1762	−0.53	.2981	−0.13	.4483
−1.32	.0934	−0.92	.1788	−0.52	.3015	−0.12	.4522
−1.31	.0951	−0.91	.1814	−0.51	.3050	−0.11	.4562
−1.30	.0968	−0.90	.1841	−0.50	.3085	−0.10	.4602
−1.29	.0985	−0.89	.1867	−0.49	.3121	−0.09	.4641
−1.28	.1003	−0.88	.1894	−0.48	.3156	−0.08	.4681
−1.27	.1020	−0.87	.1922	−0.47	.3192	−0.07	.4721
−1.26	.1038	−0.86	.1949	−0.46	.3228	−0.06	.4761
−1.25	.1056	−0.85	.1977	−0.45	.3264	−0.05	.4801
−1.24	.1075	−0.84	.2005	−0.44	.3300	−0.04	.4840
−1.23	.1093	−0.83	.2033	−0.43	.3336	−0.03	.4880
−1.22	.1112	−0.82	.2061	−0.42	.3372	−0.02	.4920
−1.21	.1131	−0.81	.2090	−0.41	.3409	−0.01	.4960
−1.20	.1151	−0.80	.2119	−0.40	.3446	0.00	.5000

TABLE A.3 *Continued*

z	Area	z	Area	z	Area	z	Area
0.01	.5040	0.41	.6591	0.81	.7910	1.21	.8869
0.02	.5080	0.42	.6628	0.82	.7939	1.22	.8888
0.03	.5120	0.43	.6664	0.83	.7967	1.23	.8907
0.04	.5160	0.44	.6700	0.84	.7995	1.24	.8925
0.05	.5199	0.45	.6736	0.85	.8023	1.25	.8944
0.06	.5239	0.46	.6772	0.86	.8051	1.26	.8962
0.07	.5279	0.47	.6808	0.87	.8078	1.27	.8980
0.08	.5319	0.48	.6844	0.88	.8106	1.28	.8997
0.09	.5359	0.49	.6879	0.89	.8133	1.29	.9015
0.10	.5398	0.50	.6915	0.90	.8159	1.30	.9032
0.11	.5438	0.51	.6950	0.91	.8186	1.31	.9049
0.12	.5478	0.52	.6985	0.92	.8212	1.32	.9066
0.13	.5517	0.53	.7019	0.93	.8238	1.33	.9082
0.14	.5557	0.54	.7054	0.94	.8264	1.34	.9099
0.15	.5596	0.55	.7088	0.95	.8289	1.35	.9115
0.16	.5636	0.56	.7123	0.96	.8315	1.36	.9131
0.17	.5675	0.57	.7157	0.97	.8340	1.37	.9147
0.18	.5714	0.58	.7190	0.98	.8365	1.38	.9162
0.19	.5753	0.59	.7224	0.99	.8389	1.39	.9177
0.20	.5793	0.60	.7257	1.00	.8413	1.40	.9192
0.21	.5832	0.61	.7291	1.01	.8438	1.41	.9207
0.22	.5871	0.62	.7324	1.02	.8461	1.42	.9222
0.23	.5910	0.63	.7357	1.03	.8485	1.43	.9236
0.24	.5948	0.64	.7389	1.04	.8508	1.44	.9251
0.25	.5987	0.65	.7422	1.05	.8531	1.45	.9265
0.26	.6026	0.66	.7454	1.06	.8554	1.46	.9279
0.27	.6064	0.67	.7486	1.07	.8577	1.47	.9292
0.28	.6103	0.68	.7517	1.08	.8599	1.48	.9306
0.29	.6141	0.69	.7549	1.09	.8621	1.49	.9319
0.30	.6179	0.70	.7580	1.10	.8643	1.50	.9332
0.31	.6217	0.71	.7611	1.11	.8665	1.51	.9345
0.32	.6255	0.72	.7642	1.12	.8686	1.52	.9357
0.33	.6293	0.73	.7673	1.13	.8708	1.53	.9370
0.34	.6331	0.74	.7704	1.14	.8729	1.54	.9382
0.35	.6368	0.75	.7734	1.15	.8749	1.55	.9394
0.36	.6406	0.76	.7764	1.16	.8770	1.56	.9406
0.37	.6443	0.77	.7794	1.17	.8790	1.57	.9418
0.38	.6480	0.78	.7823	1.18	.8810	1.58	.9429
0.39	.6517	0.79	.7852	1.19	.8830	1.59	.9441
0.40	.6554	0.80	.7881	1.20	.8849	1.60	.9452

TABLE A.3   *Continued*

z	Area	z	Area	z	Area	z	Area
1.61	.9463	1.96	.9750	2.31	.9896	2.66	.9961
1.62	.9474	1.97	.9756	2.32	.9898	2.67	.9962
1.63	.9484	1.98	.9761	2.33	.9901	2.68	.9963
1.64	.9495	1.99	.9767	2.34	.9904	2.69	.9964
1.65	.9505	2.00	.9772	2.35	.9906	2.70	.9965
1.66	.9515	2.01	.9778	2.36	.9909	2.71	.9966
1.67	.9525	2.02	.9783	2.37	.9911	2.72	.9967
1.68	.9535	2.03	.9788	2.38	.9913	2.73	.9968
1.69	.9545	2.04	.9793	2.39	.9916	2.74	.9969
1.70	.9554	2.05	.9798	2.40	.9918	2.75	.9970
1.71	.9564	2.06	.9803	2.41	.9920	2.76	.9971
1.72	.9573	2.07	.9808	2.42	.9922	2.77	.9972
1.73	.9582	2.08	.9812	2.43	.9925	2.78	.9973
1.74	.9591	2.09	.9817	2.44	.9927	2.79	.9974
1.75	.9599	2.10	.9821	2.45	.9929	2.80	.9974
1.76	.9608	2.11	.9826	2.46	.9931	2.81	.9975
1.77	.9616	2.12	.9830	2.47	.9932	2.82	.9976
1.78	.9625	2.13	.9834	2.48	.9934	2.83	.9977
1.79	.9633	2.14	.9838	2.49	.9936	2.84	.9977
1.80	.9641	2.15	.9842	2.50	.9938	2.85	.9978
1.81	.9649	2.16	.9846	2.51	.9940	2.86	.9979
1.82	.9656	2.17	.9850	2.52	.9941	2.87	.9979
1.83	.9664	2.18	.9854	2.53	.9943	2.88	.9980
1.84	.9671	2.19	.9857	2.54	.9945	2.89	.9981
1.85	.9678	2.20	.9861	2.55	.9946	2.90	.9981
1.86	.9686	2.21	.9864	2.56	.9948	2.91	.9982
1.87	.9693	2.22	.9868	2.57	.9949	2.92	.9982
1.88	.9699	2.23	.9871	2.58	.9951	2.93	.9983
1.89	.9706	2.24	.9875	2.59	.9952	2.94	.9984
1.90	.9713	2.25	.9878	2.60	.9953	2.95	.9984
1.91	.9719	2.26	.9881	2.61	.9955	2.96	.9985
1.92	.9726	2.27	.9884	2.62	.9956	2.97	.9985
1.93	.9732	2.28	.9887	2.63	.9957	2.98	.9986
1.94	.9738	2.29	.9890	2.64	.9959	2.99	.9986
1.95	.9744	2.30	.9893	2.65	.9960	3.00	.9987

TABLE A.4 Distribution of t

df	PROBABILITY					
	.20	.10	.05	.02	.01	.001
1	3.078	6.314	12.706	31.821	63.657	636.619
2	1.886	2.920	4.303	6.965	9.925	31.598
3	1.638	2.353	3.182	4.541	5.841	12.941
4	1.533	2.132	2.776	3.747	4.604	8.610
5	1.476	2.015	2.571	3.365	4.032	6.859
6	1.440	1.943	2.447	3.143	3.707	5.959
7	1.415	1.895	2.365	2.998	3.499	5.405
8	1.397	1.860	2.306	2.896	3.355	5.041
9	1.383	1.833	2.262	2.821	3.250	4.781
10	1.372	1.812	2.228	2.764	3.169	4.587
11	1.363	1.796	2.201	2.718	3.106	4.437
12	1.356	1.782	2.179	2.681	3.055	4.318
13	1.350	1.771	2.160	2.650	3.012	4.221
14	1.345	1.761	2.145	2.624	2.977	4.140
15	1.341	1.753	2.131	2.602	2.947	4.073
16	1.337	1.746	2.120	2.583	2.921	4.015
17	1.333	1.740	2.110	2.567	2.898	3.965
18	1.330	1.734	2.101	2.552	2.878	3.922
19	1.328	1.729	2.093	2.539	2.861	3.883
20	1.325	1.725	2.086	2.528	2.845	3.850
21	1.323	1.721	2.080	2.518	2.831	3.819
22	1.321	1.717	2.074	2.508	2.819	3.792
23	1.319	1.714	2.069	2.500	2.807	3.767
24	1.318	1.711	2.064	2.492	2.797	3.745
25	1.316	1.708	2.060	2.485	2.787	3.725
26	1.315	1.706	2.056	2.479	2.779	3.707
27	1.314	1.703	2.052	2.473	2.771	3.690
28	1.313	1.701	2.048	2.467	2.763	3.674
29	1.311	1.699	2.045	2.462	2.756	3.659
30	1.310	1.697	2.042	2.457	2.750	3.646
40	1.303	1.684	2.021	2.423	2.704	3.551
60	1.296	1.671	2.000	2.390	2.660	3.460
120	1.289	1.658	1.980	2.358	2.617	3.373
∞	1.282	1.645	1.960	2.326	2.576	3.291

Source: R. A. Fisher and F. Yates, Statistical Tables for Biological, Agricultural and Medical Research (6th ed.), Pearson Education Limited, copyright © 1974 Longman Group Ltd. Reprinted with permission of Pearson Education Limited.

TABLE A.5	Distribution of F

$p = .10$

	n_1*					
n_2**	1	2	3	4	5	6
4	4.54	4.32	4.19	4.11	4.05	4.01
5	4.06	3.78	3.62	3.52	3.45	3.40
6	3.78	3.46	3.29	3.18	3.11	3.05
7	3.59	3.26	3.07	2.96	2.88	2.83
8	3.46	3.11	2.92	2.81	2.73	2.67
9	3.36	3.01	2.81	2.69	2.61	2.55
10	3.28	2.92	2.73	2.61	2.52	2.46
11	3.23	2.86	2.66	2.54	2.45	2.39
12	3.18	2.81	2.61	2.48	2.39	2.33
13	3.14	2.76	2.56	2.43	2.35	2.28
14	3.10	2.73	2.52	2.39	2.31	2.24
15	3.07	2.70	2.49	2.36	2.27	2.21
16	3.05	2.67	2.46	2.33	2.24	2.18
17	3.03	2.64	2.44	2.31	2.22	2.15
18	3.01	2.62	2.42	2.29	2.20	2.13
19	2.99	2.61	2.40	2.27	2.18	2.11
20	2.97	2.59	2.38	2.25	2.16	2.09
21	2.96	2.57	2.36	2.23	2.14	2.08
22	2.95	2.56	2.35	2.22	2.13	2.06
23	2.94	2.55	2.34	2.21	2.11	2.05
24	2.93	2.54	2.33	2.19	2.10	2.04
25	2.92	2.53	2.32	2.18	2.09	2.02
26	2.91	2.52	2.31	2.17	2.08	2.01
27	2.90	2.51	2.30	2.17	2.07	2.00
28	2.89	2.50	2.29	2.16	2.06	2.00
29	2.89	2.50	2.28	2.15	2.06	1.99
30	2.88	2.49	2.28	2.14	2.05	1.98
40	2.84	2.44	2.23	2.09	2.00	1.93
60	2.79	2.39	2.18	2.04	1.95	1.87
120	2.75	2.35	2.13	1.99	1.90	1.82
∞	2.71	2.30	2.08	1.94	1.85	1.77

*n_1 = degrees of freedom for the mean square between
**n_2 = degrees of freedom for the mean square within

Source: From R. A. Fisher and F. Yates, *Statistical Tables for Biological, Agricultural and Medical Research* (6th ed.), Pearson Education Limited, copyright © 1974 Longman Group Ltd. Reprinted with permission of Pearson Education Limited.

TABLE A.5 Continued

$p = .05$

	n_1*					
n_2**	1	2	3	4	5	6
4	7.71	6.94	6.59	6.39	6.26	6.16
5	6.61	5.79	5.41	5.19	5.05	4.95
6	5.99	5.14	4.76	4.53	4.39	4.28
7	5.59	4.74	4.35	4.12	3.97	3.87
8	5.32	4.46	4.07	3.84	3.69	3.58
9	5.12	4.26	3.86	3.63	3.48	3.37
10	4.96	4.10	3.71	3.48	3.33	3.22
11	4.84	3.98	3.59	3.36	3.20	3.09
12	4.75	3.88	3.49	3.26	3.11	3.00
13	4.67	3.80	3.41	3.18	3.02	2.92
14	4.60	3.74	3.34	3.11	2.96	2.85
15	4.54	3.68	3.29	3.06	2.90	2.79
16	4.49	3.63	3.24	3.01	2.85	2.74
17	4.45	3.59	3.20	2.96	2.81	2.70
18	4.41	3.55	3.16	2.93	2.77	2.66
19	4.38	3.52	3.13	2.90	2.74	2.63
20	4.35	3.49	3.10	2.87	2.71	2.60
21	4.32	3.47	3.07	2.84	2.68	2.57
22	4.30	3.44	3.05	2.82	2.66	2.55
23	4.28	3.42	3.03	2.80	2.64	2.53
24	4.26	3.40	3.01	2.78	2.62	2.51
25	4.24	3.38	2.99	2.76	2.60	2.49
26	4.22	3.37	2.98	2.74	2.59	2.47
27	4.21	3.35	2.96	2.73	2.57	2.46
28	4.20	3.34	2.95	2.71	2.56	2.44
29	4.18	3.33	2.93	2.70	2.54	2.43
30	4.17	3.32	2.92	2.69	2.53	2.42
40	4.08	3.23	2.84	2.61	2.45	2.34
60	4.00	3.15	2.76	2.52	2.37	2.25
120	3.92	3.07	2.68	2.45	2.29	2.17
∞	3.84	2.99	2.60	2.37	2.21	2.10

*n_1 = degrees of freedom for the mean square between
**n_2 = degrees of freedom for the mean square within

TABLE A.5   *Continued*

$p = .01$

n_2**	\multicolumn{6}{c}{n_1*}
	1	2	3	4	5	6
4	21.20	18.00	16.69	15.98	15.52	15.21
5	16.26	13.27	12.06	11.39	10.97	10.67
6	13.74	10.92	9.78	9.15	8.75	8.47
7	12.25	9.55	8.45	7.85	7.46	7.19
8	11.26	8.65	7.59	7.01	6.63	6.37
9	10.56	8.02	6.99	6.42	6.06	5.80
10	10.04	7.56	6.55	5.99	5.64	5.39
11	9.65	7.20	6.22	5.67	5.32	5.07
12	9.33	6.93	5.95	5.41	5.06	4.82
13	9.07	6.70	5.74	5.20	4.86	4.62
14	8.86	6.51	5.56	5.03	4.69	4.46
15	8.68	6.36	5.42	4.89	4.56	4.32
16	8.53	6.23	5.29	4.77	4.44	4.20
17	8.40	6.11	5.18	4.67	4.34	4.10
18	8.28	6.01	5.09	4.58	4.25	4.01
19	8.18	5.93	5.01	4.50	4.17	3.94
20	8.10	5.85	4.94	4.43	4.10	3.87
21	8.02	5.78	4.87	4.37	4.04	3.81
22	7.94	5.72	4.82	4.31	3.99	3.76
23	7.88	5.66	4.76	4.26	3.94	3.71
24	7.82	5.61	4.72	4.22	3.90	3.67
25	7.77	5.57	4.68	4.18	3.86	3.63
26	7.72	5.53	4.64	4.14	3.82	3.59
27	7.68	5.49	4.60	4.11	3.78	3.56
28	7.64	5.45	4.57	4.07	3.75	3.53
29	7.60	5.42	4.54	4.04	3.73	3.50
30	7.56	5.39	4.51	4.02	3.70	3.47
40	7.31	5.18	4.31	3.83	3.51	3.29
60	7.08	4.98	4.13	3.65	3.34	3.12
120	6.85	4.79	3.95	3.48	3.17	2.96
∞	6.64	4.60	3.78	3.32	3.02	2.80

*n_1 = degrees of freedom for the mean square between
**n_2 = degrees of freedom for the mean square within

TABLE A.5 *Continued*

$p = .001$

n_2^{**}	n_1^*					
	1	2	3	4	5	6
4	74.14	61.25	56.18	53.44	51.71	50.53
5	47.18	37.12	33.20	31.09	29.75	28.84
6	35.51	27.00	23.70	21.92	20.81	20.03
7	29.25	21.69	18.77	17.19	16.21	15.52
8	25.42	18.49	15.83	14.39	13.49	12.86
9	22.86	16.39	13.90	12.56	11.71	11.13
10	21.04	14.91	12.55	11.28	10.48	9.92
11	19.69	13.81	11.56	10.35	9.58	9.05
12	18.64	12.97	10.80	9.63	8.89	8.38
13	17.81	12.31	10.21	9.07	8.35	7.86
14	17.14	11.78	9.73	8.62	7.92	7.43
15	16.59	11.34	9.34	8.25	7.57	7.09
16	16.12	10.97	9.00	7.94	7.27	6.81
17	15.72	10.66	8.73	7.68	7.02	6.56
18	15.38	10.39	8.49	7.46	6.81	6.35
19	15.08	10.16	8.28	7.26	6.62	6.18
20	14.82	9.95	8.10	7.10	6.46	6.02
21	14.59	9.77	7.94	6.95	6.32	5.88
22	14.38	9.61	7.80	6.81	6.19	5.76
23	14.19	9.47	7.67	6.69	6.08	5.65
24	14.03	9.34	7.55	6.59	5.98	5.55
25	13.88	9.22	7.45	6.49	5.88	5.46
26	13.74	9.12	7.36	6.41	5.80	5.38
27	13.61	9.02	7.27	6.33	5.73	5.31
28	13.50	8.93	7.19	6.25	5.66	5.24
29	13.39	8.85	7.12	6.19	5.59	5.18
30	13.29	8.77	7.05	6.12	5.53	5.12
40	12.61	8.25	6.60	5.70	5.13	4.73
60	11.97	7.76	6.17	5.31	4.76	4.37
120	11.38	7.32	5.79	4.95	4.42	4.04
∞	10.83	6.91	5.42	4.62	4.10	3.74

$^*n_1$ = degrees of freedom for the mean square between
$^{**}n_2$ = degrees of freedom for the mean square within

TABLE A.6   Distribution of χ^2

df	.10	.05	.01	.001
1	2.706	3.841	6.635	10.827
2	4.605	5.991	9.210	13.815
3	6.251	7.815	11.345	16.266
4	7.779	9.488	13.277	18.467
5	9.236	11.070	15.086	20.515
6	10.645	12.592	16.812	22.457
7	12.017	14.067	18.475	24.322
8	13.362	15.507	20.090	26.125
9	14.684	16.919	21.666	27.877
10	15.987	18.307	23.209	29.588
11	17.275	19.675	24.725	31.264
12	18.549	21.026	26.217	32.909
13	19.812	22.362	27.688	34.528
14	21.064	23.685	29.141	36.123
15	22.307	24.996	30.578	37.697
16	23.542	26.296	32.000	39.252
17	24.769	27.587	33.409	40.790
18	25.989	28.869	34.805	42.312
19	27.204	30.144	36.191	43.820
20	28.412	31.410	37.566	45.315
21	29.615	32.671	38.932	46.797
22	30.813	33.924	40.289	48.268
23	32.007	35.172	41.638	49.728
24	33.196	36.415	42.980	51.179
25	34.382	37.652	44.314	52.620
26	35.563	38.885	45.642	54.052
27	36.741	40.113	46.963	55.476
28	37.916	41.337	48.278	56.893
29	39.087	42.557	49.588	58.302
30	40.256	43.773	50.892	59.703
32	42.585	46.194	53.486	62.487
34	44.903	48.602	56.061	65.247
36	47.212	50.999	58.619	67.985
38	49.513	53.384	61.162	70.703
40	51.805	55.759	63.691	73.402
42	54.090	58.124	66.206	76.084
44	56.369	60.481	68.710	78.750
46	58.641	62.830	71.201	81.400
48	60.907	65.171	73.683	84.037
50	63.167	67.505	76.154	86.661

Source: From R. A. Fisher and F. Yates, *Statistical Tables for Biological, Agricultural and Medical Research* (6th ed.), Pearson Education Limited, copyright © 1974 Longman Group Ltd. Reprinted with permission of Pearson Education Limited.

Appendix B

Math Review

Name: _____   Date: _____

Worksheet 1: MATH REVIEW: ORDER OF OPERATIONS

RIDDLE: Why did the bored man cut a hole in the carpet?

Directions: To find the answer to the riddle, write the answers to the problems on the lines. The letter in the solution section beside the answer to the first problem is the first letter in the answer to the riddle, the letter beside the answer to the second problem is the second letter, and so on.

1. 5 x 10 + 6 x 2 = _____

2. 3 + 4 x 9 = _____

3. (9 + 28) x 6 = _____

4. 159 − 66 x 2 = _____

5. 15 x 14 − 8 x 20 = _____

6. 19 − 5 + 2 x 3 = _____

7. 70 − 5 x 3 x 4 = _____

8. 6 + 8 x 1 x 5 = _____

9. 33/1 + 1 x 3 = _____

10. 8/4 + (6)(0) = _____

11. 169/(12 + 1) = _____

12. (2 + 3 + 4)/3 = _____

13. (2 + 18)/(9 − 5) = _____

14. (1 + 5)(3) + (7)(2) = _____

15. (9 + 9)(10 − 1)(2) = _____

16. (15 − 4)(21/7)(63 − 59) = _____

17. (3)(1)(1) + (6/2)(9) = _____

SOLUTION SECTION:

112(B)	62(T)	39(O)	10(H)	780(Y)	222(S)	3(O)
2(L)	63(A)	27(E)	177(Z)	186(X)	13(O)	5(R)
32(S)	50(E)	4,040(D)	20(T)	46(E)	30(W)	70(F)
132(O)	102(K)	36(F)	324(H)	187(B)	1(J)	48(I)

Write the answer to the riddle here, putting one letter on each line:

___ ___   ___ ___ ___   ___ ___ ___ ___

___ ___ ___ ___ ___ ___   ___ ___ ___ ___ ___ ___

Source: Reprinted by permission from *Statistics With a Sense of Humor: A Humorous Workbook and Guide to Study Skills* by Fred Pyrczak, Publisher, P.O. Box 39731, Los Angeles, CA 90039.

Name: _____   Date: _____

Worksheet 2: MATH REVIEW: NEGATIVES

RIDDLE: What did the owner of the wreck of a car say about the noise it makes?

Directions: To find the answer to the riddle, write the answers to the problems on the lines. The word in the solution section beside the answer to the first problem is the first word in the answer to the riddle, the word beside the answer to the second problem is the second word, and so on.

1. (−10)(−2) = _____
2. (−5)(47) = _____
3. (6)(−16) = _____
4. 15/−3 = _____
5. −144/12 = _____
6. −169/−13 = _____

7. 19 + −3 = _____
8. −28 + −28 = _____
9. −88 + 18 = _____
10. 15 − −15 = _____
11. −29 − 14 = _____
12. −30 − −29 = _____

13. (−15)(−33) = _____
14. (−11)(44) = _____
15. −2178/33 = _____
16. 188 + −99 = _____
17. −279 + −188 = _____
18. −399 − 59 = _____

SOLUTION SECTION:

−20(GARAGE)   235(TWO)   340(SKY)   20(THERE'S)   −96(ONE)
−235(ONLY)   96(ROAD)   −56(THAT)   −70(DOESN'T)   −1(SORT)
−458(HORN)   −467(THE)   5(IS)   −12(ON)   −5(THING)   13(MY)
−13(USE)   16(CAR)   12(BE)   30(MAKE)   0(FIX)   22(BUS)
495(OF)   −484(NOISE)   56(AN)   −66(AND)   70(TRANSPORTATION)
89(THAT'S)   −43(SOME)   −15(ALWAYS)   −59(HIGHWAY)
−495(MECHANIC)   66(BROKEN)   484(STRANDED)   467(FREEWAY)

Write the answer to the riddle here, putting one word on each line:

_____ _____ _____ _____ _____ _____

_____ _____ _____ _____ _____ _____

_____ _____ _____ _____ _____ _____

Name: _____   Date: _____

Worksheet 3: MATH REVIEW: ROUNDING

RIDDLE: What did the psychologist put on a sign in her office to make her patients pay?

Directions: To find the answer to the riddle, write the answers to the problems on the lines. The word in the solution beside the answer to the first problem is the first word in the answer to the riddle, the word beside the answer to the second problem is the second word, and so on.

Round as usual except when rounding off a number ending in a five (5). If the number immediately preceding a five is odd, round up. If the number immediately preceding a five is even, round down. Another way to state this principle is: "round to the nearest even number all numbers ending in 5." For example, 4.85 rounds to 4.8; 4.75 rounds to 4.8. Notice, however, that 4.851, which ends in a value greater than "5," rounds to 4.9.

1. Round 10.543 to the nearest hundredth: _____

2. Round 8.67 to the nearest tenth: _____

3. Round 8.4 to the nearest whole number: _____

4. Round 9.8452 to the nearest thousandth: _____

5. Round 15.839 to the nearest tenth: _____

6. Round 29.5 to the nearest whole number: _____

7. Round 15.86 to the nearest tenth: _____

8. Round 3.945 to the nearest hundredth: _____

9. Round 8.45 to the nearest tenth: _____

10. Round 10.555555 to the nearest hundredth: _____

SOLUTION SECTION:

29(CRAZY)   15.9(THE)   8.7(THE)   30(PAY)   3.95(AM)   8(AMNESIA)

10.56(ADVANCE)   8.4(IN)   8.5(ONLY)   3.94(PSYCHOLOGIST)   15.8(MUST)

9845(IS)   15.4(BILL)   9.85(HELPS)   9.846(NEVER)   10(LOVING)

9.845(PATIENTS)   9(LIFE)   10.54(ALL)   10.5(COUNSELING)   4(DISTURBED)

Write the answer to the riddle here, putting one word on each line:

_____   _____   _____   _____   _____   _____

_____   _____   _____

Name: _____   Date: _____

Worksheet 4: MATH REVIEW: DECIMALS

RIDDLE: What did the bore do to help the party?

Directions: To find the answer to the riddle, write the answers to the problems on the lines. The letter in the solution section beside the answer to the first problem is the first letter in the answer to the riddle, the letter beside the answer to the second problem is the second letter, and so on.

   If an answer has more than two decimal places, round to two.

1. 0.02 multiplied by 1 = _____

2. 1.1 multiplied by 1.11 = _____

3. 5.999 multiplied by 0 = _____

4. 3.77 multiplied by 4.69 = _____

5. 12.4 divided into 169.38 = _____

6. 15.9 divided by 1 = _____

7. 12.1 plus 99.98 = _____

8. 3.11 plus 8.99 = _____

9. 18.3 subtracted from 25.46 = _____

10. 10.01 minus 8.873 = _____

SOLUTION SECTION:

1.22(E)	0.2(C)	0.14(X)	7.16(M)	71.6(D)	0(W)
6.00(K)	2.11(F)	0.02(H)	112.08(H)	101.19(P)	
15.9(T)	1.59(B)	13.66(N)	1.21(J)	17.68(E)	
1.366(G)	12.10(O)	0.177(R)	1.14(E)	1.111(S)	

Write the answer to the riddle here, putting one letter on each line:

___ ___   ___ ___ ___ ___   ___ ___ ___ ___

Name: _____ Date: _____

Worksheet 5: MATH REVIEW: FRACTIONS AND DECIMALS

RIDDLE: Why should you respect the lily?

Directions: To find the answer to the riddle, write the answers to the problems on the lines. The word in the solution section beside the answer to the first problem is the first word in the answer to the riddle, the word beside the answer to the second problem is the second word, and so on. Express fractions in lowest terms.

1. $1/5 + 3/5 =$ _____

2. $1/5 + 1/10 =$ _____

3. $3/9 - 1/9 =$ _____

4. $1 - 7/8 =$ _____

5. $2/3 \times 2/3 =$ _____

6. $2/5 \times 4/7 =$ _____

7. $2/9$ divided by $1/9 =$ _____

8. 5 divided into $2/3 =$ _____

9. What is the decimal equivalent of $1/2$? = _____

10. What is the decimal equivalent of $3/4$? = _____

11. What is the decimal equivalent of 2 and $2/3$? = _____

12. What is the decimal equivalent of 2 and $3/4$? = _____

13. What is the decimal equivalent of 2 and $1/10$? = _____

14. What fraction corresponds to 0.2? = _____

15. What fraction corresponds to 0.11? = _____

16. What fraction corresponds to 0.555? = _____

SOLUTION SECTION:

4/5(NEVER)   2/5(SEE)   3/10(LOOK)   11/20(IS)   0.5(DAY)

0.55(FLOWERS)   2/3(FLORIST)   4/9(A)   2/9(DOWN)   2.1(LOOK)

1/5(DOWN)   11/100(ON)   2/35(CLEAN)   8/35(LILY)   1/8(ON)

2/81(HOPE)   2(BECAUSE)   2/15(ONE)   0.75(A)   2.67(LILY)

2.75(WILL)   111/200(YOU)   8/8(EASTER)   3 1/3(BEAUTIFUL)

Write the answer to the riddle here, putting one word on each line:

_____ _____ _____ _____ _____ _____ _____ _____

_____ _____ _____ _____ _____ _____ _____ _____

Name: _____   Date: _____

Worksheet 6: MATH REVIEW: ALGEBRAIC MANIPULATIONS

RIDDLE: When do actors and actresses get stage fright?

Directions: To find the answer to the riddle, write "T" for "true" or "F" for "false" on the line to the left of each statement. The word at the end of the first true statement is the first word in the answer to the riddle, the word at the end of the second true statement is the second word, and so on.

All variables are distinct from one another; that is, no variable equals any other variable.

_____ 1. If $A = C/D$, then $C = (A)(D)$ (WHEN)

_____ 2. If $A = C/D$, then $D = C/A$ (THEY)

_____ 3. If $P/B = F$, then $P = F/B$ (GET)

_____ 4. If $X + Y = 10$, then $X = 10 - Y$ (SEE)

_____ 5. If $25 = A + B$, then $A = 25 - B$ (AN)

_____ 6. If $X + 25 = W$, then $X = W + 25$ (CURTAIN)

_____ 7. If $A = C - D$, then $D = C + A$ (APPLAUSE)

_____ 8. If $A - D = F$, then $A = F + D$ (EGG)

_____ 9. If $A = F - G - H$, then $F = A - G - H$ (STAGE)

_____ 10. If $(B)(C) = P$, then $B = P/C$ (OR)

_____ 11. If $Y = (B)(F)$, then $B = F/Y$ (SCRIPT)

_____ 12. If $X = (N)(B)(C)$, then $B = X/(N)(C)$ (A)

_____ 13. If $X + Y = B - C$, then $B = X + (Y)(C)$ (VOICE)

_____ 14 If $(B)(Y) = (X)(C)$, then $C = (B)(Y)/X$ (TOMATO)

Write in the answer to the riddle here, putting one word on each line:

_____   _____   _____   _____   _____   _____

_____   _____

CONCISE KEY

Worksheet 1: 1. 62, 2. 39, 3. 222, 4. 27, 5. 50, 6. 20, 7. 10, 8. 46, 9. 36, 10. 2, 11. 13, 12. 3, 13. 5, 14. 32, 15. 324, 16. 132, 17. 30   The answer to the riddle is: "To see the floor show."

Worksheet 2: 1. 20, 2. –235, 3. –96, 4. –5, 5. –12, 6. 13, 7. 16, 8. –56, 9. –70, 10. 30, 11. –43, 12. –1, 13. 495, 14. –484, 15. –66, 16. 89, 17. –467, 18. –458   The answer to the riddle is: "There's only one thing on my car that doesn't make some sort of noise and that's the horn."

Worksheet 3: 1. 10.54, 2. 8.7, 3. 8, 4. 9.845, 5. 15.8, 6. 30, 7. 15.9, 8. 3.94, 9. 8.4, 10. 10.56   The answer to the riddle is: "All the amnesia patients must pay the psychologist in advance."

Worksheet 4: 1. 0.02, 2. 1.22, 3. 0, 4. 17.68, 5. 13.66, 6. 15.9, 7. 112.08, 8. 12.10, 9. 7.16, 10. 1.14   The answer to the riddle is: "He went home."

Worksheet 5: 1. 4/5, 2. 3/10, 3. 2/9, 4. 1/8, 5. 4/9, 6. 8/35, 7. 2, 8. 2/15, 9. 0.5, 10. 0.75, 11. 2.67, 12. 2.75, 13. 2.1, 14. 1/5, 15. 11/100, 16. 111/200   The answer to the riddle is: "Never look down on a lily because one day a lily will look down on you."

Worksheet 6: 1. T, 2. T, 3. F, 4. T, 5. T, 6. F, 7. F, 8. T, 9. F, 10. T, 11. F, 12. T, 13. F, 14. T   The answer to the riddle is: "When they see an egg or a tomato."

:: STEP-BY-STEP KEY
Worksheet 1

Order of operations: Do all work inside parentheses first. Perform multiplication and division before performing addition and subtraction.

1. $5 \times 10 + 6 \times 2$
   $= 50 + 12$
   $= 62$

2. $3 + 4 \times 9$
   $= 3 + 36$
   $= 39$

3. $(9 + 28) \times 6$
   $= 37 \times 6$
   $= 222$

4. $159 - 66 \times 2$
   $= 159 - 132$
   $= 27$

5. $15 \times 14 - 8 \times 20$
   $= 210 - 160$
   $= 50$

6. $19 - 5 + 2 \times 3$
   $= 19 - 5 + 6$
   $= 14 + 6$
   $= 20$

7. $70 - 5 \times 3 \times 4$
   $= 70 - 15 \times 4$
   $= 70 - 60$
   $= 10$

8. $6 + 8 \times 1 \times 5$
   $= 6 + 8 \times 5$
   $= 6 + 40$
   $= 46$

9. $33/1 + 1 \times 3$
   $= 33 + 3$
   $= 36$

10. $8/4 + (6)(0)$
    $= 8/4 + 0$
    $= 2 + 0$
    $= 2$

11. $169/(12 + 1)$
    $= 169/13$
    $= 13$

12. $(2 + 3 + 4)/3$
    $= 9/3$
    $= 3$

13. $(2 + 18)/(9 - 5)$
    $= 20/4$
    $= 5$

14. $(1 + 5)(3) + (7)(2)$
    $= (6)(3) + (7)(2)$
    $= 18 + 14$
    $= 32$

15. $(9 + 9)(10 - 1)(2)$
    $= (18)(9)(2)$
    $= (162)(2)$
    $= 324$

16. $(15 - 4)(21/7)(63 - 59)$
    $= (11)(3)(4)$
    $= (33)(4)$
    $= 132$

17. $(3)(1)(1) + (6/2)(9)$
    $= 3 + (3)(9)$
    $= 3 + 27$
    $= 30$

Worksheet 2

Rules follow for working with positive and negative numbers.

Multiplication

When a negative number is multiplied by a positive number, the result is negative. When two negative numbers are multiplied, the result is positive.

1. $(-10)(-2) = 20$ 2. $(-5)(47) = -235$ 3. $(6)(-16) = -96$

Division

When two numbers with the same sign are divided, the result is positive. When two numbers with opposite signs are divided, the result is negative.

4. $15/-3 = -5$ 5. $-144/12 = -12$ 6. $-169/-13 = 13$

Addition

When numbers all have the same sign, add as usual. When numbers have different signs, first add all positive numbers together, then add all negative numbers together, and then subtract the negative sum from the positive sum.

7. $19 + -3 = 16$ 8. $-28 + -28 = -56$ 9. $-88 + 18 = -70$

Subtraction

When subtracting negative numbers, change the sign of the number being subtracted, then add:

10. $15 - -15 = 30$ 11. $-29 - 14 = -43$ 12. $-30 - -29 = -1$

For items 13 through 18, follow the rules given above.

13. 495   14. -484 15. -66 16. 89   17. -467 18. -458

Worksheet 3

See the directions on Worksheet 3 for rules on rounding numbers that end in five (5).

1. Read 10.543 as 10.5(tenths)4(hundredths)3(thousandths); therefore, to the nearest hundredth, 10.543 rounds to 10.54.
2. Read 8.67 as 8.6(tenths)7(hundredths); therefore, to the nearest tenth, 8.67 rounds to 8.7.
3. Read 8.4 as 8(whole number, ones place).4(tenths); therefore, to the nearest whole number, 8.4 rounds to 8.
4. Read 9.8452 as 9.8(tenths)4(hundredths)5(thousandths)2(ten thousandths); therefore, to the nearest thousandth, 9.8452 rounds to 9.845.
5. 15.839, to the nearest tenth, rounds to 15.8.
6. Because 29.5 ends in 5, round to the nearest even number, which is 30.
7. 15.86 rounds to 15.9.
8. Because 3.945 ends in 5, round to the nearest even number, which is 3.94. (Notice that the "4" in the hundredths place is even.)
9. Because 8.45 ends in 5, round to the nearest even number, which is 8.4. (Notice that the "4" in the tenths place is even.)

10. Beyond the hundredths place are four 5's. Therefore, at the point at which you are rounding, the number does not end in "5"; it ends in "5555," which is greater than 5. Therefore, 10.555555, to the nearest hundredth, rounds to 10.56.

Worksheet 4

1. When multiplying, the answer has the total number of decimal places as the total number in the two multipliers. Since 0.02×1 has a total of two digits to the right of the decimal place, the answer is 0.02, which also has two digits to the right.
2. 1.1×1.11 has three digits to the right; therefore, the answer is 1.221, which rounds to 1.22.
3. Any number multiplied by zero equals zero.
4. (See explanation for item 1.) $3.77 \times 4.69 = 17.6813$ (four decimal places), which rounds to 17.68.
5. When dividing with a calculator, enter the numbers as shown. When dividing by hand, first move the decimal place in the divisor to the far right. (In this case, change 12.4 to 124.) Then, move the decimal place in 169.38 the same number of places to the right, changing 169.38 to 1693.8. Then divide as usual. The answer is $13.660 = 13.66$.
6. (See explanation for item 5. Notice the difference between "divided into" and "divided by." This wording usually is not used in textbooks, but your instructor may use it in lectures.) The answer is 15.9. (Notice that division by one has no effect.)
7. Before adding, line up the decimal places one above the other and then add.

$$\begin{array}{r} 12.1 \\ +99.98 \\ \hline 112.08 \end{array}$$

8. (See explanation for item 7.) The answer is 12.10.
9. Before subtracting, line up the decimal places one above the other and then subtract.

$$\begin{array}{r} 25.46 \\ -18.3 \\ \hline 7.16 \end{array}$$

10. (See explanation for number 9. Notice the difference between "subtracted from" and "minus.")

$$\begin{array}{r} 10.01 \\ -8.873 \\ \hline 1.137 \end{array}$$, which rounds to 1.14

Worksheet 5

(General note: For most beginning students, it is best to convert fractions to their decimal equivalents as soon as permitted under the rules of mathematics. For example, to convert $\frac{1}{5}$, divide 1 by 5, which yields 0.2. This is desirable because most calculators will not allow you to operate directly on fractions. In addition, it is conventional to report statistics with their decimal equivalents for fractional parts.

   Knowledge of fractions is important for understanding the meaning of certain statistics and for understanding their derivations, however.)

1. When adding fractions with a common denominator (same denominator), add the numerators and retain the common denominator. Thus, $\frac{1}{5} + \frac{3}{5} = \frac{4}{5}$.

2. When adding fractions with unlike denominators, first convert so that they both have the same denominator. In this case, by multiplying both the numerator and denominator of $\frac{1}{5}$ by 2, the equivalent fraction of $\frac{2}{10}$ is obtained. Then follow the instructions for item 1. Thus, $\frac{2}{10} + \frac{1}{10} = \frac{3}{10}$.

3. When subtracting fractions with a common denominator, subtract the numerators and retain the common denominator. Thus, $\frac{3}{9} - \frac{1}{9} = \frac{2}{9}$.

4. When subtracting a fraction from a whole number, first convert the whole number to a fractional equivalent with the same denominator. In this case, $1 = \frac{8}{8}$. Thus, $\frac{8}{8} - \frac{7}{8} = \frac{1}{8}$.

5. When multiplying fractions, multiply the numerators, then multiply the denominators. For example, $\frac{2}{3} \times \frac{2}{3} = \frac{4}{9}$.

6. (See the explanation for item number 5.) The answer is $\frac{8}{35}$.

7. To divide one fraction by another, invert the divisor (i.e., $\frac{1}{9}$ becomes $\frac{9}{1}$). Then multiply: $\frac{2}{9} \times \frac{9}{1} = \frac{18}{9}$. To simplify when the numerator is evenly divisible by the denominator, divide the denominator into the numerator: 18 divided by 9 = 2, which is the answer.

8. (See the explanation for item 7.) Note the difference in wording of items 7 and 8. In this case, 5 is the divisor; when inverted, it becomes $\frac{1}{5}$. Thus, $\frac{2}{3} \times \frac{1}{5} = \frac{2}{15}$.

9. To find the decimal equivalent of a fraction, divide the numerator by the denominator. In this case, divide 1 by 2, which yields an answer of 0.5.

10. (See the explanation for item 9.) The answer is 0.75.

11. To find the decimal equivalent of a mixed number (i.e., a whole number plus a fractional part), retain the whole number and convert the fractional part as described in the explanation for item 9. In this case, 2 and $\frac{2}{3}$ becomes 2 and .666, which rounds to 2.67.

12. (See the explanation for item 11.) The answer is 2.75.

13. (See the explanation for item 11.) The answer is 2.1.

14. Note that 0.2 is read as "two tenths." Therefore, it is equivalent to $\frac{2}{10}$. Since both the numerator and denominator are evenly divisible by 2, divide both by 2, which yields $\frac{1}{5}$, which is the answer expressed in lowest terms.

15. Note that 0.11 is read as "eleven one hundredths." Therefore, the answer is expressed as $\frac{11}{100}$.

16. Note that 0.555 is read as "five hundred fifty-five one thousandths." Therefore, it is equivalent to $\frac{555}{1000}$. Since 5 will divide evenly into both the numerator and denominator, simplify by division. This gives an answer of $\frac{111}{200}$.

Worksheet 6

1. If $A = \frac{C}{D}$, then $C = (A)(D)$
$A = \frac{C}{D}$
$\frac{C}{D} = A$
$(\frac{C}{D})(D) = (A)(D)$
$C = (A)(D)$
Therefore, the statement is true.

2. If $A = \frac{C}{D}$, then $D = \frac{C}{A}$
$A = \frac{C}{D}$
$(A)(D) = (\frac{C}{D})(D)$
$(A)(D) = C$
$\frac{(A)(D)}{A} = \frac{C}{A}$
$D = \frac{C}{A}$
Therefore, the statement is true.

3. If $\frac{P}{B} = F$, then $P = \frac{F}{B}$
$\frac{P}{B} = F$
$(\frac{P}{B})(B) = (F)(B)$
$P = (F)(B)$
Therefore, the statement is false.

4. If $X + Y = 10$, then $X = 10 - Y$
$X + Y = 10$
$X + Y - Y = 10 - Y$
$X = 10 - Y$
Therefore, the statement is true.

5. If $25 = A + B$, then $A = 25 - B$
$25 = A + B$
$A + B = 25$
$A + B - B = 25 - B$
$A = 25 - B$
Therefore, the statement is true.

6. If $X + 25 = W$, then $X = W + 25$
$X + 25 = W$
$X + 25 - 25 = W - 25$
$X = W - 25$
Therefore, the statement is false.

7. If $A = C - D$, then $D = C + A$
$A = C - D$
$A + D = C - D + D$
$A + D = C$
$A + D - A = C - A$
$D = C - A$
Therefore, the statement is false.

8. If $A - D = F$, then $A = F + D$
$A - D = F$
$A - D + D = F + D$
$A = F + D$
Therefore, the statement is true.

9. If $A = F - G - H$, then
$F = A - G - H$
$A = F - G - H$
$F - G - H = A$
$F - G - H + G = A + G$
$F - H = A + G$
$F - H + H = A + G + H$
$F = A + G + H$
Therefore, the statement is false.

10. If $(B)(C) = P$, then $B = \frac{P}{C}$
$(B)(C) = P$
$\frac{(B)(C)}{C} = \frac{P}{C}$
$B = \frac{P}{C}$
Therefore, the statement is true.

11. If $Y = (B)(F)$, then $B = \frac{F}{Y}$
$Y = (B)(F)$
$(B)(F) = Y$
$\frac{(B)(F)}{F} = \frac{Y}{F}$
$B = \frac{Y}{F}$
Therefore, the statement is false.

12. If $X = (N)(B)(C)$, then $B = \frac{X}{(N)(C)}$
$X = (N)(B)(C)$
$(N)(B)(C) = X$
$\frac{(N)(B)(C)}{(N)(C)} = \frac{X}{(N)(C)}$
$B = \frac{X}{(N)(C)}$
Therefore, the statement is true.

13. If $X + Y = B - C$, then $B = X + (Y)(C)$
$X + Y = B - C$
$B - C = X + Y$
$B - C + C = X + Y + C$
$B = X + Y + C$
Therefore, the statement is false.

14. If $(B)(Y) = (X)(C)$, then $C = \frac{(B)(Y)}{X}$
$(B)(Y) = (X)(C)$
$(X)(C) = (B)(Y)$
$\frac{(X)(C)}{X} = \frac{(B)(Y)}{X}$
$C = \frac{(B)(Y)}{X}$
Therefore, the statement is true.

Appendix C

Suggested Responses

Self-Test for Task 1a (page 20)

Motivational Effects on Test Scores of Elementary Students (page 21)

Topic Studied.   The purpose of this study was to determine the effect of experimentally manipulated motivational conditions on elementary students' mathematical scores.

The Procedures.   Pairs of normal, heterogeneous classes at each grade level (3, 4, 6, 7 and 8) from each of three public schools were randomly chosen to participate; classes were selected for experimental and control conditions by a flip of a coin (i.e., one class of each pair became an experimental group and the other a control group). Form 7 of the Mathematics Concepts subtest of the Iowa Tests of Basic Skills (ITBS) was the measuring instrument. Prior to taking the test, all students were given the instructions from the ITBS test manual. Experimental students were also read a brief motivational script on the importance of doing well. All participating teachers were trained to administer the test, and experimental teachers were given additional training regarding the script (e.g., read it exactly as it is written).

The Method of Analysis.   An analysis of variance was run (on test scores) to test the effects of the experimental and normal (control) conditions (as well as several other variables).

The Major Conclusion.   Students asked to try especially hard did considerably better than those who were given the usual standardized test instructions only.

Self-Test for Task 1b (page 20)

A Really Good Art Teacher Would Be Like You, Mrs. C.: A Qualitative Study of a Teacher and Her Artistically Gifted Middle School Students (page 25)

Topic Studied.   The purpose of this study is to expand comprehension of *teacher effectiveness* through the in-depth study of a teacher and her artistically gifted students.

The Procedures.   The participants studied included one teacher and 26 artistically gifted sixth, seventh, and eighth graders in a middle school, members of an existing gifted art program; students had previously been formally screened. The researcher was a participant observer, interacting with students and the teacher weekly during two semesters and several summer school class sessions. Primary data collection included informal interviews, photographing and recording class interactions on audio- and videotape, and gathering slides, photos, and videos of artwork as well as class artifacts that served as secondary sources. The researcher focused on social interactions among participants and on studying the teacher's curriculum and effectiveness as a translator of the art world to her students.

The Method of Analysis. Transcripts from audio- and videotapes and field notes were analyzed using constant comparison method of analysis, producing codes and patterns. In addition, 7 graduate and undergraduate art education students rated interaction behaviors in 5 selected video clips, producing codes that were compared with the researcher's codes for the same clips, which reflected an inter-rater reliability of .91. Theoretical memos were written during analysis and linkages were found between patterns. The codes, patterns, and linkages were triangulated with interview and secondary data information and scanned for disconfirming data.

The Major Conclusion. The study described how students learned about art processes and identified themselves as real artists through substantive, effective teaching.

Self-Test for Task 1c (page 20)

1. Research Approach: Action research. Action research studies focus on ways teachers can improve their practice.
2. Research Approach: Descriptive research. Descriptive research involves collecting data to answer questions about the current status of issues or topics; a questionnaire was administered to find out how teachers feel about an issue.
3. Research Approach: Correlational research. Correlational research seeks to determine whether, and to what degree, a statistical relationship exists between two or more variables. Here, the researchers are interested in the similarity of the two tests.
4. Research Approach: Causal–comparative research. In causal–comparative research, at least two groups (fifth graders from single-parent families and those from two-parent families) are compared on a dependent variable or effect (in this case, achievement of reading).
5. Research Approach: Experimental research. Experimental research allows researchers to make cause–effect statements about a study. In addition, researchers have a great deal of control over the study; here the researchers determined the two groups (at random) and applied different treatments (the two methods of conflict resolution) to the two groups.
6. Research Approach: Ethnographic research. Ethnographic research studies participants in their natural culture or setting; the culture of recent Armenian emigrants is examined in their new setting.

Self-Test for Task 11 (pages 556–559)

Effects of Using an Instructional Game on Motivation and Performance

General Evaluation Criteria

INTRODUCTION

Problem	CODE
A statement?	Y
Paragraph (¶)7, sentence (S)1[1]	
Researchable?	Y
Background information?	Y
e.g., ¶2	
Significance discussed?	Y
e.g., ¶1	
Variables and relationships discussed?	Y
Definitions?	Y
e.g., ¶7, S3	
Researcher knowledgeable?	Y

Review of Related Literature	
Comprehensive?	?/X
Appears to be	
References relevant?	Y
Sources primary?	Y
Critical analysis?	Y
e.g., ¶6	
Relevance of each reference explained?	Y
Well organized?	Y
Summary?	N
Rationale for hypotheses?	N
References complete and accurate?	Y

Hypotheses	
Questions or hypotheses?	Y
¶7, S6 & 7	
Expected differences stated?	Y
Variables defined?	Y
Testable?	Y

METHOD

Participants	CODE
Population described?	Y&N
Very briefly.	
Accessible and target populations described?	Y
Sample selection method described?	NA
Selection method "good"?	NA
Sample described?	Y&N
Size, yes; characteristics, no	

---

[1] ¶7 refers to paragraph 7 of the introduction section of the article. The introduction section ends where "Method" begins.

	CODE
Minimum sizes?.	Y
$n^1 = 37; n^2 = 38$.	

Instruments

Guidelines met for protecting participants? Permissions obtained?.	?/X
Rationale for selection?.	N
Instrument described?.	Y
¶6 & 7	
Validity discussed?.	N
Reliability discussed?.	Y
¶6 & 7	
Appropriate?.	Y
Researcher skilled in test construction, administration?.	Y
Evidence that it is appropriate for sample?.	N
Subtest reliabilities?.	Y
¶6	
Procedures for development described?.	N
Performance posttest not described	
Administration, scoring, and interpretation procedures described?.	N
Type of instrument correct?.	Y

Design and Procedure

Design appropriate?.	Y
Procedures sufficiently detailed?.	Y
Procedures logically related?.	Y
Instruments and procedures applied correctly?.	Y
Pilot study described?.	NA
Control procedures described?.	Y
e.g., ¶9	
Confounding variables discussed?.	Y
e.g., ¶10, S2	

RESULTS

Appropriate descriptive statistics?.	Y
Table 1	
Probability level specified in advance?.	Y
e.g., ¶1	
Parametric assumptions not violated?.	Y
Tests of significance appropriate?.	Y or ?/X
Inductive logic explicit?.	NA
Appropriate degrees of freedom?.	Y or ?/X
Results clearly presented?.	Y
Tables and figures well organized?.	Y
Data in each table and figure described?.	Y

DISCUSSION (CONCLUSIONS AND RECOMMENDATIONS)

Results discussed in terms of hypothesis?.	Y
Results discussed in terms of previous research?.	Y
e.g., ¶3	
Generalizations consistent with results?.	Y
e.g., ¶1	

	CODE
Effects of uncontrolled variables discussed?	Y
e.g., ¶2	
Implications discussed?	Y
e.g., ¶7	
Recommendations for action?	Y
e.g., ¶8	
Suggestions based on practical significance?	Y
Effect sizes were presented under Results, ¶2, S4 & 5	

ABSTRACT (OR SUMMARY)

Problem restated?	Y
Participants and instruments described?	Y&N
Participants briefly; instruments indirectly	
Design identified?	Y
Not named, but described	
Procedures?	Y
Results and conclusions?	Y

Type-Specific Evaluation Criteria

Design used:
Basically a posttest-only control group design. The independent variable was type of practice.

$$R \qquad X_1O \qquad X_1 = \text{game}$$
$$R \qquad X_2O \qquad X_2 = \text{worksheet}$$
$$O = \text{Motivation scale performance posttest}$$

Because of the inclusion of a second, unmanipulated independent variable, completion versus noncompletion of reading assignment, the design was a 2 × 2 factorial design, based on a posttest-only control group design.

Design appropriate?	Y
Design selection rationale?	N
Invalidity discussed?	N
But mortality was not a problem	
Group formation described?	Y
Random assignment	
Groups formed in same way?	Y
Groups randomly formed?	Y
Treatments randomly assigned?	?/X
Extraneous variables described?	Y
e.g., ¶6, S3–5	
Groups equated?	N
Reactive arrangements controlled for?	N
But discussed, under Discussion, ¶2, S3–6	
Tables clear and pertinent?	Y
Results generalized to appropriate group?	Y

Glossary

A-B design A single-subject design in which baseline measurements are repeatedly made until stability is presumably established, treatment is introduced, and an appropriate number of measurements are made during treatment.

A-B-A design A single-subject design in which baseline measurements are repeatedly made until stability is presumably established, treatment is introduced, an appropriate number of measurements are made, and the treatment phase is followed by a second baseline phase.

A-B-A-B design A single-subject design in which baseline measurements are repeatedly made until stability is presumably established, treatment is introduced, an appropriate number of measurements are made, and the treatment phase is followed by a second baseline phase, which is followed by a second treatment phase.

abstract A summary of a study that describes its most important hypotheses, procedures, and conclusions.

accessible population The population from which the researcher can realistically select subjects. *Also called* available population. *Compare* target population.

accidental sampling *See* convenience sampling.

achievement test An instrument that measures an individual's current proficiency in given areas of knowledge or skill.

action research Any systematic inquiry conducted by teachers, principals, school counselors, or other stakeholders in the teaching–learning environment, to gather information about the ways in which their particular schools operate, the teachers teach, and the students learn.

additive design Any of the variations of A-B design that involve the addition of another phase or phases in which the experimental treatment is supplemented with another treatment.

affective characteristic A mental characteristic related to emotion, such as attitude, interest, and value.

affective test An assessment designed to measure mental characteristics related to emotion.

alternating treatments design A variation of multiple-baseline design that involves the relatively rapid alternation of treatments for a single participant. *Also called* multiple schedule design, multi-element baseline design, multi-element manipulation design, *or* simultaneous treatment design.

alternative assessment *See* performance assessment.

alternative-forms reliability *See* equivalence.

analysis of covariance A statistical method of equating groups on one or more variables and for increasing the power of a statistical test; adjusts scores on a dependent variable for initial differences on some other variable (e.g., pretest performance or IQ) related to performance on the dependent variable.

analysis of narrative In narrative research, the development of a collection of stories and the search for themes in order to develop general knowledge about the collection of stories. *Compare* narrative analysis.

analysis of variance An inferential statistics technique used to determine if there is a significant difference among the means of three or more data groups.

anonymity State of being unknown; what study participants have when their identities are kept hidden from the researcher.

applied research Research conducted for the purpose of applying, or testing, a theory to determine its usefulness in solving practical problems.

aptitude test A measure of potential used to predict how well an individual is likely to perform in a future situation.

artificial categories Categories that are operationally defined by a researcher.

assessment General term for the process of collecting, synthesizing, and interpreting information; also, the instrument used for such purposes. A test is a type of assessment.

assumption Any important fact presumed to be true but not actually verified; assumptions should be described in the procedure section of a research plan or report.

attenuation The reduction in correlation coefficients that tends to occur if the measures being correlated have low reliability.

attitude scale A measurement instrument used to determine what a respondent believes, perceives, or feels about self, others, activities, institutions, or situations.

attrition *See* mortality.

authentic assessment *See* performance assessment.

available population *See* accessible population.

baseline measures Multiple measures of pretest performance conducted in single-subject research designs to control for sources of invalidity.

basic research Research conducted for the purpose of developing or refining a theory.

bias Distortion of research data that renders the data suspect or invalid; may occur due to characteristics of the researcher, the respondent, or the research design itself.

Buckley Amendment *See* Family Educational Rights and Privacy Act of 1974.

case study The in-depth investigation of one unit (e.g., individual, group, institution, organization, program, or document).

category A classification of ideas and concepts in qualitative data analysis.

causal–comparative research Research that attempts to determine the cause, or reason, for existing differences in the behavior or status of groups of individuals. *Also called* ex post facto research.

census survey Descriptive research that attempts to acquire data from each and every member of a population.

changing criterion design A variation of the A-B-A design in which the baseline phase is followed by successive treatment phases, each of which has a more stringent criterion for acceptable (improved) behavior.

chi square A nonparametric test of significance appropriate when the data are in the form of frequency counts; compares proportions actually observed in a study with expected proportions to see if they are significantly different.

clinical replication The development and application of a treatment package, composed of two or more interventions that have been found to be effective individually, designed for persons with complex behavior disorders.

closed-ended item *See* structured item.

cluster Any location that contains an intact group of similar characteristics (population members).

cluster sampling Sampling in which intact groups, not individuals, are randomly selected.

coding The process of categorically marking or referencing units of text (e.g., words, sentences, paragraphs, and quotations) with codes and labels as a way to indicate patterns and meaning in qualitative data.

coefficient alpha (α) *See* Cronbach's alpha.

cognitive characteristic A mental characteristic related to intellect, such as mathematics achievement, literacy, reasoning, or problem solving.

cognitive test An assessment designed to measure intellectual processes.

common variance The variation in one variable that is attributable to its tendency to vary with another variable. *Also called* shared variance.

compensatory rivalry *See* John Henry effect.

concurrent validity The degree to which the scores on a test are related to the scores on a similar, preexisting test administered in the same time frame or to some other valid measure available at the same time; a form of criterion-related validity.

confidentiality Right to have information about oneself kept private; what researchers protect when they know the identities of study participants but do not disclose that information.

consequential validity The extent to which an instrument creates harmful effects for the user.

construct An abstraction that cannot be observed directly; a concept invented to explain behavior.

construct validity The degree to which a test measures an intended hypothetical construct, or nonobservable trait, that explains behavior.

content validity The degree to which a test measures an intended content area; it is determined by expert judgment and requires both item validity and sampling validity.

control Efforts on the part of a researcher to remove the influence of any variable other than the independent variable that might affect performance on a dependent variable.

control group The group in a research study that either receives a different treatment than the experimental group or is treated as usual.

control variable A nonmanipulated variable, usually a physical or mental characteristic of the subjects (such as IQ).

convenience sampling The process of using as the sample whoever happens to be available (e.g., volunteers). *Also called* accidental sampling *or* haphazard sampling.

correlation A quantitative measure of the degree of correspondence between two or more variables.

correlation coefficient A decimal number between -1.00 and $+1.00$ that indicates the degree to which two variables are related.

correlational research Research that involves collecting data to determine whether, and to what degree, a relationship exists between two or more quantifiable variables.

counterbalanced design A quasi-experimental design in which all groups receive all treatments, each group receives the treatments in a different order, the number of groups equals the number of treatments, and all groups are posttested after each treatment.

credibility A term used in qualitative research to indicate that the topic was accurately identified and described.

criterion In a prediction study or analysis of concurrent or predictive validity, the variable that is predicted.

criterion variable *See* dependent variable.

criterion-referenced scoring A scoring approach in which an individual's performance on an assessment is compared to a predetermined, external standard.

criterion-related validity Validity that is determined by relating performance on a test to performance on another criterion (e.g., a second test or measure); includes concurrent and predictive validity.

critical action research A type of action research in which the goal is liberating individuals through knowledge gathering. *Also called* emancipatory action research.

critical ethnography A highly politicized form of ethnography written by a researcher in order to advocate against inequalities and domination of particular groups that exist in society.

Cronbach's alpha (α) The general formula for estimating internal consistency based on a determination of how all items on a test relate to all other items and to the total test. The Kuder-Richardson 20 (KR-20) is a special case of the Cronbach's alpha general formula. *Also called* coefficient alpha *or* Cronbach's coefficient alpha.

Cronbach's coefficient alpha *See* Cronbach's alpha.

cross-sectional survey A survey in which data are collected from selected individuals in a single time period. *Compare* longitudinal survey.

cross-validation Validation of a prediction equation with at least one group other than the group on which it was developed; results in the removal from the equation of variables no longer found to be related to the criterion measure.

culture The set of attitudes, values, concepts, beliefs and practices shared by members of a group; a central construct in ethnographic research.

curvilinear relationship A relationship in which an increase in one variable is associated with a corresponding increase in another variable to a point, at which a further increase in the first variable results in a corresponding decrease in the other variable (or vice versa); represented graphically as a curve.

data *(sing.* datum*)* Pieces of information.

data analysis In qualitative research, an attempt by a researcher to summarize data, collected for a study, in a dependable and accurate manner; usually involves coding and finding patterns or themes in narrative data. *Compare* data interpretation.

data interpretation In qualitative research, an attempt by a researcher to find meaning in the data collected for a study. *Compare* data analysis.

data saturation A point in qualitative research when so much data are collected that it is very unlikely that additional data will add to what is already collected.

database A sortable, analyzable collection of units of information maintained on a computer.

deductive hypothesis A hypothesis derived from theory that provides evidence which supports, expands, or contradicts the theory.

deductive reasoning Reasoning that involves developing specific predictions based on general principles, observations, or experiences.

dependent variable The change or difference in a behavior or characteristic that occurs as a result of the independent variable. *Also called* criterion variable, effect, outcome, *or* posttest.

descriptive research Research that determines and describes the way things are; involves collecting numerical data to test hypotheses or answer questions about the current subject of study. *Also called* survey research.

descriptive statistics Data analysis techniques that enable a researcher to meaningfully describe many pieces of data with a small number of numerical indices.

descriptive validity The degree to which qualitative research is factually accurate.

design A general strategy or plan for conducting a research study; indicates the study's basic structure and goals.

developmental survey A study concerned with behavior variables that differentiate children at different levels of age, growth, or maturation.

diagnostic test A type of achievement test that yields multiple scores for each area of achievement measured in order to facilitate identification of a student's weak and strong areas.

Dialectic Action Research Spiral A four-step process for conducting action research: (1) identifying an area of focus, (2) data collection, (3) data analysis and interpretation, and (4) action planning.

differential selection of subjects Selection of subjects who have differences at the start of a study that may at least partially account for differences found on a posttest; a threat to internal validity.

direct replication Replication of a study by the same investigator, with the same subjects or with different subjects, in a specific setting.

directional hypothesis A research hypothesis that states the expected direction of the relationship or difference between variables.

ecological validity *See* external validity.

educational research The formal, systematic application of the scientific method to the study of educational problems.

environmental variable A variable in the setting of a study (e.g., learning materials) that might cause unwanted differences between groups.

equivalence The degree to which two similar forms of a test produce similar scores from a single group of test takers. *Also called* equivalent-forms reliability or alternate-forms reliability.

equivalent-forms reliability *See* equivalence.

ethnographic case study A form of ethnography that focuses on describing the activities of a specific group and the shared patterns of behavior it develops over time.

ethnographic research The study of the cultural patterns and perspectives of participants in their natural setting; a form of qualitative research. *Also called* ethnography.

ethnography Ethnographic research; also, the narrative produced as the result of such research.

ethnomethodolgy A qualitative approach that studies how participants make sense of everyday activities to act in a social way.

evaluation research The systematic process of collecting and analyzing data on the quality, effectiveness, merit, or value of programs, products, or practices for the purpose of making decisions about those programs, products, or practices.

evaluative validity The degree to which a qualitative researcher is able to present data objectively, without being evaluative or judgmental.

experimental group The group in a research study that typically receives the new treatment under investigation.

experimental research Research in which at least one independent variable is manipulated, other relevant variables are controlled, and the effect on one or more dependent variables is observed.

experimental variable *See* independent variable.

experimenter bias A situation in which a researcher's expectations of study results actually contribute to producing various outcomes.

experimenter effects Threats to an experiment's external validity from the researcher's unintentional or intentional influences on participants or on study procedures.

ex post facto research *See* causal–comparative research.

external observation *See* nonparticipant observation.

external validity The degree to which results are generalizable, or applicable, to groups and environments outside the experimental setting. *Also called* ecological validity.

F ratio A computation used in analyses of variance to determine whether variances among sample means are significant.

face validity The degree to which a test appears to measure what it claims to measure.

factorial analysis of variance A statistical technique that allows the researcher to determine the effect of the independent variable and the control variable on the dependent variable both separately and in combination. It is the appropriate statistical analysis if a study is based on a factorial design and investigates two or more independent variables and the interactions between them; yields a separate F ratio for each independent variable and one for each interaction.

factorial design Any experimental design that involves two or more independent variables (at least one of which is manipulated) in order to study the effects of the variables individually and in interaction with each other.

Family Educational Rights and Privacy Act of 1974 Federal law that protects the privacy of student educational records. *Also called* Buckley Amendment.

field notes Qualitative research material gathered, recorded, and compiled (usually on-site) during the course of a study.

field-oriented research *See* qualitative research.

fieldwork Qualitative data collection; involves spending considerable time in the setting under study, immersing oneself in this setting, and collecting as much relevant information as possible as unobtrusively as possible.

formative evaluation Evaluation whose function is to form and improve a program or product under development so that weaknesses that can be remedied during implementation.

generalizability The applicability of research findings to settings and contexts different from the one in which they were obtained.

grading on the curve *See* norm-referenced scoring.

grounded theory A qualitative approach in which the researcher focuses on how an individually derived theory about a phenomenon is grounded in the data in a particular setting.

halo effect The phenomenon whereby initial impressions concerning an individual (positive or negative) affect subsequent measurements.

haphazard sampling *See* convenience sampling.

Hawthorne effect A type of reactive arrangement resulting from the subjects' knowledge that they are involved in an experiment or their feeling that they are in some way receiving special attention.

historical research A qualitative approach in which the researcher focuses on collecting and evaluating data in order to understand and interpret past events.

history Any event occurring during a study that is not part of the experimental treatment but may affect performance on the dependent variable; a threat to internal validity.

hypothesis An explanation for the occurrence of certain behaviors, phenomena, or events; a prediction of research findings.

independent variable A behavior or characteristic believed to influence some other behavior or characteristic. *Also called* experimental variable, manipulated variable, cause, *or* treatment.

inductive hypothesis A generalization based on observation.

inductive reasoning Reasoning that involves developing generalizations based on observations of a limited number of related events or experiences.

inferential statistics Data analysis techniques for determining how likely it is that results obtained from a sample or samples are the same results that would have been obtained for the entire population.

instrument In educational research, a test or other tool used to collect data.

instrumentation Unreliability in measuring instruments that may result in invalid assessment of participants' performance.

interaction A situation in which different values of the independent variable are differentially effective depending upon the level of the control variable.

interjudge reliability The consistency of two or more independent scorers, raters, or observers.

internal validity The degree to which observed differences on the dependent variable are a direct result of manipulation of the independent variable, not some other variable.

interpretive research Collective, generic term for qualitative research approaches.

interpretive validity The degree to which a qualitative researcher attributes the appropriate meaning to the behavior or words of the participants being studied and therefore captures the participants' perspective.

interval scale *See* interval variable.

interval variable A measurement scale that classifies and ranks subjects, is based on predetermined equal intervals, but does not have a true zero point.

intervening variable A variable (e.g., anxiety) that intervenes between, or alters the relationship between, an independent variable and a dependent variable but which cannot be directly observed or controlled; can be controlled for.

interview An oral, in-person question-and-answer session between a researcher and an individual respondent. It is a purposeful interaction in which one person is trying to obtain information from the other.

intrajudge reliability The consistency of one individual's scoring, rating, or observing over time.

item validity The degree to which test items are relevant to the measurement of the intended content area.

John Henry effect The phenomenon in which members of a control group who feel threatened or challenged by being in competition with an experimental group outdo themselves and perform way beyond what would normally be expected. *Also called* compensatory rivalry.

judgment sampling *See* purposive sampling.

Kuder-Richardson 20 (KR-20) *See* Cronbach's alpha.

Likert scale An instrument that asks an individual to respond to a series of statements by indicating whether he or she strongly agrees (SA), agrees (A), is undecided (U), disagrees (D), or strongly disagrees (SD) with each statement.

limitation An aspect of a study that the researcher knows may negatively affect the results or generalizability of the results but over which the researcher has no control.

linear relationship A relationship in which an increase (or decrease) in one variable is associated with a corresponding increase (or decrease) in another variable; represented graphically as a straight line.

longitudinal survey A survey in which data are collected at two or more times in order to measure changes or growth over time. *Compare* cross-sectional survey.

matching A technique for equating groups on one or more variables, resulting in each member of one group having a direct counterpart in another group.

maturation   Physical, intellectual, and emotional changes that naturally occur within subjects over a period of time; poses a threat to internal validity because changes may affect subjects' performance on a measure of the dependent variable.

mean   The arithmetic average of a set of scores.

measurement   The process of quantifying or scoring performance on an assessment instrument.

measurement scale   A group of several related statements that vary by differing degrees that research participants select from to indicate their agreement or lack of agreement.

measures of central tendency   Indices that represent the typical or average score among a group of scores.

measures of variability   Indices that indicate how spread out the scores are in a distribution.

median   That point in a distribution above and below which are 50% of the scores.

meta-analysis   A statistical approach to summarizing the results of many quantitative studies that have investigated basically the same problem.

mixed methods research designs   Research designs that combine quantitative and qualitative approaches by essentially mixing both quantitative and qualitative data in a single study.

mode   The score that is attained by more subjects in a group than any other score.

mortality   A reduction in the number of research participants that occurs over time as individuals drop out of a study; poses a threat to internal validity because subjects who drop out of a study may share a characteristic, and their absence may therefore have a significant effect on the results of the study. *Also called* attrition.

multi-element baseline design   *See* alternating treatments design.

multi-element manipulation design   *See* alternating treatments design.

multiple comparisons   Procedures used following application of analysis of variance to determine which means are significantly different from which other means. *Also called* post hoc comparisons.

multiple prediction equation   *See* multiple regression equation.

multiple regression equation   A prediction equation using two or more variables that individually predict a criterion in order to make a more accurate prediction. *Also called* multiple prediction equation.

multiple schedule design   *See* alternating treatments design.

multiple time-series design   A variation of the time-series design that involves the addition of a control group to the basic design.

multiple-baseline design   A single-subject design in which baseline data are collected on several behaviors for one subject, one behavior for several subjects, or one behavior and one subject in several settings. Treatment is applied systematically over a period of time to each behavior (or each subject or setting) one at a time until all behaviors (or subjects or settings) are under treatment.

multiple-treatment interference   Phenomenon that occurs when carryover effects from an earlier treatment make it difficult to assess the effectiveness of a later treatment; a threat to external validity.

narrative analysis   In narrative research, the development of a narrative or story that focuses on particular knowledge about how or why an outcome occurred. *Compare* analysis of narrative.

narrative research   The study of how different humans experience the world around them; involves a methodology that allows people to tell the stories of their "storied lives."

National Research Act of 1974   Act that led to the establishment of federal regulations governing the protection of human subjects in research; mandates that activities involving human participants be reviewed and approved by an authorized group before execution of the research.

naturalistic inquiry   *See* qualitative research.

naturalistic research   *See* qualitative research.

negatively skewed distribution   A distribution in which there are more extreme scores at the lower end than at the upper, or higher, end.

nominal scale   *See* nominal variable.

nominal variable   A measurement scale that classifies persons or objects into two or more categories; represents the lowest level of measurement. A person can be in only one category, and members of a category have a common set of characteristics. *Also called* categorical variable.

nondirectional hypothesis   A research hypothesis that states simply that a relationship or difference exists between variables.

nonequivalent control group design   A quasi-experimental design involving at least two groups, both of which are pretested; one group receives the experimental treatment, and both groups are posttested.

nonparametric test   A test of significance appropriate when the data represent an ordinal or nominal scale, when a parametric assumption has been greatly violated, or when the nature of the distribution is not known.

nonparticipant observation   Observation in which the observer is not directly involved in the situation being observed; that is, the observer does not intentionally interact with or affect the object of the observation. *Also called* external observation.

nonprobability sampling   The process of selecting a sample using a technique that does *not* permit the researcher to specify the probability, or chance, that each member of a population has of being selected for the sample. *Also called* nonrandom sampling.

nonrandom sampling   *See* nonprobability sampling.

norm-referenced scoring   A scoring approach in which an individual's performance on an assessment is compared to the performance of others. *Also called* grading on the curve.

novelty effect   The increased interest, motivation, or participation participants develop simply because they are doing something different; a type of reactive arrangement.

null hypothesis   A hypothesis stating that there is no relationship (or difference) between variables and that any relationship found will be a chance (not true) relationship, the result of sampling error.

observer bias   The phenomenon whereby an observer does not observe objectively and accurately, thus producing invalid observations.

observer effect   The phenomenon whereby persons being observed behave atypically simply because they are being observed, thus producing invalid observations.

one-group pretest–posttest design   A pre-experimental design involving one group that is pretested, exposed to a treatment, and posttested.

one-shot case study   A pre-experimental design involving one group that is exposed to a treatment and then posttested.

one-way analysis of variance   *See* simple analysis of variance.

ordinal scale   *See* ordinal variable.

ordinal variable   A measurement scale that classifies persons or objects and ranks them in terms of the degree to which they possess a characteristic of interest.

organismic variable   A characteristic of a subject or organism (e.g., sex) that cannot be directly controlled but can be controlled for.

parameter   A numerical index describing the behavior of a population.

parametric test   A test of significance appropriate when the data represent an interval or ratio scale of measurement and other assumptions have been met.

participant effects   *See* reactive arrangements.

participant observation   Observation in which the observer actually becomes a part of, a participant in, the situation being observed.

participant variable   A variable on which participants in different groups in a study might differ (e.g., intelligence).

Pearson *r*   A measure of correlation appropriate when both variables are expressed as continuous (i.e., ratio or interval) data; it takes into account each and every score and produces a coefficient between −1.00 and +1.00.

percentile rank   A measure of relative position indicating the percentage of scores that fall at or below a given score.

performance assessment   A type of assessment that emphasizes a respondent's performance of a process or creation of a product. *Also called* authentic assessment *or* alternative assessment.

phenomenology   A qualitative approach in which the researcher focuses on capturing the experience of an activity or concept from participants' perspectives.

pilot study   A small-scale trial of a study conducted before the full-scale study in order to identify problems with the research plan.

placebo effect   Any beneficial effect caused by a person's expectations about a treatment rather than the treatment itself.

population   General term for the larger group from which a study's sample is selected or the group to which the researcher would like to generalize the results of the study. *Compare* target population *and* accessible population.

positively skewed distribution   A distribution in which there are more extreme scores at the upper, or higher, end than at the lower end.

post hoc comparisons   *See* multiple comparisons.

posttest-only control group design   A true experimental design involving at least two randomly formed groups; one group receives a new or unusual treatment, and both groups are posttested.

power   The ability of a significance test to reject a null hypothesis that is false and to therefore avoid making a Type II error.

practical action research   A type of action research that emphasizes a "how-to" approach to the processes of action research and has a less philosophical bent than critical action research.

prediction study   An attempt to determine which of a number of variables are most highly related to a criterion variable, a complex variable to be predicted.

predictive validity   The degree to which a test is able to predict how well an individual will do in a future situation; a form of criterion-related validity.

predictor   In a prediction study or analysis of concurrent or predictive validity, the variable upon which the prediction is based on.

pretest–posttest control group design   A true experimental design that involves at least two randomly formed groups; both groups are pretested, one group receives a new or unusual treatment, and both groups are posttested.

pretest sensitization   *See* testing.

pretest-treatment interaction   Phenomenon that occurs when subjects respond or react differently to a treatment because they have been pretested; a threat to external validity.

primary source   Firsthand information, such as the testimony of an eyewitness, an original document, a relic, or a description of a study written by the person who conducted it.

probability sampling   The process of selecting a sample using a sampling technique that permits the researcher to specify the probability, or chance, that each member of a defined population has of being selected for the sample.

problem statement   *See* topic statement.

prospective causal–comparative research   A variation of the basic approach to causal–comparative research; involves starting with the causes and investigating effects.

purposive sampling   The process of selecting a sample that is *believed* to be representative of a given population. *Also called* judgment sampling.

qualitative research   The collection, analysis, and interpretation of comprehensive narrative and visual data in order to gain insights into a particular phenomenon of interest. *Sometimes called* naturalistic research, naturalistic inquiry, *or* field-oriented research.

qualitative sampling   The process of selecting a small number of individuals for a study in such a way that the individuals chosen will be able to help the researcher understand the phenomenon under investigation.

quantitative research   The collection of numerical data in order to explain, predict and/or control phenomena of interest.

quartile deviation   One half of the difference between the upper quartile (the 75th percentile) and the lower quartile (the 25th percentile) in a distribution.

questionnaire   A written collection of self-report questions to be answered by a selected group of research participants.

quota sampling   The process of selecting a sample based on required, exact numbers (quotas) of persons of varying characteristics.

range   The difference between the highest and lowest score in a distribution.

rating scale   A measurement instrument used to determine a respondent's attitude toward self, others, activities, institutions, or situations.

ratio scale   *See* ratio variable.

ratio variable   A measurement scale that classifies subjects, ranks them, is based on predetermined equal intervals, and has a true zero point; represents the highest level of measurement.

raw score   The numerical calculation of the number or point value of items answered correctly on an assessment.

reactive arrangements   Threats to the external validity of a study associated with the way in which a study is conducted and the feelings and attitudes of the subjects involved. *Also called* participant effects.

realist ethnography   A form of ethnography written with an objective style and using common categories (e.g., "family life") for cultural description, analysis, and interpretation.

refereed journal   A journal in which articles are reviewed by a panel of experts in the field and are thus seen as more "scholarly" and "trustworthy" than articles from nonrefereed or popular journals.

relationship study   An attempt to gain insight into the variables, or factors, that are related to a complex variable, such as academic achievement, motivation, or self-concept.

reliability   The degree to which a test (or qualitative research data) consistently measures whatever it measures.

replication   A repetition of a study, using different subjects, or retesting of its hypothesis.

research   The formal, systematic application of the scientific method to the study of problems.

research and development (R&D)   An extensive process of researching consumer needs and then developing products specifically designed to fulfill those needs; R&D efforts in education focus on creating effective products for use in schools.

research hypothesis   A statement of the expected relationship (or difference) between two variables.

research plan   A detailed description of a proposed study designed to investigate a given problem.

response set   The tendency of an assessed individual to continually respond in a particular way to a variety of instruments, such as when a respondent repeatedly answers as he or she believes the researcher desires even when such answers do not reflect the respondent's true feelings; also, the tendency of an observer to rate the majority of observees the same regardless of the observees' actual behavior.

restorying   A process, unique to narrative research, in which a researcher gathers stories, analyzes them for key elements of the story, and then rewrites the story to place it in a chronological sequence.

retrospective causal–comparative research   The basic approach to causal–comparative research; involves starting with effects and investigating causes.

review of related literature   The systematic identification, location, and analysis of documents containing information related to a research problem; also, the written component of a research plan or report that discusses the reviewed documents.

sample   A number of individuals, items, or events selected from a population for a study, preferably in such a way that they represent the larger group from which they were selected.

sample survey   Research in which information about a population is inferred based on the responses of a sample selected from that population.

sampling   The process of selecting a number of individuals (a sample) from a population, preferably in such a way that the individuals selected represent the larger group from which they were selected.

sampling bias   Systematic sampling error; two major sources of sampling bias are the use of volunteers and the use of available groups.

sampling error   Expected, chance variation in variables that occurs when a sample is selected from a population.

sampling validity   The degree to which a test samples the total content area being tested.

Scheffé test   A conservative multiple comparison technique appropriate for making any and all possible comparisons involving a set of means.

scientific method   An orderly process that entails recognition and definition of a problem, formulation of hypotheses, collection of data, and statement of conclusions regarding confirmation or disconfirmation of the hypotheses.

secondary source   Secondhand information, such as a brief description of a study written by someone other than the person who conducted it.

selection–maturation interaction   Phenomenon that occurs when already-formed groups are used in a study and one group profits more (or less) from treatment or has an initial advantage (or disadvantage) because of maturation factors; a threat to internal validity. Selection may also interact with factors such as history and testing.

selection–treatment interaction   Phenomenon that occurs when nonrepresentative groups are used in a study and the results of the study apply only to the groups involved and are not representative of the treatment effect in the population; a threat to external validity.

self-referenced scoring   A scoring approach in which an individual's repeated performances on a single assessment are compared over time.

semantic differential scale   An instrument that asks an individual to indicate his or her attitude about a topic (e.g., property taxes) by selecting a position on a continuum that ranges from one bipolar adjective (e.g., fair) to another (e.g., unfair).

shared variance   *See* common variance.

shrinkage   The tendency of a prediction equation to become less accurate when used with a group other than the one on which the equation was originally developed.

simple analysis of variance (ANOVA)   A parametric test of significance used to determine whether a significant difference exists between two or more means at a selected probability level. *Also called* one-way analysis of variance.

simple random sampling   The process of selecting a sample in such a way that all individuals in the defined population have an equal and independent chance of being selected for the sample.

simultaneous replication   Replication done on a number of subjects with the same problem, at the same location, at the same time.

simultaneous treatment design   *See* alternating treatments design.

single-case experimental designs   *See* single-subject experimental designs.

single-subject experimental designs   Designs applied when the sample size is one; used to study the behavior change which an individual or group exhibits as a result of some intervention, or treatment. *Also called* single-case experimental designs.

single-variable design   Any experimental design that involves only one independent variable (which is manipulated).

single-variable rule   An important principle of single-subject research that states that only one variable should be manipulated at a time.

skewed distribution   A nonsymmetrical distribution in which there are more extreme scores at one end of the distribution than the other.

Solomon four-group design   A true experimental design that involves random assignment of subjects to one of four groups; two groups are pretested, and two are not; one of the pretested groups and one of the unpretested groups receive the experimental treatment; and all four groups are posttested.

Spearman rho   A measure of correlation appropriate when the data for at least one of the variables are expressed as rank or ordinal data; it produces a coefficient between -1.00 and $+1.00$.

specificity of variables   Refers to the fact that a given study is conducted with a specific kind of subject, using specific measuring instruments, at a specific time, and under a specific set of circumstances. These factors affect the generalizability of the results.

split-half reliability   A measure of internal consistency that involves dividing a test into two equivalent halves and correlating the scores on the two halves.

stability   The degree to which scores on a test are consistent, or stable, over time. *Also called* test–retest reliability.

standard deviation   The measure of variability that is most stable and takes into account each and every score in a distribution. Calculated as the square root of the variance, or amount of spread among test scores, it is the most frequently used statistical index of variability.

standard error of the mean   The standard deviation of sample means; indicates by how much the sample means can be expected to differ if other samples from the same population are used.

standard error of measurement   An estimate of how often one can expect errors of a given size in an individual's test score.

standard score   A derived score that expresses how far a given raw score is from some reference point, typically the mean, in terms of standard deviation units.

standardized test   A test that is administered, scored, and interpreted in the same way no matter where or when it is used.

stanines   Standard scores that divide a distribution into nine parts.

static-group comparison   A pre-experimental design that involves at least two nonrandomly formed groups; one receives a new or unusual (experimental) treatment, the other receives a traditional (control) treatment, and both groups are posttested.

statistic   A numerical index describing the behavior of a sample or samples.

statistical regression   The tendency of subjects who score highest on a pretest to score lower on a posttest, and of subjects who score lowest on a pretest to score higher on a posttest; a threat to internal validity.

statistical significance   The conclusion that results are unlikely to have occurred by chance–that is, that the observed relationship or difference is probably a real one.

statistics   A set of procedures for describing, synthesizing, analyzing, and interpreting quantitative data.

stratified sampling   The process of selecting a sample in such a way that identified subgroups (strata) in the population are represented in the sample in the same proportion in which they exist in the population.

stratum   (*pl.* strata) A subgroup derived from a sample; a variable that can be divided into groups.

structured interview   An interview that consists of a specified set of questions to be asked.

structured item   An item on a questionnaire that asks the respondent to choose among the provided response options (e.g., by circling a letter, checking a list, or numbering preferences). *Also called* closed-ended item.

summative evaluation   Evaluation whose function is to sum up the overall quality or worth of a program or product at its completion.

systematic replication   Replication that follows direct replication and involves different investigators, behaviors, or settings.

systematic sampling   Sampling in which individuals are selected from a list by taking every Kth name, where K equals the number of individuals on the list (population size) divided by the number of subjects desired for the sample.

***T* score**   A standard score derived from a z score by multiplying the z score by 10 and adding 50. *Also called* Z score.

***t* test**   An inferential statistics technique used to determine whether the means of two groups are significantly different at a given probability level. *See also t* test for independent samples *and t* test for nonindependent samples.

***t* test for independent samples**   A parametric test of significance used to determine whether, at a selected probability level, a significant difference exists between the means of two independent samples.

_t_ test for nonindependent samples A parametric test of significance used to determine whether, at a selected probability level, a significant difference exists between the means of two matched, or nonindependent, samples or between the means for one sample at two different times.

table of random digits *See* table of random numbers.

table of random numbers A list of multidigit numbers, arranged in a table, that have been randomly generated by a computer to have no defined patterns or regularities; used in sampling. *Also called* table of random digits.

target population The population to which the researcher would ideally like to generalize study results. *Compare* accessible population.

test A formal, systematic, usually paper-and-pencil procedure for gathering information about people's cognitive and affective characteristics.

test of significance A statistical test used to determine whether or not there is a significant difference between or among two or more means at a selected probability level.

testing A threat to experimental validity in which improved performance on a posttest is the result of subjects having taken a pretest. *Also called* pretest sensitization.

test–retest reliability *See* stability.

theoretical validity The ability of a qualitative research report to explain the phenomenon being studied in relation to a theory.

theory An organized body of concepts, generalizations, and principles that can be subjected to investigation.

time-series design A quasi-experimental design involving one group that is repeatedly pretested, exposed to an experimental treatment, and repeatedly posttested.

topic statement A statement in a research plan or report that describes the variables of interest to the researcher, the specific relationship between those variables and, ideally, important characteristics of the study participants. *Also called* problem statement.

treatment diffusion A threat to an experiment's external validity that occurs when different treatment groups communicate with and learn from each other.

triangulation The use of multiple methods, data collection strategies, and data sources in order to get a more complete picture of what is being studied and to cross-check information.

true categories Categories into which persons or objects naturally fall, independently of a research study.

trustworthiness Along with understanding, a feature essential to the validity of qualitative research; is established by addressing the credibility, transferability, dependability, and confirmability of study findings.

Type I error The rejection by the researcher of a null hypothesis that is actually true.

Type II error The failure of a researcher to reject a null hypothesis that is really false.

unobtrusive measures Ways to collect data that do not intrude on, or require interaction with, research participants; examples include observation and collecting data from written records.

unstructured interview An interview that consists of questions prompted by the flow of the interview itself.

unstructured item An item on a questionnaire that gives the respondent complete freedom of response.

validity The degree to which a test measures what it is intended to measure; a test is valid for a particular purpose for a particular group. In qualitative research, it is the degree to which qualitative data accurately gauge what the researcher is trying to measure.

variable A concept (e.g., intelligence, height, aptitude) that can assume any one of a range of values.

variance The amount of spread among scores.

_z_ score The most basic standard score; expresses how far a score is from a mean in terms of standard deviation units.

Z score *See* T score.

Author Index

Subject Index